Studies in Church History

58

(2022)

THE CHURCH IN SICKNESS
AND IN HEALTH

THE CHURCH IN SICKNESS
AND IN HEALTH

EDITED BY

CHARLOTTE METHUEN

and

ANDREW SPICER

PUBLISHED FOR
THE ECCLESIASTICAL HISTORY SOCIETY
BY
CAMBRIDGE UNIVERSITY PRESS
2022

Published by Cambridge University Press
on behalf of the Ecclesiastical History Society
University Printing House, Cambridge CB2 8BS, United Kingdom

First published 2022

ISBN 9781009284806

ISSN 0424-2084

SUBSCRIPTIONS: *Studies in Church History* is an annual subscription
journal (ISSN 0424-2084). The 2022 subscription price (excluding VAT),
which includes print and electronic access, is £106 (US $193 in the USA,
Canada and Mexico) for institutions and £66 (US $106 in the USA, Canada
and Mexico) for individuals ordering direct from the Press and certifying that
the volume is for their personal use. An electronic-only subscription is also
available to institutions at £93 (US $148 in the USA, Canada and Mexico).
Special arrangements exist for members of the Ecclesiastical History Society.

Previous volumes are available online at www.cambridge.org/StudCH

Printed in the United Kingdom by Bell & Bain Ltd
A catalogue record for this publication is available from the British Library

Contents

Preface   ix

List of Contributors   xi

List of Abbreviations   xiii

List of Illustrations   xv

Introduction   1
    Charlotte Methuen and Andrew Spicer

Contagion of the Jews: Metaphorical and Rhetorical Uses of   8
Sickness, Plague and Disease in Pseudo-Hegesippus
    Carson Bay

Bede on Sickness, Episcopal Identity and Monastic   28
Asceticism
    Jessica Collett

Healing Body and Soul in Early Medieval Europe: Medical   46
Remedies with Christian Elements
    Claire Burridge

Plague and Popular Revival: Ecclesiastical Authorities and   68
the Biachi Devotions in 1399
    Alexandra R. A. Lee

Preaching during Plague Epidemics in Early Modern   91
Germany, c.1520–1618
    Martin Christ

A Sixteenth-Century Clergyman and Physician: Timothy   112
Bright's Dual Approach to Melancholia
    Emily Betz

Godly Preaching, in Sickness and Ill-Health, in Seventeenth-   134
Century England (*President's Prize*)
    Robert W. Daniel

Contents

Healthcare and Catholic Enlightenment in the Polish-Lithuanian Commonwealth
Stanisław Witecki
150

Moral Sick Notes: Medical Exemptions to Religious Fasting in the Eighteenth-Century Spanish World
George A. Klaeren
173

Pain as a Spiritual Barometer of Health: A Sign of Divine Love, 1780–1850
Angela Platt
196

Caring for the Sick in Hamburg: Amalie Sieveking and the 'dormant strength' of Christian Women
Andrew Kloes
217

Health and Sickness as Reality and Metaphor in the Oratory Parish of F. W. Faber, 1849–63
Melissa Wilkinson
241

Ministering to Body and Soul: Medical Missions and the Jewish Community in Nineteenth-Century London (*Kennedy Prize*)
Jemima Jarman
262

The Church's Promotion of Public Health in the Southern Part of the Nineteenth-Century Austro-Hungarian Empire
Branka Gabrić and Darija Damjanović Barišić
284

'It is well with the child': Changing Views on Protestant Missionary Children's Health, 1870s–1930s
Hugh Morrison
306

Caring for the Sick and Dying in Early Twentieth-Century Anglo-Catholic Parishes
Dan D. Cruickshank
330

'Alleviating the Sum of Human Suffering': The Origins, Attributes and Appeal of Hospital Sunday, 1859–1914
Roger Ottewill
352

Contents

Hospital Sunday and the new National Health Services: An End to the 'Voluntary Spirit' in England?
    Robert Piggott — 372

From Plato to Pentecostalism: Sickness and Deliverance in the Theology of Derek Prince
    Brian Stanley — 394

Masks vs. God and Country: The Conflict between Public Health and Christian Nationalism
    Brittany Acors — 415

Preface

Studies in Church History 58 takes as its theme *The Church in Sickness and in Health*. For the first time in the history of the Ecclesiastical History Society, this volume did not arise from a summer conference: along with so many other events, the 2020 Summer Conference, due to explore 'The Church and Rites of Passage', had to be postponed. Under the extended presidency of Professor Alec Ryrie, the committee of the Ecclesiastical History Society issued a call for papers for a volume exploring the Church's approach to sickness and to health. This volume comprises twenty peer-reviewed articles selected from those submitted, some of which were presented at the 2021 Winter Meeting, held online.

These articles offer fascinating insights into the Church's response to previous pandemics, and the current one, and the way in which themes of sickness and health have shaped the self-understandings of individual Christians as well as communities. The standard of research presented here is particularly noteworthy given the difficulties in undertaking historical research during the closure of, or limited access to, libraries and archives during the pandemic. In some cases, this volume illustrates and demonstrates the academic value of the remarkable range of digitized materials now available to historians.

We are grateful to the EHS committee for their support in this endeavour, and particularly to Professor Ryrie for his engagement throughout his extended presidency. We also thank everyone who submitted papers for consideration for the volume, and those who peer reviewed the contributions, thereby helping the society to ensure that the volume is of the highest quality. Dr Tim Grass continued his meticulous work as assistant editor, joined latterly by Dr Alice Soulieux-Evans. We are particularly grateful to the Ecclesiastical History Society for funding two assistant editor posts during this period of transition. In addition, the careful planning of the society's conference secretary, Professor Elizabeth Tingle, ensured the smooth running of the first online Winter Meeting. She was supported by the society's outgoing and incoming secretaries, Dr Gareth Atkins and Dr

Jacqueline Rose, by the EHS treasurer, Simon Jenkins, and by other members of the committee.

The Ecclesiastical History Society awards two annual prizes for articles accepted for publication in Studies in Church History. The Kennedy Prize, for the best contribution by a postgraduate student, has been awarded to Jemima Jarman, for her article 'Ministering to Body and Soul: Medical Missions and the Jewish Community in Nineteenth-Century London'. The President's Prize, for the best contribution by an early career scholar, has been awarded to Robert W. Daniel, for 'Godly Preaching, in Sickness and Ill-Health, in Seventeenth-Century England'. Each author used meticulous research to offer an important contribution to this theme.

Charlotte Methuen
University of Glasgow

Andrew Spicer
Oxford Brookes University

Contributors

Brittany Acors
> Postgraduate student, University of Virginia

Carson Bay
> Postdoctoral researcher, University of Bern

Emily Betz
> Postgraduate student, University of St Andrews

Claire Burridge
> Leverhulme Trust Early Career Fellow, Department of History, University of Sheffield

Martin Christ
> Postdoctoral researcher, Max-Weber-Kolleg, University of Erfurt

Jessica Collett
> Postgraduate student, University of St Andrews

Dan D. Cruickshank
> Postgraduate student, University of Glasgow

Darija Damjanović Barišić
> Frankfurt am Main

Robert W. Daniel
> Associate Tutor, University of Warwick

Branka Gabrić
> Research Assistant, Institut für Weltkirche und Mission, Philosophisch-Theologische Hochschule Sankt Georgen, Frankfurt am Main

Jemima Jarman
> Postgraduate student, Birkbeck, University of London

Contributors

George A. Klaeren
> Research Fellow, School of Divinity, University of St Andrews

Andrew Kloes
> Washington DC

Alexandra R. A. Lee
> Postgraduate student, University College London

Hugh Morrison
> Associate Professor in Education, University of Otago

Roger Ottewill
> Southampton

Robert Piggott
> Lecturer in History, University of Huddersfield

Angela Platt
> Postgraduate student, Royal Holloway, University of London

Brian Stanley
> Professor of World Christianity, University of Edinburgh

Melissa Wilkinson
> Welwyn Garden City

Stanislaw Witecki
> Assistant Professor, Institute of History, Jagiellonian University, Kraków

Abbreviations

AHR	*American Historical Review* (1895–)
BAV	Biblioteca Apostolica Vaticana
BHM	*Bulletin of the History of Medicine* (1939–)
BL	British Library
BN	Bibliothèque nationale de France
Bodl.	Bodleian Library
CChr.SL	Corpus Christianorum, series Latina (1953–)
CHC	*Cambridge History of Christianity*, 9 vols (Cambridge, 2005–9)
ChH	*Church History* (1932–)
CSEL	Corpus Scriptorum Ecclesiasticorum Latinorum (Vienna, 1866–)
EHR	*English Historical Review* (1886–)
EME	*Early Medieval Europe* (1992–)
FOTC	Fathers of the Church (Washington DC, 1989–)
GH	*Gender and History* (1989–)
HistJ	*Historical Journal* (1958–)
HR	*Historical Research* (1986–)
IBMR	*International Bulletin of Missionary Research*, o.s. 1–10, n.s. vols 1–39 (1950–2015); *International Bulletin of Mission Research*, vol. 40 on (2016–)
JBR	*Journal of the Bible and its Reception* (2014–)
JBS	*Journal of British Studies* (1961–)
JCR	*Journal of Contemporary Religion* (1985–)
JEH	*Journal of Ecclesiastical History* (1950–)
JHCY	*Journal of the History of Childhood and Youth* (2008–)
JICH	*Journal of Imperial and Commonwealth History* (1972–)
JMedH	*Journal of Medieval History* (1975–)
JMH	*Journal of Modern History* (1929–)
JRH	*Journal of Religious History* (1960–)
JThS	*Journal of Theological Studies* (1899–)
LCL	Loeb Classical Library
MH	*Medical History* (1957–)
n.d.	no date
n.pl.	no place
n.s.	new series

Abbreviations

ODNB	H. C. G. Matthew and Brian Harrison, eds, *Oxford Dictionary of National Biography*, 63 vols (Oxford, 2004), and subsequent online versions
OHA	Rowan Strong, gen. ed., *Oxford History of Anglicanism*, 5 vols (Oxford, 2017–18)
P&P	*Past and Present* (1952–)
SC	*Seventeenth Century* (1986–)
SC	Sources Chrétiennes (Paris, 1941–)
SCH	Studies in Church History
SCJ	*Sixteenth Century Journal* (1970–2006)
SHM	*Social History of Medicine* (1988–)
s.v.	*sub verbo* ('under the word')
TCBH	*Twentieth Century British History* (1990–)
TNA	The National Archives
TRHS	*Transactions of the Royal Historical Society* (1871–)
TTH	Translated Texts for Historians
UL	University Library
UH	*Urban History Yearbook*, vols 1–18 (1974–91); *Urban History*, from vol. 19 (1991–)
VS	*Victorian Studies* (1956–)
WA	*D. Martin Luthers Werke: Kritische Gesamtausgabe*, ed. J. K. F. Knaake et al. (Weimar / Berlin / Heidelberg, 1883–2009)
WA, Br	*D. Martin Luthers Werke: Kritische Gesamtausgabe. Briefwechsel*, 18 vols (Weimar, 1930–85)
WSA	*The Works of Saint Augustine: A Translation for the Twenty-First Century* (Garden City, NY, 1990–)

Illustrations

Alexandra R. A. Lee, 'Plague and Popular Revival: Ecclesiastical Authorities, Civic Religion and the Bianchi Devotions in 1399'

Fig. 1. Lucca, Archivio di Stato, MS 107, fol. 49v: *Come fu moria grande*. Su concessione del Ministero per i beni e le attività culturali e per il turismo – Archivio di Stato di Lucca (With permission from the Ministry for Cultural Heritage and Activities and Tourism, State Archive of Luca).   74

Fig. 2. Map of Itinerant Tuscan Bianchi Procession Towns.   87

Introduction

Prepared in the midst of a global pandemic, which closed churches and universities on a scale which was familiar to many historians from their sources but until now unknown to them in practice, this volume explores the Church's response to previous epidemics and its reflections on sickness and on health. From the earliest times, the Church has been involved in caring for the sick within society. Early church communities succoured the sick and the frail as well as taking in abandoned children. Medieval monastic houses included infirmaries; leper and plague hospitals were religious establishments. Major London hospitals, such as Bart's and St Thomas's, began as religious institutions, which were then reconstituted following the dissolution of the monasteries. The Reformation brought alternative reflections on the relationship between medicine and salvation, but included reforms in medical care, such as the Reformed diaconate assisting the sick. The early modern period also witnessed the temporary closure of institutions such as schools and universities, and the evacuation or isolation of communities, due to plague. With the professionalization of medical care during the eighteenth and nineteenth centuries, both Catholic and Protestant churches established schools to train doctors and nurses as well as hospitals to treat the sick. Globally churches remain key players in the provision of healthcare: indeed, the Roman Catholic Church today is the largest non-governmental provider of healthcare in the world. At the same time, some Christian groups, including Jehovah's Witnesses and Christian Scientists, have rejected medical interventions. Such responses serve to exacerbate the perceived divide between science and religion.

The articles contained in this volume address several interconnected themes. Many of them focus on the Church's response to sickness, and specifically to the experience of pandemics, through the ages. Others explore the connection between the Church and the medical profession, and by implication the relationships between spiritual and physical approaches to sickness. An important aspect of interaction in the modern era was the involvement of churches and clergy in public health. Another group of articles considers the clerical experience of sickness, and its impact on ministry, preaching

Studies in Church History 58 (2022), 1–7   © The Author(s), 2022. Published by Cambridge University Press on behalf of Ecclesiastical History Society
doi: 10.1017/stc.2022.23

and understandings of God. Finally, they show some of the ways that sickness has served as a metaphor for understanding the church and its relationship to the world.

Largely for reasons relating to the (non-)availability of source material, the earliest articles chronologically focus on the last of these themes, although metaphors of sickness in many ways provide a leitmotif in the theological thinking of the Church. Carson Bay explores the text *De excidio Hierosolymitano*, also known as 'Pseudo-Hegesippus'. The depiction of Jewish contagion in this text can be interpreted as a historiographical solution to the Christian theological need to explain the Jews out of history. Pseudo-Hegesippus provided a language which was later applied to Christian heresy, allowing it to be seen as infection or sickness.

The metaphor of sickness is found frequently in Christian writings. Jessica Collett observes that Gregory the Great's commentary on Job identified prolonged sickness and suffering unto death as an experience in which the contemplative values of heaven can be united with an active life on earth, serving as a figure and anticipation in this life of the final union of heaven and earth at Christ's second coming. Gregory applied this insight when exploring the role of the episcopate, and Bede drew on his writings to frame and present the episcopate of Columba. For Bede, Columba, like Job, did not endure sickness and suffering for its own sake, but in the hope of his future union with Christ and for the sake of the cleansing renewal of the church's leadership. Collett's analysis offers an important reminder that, like miracles, sickness was one of the tropes of a holy life.

The use of sickness to understand, and share more deeply in, Christ's suffering is common in medieval and early modern piety, but also permeates the nineteenth-century evangelical writings examined by Angela Platt. Pain in the Christian life was often understood theologically as a quotidian display of divine love, rooted in the atonement as a loving aspect of God's providence. The meaning and purpose of pain was sanctification, a retributive though mainly redemptive implement of God's fatherly love. Platt shows how those who experienced pain struggled to accept it as an expression of God's love, finding that Baptists and Congregationalists emphasized the sin that necessitated the atonement, whilst Quakers focused on suffering with Christ.

The practical applications of metaphors of sickness and health are explored in Brian Stanley's study of the influence of Derek Prince

(1915–2003). Prince, a former philosophy fellow of King's College, Cambridge, became a globally influential Pentecostal teacher and author with a strong belief in the invisible realm of spiritual powers and its impact on the health and material well-being of Christians. Prince's teaching on ancestral curses and the vulnerability of Christians to demonization has been widely received in Africa and other parts of the non-Western world, approaches which, as Stanley shows, are often seen as providing solutions to endemic problems of chronic sickness and impoverishment.

The Church's response to actual experiences of sickness, and specifically to the experience of pandemics down the ages, is an important theme of this volume. The medieval church devised rituals to help it cope with plague, or the threat of plague, such the Bianchi devotions of late fourteenth-century northern Italy discussed by Alexandra R. A. Lee. These processions were sometimes restricted to particular towns, particularly when plague had already broken out; in other cases they progressed through the local region. Dressed in white, the participants moved from church to church, holding services and singing. Prayer and religious ritual were perceived as helping to ward off plague or to reduce its effects.

An outbreak of plague faced churches and individuals with many pragmatic decisions. Martin Christ presents Martin Luther's deliberations about his own response to such an outbreak in Wittenberg: should he remain in Wittenberg or should he leave? On the whole, Luther thought, preachers and those who had civic responsibilities should stay, unless they could appoint a deputy. He himself was, he remarked, 'willing to take medicine, air rooms and avoid places where he was not needed, but if God called on him to help, he would not avoid any person or place'. Luther's advice about how people should respond to the plague combined practical, moral and theological or spiritual aspects: they should pray, avoid dancing and drinking, and keep their homes and towns clean. For Luther, however, the suffering caused by plague was to be understood primarily as divine punishment: the plague had been sent by God to call people to repentance.

The relationship between Christian ritual and care for the sick is discussed further in Dan D. Cruickshank's exploration of how Anglo-Catholic clergy and parishes cared for the sick and dying in the early twentieth century. Drawing on evidence submitted to the Church of England's Royal Commission on Ecclesiastical Discipline (1904–6), he concludes that the provision of communion for the sick was often cited as the reason for the reservation of the sacrament; the need to draw in those who could not attend church because they were unwell was used to justify the ringing of a sanctus bell – generally the church bell – at the point of consecration.

Hugh Morrison shows how, amongst nineteenth-century mission-ary families, the missionaries' ill-health and early death, as well as that of their spouse and children, were understood in both private and public discourse as being 'reflexive of and contributory to a specifi-cally missionary identity'. However, this attitude gradually changed to an expectation that missionary families' health and welfare be exemplary. This gave rise to a complex balance between a religiously motivated rhetoric that expected illness and death, particularly of children, to be part of missionary experience, and an emerging professionalized discourse that redefined these families as paragons of health and well-being.

Morrison's study reflects the Church's response to sickness, but also another theme explored in this volume: the changing relationship between the Church and the medical profession, and thus between spiritual and physical approaches to healing. However, this was not only a modern phenomenon. Evidence for the Christianizing of clas-sical medical recipes is considered in Claire Burridge's study of the incorporation of spiritual practices into the preparation of cures and remedies during the ninth century. These might include saying the Lord's Prayer while collecting herbs for these preparations, the addition of holy water or chrism to a medicine, or the association of the treatments with other Christian rituals, such as instructions to make the sign of the cross or to say mass. This evidence is not easy to interpret: are these interventions simply intended to increase the efficacy of the treatment? Are they affirmations of the scribe's faith, or of the faith of practitioners? Are they conscious attempts to make potentially controversial writings more acceptable to a ninth-century audience?

The complexity of the line between spiritual and physical care is highlighted also by Emily Betz's consideration of Timothy Bright's *A Treatise of Melancholie* (1586). Melancholia was commonly recog-nized to have both corporeal and spiritual aspects, and was therefore a disease generally treated by both medical practitioners and the clergy. Bright recognized the importance and the distinctive contribution of both, but also that melancholy and affliction of conscience were closely connected. Clergymen and physicians in this period might clash, particularly as the medical profession became more professionalized and regulated. Bright's discussion of melancholia, however, offers examples of how the two professions might also cooperate.

Further evidence of the interplay between spiritual and physical assessments of sickness and health is offered by George A. Klaeren's exploration of eighteenth-century Spanish debates about ecclesiastical regulations surrounding fasting. The requirement to fast could be lifted on medical grounds. What constituted a medical exemption, and who had the authority to make this decision? Klaeren finds that the opinions of both a 'spiritual doctor' and a 'medical doctor' were required.

The eighteenth century also saw the beginnings of church involvement in what we might now call public healthcare provision, another aspect of the interplay between spiritual and physical approaches to sickness and health. Stanisław Witecki considers the interventions of Polish bishops who, influenced by the Catholic Enlightenment, encouraged their clergy to take responsibility for medical education and the organization of healthcare, and sought to reform customs which they had come to view as detrimental to health. Healthcare issues were increasingly important for Catholic enlighteners in the Polish-Lithuanian Commonwealth, and priests could play a significant role in promoting healthcare. Branka Gabrić and Darija Damjanović Barišić observe similar patterns of engagement in the nineteenth-century kingdom of Slavonia, part of the Austro–Hungarian Empire, where bishops supported measures to provide access to clean water and hygienic measures in cemeteries, alongside opening hospitals and schools. In both cases, these reforms were legitimated by the theological understanding that disease was due to natural causes rather than being a punishment sent by God. Nonetheless, there could be tensions between these reforms and the practices of lived religion, especially around funerals and burial practices.

Public health might also be supported by local faith-based organizations. Andrew Kloes describes the foundation of the *Weiblicher Verein für Armen- und Krankenpflege* ('Women's Association for the Care of the Poor and the Sick') by Amalie Sieveking in connection with an outbreak of cholera in Hamburg in 1831. Members of the Women's Association visited the homes of the sick, seeking to promote the well-being of those whom they assisted by providing food, clothing, paid employment and housing, as well as opportunities to cultivate their spiritual life. A similarly local approach is observed by Jemima Jarman in her study of late nineteenth-century medical missions established by evangelical Protestants and aimed specifically at Jews in the East End of London. These offered free health care, provided by doctors and nurses who were encouraged to learn Yiddish. Intended as a form of evangelization, these medical missions were markedly unsuccessful in converting their clients, but the provision they offered was a valuable resource for the immigrant Jewish community.

The importance of medical provision to local communities was recognized in many towns and cities across England by the institution of 'Hospital Sunday' in the mid-Victorian era. This designated one Sunday each year to support and raise funds for the work of local hospitals and dispensaries. Roger Ottewill shows that it was often an ecumenical event and something of a gala Sunday. Robert Piggott observes that in many areas Hospital Sunday continued for some time after the foundation of the NHS in 1948, witnessing to the deep and ongoing relationships between local clergy, congregations and healthcare.

However, the relationship between the church and public health remains vulnerable. This is demonstrated by Brittany Acors, who shows how the current COVID-19 pandemic has witnessed protests against public health guidelines. In the USA these arise particularly amongst some evangelical groups who use religious language to defend what they see as their civil and God-given rights.

Finally, sickness was also frequently part of the experience of the minister or preacher, and this often shaped their theology and their ministry. As Hugh Morrison observes of missionary families, so too Robert W. Daniel finds that the experience of sickness was a part of a clergyman's vocation. A minister's sufferings were to be seen publicly rather than concealed privately, to build faith and serve as a living exemplar. Practical considerations did arise: if ministers preached while suffering from colds, agues and fevers, they risked infecting others and exacerbating their own pain and discomfort, or worse. When congregants followed their example, attending church with all manner of ailments, they too risked making themselves and others sicker. Nonetheless, belief in divine providence, the power of preaching, and strict Sabbatarianism held powerful sway throughout the seventeenth century. Preaching when unwell could hamper a sermon's audibility, but the physical presence of an ill minister could have a powerful and inspiring impact. The understanding that illness was an aspect of God's providential action was an important factor.

Similarly, although in a very different context, Melissa Wilkinson shows how the chronic ill-health of F. W. Faber, the founder in 1849 of the first London Oratory (the precursor to the Brompton Oratory) informed his ministry. Faber drew on his own illness, and that which pervaded the area where his church building was located, to present sickness and health as a profound metaphor for the spiritual life.

The essays in this volume therefore demonstrate the extensive and interconnected associations of the Church with sickness and health at both practical and theoretical levels. While these contributions have tended to focus more on the response of ecclesiastical institutions and clergy to sickness, their concern to bolster public and spiritual health is also evident. Furthermore, a striking number of themes and questions which have been of concern to churches and institutions as they grapple with the current pandemic are shown to have exercised the minds of theologians and clergy across the ages.

Charlotte Methuen and Andrew Spicer

Contagion of the Jews: Metaphorical and Rhetorical Uses of Sickness, Plague, and Disease in Pseudo-Hegesippus

Carson Bay*
University of Bern

Drawing upon discourses developed in earlier Graeco-Roman and Judaeo-Christian antiquity, the little-known text De excidio Hierosolymitano, *also dubbed 'Pseudo-Hegesippus', develops a discourse of Jewish disease within a history of Jerusalem's destruction by the Romans in 70 CE. Based upon Flavius Josephus's Greek* Jewish War, *this Latin Christian text of Late Antiquity thus deploys a rhetoric of Jewish contagion within its historiographical solution to the Christian theological exigency of explaining the Jews out of history. Far from being an incidental or merely aesthetic component of this work, this article shows that a discourse of Jewish sickness constitutes a central component of Pseudo-Hegesippus's conceptualization and presentation of the end of Jerusalem and the historical demise of the Jews.*

Christian authors of Late Antiquity, particularly in the fourth century, had many things to say about the Jews. They also had many ways of saying them. The most pressing dilemma for many was to explain how the Jews, the cultural and genealogical descendants of the ancient Hebrews or Israelites, had once been the covenant people of God but were so no longer. The former claim was undeniable, codified in the Christians' own Scriptures (their 'Old Testament'). The latter claim Christians took as axiomatic: the Christians alone were (now) God's chosen collective. Explaining how the Jews had lost their privileged place as God's people was thus of fundamental importance for Christians seeking to establish their own place within a theological understanding of history. One way of delegitimizing the Jews involved capitalizing on a complex of ideas familiar to the Roman world: namely, those of sickness, plague and disease.

* Gantrischstrasse 43, 3006 Bern, Switzerland. E-mail: Carson.bay@theol.unibe.ch.

Studies in Church History 58 (2022), 8–27 © The Author(s), 2022. Published by Cambridge University Press on behalf of Ecclesiastical History Society
doi: 10.1017/stc.2022.1

Christians have always tended to see what we call the first century CE as definitive for Jewish and Christian identity: this period witnessed the birth of Christianity and its Scriptures, as well as the demise of the Jews in the Roman destruction of Jerusalem and its Temple in 70 CE. Ancient Christians generally understood the latter as a direct result of the Jews' rejection and crucifixion of Jesus Christ. Jerusalem's destruction, and the larger Roman-Jewish War (66–70 CE), came to be seen as the provoked and purposeful rejection (and cursing) by God of his former people. Perhaps the most forceful articulation of this perspective came in a work fittingly titled *On the Destruction of Jerusalem* (*De excidio Hierosolymitano*).[1] This work employs the themes of sickness, disease and plague to help 'write the Jews out of history', as it were. That is, it uses a discourse of disease to signal a process of Jewish 'dying' in the course of the catastrophic events of the later first century.

The present article argues that *De excidio* uses a rhetoric of sickness, disease and plague to do two specific things: first, to stereotype the (first-century) Jews of the author's narrative as a people who are 'sick' or 'diseased' in certain critical ways; second, to present that sickness as a key causal and explanatory factor in the destruction of Jerusalem and its Temple. In cataloguing this rhetoric of contagion, we see that 'Pseudo-Hegesippus', the name given to the anonymous author of this work,[2] drew upon, and was inspired by, various categories of sources – biblical, classical and Josephan – but also that these influences were marshalled into a thoroughly Christian conception of supersessionist theology and anti-Jewish historiography ('supersessionism' being the biblically-based Christian self-understanding and

---

[1] The Latin text of *De excidio* is taken from Vincenzo Ussani's standard critical edition, *Hegesippi qui dicitur Historiae libri v*, 1: *Textum criticum continens* (CSEL 66.1). All translations are my own. Texts and translation of Josephus's Greek works are from the LCL editions.

[2] The name 'Hegesippus' constitutes a historical conflation between the author of *De excidio* and the second-century, Greek-writing Hegesippus who penned a five-book *Hypomnēmata* (*Memoirs*) and was a major source for Eusebius's *Ecclesiastical History*, a conflation which first appears in manuscripts during the ninth and tenth century, which coincides with a subtle orthographical move from the Latin phrase *ex iosippi* ('of Josephus') to the similar *egesippi* ('of Hegesippus'), as in Milan Codex Ambrosianus C105 inf., fol. 67v. In any case, it is best practice to refer to *De excidio*'s author as Pseudo-Hegesippus to avoid confusion and to signal that the author of *De excidio* was almost certainly not named 'Hegesippus' (something that many, including the Thesaurus Latinae Linguae at Munich, continue not to do).

claim to have displaced the Jews as God's covenant people within history). As today, in the ancient world disease and contagion were widely used as metaphors for moral, social and conceptual realities (the 'spread' of ideas, the notion of a social 'disease'). Drawing upon such metaphor as it appears in the literature of traditions both 'Graeco-Roman' and 'Judaeo-Christian', Pseudo-Hegesippus articulated an early and significant iteration of a multifaceted, widespread and long-enduring Christian rhetoric: that of the contagion of the Jews.

PSEUDO-HEGESIPPUS AS AN OBJECT OF STUDY

De excidio, and its anonymous author dubbed 'Pseudo-Hegesippus', have received little attention during the past century.[3] This marginalization has several interrelated causes,[4] but suffice it to say that recent scholarship has begun to appreciate anew *De excidio*'s significance as a literary artefact of Christian Late Antiquity.[5] Despite its authorial anonymity, unknown date (probably *c*.370–380 CE), and unknown provenance (probably Antioch, possibly Rome or Italy),[6] *De excidio* is an interesting text and in some ways may act as a cultural barometer of later fourth-century Christian thought.[7] Unlike any other extant ancient Christian text, it provides a type of historiography more reminiscent of Sallust or Livy than any other Christian

---

[3] The only monograph on the work to date, an excellent but brief overview of its primary features, is in Italian: Chiara Somenzi, *Egesippo – Ambrogio. Formazione scolastica e Cristiana a Roma alla metà del IV secolo*, Studia Patristica Mediolanensia 27 (Milan, 2009).
[4] See Albert A. Bell Jr, 'Classical and Christian Traditions in the Work of Pseudo-Hegesippus', *Indiana Social Studies Quarterly* 33 (1980), 60–4.
[5] More or less beginning with Albert A. Bell Jr, 'An Historiographical Analysis of the *De Excidio Hierosolymitano* of Pseudo-Hegesippus' (Ph.D. dissertation, University of North Carolina at Chapel Hill, 1977); idem, 'Josephus and Pseudo-Hegesippus', in Louis H. Feldman and Gohei Hata, eds, *Josephus, Judaism, and Christianity* (Detroit, MI, 1987), 349–61. See now, for example, Carson Bay, 'The Bible, the Classics, and the Jews in Pseudo-Hegesippus: A Literary Analysis of *De Excidio Hierosolymitano* 5.2' (Ph.D. dissertation, Florida State University, 2018).
[6] On the text's provenance and (briefly) its date and authorship, see Carson Bay, 'Pseudo-Hegesippus at Antioch? Testing a Hypothesis for the Provenance of *De Excidio Hierosolymitano*', *Bulletin de l'Académie Belge pour l'Étude des Langues Anciennes et Orientales* 8 (2019), 97–128.
[7] I draw loosely on the notion of 'cultural biography' as discussed in Andrew S. Jacobs, *Epiphanius of Cyprus: A Cultural Biography of Late Antiquity* (Berkeley, CA, 2016).

modification of that genre.[8] Following Josephus in terms of literary genre, it is actually much like Thucydides in that it is a 'war monograph', expressing interests which are largely martial, geographical and political. As a distinctive and little-studied text, *De excidio* has a significant contribution to make to the growing body of work on the development and diversity of historiographical literature in Late Antiquity.[9]

Pseudo-Hegesippus cited, and was familiar with, the classical tradition, including its historiography; thus the text often quotes Sallust, for instance. Whilst overtly Christian in outlook and rhetoric, Pseudo-Hegesippus produced a history that in many ways feels more classical than its Christian counterparts,[10] although this distinction itself is not unproblematic. In writing Jewish history in a classical tone (albeit from a Christian perspective), Pseudo-Hegesippus was following the lead of his primary source, Flavius Josephus, of whose *Jewish War*, a seven-book history written in Greek in the first century CE, *De excidio* was essentially a Latin rewriting.[11] *De excidio*'s classical genealogy, including its more immediate predecessor, the *Jewish War*, proves a helpful framework for understanding Pseudo-Hegesippus's traditional yet novel configuration of contagion rhetoric within his larger project of anti-Jewish historiography.

JEWISH DISEASE FROM JOSEPHUS TO PSEUDO-HEGESIPPUS

In the *Jewish War*, Josephus speaks of the ills of Jewish factionalism in terms of the metaphor of sickness, referring to the capacity of the Sicarii (dagger-carrying Jewish rebels) to foment rebellion as a 'madness akin to disease'.[12] More than once, Josephus refers to the Jewish

---

[8] 'Die literarische Tradition, an die Ps.-Hegesipp anknüpft, ist die eines Sallust. Er schreibt, wie Sallust, eine Monographie': Markus Sehlmeyer, *Geschichtsbilder für Pagane und Christen. Res Romanae in den spätantiken Breviarien* (Berlin, 2009), 222.

[9] See Carson Bay, 'Pseudo-Hegesippus and the Beginnings of Christian Historiography in Late Antiquity', *Studia Patristica* 126 (2021), 255–66.

[10] Dominique Estève, 'L'Oeuvre historique du Pseudo-Hegésippe: "De Bello iudaico", livre I à IV' (Ph.D. thesis, Université Paris Nanterre, 1987).

[11] See Carson Bay, 'On the Multivocality of the Latin Josephus Tradition: A Comparison between the Latin *War*, Latin *Antiquities*, Pseudo-Hegesippus, and Rufinus based on the Egyptian Pseudo-Prophet Episode (*War* 2.261–263, *Antiquities* 20.169–172a)', *Medaevalia et Humanistica* 46 (2020), 1–36.

[12] 'ἀπόνοια καθάπερ νόσος': Josephus, *Jewish War* 7.437 (LCL 210, 428); cf. Herodotus 3.76.2, 3.127.1, 5.28. It is worth noting that Josephus's comment here

uprisings that fuelled civil dissension during the Roman-Jewish War by using the language of disease, particularly the noun νόσος ('sickness, disease, plague') and corresponding verb νοσέω ('to be sick / diseased, to suffer [from plague]').[13] In so doing, Josephus plays on the established historian's habit of describing undesirable social movements, which often carried strong ethnic associations, in terms of disease.[14] Livy had done the same thing in Book 39 of his *Ab vrbe condita* when he described the foreign (Greek) cult of the Bacchanalia as a dangerous movement which was spreading through Italy 'like a contagious disease'.[15] Further, this figurative portrayal of disease played on the already important place of plague in ancient historiography – Thucydides' description of the plague at Athens (430–426 BCE) in Book 2 of his *History of the Peloponnesian War* is one of the more popular pericopes of ancient history-writing[16] – by imputing to human social action what had already been observed (by some) of epidemiological reality: the capacity to 'catch,' spread and harm.[17] Such metaphors became particularly prominent in the work of Roman authors such as Sallust and Lucan, who discussed civil war in terms of a 'disease' of state;[18] Josephus will have been

---

appears nearly at the end of his seven-book *Jewish War*, suggesting that the correlation of sedition and disease may have formed a core part of how he understood the Judaean uprising that led to the Roman-Jewish War, or at least the eventual Jewish 'death' it effected.

[13] Josephus, *Jewish War* 2.11, 2.264, 3.443, 4.376, 6.337; see Steve Mason, *Flavius Josephus: Translation and Commentary, Volume 1B – Judean War 2* (Leiden, 2008), 214 n. 1660.

[14] Steve Mason, *A History of the Jewish War: AD 66–74* (Cambridge, 2016), 14.

[15] 'Velut contagione morbi': Livy 39.9.1 (LCL 313, 230). Benjamin Isaac notes that such Roman 'attacks on Greek culture and Asiatic customs' were extended to the Jews as well: *The Invention of Racism in Classical Antiquity* (Princeton, NJ, 2004), 385, cf. 479; see also Livy 28.34.4.

[16] Thucydides' description 'has been immensely influential to subsequent plague narratives in Western literature', not least in its literary function of using plague to discuss religious and moral decay: Peter Hunt, 'Thucydides on the First Ten Years of War (Archidamian War)', in Ryan K. Balot, Sara Forsdyke and Edith Foster, eds, *The Oxford Handbook of Thucydides* (Oxford, 2017), 125–45, at 139.

[17] 'Individuals probably noticed contagion well before recorded history and Thucydides makes it clear that some people were afraid to approach plague victims for fear of catching the disease (Thucy. 2.51.5). Nevertheless, the historian himself deserves the credit of being the first writer clearly to operate within a model of contagion, something that was not formally proposed again until the sixteenth century and not fully accepted until the nineteenth century': Hunt, 'First Ten Years', 139.

[18] For example, Sallust *Bellum catilinae* 10.6; Lucan *Bellum civile* 3.322; cf. Livy 28.27.11, 29.6.3.

influenced by such a milieu as a historian in Rome writing explicitly about (Jewish) civil war. Pseudo-Hegesippus, who also knew both Sallust and Lucan, goes even further, building upon Josephus's characterization of Jewish factionalism as a sickness to portray not just the Jewish rebels, but the Jews in general as a diseased, and thus dying, people.

This article will show how Pseudo-Hegesippus develops an original 'rhetoric of contagion', moving far beyond his major source, by referencing a series of passages which have no direct parallel in Josephus's *Jewish War*. This is significant, because much of *De excidio*'s narrative consists in loose translations or paraphrases of Josephus's earlier Greek work. Just as significant is the literary nature of the passages to be discussed: we find Pseudo-Hegesippus's rhetoric of the 'contagion of the Jews' expressed most frequently and most fully in character speeches.

Speeches attributed to various characters in the narrative were a constituent and important feature of ancient historiography.[19] They allowed historians to frame, explain and interpret their narratives in terms of variegated perspectives and possibilities. Numerous scholars have contributed to our understanding of ancient historiographical speeches in recent decades.[20] The most important points to note here are that speeches in ancient histories were not what such speeches would be expected to be in modern histories: they were not presented as verbatim transcripts of things said, but were understood as the kinds of things that particular people would, should or could have said in particular scenarios. Such speeches were evaluated in terms of plausibility, as well as aesthetic quality and rhetorical style, not what we would dub 'accuracy'.[21] Thus, although the passages treated below are imputed to various characters within *De excidio*'s narrative, they evince ways in which

[19] See Dennis Pausch, ed., *Stimmen der Geschichte. Funktionen von Reden in der antiken Historiographie* (Berlin, 2010).
[20] John Marincola, 'Speeches in Classical Historiography', in idem, ed., *A Companion to Greek and Roman Historiography*, 2 vols (Malden, MA, 2007), 1: 118–32.
[21] The best known presentation of this argument is A. J. Woodman, *Rhetoric in Classical Historiography: Four Essays* (Portland, OR, 1988), which deals at length with speeches in Thucydides surrounding the plague at Athens (ibid. 32–9); see also M. J. Wheeldon, '"True Stories": The Reception of Historiography in Antiquity', in Averil Cameron, ed., *History as Text: The Writing of Ancient History* (London, 1989), 33–63.

Pseudo-Hegesippus constructed meaning via the interplay between imagined authorial and character perspectives.

THE DISCOURSE OF JEWISH DISEASE IN *DE EXCIDIO*

Early in his work, in Book 1, Pseudo-Hegesippus alters a fundamental aspect of Josephus's own disease discourse, thereby signalling the anti-Jewish rhetoric of contagion to be developed throughout *De excidio*. In describing the reign of the little-loved Judean king Alexander Jannaeus (103–76 BCE), Pseudo-Hegesippus speaks of a *domestica seditio* and *contentio* which led to war, and he calls these uprisings *pestis* ('a plague'),[22] following Josephus's metaphorical model. But Pseudo-Hegesippus goes beyond Josephus when he identifies this 'sickness' as a kind 'familiar to the Jews'.[23] Now, instead of just describing Jewish factions, the metaphor of sedition as disease becomes a pockmark of the Jews in general: in *De excidio*, the Jews are stereotyped as a people who carry the contagion of civil unrest.

While Pseudo-Hegesippus attributes the disease of sedition to the Jews in general, we will explore further below how the manifestation of this 'illness' is also shown to be specifically symptomatic of the Jewish factions and their rebel leaders per se,[24] again as in Josephus's oeuvre. Thus, in Book 4, where Pseudo-Hegesippus reports how John of Gischala fled Galilee and entered Jerusalem, there to stir up trouble, he describes him as doing so 'like some kind of disease' (*quasi quaedam pestis*) which 'infected' (*infecit*) the minds of many.[25] Elsewhere John is called a 'pestilential virus'

---

[22] See briefly Estève, 'L'Oeuvre historique', xxii.

[23] 'Hos bellandi successus domestica seditio interpolauit, et orta conuiuiis usque ad bellum contentio processit familiari peste huiusmodi Iudaeorum uiris, ut de epulari ludo sese in arma excitant' ('A domestic rebellion interrupted these successes in war, and the dispute, having arisen in social gatherings, advanced to war by a plague of the sort familiar to the men of the Jews, that they stir themselves to arms from festive play'): *De excidio* 1.9.3. This is a creative and subtle expansion of Josephus, *Jewish War* 1.88. The dative plural *uiris* here ('[to] the men') may also be playing on the Latin term *uirus*, which can mean 'virus'. On ideology as a disease (*pestis*) or contagion (*contagio*) which may spread, see also *De excidio* 1.39.1, cf. 1.37.6–7.

[24] See also ibid. 3.22.1, 4.11.1.

[25] 'Fugiens ut supra diximus, de Galilaeae partibus Iohannes ad Hierosolymitanam urbem se contulit et quasi quaedam pestis infecit animos conplurium, qui ex diuersis regionibus principes flagitiorum eo quasi in sentinam confluxerant' ('Fleeing the regions of Galilee, as we explained above, John betook himself to the city of Jerusalem and, as if some kind of disease, he infected the minds of many, who, leaders of the scoundrels from

(*pestilens uirus*).[26] Nor is John's 'sickness' incidental to Pseudo-Hegesippus's narrative. The very next sentence begins: 'this, therefore, was the cause of the destruction of that great city'.[27] In other words, the seditious contagion of which John was a representative was the primary cause of Jerusalem's destruction. In this Pseudo-Hegesippus agrees with Josephus, who also identified Jewish sedition as the effective cause of the destruction of both Jerusalem and the Temple.[28] Josephus even allowed what we will soon see Pseudo-Hegesippus aver: that this internal self-destruction had a level of prophetic inevitability to it.[29] However, as an examination of Pseudo-Hegesippus's rhetoric of contagion will reveal, the Christian author drew rather different conclusions from these events than had his Jewish predecessor.

It is at this point that we begin entering territory within *De excidio* which does not have parallels in Josephus's earlier Greek work. The passages discussed below occur in speeches which *De excidio* creatively reworked and expanded what the author had found in Josephus (when he found anything at all), so that the passages themselves are original to Pseudo-Hegesippus. Thus they not only illustrate how *De excidio*'s anti-Jewish rhetoric of contagion functions within the narrative's broader logic, but they also demonstrate that Pseudo-Hegesippus wielded this discourse as an original and independent historian in his own right.

We begin with *De excidio* 5.2.1, arguably the most striking and important speech in the entire work.[30] In that speech, a second-person address by the author or narrator to the city of Jerusalem (and by proxy to the Jews), Pseudo-Hegesippus dramatizes, describes, explains and frames the destruction of Jerusalem, which the remainder of the work will narrate. The address begins, notably, by

---

diverse regions, had come together there even as in a cesspool'): ibid. 4.6.1 (paralleled in Josephus, *Jewish War* 4.122).
[26] *De excidio* 4.4.5.
[27] 'Hoc enim illi urbi maioris causa excidii fuit': ibid. 4.6.1.
[28] Nicolas Wiater, 'Reading the Jewish War: Narrative Technique and Historical Interpretation in Josephus's *Bellum Judaicum*', *Materiali e discussioni per l'analisi dei testi classici* 64 (2010), 145–85.
[29] Like Jesus in the gospels of Matthew and Luke: see William den Hollander, 'Jesus, Josephus, and the Fall of Jerusalem: On doing History with Scripture', *HTS Theological Studies* 71 (2015), 1–9.
[30] As argued in Bay, 'The Bible, the Classics, and the Jews'.

summoning five biblical figures as a kind of cloud of witnesses to behold the Jerusalem and Jews to, about and over whom Pseudo-Hegesippus speaks. These are Moses, Aaron, Joshua, David and Elisha.[31] Each hero is introduced with reference to one or more of his most famous legacies within biblical tradition. In introducing Aaron, Moses's brother and Israel's celebrated inaugural high priest, Pseudo-Hegesippus says: 'Arise, Aaron, you who once, when death was devouring the majority of the people because they had offended the omnipotent God, stood between the living and the dead, and death was stayed and the plague clung to your body, which was thrown forward, nor was it able to become a contagion among the living'.[32] Pseudo-Hegesippus introduces Aaron as an ancestral *exemplum* in terms of his heroic actions in Numbers 16: 41–50: there, following yet another rebellion on Israel's part against God's ordained leaders (Moses and Aaron), God strikes the people with a plague, which Aaron must check, censer and incense in hand. Pseudo-Hegesippus recalls this major moment of Aaron's priestly mediation by way of introduction: Aaron was one who prevented death (*mors*) from plague (*lues*), which could have become a contagion (*contagio*) among God's people.

Why does Pseudo-Hegesippus introduce Aaron this way? One answer seems to be that this scene was in Pseudo-Hegesippus's mind a key episode from the Bible, relevant to later Jews in several respects. Out of seven passages in *De excidio* in which Aaron is mentioned, three specifically reference this story from Numbers 16.[33]

---

[31] See on this passage Carson Bay, 'Jewish National Decline and Biblical Figures as Classical Exempla in Pseudo-Hegesippus: Moses, Aaron, Joshua, David, and Elisha at *De Excidio* 5.2.1', *JBR* 7 (2020), 167–204.

[32] 'Exsurge, Aaron, qui aliquando, cum propter offensam dei omnipotentis mors plurimos populi depasceretur, stetisti inter uiuentes ac mortuos, et mors stetit atque obiectu corporis tui haesit lues nec transire potuit ad contagionem uiuentium': *De excidio* 5.2.1.

[33] Ibid. 3.16–17, 5.2.1. Aaron is also mentioned in 2.12 (twice), 2.13 (twice), 5.9, 5.16. Even beyond this, the rebellions of Numbers 16 seem to have loomed large in Pseudo-Hegesippus's memory, as they emerge again in a mention of Dathan and Abiram (Numbers 16: 1–27) as models of divine judgment in Antipater's speech: *De excidio* 1.44.8. At 3.16.1, Josephus's Jewish comrades cite Aaron as an example of willingness to die as a good leadership trait, as part of an attempt to dissuade Josephus from capitulating to the Romans, recently victorious at Jotapata: 'Vbi est Aaron, qui inter uiuos ac mortuos medius stetit, ne mors uiuentem populum saeuo contagio depasceretur' ('Where is Aaron, who stood in the middle between the living and the dead, lest death consume the living populace with a savage infection?'). In 3.17.1, Josephus responds that Aaron's action was an instance of *uirtus*, not *temeritas*.

Another answer, however, appears inductively from an examination of the speech of *De excidio* 5.2.1 which follows Aaron's introduction. There it becomes clear that what Aaron represents in the speech is a kind of national priestly leadership that is willing and able to stave off death and disease from God's people. The ancient Israelites had this in Aaron; the first-century Jews manifestly lacked it, at least after killing their own legitimate priests Ananus and Jesus (not the Jesus of the gospels) and then rejecting and crucifying the true high priest (from a Christian perspective), Jesus Christ. Indeed, Pseudo-Hegesippus alludes to Aaron again in delineating this with reference to Aaron's staff, whose miraculous budding (Numbers 17) is explicitly said to have characterized ancient Israel's divine blessing, and whose present (figurative) absence embodies the divinely abandoned state of the first-century Jews:

> Ananus and Jesus – chief priests – lay unburied within you, and these men who not long ago were clothed in priestly robes, who were held in honour even by foreigners, lay with deformed corpses, fodder for birds and food for dogs, with their limbs removed and scattered throughout the whole city, so that a spectacle of ancient sanctity might be seen to mourn such an affront of the sacred name and such deformity of the once brilliant office [of priest]. ... And previously the priestly staff blossomed even though cut off from its wooden root, but now faith withers and piety has been buried and all emulation of virtue is departed. It is no wonder if a people which has turned away from God and follows after the vile spirit of opposition has been divided against itself. For how would he have been able to hold onto his peace who had repudiated the peace of God? Christ is the peace of God who made the two one. For this reason, from one people many have rightly been turned against themselves, because, divided, they did not want to follow Jesus, who was bringing harmony, but rather, united, they followed the divisive spirit of fury. Therefore you were receiving a just reward for your faithlessness, Jerusalem, when you destroyed your ramparts with your own hands, when you tore out your entrails with your own swords, so that the enemy had pity on you, and he spared you so that you might rage.[34]

---

[34] 'Iacuerunt in te Ananus et Iesus insepulti sacerdotum principes, et illi dudum sacerdotalibus amicti stolis, qui uenerationi etiam exteris fuerant, deformi iacuerunt cadauere, escae uolatilium et deuoratio canum, membra laceri et tota dispersi urbe, ut deplorare ueteris sanctitatis species uideretur tantam sacri nominis contumeliam et speciosi quondam muneris deformitatem. ... Ante et uirga sacerdotalis floruit recisa de siluestri radice, nunc et fides aret et sepulta est pietas et abiit omnis uirtutis aemulatio. Nec mirum si populus, qui a deo recessit et improbum contradictionis spiritum sequitur, in se ipsum

In other words, Aaron – or his staff – provided what might be understood as a sacerdotal vaccine to ancient Israel whereby that people was able to avoid the disease of civil dissent (what Pseudo-Hegesippus here calls the 'vile spirit of contradiction', *improbus contradictionis spiritus*). *De excidio* 5.2.1, therefore, evinces a creative interpolation of biblical imagery, Christian theology and rhetorical exemplarity: the cultural practice, perfected by the Romans, of using ancient figures to embody ideals and thus interpret and evaluate current events.[35] This complex serves to illustrate how Aaron, who historically shielded Israel from a literal plague caused by sedition, provides a sharp contrast to the unprotected Jews of 70 CE, who in Pseudo-Hegesippus's narrative are dying of a disease comprised of sedition.

De excidio 5.2.1 perpetuates Pseudo-Hegesippus's rhetoric of Jewish contagion by playing on various kinds of sickness, both historically and in his narrative present.[36] Aaron had defended Israel from a plague in Hebrew antiquity, which provides a contrast to the situation of the narrative's present-day Jews, who were 'consumed by a very severe disease' (*grauiore morbo consumerentur*) while they were besieged inside Jerusalem's walls.[37] But even this sickness during siege experienced by the Jews emerges within a larger description of a polluted Jerusalem and Temple precincts, whose smell (and even taste) Pseudo-Hegesippus describes in detail. The dead bodies around the Temple had created a twofold ill, one which was both medical and ritual, such that 'human and divine things were equally spoiled and

---

diuisus est. Quomodo enim pacem suam tenere poterat qui pacem dei repudiauit? Pax dei Christus est qui fecit utraque unum. Merito ergo ex uno populo plures aduersum se facti sunt, quia noluerunt sequi diuisa consociantem Iesum, sed secuti sunt coniuncta diuidentem furoris spiritum. Soluebas igitur, Hierusalem, mercedem perfidiae tuae, cum ipsa tuis manibus destrueres munimina tua, cum tuis mucronibus foderes uiscera tua, ita ut hostis misereretur, ut ille parceret tu saeuires': ibid. 5.2.1.

[35] See Rebecca Langlands, *Exemplary Ethics in Ancient Rome* (Cambridge, 2018); Matthew B. Roller, *Models from the Past in Roman Culture: A World of* Exempla (Cambridge, 2018).

[36] Significantly, *De excidio* 5.2.1 is written in the style of a funeral oration, and it resembles in more ways than one the funeral oration Thucydides puts in Pericles's mouth immediately preceding the account of the plague of 430 BCE.

[37] When, a few lines later, Pseudo-Hegesippus speaks of a 'fury that was transferred from the dead to those who were still living' (*a mortuis in eos qui adhuc uiuerent furor transferebatur*), he may well have in mind the avenging plague said to have killed so many Israelites in Numbers 16, as discussed above. Pseudo-Hegesippus also describes the diseases spread among the Jews holed up in Jerusalem: ibid. 5.18.2.

polluted together, with all things being mixed' (*humana pariter atque diuina maculari ac pollui, permixta omnia*). Both epidemiological-physical and theological-religious disease characterize the plight of the first-century Jews, which, according to Pseudo-Hegesippus, related to, and was accompanied by, the contagion of civil dissent.[38] Nor does Pseudo-Hegesippus refrain from mentioning the would-be cure (*remedium*) which existed for the Jews: namely, Jesus Christ. In so doing, *De excidio* fuses Christian theology with the Roman historiographical habit, exemplified in Tacitus, of speaking of societal boons as *remedia*.[39]

De excidio 5.2.1 clarifies that different kinds of disease were, in the author's mind, causal factors in Jerusalem's demise. Ritual pollution, physiological ailments and civic sickness were interrelated parts of the diseased Jewish body politic which is the object and addressee of the speech in that chapter. But there was also another, contiguous party to these events: the Romans. At one point in the address, Pseudo-Hegesippus discusses how the Romans at times refrained from their active siege of Jerusalem because the Jews were doing their work for them by warring amongst themselves. However, Pseudo-Hegesippus explains this by saying of Jewish unrest, which might be viewed as a standard military tactic, that 'it was for this reason that the Romans preferred to be spectators rather than fighters, lest within your internally raging innards there be perceived a force at work more of contagion than of strength'.[40] Pseudo-Hegesippus's sideways attribution of a *manus contagionis* to the Jews here is a way of saying that the Romans' occasional abstention from battle was due, at least sometimes, not to the military threat the Jews posed, but to their 'viral' threat. Just before this Pseudo-Hegesippus describes Jerusalem as a body tearing itself apart, a rhetorical trend in Roman historical analysis epitomized in Lucan's *Pharsalia* (i.e. *De bello civili*).[41] Is Jerusalem's metaphorical sickness therefore

---

[38] See Bay, 'The Bible, the Classics, and the Jews', 148–99.

[39] See Tacitus, *Histories* 1.14.1, 1.20.3, 1.29.1, 1.37.4, 1.63.1, 1.83.1, 2.68.3, 3.54.1, 4.9.1, 4.46.4, 4.81.2; cf. Bay, 'The Bible, the Classics, and the Jews', 280–4; Rebecca Edwards, '*Deuotio*, Disease, and *Remedia* in the Histories', in Victoria Emma Pagán, ed., *A Companion to Tacitus* (Malden, MA, 2012), 237–59.

[40] 'Et ideo spectatores malebant esse Romani quam percussores, ne furentibus tuis inter se uisceribus manum admouere contagionis magis quam fortitudinis aestimaretur': *De excidio* 5.2.1.

[41] See Martin Dinter, *Anatomizing Civil War: Studies in Lucan's Epic Technique* (Ann Arbor, MI, 2013).

physiological or psycho-social?[42] In any case, Pseudo-Hegesippus adds to this, in the line directly preceding the one cited above, a theological element, saying to Jerusalem that God had fought against it as well. The suggestion in all of this is that the Jews of Jerusalem were understood by the Romans to be in some way 'contagious', sick with a disease whose symptoms were civil unrest and infighting and whose causes, it seems, were at least in part divinely sent.

DISEASE, THE DESTRUCTION OF JERUSALEM AND THE DEMISE OF THE JEWS

In this final section we follow the Roman and divine components of Jewish sickness as diagnosed by Pseudo-Hegesippus, introduced above, into what is arguably the most serious aspect of Jewish contagion in *De excidio*. We have already seen that Pseudo-Hegesippus's understanding of the Jews' diseased state was multifaceted and involved a theological component. We have also seen that *De excidio* presents the Romans as having recognized, and having tried to avoid, this Jewish epidemic. These features of the discourse become even more explicit and grave in a speech made by the Roman general (and future emperor) Titus towards the end of the work.

De excidio 5.40 is in many ways the most disturbing chapter in a generally disturbing history. There, we read Pseudo-Hegesippus's rewriting of a story recorded previously in Josephus's *Jewish War* (6.199–213), sometimes called the 'Maria Story'; it is the story of a mother caught up in the Roman siege of Jerusalem who, driven mad by starvation and harassment, proceeds to kill, cook and eat her infant son.[43] When Titus hears news of this, he is horrified. In *De excidio* he

---

[42] The connection between physical plague and self-mutilation was immortalized in the discussion of the Athenian plague in Lucretius, *De rerum natura*, e.g. 6.1199–1214, as discussed by Catharine Edwards, *Death in Ancient Rome* (New Haven, CT, 2007), 82–3, who notes that 'these references to self-mutilation have no precedent in Thucydides. For Lucretius, plague is a physical disaster but also – much more than for Thucydides – a moral calamity. … Social structures are undermined, moral values and ritual practices abandoned'. Edwards could be describing *De excidio*'s portrayal of Jerusalem at 5.2.1.

[43] See Carson Bay, 'The "Maria Story" in Greek, Latin, & Hebrew: The *Teknophagia* Episode (BJ 6.201–13) in Josephus, Latin Josephus, Rufinus, Pseudo-Hegesippus, and *Sefer Yosippon* with Introduction, Texts, Translations, Notes, & Commentary', *Judaica* 3 (2022), 1–105; Honora Howell Chapman, 'Josephus and the Cannibalism of Mary (*BJ* 6.199–219)', in Marincola, ed., *Companion to Greek and Roman Historiography*, 2: 419–26; eadem, '"A Myth for the World": Early Christian Reception of Infanticide

responds with an extended prayer-speech hybrid which, among other aspects, brings Pseudo-Hegesippus's rhetoric of contagion to new heights. The way that Pseudo-Hegesippus introduces Titus's reaction to the report is one of the more telling instances of anti-Jewish contagion rhetoric to be found in the whole of *De excidio*. We read:

> Upon hearing this [i.e. news of Maria's deed], Caesar cursed the contagion of the unhappy country and, lifting his hands to heaven, declared as follows: '... I, blameless, absolve myself to you from this contagion, whatever power you are who exists in heaven. ... May their own ruins cover it and hide it, lest the sun look upon the disease of the earth itself, lest the sphere of stars behold it; lest the breeze of the wind be defiled, and that cleansing fire arise.'[44]

The Latin term *contagium*, like *contagio* (with which it is often semantically and grammatically interchangeable), refers to 'contact' and carries the idea of 'infection, contagion, taint'.[45] Therefore Titus is here deploring not only Roman contact with the Jews, but the taint of that contact: the Jews are sick, and they threaten to infect the Romans. Maria's unthinkable deed becomes an embodiment of Jewish sickness that now threatens Roman civil health. Titus tries to deal with the disease by means of prayer, a kind of ad hoc apotropaic cure, absolving himself to 'whatever power exists' in heaven from the Jewish contagion he beholds before him in Jerusalem (*ab hoc contagio tibi me absoluo*). In Titus's speech we find again the correlation between epidemiology and theology (or, better, theodicy): the Jews are sick with an illness that manifests itself in self-harm, but this ailment also has divine implications. Titus does not want to 'catch' it, nor to appear before the divinity as if he had. But Titus's reaction to Maria's deed does not end with prayer.

---

and Cannibalism in Josephus, *Bellum Judaicum* 6.199–219', *Society of Biblical Literature Seminar Papers* 39 (2000), 359–78; eadem, 'Spectacle and Theater in Josephus's *Bellum Judaicum*' (Ph.D. dissertation, Stanford University, 1998), 58–121.

[44] 'Quo conperto Caesar exsecratus infelicis terrae contagium, manus ad caelum eleuans, talia protestabatur: ... Mundus ego ab hoc contagio tibi me absoluo, quaecumque in caelo potestas es. ... Operiant eam ruinae suae atque abscondant, mundi ipsius contagionem ne sol uideat, ne stellarum globus spectet; ne maculentur aurarum spiramina, purgatorius quoque ille exsurgat ignis': *De excidio* 5.41.2.

[45] Charlton T. Lewis and Charles Short, *A Latin Dictionary* (Oxford, 1879), *s.vv.* 'contagio', 'contagium'.

The final statement in Titus's quotation above comes near the end of his speech. To my mind it is among the most important manifestations of what is here referred to as Pseudo-Hegesippus's rhetoric of contagion. In the interim between the earlier statements quoted above and this final statement, Titus delivers a lengthy speech in which he explicitly stereotypes the Jews as a people – they are twisted, self-harming and destructive[46] – and considers and justifies at length what he sees as a necessary course of action: the destruction of Jerusalem, and thus the effective decimation of the Jews. This event is, of course, what *De excidio* is all about, as its title overtly suggests. What is important for present purposes is that Titus casts Jerusalem's destruction as necessary partly in the terms of Pseudo-Hegesippus's overarching Jewish-disease discourse: 'let the sun not look upon the contagion of the earth itself'. The land of Judaea, the Jewish people, constitute a plague that must be quarantined, quashed, lest it infest the elements and the universe itself. This fits well with the statement of Pseudo-Hegesippus mentioned earlier that the *pestis* embodied in John of Gischala is said to have been the *causa* of Jerusalem's destruction.[47] In the passage at hand, Pseudo-Hegesippus uses the Roman general Titus as a mouthpiece to reinforce his own perspective as a historian that the destruction of Jerusalem, the effective end of the Jews, represented the needful hygienic eradication of a diseased people. World history is not unacquainted with those who have viewed such group or ethnic eliminations as 'cleansings'. Titus's final statement about a 'cleaning fire' (*purgatorius ignis*), an ancient Stoic idea, somehow resonates uncomfortably with such a notion. But the point here is that Titus's speech marks the Jewish 'disease' not only as the ultimate cause of Jerusalem's destruction, but also as a visible reality whose symptoms sparked the Roman response to the epidemic.

The fact that Titus prays to some undefined deity in his speech at *De excidio* 5.41.2 introduces a final, though no less important, element into the equation. Like Josephus, Pseudo-Hegesippus recognizes in Jerusalem's destruction a divine hand linked to ancient

---

[46] This involves the example of Abraham and his infamous near-sacrifice of his son Isaac (the *Aqedah* from Genesis 22), as ancestors definitive of the national character: see Carson Bay, 'Exemplarity, Exegesis, & Ethnography: Abraham in Pseudo-Hegesippus as a Test Case for Biblical Reception in Christian Late Antiquity', *JBR* 8 (2021), 35–59.

[47] *De excidio* 4.6.1.

prophecy.[48] But the couching of this viewpoint in contagion language sets *De excidio*'s theological perspective apart. At *De excidio* 5.16.1, Pseudo-Hegesippus scripts the second of two consecutive speeches given by Josephus qua historical actor (former Jewish general turned Roman captive-client-ambassador) to his Jewish countrymen trapped behind the walls of Jerusalem (in what follows Josephus is discussed as the historical character of *De excidio*'s narrative, not as author of the *Jewish War*). In an effort to convince his comrades to lay down arms and bow to the inevitable Roman *imperium*, Josephus in these speeches is made to present extensive, sweeping recollections of Hebrew history to make his case that resistance is futile and capitulation is the virtuous, right and only option. Josephus also states unequivocally the cause of the current Jewish plight: internal strife and sedition. Eventually his argument turns theological. Using biblical *exempla* who are, as we already saw above, rather familiar to *De excidio* and especially to its discourse of Jewish contagion, Pseudo-Hegesippus has Josephus wax eloquent:

> No wonder if divine favour has departed from the Jews, whom so many shameful things had walled in. For surely, a good man will flee his home and desert his house, full of horror, if he learns that some crime has been committed in it – he refuses to be associated with a dishonourable household, and he abhors the iniquities of those who abide there; and shall we doubt concerning the highest and immaculate God, that he would abhor the taint of such shameful things, and that he would turn away from such deadly crimes, lest he be delayed within the marketplaces of murderers, he who commanded that Dathan and Abiram be separated from the innocent, because they had challenged Moses and Aaron for claiming the priestly office, lest either their stain contaminate the pious by their proximity to the innocent or their punishment engulf them?[49]

---

[48] *De excidio* 1.16.3, 5.2.1, 5.31.2, 5.32.1.

[49] 'Nec mirum est si recessit a Iudaeis diuina gratia, quos tanta flagitia circumuallarunt. An uero bonus uir plenum horroris refugit diuersorium et domum suam deserit, si quid in ea commissum sceleris agnouerit, declinat indignae habitationis consortia, execratur conuersantium iniquitates: et dubitamus de summo et immaculato deo, quod abhorreat tantorum contagia flagitiorum, et funestorum scelerum auersetur atrocitatem, nec demoretur in parricidarum conciliabulis, qui Dathan et Abiron, quia Moysen et Aaron praeripiendo sacerdotii munere lacessiuerant, separari ab innoxiis praecepit, ne pios aut macula contaminaret de consortio noxiorum aut poena inuolueret?': ibid. 5.16.1. This part of this speech, based upon a shorter and rather different speech in Josephus, *Jewish War*

Here Pseudo-Hegesippus takes ideas found in Josephus, *Jewish War* 5.412–15, and couches them in the language of contagion, adding key biblical *exempla* as illustrations of the argument. The picture painted by Josephus's *sententia* here is of a God who is *immaculatus* and as such fundamentally averse to the *contagium* of the Jews' shameful deeds. As a historical illustration of what God is like, furthermore, Josephus cites the rebellion of Dathan and Abiram against Moses and Aaron, a rebellion which resulted in the divinely mandated quarantining, and then the exceptional destruction, of the offending party.[50] The upshot of this section of Josephus's speech is that God, the final historical cause of Jerusalem's destruction, is presented as having abandoned the Jews for reasons of sanitation and hygiene: like the disease of rebellion evinced by Dathan and Abiram, the Jews are diseased and thus have the potential to contaminate (*contaminare*). For this reason, Pseudo-Hegesippus has Josephus say that it is 'no surprise' that *diuina gratia* has departed from the Jews.

The above passage appears in one of the sections of *De excidio* where Pseudo-Hegesippus is at his most creative and most expansive as a historian in departing from his historical source. In other words, it is a passage of great import for understanding Pseudo-Hegesippus in general. The section quoted above, along with other passages discussed earlier, suggests that at a basic level Pseudo-Hegesippus understood the divine rejection of the Jews to be an attempt to reduce contagion. The Jews of the first century, whom *De excidio* effectively depicts as the 'final Jewish generation' in history, were diseased. Their sickness exhibited interrelated symptoms, including civil war, ritual pollution and at times even literal, physiological disease. Pseudo-Hegesippus implies that such sickness was communicable and that it was understood as such both by the Romans (embodied in Titus) and by God. Clearly this lies at the centre of *De excidio*'s historiographical logic, inasmuch as it speaks directly to the ultimate and

---

5.376–419, builds upon certain theological ideas presented there: see 5.392, 413, and specifically 5.413–15.

[50] After Dathan and Abiram, along with Korah, rejected the authority of Moses and Aaron in Israel, the Lord prescribes their punishment. The first thing Moses says to the congregation is: 'Depart now from the tents of these wicked men, and touch nothing that belongs to them, or you will be swept away in all their sin' (Numbers 16: 26, NASB). Thereafter Dathan, Abiram and all their goods and relatives are swallowed alive by the earth.

mediate causes of Jerusalem's destruction. Pseudo-Hegesippus's anti-Jewish rhetoric of contagion is not a peripheral part of *De excidio*; it is the very germ of the work's historical logic and narrative rhetoric.

CONCLUSION

Even aside from a rather impressive argot related to disease,[51] *De excidio* demonstrates an apparent familiarity with the institutions related to health and sickness in the author's day.[52] Furthermore, the later Roman world in which this text was written was one familiar with the realities of plague, disease and epidemic, even if the fourth century was something of a 'golden age' which largely avoided such devastations.[53] Thus, Pseudo-Hegesippus's rhetoric of Jewish disease is in some ways unsurprising to find in *De excidio* as a work, and within the late Roman Empire as a culture. Further, as noted above, Pseudo-Hegesippus was writing within an ancient Mediterranean *koinê* which had already developed many of the metaphorical tools that he applies to his discourse of Jewish disease. In a way, then, Pseudo-Hegesippus's deployment of disease language to realize anti-Jewish depiction is an extension of discursive habits, informed by his own *habitus*, that extend far beyond these particular rhetorical aims. As a Christian text of the late fourth century, *De excidio* is in good company in presenting his anti-Jewish rhetoric of contagion: John Chrysostom is another Christian author who routinely refers to Jewish ritual and Jewishness as a disease in his *Discourses against*

[51] In *De excidio* one finds the terms *aeger / aegra / aegrum* and *aegritudo* twelve times each, *contagio / contagium* fourteen times, *febris* four times, *medicabilis* once, *medicamentum* four times, *medicinus / medicina* three times, *morbus* eleven times, *noxius / noxia / noxium* eleven times, *pestilens* once, *pestis* seventeen times, *pestilentia* five times and *plaga* seven times. Sometimes these terms are used literally, sometimes figuratively. The brevity of this article prevents a full survey of this vocabulary of sickness within *De excidio*.
[52] An interesting and accidental example is in Pseudo-Hegesippus's mistranslation of the Greek verb ξενοτροφεῖν ('to hire foreign troops') from Josephus, *Jewish War* 1.61 by the Latin *xenodocheia*, a reference to a system of institutional healthcare whereby the poor and indigent were cared for and which emerged, apparently, in the mid-fourth century CE: see Mark Anderson, 'Mistranslations of Josephus and the Expansion of Public Charity in Late Antiquity', *EME* 25 (2017), 139–61, discussed in Bay, 'Pseudo-Hegesippus at Antioch?', 116.
[53] See Kyle Harper, *The Fate of Rome: Climate, Disease, & the End of an Empire* (Princeton, NJ, 2017).

Judaizing Christians.[54] All these things – intertextual evidence, context of writing, sources and inspirations, broader literary-rhetorical milieu – help make sense of Pseudo-Hegesippus's discourse of Jewish contagion. In a text such as *De excidio*, such a discourse is unsurprising, even *de rigeur*.

At the same time, however, Pseudo-Hegesippus's rhetoric of Jewish contagion marks a singularity within ancient Christian literature. For *De excidio* applies its discourse of Jewish disease to the widespread Christian historiographical dilemma of explaining the Jews out of history, as it were. Many authors may have talked about Jews and Jewishness in terms of disease – ironically, for Pliny the Younger had said the same of Christians in his famous tenth *Letter*[55] – but far fewer constructed a historicized rhetoric of Jewish contagion as a way of diagnosing the effective end of the Jews. Pseudo-Hegesippus was far from unique in making figurative use of disease language; but his specific application of that language is distinctive: *De excidio* exudes an original and pointed play on this extant trope which serves poignantly and multifariously to imbue an anti-Jewish historiographical vision.

Noting the antiquity of the figurative use of disease in his essay 'Culture and Contagion', Marvin Pernick makes a critical note about interpreting such metaphorical usage:

Although *contagion* has served as a metaphor for centuries, distinguishing the figurative from the literal usages depends on the specific historical and literary contexts. It is anachronistic to assume that every use that does not fit modern bacteriologic meanings must have been intended metaphorically. Since Greek and Roman antiquity, religion, ideas, and emotions have often been seen as literally linked with physical health. Calling sin or grief 'contagious' could be a metaphor, but it could also be meant quite literally. Since imbalances of the mind and soul were widely believed to cause and reflect physical disease, mental states might be seen as transmitted by a physical *contagion* or might themselves actually be the poison of disease *contagion*.[56]

---

[54] See *Contra Iudaeos* 1.1.5, 1.4.4, 2.1.1, cf. 8.7.8–12; also *St John Chrysostom: Discourses against Judaizing Christians*, ed. Paul W. Harkins (FOTC 68), especially xxxix, 267.
[55] Pliny the Younger, *Epistula* 10.96.9 refers to Christians as a *contagium* and as a *superstitio*; cf. Tacitus, *Annals* 44.4.
[56] Martin S. Pernick, 'Contagion and Culture', *American Literary History* 14 (2002), 858–65, at 860.

In other words, we should beware of mapping our own modern assumptions and worldview onto a metaphor-employing discourse such as Pseudo-Hegesippus's rhetoric of Jewish contagion. Adjectives such as 'literal' and 'metaphorical' used in this article may in reality be misleading, for it seems very likely that Pseudo-Hegesippus would not have recognized a reading of (say) civil dissension as disease as anything other than literal. And indeed, as George Lakoff and Mark Johnson have most famously shown, the way that we as humans apprehend the world is, quite literally, usually a matter of metaphor.[57] When Pseudo-Hegesippus talks about what he perceives as problems within the social history of the Jews in terms of disease and contagion, he is merely betraying the fact that he is human: human minds function in terms of metaphors; it is their fundamental *modus operandi*.[58]

For Pseudo-Hegesippus, the corporate sins of the Jews – moral, ritual and religious – constitute a 'disease'. But there is no good reason to assume that Pseudo-Hegesippus would have disassociated such an idea from, say, physical disease. Indeed, as this essay has shown, his disease rhetoric itself ignores any real boundary between physical and conceptual sickness: the contagion of the Jews, witnessed by Titus and God, was what we would call a 'metaphor' but is presented as having literal physiological correlates and real historical consequences. *De excidio*'s anti-Jewish discourse of contagion is 'real' and had real implications as well, carried as it was by one of the more popular and influential texts of Late Antiquity.[59] Inasmuch as such an idea spread through subsequent streams of Christian thought and discourse, we might be justified in seeing Pseudo-Hegesippus's discourse of Jewish contagion as a kind of ideological disease all its own.

---

[57] George Lakoff and Mark Johnson, *Metaphors we live by* (Chicago, IL, 1980).
[58] Steven Pinker, *How the Mind works* (New York, 1997), 355–62.
[59] See Richard Matthew Pollard, 'The *De Excidio* of "Hegesippus" and the Reception of Josephus in the Early Middle Ages', *Viator* 46 (2015), 65–100.

Bede on Sickness, Episcopal Identity and Monastic Asceticism

Jessica Collett*

University of St Andrews

The value of bodily affliction as a means for integrating an active life of good works on earth with the contemplative values of heaven, prior to the return of Christ and the world's end, remains relatively unexplored, despite suffering saints being a common medieval trope. Using the work of Gregory the Great and the Venerable Bede, this article seeks to explore the interrelation of an active contemplative life and bodily affliction to shed light upon Bede's use of Gregory and his presentation of Cuthbert's episcopate to forge a distinctive understanding of the links between bodily illness, episcopal identity and the biblical ordering of time, as that ordering finds expression in biblical eschatology and apocalyptic.

Bodily suffering and physical affliction are rarely seen as an affirmation of one's identity in our contemporary world. In contrast, early medieval monasticism viewed bodily sickness and affliction as hallmarks for the identification of saints in the church and to the world. Physical suffering places the saints on an interior stairway or pathway of ascent to God, transforming it from a burden to a means of personal assurance that one is God's own. While this view appears to be commonly recognized in medieval scholarship,[1] the value of bodily affliction as a means for integrating an active life of good works on earth with the contemplative values of heaven, prior to the return of Christ and the world's end, remains relatively unexplored.

* 31 Lamberton Place, St Andrews, Fife, KY16 8YE. E-mail: jrc29@st-andrews.ac.uk.
[1] See Donald Mowbray, *Pain and Suffering in Medieval Theology: Academic Debates at the University of Paris in the Thirteenth Century* (Woodbridge and Rochester, NY, 2009); Caroline Walker Bynum, *Holy Feast and Holy Fast: The Religious Significance of Food to Medieval Women* (London, 1987); eadem, 'The Female Body and Religious Practice in the Late Middle Ages', in M. Feher, ed., *Fragments of a History of the Human Body Part 1* (New York, 1989), 160–220, where she argues that bodily affliction offers union with the divine; E. M. Ross, *The Grief of God: Images of the Suffering Jesus in Late Medieval England* (Oxford, 1997).

Studies in Church History 58 (2022), 28–45 © The Author(s), 2022. Published by Cambridge University Press on behalf of Ecclesiastical History Society
doi: 10.1017/stc.2022.2

In his *Life of St Cuthbert*, the Venerable Bede draws upon the concept of *longa aegritudo* (prolonged sickness) and martyrdom in Gregory the Great's *Dialogues* to mediate a Joban model of suffering piety by presenting Cuthbert's illness and death as a pedagogical model for advancing Gregory's vision of the active contemplative life for church leadership.[2] For example, Gregory's *Moralia in Iob* and *Regula pastoralis* use the biblical story of Job as an interpretative model for uniting works of piety with contemplative reflection on the theological realities of final judgment and the next life.[3] Bede extends this Joban ideal to the question of episcopal identity and church leadership in the context of monastic asceticism, with Cuthbert's life serving as a case in point. Bede's portrayal of Cuthbert exemplifies the widespread medieval trope that physical sickness and suffering is the route to God and the source of one's personal assurance of salvation, but it also provides a model for the shaping of episcopal identity and the reform of monastic asceticism in Bede's own day. This article seeks to explore the interrelation of these threads to shed light upon Bede's use of Gregory and his presentation of Cuthbert's suffering to forge a distinctive understanding of the links between bodily illness, episcopal identity and the biblical ordering of time, as that ordering finds expression in biblical eschatology and apocalyptic writings.

It is helpful to begin with the Joban ideal which Bede inherited from Gregory, in order to appreciate his use of models for shaping

---

[2] *Vita sancti Cuthberti prosaica auctore Beda*, in Bertram Colgrave, transl. and ed., *Two Lives of Saint Cuthbert* (Cambridge, 1940; reprinted 1985), 142–307 (hereafter: *Vita Cuthberti prosaica*). *Gregorii Magni Dialogi*, ed. U. Moricca (Rome, 1924; hereafter: *Dialogi*).

[3] Gregory's *Regula pastoralis* (SC 381–2) was completed in the same time frame as the *Moralia* and advances many of the same directives to church leaders. See R. A. Markus, *Gregory the Great and his World* (Cambridge, 1997), 19–21, 29, who observes that 'a fair number of mini-treatises in the *Moralia* anticipate the pastoral advice' of the *Pastoral Rule*, much of which 'had been foreshadowed in the scarcely penetrable jungle of the *Moralia*' (ibid. 20–1); cf. George Demacopoulos, 'Gregory's Model of Spiritual Direction in the *Liber Regulae Pastoralis*', in Bronwen Neil and Matthew Dal Santo, eds, *A Companion to Gregory the Great* (Leiden, 2013), 205–24, at 211. The most prominent of these shared directives is Gregory's concern to balance 'the *contemplatio* of the isolated ascetic and the *actio* of the well-trained administrator': idem, *Five Spiritual Models of Spiritual Direction in the Early Church* (Notre Dame, IN, 2007), 135; see also Carole Straw, *Gregory the Great: Perfection in Imperfection* (Berkeley, CA, 1988), 247–51, especially 250; Straw, 'Gregory's Moral Theology: Divine Providence and Human Responsibility', in Neil and Dal Santo, eds, *Companion to Gregory*, 177–204, at 191–2. For examples, see Gregory, *Regula* 1.2, 1.5, 2.7.

church leadership through illness and suffering. Commonly known as St Gregory the Great, Pope Gregory I was a well-known figure in the early medieval church. He was bishop of Rome from September 590 until his death in March 604 and is most remembered for his writings and instigation of the Gregorian mission, an effort to convert the pagans of England to Christianity. Although one might run into trouble in some circles by claiming him as a medieval pope, rather than a pope of Late Antiquity, his continuing influence in the Middle Ages cannot be questioned: 'Throughout the Middle Ages, Gregory was acknowledged as a master of the spiritual life. The *Moralia in Iob*, a commentary in the Old Testament Book of Job and Gregory's longest work, was copied and circulated for centuries across medieval Europe.'[4] The key to Gregory's continuing influence lay in his 'minute exposition of self-control, in his ability to transform suffering and trial into spiritual progress ... Does not the Lord chasten every son he receives?'[5] For Gregory, suffering has value, not only because of the transience of this world, but because in suffering the saints find the fortification and renewal of their relationship with God: 'The suffering of the flesh improves the welfare of the soul; wounds inflicted on the body cure wounds of the soul.'[6]

Bede's awareness of Gregory's *Moralia* has been documented by Michael Lapidge and is evident from the many references to it in Bede's expositions and commentaries on Genesis, Samuel, Proverbs, the Song of Songs, Ezra, Mark, Luke, Acts, the Catholic Epistles and Revelation, as well as Tobit, and his *De tabernaculo*.[7]

---

[4] Neil and Dal Santo, 'Editors' Preface', in eidem, eds, *Companion to Gregory*, xvii–xxv, at xviii.

[5] 'The passage Gregory cites of Paul expresses his acceptance of life's ambivalence, and the love enabling him to endure it: "I know both how to be brought low, and I know how to enjoy abundance: everywhere and in all things I am instructed both to be full and to be hungry; both to abound and to suffer need. I can do all things through Christ who strengthens me" [Phil. 4: 12–13]': Straw, *Gregory the Great*, 27; cf. Gregory, *Homiliae in Hiezechielem* 2.7.15 (CChr.SL 142, 329; hereafter *Homiliae*).

[6] Straw, *Gregory the Great*, 45; Gregory, *Moralia* 33.19.35 (CChr.SL 143B, 1705–6).

[7] Michael Lapidge, *The Anglo-Saxon Library* (Oxford, 2005), 210–11. Bede was aware of Philipp the Presbyter's earlier commentary on Job, as is evident from a reference in his *De temporum ratione*: Lapidge, *Anglo-Saxon Library*, 222. Philipp, a student of Jerome, may have influenced Gregory's *Moralia*. Although it remains speculation, some scholars believe that Bede produced his own version of a commentary on Job by reworking Philipp's commentary: see Kenneth B. Steinhauser, 'Job in Patristic Commentaries and Theological Works', in Francis T. Harkins and Aaron Canty, eds, *A Companion to Job in the Middle Ages* (Leiden, 2017), 34–70, at 43–51, 69–70, especially 45. On Bede's library,

Bede's affection for Gregory's pastoral vision runs deeply throughout his works, which can make it difficult for Bede's interpreters to isolate the strands of Gregory's influence in his writing, especially his exegesis.[8] Nevertheless, an understanding of the influence which Gregory's view of active spirituality had within the church of Bede's day can help the modern reader discover these strands. Carole Straw argues that Gregory overcomes the dualistic tensions in Paul's 'dialectic of flesh and spirit to stress the reciprocity and complementarity of the carnal and spiritual sides of experience, whether in active and contemplative lives, adversity and prosperity, virtue and sin, or even God and the devil'.[9] For Gregory, the elect are those who glow with the light of the love and grace of God, in contrast to those who dwell in 'an inner darkness that nothing can illumine'.[10] Such favour is not capable of being earned through word or deed. Rather, as Jane Baun rightly observes, it is by God's grace that the saints are his elect, although this should not encourage presumption on their part: 'And none should presume certainty as to his own status, or that of others – an oft-repeated theme in the homilies, which emphasize the hidden nature of the identity of the elect. Jesus' chilling saying, "Many are called, but few are chosen" (*multi sunt uocati, pauci uero electi*) runs like a mantra through the final sections of Homily 38.'[11] As these observations anticipate, and this article hopes to show, Gregory's use of Job's bodily sickness as a model for promoting his episcopal vision seeks to integrate the contemplative graces of heaven enjoyed by the elect with the active life of good works on earth. Because this union serves as a figure of the coming union of heaven and earth at Christ's return, Gregory's approach to physical illness cannot be

---

see Lapidge, *Anglo-Saxon Library*, 34–7; Rosalind Love, 'The Library of the Venerable Bede', in Richard Gameson, ed., *The Cambridge History of the Book in Britain*, 1: c.*400–1100* (Cambridge, 2012), 606–32.

[8] Dom Paul Meyvaert, *Bede and Gregory the Great,* Jarrow Lecture 1964, in Michael Lapidge, ed., *Bede and His World*, 1: *The Jarrow Lectures, 1958–1993* (Aldershot, 1994), 103–32; Scott DeGregorio, 'The Venerable Bede and Gregory the Great: Exegetical Connections, Spiritual Departures', *EME* 18 (2010), 43–60.

[9] Carole Straw, 'Gregory's Moral Theology', 179.

[10] Jane Baun, 'Gregory's Eschatology', in Neil and Dal Santo, eds, *Companion to Gregory*, 157–76, at 170; see Gregory, *Moralia in Job* 4.11.19 (CChr.SL 143, 176–7), 9 (CChr.SL 143, 456–533), 15 (CChr.SL 143A, 749–98), 16.26.31–27.33 (CChr.SL 143A, 817–18).

[11] Baun, 'Gregory's Eschatology', 170; cf. Matt. 22: 2–14, 20: 1–16.

appreciated apart from the eschatological framework in which he locates the realities of bodily suffering and death.

The Interpretive Framework of Gregory's Moralia

To appreciate further Bede's use of Gregory, it is important first to clarify the interpretative context in which he approaches the nature of Job's sickness and suffering, along with its value for monastic life.[12] Building upon the work of Carole Straw, Susan Schreiner argues that the 'rule' or interpretative framework through which Gregory reads Job consists of two presuppositions that we must be aware of if we are to understand Gregory's motivations.[13] The first is that reality exists within a hierarchical scale and ontological continuum that links the lower historical levels of existence with the highest level (God) in order to create a chain of being. The second is that an understanding or perception of the true nature of reality can only be gained by an inward ascent from the lowest to the highest level of reality, which is made possible through suffering.[14]

Although Schreiner's reading of Gregory offers some important insights, it has a tendency to locate the pressures at work in Gregory's reading of Job's suffering and bodily affliction within the thought world of Neoplatonism. For Gregory, however, the book of Job is a theological reflection on the suffering of a particular man viewed within the biblical eschatology of creation, and his exegesis reflects this perspective. Indeed, as Baun affirms, his eschatological exegesis 'lifts the book above all the unresolved questions that plague a literal reading, offering the believer a life's model, and a way of understanding, that can turn doubt into trust, lament into praise, desolation into consolation, and despair into hope'.[15] The contrast we see in the *Moralia* between this world and the next is

<hr/>

[12] For more on Gregory and his work, see George E. Demacopoulos, *Gregory the Great: Ascetic, Pastor, and First Man of Rome* (Notre Dame, IN, 2015); Markus, *Gregory the Great*; Jeffrey Richards, *Consul of God: The Life and Times of Gregory the Great* (London, 1980); Straw, *Gregory the Great*.
[13] Straw, *Gregory the Great*, 28–46; cf. Susan Schreiner, *Where shall Wisdom be found? Calvin's Exegesis of Job from Medieval and Modern Perspectives* (Chicago, IL, 1994), 24; Straw, 'Gregory's Moral Theology', 179–82, especially 180: 'The two worlds are joined materially, being literally continuous.'
[14] Schreiner, *Where shall Wisdom be found*, 23.
[15] Baun, 'Gregory's Eschatology', 163.

not a vertical or ontological contrast between the temporal and eternal worlds of Neoplatonism, but a horizontal and historical contrast between this world and the eternal world to come, a contrast rooted in the New Testament and the eschatology of the apostle Paul.[16] This rule for reading history makes a distinction between this transient world,[17] which is passing away under the sentence of sin and death, and the world to come, where the saints of God will experience the *visio Dei* or beatific vision of God. The contrast between these two worlds is not metaphysical but ethical: this world is passing away, not because its transience marks it as a less real world, but because it is under God's judgment. Commenting on Job 3: 18, Gregory writes:

> Thus it is well said by Paul, For the creation is made subject to vanity, not willingly, but for the sake of him who subjected it in hope; because the creation itself will be liberated from the bondage of corruption, into the glorious liberty of the children of God [Rom. 8:20–1]. For 'the creation is made subject to vanity, not willingly', because human beings, who willingly deserted the state of inborn constancy, being pressed down by the weight of a deserved mortality, involuntarily serve the corruption of their mutable condition. But this creation is then rescued from the bondage of corruption, when it will be raised by being elevated to the incorruptible glory of the children of God.[18]

For Gregory, it is not the transient character of the world that brings about the deserved mortality and ethical corruption of humankind, but the fact that Adam '*willingly* deserted the footing of *inborn constancy*'. Given the passing character of this world and the certainty of its end in God's final judgment, Gregory's main concern is with the object of our desires in this world, rather than with a hierarchical view of reality. What is the object of our desires? Are they focused on that

---

[16] According to the letters of Paul, Christ's death and resurrection usher in the new reality of heaven and earth. For example, Rom. 8: 22–5 NRSV: 'We know that the whole creation has been groaning in labour pains until now; and not only the creation, but we ourselves, who have the first fruits of the Spirit, groan inwardly while we wait for adoption, the redemption of our bodies. For in hope we were saved. Now hope that is seen is not hope. For who hopes for what is seen? But if we hope for what we do not see, we wait for it with patience.'

[17] Gregory, *Moralia* 17.9.11 (CChr.SL 143A, 857–8).

[18] Gregory, *Moralia* 4.34.68 (CChr.SL 143, 213), cf. 8.8.13 (CChr.SL 143, 390–1), 8.10.19 (CChr.SL 143, 395–6), 12.13.17 (CChr.SL 143A, 638–9). In these passages Gregory appeals to Rom. 8: 20–2, describing the world as 'corruptible' and under the bondage of sin. All translations of the *Moralia* are mine unless otherwise noted.

which is passing and subject to the bondage of corruption, or that which is eternal?

The focus of our desires lays bare what we are truly living for, whether that is this world and its passing desires, or the world to come.[19] The problem arises from the disordered desires with which the saints of God continue to struggle due to the corruption of the flesh. As a result, the object of their desires is divided, and a holy conflict arises even within the saints between their desire for the things of this passing world and their desire for the beatific vision of God in the world to come, as Gregory observes: 'Are they not firmly bound by an inflexible chain of vexation, who, when their inflamed soul draws them with full desire into the bosom of inner peace, suffer disturbance from the flesh in the heat of the conflict?'[20] For this reason, as James Palmer observes, worldliness is the real problem for Gregory, rather than the world's imminent end:

> Gregory the Great repeatedly urged his audiences not to fear the world's passing for this reason: the world was transitory and not worth loving … In many ways, the imminence or not of the end is irrelevant in this mode of living: one has already divorced oneself from the things that will fall away in the End Times.[21]

Palmer rightly recognizes that biblical eschatology forms the primary force that motivates Gregory's approach to reform through suffering and apocalyptic. At the level of Gregory's basic commitments, neither Neoplatonism nor socio-political upheaval served to motivate his worldview or the value he placed upon suffering, although this is not to deny that they were contributing factors on some level. Rather, for Gregory, suffering is inherently linked to the passing character of

---

[19] Gregory, *Moralia* 1.25.34 (CChr.SL143, 43–4), 1.31.43 (CChr.SL143, 48), 17.9.11 (CChr.SL 143A, 857–8), 20.15.39 (CChr.SL143A, 1030–2), 27.17.33 (CChr.SL 143B, 1355–6); cf. 1 Cor. 7: 29–31 NRSV: 'I mean, brothers and sisters, the appointed time has grown short; from now on, let even those who have wives be as though they had none, and those who mourn as though they were not mourning, and those who rejoice as though they were not rejoicing, and those who buy as though they had no possessions, and those who deal with the world as though they had no dealings with it. For the present form of this world is passing away'; 1 John 2: 17 NRSV: 'And the world and its desires are passing away, but those who do the will of God live for ever.'

[20] Gregory, *Moralia* 4.34.68 (CChr.SL 143, 212).

[21] James T. Palmer, 'To be found Prepared: Eschatology and Reform Rhetoric *ca.*570–*ca.*640', in Matthew Gabriele and James T. Palmer, eds, *Apocalypse and Reform from Late Antiquity to the Middle Ages* (London, 2019), 31–49, at 42.

this world and its final judgment, which means that the value it has for reordering our desires and preparing us for the world to come cannot be separated from his views on biblical eschatology. The eschatological and apocalyptic narrative at work in the biblical ordering of time are what contribute to the Gregorian ideal of reform by serving a practical role and function in the life of the church. Commenting on Job 6: 19, Gregory therefore writes:

> But it is well said, wait a little; for it is often the case, that while the brevity of the present life is loved as if it were for a long time, the soul is broken loose from its eternal hope, and being seduced by present things, is thrown back by the darkness of self-despair ... They of course 'lose patience', who, while they reckon to dwell long among visible things, abandon the hope of the invisible. And while the mind is fixed on present things, life ends, and they are suddenly brought to unforeseen punishments, which, being deceived by their presumptions, they believed they would never meet with, or not until later. Hence the Truth says: Watch therefore, for you know neither the day nor the hour [Matt. 25: 13]. Hence it is written again, The Day of the Lord will come like a thief in the night [1 Thess. 5: 2]; for since it is never seen drawing near to seize the soul, it is compared to a thief in the night. It ought therefore to be understood as always coming, since it cannot be foreknown by us when it is about to come. Whence holy men also, since they incessantly gaze on the brevity of life, live daily as if they were dying; and thus prepare themselves more solidly for the things that will endure, in proportion as they are always meditating until the end that transitory things are nought.[22]

It is important to recognize that Gregory believed that the world in his own day was near its end.[23] Rome was in decline and the threat of the Lombards and the Greeks meant that the fate of Rome was

---

[22] Gregory, *Moralia* 7.30.45 (CChr.SL 143, 368–9), cf. 19.8.14 (CChr.SL 143A, 966), on Job 28: 28: 'Hence also it is said by the Psalmist: *The beginning of Wisdom is the fear of the Lord* [Psalm 111: 10], because it then begins to penetrate the heart, when it disturbs the heart by dread of the final judgment.' See also ibid. 3.21.41 (CChr.SL 143, 141–2), 8.8.14 (CChr.SL 143, 391–2), 27.17.33 (CChr.SL 143A, 869).

[23] 'Quia enim mundi iam tempora malis crebrescentibus termino adpropinquante turbata sunt, ipsi nos, qui interius mysteriis deseruire credimur, curis exterioribus implicamur': Gregory, *Epistola reverendissmo et sanctissimo fratri Leandro coepiscopo Gregorius servuus servorum Dei* 27 (CChr.SL143); cf. Gregory, *Dialogi* 4.43.

hanging in the balance.[24] This apocalyptic conviction greatly shaped Gregory's thoughts on the worth of suffering, the nature of the church and especially the shaping of its leadership. But the framework in which Gregory understands the interrelation of these things is strictly tied neither to political strife or social upheaval nor to the precise timing of the judgment, as Palmer observes: 'Apocalypse has also been taken seriously as part of traditions of biblical exegesis, many of which centred on ecclesiology (what the imagery said about the nature of the church) rather than on the timing and events of the Last Days specifically.'[25] Citing Bernard McGinn, Palmer also notes that apocalyptic thought is a continuous presence in the early church and medieval world, and not always tied to the presence of social upheavals or widespread bodily sickness, such as the plagues during the reign of Justinian in the sixth century. This suggests that there is not a direct correspondence between social-physical crises and the appeal to apocalyptic as a way to motivate behaviour and promote reform:

> Crucially, Gregory also saw little distinction between apocalyptic thought and the 'everyday eschatology' in which people were encouraged to be penitent for their sins so that they might still gain salvation. The pope saw the urgent need for people to prepare themselves for Judgement Day: whether those people died sooner or later, it was coming.[26]

The saints were to be prepared whether judgment was upon them today or tomorrow, which suggests that the precise timing of the end, while a topic for continuing speculation,[27] did not form the primary motivation for Gregory's interest in the world's end as a means of behavioural reform.

---

[24] Straw, 'Gregory's Moral Theology', 177; Gregory, *Regula* 3.29, 61 (CChr.SL 140, 175, 209–11), 11.37 (CChr.SL 140A, 931–2).
[25] Palmer, 'To be found Prepared', 32.
[26] Ibid. 31–2. See also Baun, 'Gregory', 157–8: 'Whether teaching, dispensing pastoral advice, responding to queries, ruling on papal matters, or writing to intimate friends, Gregory's conviction that all must face the Judge – *soon* – infused his every word and deed with urgency. Throughout his pontificate, Gregory's focus on the End and its implications for present-day behaviour was consistent, no matter who the audience; none escaped his call for increased eschatological mindfulness.'
[27] E. Ann Matter, 'Exegesis of the Apocalypse in the Middle Ages', in Michael Frassetto, ed., *The Year 1000: Religious and Social Response to the Turning of the First Millennium* (New York, 2002), 29–40, especially 36–7.

BEDE'S USE OF GREGORY ON SICKNESS AND SUFFERING

How did Bede appropriate these Gregorian Joban ideals, and in what ways do they shed light upon his understanding of the value of bodily sickness and affliction in this life? A useful lens for exploring these questions can be found in Bede's reworking of the earlier account of Cuthbert's life. Bede's prose reworking of the *Life of St Cuthbert* in 721, while a notable improvement on the style of an earlier anonymous *Life*, also included the addition of ten new chapters of material.[28] Cuthbert's enduring popularity from the Middle Ages to the present serves as an example of Bede's 'superior narrative gifts, his theological depth, and his ability to portray so arrestingly Gregory's idea of sanctity', as Foley puts it, providing a portrait of Cuthbert as one who embodies the Gregorian ideal of suffering unto death for the sake of union with Christ.[29] To this end, Bede's *Life* adds considerable detail in order to produce a longer account of Cuthbert's illness and death,[30] sharing 'verbal reminiscences' with Gregory's *Dialogues*, a work that Bede held especially dear.[31] Living during a time when persecution of the saints was largely a past reality, Bede looked to the *Dialogues* for models of martyrdom and saintly suffering which he could appropriate in his account of Cuthbert's life. In Bede's 'longer, grimmer, and more agonising account', we are presented with a struggling Cuthbert who stood firm against both physical and mental assault in the form of

---

[28] Bede wrote two versions of the *Life of St Cuthbert*. The first, written in metre, followed approximately seven years after the anonymous *Life*. Fourteen years later, Bede produced the prose *Life*. Bede's metrical *Life* expanded the treatment in the anonymous *Life* of Cuthbert's death, while the second prose *Life* expanded even further that of Cuthbert's illness and death. For more on the differences between Bede's earlier and later *Lives*, see Colgrave's introduction to *Two Lives*, 11–16; W. Berschin, '*Opus deliberatum ac perfectum*: Why did the Venerable Bede write a second prose Life of St Cuthbert?', in Gerald Bonner, David Rollason and Clare Stancliffe, eds, *St Cuthbert: His Cult and his Community to A.D. 1200* (Woodbridge and Rochester, NY, 1989), 95–102; W. Trent Foley, 'Suffering and Sanctity in Bede's *Prose Life of St Cuthbert*', *JThS* n.s.50 (1999), 102–16, at 102–5; Alan Thacker, 'Bede's Ideal of Reform', in Patrick Wormald, Donald A. Bullough and Roger Collins, eds, *Ideal and Reality in Frankish Anglo–Saxon Society* (Oxford, 1983), 130–53, especially 136–43.

[29] See *Vita Cuthberti prosaica* 28, 37–9, 43, where the Christian virtue of prolonged illness issuing in death is discussed with reference to the cases of Hereberht, Cuthbert and Eadberht; cf. Foley, 'Suffering and Sanctity', 114–15.

[30] Foley states that Bede's version of Cuthbert's ailments and death is almost twenty times longer than its counterpart: 'Suffering and Sanctity', 105.

[31] Colgrave notes Bede's debts to Gregory's *Dialogues* and describes it as 'a favourite work of Bede': *Two Lives*, 14, 16.

bodily affliction and demons.[32] What is surprising about Bede's account is the sheer quantity of examples of bodily ailments to which Bede alludes, 'ailments which are not miraculously cured, but typically end in death'.[33]

In his helpful study of Bede's prose *Life*, W. Trent Foley argues that Bede took over Gregory's theological reading of bodily affliction, noting that the Latin phrase *longa aegritudo* used in Gregory's *Dialogues* to describe the paralysed man named Servulus is used three times by Bede in the prose *Life* to describe prolonged bodily illness, leading to death in two cases (Hereberht and Eadberht).[34] This verbal link with Gregory's account of Servulus, as well as Gregory's description of Servulus's suffering unto death, appears to be the model on which Bede drew to present the deaths of Hereberht and Eadberht in his prose *Life*, both of whom are identified with Cuthbert in their deaths.[35] Thus, while Bede does not explicitly refer to Gregory's *Moralia* or the book of Job in his prose *Life*, the influence of Gregory's *Dialogues* in Bede's prose *Life* serves to mediate Gregory's Joban ideals of suffering in the form of the concept of *longa aegritudo* (prolonged illness), especially its theological application to illness, affliction and sanctity.[36]

These observations shed light upon the Gregorian ideal of sainthood and its influence on Bede. However, they do not explore the interpretative rationale that links the prose *Life* with Gregory's *Moralia* via the *Dialogues*. Neither the biblical figure of Job nor Cuthbert the martyr suffered for suffering's sake. Instead, their suffering serves as an embodiment of Christ's suffering unto

---

[32] See *Vita Cuthberti prosaica* 22, 37, 39–40, where Cuthbert is described as being stricken with agonizing pain in his limbs while also being under attack by demons; cf. Foley, 'Suffering and Sanctity', 102.

[33] Foley, 'Suffering and Sanctity', 103.

[34] The phrase is used to describe Servulus in Gregory, *Dialogi* 4.15. For references in the prose *Life*, see *Vita Cuthberti prosaica* 28, 32, 43, cf. ibid. 44, cited in Foley, 'Suffering and Sanctity', 110 n. 30. For references on *longa aegritudo* in Gregory's *XL homiliae in Euangelia 15*, see Foley, 'Suffering and Sanctity', 109 n. 38.

[35] Colgrave observes that the Anonymous *Life* 'has nothing to say of the sufferings endured by Hereberht in order that he might be accounted worthy to die on the same day as Cuthbert': *Two Lives*, 352.

[36] While Bede's prose *Life* does not cite the *Moralia*, the influence of its eschatology upon Bede's presentation of Cuthbert's theological values may be seen in *Vita Cuthberti prosaica* 22, where Cuthbert is described as one who knows how to refresh those who are afflicted in this life by reminding them of the joys of heavenly life in contrast to the fleeting pleasures and sorrows of this transient world.

death,[37] for it is the union of head (Christ) and body (Church) that gives theological and practical value to physical illness and suffering unto death in this life. The text of Colossians 1: 24 was often cited in Gregory's *Moralia* to justify this understanding of the relation between Christ's suffering and that of the Church.[38] This suffering unto death may be the result of external physical persecution or of bodily illness: according to Gregory both are to be viewed as forms of martyrdom. In the *Dialogues* he argues that the Gospels assure us that martyrdom is possible without external or public suffering, for there are two kinds of martyrdom: outward and one inward. Citing the examples of James and John in Matthew 20, Gregory reasons that although James was put to death, John was also made to drink from the cup of the Lord's suffering, even though he did not die as the result of persecution.[39] In this way Gregory reinterprets the earlier history of the deaths of martyrs, most of which were external and public, in order to appropriate that history for the monasticism of his day, along with its ideals. As Felice Lifshitz has argued, Bede later receives this history of martyrdom in the form of lists and transforms it into a narrative to serve as 'the liturgical pendant' to his *Historia ecclesiastica*.[40]

Building upon Gregory's account of martyrdom, Cuthbert's *longa aegritudo* is characterized by Bede as a sickness unto death in which God's elect experience the inward death of

[37] Bernard Green, 'The Theology of Gregory the Great: Christ, Salvation and the Church', in Neil and Dal Santo, eds, *Companion to Gregory*, 135–56, at 154–6.

[38] 'I am now rejoicing in my sufferings for your sake, and in my flesh I am completing what is lacking in Christ's afflictions for the sake of his body, that is, the church' (NRSV). For references in Gregory's *Moralia*, see Praefatio 6.14 (CChr.SL 143, 19–20), 1.24.33 (CChr.SL 143, 43), 3.13.25 (CChr.SL 143, 130–1), 6.1.1 (CChr.SL 143, 284), 23.1.2 (CChr.SL143B, 1144–5). Both Bede and Gregory follow the head / body principle in the exegesis of biblical texts, a principle used by Tyconius the Donatist and modified by Augustine. In his early work *De schematibus et tropis*, Bede appeals to Gregory's *Moralia* as a precedent for reading the church as an allegory of Christ's body: Gussie Hecht Tanenhaus, 'Bede's *de schematibus et tropis*: A Translation', *Quarterly Journal of Speech* 48 (1962), 237–53, at 252. For discussions of Augustine's use of the 'prosopological' exegesis founded upon this principle, see Michael Cameron, *Christ meets me everywhere: Augustine's Early Figurative Exegesis* (Oxford, 2012), 165–212; cf. Michael Fiedrowicz, 'General Introduction' to 'Expositions of Psalms 1–32', transl. Maria Boulding, *WSA* III/15, 13–66, at 50–60.

[39] Gregory, *Dialogi* 3.26; cf. Colgrave, ed. and transl., *Two Lives*, 315–16.

[40] Felice Lifshitz, 'Bede, Martyrology', in eadem, transl., Thomas Head, ed., *Medieval Hagiography: An Anthology* (New York, 2000), 169–97, especially 171–3.

martyrdom.[41] Prolonged suffering even to the point of death is a means through which a believer shares in the experience of Christ's incarnation and death on the cross, and thus to be martyred is to follow in the footsteps of Christ. Martyrdom is thus caught up in the mystery of Christ's death and the end of the world. Because Christ ascended to heaven after his death, foreshadowing the union of heaven and earth through his suffering unto death, the death of his saints also anticipates the union of heaven and earth at the end of time.[42] Like Gregory before him, Bede interprets suffering and martyrdom in the biblical framework of eschatology and apocalyptic.[43] However, according to Ann Matter, the early church espoused the 'radical assumption of the imminent end evident in the Apocalypse', while Bede's world and the Carolingian world that followed tended to read the Apocalypse as an allegory of the church in the present world: 'All the Apocalypse commentaries from the Carolingian world thus show the continuing assumption of the text as an allegory of the Church, and a continuing process of filtering specific interpretations from earlier commentaries to support that assumption.'[44] If 'apocalyptic' is understood to mean a concern with the imminent end of the world, rather than the shape of ecclesial life in the present world, then on Matter's reading of things it would be better to describe early medieval readings of Revelation as *anagogic* rather than *apocalyptic*. This helps us distinguish between the concern of Gregory and Bede to understand the nature of the Church in light of history's end (ecclesiological symbolism), and apocalyptic concerns with the timing of that end (apocalyptic symbolism). While these apocalyptic concerns were always present to some degree in the early medieval world, they become dominant only after Gregory and Bede.[45]

[41] Cuthbert is called a martyr by Bede in two places: *Vita Cuthberti prosaica* 15, 17.
[42] For general examples, see Gregory, *Dialogi* 4.49; cf. his account of the death of Benedict, ibid. 2.37; and Bede's account of the death of Cuthbert in *Vita Cuthberti prosaica* 39.
[43] *Bede: Commentary on Revelation*, transl. Faith Wallis, TTH (Liverpool, 2013); Robert Boenig, 'The Apocalypse in Medieval England', in Michael A. Ryan, ed., *A Companion to the Premodern Apocalypse* (Leiden, 2015), 297–330; George Hardin Brown, *A Companion to Bede* (Woodbridge, 2009), 69–70; Peter Darby, *Bede and the End of Time* (Farnham, 2012).
[44] Matter, 'Exegesis of the Apocalypse', 36.
[45] Ibid. 37.

These observations provide insight into the reason why the biblical account of Job's sickness and suffering was valued by both Gregory and Bede. On the practical level of human existence in this world, suffering is the means through which the contemplative values of the world to come are united with the active values of this present world. The actualization of this union through suffering, read in the light of the world's end, is thus a microcosm or anagogic figure of the final joining of heaven and earth at Christ's return,[46] as suggested by Matter's study of early medieval exegesis of the Apocalypse. The concern of Gregory and Bede with bodily sickness and the world's end thus arose out of a distinctly ecclesiological concern, namely, the integration of the active and contemplative life, a union which 'pulls' the contemplative values of heaven into the midst of this passing world. This is perhaps why both Gregory and Bede found in the book of Job a helpful model for reforming monasticism and shaping pastoral leadership in the church. The providential trial and suffering God brought upon Job, the man of action and good works (Job 1: 1–5), forced him to contemplate and reflect theologically on what those good works said about the nature of his piety. Was Job serving God for gain, as his accuser asserted? It was in his suffering that Job was forced to reflect on his actions and what they said about the nature of his service and obedience to God, and in this way he serves as a model of the active contemplative life by promoting their integration.[47] In its usefulness for integrating the contemplative and active spheres of existence in the life of the church, suffering anticipates in this life the 'expectation of the final joining of the spiritual and physical churches' made possible by Christ's passion on the cross.[48]

Bede's own model for illustrating this union finds expression in his *Life of St Cuthbert*. For Bede, Cuthbert was virtually a textbook example of Gregory's Joban ideals in practice, and also on a par with Benedict of Nursia, one of Gregory's heroes in the

---

[46] Cf. Straw, *Gregory the Great*, 39: 'In this traditional view of man as microcosm, Gregory sees man as an image of the whole universe and as a mediator participating in its various levels of existence.'

[47] See Demacopoulos, *Gregory the Great*, 57–60, especially 60: 'It is particularly significant that even though Job was not a priest, Gregory is able to emphasise Job's role as "preacher" and "holy man" precisely because he struck the proper balance of action and contemplation'; cf. Gregory, *Moralia* 6.37.56 (CChr.SL 143, 325–6).

[48] Matter, 'Exegesis of the Apocalypse', 36.

Dialogues.[49] Like Gregory before him, Bede held strongly to the belief that monastic spirituality is to be an active spirituality. Through the model of Cuthbert's episcopate, Bede sought to stress the importance of teaching *and* leading by example rather than by word alone. Both action and contemplation are needed, which required Bede to interpret Cuthbert's own spirituality along these same lines: 'In his prose *Life of Cuthbert*, for example, he removed many of the details from the earlier anonymous life depicting Cuthbert as a contemplative and instead stressed his role as an active and prayerful preacher.'[50] The means for this reinterpretation of Cuthbert, along with the editorial activity it produced, are found in Gregory's concept of *longa aegritudo* and Bede's shared concern to shape the church's episcopal leadership in light of biblical eschatology.

Sickness and Suffering in Bede's Portrayal of Cuthbert and Wilfrid

Bede's account of bodily sickness in the *Life of Cuthbert* allows him to bring together the active and contemplative life made possible through suffering, the glue that holds together word and deed in the life of the church. In this way, Cuthbert's life becomes the ideal embodiment of Gregory's teachings, over against Bede's near contemporary, Bishop Wilfrid, whose active life as a bishop lacked the needed inner dimension of 'suffering unto death' required for the proper integration of word and deed. Wilfrid functioned as an example of a bishop whose primary function was that of an administrator, rather than as a child and servant of the word who, through bodily illness and suffering, has learned how to integrate contemplation and action. Like Wilfrid, Cuthbert suffered persecution from worldly church leaders. But in addition to suffering persecution from Celtic schismatics and wicked monks, Cuthbert and his fellow brethren were also subject to prolonged bodily affliction.[51] By the theological standards Bede inherited from Gregory, this distinguished him from Wilfrid.[52]

[49] Alan Thacker, 'Bede and History', in Scott DeGregorio, ed., *The Cambridge Companion to Bede* (Cambridge, 2010), 170–89, at 182.
[50] Scott DeGregorio, 'The Venerable Bede on Prayer and Contemplation', *Traditio* 54 (1991), 1–39, at 6.
[51] Bede, *Vita Cuthberti prosaica* 22, 37, 39.
[52] Foley, 'Suffering and Sanctity', 114–15.

Bede depicted Cuthbert's relationship with Bishop Wilfrid as somewhat less than cordial.[53] Others suggest that Bede's 'frosty' demeanour towards Wilfrid in his *Historia Ecclesiastica* is the product of our own modern reading.[54] In light of the arguments put forth here, a more plausible explanation is that Bede's portrait of Wilfrid stems from his Gregorian ideals of what a bishop should be. It is not that Bede has a personal dislike for Wilfrid, or that we are committing the *faux pas* of a Whig historian by reading our own modern notions into the actions of an early medieval scholar and saint. Instead, the spiritual distance one senses between Cuthbert and Wilfrid in Bede's writings is a matter of the spiritual and moral compass Bede inherited from Gregory. Just as the Gregorian ideal calls for the integration of contemplative and active spirituality, so also it requires the integration of official and personal sanctity. Foley suggests that the scarcity of miracles attributed to Wilfrid's ministry in the *Historia Ecclesiastica* is due to the fact that for Bede, Wilfrid's piety was largely an 'official' sanctity, arising from the execution of his public duties as bishop, while Cuthbert's sanctity was not merely official, but also personal.[55] In Bede's eyes, Wilfrid failed to live up to the integrated piety of the Gregorian ideal found in bishops such as Cuthbert. The lack of this integration in the life of Wilfrid, at least when measured according to the Gregorian ideal Bede inherited from Gregory, helps explain the relative lack of miraculous attestation in Bede's account of Wilfrid's episcopate when compared to that of Cuthbert. Yet this does not make Wilfrid a bad bishop. He is merely not the *ideal* bishop.[56]

That the ideal for bishops forged by Gregory and inherited by Bede was not limited to the early mediaeval church is evident from Katherine Harvey's study of the thirteenth-century bishop Richard

[53] See Bertram Colgrave, introduction to *The Life of Bishop Wilfrid* (Cambridge, 1985), xii.
[54] See J. M. Wallace-Hadrill, 'Bede and Plummer', in Gerald Bonner, ed., *Famulus Christi: Essays in Commemoration of the Thirteenth Centenary of the Birth of the Venerable Bede* (London, 1976), 366–85, at 380.
[55] See W. Trent Foley, 'Suffering and Sanctity in Bede's *Prose Life of St Cuthbert*', 102–16. Foley's arguments grow out of his earlier study, *Images of Sanctity in Eddius Stephanus' Life of Bishop Wilfrid, an Early English Saint's Life* (Lewiston, ME, 1992).
[56] Foley tends to contrast official and personal forms of sanctity, while for Bede they are integrated. Bede did not think official sanctity was unimportant, but simply insufficient.

of Chichester.[57] Harvey's essay suggests that the genre of the *Vita* continued to serve as a model for sanctity well into the high Middle Ages, citing the thirteenth-century author Ralph Bocking's *Life of St Richard, Bishop of Chichester* as a notable case in point. While she does not mention Bede's writings on Cuthbert, his *Vita sancti Cuthberti* and Bocking's *Vita Sancti Ricardi* share in common the idea that the sanctity which arises from performing the duties of the office of bishop (official sanctity) is not enough to qualify a bishop to serve as a model of episcopal sanctity for future generations. In order for a particular bishop to qualify as a model and have a *Vita* written about them, a bishop must also possess personal sanctity. Someone can be a bishop who faithfully executes the duties of one's episcopal office in a way that is commendable, but in order to qualify as a 'Saint-Bishop' and not merely a good bishop, he also needs personal piety.[58]

Harvey also discusses the way in which this personal sanctity was achieved in Richard's life through his cultivation of proper attitudes toward food, drink and sleep. These mostly took the form of abstinence of some kind, for example, fasting from food and drink, as well as denying oneself sleep. Because these practices were integral to the idea of masculinity in Richard's day, they defined what the idea of a 'perfect man' consists in, namely, one who is able to control his body and its desires.[59] These practices demonstrated personal sanctity by showing that a man had mastery of his body and its desires. This aspect of sanctity had to be present, as well as the aspect of official sanctity. The two realms of the official and the personal must be integrated, hence the title of Harvey's essay: 'Perfect Bishop, Perfect Man.'

CONCLUSION

Just as the question of Job's sickness and suffering[60] was theologically significant for Gregory's vision of the episcopate, so also the question

[57] Katherine Harvey, 'Perfect Bishop, Perfect Man? Masculinity, Restraint and the Episcopal Body in the Life of St Richard of Chichester', *Southern History* 35 (2013), 1–22. I am indebted to the editors of SCH for this reference.
[58] Ibid. 3.
[59] Harvey notes that another historical factor shaping the ideal of the perfect man stemmed from the state of medical theory in Richard's day, which sought to eliminate sexual lust through immersion in cold water and bloodletting: ibid. 8.
[60] The continuing influence of Gregory's episcopal vision during the Reformation era is evident from Calvin's lengthy discussion of this vision in Book Four of his *Institutes of the Christian Religion*.

of why Cuthbert suffered was significant for Bede's monastic ideal for church leadership. Job and Cuthbert did not endure sickness and suffering for their own sake, but for the sake of their union with Christ, their head, and also for the sake of the cleansing renewal of the church's leadership. In the *Moralia* and the *Dialogues*, Bede found the needed resources for addressing the question of the value of suffering and bodily affliction, and his solution took the form of an interpretative rule that integrated the active and contemplative life through suffering, even prolonged suffering unto death (*longa aegritudo*). In this visionary and Joban ideal forged by Gregory for episcopal identity, Bede recognized his own belief that the active contemplative life should define monastic spirituality, an ideal that Bede also extended to the integration of official and personal sanctity in his *Life of St Cuthbert*.

Prolonged sickness and suffering unto death unite the contemplative values of heaven with our active life on earth, serving as a figure and anticipation in this life of the final union of heaven and earth at Christ's return. The integrative capacity of bodily sickness is a distinct quality of Gregory's exegesis that is also harnessed by Bede, especially in his prose *Life* of Cuthbert's episcopate, and also motivates his portrait of Cuthbert as a compelling example of this integrative model and Joban ideal. In this Gregorian vision of church leaders as the suffering servants of God, the experience of *longa aegritudo* and suffering unto death in this life prefigures the union of heaven and earth at Christ's return. Here biblical eschatology serves as the interpretative framework in which the integrative qualities of suffering are given purpose in this present life. In this way, the biblical ordering of time served the end of reforming the church's episcopal leadership, as well as the nature and desires of the saints in this life. In this reordering of desire through bodily suffering, Gregory's *Moralia* and *Dialogues*, along with Bede's *Life of St Cuthbert*, were literary tools by which to accomplish this purpose and promote its ideals.

Healing Body and Soul in Early Medieval Europe: Medical Remedies with Christian Elements

Claire Burridge*
University of Sheffield

The early medieval period has been traditionally cast as the nadir of medicine in the West. Such an image stemmed in part from the negative perceptions of 'superstitious' charms and incantations, in which medicine was seen to be detrimentally affected by Christian and pagan influences alike. This outdated view has been revised substantially, and the intersections between medicine and religion are now understood to reflect a complex, multivalent approach to healing. However, this re-evaluation of early medieval medicine, and especially of recipe literature, has concentrated primarily on Old English material. As a result, the substantial corpus of early medieval Latin continental recipes found outside the established canon of classical and late antique texts has largely been overlooked. This article seeks to redress this imbalance, offering the first systematic investigation into the ways in which Christian elements appear in these comparatively understudied pharmaceutical writings. The article's findings have significant implications for our understanding of Latin recipe literature and of the evolution of medical knowledge in early medieval Europe.

'[Collect] the herb betony with the Lord's Prayer. Let [the patient] take two ounces with honey for nine days.'[1]

These instructions, found in a ninth-century medical manuscript (St Gallen, Stiftsbibliothek, Cod. sang. 751), are located within a large, anonymous recipe collection that contains pharmaceutical

* Department of History, The University of Sheffield, Jessop West, 1 Upper Hanover Street, Sheffield S3 7RA. E-mail: c.burridge@sheffield.ac.uk.
I would like to extend my sincere thanks to the organizers of the 2021 EHS Winter Meeting for providing the original platform for this piece, as well as to Rosamond McKitterick, Meg Leja, the anonymous reviewers and the editors for their immensely valuable feedback.

[1] '[E]rba uittonica cum oratione dominica unci̲a. ii. ex melle accipiat /per dies viiii\': St Gallen, Stiftsbibliothek, Cod. sang. 751, p. 409. All translations and transcriptions are my own unless otherwise stated.

Studies in Church History 58 (2022), 46–67 © The Author(s), 2022. Published by Cambridge University Press on behalf of Ecclesiastical History Society
doi: 10.1017/stc.2022.3

information from a range of sources. The recipe is the final entry in a group of recipes derived from the late antique herbal *De herba vettonica liber*. Although it lacks a title in Cod. sang. 751, the parallel treatment in *De herba vettonica liber*, 'Ad tussim', offers a cure for cough. The two prescriptions provide the same pharmaceutical information, but their instructions differ in one respect: the original does not include the Lord's Prayer.[2] How should the addition of such an explicitly Christian feature be interpreted? Is this evidence for the symbolic Christianization of pre-Christian medical knowledge, an attempt to make potentially controversial writings more acceptable to a ninth-century readership? Did a scribe include this feature with the hope that it would increase the efficacy of the cough treatment, strengthening an existing recipe through the power of prayer? Could this simply be a statement of the scribe's faith? Or does it represent a combination of all these possibilities?

Prayers are not the only overtly Christian material to appear in early medieval recipes: some treatments include sacred ingredients, such as holy water or chrism; some involve other Christian rituals, such as instructions to make the sign of the cross or to prepare the recipe while mass is being said; and a number of recipes integrate multiple Christian elements within a single treatment. While these features do not appear with great frequency in early medieval recipe literature, their presence is noticeable and noteworthy. This article offers the first systematic study of Christian elements recorded in early medieval Latin recipes found outside established classical and late antique medical writings. It considers the types of Christian elements included in such recipes, the ways in which they are used and the ailments these recipes attempt to treat. This analysis, although not comprehensive, highlights patterns concerning the appearance of this material and uncovers significant individual findings. These results provide another perspective on the intersections between health, healing and Christianity – medicine and the church – in the early

---

[2] Pseudo-Antonius Musa, *De herba vettonica liber*, ed. Ernst Howald and Henry E. Sigerist, Corpus Medicorum Latinorum 4 (Leipzig, 1927), 3–11, at 7: 'Ad tussim: Herbae vettonicae uncias II cum melle accipiat per dies IX'. Note that the recipe in Stiftsbibliothek, Cod. sang. 751 uses the phrase *ex melle* instead of *cum melle* and could therefore mean 'let the patient take two ounces from a honey-based mixture'; I have translated it as 'with honey' since it seems plausible that this represents a deviation in the Latin due to the indirect transmission of the text.

medieval West, while simultaneously enriching our understanding of the place and evolution of medical knowledge in the Carolingian world.

Framing the Analysis

Although negative, reductive depictions of early medieval medicine remain common in popular culture, these outdated stereotypes have been effectively challenged and overturned by recent generations of scholars, and writings surviving from this period are no longer seen to offer only a simplified version of classical medical knowledge adulterated by 'primitive' folkloric or religious healing traditions.[3] Relatedly, many studies have demonstrated the inappropriateness of classifying medieval medical texts according to a modern, Western conceptual framework that distinguishes rigidly between 'medicine', 'religion', 'magic' and other familiar categories.[4] The present article offers another route into exploring these intertwined concepts by focusing on a traditionally overlooked genre of medical writing: Latin recipes recorded outside known classical and late antique texts or textual families, either as marginal additions or as independent recipe collections.

The long-standing focus on the inheritance and reception of classical and late antique medical texts has limited research into material that exists beyond this canon. Stemming from (and perpetuating) this preoccupation with the medical classics, the standard manuscript catalogues often label recipes and recipe collections outside this textual framework as 'miscellaneous', a term that obscures not only the

---

[3] Contrast, for example, John H. G. Grattan and Charles Singer, *Anglo-Saxon Magic and Medicine: Illustrated specially from the Semi-Pagan Text* Lacnunga (Oxford, 1952) with Katherine Park, 'Medicine and Society in Medieval Europe, 500–1500', in Andrew Wear, ed., *Medicine in Society: Historical Essays* (Cambridge, 1992), 59–90; John M. Riddle, 'Theory and Practice in Medieval Medicine', *Viator* 5 (1974), 157–84; Anne Van Arsdall, 'Challenging the "Eye of Newt" Image of Medieval Medicine', in Barbara S. Bowers, ed., *The Medieval Hospital and Medical Practice* (Aldershot, 2007), 195–206; Linda Ehrsam Voigts, 'Anglo-Saxon Plant Remedies and the Anglo-Saxons', *Isis* 70 (1979), 250–68.

[4] A few important studies are Peregrine Horden, 'Sickness and Healing', in Thomas F. X. Noble and Julia M. H. Smith, eds, *CHC, 3: Early Medieval Christianities, c.600–1100* (Cambridge, 2008), 416–32; idem, 'What's Wrong with Early Medieval Medicine?', *SHM* 24 (2011), 5–25; Lea T. Olsan, 'Charms and Prayers in Medieval Medical Theory and Practice', *SHM* 16 (2003), 343–66.

texts themselves but also their potential relationships with other writings.[5] Although these recipe collections are not attributed to any specific (late) ancient authority, their contents are closely related to earlier texts; as the example from Cod. sang. 751 with which this article opened illustrates, early medieval compilers brought together a range of sources in the creation of new collections. Classical and late antique texts, however, were not the only sources used to produce new compilations. Many works contain signs of non-classical influences, including the use of ingredients unrecorded in earlier Western medical traditions as well as the appearance of Christian rituals, incantations and ingredients.[6] Although a substantial number of these unattributed recipe collections survive (totalling thousands of recipes), few have been analysed in depth and the genre has received little attention overall given the traditional preference for studying the transmission of classical writings.[7]

In contrast, the much smaller corpus of early medieval recipes recorded in Old English has been comparatively well studied.[8]

---

[5] For a list of 'miscellaneous' medical material, including recipes, extracts and dietary notes, see Augusto Beccaria, *I codici di medicina del periodo presalernitano (secoli ix, x e xi)* (Rome, 1956). On additional problems with the traditional philological approach to studying early medieval medical writings, see also Faith Wallis, 'The Experience of the Book: Manuscripts, Texts, and the Role of Epistemology in Early Medieval Medicine', in Don Bates, ed., *Knowledge and the Scholarly Medical Traditions* (Cambridge, 1995), 101–26.

[6] On ingredients, see John M. Riddle, 'The Introduction and Use of Eastern Drugs in the Early Middle Ages', *Sudhoffs Archiv für Geschichte der Medizin und der Naturwissenschaften* 49 (1965), 185–98; Michael McCormick, *Origins of the European Economy: Communications and Commerce AD 300–900* (Cambridge, 2002), especially 708–19; Claire Burridge, 'Incense in Medicine: An Early Medieval Perspective', *EME* 28 (2020), 219–55.

[7] It is difficult to estimate the total number of surviving recipes, since many have yet to be transcribed. The present article is based on a sample of over six thousand recipes from twenty-nine manuscripts.

[8] Only six major recipe collections survive in Old English: three *Leechbooks* (*Bald's Leechbook I*, *Bald's Leechbook II* and *Leechbook III*), the *Lacnunga*, and translations of two late antique Latin recipe collections (the *Herbarius* of Pseudo-Apuleius and *Medicina de quadrupedibus* of Pseudo-Sextus Placitus). On these texts and their contexts, see, for example, Malcolm L. Cameron, *Anglo-Saxon Medicine* (Cambridge, 1993); Maria Amalia D'Aronco, 'The Transmission of Medical Knowledge in Anglo-Saxon England: The Voices of Manuscripts' in Patrizia Lendinara, Loredana Lazzari and Maria Amalia D'Aronco, eds, *Form and Content of Instruction in Anglo-Saxon England in Light of Contemporary Manuscript Evidence* (Turnhout, 2007), 35–58; Emily Kesling, *Medical Texts in Anglo-Saxon Literary Culture* (Woodbridge, 2020); Audrey L. Meaney, 'The Practice of Medicine in England about the Year 1000', *SHM* 13 (2000), 221–37;

Research into this material has played a central role in countering the negative stereotypes that surrounded early medieval medicine and the inappropriate application of modern conceptual categories, such as 'medicine', 'magic' and 'religion', to medieval medical writings. Detailed analyses of the 'extra-medical' aspects of recipes, including charms, incantations and symbolically significant ingredients, have addressed how these features appear in pharmaceutical texts and their importance for understanding the evolving healthscape of early medieval England.[9] In particular, Audrey Meaney's thorough assessment of extra-medical elements within Old English recipe collections has revealed that the texts most closely related to Latin exemplars include significantly less Christian material than those more loosely based on Latin sources.[10]

Problematically, however, when Old English recipe literature is compared to Latin continental recipe literature, the latter is generally treated as a single entity, and one based on the recognized, inherited texts of (Late) Antiquity without considering recipes found beyond this corpus. While the traditionally studied classical and late antique recipe collections, such as the Plinian family of texts or the herbals and bestiaries of the *Herbariencorpus*, include many extra-medical rituals, charms and incantations, they lack explicit references to Christianity or Christian(ized) material.[11] The handful of exceptions to this general picture, such as the two recipes within Marcellus's *De medicamentis liber* with Christian connections or the two recipes in the anonymous *De taxone liber* that contain Christian invocations,

---

eadem, 'Extra-Medical Elements in Anglo-Saxon Medicine', *SHM* 24 (2011), 41–56; Anne Van Arsdall, *Medieval Herbal Remedies: The Old English Herbarium and Anglo-Saxon Medicine* (New York, 2002).

[9] See especially Meaney, 'Practice of Medicine'; eadem, 'Extra-Medical Elements'. I follow Meaney in using 'extra-medical' as a more neutral term to describe this type of material: 'Extra-Medical Elements', 42.

[10] Ibid. 55.

[11] *Plinii Secundi Iunioris qui feruntur de medicina libri tres*, ed. Alf Önnerfors, Corpus Medicorum Latinorum 3 (Berlin, 1964); Yvette Hunt, *The* Medicina Plinii: *Latin Text, Translation, and Commentary* (Abingdon, 2020); *Physica Plinii Bambergensis (Cod. Bamb. Med. 2, fol. 93v–232r)*, ed. Alf Önnerfors (Hildesheim, 1975); Gerhard Baader, 'Die Anfänge der medizinischen Ausbildung im Abendland bis 1100', in *La scuola nell'Occidente latino dell'alto medioevo*, Settimane di studio del Centro italiano di studi sull'alto medioevo 19, 2 vols (Spoleto, 1972), 2: 669–718; John M. Riddle, 'Pseudo-Dioscorides' *Ex herbis femininis* and Early Medieval Medical Botany', *Journal of the History of Biology* 14 (1981), 43–81.

have been debated and do not offer unambiguous examples of Christian influence.[12] In short, the surviving classical and late antique recipe collections copied in the early Middle Ages lack Christian references within their prescriptions. This differs from much of the Old English material, where extra-medical elements incorporate Christian rituals and symbolism. From this perspective, early medieval recipe literature could be divided into the following groups:

a) Latin recipe literature from the Continent, consisting primarily of classical and late antique texts (and thus devoid of Christianized content);

b) Old English translations of this Latin material (correspondingly lacking Christianized content);

c) Old English recipe collections that combine a variety of sources, drawing on 'a common reservoir of medicines native to Europe generally' (including Christian elements).[13]

Yet, as the opening example shows, a division along these lines ignores many Latin continental recipes, namely those recorded outside established classical and late antique recipe collections. The remainder of this article investigates how Christian elements appear in this previously overlooked body of knowledge, analysing a sample of over six thousand recipes found in nearly thirty early medieval manuscripts, the vast majority of which have been dated to the ninth century (see Appendix 1 for a detailed description of the manuscripts under consideration). These codices were produced in writing centres across western continental Europe, with particular concentrations in the Rhineland, the area around Lake Constance and northern Italy, and thus offer a large and diverse sample. Only a relatively small percentage of the recipes under analysis have received much attention to date, and previous

[12] Regarding debates surrounding Marcellus's beliefs and the possible Christian elements in his work, see Miriam Ewers, *Marcellus Empiricus: 'De medicamentis.' Christliche Abhandlung über Barmherzigkeit oder abergläubische Rezeptsammlung?* (Trier, 2009); Anthony Corbeill, 'Miriam Ewers, *Marcellus Empiricus: 'De medicamentis.' Christliche Abhandlung über Barmherzigkeit oder abergläubische Rezeptsammlung?*', *Bryn Mawr Classical Review 2010*, online at: <https://bmcr.brynmawr.edu/2010/2010.06.10/>, last accessed 19 January 2022. Notably, the two Christian invocations found in *De taxone liber* appear only in the manuscripts of recension α, which includes the Old English translation, and are mentioned by Meaney ('Extra-Medical Elements', 43) as exceptions in the *Medicina de quadrupedibus*; for the recensions, see *De taxone liber*, ed. Ernst Howald and Henry E. Sigerist, Corpus Medicorum Latinorum 4 (Leipzig, 1927), 227–32.
[13] Cameron, *Anglo-Saxon Medicine*, 36.

work has generally concentrated on individual codices rather than multi-manuscript studies.[14]

CHRISTIAN ELEMENTS IN EARLY MEDIEVAL LATIN RECIPES

In this article, a recipe is described as including explicitly Christian features if it incorporates extra-medical elements that are unequivocally related to Christian rituals, spaces or substances. This definition is intentionally broad and flexible given the varied nature of this material; as delineated below, recipes present a diverse assortment of such Christian material, from prayers and rituals to holy ingredients. The following survey presents an overview of the data before considering what, where and how Christian elements were included in recipes as well as the ailments that these recipes were intended to treat.

First, nearly one hundred explicitly Christian features have been identified in sixty-four treatments, roughly one per cent of the recipes under analysis.[15] While this percentage may seem insignificant, it documents a major break with the classical material and a new development within pharmaceutical writing. Even if the handful of exceptions in late antique texts are taken into account, they represent such a miniscule fraction (the two recipes from *De medicamentis liber*, for example, comprise less than 0.1 per cent of the treatise's total number of recipes), that the sixty-four recipes within this sample still bear witness to a significant change.

When considering these examples in more detail, it becomes evident that Christian features appear at two primary stages within the

---

[14] Consider, for example, research on Bamberg, Staatsbibliothek, Msc.Med.1, including *Das Lorscher Arzneibuch: Ein medizinisches Kompendium des 8. Jahrhunderts (Codex Bambergensis Medicinalis 1). Text, Übersetzung und Fachglossar*, ed. and transl. Ulrich Stoll (Stuttgart, 1992); Gundolf Keil and Paul Schnitzer, eds, *Das Lorscher Arzneibuch und die frühmittelalterliche Medizin: Verhandlungen des medizinhistorischen Symposiums im September 1989 in Lorsch* (Lorsch, 1991); Klaus-Dietrich Fischer, 'Das Lorscher Arzneibuch im Widerstreit der Meinungen', *Medizinhistorisches Journal* 45 (2010), 165–88; Joel L. Gamble, 'A Defense of the Carolingian "Defense of Medicine": Introduction, Translation, and Notes', *Traditio* 75 (2020), 87–125. Although recipe collections in several early medieval manuscripts were transcribed by Henry Sigerist and Julius Jörimann in the early twentieth century, surprisingly little research has engaged with these publications: Henry Sigerist, *Studien und Texte zur frühmittelalterlichen Rezeptliteratur* (Leipzig, 1923); Julius Jörimann, *Frühmittelalterliche Rezeptarien* (Zurich, 1925).

[15] Since a single recipe may include multiple Christian elements, the numbers of recipes belonging to the various categories described below do not add up to sixty-four.

treatment process: (a) preparation, and (b) application and administration. The former, represented by (for example) rituals relating to the collection of ingredients, are seen in thirty-one recipes, while the latter, exemplified by the use of symbolic ingredients, are recorded in thirty-two recipes. In ten recipes, such as those ending with a Christian phrase (*in Christi nomine, in nomine domine*, etc.), Christian elements appear to play a less active role in the treatment process.[16] While these features are deserving of further research, the rest of the present analysis concentrates on the two main contexts in which Christian elements appear.

Instructions to say the Lord's Prayer, an example of which was seen in the opening recipe, are given in twenty-one recipes and represent the most frequently recorded Christian element in the preparation stage. Several additional instances can also be found in Cod. sang. 751, including a recipe intended to treat haemorrhoids: 'you collect a bundle of *losera*, which [others] call *mentastrum*, which is white mint, on a Thursday with a waning moon [and] with the Lord's Prayer. You mix [it] with thirty pepper grains and thirty grains of mastic in wine and let [the patient] drink [it] for three days. It is a cure.'[17] The instructions for collecting *losera* also provide directions regarding the timing of this activity. Similar extra-medical guidance naming specific days of the week, seasons, phases of the moon and other calendrical or astronomical information is found in just over half of the recipes that include the Lord's Prayer, a topic discussed below.

An entry in Cod. sang. 44 entitled *Ad lunaticos et cadiuos* ('for lunatics and epileptics') provides a further example of this connection between the Lord's Prayer and calendrical or astronomical information: 'ribwort, mistletoe from oak, agrimony, milfoil – you collect all this with the Lord's Prayer and, for four lunar cycles, give [it] to the fasting person to drink with holy water'.[18] The recipe showcases

---

[16] The *Antidotum sotira* of Stiftsbibliothek, Cod. sang. 44, pp. 234–6, ends with the phrase 'in nomine domini', for example, while a recipe on pp. 339–40 opens with 'IN CHRISTI NOMINE'.

[17] 'ITEM AD FICO erba losera que dicunt mentastrum idest menta alba collegis die iouis luna decurrente fasciculum cum oratione dominica piper grana. xxx. mastice grana xxx. \in/ uino distemperas et per tres dies bibat remedium. est': Stiftsbibliothek, Cod. sang. 751, p. 383.

[18] 'AD LUNATICOS. ET CADIUOS. Herba lanciolata. uiscu. ruborio agrimonia. milfolio. ista. omnia cum oratione dominica colligis. et per quattuor lunaciones das bibere ieiuno cum aqua benedicta': Cod. sang. 44, p. 358.

two other striking features that will be elaborated below but deserve a brief mention here. First, this is a treatment for madness and epilepsy, which, as following examples demonstrate, is a recurring trend. Secondly, the herbal ingredients are to be liquefied by the addition of holy water, *aqua benedicta*. This recipe thus combines Christian elements during both phases of the treatment process: the preparation incorporates a Christian ritual and the end product contains an explicitly Christian ingredient, not simply water but *holy* water.

A recipe to expel demons, recorded in Paris, BN, Lat. 9332, also involves multiple Christian elements; here, both occur during the treatment's preparation. The Lord's Prayer is again linked to the initial ingredient collection, and then the recipe describes how to make the potion, instructing the reader to mix an egg-full of the juice of danewort or dwarf elder with an egg-full of oil and an egg-full of old wine while a priest sings mass.[19]

A wide range of other types of Christian features can be seen during the preparation stage in addition to, or alongside, the Lord's Prayer. Some recipes suggest making a physical gesture, usually the sign of the cross. A remedy for stomach pain in Cod. sang. 44, for example, instructs that the sign of the cross should be made over an ingredient when preparing an ointment that will be applied topically to the stomach.[20] Other recipes include instructions for where or when to prepare a treatment related to spiritually significant places and times. Another remedy for demon possession found in Cod. sang. 44, for instance, states that the 'herb that is called *paniscardi*' should be collected at Easter and then put on the altar where mass is said that day.[21] The scribe left no doubt that Easter was the appointed day for this preparation to take place, writing that this process should occur on *dies resurrectionis domini* and adding *hoc est prima pascha*.

[19] 'Item collegis odecum idest euolus aput oratione dominica. et facis exinde ius ouo pleno oleo ouo pleno uino uetus ouo pleno totum insimul mitis et super sacerdos missa cantat ante a qui patitur triduana faciat et sic ieiunus bibat probatissimum est.' The recipe is one of several listed under the heading 'Ad demonio expellendo': Paris, BN, Lat. 9332, fol. 233va.
[20] 'AD STOMACHI dolorem. facis crucem christi. super herba ceruis lingua et ipsam de mel unguis. et super stomachum ponis': Stiftsbibliothek, Cod. sang. 44, p. 349.
[21] 'Remedium ad inmissiones diaboli. Herba quae dicitur paniscardi dies resurrectionis domini. hoc est prima pa\s/cha colligis ipsum cardo sine ferro uerticulo habet in suma radice et sit in altario. ubi ipsa die missa dicitur. et postea cui necesse fuerit. in aqua. aut in uino bibat. sanat': ibid., pp. 346–7.

Turning to the application stage, the use of ingredients with Christian significance has already been noted: holy water was named as an ingredient in a recipe in Cod. sang. 44.[22] Of the various ingredients derived from or associated with Christian rituals that are listed in recipes, holy water and incense occur most frequently. The former can also be found in two recipes from Cod. sang. 751; BAV, Pal. lat. 1088; and Bamberg, Staatsbibliothek, Msc.Med.1. Incense appears once in four different manuscripts: Cod. sang. 759; BAV, Pal. lat. 1088; BAV, Reg. lat. 1143; and Bamberg, Staatsbibliothek, Msc.Med.1.[23] Other substances associated with Christian rituals named as ingredients include chrism and the oil from holy candles. An entry in Msc.Med.1, for example, uses red incense, chrism and holy water in another treatment for epilepsy.[24]

In addition to these ingredients, Christianized rituals occasionally appear as active components in the administration of treatments. Like the rituals involved in the preparation phase, they most frequently take on spoken forms, varying in their level of detail. In one case, to help someone with something stuck in their throat, the reader (or whoever performs the cure) is instructed to say slowly 'Christ is from the virgin Mary born' into the patient's ear three times.[25] Most incantations and charms, however, are longer and more complex, such as a treatment in Cod. sang. 759 that offers protection against demons and fevers that covers half a folio.[26] It opens with a

---

[22] Ibid., p. 358.

[23] For holy water, see Stiftsbibliothek, Cod. sang. 751, p. 396: 'AD CADUCOS', p. 419: 'Ad caducas'; BAV, Pal. lat. 1088, fol. 33v: 'Ad lunaticos et cadiuos', fol. 62r: 'Curatio ad omnes febres uel typos' (specifically, the eighth recipe within a cluster under this title); Bamberg, Staatsbibliothek, Msc.Med.1, fols 39r–39v: 'AD EPILEMTICOS' (both recipes are found within a group of recipes under this title). For incense, see Bamberg, Staatsbibliothek, Msc.Med.1, fols 39r–39v: 'AD EPILEMTICOS'; Stiftsbibliothek, Cod. sang. 759, pp. 67–8: 'Ad mulierem ut partum eiciat'; BAV, Pal. lat. 1088, fol. 47v: 'Ad omnes typos'; Reg. lat. 1143, fol. 109r: 'Ad cadiuo homine'.

[24] 'Item incenso rubeo quantum duo dinarius pensant piper grana viiii gramastici granas viiii oleum benedictum quantum aestimaueris inter aqua exorcizata et uinum calices iii totum insimul mittat et deficiente luna ipsa die quando quinta est aut quando no[n]\u/ a euenit quinta sic bibat': Bamberg, Staatsbibliothek, Msc.Med.1, fol. 39v, in *Das Lorscher Arzneibuch*, ed. and transl. Stoll, 226–7.

[25] 'ITEM. aliut ad aurem eius. qui patitur in guttere spinam. dicis tercio. lenti. christus. de maria uirgi natus est': Stiftsbibliothek, Cod. sang. 217, p. 260a.

[26] 'Breue quod facit pro temtamenta diaboli uel frigoras portit super se hec scriptura. Per crucem domini nostri iesu christi parce per sanguinem domini nostri iesu christi parce per resurrexionem domini nostri iesu christi parce per ascentionem domini nostri iesu christi

Claire Burridge

series of formulaic expressions beseeching 'our Lord Jesus Christ' and
then lists a host of protective powers attributed to the cross, including
its ability to conquer venom, swords and the devil. Before closing, the
scribe names the archangels, who, in addition to the standard
Michael, Gabriel and Raphael, also feature Uriel, Raguel and Tubel.

Christian rituals that take a physical form may also be directly
involved in therapy. A recipe to treat an itchy skin condition, 'Ad sca-
bies', in Paris, BN, Lat. 13955, instructs that the afflicted area should
be 'baptized' (*baptizetur*).[27] Could this term have been used without
Christian overtones, simply meaning that the affected area should be
fully immersed? Given the word's general absence from the recipe literature in the context of bathing or washing, it seems highly unlikely
that its use here is entirely detached from a Christian meaning; rather,
labelling this therapeutic act as a baptism links the treatment to a
Christian context.

Finally, remedies may describe where or when a treatment should
occur, specifying a location or time with Christian significance. A
treatment for kidney pain in Cod. sang. 751, 'Contra renes dolorem',
offers one such example: after providing the instructions for a potion
involving *herba sancta*, Venus's hair, wine and pepper grains, the
reader is informed that the patient should drink this potion for six
days, starting on a Sunday, 'the day of the Lord [when] mass is performed in church'.[28] While these instructions about timing could
serve a purely practical function by helping the patient count the
days, the scribe's emphasis on the particular spiritual significance of

---

parce non percutias famulo di illo neque omnes homines habitantes mecum inter dico tibi per
patrem et filum et spiritum sanctum. Crux domini est signum mihi contra insidias tuas + crux
quam ego semper adoro + Crux mihi refugium + crux uincit uenenum + crux superet gladio +
crux uincit diabolo + crux aperit ianuas celi + crux adoranda per omnia deus benedictus in sec-
ula. obsecro uobis fortisimi et beatisimi harcahenli dei. michael gabriel rapahel oriel raguel
tubel et cum uirtut[u]is dei et potentia spiritus sancti iubet <.>tis illo saluare noctibus ac
diebus horis atque monementis de gladio maligno et de pustula et de omne contagione mor-
borum ds [note: 'ds' is lacking a mark of abbreviation but is probably intended to be read as
'deus'] forsimi adiuua illi': Stiftsbibliotek, Cod. sang. 759, p. 91.
[27] 'Item rubus elixa et trita hoc facit. Post allei combusti puluerem uulneri asperge. sal
tritum et in linteo ligatum et in aceto infusum. si ex hoc baptizetur uulnus uel infundatur.
sanguinem eicit': BN, Lat. 13955, fol. 147v.
[28] 'CONTRA RENES DOLOREM Erba sancta manipulos. iii. capillos ueneris manipulos
de uino staupos. vi. de piper grana. lvii. teris et distemperas et potionem exinde facias et per
sex manes bibis prima die dominico missa peracta in ecclesia bibat pleno staupo calido et
postea a per ebdoma da et multum adiuuat': Stiftsbibliothek, Cod. sang. 751, p. 407.

56

this day, through the explicit reference to the celebration of mass in a church, suggests that this specification simultaneously introduces a layer of Christian symbolism into the process.

This review of Christian elements has highlighted recipes that aim to cure a range of ailments, from kidney pain to throat obstruction. Within the examples above, treatments targeting epilepsy, madness and demon possession have been noted most frequently: twelve recipes with Christian features target these conditions. Particularly striking is that five of the six recipes that name holy water as an ingredient are intended to treat those suffering from this group of conditions. Although modern medicine may not see a connection between these afflictions, they are often grouped together in early medieval recipe literature: epilepsy, also known as the 'falling sickness', and madness were sometimes associated with demonic possession.[29] The strong correlation between demon-related conditions and holy water suggests that this Christian ingredient was noted for its properties in combatting demonic influences, perhaps being perceived as imbuing the treatment with a higher power. This medieval aetiology and use of symbolically enriched ingredients offer useful reminders regarding the inappropriateness of attempting to understand past medical writings from a modern medical perspective. Relatedly, these findings emphasize an integrated approach to healing that was designed to heal both body and soul as it was predicated on the perceived inseparability of body and soul.[30] The linked nature of corporal and spiritual health reinforces the centrality of the church to the practice of medicine: spiritual guidance and proper beliefs were essential ingredients in the maintenance of health.

Returning to the dataset, four other distinct clusters emerge: eight recipes with Christian elements are intended to treat fevers, five recipes can be classified as general panaceas (non-specific antidotes), five target haemorrhoids and four aim to heal wounds.[31] The remaining

---

[29] Siam Bhayro and Catherine Rider, eds, *Demons and Illness from Antiquity to the Early Modern Period* (Leiden, 2017); Claire Trenery, *Madness, Medicine and Miracle in Twelfth-Century England* (Abingdon, 2019); although epilepsy and madness often occur together in early medieval recipes, they appear to have been perceived as distinct conditions in later sources.

[30] Meg Leja, 'The Sacred Art: Medicine in the Carolingian Renaissance', *Viator* 47 (2016), 1–34.

[31] Recipes with Christian elements intended to combat fevers can be found in Stiftsbibliothek, Cod. sang. 751, pp. 401, 407, 410; Cod. sang. 899, p. 84; BAV, Pal.

recipes, just under half of the sixty-four, present an eclectic mix of treatments. While the examples reviewed above have already illustrated that Christian features can be found in recipes that target coughs, stomach pains, kidney pains, skin conditions and throat obstruction, similar Christian material can also be found in recipes intended to alleviate toothache, cure head pain, staunch blood-flow, help with birthing difficulties, resolve incontinence, and so on.[32]

Assessing the Data and their Implications

The Question of Christianization

As noted earlier, many recipes with instructions to say the Lord's Prayer also include extra-medical information, not overtly Christian, specifying the time at which ingredients should be collected. Indeed, one of the examples named above, a treatment for haemorrhoids found in Cod. sang. 751, is one of seven recipes in this manuscript alone that combine instructions to say the Lord's Prayer with timing specifications that are probably pre-Christian.[33] Timing information is most often framed around the days of the week and the movements of the sun and moon. Given the similarities of this material with that recorded in classical and late antique herbals, such as Pseudo-Apuleius's *Herbarius*, these timing instructions likely have ancient origins.[34] The addition of prayers to pre-Christian calendrical rituals could suggest

---

lat. 1088, fols 47v, 61r, 62r. For non-specific treatments and general panaceas, see Stiftsbibliothek, Cod. sang. 44, pp. 284, 234–6, 339–40; Cod. sang. 751, pp. 398–9, 499. For haemorrhoids, see Cod. sang. 44, p. 242; Cod. sang. 751, p. 383; Cod. sang. 759, p. 67; Glasgow, UL, Hunter 96 (formerly T.4.13), fol. 156r (see Sigerist, *Studien und Texte*, 126). For wounds, see Stiftsbibliothek, Cod. sang. 44, p. 242; Cod. sang. 751, pp. 367–8, 399; BN, Lat. 6882A, fol. 8r.

[32] A recipe for toothache, 'Ad dentes ut numquam doleant', with a Christian element (here, the Lord's Prayer) can be found in Stiftsbibliothek, Cod. sang. 759, p. 73. For headache, see Cod. sang. 751, p. 404, 'Ad capitis dolorem'. To stop bleeding, see BAV, Reg. lat. 1143, fol. 150v, 'Ad sanguine sta[n]gnandum'. For birthing difficulties, see Stiftsbibliothek, Cod. sang. 759, pp. 67–8, 'Ad mulierem ut partum eiciat'. For incontinence, see Cod. sang. 899, p. 141, recipe added after 'Ad eos qui urinam non continent'.

[33] Additional examples appear in Stiftsbibliotek, Cod. sang. 751: p. 378: 'Ad nesc<i>a rem probata', p. 392: 'De birbina dicitur', p. 407: 'Contra frigolas', p. 410: 'Ad frigoras cotidianas tercianas', pp. 412–13: 'Ad nescia rem probatam', pp. 413–14: 'Potio ad oua colobrina'.

[34] Pseudo-Apuleius, *Herbarius*, ed. Howald and Sigerist, 15–225.

that those responsible for compiling recipe collections intentionally Christianized ancient medical traditions.[35]

However, this type of pre-Christian, extra-medical material occurs with some regularity in simple herbal remedies and in many cases is not accompanied by Christian elements. The continued presence of extra-medical material from earlier traditions without accompanying Christian elements indicates that this content was not necessarily seen as in need of a Christian addition to make it acceptable, challenging the idea that early medieval scribes routinely Christianized recipes with pre-Christian extra-medical information. Given the vast range of calendrical information that circulated in early medieval manuscripts, from computistical texts to treatises on Egyptian Days (days thought to be unlucky, especially in the context of bloodletting), it seems possible that instructions regarding the timing of a treatment based on the seasons, sun and moon may not have appeared to transmit illicit knowledge.[36] While there is no question that Christian elements were introduced to some recipes in this period, it cannot be said with certainty that the primary motivation for their inclusion was to Christianize recipes that contained pre-Christian extra-medical content. Although a modern reader may recognize the different traditions behind these rituals and be tempted to interpret their association as indicative of a Christianizing reflex, the targeted Christianization of pre-Christian content remains one of many possible explanations for the appearance of Christian elements.

The opening example from a large recipe collection in Cod. sang. 751 offers another perspective on the Christianization of pre-Christian sources. Here a two-page cluster of nearly twenty recipes is derived from the late antique herbal *De herba vettonica liber*.[37] Although the standard edition of the herbal, a treatise dedicated to the medical uses of betony (*Stachys officianalis*), contains twice as

---

[35] Gary B. Ferngren, *Medicine and Religion: A Historical Introduction* (Baltimore, MD, 2014), 95.
[36] Don C. Skemer, '*Armis Gunfe*: Remembering Egyptian Days', *Traditio* 65 (2010), 75–106; Faith Wallis, 'Medicine in Medieval Calendar Manuscripts', in Margaret R. Schleissner, ed., *Manuscript Sources of Medieval Medicine: A Book of Essays* (New York, 1995), 105–43.
[37] Stiftsbibliothek, Cod. sang. 751, pp. 408–9. This cluster is bisected by a short group of recipes that use various parts of vultures as ingredients: see L. C. MacKinney, 'An Unpublished Treatise on Medicine and Magic from the Age of Charlemagne', *Speculum* 18 (1943), 494–6.

many recipes as the group in Cod. sang. 751 (and presents them in a different order), the individual recipes are nearly identical. The final recipe of the excerpt, however, provides a conspicuous exception: it includes an instruction to say the Lord's Prayer, a command lacking in the late antique original. This example reveals an important difference between established classical and late antique textual traditions and early medieval compilations: copies of the former remained (relatively) stable and unmodified, but when scribes used these writings as the building blocks of new compositions they adapted and updated their contents. That is, Christian elements were not added to copies of classical texts, but they could be introduced to the same material outside its original context, such as the excerpts found within newly created recipe collections.

Was the excerpt from *De herba vettonica liber* recognized as being derived from a pre-Christian source and thus seen as in need of a Christianized closing recipe? While this is possible, as with the previous example, Christian elements may have been added for numerous reasons. Perhaps such features were included with the expectation that they would increase a recipe's potency by incorporating rituals or ingredients connected to a higher power. The correlation between demon-related conditions and Christian elements may reflect an understanding that certain ailments, particularly those seen to relate to demonic possession, were perceived as benefiting from treatments that involved a Christian component, curing body and soul concurrently. Ultimately, multiple overlapping reasons may have inspired the incorporation of Christian elements and these motivations probably varied between different contexts and scribes. Although it remains impossible to determine precisely why these features were included in individual recipes, their introduction in early medieval Latin recipe literature marks a break with the classical and late antique traditions on which they build.

The Sacralization of Recorded Medical Knowledge

One of the most striking patterns to emerge in the preceding analysis is, paradoxically, the lack of more patterning in the data: the sixty-four recipes that include explicitly Christian elements present an immense degree of variation in all respects. The specific Christian features range from sacred ingredients to symbolic rituals; they take on a multiplicity of formats (including spoken, written, performative, location-based and chronological); they occur at different points in the treatment process; and they can be found in treatments for a vast assortment of conditions. Another aspect of this diversity concerns the manuscripts in which these recipes are found: these codices were produced in writing centres across western Europe, from Italy to Brittany.[38] The variety of the material, combined with the wide-ranging origins of the manuscripts themselves, indicates that the incorporation of Christian elements in recipe literature was neither an isolated development nor a regional phenomenon but a change that should be seen within a much wider framework, that of the intellectual and ecclesiastical landscape of the Carolingian world.

Although the concept of a Carolingian 'renaissance' has been revised in recent years, the intellectual culture that developed in the wake of the reforms stemming from Charlemagne's court provides the framework within which written sources must be understood.[39] Medicine has traditionally been viewed as a field relatively unaffected by this reforming environment, feeling its impact only with respect to the general increase in manuscript production.[40] Recent research, however, has begun to challenge this view, arguing that medical writings were strongly influenced by and, in turn, contributed to the intellectual discourses of the period.[41] Meg Leja has shown that medical texts exhibit many of the same characteristics linked to the project of *correctio* that have been observed in writings from other genres, such as an interest in recovering classical knowledge, a strong focus on presentation and order, and the centrality of Christian rhetoric, symbolism and motifs.

The present article's review of Christian elements in recipes supports the idea that medical knowledge felt the impact of *correctio* as part of

---

[38] On the origins and movements of Carolingian manuscripts containing medical texts, see especially Florence Eliza Glaze, 'The Perforated Wall: The Ownership and Circulation of Medical Books in Medieval Europe, ca.800–1200' (Ph.D. thesis, Duke University, 1999).

[39] Janet L. Nelson, 'Revisiting the Carolingian Renaissance', in Jamie Kreiner and Helmut Reimitz, eds, *Motions of Late Antiquity: Essays on Religion, Politics, and Society in Honour of Peter Brown* (Turnhout, 2016), 331–46.

[40] Horden, 'What's Wrong?', 17. On medicine in the early Middle Ages, and especially the Carolingian period, see, for example, John J. Contreni, 'Masters and Medicine in Northern France in the Reign of Charles the Bald', in Margaret T. Gibson and Janet L. Nelson, eds, *Charles the Bald: Court and Kingdom. Papers based on a Colloquium held in London in April 1979*, 2nd edn (Aldershot, 1990), 267–82; Glaze, 'Perforated Wall'; Peregrine Horden, 'The Millennium Bug: Health and Medicine around the Year 1000', *SHM* 12 (2000), 201–19; Wallis, 'Experience of the Book'; eadem, 'Signs and Senses: Diagnosis and Prognosis in Early Medieval Pulse and Urine Texts', *SHM* 13 (2000), 265–78.

[41] Leja, 'Sacred Art'.

broader intellectual and ecclesiastical currents. The addition of explicitly Christian material in early medieval recipes fits into this intellectual climate, not only marking a break with classical and late antique pharmaceutical collections (works essentially devoid of Christian references), but also demonstrating that scribes and compilers modified the information they inherited from earlier medical texts to suit the needs and tastes of their contexts. More specifically, this evidence argues for the sacralization of medical writings in this period rather than of the field of medicine as a whole. Sources other than medical texts bear witness to a healthscape that had long engaged with Christianity: from histories and hagiographies to archaeology, there is abundant textual and material evidence in support of a sacralized medicine from Late Antiquity onwards.[42] The key development isolated in this article is that, during the early Middle Ages, the medical literature began to reflect this aspect of the healthscape. The use of ingredients produced by or associated with Christian rituals and sites, for example, strongly parallels similar practices that had been recorded in other types of writings for centuries. Its inclusion in pharmaceutical writings thus appears to be the next stage in the evolution of recorded medical knowledge, codifying and legitimizing these practices by presenting them alongside ancient authorities.

Not only does the timing of this transformation fit within the Carolingian intellectual and ecclesiastical framework, but the transformation itself plays an active role in the construction of this framework, partaking in the process of *reformatio* by updating the recorded medical knowledge. Scribes adapted pharmaceutical literature by reworking earlier sources to align better with a Christian community intent on correcting their beliefs and practices while simultaneously integrating contemporary approaches to healing within the learned traditions of medicine. Overall, the picture that emerges points to a shared drive that, although it produced many different individual responses, exhibits related impulses.

CONCLUSION

This article has presented the initial results and conclusions of the first large-scale analysis of Christian elements in early medieval Latin

[42] Gregory of Tours, *The History of the Franks*, transl. Lewis Thorpe (London, 1974); David Knipp, 'The Chapel of the Physicians at Santa Maria Antiqua', *Dumbarton Oaks Papers* 56 (2002), 1–23; Gary B. Ferngren, *Medicine & Health Care in Early Christianity* (Baltimore, MD, 2009).

recipe literature. The investigation identified sixty-four recipes that included at least one explicitly Christian feature, although a sizeable proportion of these recipes combined multiple Christian features. The types of Christian elements, such as prayers and holy ingredients, and the ways in which these elements appear in treatments have strong parallels to the insular material analysed in earlier studies.

While recipes with Christian features remain a small percentage of the recipe literature overall, totalling roughly one per cent of treatments in the sample of recipes under analysis in the present study, their existence is significant, marking a distinct development in early medieval medical writing, since (late) ancient medical texts were essentially devoid of Christian content. It should not, however, be expected that the introduction of Christian elements would result in a straightforward replacement of existing pharmaceutical knowledge. While it may have replaced material in some cases, Christian elements more often appear to augment earlier writings: a recipe using Christian ingredients, for example, could offer one of several possible treatments for a certain condition, or Christian features could be added to a prescription, expanding it rather than eliminating its non-Christian content. Thus the recording of Christian elements in pharmaceutical writings generally appears to offer additional approaches to healing instead of a substitution of medical traditions.

From the analysis, it has become evident that the inclusion of Christian elements could stem from myriad motivations, such as the perceived potency of treatments involving a higher power, the need for explicitly Christian cures for certain ailments (especially those thought to be caused by demons) or the aim to Christianize non-Christian medical knowledge. Regardless of the rationale behind each individual Christian element, their diversity and widespread appearance indicates that these developments were known throughout the Carolingian world. Ultimately, the introduction of Christian features documents the adaptation of recorded medical knowledge, aligning with the reforming dynamics of the period and updating the written record to fit with the Christianized healthscape of the early medieval West.

These findings touch on major topics and themes at the intersections of Carolingian history, the history of Christianity and the history of healthcare and medicine. More research is needed in all directions, especially in connection to the wider society of early medieval Europe and the contexts in which the manuscripts containing these recipes were produced and used (remembering, however, that therapy represents just one of the possible ways in which medical

Claire Burridge

texts could have been used).[43] In particular, it is essential to explore the relationships between medical texts incorporating Christian elements, healing practices involving Christian rituals, and Christian spaces and communities. The origins of these manuscripts demand that these medical writings be investigated further in relation to monastic communities (as sites of learning, manuscript production and knowledge exchange) and the intellectual, ecclesiastical and political networks that connected them.[44] Additional research into recipes and their manuscripts is thus needed in order to pursue these important topics. As an initial study of Christian elements in Latin recipes, this article has aimed to cast fresh light on the evolution of recipe literature within the context of the Carolingian world, offering a new perspective on the relationship between medicine and the church and pointing the direction for future research.

APPENDIX 1: MANUSCRIPTS[45]

Note regarding dating: If a superscript fraction follows the century in which a manuscript was written, it indicates that a more precise date has been suggested for the manuscript's composition. The bottom half of the fraction breaks the century into that fraction of time (so '2' breaks it into halves and '4' into quarters); the top half of the fraction then specifies which time (i.e., which half, third or quarter). So '2/4' represents the second quarter of the century in question, '2/2' is the second half and '2–4/4' indicates that it was written between the second and fourth quarters (which can be useful if the manuscript was added to over time or if its dating is more ambiguous). In other cases (also written in superscript), 'in', 'med' or 'ex' are used to indicate that a manuscript was written at the beginning, middle or end of the century in question.

---

[43] Peregrine Horden, 'Prefatory Note: The Uses of Medical Manuscripts', in Barbara Zipser, ed., *Medical Books in the Byzantine World* (Bologna, 2013), 1–6.
[44] Glaze, 'Perforated Wall'.
[45] Regarding the dating and origins of these manuscripts, I have consulted Bischoff, *Katalog der festländischen Handschriften*; Beccaria, *I codici*; Ernest Wickersheimer, *Les Manuscrits latins de médecine du haut moyen age dans les bibliothèques de France* (Paris, 1966). See Sigerist, *Studien und Texte* for published transcriptions of recipe collections in Bamberg, Staatsbibliothek, Msc.Med.2; Berlin, Staatsbibliothek, Phill. 1790; Glasgow, UL, Hunter 96; Karlsruhe, Badische Landesbibliothek, Cod. Aug. perg. 120; London, BL, Harley MS 5792; St Gallen, Stiftsbibliotek, Cod. sang. 44. See Jörimann, *Frühmittelalterliche Rezeptarien* for additional recipe collections in Bamberg, Staatsbibliothek, Msc.Med.2; cod. sang. 44. See *Das Lorscher Arzneibuch*, ed. and transl. Stoll, for Bamberg, Staatsbibliothek, Msc.Med.1.

64

Appendix

Manuscript	Date	Origin	Recipes with Christian elements	Digital facsimile
Bamberg, Staatsbibliothek				
Msc.Med.1	c.800	Lorsch	Yes	http://digital.bib-bvb.de/view/bvbmets/viewer.0.6.4.jsp?folder_id=0&dvs=1612036768701~842&pid=4685473&locale=de&usePid1=true&usePid2=true
Msc.Med.2	s.IX–X	Northern Italy		https://zendsbb.digitale-sammlungen.de/db/0000/sbb00000138/images/index.html?id=00000138&fip=84.86.241.245&no=0&seite=0&signatur=Msc.Med.2
Berlin, Staatsbibliothek				
Phill. 1790	s.IX$^{2-4/4}$	Eastern France		https://bvmm.irht.cnrs.fr/consult/consult.php?reproductionId=4528
Glasgow, University Library				
Hunter 96 (formerly T.4.13)	s.VIII–IX	Southern France	Yes	No digital facsimile available
Karlsruhe, Badische Landesbibliothek				
Cod. Aug. perg. 120	s.IX–X	Northern Italy, probably Verona		https://digital.blb-karlsruhe.de/blbhs/Handschriften/content/titleinfo/64141
London, BL				
Harley MS 5792[46]	s.VIII$^{2/2}$	Italy		No digital facsimile available
Paris, BN				
Lat. 2849A	s.IX$^{3/4}$	France or Italy		https://gallica.bnf.fr/ark:/12148/btv1b9067647m/f4.image

Continued

[46] Composite manuscript: the information regarding this manuscript's composition concerns fols 273r–276v.

Appendix continued

Manuscript	Date	Origin	Recipes with Christian elements	Digital facsimile
Lat. 6882A[47]	s.IX$^{1/2}$	Southwest France (probably)	Yes	https://gallica.bnf.fr/ark:/12148/btv1b9076757/9.r=6882a?rk=21459;2
Lat. 7021	s.IX$^{1-2/4}$	Paris region		https://gallica.bnf.fr/ark:/12148/btv1b100352360/f1.image#
Lat. 9332	s.IX^{in}	Western France (probably Fleury)	Yes	https://gallica.bnf.fr/ark:/12148/btv1b60004321/f2.image
Lat. 11218	s.VIII–IX	Burgundy (possibly)		https://gallica.bnf.fr/ark:/12148/btv1b9066936j/f1.image
Lat. 13955	s.IX$^{mid-3/4}$	Corbie	Yes	https://gallica.bnf.fr/ark:/12148/btv1b9066978w?rk=21459;2
St Gallen, Stiftsbibliothek				
Cod. sang. 44[48]	s.IX$^{2/2}$	Northern Italy (probably)	Yes	https://www.e-codices.unifr.ch/de/list/one/csg/0044
Cod. sang. 217	s.IX^{in}	Northern Italy (probably)	Yes	https://www.e-codices.unifr.ch/de/list/one/csg/0217
Cod. sang. 550	s.IX$^{2/2}$	Southern German region	Yes	https://www.e-codices.unifr.ch/de/list/one/csg/0550
Cod. sang. 751	s.IX$^{2/2}$	Northern Italy (probably)	Yes	https://www.e-codices.unifr.ch/de/list/one/csg/0751
Cod. sang. 752	c.900	St Gallen	Yes	https://www.e-codices.unifr.ch/de/list/one/csg/0752
Cod. sang. 759	s.IX^{in}	Brittany	Yes	https://www.e-codices.unifr.ch/de/list/one/csg/0759
Cod. sang. 761	s.IX^{in}	Fulda		https://www.e-codices.unifr.ch/de/list/one/csg/0761
Cod. sang. 878	s.IX$^{2/4}$	Reichenau		https://www.e-codices.unifr.ch/de/list/one/csg/0878

47 Composite manuscript: the information regarding this manuscript's composition concerns fols 1v–26v.
48 Composite manuscript: the information regarding this manuscript's composition concerns pp. 186–368.

Cod. sang. 899	s.IX–X	St Gallen	Yes	https://www.e-codices.unifr.ch/de/list/one/csg/0899
Cod. sang. 1396[49]	s.IX^{in}	Northern Italy (probably)		No digital facsimile available
Vatican City, BAV				
Pal. lat. 187	s.VIII$^{2/2}$	Northern Italy (probably)		https://digi.vatlib.it/view/bav_pal_lat_187
Pal. lat. 1088	s.IX$^{mid-3/4}$	Lyon area	Yes	https://digi.vatlib.it/view/MSS_Pal.lat.1088
Reg. lat. 598[50]	c.900	Unrecorded		https://digi.vatlib.it/view/MSS_Reg.lat.598
Reg. lat. 1143	s.IX^{in}	Mainz (possibly)	Yes	https://digi.vatlib.it/view/MSS_Reg.lat.1143
Vat. lat. 5951	s.IX$^{1/4}$	Italy (possibly Nonantola) or southern Burgundy		https://digi.vatlib.it/view/MSS_Var.lat.5951
Wolfenbüttel, Herzog August Bibliothek				
Cod. 56.18. Aug. 8	s.IX^{mid}	Ferrières		http://diglib.hab.de/mss/56-18-aug-8f/start.htm
Wrocław, Biblioteka Cyfrowa				
Cod. III.F.19	s.IX^{in}	Metz (probably)		https://www.bibliotekacyfrowa.pl/dlibra/publication/edition/15474?id=15474&from=publication&

[49] Collection of fragments: the information regarding this manuscript's composition concerns pp. 9–16, 19–22.
[50] Collection of fragments: the information regarding this manuscript's composition concerns fols 26r–33r, 124r–125r.

Plague and Popular Revival: Ecclesiastical Authorities and the Bianchi Devotions in 1399

Alexandra R. A. Lee*

University College London

Religious processions were commonly held during plague outbreaks in medieval Europe to provide succour against disease. The Bianchi of 1399, a popular religious revival, is one such example. This article addresses the Bianchi in Tuscany, demonstrating the crucial role of ecclesiastical authorities in moulding this response to plague, and contributing to both religious history and the history of medicine. It first problematizes the connection between the Bianchi and a punitive plague which could purportedly be remedied by religious devotions. The role of the clergy in the movement is then examined, demonstrating their prominence in preparing the populace, preaching and even leading processions. An assessment of Bianchi processional composition and routes reveals exploitation of pre-existing liturgical traditions. This localized, comparative analysis demonstrates how individual Tuscan towns organized and supported these devotional activities, successfully managing the popular response to plague expressed in the Bianchi devotions.

During times of crisis, and perhaps especially epidemics, society employs any means possible to find succour and hope. An explanation of such outbreaks and a solution to them can both be sought in religion. When epidemics hit in medieval Europe, the populace often participated in ritual processions led by members of the church. During the Black Death of 1347–52, for example, a flagellant revival occurred, although this was condemned by church authorities as it descended into anti-clerical violence.[1] In 1399, the populace of the

* E-mail: a.r.a.lee@ucl.ac.uk.

I wish to thank Catherine Keen and Melissa Benson for their insightful comments on this article, as well as the reviewers and editors for their suggestions. I also wish to thank the Arts and Humanities Research Council, who funded my doctoral research which included this topic.

[1] Mitchell B. Merback, 'The Living Image of Pity: Mimetic Violence, Peace-Making and Salvific Spectacle in the Flagellant Processions of the Later Middle Ages', in Debra Higgs Strickland, ed., *Images of Medieval Sanctity: Essays in Honour of Gary Dickson* (Leiden, 2007), 135–80, at 155.

Studies in Church History 58 (2022), 68–90 © The Author(s), 2022. Published by Cambridge University Press on behalf of Ecclesiastical History Society

doi: 10.1017/stc.2022.4

northern and central Italian peninsula responded to the threat of plague by dressing in white and joining a series of nine-day circular itinerant processions: the Bianchi movement.[2] Participants would sing *laude* (songs of praise), pray, visit churches and fast. Rather than being condemned, this popular revival was endorsed by church authorities at various levels, contributing to its successful spread throughout the central Italian peninsula.

The Bianchi have until now been assessed as a whole, or in terms of individual case studies. Following Tognetti's book-length article and a series of smaller studies in Italian, Daniel Bornstein's monograph brought the Bianchi into Anglophone scholarship in 1993, providing a substantial overview of the devotions.[3] His brief treatment of ecclesiastical officials is developed here in the exploration of their role during the processions. A volume of essays arising from a major conference on the Bianchi in 1999 added a series of individual case studies to Italian Bianchi scholarship.[4] I shall argue that considering such case studies in parallel reveals key differences in the practice of Bianchi devotions in each town. This in-depth, comparative analysis reveals the intricate, individual ways in which towns responded to the advent of these novel processions, specifically through examining the roles played by ecclesiastical authorities.

The Bianchi devotions began in Genoa, gaining a mass following on 5 July 1399 and spreading east towards Venice and south in the direction of Rome. Each circular procession would undertake about four and a half days' travel from its starting point before turning around to complete the loop. Thus Bianchi participants did not travel (for example) from Genoa to Rome; rather, each town that was successfully proselytized took up the devotions and sent out its own groups, meaning that the devotions spread gradually throughout the northern and central Italian peninsula. The focus of this article is on the Bianchi in Tuscany, specifically Lucca, Pistoia and

---

[2] For an overview of the movement, see Giampaolo Tognetti, 'Sul moto dei Bianchi nel 1399', *Bullettino dell'Instituto Storico Italiano* 78 (1967), 205–343.

[3] Tognetti, 'Sul moto dei Bianchi'; Arsenio Frugoni, 'La devozione dei Bianchi del 1399', in *L'attesa dell'età nuova nella spiritualità della fine del medioevo* (Turin, 1962), 232–48; Daniel Bornstein, *The Bianchi of 1399: Popular Devotion in Late Medieval Italy* (Ithaca, NY, 1993).

[4] Francesco Santucci, ed., *Sulle orme dei Bianchi. Dalla Liguria all'Italia centrale. Atti del convegno storico internazionale, Assisi, Vallo di Nera, Terni, Rieti, Leonessa (18–20 giugno 1999)* (Assisi, 2001).

Florence, with reference to Padua for a northerly comparison. These towns can be considered hubs of Bianchi activity. In addition to sending out groups on itinerant processions and receiving Bianchi participants from nearby locations, these towns also offered an intra-urban alternative for those unable to leave home. Participants in these less arduous processions returned home each evening, and often remained within the walls of their town.

The detailed chronicles of Giovanni Sercambi[5] and Luca Dominici[6] elucidate the Bianchi experience in Lucca and Pistoia respectively. More of a patchwork of sources survives for Florence, including the diary and letters of Francesco di Marco Datini[7] and devotional poetry by Andrea Stefani[8] and Franco Sacchetti.[9] Giovanni Conversini da Ravenna's chronicle provides similarly detailed evidence for Padua.[10] This cross-comparison of the

---

[5] Giovanni Sercambi, *Le croniche di Giovanni Sercambi, Lucchese*, ed. Salvatore Bongi, 3 vols (Lucca, 1892). The text details life in Lucca from the twelfth century until Sercambi's death in 1423. Sercambi began his career as an apothecary, and then worked as a notary in the employ of the Guinigi family, who staged a successful coup in 1400 and for whom he composed the chronicle: Robert A. Pratt, 'Giovanni Sercambi, Speziale', *Italica* 25 (1948), 12–14. Sercambi is also known for his *Novelliere* written in the style of Boccaccio: *Il Novelliere*, ed. Luciano Rossi (Rome, 1984).

[6] Luca Dominici, *Cronache di ser Luca Dominici. Cronaca della venuta dei Bianchi e della moria 1399–1400*, ed. Carlo Gigliotti (Pistoia, 1933). Dominici was also a notary, in his native Pistoia, and composed two chronicles around the turn of the fifteenth century, the first on the Bianchi and the second treating the civil war in Pistoia shortly after: Luca Dominici, *Cronache di ser Luca Dominici. Cronaca seconda*, ed. Carlo Gigliotti (Pistoia, 1937). For more on Dominici, see Gigliotti's detailed introductions to these editions.

[7] Federigo Melis, *Aspetti della vita economica medievale. Studi nell'archivio Datini di Prato* (Florence, 1962), 101; Prato, Archivio di Stato, Fondo Datini, Fondaco di Barcellona, 864.13.903012 27/09/1399. Datini is best known as the Merchant of Prato, whose business records and letters provide a substantial picture of his life: see, for example, Giampiero Nigro, ed., *Francesco di Marco Datini. L'uomo il mercante* (Florence, 2010).

[8] Florence, Biblioteca Marucelliana, MS C.152, fols 53v–55v; Ugo Scoti-Bertinelli, ed., *Note e documenti di lettertura religiosa* (Florence, 1908), 35–62. Stefani was probably a composer and poet, although no further details are known about his life: Guglielmo Volpi, *Una lauda di Andrea Stefani fiorentino* (Florence, 1908).

[9] Franco Sacchetti, *Il libro delle rime*, ed. Franca Brambilla Ageno (Florence, 1990). Sacchetti was well known for his literary works, which also included *Novelle*, written alongside a political career: Natalino Sapegno, 'Sacchetti, Franco', *Enciclopedia Italiana* (1936), online at: <https://www.treccani.it/enciclopedia/franco-sacchetti_%28Enciclopedia-Italiana%29/>, accessed 17 June 2021.

[10] Giovanni Conversini da Ravenna, *La processione dei Bianchi nella città di Padova (1399)*, ed. Libia Cortese and Dino Cortese (Padua, 1978). Da Ravenna had a varied, peripatetic career involving teaching rhetoric at Florence and notarial positions for northerly Italian governments such as Venice, Udine and Padua: Remigio Sabbadini, 'Giovanni

Bianchi experience highlights elements of continuity as well as key areas of local difference, moving beyond traditional studies of the movement that focus on a single location, or on a specific practice such as peacemaking.[11]

To demonstrate this, we shall explore the relationship between the Bianchi and the plague epidemic at the turn of the fifteenth century. The article then examines three facets of local, ecclesiastical support for the Bianchi. Firstly, the role of the clergy will be assessed, particularly their involvement in preparing and motivating the populace. The composition of the processions will then be discussed, with a focus on the different groups of individuals participating in the Bianchi processions. Finally, the routes will be evaluated, considering both itinerant and intra-urban devotional activities. This will demonstrate the way that the Bianchi devotions were moulded by each town to suit local traditions, and the importance of ecclesiastical authorities in facilitating the processions.

PLAGUE AND THE BIANCHI

Plague was a crucial motivating factor for participants in the Bianchi devotions. The most prevalent origin narrative, the *tre pani* story, explained that a punitive pandemic was ordained on account of the sins of humankind, but that the Bianchi processions could prevent, or at least mitigate, this outbreak.[12] Many versions of the narrative included detailed instructions for the Bianchi processions as the act

---

da Ravenna', *Enciclopedia Italiana* (1933), online at: <https://www.treccani.it/enciclopedia/giovanni-da-ravenna_%28Enciclopedia-Italiana%29/>, accessed 2 June 2021.

[11] See, for example, Amleto Spicciani, ed., *La devozione dei Bianchi nel 1399. Il miracolo del crocifisso di Borgo a Buggiano* (Pisa, 1998). For more on Bianchi peacemaking, see Katherine L. Jansen, *Peace and Penance in Late Medieval Italy* (Princeton, NJ, 2018), 48–54; Glenn Kumhera, *The Benefits of Peace: Private Peacemaking in Late Medieval Italy* (Leiden, 2017), 161–2; Diana Webb, 'Penitence and Peace-Making in City and Contado: The Bianchi of 1399', in Derek Baker, ed., *The Church in Town and Countryside*, SCH 16 (Oxford, 1979), 243–56.

[12] The *tre pani* narrative is reproduced in numerous textual and visual sources, such as Dominici, *Cronaca dei Bianchi*, ed. Gigliotti, 50–4. Briefly, a peasant miraculously found three pieces of bread, as directed by Christ (disguised as a pilgrim). The peasant went to moisten the bread and met a woman dressed in white, the Virgin in disguise. One piece of bread was thrown into the water, condemning a third of humanity to die by plague, but the Virgin then provided instructions for the Bianchi processions as a means to remedy this threat.

of devotion required to prevent the outbreak. The chronicles suggest that this narrative was preached, and the existence of numerous *laude* also telling the *tre pani* story suggests that they constituted another mode of its transmission.[13] It is therefore likely that participants in the devotions would have been aware of this connection to plague. As the processions spread, the threat of a 'great death' (*gran moria*) was further reinforced by visions in towns the Bianchi were trying to convert.[14] In addition to *laude* telling the *tre pani* story, Bianchi participants also sang a variety of devotional hymns. Some of these also emphasized their connection to plague, such as *Misericordia etterno Dio*, described as 'a *lauda* that was sung to placate God for the plague'.[15] In this way, the relationship between the forthcoming plague and the necessity for the Bianchi processions was highlighted at various levels.

However, the correlation between the Bianchi and the reality of the plague spreading through the Italian peninsula at the turn of the fifteenth century was more complicated. By this period, plague was a frequent occurrence; after the Black Death of 1347–52, the disease recurred roughly once a decade. However, different locations were not affected in the same way. For example, Umbrian Orvieto endured two outbreaks in the 1370s, whereas Lucca and Pistoia only experienced one.[16] Governmental edicts permitted town councils to convene with lower quora or to appoint emergency committees (*balìa*) during outbreaks, as well as regulating public health matters such as the burial of the dead and the slaughter of animals.[17] Processions also took place: the bishop in Pistoia led plague

[13] For example, Sercambi, *Croniche*, ed. Bongi, 2: 320. *Laude* narrating the *tre pani* narrative were composed both in the vernacular and in Latin, for example *Se peccatore te vol salvare*, in Gennaro M. Monti, *Un laudario umbro quattrocentista dei Bianchi* (Città di Castello, 1920), 124–7.

[14] Dominici, *Cronaca dei Bianchi*, ed. Gigliotti, 184–5, 174. All translations are my own.

[15] 'Una lauda già cantata per placare Idio sopra la pestilenzia': Dominici, *Cronaca dei Bianchi*, ed. Gigliotti, 234.

[16] 'Cronaca Urbevetana (1294–1505)', in Luigi Fumi, ed., *Ephemerides urbevetanae dal cod. vaticano urbinate 1745* (Bolgona, 1929), 198–210, at 208; Cipriano Manenti, 'Estratti dalle Historie di Cipriano Manenti (1325–1376)', ibid. 415–71, at 468; Pistoia, Archivio di Stato, MS Provvisioni Comune 16, fol. 65v; Sercambi, *Croniche*, ed. Bongi, 1: 206.

[17] Animal slaughter was regulated to reduce putrid smells, which were connected to the spread of disease: Pistoia, Archivio di Stato, MS Provvisioni Comune 9, fol. 166r; Alberto Chiappelli, 'Gli ordinamenti sanitari del comune di Pistoia contro la pestilenza del 1348', *Archivio Storico Italiano* 20 (1887), 3–4. For more on medieval public health, see Guy

processions behind a reportedly miraculous crucifix.[18] Each epidemic outbreak was met with a combination of communal edicts and religious actions.

The belief that divine anger was a key cause of disease is reinforced in Sercambi's account of Bianchi activity in Lucca.[19] The chronicler details six outbreaks of plague, and each is accompanied by a very similar illustration (Figure 1).[20] For example, in the first, accompanying the Black Death of 1348, humanity lies prostrate on the ground, with angels or demons bearing weapons and raining down arrows and oil. Louise Marshall suggests that the fact that these creatures are not prevented from their attacks demonstrates divine anger, as God does not mercifully intervene.[21] These images are reinforced by Sercambi's explanation in the text of the disease as a result of the sins of humankind. They also create continuity within the manuscript between each outbreak in terms of cause and the devastation wrought. The threat of plague for non-participants in the Bianchi devotions was grounded in at least half a century of coping with the disease. Those who participated would – at least theoretically – be spared the terrors of the epidemic.

The plague at the turn of the fifteenth century is described in detail by Sercambi and Dominici, providing comparative evidence for Lucca and Pistoia. The so-called *moria dei Bianchi* ('plague at the time of the Bianchi') began in Genoa in 1397, striking central Italy in late 1399, where it reached a peak in the summer of 1400.[22] The

---

Geltner, 'The Path to Pistoia: Urban Hygiene before the Black Death', *P&P* 246 (2020), 3–33.

[18] Giuseppe M. Guidi, *Vita del beato fra Andrea Franchi dell'ordine di S. Domenico* (Pistoia, 1839), 43–5. Religious processions during plagues were not unique to Pistoia, and occurred frequently during epidemics: Jussi Hanska, *Strategies of Sanity and Survival: Religious Responses to Natural Disasters in the Middle Ages* (Helsinki, 2002), 21–2.

[19] Lucca, Archivio di Stato, MS 107.

[20] For the other images, see Ottavio Banti and Maria Cristiani Testi, *Le illustrazioni delle croniche nel codice lucchese* (Genoa, 1978), 18 (1348), 26 (1363), 56 (1371), 78 (1383), 85 (1390), 154 (1397), 209 (1400).

[21] Louise Marshall, 'God's Executioners: Angels, Devils and the Plague in Giovanni Sercambi's Illustrated Chronicle (1400)', in Jennifer Spinks and Charles Zika, eds, *Disaster, Death and the Emotions in the Shadow of the Apocalypse, 1400–1700* (London, 2016), 177–99.

[22] For a basic overview, see also Alfonso Corradi, 'Del movimento de' Bianchi e della peste del 1399 e 1400', *Rendiconti del Reale Istituto Lombardo di Scienze e Lettere* 24 (1891), 1055–8.

Figure 1. Lucca, Archivio di Stato, MS 107, fol. 49^v: *Come fu moria grande*. Su concessione del Ministero per i beni e le attività culturali e per il turismo – Archivio di Stato di Lucca (With permission from the Ministry for Cultural Heritage and Activities and Tourism, State Archive of Luca).

Tuscan devotions therefore began before the advent of the plague in that region, although under the shadow of the plague in the north. Sercambi places the initial outbreak in Lucca in September 1399, about a month after the Bianchi devotions began in the town, but still during the height of the processions.[23] He has a second entry for the disease in May 1400, indicating that a hundred and fifty people were dying each day.[24] The *Podestà* led a plague procession in 1400, a completely separate event from the Bianchi processions the previous year. Council records show significant numbers of deaths, and emergency measures were implemented.[25]

Dominici references the disease as early as 17 August 1399, just five days after Bianchi processions began in Pistoia. The highest numbers of deaths are reported between May and August the following year.[26] The statistics presented in Dominici's chronicle indicate

[23] Sercambi, *Croniche*, ed. Bongi, 2: 397.
[24] Ibid. 3: 4–5.
[25] Christine Meek, *Lucca, 1369–1400: Politics and Society in an Early Renaissance City-State* (Oxford, 1978), 336.
[26] Figures at the end of Dominici's chronicle recorded by his brother Paolo show this clearly for Pistoia: *Cronaca dei Bianchi*, ed. Gigliotti, 71, 238–85.

that roughly half of the Pistoiese population perished. Plague processions were held in May 1400, organized by the bishop and town officials. As seen with Lucca, the Bianchi processions preceded and then coincided with the outbreak of plague, yet there is no mention of the Bianchi in connection to the actual outbreak of the disease.

Turning to the north, again, there is no detailed evidence for the plague in Padua, although other cities offer a comparison. Sercambi describes plague hitting Bologna in October 1399 with a population loss of between fifty and two hundred each day, due not only to deaths but also to people fleeing.[27] Milan legislated ruthlessly during times of plague, prohibiting movement of foreigners into the territories it governed, specifically to avoid the contagion of the plague.[28] This had an impact on the Bianchi processions, since it meant that the Milanese were only allowed to participate in intra-urban processions.

While plague is presented in the origin stories and the *laude* as a key motivator for participants in the Bianchi processions, the relationship of the movement to the epidemic of 1399–1400 is less straightforward. Chronicles are frustratingly silent on the link, sometimes even reporting the plague in separate sections of the text, as Sercambi does, for instance. Nevertheless, the Bianchi devotions were portrayed as a method through which humankind could prevent or ameliorate an epidemic outbreak, as indicated through the origin narratives and the frequent mentions of plague in the *laude* and chronicles as the processions spread. Despite their proximity to an actual epidemic of plague, it seems that the Bianchi activities were understood as plague-prevention processions, rather than the more traditional plague processions which were utilized during outbreaks. The devotions can consequently be understood as an important reaction, in each town they reached, to the threat of epidemic disease.

THE ROLE OF THE CLERGY

The duties of clerics during the Bianchi devotions could range from saying mass and preaching to taking part in itinerant processions. Their actions provided endorsement for the popular religious revival,

---

[27] Sercambi, *Croniche*, ed. Bongi, 2: 391.
[28] *I registri dell'ufficio di professione e dell'ufficio dei sindaci sotto la dominazione viscontea* (Milan, 1929), 164.

Alexandra R. A. Lee

helping to maintain its momentum. In addition to putting on white garments, participants were required to confess and take communion.[29] Datini records taking communion; the prerequisite of confession is implicit.[30] While the laity attended mass regularly, under normal circumstances communion was generally only taken at Easter, marking the Bianchi devotions as exceptional. Sercambi describes how both parish priests and mendicants struggled to keep up with the demand for the sacraments,[31] While this may be an exaggeration, it highlights the popularity of the Bianchi devotions and the large number of individuals preparing to participate in the plague-prevention processions. These requirements essentially made the clergy into spiritual gatekeepers for participation. Their sacramental support established a penitential prerequisite for the Bianchi participants, and demonstrated ecclesiastical endorsement for the processions.

As seen above, preaching was crucial for spreading the Bianchi origin narratives, instructing participants, and communicating the urgency of participation. Clergy used preaching to communicate with the laity who, by the turn of the fifteenth century, had increasingly high expectations from sermons.[32] This was in no small part due to the Franciscans and Dominicans, who were trained to preach in an engaging way.[33] Urban spaces were given over to preachers, for whom special platforms were sometimes constructed, and exceptional orators could even be paid.[34]

All Bianchi participants were expected to attend mass daily, and preaching formed a crucial part of their devotional experience.[35] Sercambi describes the sermon of a *frate* who provided detailed instructions about what was required during the processions.[36] The

[29] Sercambi, *Croniche*, ed. Bongi, 2: 320.
[30] 'Prexi la comunione del corpo del nostro Signore Gieso Cristo': Melis, *Aspetti*, 101.
[31] Sercambi, *Croniche*, ed. Bongi, 2: 305.
[32] David d'Avray, *The Preaching of the Friars: Sermons diffused from Paris before 1300* (Oxford, 1985), 6, 127; Nicole Bériou, *Religion et Communication. Un Autre Regard sur la prédication au Moyen Âge* (Geneva, 2018).
[33] D'Avray, *Preaching of the Friars*, 28, 66.
[34] Augustine Thompson, *Revival Preachers and Politics in Thirteenth-Century Italy: The Great Devotion of 1233* (Oxford, 1992), 52.
[35] Melis, *Aspetti*, 102.
[36] Sercambi, *Croniche*, ed. Bongi, 2: 319–21. All those who wished to join the processions were to confess and communicate, and then don the white Bianchi garments. These were to cover their whole person except their face and hands. Participants were

involvement of various ranks of the clergy, including priests, friars and bishops, indicates an endorsement of the Bianchi by the church hierarchy. Their actions both literally and figuratively aided the spread of the devotions, maintaining momentum and ensuring that other towns were more open to the processions. The fact that individual clergy were also responsible for instructing people on how to participate in the processions provided an additional method of control, and also a way to mould Bianchi devotions according to local traditions.

In Pistoia, Dominici often names the mass celebrant and the preacher. For example, on 13 August, mass was said by a canon, Giovanni di Simone Cibicci Cancellieri, a member of a prominent Pistoiese family, and the preacher was *frate* Giovanni da Carmignano.[37] Dominici frequently emphasizes the role of high-status individuals, demonstrating that the Bianchi were seen as a suitable endeavour even for the elite of society. The most frequent preacher in Dominici's account is the Dominican bishop Andrea Franchi, who also sometimes said the accompanying mass, as well as granting indulgences of forty days to Bianchi participants who visited particular crucifixes or participated in the itinerant processions.[38] Franchi also made announcements, reiterating that pregnant women or children under twelve years old were excused from the itinerant processions and reinforcing the importance of the processions for plague prevention.[39] He announced the progress and return of the itinerant Pistoiese Bianchi while remaining within the town. The bishop thus directed the discourse about the Bianchi in Pistoia. Franchi's pronouncements also demonstrate that those in Pistoia had a clear sense of where the itinerant participants were, using this knowledge for practical purposes such as food provision, although it is unclear

---

to process for nine days, not sleeping in walled towns or in beds but in churches. They were to refrain from eating meat and remain chaste, fast on bread and water on Saturdays, and sing *laude*, including the *Stabat Mater*.

[37] Dominici, *Cronaca dei Bianchi*, ed. Gigliotti, 59. The latter's order is not noted.

[38] Ibid. 71, 143, 162. For more on Franchi, see Giuseppe M. Guidi, *Vita del beato fra Andrea Franchi dell'ordine di S. Domenico* (Pistoia, 1839); Paolo Franzese, 'Franchi, Andrea', *Dizionario Biografico degli Italiani* (1998), online at: <https://www.treccani.it/enciclopedia/andrea-franchi_(Dizionario-Biografico)>, accessed 18 November 2020.

[39] Dominici, *Cronaca dei Bianchi*, ed. Gigliotti, 77.

how this information was communicated.[40] Datini describes how the bishop of Fiesole, the Dominican Jacopo Altovita, led the itinerant Florentine procession in which he participated.[41] This involvement of bishops in both itinerant and intra-urban processions demonstrates their support for various Bianchi activities. Moreover, their direct involvement, particularly in terms of leadership and preaching, helped to shape the devotions.

One particularly remarkable example is Grazia di Santo Spirito, an Augustinian from Santo Spirito in Florence who is explicitly named in two separate sources.[42] Dominici reports that Grazia accompanied an itinerant procession from Florence, on one day of which he preached a Bianchi origin at Pacciana, near Pistoia.[43] In the Florentine *laudario* MS Chigiano L.VII.266, he is credited as the author of the Bianchi *lauda*, *Vedete, o peccatori* ('See, O you sinners').[44] The rubric even dates the composition of the *lauda* specifically to August 1399, suggesting it was written in the midst of the processions. It is unusual for a preacher to feature cross-textually in this manner, although this could reflect his reported fame as an excellent orator.[45] These examples demonstrate the important role of a series of individuals in creating motivation and momentum for the Bianchi movement.

To sum up, there was considerable space for members of the church hierarchy during the Bianchi processions. They contributed to the successful adoption and spread of the processions in all the locations under consideration here. The clergy determined whether the processions could occur; secular leaders could decide whether or not to let the processions in, as seen with Milan above, but

[40] Alms for the itinerant groups were collected outside the church of San Giovanni di Rotondo and sent out: ibid. 83.
[41] Giorgio Stella, *Annales Genuenses ab anno 1298 usque ad finem anni 1409*, ed. Giovanna Petti Balbi (Bologna, 1975), 240; Melis, *Aspetti*, 102.
[42] Gary Dickson, 'Encounters in Medieval Revivalism: Monks, Friars, and Popular Enthusiasts', *ChH* 68 (1999), 265–93, at 288.
[43] In this tale, an Irish recluse, Capperledis, had a vision of the heavenly court, and was told to spread the Bianchi devotions to prevent total world annihilation. Dominici's chronicle is the only source to include this narrative: *Cronaca dei Bianchi*, ed. Gigliotti, 168.
[44] Vatican City, BAV, MS Chigiano L.VII.266, fols 21r–v, reproduced in Bernard Toscani, ed., *Le laude dei Bianchi contenute nel codice Vaticano Chigiano L. VII 266. Edizione critica* (Florence, 1979), 82–5.
[45] Dominici, *Cronaca dei Bianchi*, ed. Gigliotti, 164.

ecclesiastical authorities were necessary to confess and communicate the populace as part of their spiritual preparation. Preaching allowed the clergy to shape the regulations for the Bianchi participants. This visible role of members of the church hierarchy in the Bianchi devotions provided legitimation, as well as allowing the processions to be shaped according to local norms. Indeed, communal actions such as providing food and drink for the Bianchi often took place behind the scenes, making the clergy the face of communal control.[46] Examining ecclesiastical authorities at this local level provides a more detailed picture of their role in the Bianchi devotions; while they formed a key part of the community, their elevated position in these processions maintained the distinction between laity and clergy. Moreover, this accorded them a significant amount of control during the processions, moulding them to local expectations.

PROCESSIONAL COMPOSITION

Medieval towns played host to a variety of annual feast day processions, including those celebrating major festivals such as Easter and Christmas.[47] These processions could be centred around guilds, confraternities or even military companies.[48] The routes and composition of these processions were often codified in town statutes, which also dictated fines for non-participation.[49] The events were inherently local to each town, combining civic pride and religious devotion.[50]

---

[46] See, for example, Lucca, Archivio di Stato, Raccolte speciali, MS Consiglio Generale 13, 263 (this manuscript is paginated); Pistoia, Archivio Capitolare, MS M6, fol. 15r.

[47] For example, the procession for the patron of Pistoia, St James, was on 25 July. Gai describes a composition centred around guilds, led by *il clero*: Lucia Gai, 'Le feste patronali di S. Jacopo e il palio a Pistoia', *Incontri Pistoiese di storia arte cultura* 39 (1987), 1–29, at 8–15.

[48] Almerico Guerra, *Notizie storiche del volto Santo di Lucca* (Lucca, 1881), 121; Lucca, Archivio di Stato, MS Statuti del Comune di Lucca 5, fols 46v–51r; Richard Trexler, *Public Life in Renaissance Florence* (New York, 1994), 219; Franklin Toker, *On Holy Ground: Liturgy, Architecture and Urbanism in the Cathedral and the Streets of Medieval Florence* (London, 2010), 120–2.

[49] For example, in Lucca, the celebrations for the annual feast for the *Volto Santo* were codified in 1308, and there was a fine of 40 *soldi* for non-participation: Guerra, *Notizie storiche*, 121.

[50] The combination of secular and religious activities incorporated in these processions can be described as 'civic religion'. For an overview of this complicated concept, see Nicholas Terpstra, 'Civic Religion', in John H. Arnold, ed., *The Oxford Handbook of Medieval Christianity* (Oxford, 2014), 148–63; Patrick Boucheron, 'Religion civique,

Alexandra R. A. Lee

These religious rituals in communal spaces provided a template for those organizing the Bianchi processions, allowing the novel devotions to employ familiar local liturgical practices. Hanska suggests that the use or adaptation of traditional liturgical practices during times of crisis was not unusual.[51] We shall examine the composition of several Bianchi processions, treating each town individually in order to compare the different arrangements. This will demonstrate that the processions were not simply adopted indiscriminately in every new location: they were carefully managed.

Among the various Bianchi activities Dominici describes is a nine-day intra-urban procession which began on 18 August in Pistoia. This included ranks of the clergy: the bishop, priests, friars and prelates; followed by men, women and children; then *Battuti* and *Ingesuati* (flagellants and members of an order founded by Giovanni Colombini) and finally whoever was left over.[52] This suggests that despite the white garments worn by the participants, there was clear demarcation between these different groups, in particular a separation between the ecclesiastical and lay sections. Dominici also highlights the high social status of some of the individuals, citing knights and nobles among the throng, indicating that the processions were for everyone.[53]

An even more detailed order was reported for another procession in Pistoia on 7 September. Dominici cites three high-status leaders followed by the *Battuti*, then the rector of Santa Maria, a singer with a viol and men clad in white. Then followed the priests, friars, prelates, abbots, masters of theology, the general (*lo generale*) of the Augustinians and the bishop. Behind them was a group not dressed in white, followed by religious confraternities.[54] The traditional

religion civile, religion séculière. L'Ombre d'un doute', *Revue de synthèse* 134 (2013), 161–83; Andrew Brown, 'Civic Religion in Late Medieval Europe', *JMedH* 42 (2016), 338–56; Alexandra R. A. Lee, *The Bianchi of 1399 in Central Italy: Making Devotion Local* (Leiden, 2021), 146–216.
[51] Hanska, *Strategies*, 55, 63.
[52] Dominici, *Cronaca dei Bianchi*, ed. Gigliotti, 64.
[53] Ibid. 150.
[54] 'Tre guidatori, grandi cittadini … tutti li torchi de' Battuti … poi il crocifisso … di S. Maria a Ripalta: portollo il rettore di S. Maria … uno cantatore con una viola … uomini vestiti tutti di bianco, poi li preti, frati, prelati e abati, maestri in sacra teologia, lo generale de' frati di S. Augustino … poi m. lo Vescovo … poi molta gente non vestita di bianco, poi certi Ingiesuati, Apostoli e simili, poi Battuti': ibid. 129–30.

Pistoiese processional structure, which centred around guilds, was exchanged for one focusing on religious groups; the model was adapted rather than merely adopted.[55] This level of specificity in terms of processional composition suggests communal oversight, as traditions traditionally overseen by civic authorities were transposed onto the novel devotions.

One of the intra-urban processions Sercambi describes in Lucca was composed of lay men, lay women, members of the *Anziani* (a town council of nine members) and the bishop.[56] This highlights the combined presence of secular and religious authorities as key groups within the processions, separated from the laity at large. The specificity of these demarcations within a rapidly organized procession again suggests reliance on a pre-existing order connected to the town's annual celebrations. Sercambi's illustrations offer a small amount of information about processional composition.[57] The individuals at the heads of each procession depicted carry crucifixes or large candles.[58] Some differentiation is offered in that many of those leading the processions wear beards, although they wear the same, raised white hoods as the other participants. While Sercambi's text suggests a great diversity of participation from various levels of society, including men and women, the images do not provide visual reinforcement of this diversity.

Andrea Stefani's report of Florentine processions included the bishop and the Signoria together announcing the Bianchi processions and encouraging participation, thus uniting these authorities. The participants included men and women, adults and children, and Stefani highlights those leading the singing: priests, school children and nuns.[59] He includes no further information about how the participants were ordered, except that they were to walk four by four. Datini reports an itinerant procession beginning in Florence in which the groups were arranged by parish.[60] This less complex

[55] Gai, 'Feste patronali', 8–15.
[56] Sercambi, *Croniche*, ed. Bongi, 2: 354.
[57] While it was initially believed that Sercambi created the images himself, recent scholarship has noted the professional nature of the illustrations, although it is likely that Sercambi had some oversight: Banti and Cristiani Testi, *Le illustrazioni*, 70–4.
[58] Ibid. 199 (image 470).
[59] 'Preti o scolari o monache o scolare femmine': Biblioteca Marucelliana, MS C.152, fol. 54r. Singing *laude* such as the *Stabat Mater* was a crucial requirement for Bianchi participants.
[60] Melis, *Aspetti*, 101.

processional composition would presumably have been more practical for those travelling from town to town. The Florentine sources do not mention the presence of communal authorities, but this does not mean they were not there. Indeed, it is likely that processional orders from annual processions would have been co-opted in Florence, as in Lucca and Pistoia, and perhaps they were simply so well known that Stefani and Datini did not feel they needed repeating.

Giovanni Conversini da Ravenna's report on the Bianchi in Padua demonstrates that processional composition was not solely a Tuscan concern.[61] Like Datini, Da Ravenna reports organization by parish, although the Paduan Bianchi were to walk three by three. The processions were led by the mendicants, followed by other religious orders, and then the laity organised by *quartiere*: children and women, and finally men.[62] For the intra-urban processions, which lasted nine days, a different parish led the procession each day. This is an extra level of detail not present in Tuscan sources, suggesting a slightly more complicated composition in Padua.

These detailed processional compositions account mainly for the intra-urban processions; much less detail is provided for the itinerant devotions. The participants in these intra-urban examples were ordered according to local norms, as pre-existing processional orders were adapted. This meant that the whole community was involved: the laity, alongside ecclesiastical and secular authorities. Notwithstanding, usual social distinctions were maintained; while everyone was to participate, they were not accorded equal status within the processions. This local, comparative analysis reveals the crucial role of ecclesiastical authorities in providing practical support to manage and facilitate these important processions to prevent the plague. Their intervention encouraged orderly participation from as much of the populace as possible.

PROCESSIONAL ROUTES

Another key concern for the Bianchi processions was the nine-day routes taken within towns for intra-urban processions, and those followed by the itinerant participants. The routes for annual liturgical

---

[61] Da Ravenna, *Processione*, ed. Cortese and Cortese, 66–8.
[62] *Quartieri* were the official divisions of the city, and each *quartiere* usually had a main parish church.

processions were usually well established, reinforcing the idea of the city as a sacred landscape, although little information about these routes survives.[63] For the Bianchi, reports of intra-urban processions focus on the church or churches visited each day, sometimes complemented by detailed itineraries of the processions' progress through the streets of the town. Reports of itinerant processions tend to focus instead on the town or towns visited each day, meaning that we can only speculate about the precise route taken through these urban spaces to visit the requisite daily church or churches. The chronicles do not elucidate how routes were selected, although the practical use of space and achievable daily distances suggest a degree of oversight. I will first consider intra-urban processions, then itinerant examples. Chroniclers often describe a multitude of processions within their treatment of the Bianchi, so particularly detailed examples have been selected.

In Lucca, the populace prepared for the Bianchi devotions by confessing and receiving communion. However, the secular authorities decided against letting anyone leave the town to participate in an itinerant procession. Even so, some individuals managed to 'escape' before the town gates could be shut, and could not be convinced to return. A single day of intra-urban processions was staged on 13 August 1399 for those who remained within the town, but the populace judged this insufficient in comparison to the nine-day itinerant tour of their fellow Lucchese who had managed to leave the town.[64]

Consequently, a *novena* was begun on 15 August, coinciding with the feast of the Assumption. On each of the nine days, the intra-urban Lucchese Bianchi met at a specific church for mass; thereafter they processed to the cathedral of San Martino, and then returned home, moving between two churches each day.[65] All but one of the churches visited were within the town walls, and they included the main Franciscan and Dominican churches. While the churches are named, the routes from each church to the cathedral are not elucidated. However, some churches, such as San Frediano, had well-established processional traditions from annual liturgical feast days

---

[63] Philip Sheldrake, *The Spiritual City: Theology, Spirituality, and the Urban* (Chichester, 2014), 70.

[64] Sercambi, *Croniche*, ed. Bongi, 2: 348.

[65] Ibid. 2: 353–7. The churches were Santa Maria Forisportam, San Frediano, San Salvatore, San Michele, San Francesco, San Romano, Santa Maria dei Servi and San Giovanni.

and these may have been followed.[66] When exiting the baptistry church of San Giovanni, the cathedral is visible, so this would have been a very short procession indeed had the participants gone straight from one to the other. It is therefore possible that more circuitous routes were taken. Another issue was practicality: all these churches were relatively large, and most had a piazza outside into which Bianchi participants could overflow if required. This was not a fixed set of Bianchi churches, however, and itinerant Bianchi from other places would visit other locations, suggesting a level of oversight in directing the different groups of participants.[67]

The situation for a procession in August in Pistoia was similar, with the participants meeting at a named church each day for mass before processing to the cathedral of San Zeno. The churches were all within the town walls, and again included those of the Franciscans and Dominicans.[68] A route is indicated for the first day of the processions, which also involved the Pistoiese Bianchi who were beginning an itinerant procession, but the remainder of the days specify only a named church.[69] The route for the initial day focuses on the churches visited by the participants, as well as naming secular landmarks such as *Porte* and the palazzo of Piero Cancellieri.[70] Another contrast with Lucca is that each of the named churches is roughly equidistant from the cathedral, providing a similar journey for each day of the intra-urban Pistoiese Bianchi if a direct route were taken.

Two perspectives on Florence are provided by Stefani's account of an intra-urban procession there and Datini's account of the use of Florence as the starting point for an itinerant procession. The churches described by Stefani cover a broader geographical area than those visited by the intra-urban processions in Lucca and Pistoia, but remain within the bounds of Florentine

[66] There is no record of the route taken: Kasimir Edschmid, *La Processione di Lucca* (Lucca, 1991).
[67] For example, a group of itinerant Bianchi participants from Montemagno visited Sant'Agostino: Sercambi, *Croniche*, ed. Bongi, 2: 319.
[68] Dominici, *Cronaca dei Bianchi*, ed. Gigliotti, 80–101. The churches were San Zeno, San Francesco, San Lorenzo, San Giovanni Fuorcivitas, San Paolo, Servi, San Bartolomeo, San Domenico and San Francesco.
[69] Gai states that the annual *Volto Santo* procession began at San Francesco and ended at the cathedral, but that no sources record the route: 'Feste patronali', 14.
[70] A member of a high-ranking family in Pistoia: Dominici, *Cronaca dei Bianchi*, ed. Gigliotti, 80.

territory.[71] This could reflect the dominion of Florence over a broader area, coupled with the fact that there was no issue of participants trying to leave the city, as in Lucca. There is significant overlap in the spaces traversed by Datini, although the merchant relied more on secular landmarks like *Porte* and bridges.[72] This focus on entry points to, and bridges within, Florence may reflect its position as the start of an itinerant procession, as seen above with Dominici's description of the Bianchi at Pistoia. The specificity of this route suggests that the leaders knew where to take the Bianchi participants as they were led out of Florence for their itinerant journey.

Again, Padua provides a useful northern point of contrast. Da Ravenna notes a series of churches and secular landmarks to be visited and passed through, recording an impressive level of detail for each of the different, circular processions.[73] Each of the nine days began and ended at the cathedral, with the exception of the final day, which focused on the church of Santa Giustina, whose patronal festival it was. Da Ravenna even indicates whether participants should turn left or right down particular streets, as well as suggesting distances.[74] He also shows how access to the sacred spaces was facilitated by the commune: certain individuals would lead the way, open (*aprire*) streets and fill in holes in the roads.[75] This demonstrates the chronicler's detailed knowledge of these routes, as well as highlighting a different mode of practice to the Tuscan examples. Several churches were reportedly visited each day, with some visited more than once throughout the nine-day period. Again, this differs from the

[71] Biblioteca Marucelliana, MS C.152, fol. 53v. The notation '∧' in the manuscript indicates that the fifth day's location is missing. The churches named are: San Ghaggio, Santo Antonio a Ricorboli and San Miniato, Verzara, 'il tempio', San Salus, San Ghallo, the monastery at Montedomini, San Giovanni Trallarcora and San Bartolo fuori della porta al Prato.
[72] Melis, *Aspetti*, 101–2. After the participants gathered at Santa Maria Novella, this procession went through the Porta a San Gallo, the Porta alla Crocie and the Porta alla Giustizia before reaching Santa Croce, then crossing the Ponte Rubaconte and going on to the Piazza de' Mozzi, the Porta a San Niccolò, and then to Ricorboli.
[73] Da Ravenna, *Processione*, ed. Cortese and Cortese, 68–89. For example, the first procession left the cathedral and went to Sant'Agostino, San Michele (whose feast it was), Santa Maria Maddalena, the convent of San Francesco piccolo and San Prosdocimo: ibid. 68–71. The granular level of detail offered by Da Ravenna suggests a different approach to recording the processions.
[74] For example, 'octo prope stadia emensi … ordines processerunt' ('so, the processions went forward for eight *stade*'): ibid. 87. This distance is roughly equal to 1.5 kilometres.
[75] Da Ravenna, *Processione*, ed. Cortese and Cortese, 75–7.

Tuscan intra-urban Bianchi processions which focused on one church each day. However, like Datini and Dominici, Da Ravenna includes a mixture of sacred and secular markers for the participants to follow as they navigated the processional route through the town, making these intra-urban processions more like the reported Tuscan itinerant processional beginnings.

The distribution of churches in each town meant that the Bianchi participants covered a significant amount of urban space. Hanska suggests that circular processional routes were common, making a 'sphere of protection'.[76] Indeed, it is possible that this is what the Bianchi participants were aiming to achieve through their various intra-urban routes. Da Ravenna notes that the routes were always circular within Padua, and the spread of churches in Lucca and Pistoia creates a circle around the cathedral, as does Stefani's route for Florence. Datini's route however is more linear, simply leading out of the town rather than making the town a key focus. This appears to constitute a difference in aim between the itinerant and intra-urban processions: those which remained within the towns sought as much divine protection as possible for the town itself, whereas itinerant processions were more focused on the journey from town to town to secure salvation. It is to these itinerant journeys that we now turn.

Accounts describing the nine-day itinerant processions tend to focus solely on the towns visited each day. Figure 2 shows the area of Tuscany covered by the processions under discussion. Sercambi reports a group of Lucchese Bianchi visiting Castelfranco, San Miniato, Vicopisano, Calci, Cigoli, Vorno, Vico, Bu(i)ti, Badia di Guamo (Cantignano) and Pontectio (Pontetetto), before returning to Lucca.[77] If Sercambi's route is to be taken as the one followed by these Bianchi, it is not especially direct, although the distance to be covered each day was roughly 25 kilometres. The Pistoiese route is much more circular, visiting Quarrata, Tizzana, Carmignano, Signa, Fiesole, Florence, Peretola, Campi, Prato and Pacciana, before arriving back in Pistoia.[78] While no specific churches are mentioned, the fact that Dominici mentions the *cintola*, a relic of the Virgin, suggests that the Prato cathedral (where it was kept) was a stopping point. Dominici also records that the procession stopped in more than

[76] Hanska, *Strategies*, 58.
[77] Sercambi, *Croniche*, ed. Bongi, 2: 360–6.
[78] Dominici, *Cronaca dei Bianchi*, ed. Gigliotti, 73–100.

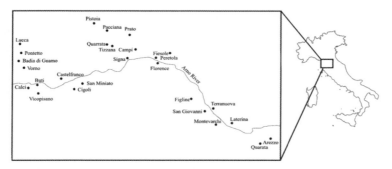

Figure 2. Map of Itinerant Tuscan Bianchi procession towns.

nine towns, although the distance between some stops is very short: for example, Quarrata and Tizzana are only 3.4 kilometres apart. It would therefore have been possible to visit more than one town each day, spreading the Bianchi message in the hope of preventing the forthcoming plague. As Datini describes a procession in which he took part, rather than just providing a report, it is perhaps unsurprising that the route is the neatest. Beginning at Florence, the procession went to Figline, San Giovanni, Montevarchi and Quarata, reaching Arezzo before turning back northwards through Laterina and Terranuova on the way back to Florence. There was a distance of between ten and fifty kilometres between each town. Some towns lay at intersections between different routes: for example, a Bianchi group left from Florence on 28 August 1399, six days after the itinerant Pistoiese Bianchi had visited the town.

The more northerly sources provide less detail on itinerant activities. Da Ravenna does not provide any information on itinerant routes taken by the Paduan Bianchi. However, sources from Milan suggest that there were prohibitions on movement which had an impact on Bianchi processions in Milanese territories; indeed, routes were curtailed specifically to avoid spreading the plague.[79] As such, the Milanese were only allowed to participate in intra-urban processions and were stringently separated by *quartiere*. In Venice, the Bianchi were not allowed in, for political rather than public health

---

[79] Bornstein, *Bianchi*, 64–82; Giuliana Albini, *Guerra, fame, peste. Crisi di mortalità e sistema sanitario nella Lombardia tardomedioevale* (Bologna, 1982), 24.

reasons. The authorities believed that that there were already sufficient religious processions in the city and were also suspicious of
the problematic Dominican Giovanni Dominici who was leading
this procession.[80] The Tuscan Bianchi did sometimes meet with
issues, as seen in Lucca, but the sources suggest that there was
more significant opposition to the Bianchi processions in Milan
and Venice.

A variety of considerations were therefore involved in establishing
processional routes. While there are no written accounts of communal intervention in route planning, it seems likely that there must
have been some oversight to ensure that the distances were feasible
and churches would not be overwhelmed. Moreover, political and
public health issues had to be addressed. For the intra-urban processions, popular spaces were used, activating sacred spaces used for feast
days. This would have made it easier for the populace to understand
the expectations for the Bianchi devotions, and for those leading and
marshalling the processions. Control over the itinerant devotions was
more difficult than with the intra-urban alternatives, but oversight
remained crucial. This is particularly visible in the way that towns
provided for their itinerant participants, as demonstrated with the
organization of food provision for the Pistoiese procession discussed
above. This meant that someone within Pistoia needed to know
where the where the groups would be in order to arrange for the supplies to reach them. Overall, this examination of the evidence from
several towns demonstrates the involvement of communes in ensuring that the Bianchi participants followed ordered routes as they
attempted to prevent the threatened epidemic of plague.

CONCLUSION

As usual during times of epidemic, Italian ecclesiastical authorities
mobilized to lead the populace in religious processions with the
hope of securing salvation from the disease. The Bianchi processions
were an amplified version of these usual devotions. Plague was presented as the motivation for the Bianchi devotions from the origin

---

[80] Daniel Bornstein, 'Giovanni Dominici, the Bianchi and Venice: Symbolic Action and
Interpretive Grids', *Journal of Medieval and Renaissance Studies* 23 (1993), 143–71.
Giovanni Dominici, while initially supported by the church, created enmity between
the Dominican order and in Venice by his actions.

stories that were narrated by preachers, and circulated in the form of *laude*. Clerical endorsement meant that participants could prepare spiritually for the plague-prevention processions through confession and communion, and visit numerous sites of worship, either within their own town or on itinerant processions. The plague began to arrive in Tuscany in the late summer and autumn of 1399, but the chroniclers do not comment on the advent of the disease in connection with the efforts of the Bianchi participants.

Ecclesiastical endorsement undoubtedly contributed to the successful spread of the Bianchi devotions. Indeed, previous popular religious revivals such as the flagellants at the time of the Black Death and the Shepherds' Crusades were unsuccessful in this, due to their condemnation and other practical issues, compared to those which involved members of the church, such as the Great Hallelujah, which spread more easily.[81] The Bianchi belong with the more successful revivals, in that they were not condemned and enjoyed a significant geographical spread, and the church's visible role in the devotions provided an ecclesiastical seal of approval. Indeed, even the pope endorsed the processions once they reached Rome.[82] Local authorities were able to exploit traditional processional norms for the Bianchi devotions, particularly processional composition. There is more work to be done on mapping the routes involved, and particularly in exploring the sometimes minutely described use of urban space. Preaching played a key role, not just in disseminating the need for the devotions, but also for clarifying local expectations in terms of what participants were supposed to do. Bishops and other clergy also led certain processions, further underscoring ecclesiastical support. Thus, unlike previous revivals which had a single leader throughout their spread, the Bianchi were shaped at a local level with local leaders, allowing an unprecedented level of control.

Members of the church therefore played a crucial role in supporting the populace through a moment of crisis. They prepared them, marshalled them and provided daily input through sermons. This support moved with the participants, both notionally in terms of

---

[81] Malcolm Barber, 'The Pastoureaux of 1320', *JEH* 32 (1981), 143–66; Augustine Thompson, *Revival Preachers and Politics in Thirteenth-Century Italy: The Great Devotion of 1233* (Oxford, 1992).
[82] After initial hesitation, Pope Boniface IX showed the Bianchi various relics in September 1399: Sercambi, *Croniche*, ed. Bongi, 2: 370–1.

the regulations and physically as bishops and preachers joined the processions. Such actions were not dissimilar to those which formed part of annual liturgical processions. However, the support that the clergy demonstrated for the novel Bianchi procession in 1399 was a significant factor in their spread throughout Tuscany, allowing the populace to attempt to prevent the foretold plague epidemic. Church authorities tempered the fervour of this popular religious revival, intervening not in a malicious manner but to shape the processions and control their impact.

Preaching during Plague Epidemics in Early Modern Germany, *c.*1520–1618

Martin Christ*

University of Erfurt

This article considers preaching during plague epidemics in early modern Germany, tracing how preachers and priests engaged with the crisis that befell their towns. It does so by discussing three important features of preaching during plague epidemics to illustrate the arrangements made during outbreaks of plague and what they can tell us more broadly about preaching during times of crisis. First, it shows the changes and continuities in personnel during plague epidemics. Second, it considers the contents of the sermons and how plague was a continuous feature of many early modern sermons. Third, the article discusses spaces and how they were used for preaching during outbreaks of plague. The article shows the malleability of sermons and how Protestants and Catholics adapted recurring themes to illustrate divine punishment and mercy.

In 1527, plague broke out in Wittenberg.[1] In his recommendations following this epidemic, Martin Luther (1483–1546) started by exploring two possibilities. When plague strikes a town, he wrote,

> [S]ome people are of the firm opinion that one need not and should not run away from the deadly plague. But rather, as death is God's punishment, which he sends to us for our sins, we must submit to God and with true and firm faith patiently await our punishment. ... Others

* Max-Weber-Kolleg, Steinplatz 2, 99085 Erfurt, Germany. E-mail: martin.christ@uni-erfurt.de.
This article was written as part of the KFG 'Religion and Urbanity: Reciprocal Formations' (DFG, FOR 2779). I wish to thank the editors and anonymous reviewers for their helpful comments and suggestions.

[1] See Lyndal Roper, 'When plague came to Wittenberg', *London Review of Books blog*, 6 July 2020, online at: <https://www.lrb.co.uk/blog/2020/july/when-plague-came-to-wittenberg>, accessed 31 January 2021. For a later outbreak of plague in Wittenberg, see also Rudolph Zaunick, 'Ein Neuer Melanchthon-Brief. Zugleich ein Beitrag zur Geschichte der Pest in Wittenberg in den Jahren 1538/39', *Archiv für Geschichte der Medizin* 14 (1923), 114–24.

Studies in Church History 58 (2022), 91–111   © The Author(s), 2022. Published by Cambridge University Press on behalf of Ecclesiastical History Society
doi: 10.1017/stc.2022.5

take the position that one may properly flee, particularly if one holds no public office.[2]

The reformer makes distinctions in terms of those who flee and those who stay, but seems to leave some leeway in his assessment of the two options, writing that 'but since amongst the Christians there are few who are strong and many who are weak, one cannot simply place the same burden on everyone'.[3] He applied the same logic to himself, affirming that he was willing to take medicine, air rooms and avoid places where he was not needed, but if God called on him to help, he would not avoid any person or place.[4]

However, while Luther recognized the weakness of some, he argued that 'those engaged in preaching and pastors must remain steadfast in the face of death. We have a plain command from Christ, "a good shepherd lays down his life for his sheep"'.[5] These instructions meant that preachers in particular had to stay in towns, even if plague broke out, an assessment that was also shared by many Catholics.[6] Luther expanded on this idea by including groups of people whom he thought should also stay in the towns. Fathers and mothers should help their children, and children their parents; those with sick neighbours and 'paid public servants such as city physicians, town scribes, constables, or whatever their titles,

[2] 'Auffs erste stehen etliche feste drauff, Man musse und solle nicht fliehen ynn sterbens leufften, sondern weil das sterben ist eine straffe Gottes, uns zugeschickt umb unser sunden willen, solle man Gott stil halten und der straffe gedültiglich erwarten ynn rechtem festen glauben ... Die andern aber halten, Man muege wol fliehen, sonderlich die, so nicht mit empten verhafftet sind': Martin Luther, 'Ob man vor dem Sterben fliehen möge', *WA* 23: 321–86, at 338–41. All translations are mine unless otherwise stated.
[3] 'Aber weil es unter den Christen so gethan ist das der starcken wenig und der schwachen viel sind, kann man fur war nicht einerley allen auffladen zu tragen': ibid. 340–1.
[4] See also Luther's 1519 sermon, 'Ein Sermon von der Bereitung zum Sterben': *WA* 2: 680–97; and his letter to Spalatin during the period of plague: *WA*, Br 3: 191–2; Johannes Brenz, 'Die erst sermon von bereyttung zu dem sterben' (1529), in idem, *Frühschriften Teil 2*, ed. Martin Brecht et al. (Tübingen, 1974), 67–79; Andreas Osiander, *Wie vnd wohin ein Christ die grausamen plag der pestilentz fliehen soll* (Nuremberg, 1533).
[5] 'Desselbigen gleichen, die so ym geistlichen ampt sind, als prediger und seelsorger, sind auch schuldig zu stehen und bleiben ynn sterben und tods noten. Denn da stehet ein öffentlicher befelh Christi: 'Ein guter hirt lest sein leben fur sein schaff': *WA* 23: 340–3.
[6] See, for example, Jakob Hornstein, *Sterbensflucht: Das ist, Christlicher vn[d] Catholischer Bericht von Sterbensläuff der Pest: Sampt angehengter frag vnd antwort, ob man derselbigen Zeit fliehen soll oder nit* (Ingolstadt, 1593).

should not flee unless they provide capable replacements who are acceptable to their lords'.[7]

Outbreaks of disease, and responses to them, always reveal much about a society and Luther's comments are no exception.[8] This article looks at preaching as a particularly important feature of early modern clerical provision to trace how Protestant pastors and Catholic priests engaged with the crisis that befell their communities. As indicated by Luther's advice, there was no clear behavioural norm defining whether someone was supposed to stay or leave during a plague, as even Luther added the caveat that officeholders should be allowed to leave if they provided a suitable replacement. This article explores these dynamics by showing the difficult line early modern clerics had to negotiate when it came to preaching during outbreaks of plague.[9]

It does so by discussing three important features of preaching during plague epidemics to illustrate the arrangements made during outbreaks of plague and what they can tell us about preaching during times of crisis more broadly. First, the article considers the preachers themselves and introduces the figure of the 'plague preacher', a preacher employed specifically during plague epidemics to supplement preaching and pastoral provision in a town. Second, it looks at a selection of sermons, either specifically on the plague or delivered during plague epidemics, which focus on disease and its prevention. This section shows how malleable sermons were when it came to admonishing the urban community, and how preachers used plague to illustrate both divine punishment and mercy.[10] This part is based on a selection of plague sermons and other texts related to the plague,

---

[7] '[W]as gemeine personen sind, auff sold und lohn gedingt, als ein stad artzt, stad diener, soldener, und wie die mogen genennet werden, mugen nicht fliehen, sie bestellen denn andere tuchtige und gnugsame an yhre stat, die von den herren angenomen werden sollen': *WA* 23: 344–5.

[8] See Neithard Bulst, 'Krankheit und Gesellschaft in der Vormoderne. Das Beispiel der Pest', in idem and Robert Delort, eds, *Maladies et Société (XIIe–XVIIIe siècles). Actes du colloque de Bielefeld* (Paris, 1989), 17–47.

[9] For a long-term view, see Franco Mormando and Thomas Worcester, eds, *Piety and Plague: From Byzantium to the Baroque* (Kirksville, MO, 2007).

[10] On urbanity and religion more broadly, see Jörg Rüpke and Susanne Rau, eds, 'Religion and Urbanity: Reciprocal Formations', *Religion and Urbanity Online* [online database], 2020, at: <https://www.degruyter.com/database/URBREL/entry/urbel. 13230336/html>, accessed 21 October 2021; Susanne Rau and Jörg Rüpke, 'Religion und Urbanität. Wechselseitige Formierungen als Forschungsproblem', *Historische Zeitschrift* 310 (2020), 654–80.

which are recorded in the *Verzeichnis der deutschsprachigen Drucke des 16. Jahrhunderts* and *Verzeichnis der deutschsprachigen Drucke des 17. Jahrhunderts*. This focus on printed sources results in a bias towards major political and administrative polities. Further archival research is required to establish whether manuscript sources point in a similar direction to that of the printed works discussed here. Finally, the article considers whether the spaces where preachers delivered their sermons changed during plague epidemics, and explores what other unique factors can be detected when preachers gave sermons in these extraordinary times. Looking at plague epidemics through the lens of preachers and their sermons allows us to better understand how clerics had to adapt and how plague fitted into broader theological patterns.

The article focuses on towns in the Holy Roman Empire, a loose collection of territories, bishoprics, imperial free cities and other polities, which was nominally ruled by an emperor, appointed by seven electors.[11] There was great diversity in the empire, politically, culturally and from the mid-1550s also confessionally; Lutheranism was officially recognized alongside Catholicism under the Peace of Augsburg in 1555.[12] This article considers the period from the introduction of the Reformation in German-speaking Europe around 1520, to the beginning of the Thirty Years' War (1618–48).[13] This period witnessed a number of local outbreaks of plague, though none as widespread as those of the Middle Ages, nor as catastrophic as later ones, such as the London plague of 1665–6.[14] This focus makes it

[11] For an overview, see Peter H. Wilson, *The Holy Roman Empire: A Thousand Years of Europe's History* (London, 2016); Joachim Whaley, *Germany and the Holy Roman Empire (1493–1806)*, 2 vols (Oxford, 2012).

[12] The Peace of Westphalia (1648) would later recognize Reformed towns and regions.

[13] For a discussion of a later period, see Jörg Zapnik, *Pest und Krieg im Ostseeraum, Der Schwarze Tod in Stralsund während des Großen Nordischen Krieges (1700–1721)* (Hamburg, 2007); Otto Ulbricht, 'Gelebter Glaube in Pestwellen 1580–1720', in Hartmut Lehmann and Anne-Charlott Trepp, eds, *Im Zeichen der Krise. Religiosität im Europa des 17. Jahrhunderts* (Göttingen, 1999), 159–88.

[14] A. Lloyd Moote and Dorothy C. Moote, *The Great Plague: The Story of London's most Deadly Year* (London, 2008). See also the works of Vanessa Harding, for example her 'Plague in Early Modern London: Chronologies, Localities, and Environments', in Lukas Engelmann, John Henderson and Christos Lynteris, eds, *Plague and the City* (London, 2018), 39–69; 'Reading Plague in Seventeenth-Century London', *SHM* 32 (2019), 267–86.

possible to explore individual responses to plague epidemics, and to see how urban magistrates and preachers responded to the challenges posed by outbreaks of plague in a period that has received little scholarly attention in terms of outbreaks of disease.[15] The time-span, from the early 1520s to the Thirty Years' War, shifts the focus away from the main epidemics of the Middle Ages and later seventeenth century.[16] The dramatic outbreak of the Thirty Years' War is a suitable endpoint, as the developments the war brought about also changed how people perceived and wrote about the plague and related disasters.

As has often been observed, it is hard to say what exactly plague was in an early modern context, as exemplified in the London 'Bills of Mortality', which use various terms in connection to the plague.[17] The first 'Bills of Mortality' were published in 1592 and they continued until the middle of the nineteenth century, using different words for plague over this period. Pestilence, plague or fever, and their German equivalents (*Pestilenz, Pest, Fieber*), or even just 'times of death' (*Sterbenszeiten*), could be used interchangeably.[18] Rather than seeking to determine what exactly *Pest* was, this article focuses on early modern interpretations of plague and what that can tell us about theology and society more broadly.

---

[15] Andrew Cunningham and Ole Peter Grell, *The Four Horsemen of the Apocalypse: Religion, War, Famine and Death in Reformation Europe* (Cambridge, 2000), 274–95. For research on a specific town during this period, see, for example, Monika Höhl, *Die Pest in Hildesheim. Krankheit als Krisenfaktor im städtischen Leben des Mittelalters und der Frühen Neuzeit (1350–1750)* (Hildesheim, 2002).

[16] There is a vast amount of literature on medieval plagues, see, for example, Samuel K. Cohn Jr, 'The Black Death: End of a Paradigm', *AHR* 107 (2002), 703–38; idem, *The Black Death transformed: Disease and Culture in Early Renaissance Europe* (London and New York, 2002); William G. Naphy and Andrew Spicer, *The Black Death and the History of Plagues 1345–1730* (Stroud, 2000); David Herlihy, *The Black Death and the Transformation of the West*, ed. Samuel K. Cohn Jr (Cambridge, MA, 1997).

[17] Roy Porter, *London: A Social History* (Cambridge, MA, 2001), 2–4, 66–92.

[18] It is now the consensus amongst historians and biologists that the plague of the early modern period was caused by the same pathogen as modern variants of the disease: see Monica Green, 'The Four Black Deaths', *AHR* 125 (2020), 1601–31; John Aberth, *The Black Death: A New History of the Great Mortality in Europe, 1347–1500* (New York, 2020), 10–13; Guido Alfani and Tommy Murphy, 'Plague and Lethal Epidemics in the Pre-Industrial World', *Journal of Economic History* 77 (2017), 314–43, especially 315–18.

Preachers

One of the most noticeable changes to clerical hierarchies during plague epidemics was the employment of plague preachers (*Pestprediger* or *Pastores Pestilentarius*) to support local clergy, especially those who had contracted the disease themselves, or to enable local clergy to leave the town. These preachers, who also administered the sacraments and (at least in Catholic areas) the last rites, would enter into life-threatening situations and many of them died quickly due to their exposure to the plague. People living in the early modern period realized that the plague spread rapidly among those in contact with victims, such as doctors and grave diggers, but also clerics.[19] In line with Luther's recommendations, some urban magistrates and preachers wanted to stay safe while providing spiritual guidance for their congregations, and the employment of plague preachers was one way of doing so.

Many plague preachers were low down the clerical hierarchy and died quickly, so few sources written by or about them survive, making it hard to determine how widespread their employment was. The range of terms used to describe them adds to this difficulty, as some terms, such as assistant preachers (*Hilfsprediger*), were not used exclusively for plague preachers. Nineteenth-century lists of preachers composed by antiquarians and church historians, who had access to some documents which no longer exist, give us a sense of the short-lived nature of many of the plague preachers' appointments. Martin Schwarzbach, for example, was *Pastor Pestilentarius* for only one year in Zittau (1608), before he 'went mad' and had to be locked up, probably because he had contracted the plague.[20] Others were more fortunate. Adam Rodiger, or Radiger, replaced the deacon (*Diakon*), the lowest-ranking cleric in Bautzen, in order to take care of the citizens infected with plague. He was also called 'doctor of the soul' (*Seelarzt*), probably another term for a plague preacher, and was called to the quarantined houses of those infected along with a doctor. He held this position between 1612 and 1617 and his 'trial sermon' (*Probepredigt*) was simultaneously dubbed his 'farewell sermon' (*Valepredigt*), as people expected him to die. He survived, however, and became archdeacon of Bautzen

[19] Cohn, *Black Death transformed*, 123.
[20] Karl Gottlob Dietmann, *Die gesamte der ungeänderten Augsb. Confession zugethane Priesterschaft in dem Marggrafthum Oberlausitz* (Lauban and Leipzig, 1777), 405.

(*Archidiakon*) from 1617 to 1621.[21] Elsewhere, Lutheran preachers' decision to remain in the towns they served echoed Luther's choice to remain in Wittenberg when plague struck there in 1527 (although his later correspondence indicates that he left town during further outbreaks); however, in the examples I was able to find, and despite these Lutheran preachers' decision to remain in plague-stricken towns, their own works do not explicitly cite Luther's example as a motive for doing so.

The gradual development of the office of plague preacher suggests an increasing awareness by urban communities of the importance of providing care for victims of plague, not only to comfort them and their families, but for the continued functioning of their towns by providing medical as well as spiritual remedies during outbreaks of plague. While in the earlier sixteenth century, plague preachers could simply be the most junior members of the clergy or preachers employed quickly to fulfil a specific need, later plague ordinances suggest a slightly different picture. The increasing regulation of these offices indicate that, in the seventeenth century, the office of plague preacher received specific and more clearly defined tasks, relating to the provision of last rites and other deathbed rituals. A plague instruction from 1680, aimed especially at rural communities, recommended that preachers should keep medicine with them, provide opportunities for communion (especially in case victims were to die unexpectedly) and preach frequently and in the open, so that 'the wind [that is, the sound] of the preacher will travel to the people'.[22] Once a preacher returned home, he was to take off and air his clothes in order to avoid infecting others.[23] Through such instructions, clergy became more differentiated, as fulfilling specific tasks. We know from the works of Liliana Górska and others that, in the eighteenth century, town councils appointed plague preachers to visit the sick, while regular preachers continued to deliver sermons, and that plague preaching was tied to strict quarantine rules, illustrating the increasing professionalization of the office of plague preacher, especially in urban settings.[24]

---

[21] Ibid. 76–7.
[22] '[D]er Wind vom Prediger zu den Leuten gehe': Johann Georg Schiebel, *Pest-Apothecke Vor Einfältige Bauern und andere Arme Leute* (n.p., 1680), 20–1.
[23] Ibid. 21.
[24] See Liliana Górska, 'Das frühneuzeitliche Pestpredigeramt', *Barok* 16 (2009), 127–47, at 137–8, 140; see also eadem, *Theatrum atrocissimorum fatorum: Religiöse Pestbewältigung in Danzig 1709* (Tönning, 2010).

Most of the examples I was able to find come from such urban settings. While this could, in part, be due to the lower survival rate of sources from villages and the countryside, it is probably due to urban clergy being generally more differentiated, both in terms of their number and of the tasks they had to fulfil, making the employment of clergy specifically responsible for plague preaching more likely. Furthermore, the more regulated regimes of dealing with plague in towns would explain the greater importance of the office in urban settings. Indeed, the generally smaller number of clergy in villages suggests that, in these settings, a local cleric or his deputy – provided they did not flee from the plague or die of it – would be the ones to provide support for plague victims. While there are cases of plague preachers working in villages or the countryside, normally they came from a local town, once again explaining the stronger connection to urban locales.

The scarcity of sources also makes it difficult to detect specifically Catholic, Lutheran or Reformed trends in the employment of plague preachers. Major theologians of all confessions grappled with questions regarding the correct behaviour during epidemics. The few examples we have suggest that, in general, the appointment of plague preachers cut across confessions, but more sources survive from Lutheran territories, suggesting that the practice might have been more common in these areas. However, this might also be connected to the greater number of sermons delivered by Lutherans compared to Catholics.[25] As discussed above, the patchy record is also an indication of the short-lived nature of many of the appointments and many of the men who took up these posts had previously been employed in less favourable positions or not employed at all.

While it was possible for urban magistrates to employ a plague preacher, either on a short-term basis or on the understanding that he would stay in the town permanently if he survived, it was equally possible for regular preachers to stay in a town and preach there during outbreaks of plague. One of the most interesting examples of this is to be found in the Lusatian town of Görlitz, where Franz Rotbart was the principal preacher. The council initially employed him because they wanted a preacher who would not cause any trouble and would stick to Catholic doctrine. When plague struck the town, the councillors fled to the countryside, while Rotbart stayed,

---

[25] Górska, 'Das frühneuzeitliche Pestpredigeramt', 129–30.

introducing key Reformation changes.[26] No sermons by Rotbart are extant, but it is clear that the flight of the council enabled him to introduce services containing liturgical elements advocated by Luther, which the council would presumably have opposed. On their return, the councillors tried to roll back the changes, but in the end, they could not stop the introduction of some Lutheran elements. The decision of key protagonists to stay in a town or to leave during a plague epidemic could therefore have wide-ranging consequences for the religious outlook of the whole town.

However, regular priests or preachers could also stay with their congregations and preach if they were especially committed to providing for the sick. One especially striking example is that of Justus Zimmermann, the preacher of the hospital (*Spitalprediger*) in Bayreuth in Franconia, who delivered a sermon on the plague in 1602.[27] In it, Zimmermann mentions having contracted plague (*Pest*) himself, and how he had had to refrain from preaching for many weeks.[28] He had lost his wife and only son to the plague and almost died of it himself. He wrote in the preface that he longed to see his dear wife in heaven, where she was with Christ, but that instead, God had called him to continue doing his work. This theme of resilience and continuity has also been observed in English plague

---

[26] On Rotbart, see Martin Christ, 'The Town Chronicle of Johannes Hass: History Writing and Divine Intervention in the Early Sixteenth Century', *German History* 35 (2017), 1–20. On Lusatia more generally, see idem, *Biographies of a Reformation: Religious Change and Confessional Coexistence in Upper Lusatia, c.1520–1635* (Oxford, 2021). See also Johannes Hass, *Goerlitzer Rathsannalen*, ed. E. E. Struve (Görlitz, 1870), 16.

[27] Only two further sermons by Zimmermann are extant, neither of which discusses the 1602 outbreak: Justus Zimmermann, *Dialogus Dialogorum. Das ist: ein Gesprech uber alle Gesprech / Unser Hochverdienten Herrn und Heilands Jesu Christi / mit Martha von Bethanien Von allgemeiner Aufferstehung von den Todten am Jüngsten Tag* (Bayreuth, 1602); idem, *Zu einer Christlichen Leichpredigt: Bey dem Volckreichen Leichbegänguß Des Herrn Conradi Paurschmids* (Bayreuth, 1603).

[28] '[M]ich dieses Predigstuhls unnd aller meiner Priesterlichen Ambtsverrichtungen ettliche Wochen bißanhero enthalten müssen': Justus Zimmermann, *Eine Christliche Klag Trost und LehrPredigt Von der Wittib zu Naim vnd [und] ihrem durch Christum vom Todt erweckten Son*, 6. The printed sermon is unpaginated, so I follow the pagination of the digitized version: Universitätsbibliothek Erlangen-Nürnberg (shelfmark: H00/4 THL-(XVIIII 201)-434), online at: <urn:nbn:de:bvb:29-bv040630577-0>, last accessed 4 February 2022. See also Karl Hermann Zwanziger, 'Bericht des Spitalpredigers Justus Zimmermann über die Pest des Jahres 1602 in Bayreuth', *Archiv für Geschichte von Oberfranken* 24 (1909), 139–69.

sermons.[29] Sermons during times of crisis could provide a crucial sense of continuity for the congregation and town at large, something that Zimmermann also stressed when emphasizing that God had provided him with the opportunity to return to preaching.[30]

In his suffering, Zimmermann found biblical precedents, to which his congregation could also relate. He quoted king Hezekiah as a biblical figure who had also lived through the plague.[31] Zimmermann commented that Sirach 40: 1–4 was a particularly useful text, as were the verses he preached on, the raising of the son of the widow of Nain (Luke 7: 11–17). He also compared himself to Job, having suffered the loss of his wife and son, as well as his own serious illness.[32] Other sermons included passages, such as the raising of Lazarus and similar verses, linked specifically to divine grace and the raising of the dead. In most cases, these were understood to stand for the possibility of recovery from serious disease with divine help. For Zimmermann, these verses were especially relevant because he had been certain that he would die of the plague, and had already drafted his own epitaph.[33]

For Zimmermann, the plague that had torn his family apart was especially painful because he had been unable to be with his wife, his treasure (*Eheschatz*), during her last moments. He deeply regretted that he had not been able to 'close the eyes of my dear wife', but also that, for eight weeks, he had been unable to enter the church despite wanting to preach and do God's work. In the midst of the plague, Zimmermann wrote, he would have been glad to help his 'little sheep'. He thanked his congregation and other citizens for praying for him, not only in the churches, but also in their homes.[34] Whether or not this was a rhetorical point, it shows that concern for a sick preacher transcended a particular congregation and was

---

[29] Olivia Formby, '"Woe unto us": Divine Wrath and Godly Sorrow in an English Plague Sermon (1637)', *SC* 36 (2021), 1–20.

[30] Zimmermann, *Eine Christliche Klag Trost und LehrPredigt*, 10.

[31] For rhetorical tropes connected to plague, see also Rebecca Totaro and Ernest B. Gilman, eds, *Representing the Plague in Early Modern England* (New York and London, 2010).

[32] '[Ich habe] unter dessen practiciret und erfaren / was König Hiskias in dergleichen Pestilenzischen seuch un[d] schwachheit [getan hat]': Zimmermann, *Eine Christliche Klag Trost und LehrPredigt*, 9–10.

[33] Ibid. 8.

[34] Ibid. 9.

discussed in many people's homes, illustrating how an outbreak of plague could also influence domestic settings.

Zimmermann, deeply affected by his own dramatic experiences, wanted to instruct his congregation in how to behave, both in times of trouble and if they recovered, showing them how to lead a pious life.[35] He wrote in his sermon about the loss of his wife and children and pointed out how much such a loss increased the suffering of the bereaved, clearly speaking from experience.[36] The publication of the sermon made it accessible to a broader public and, on the title page, Zimmermann presented the main elements of his story, mentioning the death of his wife and that he had not been able to preach for many weeks. The sermon was dedicated to Zimmermann's mother and mother-in-law, whom he praised for their steadfastness and pitied for their loss, which was also his.

Zimmermann saw his experience as exemplifying how God worked during plagues, arguing that the Lord had not only 'cast him into hell' (*in die Hölle gestossen*), but had also saved him. Out of mercy, the Lord had called him back into his house to do his work once again.[37] Zimmermann wrote that he survived thanks to divine mercy.[38] With this interpretation of divine punishment and redemption, Zimmermann's sermon was typical of early modern plague sermons.

SERMONS

The understanding of plague as a divine punishment was shared by preachers, regardless of confession, across Europe.[39] It included major outbreaks, such as the 'dancing plague' in Strasbourg in 1518 and the Great Plague in London (and England) in 1665–6.[40] Sermons were

---

[35] Ibid. 24–8.

[36] For a cross-temporal approach on suffering in religion, see John R. Hinnells and Roy Porter, eds, *Religion, Health and Suffering* (London and New York, 1998).

[37] Zimmermann, *Eine Christliche Klag Trost und LehrPredigt*, 9.

[38] 'Aber die Güte des HERRN ists / daß wir nicht gar aus sindt. So Gott ist meine Zuversicht und Sterck gewesen': ibid. 8.

[39] See, for example, Andreas Mühling, '"Welchen Tod sterben wir?" Heinrich Bullingers "Bericht der Kranken" (1535)', *Zwingliana* 29 (2002), 55–68, at 61.

[40] Lynneth J. Miller, 'Divine Punishment or Disease? Medieval and Early Modern Approaches to the 1518 Strasbourg Dancing Plague', *Dance Research* 35 (2017), 149–64; J. A. I. Champion, ed., *Epidemic Disease in London* (London, 1993). This explanation for disease continued in sermons throughout the early modern period. See Sabine Holtz,

the primary way of reminding citizens of their sins and of stressing that this was a harsh, but ultimately justified, divine punishment. During a plague epidemic in Blomberg in Westphalia in 1580–2, the Lutheran pastor Justus Piderit delivered a total of eighteen sermons, which were published in Lemgo in 1582.[41] According to Piderit, the plague was not only a punishment from God of sinful mankind, but also an admonition to repentance, providing the opportunity to receive God's grace. Piderit also wrote about the futility of fleeing from the plague, arguing that God's punishment would reach sinners anywhere.

This theme of death coming as it pleases God had been explored by Luther two generations earlier in his sermon on Mark 5: 21–43, where he wrote that he did not fear death through plague because if it was Jesus's will, the plague would harm him less than an attempt to flee. At the same time, he expressed the conviction that if it was God's will to call someone away from this earthly life, this should be accepted willingly.[42] An interpretation of the plague as divine punishment was also shared by Catholics. In his 1593 advice on the plague, for example, Jakob Hornstein, a Catholic priest, wrote that war, pestilence and famine were all divine punishments.[43] The focus on penance was also taken up directly in the title of some sermons: D. G. Lehmann, superintendent in Leipzig in the latter decades of the seventeenth century, called his sermon a 'penitence and plague sermon' (*Buß- und Pest-Predigt*).[44] Reformed theologians similarly argued that disease was a form of divine punishment: in his instructions for the sick and dying, first published in 1535, Heinrich Bullinger argued that disease helped humans to better themselves

---

'Predigt: Religiöser Transfer über Postillen', Europäische Geschichte Online, 2 February 2011, at: <http://www.ieg-ego.eu/holtzs-2011-de>, accessed 8 June 2021.

[41] Justus Piderit, *Tractat von der Pestilentz: in 18 Predigten abgefaßt* (Lemgo, 1582); Neithard Bulst, 'Die Pestpredigten des Justus Piderit', *Lippische Mitteilungen aus Geschichte und Landeskunde* 80 (2011), 99–116.

[42] Luther, 'Predigt am 24. Sonntag nach Trinitatis', *WA* 5: 21–43. This is also articulated in early modern *artes moriendi*: see Volker Leppin, 'Preparing for Death: From the Late Medieval *ars moriendi* to the Lutheran Funeral Sermon', in Tarald Rasmussen and Jon Øygarden Flæten, eds, *Preparing for Death, Remembering the Dead* (Göttingen, 2015), 9–24; Herman J. Selderhuis, '*Ars Moriendi* in Early Modern Calvinism', ibid. 109–22.

[43] Hornstein, *Sterbensflucht*, 14.

[44] D. G. Lehmann, *P.P. Buß- und Pest-Predigt auff Begehren zum Druck befördert worden Von Christoph Wilhelm Streng* (Leipzig, 1680).

and came from God's 'fatherly loyalty and love' (*vß vätterlicher trüw vnd liebe bschähe*).[45] Since God was omnipotent and would punish sinners, Piderit recommended that his listeners stay in the town, pray and repent. 'Through the plague', he wrote, 'God took away many godless people so that the pious are protected and saved from their tyranny and evil actions'. But Piderit also recommended that his readers follow doctors' instructions and take the appropriate medicines.[46] Like Zimmermann after him, he also referred to Sirach as a particularly useful biblical book for those seeking to understand how to behave during plagues.

Piderit was not alone in discussing more practical measures to prevent plague as part of his sermons, at least in their printed form. Many preachers stressed that while it was good to pray and do penance for sins and past transgressions, if one was struck by plague, it was also important to take medicine, as all medicine ultimately derived from God.[47] In this way, many clerics followed the advice of Luther, who had made clear, as quoted at the beginning of this article, that he would take any medicine to ensure a speedy recovery. But while many preachers recognized that the sick should take medicine, they usually also emphasized that it was not sufficient to focus solely on these physical measures; those suffering also had to call on Jesus.[48]

The priest Jakob Hornstein provides a good example of this in his recommendations on how to treat the plague in his 1593 *Sterbensflucht*, which discusses whether people should flee from plague:

> The people should daily pray and attend service, do penance and repent: get rid of all earthly pleasures and desires, jumping, dancing and unnecessary drinking and excessive eating. Most importantly, all inns, houses, flats, streets and alleys should be kept clean and tidy,

---

[45] Heinrich Bullinger, *Bericht der Kranken* (Zurich, 1535), unpaginated [9].

[46] 'So nimpt auch unterweilen unser Herr Godt durch die Pest viell gotloser wegk / uff das de fromen für jrer Tyranney und bösem fürnemen geschutz und darvon erlöset': Piderit, *Tractat von der Pestilentz*, unpaginated preface.

[47] Heribert Smolinsky, 'Volksfrömmigkeit und religiöse Literatur im Zeitalter der Konfessionalisierung', in Hansgeorg Molitor, ed., *Volksfrömmigkeit in der frühen Neuzeit* (Münster, 1994), 27–35, at 32–3. This was also the case for Bullinger, who recommended taking the medicine doctors prescribed: Mühling, '"Welchen Tod sterben wir?"', 59.

[48] Hornstein, *Sterbensflucht*, 5–7.

all foul and bad-smelling filth and things should be moved away quickly.[49]

In these recommendations, Hornstein combined an admonition against a sinful lifestyle with practical instructions on keeping streets and houses clean.[50] Many preachers reinforced the medical recommendations promulgated by town magistrates and physicians, linking them to spiritual advice on appropriate behaviour during plague epidemics.

One Danzig plague ordinance from 1565, for instance, lays down that 'those who die of plague should not be kept in their houses over night, but should quickly be buried in a deep grave'.[51] This timeframe was much shorter than that stipulated in previous ordinances, which called for the dead to be buried within three days or two nights. Just as preachers used recommendations by urban magistrates, so too magistrates invoked religious themes to justify their measures. The Danzig ordinance affirmed that the outbreak of the plague was a result of divine punishment. God had brought this plague onto the town because of the sins of its inhabitants.[52] These connections between clerical and urban actors are also present in other towns. In 1521, the council of Augsburg instructed all town preachers to remind their listeners to give generously to the plague hospital.[53]

Within this complex interplay of preachers and councils, physicians and apothecaries used similar methods, including elements normally associated with church rituals in their advice for the plague.[54]

---

[49] '[D]as Volck zu täglichem Gebett vnd Gottesdienst / Penitentz vnd Buß gehalten: Alle Weltfrewd vnd Wollust / Springen / Tantzen / vberflüßiges Sauffen vnnd Fressen abschaffen: Zuvorderst der Zeit alle Herbergen / Häuser / Wohnu[n]e / Strassen vn[d] Gassen / sauber vnd rein gehalten / aller faulender vn[d] vbelschmeckend[er] Unrath und Wust bey zeit hinwegk geschafft werde': ibid. 57.

[50] Ibid.; see also Smolinsky, 'Volksfrömmigkeit und religiöse Literatur', 32–3.

[51] 'Das auch die verstorbenen an Peste / nicht uber eine nacht in den Heusern gehalten / sondern in zeiten zur Erden in tieffe greber': Bartholomäus Wagner, *Von der Pestilentz / Nützliche vnd gründliche vnterrichtunge wie man sich mit Gottes hülffe vor der vergifftung bewaren / vnd auch den krancken / welche eingefallen / wieder helffen soll* (Danzig, 1565). On the Danzig ordinances, see Edmund Kizik, *Die reglementierte Feier. Hochzeiten, Taufen und Begräbnisse in der frühneuzeitlichen Hansestadt* (Osnabrück, 2008).

[52] Wagner, *Von der Pestilentz / Nützliche vnd gründliche vnterrichtunge*, unpaginated (section entitled 'Von ursachen der Pestilentz').

[53] Mariusz Horanin, 'Die Pest in Augsburg um 1500. Die soziale Konstruktion einer Krankheit' (Ph.D. thesis, Georg-August Universität Göttingen, 2019), 142.

[54] See, for example, Andreas Ellinger, *Rathschlag Herrn D. Andreae Ellingers zu Jehna seligen/ wie man sich zur zeit der Pest praeseruiren* (Leipzig, 1587).

Thus the Lemgo doctor Konrad Heinrich quoted Sirach 38 in the frontispiece of his treatise:[55]

The Lord created medicines from the earth, and a sensible person will not hesitate to use them. Didn't a tree once make bitter water fit to drink, so that the Lord's power might be known? He gave medical knowledge to human beings, so that we would praise him for the miracles he performs. The druggist mixes these medicines, and the doctor will use them to cure diseases and ease pain.[56]

As already seen, Sirach was a favourite book for many plague preachers.[57] Heinrich used this Bible passage to justify his profession as a physician, and drew attention to the instructions that followed to determine proper treatment of the plague. In many cases, instructions for the sick included prayers or hymns which reinforced the content of the sermons preached by the clergy.

In their plague sermons, preachers developed themes of sin and redemption further by adapting them to specific circumstances. These adaptations included biblical verses and their exegesis but also specific advice, for example, on appropriate behaviour or the uses of medicine.[58] Even passages that did not include direct references to disease could be interpreted in a way that made them more relevant for the audience in this time of trial.[59]

Sermons could take on more distinctly confessional tones, especially in Catholic contexts. As well as being associated with other means of penance, such as good works, confession or

---

[55] Heinrich mentions Sirach 38 but without referring to specific verses (the relevant ones are verses 4–7 and part of verse 8). In some Bible translations, this passage is entitled 'Praise of the Doctor' ('Lob des Arztes').

[56] 'Der HERR lest die Artzney aus der Erden wachsen / vnd ein vernüfftiger [sic] verachtet sie nicht / Vnd er hat solche Kunst den Menschen gegeben / das er gepreiset werde in seinen Wunderthaten / Damit heilet er vnd vertreibet die schmertzen / vnd der Apoteker machet Artzney daraus': Konrad Heinrich, *Bericht von der Pest / so dieses lauffenden 80. Jars zu Soist im schwang* (Lemgo, 1580), frontispiece.

[57] For another example, see Simon Gedik, *Gülden Kleinod Für betrübte Hertzen / Oder Trostbüchlein: Auß den fürnembsten Heuptpuncten* (Leipzig, 1608), 384.

[58] Joachim Cirenberger, *Wider alle Pestilenzische geschwinde und gifftige Fieber, Ein gründtlicher volkömlicher Bericht raht und hülffe* (Leipzig, 1564).

[59] See Sabine Holtz, 'Die Unsicherheit des Lebens. Zum Verständnis von Krankheit und Tod in den Predigten der lutherischen Orthodoxie', in Hartmut Lehmann and Anne-Charlott Trepp, eds, *Im Zeichen der Krise. Religiosität im Europa des 17. Jahrhunderts* (Göttingen, 1999), 135–58.

pilgrimages,[60] many Catholic sermons preached during plague epidemics featured elements such as the intercession of saints. In terms of pastoral provision, Catholic priests needed to administer the last rites, whereas Lutherans did not. Some Catholic plague sermons had confessionally distinctive elements, such as references to saintly intercession or papal authority, revealing different theological approaches.

When a town, whether Catholic or Protestant, was recovering from plague and its preachers thought that the worst of the outbreak was over, the tone of the sermons generally shifted. The overarching theme became one of divine mercy and even gratitude to God for teaching the town's inhabitants a lesson.[61] There were still elements of penitence, and many sermons reminded parishioners to remember the divine punishment they had experienced and lead a good life in order to prevent further divine wrath. However, the overwhelming emphasis was one of celebration that the plague had been lifted. In Ulm, the council even decreed a festivity (*Dankfest*) to mark the end of the plague, which also included the delivery of a sermon which was subsequently printed.[62] Preaching to mark the end of an epidemic continued throughout the seventeenth century. In Saxony in 1681, a series of sermons was delivered in Leipzig and Dresden to thank God for turning the plague away from the area.[63] Similarly in 1681, Johann Gottfried Lembacher thanked God for delivering Saxony from further punishment after the plague.[64]

The ongoing threat of epidemics meant that the fear of plague and the memory of recent outbreaks were constantly on people's minds.

---

[60] See Neithard Bulst, 'Heiligenverehrung in Pestzeiten. Soziale und religiöse Reaktionen auf die spätmittelalterlichen Pestepidemien', in A. Löther, ed., *Mundus in Imagine. Bildersprache und Lebenswelten im Mittelalter* (Munich, 1996), 63–97. For a later example, see Franz Xaver Hallauer, *Pest-Predig Bey der, von einer Löblichen S. Michaels Bruderschafft zu Berg ... Von München nach Ebersperg, zu dem Heiligen Martyrer Sebastiano, Umb Abwendung der laydigen Sucht, auf den ersten Sonntag in dem Advent angestellten heiligen Wahlfahrt* (Cölln, 1720).

[61] See, for example, Piderit, *Tractatus von der Pestilentz*, unpaginated preface.

[62] Conrad Dieterich, *Ulmische Dancksagungspredig Wegen gnädiger Abwendung der grausamen geschwinden Seuche der Pest/ Auß dem 107. Psalmen* (Ulm, 1636).

[63] See, for example, Johann Georg III, *Anordnung / Welcher massen Für Die gnädige Erhaltung / und gäntzliche Befreyung dieser Lande von der Pest* (Dresden, 1681); Christoph Zeisseler, *Lob und Danck Opffer Nach überstandener gefährlicher Pest-Zeit* (Leipzig, 1681).

[64] Gottfried Lembach, *O Herr hilff! O Herr laß wohl gelingen! Eine Christliche Danck-Predig* (Dresden, 1681).

So, even when there was no plague, preachers might refer to it as an example of divine punishment. Rhetorical tropes relating to disease and healing were prominent in early modern sermons and preachers knew how to deploy these in order to call parishioners to repentance. In Johann Junghans's collection of sermons, each of which had a theme (such as roses, cold, fire or St Martin's goose) one sermon was dedicated to plague (*Pest*).[65] Junghans stressed that a pious and God-fearing life could prevent plague and that one should be grateful if God did not visit his divine wrath on a town. Andreas Richter's *Ancilis Christianorum*, delivered in 1611 in the village of Wülflingroda in the duchy of Hohnstein in the Harz mountains, was even more explicit in describing how God could protect a town from plague, if – and only if – the inhabitants behaved properly.[66] He told the congregation (and later his readers) about God's protective powers against plague, both real and metaphorical, and how, through a pious life, it was possible for people to prevent this kind of punishment, both for themselves and for the urban community at large. God, he wrote, protected his children from his punishment.[67] The plague thus played an important role in sermons during this period, whether or not there was a local outbreak.

SPACES

Outbreaks of plague also influenced urban spaces, for example when citizens were no longer allowed to leave their houses or had to quarantine in order to avoid infecting other members of the community.[68] Most of the sermons given during outbreaks of plague seem to have been delivered as regular sermons from the pulpit of the parish church. In some cases, the main sermons were delivered by the town preachers

---

[65] Johann Junghans, *M. Johann Junghanßens Gerani, Weiland Pastoris zu Cösteritz/ Sermonum De Tempore* (Erfurt, 1669).

[66] Andreas Richter, *Ancilis Christianorum. Gleubiger Christen Schildt und Wapen/ wider itzt schwebender Straffruthen Gottes* (Mühlhausen, 1611).

[67] Ibid., title page. Processions in Catholic territories expressed a similar wish for divine protection from plague: see Susanne Rau, 'Canons, Councillors and Confrères: Changing Power Constellations in the City of Lyon (Late Middle Ages, Early Modern Times)', Religion and Urbanity Online [online database], 2021, at: <https://www.degruyter.com/database/URBREL/entry/urbrel.13901209/html>, accessed 15 December 2021.

[68] Paul Slack, 'Responses to Plague in Early Modern Europe: The Implications of Public Health', *Social Research* 55 (1988), 433–53.

and the plague preachers gave other sermons and provided pastoral care.[69] At least for the later seventeenth century, there were more listeners in the church, regardless of sickness or quarantine regulations.[70] From extant sermons, we know that preachers recommended that inhabitants of the towns attend church at least once a day.[71] In certain cases, however, the spaces where sermons were delivered changed. Some parishes established plague pulpits (*Pestkanzeln*), for example in Weida in Thuringia or at St Bartholomew's church, Dresden, where it was attached to the outside.[72] In the case of the latter, the pulpit was connected both to the parish church and to the hospital. It was mainly used when there was not enough space in the church for everyone wanting to attend.

While preaching generally took place only in churches or from pulpits, in extreme situations, certain aspects of sermon-giving could be transposed to places infected by plague. Clerics had to provide solace in bedchambers, for instance, and while they normally did not give sermons there, they did read biblical passages and say prayers, just as they would in a sermon.[73] Although this also happened in normal times, it was especially important during plague outbreaks.

There are also indications that preaching took place in plague cemeteries (*Pestfriedhöfe*).[74] Some of these had open air pulpits, as we know from surviving examples. Dead bodies continued to be buried in parish cemeteries and it was normally only when there was no alternative that dedicated plague cemeteries were opened on the outskirts of the town, usually outside its walls or gates.[75] In 1565, the Danzig

---

[69] See Górska, 'Das frühneuzeitliche Pestpredigeramt', 127–8, 130.

[70] Ibid. 127.

[71] Piderit, *Tractat von der Pestilentz,* unpaginated preface.

[72] Anton Weck, *Der Chur-Fürstlichen Sächsischen weitberuffenen Residentz- und Haupt-Vestung Dresden Beschreib- und Vorstellung* (Nuremberg, 1680), 272.

[73] On a Lutheran deathbed and the provision of solace, see Susan C. Karant-Nunn, *The Reformation of Feeling: Shaping the Religious Emotions in Early Modern Germany* (Oxford, 2010), 189–214. See also Benedikt Brunner, 'Madensack oder Tempel Gottes? Lutherische Bewertungen des Leibes im Angesicht des Todes', *Ebernburg-Hefte* 54 (2020), 9–31.

[74] Reiner Sörries, 'Leprosen- und Pestfriedhöfe und ihre Bedeutung für die nachmittelalterlichen Friedhöfe', in idem, ed., *Raum für Tote: die Geschichte der Friedhöfe von den Gräberstraßen der Römerzeit bis zur anonymen Bestattung* (Braunschweig, 2003), 53–62.

[75] Max Heitzer, *Vom Pestfriedhof 1636 zum Kolmsteiner Kircherl* (Haibühl, 1980); Josef Heinzmann, *Die Ringackerkapelle. Das barocke Marienheiligtum auf dem ehemaligen Pestfriedhof bei Leuk-Stadt / VS (Schweiz). Ihre Geschichte, ihre Sehenswürdigkeiten* (Leuk, 1968); Lorena Burkhardt, *Domat/Ems, Sogn Pieder. Vom frühmittelalterlichen*

plague ordinance instructed that 'as many as possible should be buried outside the town'.[76] The focus on the area 'beyond the city wall' is striking; the same regulation stipulated that no 'borrowed shrouds' (*Leylacken*) should be sold inside the city, and that the clothes of the deceased should be washed outside the city gates.[77]

The spatial separation of at least some of the preaching when plague broke out in towns speaks to broader concerns about hygiene and medicine, illustrating at least a rudimentary awareness of the causes of the spread of disease. According to early modern medical theories, polluted air spread the disease and, as such, plague victims had to be buried quickly. In the plague cemeteries, temporal aspects also came into play when the number of burials increased dramatically, so burials and any sermons associated with them had to take place rapidly. This concern to prevent the spread of disease was also expressed in treatises by town physicians, who provided guidance on remedies.[78]

CONCLUSION: PREACHING DURING TIMES OF CRISIS

Although this article has focused on preaching during outbreaks of plague, similar patterns of change can be detected during other times of crisis. Serious fires, for example, elicited similar sermons about divine punishment. Moreover, once a town had survived a serious natural disaster, preaching revolved around gratitude towards God and repentance to prevent further catastrophe.[79] These trends

---

Herrenhof zum neuzeitlichen Pestfriedhof (Chur, 2020). For a medieval example, see Hansueli Etter and Jürg Schneider, *Die Pest in Zürich: ein Pestfriedhof des 14. Jahrhunderts im ehemaligen Augustinergarten am Münzplatz* (Zürich, 1982).

[76] On the movement of cemeteries during the Reformation, see Craig M. Koslofsky, *The Reformation of the Dead: Death and Ritual in Early Modern Germany, c.1450–1700* (London, 2000), 40–77; Wagner, *Von der Pestilentz,* unpaginated.

[77] Wagner, *Von der Pestilentz,* unpaginated. In Augsburg around 1494, the council employed a temporary preacher during epidemics, who was responsible for taking care of the infected in the 'plague houses' (*Pesthäuser*) and recording those who died of plague, so that the citizens could pray for them: Horanin, *Die Pest in Augsburg,* 130.

[78] See, for example, Rat der Stadt Elbing, *Kurtze Verordnung / Wie ein Jedweder bey dieser Zeit / wegen besorglicher Pest-Gefahr / Negst Göttlicher Hülffe sich præserviren / und in der Cur verhalten solle: Mit Zulaß E. Wol Edl. und Hochw. Rahts der Königl. Stadt Elbing* (Elbing, 1708).

[79] See, for example, Zacharias Rivander, *Eine Christliche Predigt Vom schrecklichen Fewer vnd grossen Brandschaden zum Forst in Niederlaussnitz* (Eisleben, 1590). On the intersections of war and plague, see Zapnik, *Pest und Krieg im Ostseeraum.*

show how preaching adapted to specific circumstances and, while many aspects remained the same (such as the structure of the sermon or liturgy), there was a significant degree of flexibility in terms of the personnel, content and space involved in the production and delivery of a sermon. As the example of Justus Zimmermann has shown, this could even include personal experiences of plague, which preachers used in their sermons. Sermons could therefore stand both for continuity, in that preaching was a regular feature of early modern life, and for change, by adapting to specific circumstances.

Some features of these sermons were shared by both confessions, including a focus on divine punishment and redemption, or biblical verses which seemed especially appropriate, such as those from Sirach. One recurring theme in plague sermons across the confessional divide was the question of whether one should flee or remain. We can also detect a joint effort between urban, clerical and medical actors when it came to the prevention and cure of plague. Sermons contained recommendations on how to behave and admonitions to use appropriate medicine, while urban magistrates and physicians used biblical justifications for their instructions.

But there were also important differences, such as the Catholic emphasis on the intercession of saints. There are some indications that Catholic plague sermons were also preached in the New World during outbreaks of serious disease. However, the only example I was able to find comes from the mid-seventeenth century.[80] These missionary sermons, which were supposed to demonstrate divine power to indigenous populations and illustrate key concepts connected to Catholic doctrine, may form an interesting counterpart to the European examples discussed in this article, but further research is needed to determine whether there are enough such sermons to enable a meaningful comparison.

Preachers and parishioners were clearly influenced by disaster. In the case of the clergy, they could draw on their theological knowledge and personal experiences to relate to the members of their congregation and offer advice. These made their sermons more relevant by using points of reference immediately applicable to the situation. Plague was so important that preachers could even invoke ideas about the disease when a town was not immediately affected by it.

[80] See Heinz Willi Wittschier, ed., *Antonio Vieiras Pestpredigt* (Aschendorff, 1973), for an edition of this 1649 sermon.

Many of them focused on three features, depending on when during a plague epidemic the sermons were delivered. At the outset, they emphasized that God was punishing a town or region for its sinful behaviours. In a second stage, the clergy sought to provide a remedy, emphasizing the importance of repentance and the saving power of divine grace. Here, the preacher might also offer more practical or medical advice as part of his sermon. They could also comfort their flock by emphasizing the hope of salvation. Finally, when the plague was over, many of the clergy thanked God for his mercy, arguing that God provided both punishment and cure, and that he ruled supreme over life and death.

A Sixteenth-Century Clergyman and Physician: Timothy Bright's Dual Approach to Melancholia

Emily Betz*

University of St Andrews

This article explores the nexus of healing between clergy and physicians in late sixteenth- and early seventeenth-century medicine by focusing on the disease of melancholia, and in particular on the earliest extant English monograph on that subject, A Treatise of Melancholie *(1586), by Timothy Bright. Melancholia was a disease especially apt to be treated by both medical practitioners and the clergy as it was widely defined as both corporal and spiritual in origin. What makes Bright's treatise particularly noteworthy is the vocation of the author: Bright was both doctor and cleric, and his work straddled both occupations as he defined, diagnosed and attempted to cure melancholy in his reader. By examining what Bright wrote about the various aspects of the disease, this article provides further insight into the clashes, conciliations and cooperation between early modern medical practitioners.*

In 1586 the physician (and soon-to-be cleric) Timothy Bright published the earliest extant English work dedicated to the condition of melancholia, entitled *A Treatise of Melancholie*. Designed as a guide for readers who were suffering from symptoms of melancholy, Bright divided his book into two main sections: the first chapters focused on the physical origins of melancholia, while later chapters revolved around a religious malady which Bright termed affliction of conscience. These conditions resembled each other in symptoms and were often conflated into one affliction, but according to Bright they were separate ailments because of their distinct aetiologies: one was corporal, one was spiritual.[1]

* School of History, University of St Andrews, 71 South St, St Andrews, KY16 9QW. E-mail: eb261@st-andrews.ac.uk.
I am very grateful to Colin Kidd, Justine Firnhaber-Baker, Chelsea Reutcke and the anonymous reviewers for their helpful feedback on earlier versions of this article.
[1] Timothy Bright, *A Treatise of Melancholie containing the Causes thereof … with the Phisicke Cure, and Spirituall Consolation for such as haue thereto adioyned an Afflicted Conscience* (London, 1586), 187.

Studies in Church History 58 (2022), 112–133   © The Author(s), 2022. Published by Cambridge University Press on behalf of Ecclesiastical History Society
doi: 10.1017/stc.2022.6

This article shows how Bright's separation of these conditions reflected the healing practices and relationships between physicians and clergy in late sixteenth- and early seventeenth-century England. It argues that Bright's division of melancholia and affliction of conscience into secular and physiological ailments respectively should not be viewed as a commentary on the exclusivity of the spheres of influence delegated to clergy and trained medical practitioners, but rather as a way of legitimizing the use of both groups in the treatment of melancholia. Furthermore, in highlighting the acceptable areas of cooperation between physicians and clergy, less accepted therapeutic practitioners also come into focus in the form of mountebanks. Bright scorned this group of healers both for their lack of traditional medical education and their seemingly superstitious cures, which sat uncomfortably close to what Protestants viewed as 'popish' practices of healing.[2] As a physician with extensive medical training and later as a Church of England clergyman, Bright's views of appropriate and inappropriate medical practice in *The Treatise of Melancholie* allow a deeper insight into the realities of healing in the early modern medical and religious landscape.[3]

Bright's separation in his treatise of the corporal disease of melancholy and the spiritual condition of affliction of conscience superficially upholds much of the conventional historiography on doctor-clergy relations. Scholars such as Michael MacDonald, Andrew Wear and Ian Mortimer have explored the boundaries between, and struggles amongst, early modern learned physicians and members of the clergy, postulating a division between corporal and spiritual physicians that in reality was not as pronounced in sixteenth- and early seventeenth-century daily life. Both Wear and MacDonald have theorized that in the relationship between religious and secular modes of healing, physicians practised medicine that was mostly secular and were generally left free of interference, especially in

---

[2] William Perkins, *A Salve for a Sicke Man* (London, 1638; first published 1595), 132–3.
[3] Although Bright did not leave a complete record of his own religious beliefs, his treatise fits within the tradition of consolation literature inspired by the moderate Calvinist theology of the Elizabethan and Jacobean Church of England: Nicholas Tyacke, *Anti-Calvinists: The Rise of English Arminianism c.1590–1640* (Oxford, 1987), 1–7. For more on the theology of the Church of England at the turn of the seventeenth century, see Patrick Collinson, *The Elizabethan Puritan Movement* (London, 1967); Diarmaid MacCulloch, *The Later Reformation in England, 1547–1603* (London, 2001); Alec Ryrie, *Being Protestant in Reformation Britain* (Oxford, 2013).

the later seventeenth century. This 'secularization' model argues that most physicians hesitated to combine religious and secular methods of treatment.[4] Ian Mortimer's exploration of deathbed expenditures on healthcare likewise concludes that the seventeenth century was a time of turning away from ecclesiastical intervention towards 'professional' medical help.[5] These theories of physicians and clergy enviously guarding their claims to healing rights fit squarely within a historiography that focuses more on the clashes than the conciliations of the 'medical marketplace', as Harold Cook has termed it. Works by Cook and Margaret Pelling have produced a vivid picture of a variety of intersecting, and often disputing, healers.[6] There is certainly a rich source base from which it can be concluded that there were at times professional jealousies between clergy and medical healers, particularly amongst the latter. The Northampton physician John Cotta, for example, attacked 'Ecclesiasticall persons, vicars and parsons' in a 1612 treatise on 'unconsiderate and ignorant practisers of physicke', while the Scottish physician James Hart warned in 1633 against ministers who 'wrongfully and injuriously ... intrude upon another weighty profession' by administering medicine.[7]

However, the complexities of the physician-priest professional relationship cannot be simplified to a binary between corporal and spiritual, and this becomes clear when looking at ailments such as melancholia which cross the boundaries of physical and spiritual. Scholars including Jeremy Schmidt, Andrew Cunningham and Sophie Mann have worked to integrate religious history more closely

---

[4] Michael MacDonald, *Mystical Bedlam: Madness, Anxiety, and Healing in Seventeenth Century England* (Cambridge, 1982); Andrew Wear, 'Puritan Perceptions of Illness in the Seventeenth Century', in Roy Porter, ed., *Patients and Practitioners: Lay Perceptions of Medicine in Pre-Industrial Society* (Cambridge, 1986), 55–100.

[5] Ian Mortimer, 'The Triumph of the Doctors: Medical Assistance to the Dying, c.1570–1720', *TRHS*, 6th series 15 (2005), 97–116.

[6] Harold Cook, *The Decline of the old Medical Regime in Stuart London* (Ithaca, NY, 1986); Margaret Pelling, *Medical Conflicts in Early Modern London: Patronage, Physicians and Irregular Practitioners, 1550–1640* (Oxford, 2003).

[7] John Cotta, *A Short Discoverie of the Unobserved Dangers of Severall Sorts of ignorant and unconsiderate Practisers of Physicke in England* (London, 1612), 86; James Hart, *ΚΛΙΝΙΚΗ, or the Diet of the Diseased. ... Wherein is set downe at length the whole Matter and Nature of Diet for those in Health, but especially for the Sicke; the Aire, and other Elements; Meat and Drinke, with divers other things; ... besides many pleasant practicall and historicall Relations, both of the Authours owne and other Mens* (London, 1633), 12.

with an understanding of the past medical landscape.[8] Schmidt takes issue with the 'secularization' thesis put forward by scholars such as MacDonald, arguing that religious consolation did remain important well into the eighteenth century.[9] Likewise, Mann has illustrated how deeply embedded religious frameworks were in early modern medical practices by exploring how prayer was used as a physical therapeutic exercise and how physicians' faith could inform occupational practices in day-to-day life.[10] Andrew Cunningham has also investigated the connection between faith and medical science in his research on the theological claims of Sir Thomas Browne's famous *Religio Medici* (1642), finding that this connection was bridged through the application of reason. Indeed, Browne considered physicians to be especially well suited to witness God's workings due to their study of humanity and background in logic.[11] These studies complement the work of scholars such as Patrick Wallis and Jonathan Barry who have highlighted the opportunities for cooperation and collaboration of various medical practitioners in the early modern period.[12]

These closer understandings of religion and medicine have laid the groundwork for the present study. By exploring a treatise written by a professional physician-turned-cleric, it is possible not only to show how meanings of melancholia varied by context, but also to attain a deeper understanding of everyday healing practices in contested medical and religious spaces.[13] This article contends that Bright's

[8] Sophie Mann, 'Physic and Divinity: The Case of Dr John Downes M.D. (1627–1694)', *SC* 31 (2016), 451–70; David Harley, 'The Good Physician and the Godly Doctor: The Exemplary Life of John Tylston of Chester (1663–1699)', *SC* 9 (1994), 93–117; David Gentilcore, *Healers and Healing in Early Modern Italy* (Manchester, 1998).
[9] Jeremy Schmidt, *Melancholy and the Care of the Soul: Religion, Moral Philosophy and Madness in Early Modern Europe* (London, 2007), 6.
[10] Sophie Mann, '"A Double Care": Prayer as Therapy in Early Modern England', *SHM* 33 (2019), 1055–77; Mann, 'Physic and Divinity'.
[11] Andrew Cunningham, 'Sir Thomas Browne and his *Religio Medici*: Reason, Nature and Religion', in Ole Peter Grell and Andrew Cunningham, eds, Religio Medici: *Medicine and Religion in Seventeenth-Century England* (Brookfield, VT, 1996), 12–61.
[12] Patrick Wallis, 'Competition and Cooperation in the Early Modern Medical Economy', in Mark Jenner and Patrick Wallis, eds, *Medicine and the Market in England and its Colonies, c.1450–c.1850* (London, 2007), 47–68; Jonathan Barry, 'John Houghton and Medical Practice in London c.1700', *Bulletin of the History of Medicine* 92 (2018), 575–603.
[13] Bright continued to practise medicine after taking holy orders and becoming the rector of Methley in Yorkshire in 1591 and nearby Barwick-in-Elmet in 1594. Several complaints lodged against him by his congregations indicate that his medical practice was

treatise exemplifies how physicians and clergy for the most part allowed each other space to practise healing in their own respective ways, even recommending each other for various healing needs, but also how they collectively disdained irregular practitioners and used similar explanations to warn their readers to refrain from utilizing their services.

THE ENGLISH MEDICAL LANDSCAPE

In Bright's lifetime the medical world comprised a plethora of practitioners, including physicians, apothecaries, surgeons, midwives, cunning men and women, quacks and clerics. The line between professional healers and empirics was often blurred, and it was not necessary to have a medical degree to practise the art of healing. In fact, Paul Slack has estimated that two-thirds of medical works produced in Tudor England were written by authors practising professions outwith medicine.[14] In the multiplicity of healers in early modern England there were many options from which patients could choose.

Among the various types of healers available, Bright's profession as a physician was the most exclusive. In the decades either side of 1600, physicians were more limited in number than other groups of healing professionals but constituted the most prestigious of the three main groups, the other two being apothecaries and surgeons. Physicians underwent lengthy medical training based largely on traditional authorities such as Galen and Hippocrates, with a typical English MD taking seven years or more to earn.[15] In the city of London, the Royal College of Physicians had constituted the most eminent institution for medical practitioners since its establishment in 1518, although until the late sixteenth century it contributed little to new research. Instead, the college focused on medical licensing and on protecting the prerogative of physicians in the capital and

---

sometimes felt to be detrimental to his parishioners' needs: Geoffrey Keynes, *Dr Timothie Bright, 1550–1615: A Survey of his Life with a Bibliography of his Writings* (London, 1962), 19–20; H. Armstrong Hall, 'Dr Timothy Bright: Some Troubles of an Elizabethan Rector', *Publications of the Thoresby Society* 15 (1909), 30–7, at 33.

[14] Paul Slack, 'Mirrors of Health and Treasures of Poor Men: The Uses of the Vernacular Medical Literature of Tudor England', in Charles Webster, ed., *Health, Medicine and Mortality in the Sixteenth Century* (Cambridge, 1979), 237–74, at 252–4.

[15] Margaret Pelling and Charles Webster, 'Medical Practitioners', ibid. 165–236, at 189.

surrounding areas. It sought to ensure that only well-educated and licensed professionals be allowed to practise medicine within a seven-mile radius of London.[16] However, this was impossible to enforce effectively in a large capital city, and innumerable unlicensed practitioners continued to see the sick, even highly qualified physicians who did not feel the need to pay expensive college fees for licensing.[17] Bright himself remained unlicensed by the College of Physicians throughout the period that he worked in London, despite his lengthy education and prestigious post as chief physician to the Royal Hospital of St Bartholomew from 1585.[18]

In addition to his work as a physician, Bright was instituted as rector of the Yorkshire parishes of Methley and Barwick-in-Elmet in the early 1590s.[19] In that role, he joined another major constituency of healers which consisted of clergy, ministers and priests. Traditionally, the clergy played a significant role in the healing arts. Illness and accidents were commonly believed to have been sent from God as punishment for sin, or (conversely) as a sign of elect status. Theologians wrote of the necessity of disease and pain in the relationship between God and humankind.[20] Due to the perceived spiritual dimensions of many medical ailments in this theologized and moralized universe, the clergy were a vital part of the therapeutic landscape. In fact, many considered the spiritual aspect to be the most important facet of healing, especially when the affliction was manifested in mental anguish, or in times of particular crisis such as plague and other epidemics.[21] Robert Wright, bishop of Bristol (1623–32), published a sermon under the medical-sounding title *A Receyt to stay the Plague*

---

[16] Pelling and Webster, 'Medical Practitioners', 168–71.

[17] Andrew Wear, *Knowledge & Practice of English Medicine, 1550–1680* (Cambridge, 2000), 27.

[18] Bright's refusal to comply with the College of Physicians' licensing statutes led it to take punitive action against him, even issuing a warrant to commit him to the Fleet prison for his continued unlicensed practice. Bright, however, had connections in high places and was able to ignore the college's threats without consequence: Andrew Wear, 'The Popularization of Medicine in Early Modern England', in Roy Porter, ed., *The Popularization of Medicine 1650–1850* (London, 1992), 17–41, at 26; William J. Carlton, *Timothe Bright, Doctor of Phisicke: A Memoir of 'the Father of modern Shorthand'* (London, 1911), 35–6, 69–70.

[19] Carlton, *Bright*, 130, 144.

[20] Doreen Evenden Nagy, *Popular Medicine in Seventeenth-Century England* (Bowling Green, OH, 1988), 35.

[21] David Lederer, *Madness, Religion, and the State in Early Modern Europe: A Bavarian Beacon* (Cambridge, 2006), 1.

Emily Betz

(1625), in which he exhorted the reader that 'there is no such Physick as *Prayer and Penitence*, thereby to make an *Attonement between God and our sinnes*'.[22] For many, prayer and repentance were the best medicine and the surest deliverance from disease. Without them, God could render physicians' advice incorrect and physical cures ineffective.[23]

It was perhaps owing to his dual status as physician and clergyman that Bright was drawn to write a volume on melancholia. This ailment had arguably the most overlap between corporal and spiritual healing. It was also a widespread disorder throughout Europe, becoming particularly prevalent in England during the latter years of Queen Elizabeth's reign.[24] Both medical and religious works frequently commented on the ubiquity of the condition. In *A Discourse of the Preservation of Sight* (1599), the French physician André du Laurens wrote of melancholy that it 'is so often happening in these miserable times, as that there are not many people which feele not some smatch thereof', while the English divine Robert Burton asserted in the immensely popular *Anatomy of Melancholy* (1621): 'from these melancholy dispositions, no man living is free'.[25] It was in this environment of pervasive melancholy that Bright decided to write his treatise on the disease.

A TREATISE OF MELANCHOLIE: MELANCHOLIA AND AFFLICTION OF CONSCIENCE

A Treatise of Melancholie was first published in 1586, appearing in a second edition the same year and a third edition in 1613. Although most of the enduring influence of Bright's treatise would come from its use in later, more famous works, it is an ideal book for exploring

---

[22] Robert Wright, *A Receyt to stay the Plague* (London, 1636), 22–3.
[23] David Harley, 'Spiritual Physic, Providence and English Medicine, 1560– 1640', in Ole Peter Grell and Andrew Cunningham, eds, *Medicine and the Reformation* (London and New York, 1993), 101–17, at 107.
[24] Angus Gowland, 'The Problem of Early Modern Melancholy', *P&P* 191 (2006), 77–120, at 80; George Rosen, *Madness in Society: Chapters in the Historical Sociology of Mental Illness* (Chicago, IL, 1968), 8.
[25] André du Laurens, *A Discourse of the Preservation of Sight; of Melancholike Diseases; of Rheumes, and of Old Age*, transl. Richard Surphlet (London, 1599), 140; Robert Burton, *The Anatomy of Melancholy: What it is, with all the Kinds, Causes, Symptoms, Prognostics, and Several Cures of it. In Three Partitions* (New York, 1862; first published 1621), 191.

118

the nexus between the healing groups of clergy and physicians due to the very typicality of its ideas on melancholia. Bright's theorization of the disease used traditional conceptualizations of melancholy and affliction of conscience, which made his contribution more a synthesis of existing knowledge than a creation of new theories.

Bright constructed the *Treatise of Melancholie* on the pretence of offering consolation to his fictitious friend 'M.', who claimed to be suffering from melancholy and religious terrors. Bright sought to help him and others who struggled with these conditions by writing a book on the superficially similar but aetiologically different diseases of melancholy and affliction of conscience. Bright's separation of these conditions was not unique: many other writers of the late six-teenth and early seventeenth centuries, including such influential theologians as Robert Yarrow, William Perkins and Richard Greenham, differentiated them in an effort to avoid insinuating that religious observance could lead to disease.[26] Noel Brann's influential study of melancholy and religious guilt found that sixteenth- and early seventeenth-century authors were concerned primarily with distinguishing these conditions into separate categories and justifying this, although he argues that they found no satisfactory and lasting distinctions. As the seventeenth century progressed, authors became less concerned about maintaining strict divisions between the often conflated conditions; however, in Bright's era the majority of consolation literature was divided into physical and spiritual afflictions.[27] Therefore it was natural for Bright to contrast the two conditions in his *Treatise*, that 'it may easily appear the affliction of soule through conscience of sinne is quite another thing then melancholy'.[28]

---

[26] Angus Gowland, *The Worlds of Renaissance Melancholy: Robert Burton in Context* (Cambridge, 2006), 175; Katherine Hodgkin, *Madness in Seventeenth-Century Autobiography* (Basingstoke, 2007), 64; Robert Yarrow, *Soveraigne Comforts for a Troubled Conscience* (London, 1634), 16; William Perkins, *A whole Treatise of Cases of Conscience: Distinguished into Three Bookes* (London, 1608), 194; Richard Greenham, *The Workes of the reverend and dauthfull Servant of Jesus Christ M. Richard Greenham, Minister and Preacher of the Word of God*, 5th edn (London, 1612), 106–7; John Stachniewski, *The Persecutory Imagination: English Puritanism and the Literature of Religious Despair* (Oxford, 1991), 226.
[27] Noel L. Brann, 'The Problem with distinguishing Religious Guilt from Religious Melancholy in the English Renaissance', *Quidditas* 1 (1980), 63–72.
[28] Bright, *Treatise*, 106.

The first part of the *Treatise of Melancholie* focused on the material aspects. Bright described the somatic condition of melancholy as a disease which induced in its sufferers 'either a certayne fearefull disposition of the mind altered from reason, or else an humour of the body, comonly taken to be the only cause of reason by feare in such sort depraued'.[29] The main symptoms of fear and sadness identified by Bright were regarded as the hallmark of melancholy throughout the early modern period. The disease was thought to occur when the melancholy humour was imbalanced, usually through an overheating of the blood, causing splenetic vapours to rise to the mind and cloud it with 'monstrous fictions'.[30] Traditional Galenic medicine, to which Bright subscribed, taught that the body was governed by four humours – phlegm, blood, choler and black bile – and that optimal health (*crasis*) was the result of a perfect balance between them.[31] Achieving *crasis* was more of a theoretical goal than a realistic target, for each individual had a dominant humoral complexion. This innate complexion was not static, however; it could change with age, circumstance or any number of bad habits on the part of the patient, such as improper diet, disordered sleep, immoderate study, too much or too little exercise or poor habitation.[32] An imbalance of these humours resulted in physiological and temperamental changes, potentially causing disease: thus black bile led to melancholia. Bright therefore situated melancholy strictly within the physical realm, recommending cures aimed at bodily healing. These included bleeding, purging and evacuations, as well as a diet which avoided any so-called 'melancholic' foods, such as pulses, pork, beef, freshwater fish and red wine.[33] As in many other texts of the late sixteenth and early seventeenth centuries, Bright described the symptoms of melancholy in 'unequivocally negative terms'.[34]

In contrast to melancholy, affliction of conscience was a spiritual ailment. Defined as a condition of serious religious anxiety over the condition of one's eternal estate and often believed to result from sin,

[29] Ibid. 1.
[30] Jennifer Radden, *The Nature of Melancholy: From Aristotle to Kristeva* (Oxford, 2000), 120.
[31] Mary Floyd-Wilson, *English Ethnicity and Race in Early Modern Drama* (Cambridge, 2003), 28.
[32] Bright, *Treatise*, 236.
[33] Ibid. 26–31, 289, 292.
[34] Gowland, *Worlds*, 159.

it was described by Bright as a most unbearable affliction: 'Of all kinds of miseries that befall unto man, none is so miserable as that which riseth of the sense of Gods wrath, and revenging hand against the guilty soul of a sinner'.[35] Conversely, it could be visited upon the sufferer as a sign of elect status, in which case it brought 'plenty of heavenly joy, and comfort'.[36] Either way, Bright insisted that affliction of conscience had nothing to do with physical deterioration but only with an affected soul.[37] The afflicted conscience could cause physiological changes in the body leading the sufferer into melancholy as well, but the reverse was impossible because the state of the body could not impact the soul.[38] However, Bright did acknowledge that those with a melancholic complexion, such as his friend 'M.' whom he sought to comfort, might experience heightened terror and find it harder to feel consoled when they were 'under the disadvantage of the melancholicke complexion': 'As their brains are thus evill disposed, so their harts in no better case, & acquainted with terror, & overbrown [overblown] with that fearful passion ... hardly yeeld to persuasion of comfort what soever it bringeth of assurance'.[39] Despite the inherent difficulties of consoling the afflicted conscience, Bright nevertheless dedicated the second part of his treatise to the topic. In this sense, this work was part of a genre of consolation that developed from the mid-sixteenth century, written mainly by clergy to help those who suffered from religious worries.[40]

These anxieties came to the fore as a moderate Calvinism permeated the Church of England in the post-Reformation landscape. The doctrine of predestination, whilst also taught by Thomas Aquinas and Martin Luther, had become closely associated with Calvin's theology in England; it was frequently believed by its adversaries and even some of its adherents to induce excessive religious despair.[41] The fear of not being one of God's elect struck terror into the hearts of some believers, and this conviction was not infrequently censured

[35] Bright, *Treatise*, 184.
[36] Ibid. 219–22.
[37] Ibid. 193.
[38] Ibid. 195–7.
[39] Ibid. 192, 196.
[40] Elizabeth Hunter, 'Melancholy and the Doctrine of Reprobation in English Puritan Culture' (D.Phil. thesis, University of Oxford, 2012), 108.
[41] Gowland, 'Early Modern Melancholy', 105–8.

for causing intense religious suffering.[42] However, predestination was not only preached from the pulpits as a warning to the sinful, but also, as recent scholarship has shown, as a comfort to those unsure of their spiritual status.[43] According to such theologians as William Perkins, Robert Bolton and Calvin himself, the doctrine of predestination could assuage religious guilt and despair, for believers who were of the elect could rest in the assurance of their salvation, regardless of their emotional state.[44] Following the logic of predestination, the elect who suffered from religious guilt could feel comforted that their 'crosses and troubles come from God': these were miseries sent to strengthen their faith rather than as a sign of damnation.[45] While Pauline doctrine had long since established the propriety of expressing sorrow over sins when turning to God for salvation, the doctrine of double predestination, in which God preordains the elect as well as the reprobate, tended to intensify feeling further.[46] Indeed, Reformed ministers frequently encouraged strong feelings, including sorrow and terror of conscience, in their congregations. These strong feelings were believed to stimulate introspection and repentance and were seen as potentially helpful to believers' spiritual journeys, as long as they did not develop into a settled despair.[47]

Bright recognized predestination's ability both to console and to cause religious despair. Understood and utilized correctly, predestination was 'the most strong rock of assurance, in all storms of

[42] Stachniewski, *Persecutory Imagination*, 27–8, 56–7.
[43] Leif Dixon, *Practical Predestinarians in England, c.1590–1640* (Farnham, 2014), 2.
[44] Ibid. 66; Robert Bolton, *Instructions for a right comforting Afflicted Consciences* (London, 1631), 198, 206–7. Predestination was arguably not a central tenet of Calvin's theology, but it was a comforting doctrine to him when utilized within reason: 'For as a fatal abyss engulfs those who, to be assured of their election, pry into the eternal counsel of God without the word, yet those who investigate it rightly, and in the order in which it is exhibited in the word, reap from it rich fruits of consolation': John Calvin, *Institutes of the Christian Religion*, 3.24.4 (transl. Henry Beveridge, 3 vols [Edinburgh, 1845–6], 2: 585).
[45] William Perkins, 'A Treatise of Mans Imaginations', in *The Works of William Perkins*, 2nd edn (London, 1631), 456. For more on the utility of emotions, particularly sorrow, in the spiritual life of Calvinists, see Michael MacDonald and Terence Murphy, *Sleepless Souls: Suicide in Early Modern England* (Oxford, 1990); Erin Sullivan, *Beyond Melancholy: Sadness and Selfhood in Renaissance England* (Oxford, 2016); Ryrie, *Being Protestant*; Schmidt, *Melancholy*; Dixon, *Practical Predestinarians*.
[46] Brann, 'Problem', 65.
[47] Schmidt, *Melancholy*, 50.

temptations that can befall unto body or soul'.[48] However, when misunderstood, either through ignorance of God's word, inordinate curiosity about holy secrets or a hardened heart, Bright knew it could create a stumbling block for believers: 'For as a sword taken at the wrong end is ready to wound the hand of the taker ... the doctrine of predestination being preposterously conceived, may through the fault of the conceiver procure hurt'.[49] The doctrine of election could be especially harmful to those who were melancholic, not because of the humour itself or any physiological changes within the downcast, but because the melancholy were more likely to be contemplative and curious. Bright's medical background lent authority to his explanation of why melancholic sufferers of affliction of conscience might find it more difficult than others to recover from the ailment. Their temperament increased the terror in their minds and jumbled reasonable messages of consolation in their 'evil disposed' brains and hearts.[50] However, all was not lost. Bright ended his discourse on election on a comforting note for sufferers of religious despair. When God's will was accepted and his mercy received through a sound understanding of predestination, the doubts and temptations that seemed 'to be nothing else but the gate of destruction' were in fact (much like Luther's *Anfechtungen*) 'the very course and way where through God doth lead his dearest children'.[51] Bright assured his readers that it was impossible to determine signs of reprobation in the living, meaning that affliction of conscience should normally be read as nothing 'but a storme of temptation, and no marke of perdition'.[52]

Although Calvinism was not the only source of religious despair, public discourse clearly linked the tenets of Calvinism and excessive worry.[53] Clergy and parishioners alike worried about the dangers of

---

[48] Elizabeth Hunter, 'The Black Lines of Damnation: Double Predestination and the Causes of Despair in Timothy Bright's *A Treatise of Melancholie*', *Etudes Epistémè* [online journal] 28 (2015), at §40, online at: <https://journals.openedition.org/episteme/811>, last accessed 13 January 2022; Bright, *Treatise*, 201.

[49] Ibid. 200–1.

[50] Ibid. 196.

[51] Ibid. 204–5. For more on Martin Luther's concept of *Anfechtungen*, loosely translated into English as 'temptations', and their importance to the Christian spiritual journey, see David P. Scaer, 'The Concept of *Anfechtung* in Martin Luther's Thought', *Concordia Theological Quarterly* 47 (1983), 15–30, at 15–17, 19.

[52] Bright, *Treatise*, 210, 214.

[53] Stachniewski, *Persecutory Imagination*, 46.

'inordinate sorrow' over sin.[54] Although the Church of England clergyman John Donne expounded on the usefulness of 'godlie sorrow', in a Trinity Sunday sermon in 1621 he also elaborated that sorrow should not be overindulged:

Blessed are they that mourn, sayes Christ: But the blessednesse is not in the mourning, but because they shall be comforted. Blessed am I in the sense of my sins, and in the sorrow for them, but blessed therefore, because this sorrow leads me to my reconciliation to God, and the consolation of his Spirit. Whereas, if I sinke in this sorrow, in this dejection of spirit, though it were Wine in the beginning, it is lees, and tartar in the end; Inordinate sorrow growes into sinfull melancholy, and that melancholy, into an irrecoverable desperation.[55]

Similarly, both the casebooks of the clergyman and medical practitioner Richard Napier and Burton's *Anatomy of Melancholy* revealed their concerns about the effects of puritan culture on the mentally distressed.[56] Although Bright labelled affliction of conscience worse than 'any other kind of calamity whatsoever' to plague humanity, he too was resolute in warning his readers from abandoning themselves to its sadness. He counselled his friend 'M.' not to wallow in despair, lest he accidentally dishonour 'the God of peace and comfort' with disproportionate sorrow.[57] Religious despair became such a problem in the seventeenth century that it was often linked to a perceived epidemic of suicide in England.[58]

Thus affliction of conscience was a serious and potentially fatal condition requiring practitioners' careful ministrations. Medicine was ineffectual in curing religious despair, and in these cases Bright believed it necessary to look to a spiritual healer rather than to physic. 'Here no medicine, no purgation, no cordiall, no treacle or balm are able to assure the afflicted soul and trembling heart', he wrote, for the affliction was not derived from the body.[59] Bright here shared the

[54] John Donne, 'Preached upon Trinity-Sunday', in George Reuben Potter and Evelyn Spearing Simpson, eds, *The Sermons of John Donne*, 10 vols (Berkeley, CA, 1953–62), 3: 1–18 (no. 12), at 15.
[55] John Donne, 'Preached at White-Hall', in Potter and Simpson, eds, *Sermons of Donne*, 10: 1–21 (no. 6), at 20; Donne, 'Preached upon Trinity-Sunday', 15.
[56] MacDonald, *Mystical Bedlam*, 31.
[57] Bright, *Treatise*, 184–5, 207.
[58] Stachniewski, *Persecutory Imagination*, 46.
[59] Bright, *Treatise*, 189, 197.

approach of other writers on the condition, including Perkins, Bolton and John Abernethy, who similarly stressed the necessity of strong spiritual guidance and prayer above physic in treating an affliction of conscience.[60]

PHYSICIANS VS. CLERGYMEN? CONCILIATIONS AND COOPERATION

The distinction between melancholia and affliction of conscience in Bright's treatise, along with his different approaches to their respective cures, reflected separate spaces for physicians and clergymen in healing patients, according to which doctors were concerned with physical issues while ministers and preachers grappled with spiritual ailments. However, these spaces were never mutually exclusive. As Bright himself exemplified, as a practitioner of both fields, the boundaries between them were quite porous.

The similarities between the vocations were much commented upon by divines and physicians alike. The clergyman Thomas Adams wrote of the 'neere affinitie' between physic and divinity:

> Let the professions be *heterogena*, different in their kindes; onely *respondentia*, semblable in their proceedings. The Lord *created the Physitian* ... The good Physitian acts the part of the Divine. They shall pray unto the Lord, that he would prosper that which they give, for ease & remedy to prolong life. The good Minister, after a sort is a Physitian. Onely it is enough for the Sonne of God to give both naturall and spirituall Physicke. ... so wee may say of Physicke, it is conterminate to Divinitie; so farre as a Handmaid may follow her Mistresse. You see the willing similitude of these professions.[61]

Adams, although clear in his belief that the clerical profession was superior in spiritual matters, asserted that healing patients was a responsibility which was interchangeable between physicians and clergymen. In this context, the physician should pray and try to convert any patients who had fallen from belief, for '[w]ho may better

[60] William Perkins, *The Works of that Famous and Worthy Minister of Christ in the Universitie of Cambridge, M. William Perkins*, 3 vols (London, 1631), 2: 47; Bolton, *Instructions*, 198; John Abernethy, *A Christian and Heavenly Treatise: Containing Physicke for the Soule: very necessary for all that would enjoy true Soundnesse of Minde and Peace of Conscience* ... (London, 1630), sig. A4r.
[61] Thomas Adams, *The Divells Banket described in Sixe Sermons* (London, 1614), 221–4.

speake to the soule, then hee that is trusted with the body?'[62] These reminders seem to have been effective, as there are numerous examples of doctors incorporating prayer into their practices. Sir Thomas Browne, for example, wrote in his *Religio Medici* that it was the doctor's duty to help the soul of his patients: 'I cannot goe to cure the body of my Patient, but I forget my profession, and call unto God for his soule; I cannot see one say his Prayers but instead of imitating him, I fall into a supplication for him.'[63]

Similarities between clergy and physicians also appear in their advice for the healing of melancholia. Many authors, both secular and religious, recommended using all available methods of healing. Consolatory writers, including the most famous of late Elizabethan authors on the subject, the cleric Richard Greenham, found it indispensable to care for not only the spirit but also the body of their parishioners.[64] Greenham advocated a spiritual and physical approach to healing:

> If a man troubled in conscience come to a Minister, it may be he will looke all to the soule and nothing to the body: if he come to a Physition, he only considereth of the body and neglecteth the soule. For my part, I would neuer haue the Physitions counsell seuered, nor the Ministers labour neglected; because the soule and body dwelling to|gether, it is conuenient, that as the soule should be cured by the word, by prayer, by fasting, by threatning, or by comforting; so the body also should be brought into some temperature by Physicke, by purging, by diet, by restoring, by musicke, and by such like meanes ...[65]

Similarly, Abernethy advised that if the patient was afflicted with a combination of both melancholy and spiritual despair, 'the cure must be also wisely mixed. Help not the body first, and leave the soule in anguish; neither goe about to finish the cure of the soule first, for then the distempered body shall mightily marre thy proceeding.'[66]

Medical writers, too, advocated in such cases both physic and prayer. Although some who treated the mentally ill, such as the

[62] Ibid. 224.
[63] Thomas Browne, *Religio Medici* (London, 1642), 154.
[64] Hunter, 'Melancholy', 125.
[65] Greenham, *Workes*, 107.
[66] Abernethy, *Christian and Heavenly Treatise*, 136.

physician Edward Jorden and the medical clergyman Richard Napier, insisted that religious afflictions were simply a manifestation of melancholy, for most other medical practitioners the consensus seemed to be that such cases needed spiritual as well as physical care.[67] Indeed, physicians espoused the utility of prayer in the majority of written medical works on all diseases through the seventeenth century. While atheism was a charge sometimes levelled against physicians, perhaps because of their reliance on classical pagan sources such as Galen, it was not evidenced in their medical treatises, which more often than not called for the necessity of prayer in healing.[68] Richard Baxter wrote of physicians: 'It is strange that Physicions should be so much suspected of Atheism as commonly they are … For I have oft been very thankful to God, in observing the contrary, even how many excellent pious Physicions there have been … and how much they promoted the work of Reformation.'[69] Physic in most cases was seen not as a rival to religion, but as a supplement to it.

The allowance for overlap in therapeutic practices demonstrated in these theological and instructional texts seems also to have been permissible in everyday life, as indicated in the records of the Royal College of Physicians. Their annals recorded cases of irregular medical practitioners who were brought for examination before the college for practising without a licence. Between 1550 and 1640 there were 714 of these irregulars brought before the board, over 88 per cent of whom were identified with 'primary occupations' beside their names. On the basis of this information, Margaret Pelling observes that only 2 per cent (i.e. 14) of the irregular practitioners brought before the College of Physicians were classified as members of the clergy.[70] This is a much smaller percentage than those in medical occupations broadly defined (66 per cent) or in other non-medical occupations (11 per cent).[71] The low number of ministers, preachers and clergymen pursued in licensing cases by the college indicates that

---

[67] Hunter, 'Melancholy', 269.

[68] Paul Kocher, 'The Physician as Atheist in Elizabethan England', *Huntington Library Quarterly* 10 (1947), 229–49, at 240.

[69] Richard Baxter, *A Christian Directory, or, a Summ of Practical Theologie and Cases of Conscience directing Christians how to use their Knowledge and Faith, how to improve all Helps and Means, and to perform all Duties, how to overcome Temptations, and to escape or mortifie every Sin* (London, 1673), 43.

[70] Pelling, *Medical Conflicts*, 155.

[71] Ibid. 154.

they were not viewed as standing in competition with physicians. Although clerics may have taken some cases needing healing away from professional medics, few were willing to deny them the traditional ecclesiastical duty of ministering to the sick, and the college mostly left the clergy alone. In fact, prior to 1640 it is difficult to find evidence of physicians expressing resentment towards clergy for interfering in their work.[72] Rather than harrying the clergy, the college was more interested in identifying unlicensed physicians, apothecaries, surgeons and cunning men and women who were deemed 'ignoraunt'.[73]

A COMMON ENEMY: IRREGULAR PRACTITIONERS

Bright's writing reflected a similar anxiety about quacks. Although his work sought to create a holistic healing environment, open to both physicians and clergymen, it was explicit in warning the reader which healers to avoid. Alongside his definition of a set of approved practitioners in the *Treatise of Melancholie*, Bright reflected the common prejudice against irregular medical healers, shared not only by learned practitioners but also by clergymen such as William Perkins in the late sixteenth to mid-seventeenth century.[74] When Bright warned his reader that using medicine without 'that cunning which thereto appertaineth' could 'bring present perill in steade of health', he was not thinking of the clergy's medical ministrations, but rather the irregular practitioners and uneducated healers that competed for patients. Bright warned of such mountebanks' lecherous and harmful ways: 'The abuse at this day is great, and common, defrauding the simple sorte in their substance and hurting of their bodies under the pretence of experience, of secretes and hid misteries of remedies, which these masked theeves, & murtherers alleage for color of their lewdnes'.[75] Going to these healers for physic, Bright cautioned, was certain to hurt more than help.[76] His disdain toward these

---

[72] Peter Elmers, 'Medicine, Religion and the Puritan Revolution', in Roger French and Andrew Wear, eds, *The Medical Revolution of the Seventeenth Century* (Cambridge, 1989), 10–45, at 13–14.

[73] Pelling and Webster, 'Medical Practitioners', 184–5.

[74] Perkins, *Salve*, 132–3. Perkins believed it was 'better for a man to die of his sicknesse, then to seek recovery by such wicked persons', as he called cunning men and women.

[75] Bright, *Treatise*, 267–8.

[76] Ibid. 268.

practitioners was not unique but was also commonly found in other Galenic medical and religious writings.[77]

Condemning irregular practitioners, however, was often easier than identifying who exactly was meant by that term amongst the multiplicity of healers in early modern England. Healers often tried to prove their own legitimacy while casting doubts on the abilities of their peers, and in a time of limited medical licensing, the empiric and the physician were not always easily differentiated.[78] As evidenced by Bright's own unlicensed practice, it was not necessarily a lack of recognition by the Royal College of Physicians or other medical associations that would label a practitioner as a dangerous healer. In fact, out of the unlicensed practitioners who were questioned before the College of Physicians, Pelling has found that there were at least 43 practitioners (17 per cent) who, like Bright, held MDs.[79] Bright, as one of these highly educated men, would not consider these healers a threat to patients. Nor would he consider everyone in economic competition with him to be an irregular practitioner. Although economic self-preservation was undoubtedly one motivation for publicly disparaging other types of medics, it cannot have been the only consideration.[80] Instead, as has been shown in this article, consolation literature, whether authored by clergy or physicians, often explicitly pointed patients in the direction of the other group for healing. This raises the question of how physicians and theologians distinguished empiric practitioners and why they were united in their disparagement of empirical medical systems and practitioners.

It seems that for Bright and other medical authors such as William Bullein, John Cotta and John Securis, the distinction between themselves and mountebanks was rooted in an education based on traditional medicine.[81] Like many other authors on medical ailments,

[77] David Harley, 'James Hart of Northampton and the Calvinist Critique of Priest-Physicians: An unpublished Polemic of the early 1620s', *MH* 42 (1998), 362–86.
[78] Wear, 'Popularization of Medicine', 19.
[79] Pelling, *Medical Conflicts*, 144.
[80] Andrew Wear, 'Discourses of Practitioners in Sixteenth- and Seventeenth-Century Europe', in Robert Baker and Laurence McCullough, eds, *The Cambridge World History of Medical Ethics* (Cambridge, 2009), 379–90, at 380.
[81] William Bullein, *The Gouernment of Health: A Treatise written by William Bullein, for the especiall Good and healthfull Preseruation of Mans Bodie from all noysome Diseases, proceeding by the Excess of euill Diet, and other Infirmities of Nature: Full of excellent Medicines, and wise Counsels, for conseruation of Health, in Men, Women, and Children. Both plasant and profitable to the industrious Reader* (London, 1595), 12–13; John Cotta, *A short*

Bright considered empirics to be those who lacked Galenic learning and practised superstitious, sometimes borderline heretical, healing methods.[82] For centuries, physicians had been trained in the *ars et scientia* of Hippocratic and Galenic texts that emphasized humoral theory to explain man's body and health. Those without extensive medical training were unequivocally condemned by Bright as 'masked theeves' and 'lewde cousoning varlets' whose healing could not be trusted. He explicitly stated that anyone who had not gone through the whole discipline of liberal sciences should avoid attempting to cure melancholy: 'neither ought any to be admitted to touch so holy thinges, that hath not passed the whole discipline of liberall sciences, and washed himselfe pure and cleane in the waters of wisedome, and understanding.'[83] Even for those who enjoyed reading and were versed in philosophy, Bright recommended seeking the advice of a physician for medical issues. As he wrote to his friend 'M', 'Although I remember your travaile in philosophie, and studie of phisick, to which both you have had a naturall disposition, and take pleasure in reading our writings of precept & rule take advise of some learned, and vertuous phisician about you, and adventure not upon any part of evacuation without his direction'.[84] Well-educated clergymen would also be learned in natural philosophy and the liberal arts, so they were certainly included in Bright's conceptualization of appropriate medical practitioners. Those who were excluded from the list of suitable healers were the uneducated, the 'common sort', who practised medicine without having studied the underpinning philosophy.[85] Generally professional physicians bemoaned the practices of irregular healers for two reasons: economic encroachment and safety. Bright was particularly concerned about the latter; he emphasized that in the long run seeking treatment for melancholy from quacks was likely to leave the afflicted worse, for it might 'leave the body crased [crazed]'.[86]

Discovery of the unobserved Dangers of severall sorts of ignorant and unconsiderate Practisers of Physicke (London, 1612); John Securis, *A Detection and Querimonie of the daily Enormities and Abuses committed in Physic* (London, 1566).

[82] Bright, *Treatise*, 267–8.
[83] Ibid. 267.
[84] Ibid. 283.
[85] Ibid. 267–8.
[86] Ibid. 260.

Religious authors likewise condemned irregular practitioners for their refutation of learned medicine, particularly those who resorted to supernatural methods of healing which many Protestants believed to have been acceptable under Catholicism.[87] Instead of empirical practices, they considered the Galenic tradition of medicine (and occasionally the new chemical and Christian-based theories of medicine such as Paracelsianism and Helmontianism) as the best substitute for Catholic healing practices until the 1640s.[88] The Protestant rejection of Catholicism's trust in the effectiveness of the sacraments and relics translated into an increased reliance on learned medical men. With the belief that God acted primarily through secondary (natural) causes came an increasing approval of professional medical practitioners. As David Harley has shown, '[t]he moral approval of godly practitioners helped to justify campaigns against irregular competitors by freeing medical men from the humanist accusation that they were only concerned with lining their own pockets'.[89] Therefore astrological practitioners and those who practiced urinoscopy, charms and other forms of so-called 'cunning' healing were the most common targets of both theologians and physicians.[90] Perkins disparaged those who used healing charms as 'inchanters, and sorcerers', whose methods, if they did work, were 'wrought above ordinarie meanes by the work of Satan'. He compared this type of healing to the 'superstitious' practices of the Catholic Church, and urged the sick to attend physicians instead.[91] Similarly the puritan physician John Cotta wrote against the heterodox medical practices of the astrological physician and clergyman Richard Napier, who frequently used horoscopes, charms and ritual exorcisms, even though he was an Oxford-trained theologian who also incorporated more

---

[87] Harley, 'Spiritual Physic', 112.

[88] Harley, 'James Hart', 364; Andrew Wear, *Knowledge and Practice in English Medicine, 1550–1680* (Cambridge, 2000), 32. For more on Paracelsian and Helmontian medical theory, see Wear, *Knowledge & Practice*; Charles Webster, 'Alchemical and Paracelsian Medicine' in idem, ed., *Health, Medicine and Mortality*, 301–34; Hugh Trevor-Roper, 'The Court Physician and Paracelsianism', in Vivian Nutton, ed., *Medicine at the Courts of Europe, 1500–1837* (London, 1990), 79–95; Elmers, 'Medicine, Religion and the Puritan Revolution', 10–45.

[89] Harley, 'Spiritual Physic', 112.

[90] Wear, 'Discourses of Practitioners', 384.

[91] Norman Gevitz, 'Practical Divinity and Medical Ethics: Lawful versus Unlawful Medicine in the Writings of William Perkins (1558–1602)', *Journal of the History of Medicine and Allied Sciences* 68 (2012), 198–226, at 221–4.

traditional Galenic techniques into his medical practice.[92] Thus the animosity for empirics that we witness in Bright's *Treatise* expressed the desire of both clergy and physicians to retain learned medicine's supremacy in an era of challenges to medical and religious authority.

CONCLUSION

As scholars commemorate the quatercentenary of Burton's exhaustive *Anatomy of Melancholy* at the time of writing this article in 2021, assumptions about early modern melancholia are once again under debate. Burton's masterpiece on melancholia has inspired, comforted and entertained innumerable readers since it was published in the seventeenth century. As one of the few English sources that Burton included in *The Anatomy*, a re-examination of Bright's *Treatise of Melancholie* could not be timelier.

An analysis of Bright's *Treatise of Melancholie* provides a better picture not only of what melancholy was and was not, but also of the divisions and cooperation that medical practitioners and the clergy used in treating emotional disorders. This article contends that Bright recognized the need for, and the influence of, both sets of practitioners and encouraged their cooperation. Despite his attempts to distinguish between melancholy and the affliction of conscience, the inclusion of both afflictions in one volume highlighted the porous nature of these conditions and by extension the healers meant to cure them. Bright's attempts to clarify the distinct physical and religious aetiologies of emotional conditions and their practitioners paradoxically underscored many similarities in the healing practices of physicians and clergy in curing such distress. Religious and medical practitioners often recommended the same types of therapy for most diseases: prayer and natural herbal remedies, both supplied by the grace of God. Both groups also largely recognized the boundaries of their own approach to medical care and recommended each other's expertise when a patient had an affliction outside the scope of their own.

In calling attention to the general cooperation between Elizabethan physicians and clergy in the healing of emotional

[92] Harley, 'James Hart', 264. Note: For his part, and perhaps unsurprisingly, Richard Napier wrote against the dangers of a strict Calvinist theology causing melancholy in his medical casebooks: Schmidt, *Melancholy*, 50.

afflictions, Bright's work also displays these practitioners' mutual disdain of empirical healers. This article has shown how both physicians and theologians censured those who lacked a proper medical education or worked cures through charms, incantations or other potentially heretical practices. Bright's text shows how learned physicians expressed worry over patient safety, while Protestant beliefs elevated scientific reasoning over curative methods which could evoke superstitious and ostensibly papistical means. For Protestants and admirers of Galen alike, quacks endangered body and spirit, and they worked in parallel to discredit them.

Godly Preaching, in Sickness and Ill-Health, in Seventeenth-Century England

Robert W. Daniel*

University of Warwick

This article examines the myriad ways that sickness affected, and was exacerbated by, puritan preaching in seventeenth-century England. The term 'puritan' is deployed here to encompass Church of England, and later Nonconformist, ministers who espoused the significance of preaching God's word as a pastoral duty. By exploring occasions of, and motivations for, sermonizing when sick, such a study reveals that illness played a much larger role in the pulpit performances of England's preachers, especially amongst puritan clerics, than has hitherto been acknowledged.

[H]e hath often gone upon Crutches unto the Congregation of his own people … scarce able to get into the Pulpit, and his Friends with much difficulty holp him out of the Church homewards … Many times these were his words, *If I could but preach, I should be much better*; and he would rejoyce with cheerfulness and thankfulness, when in the times of his weakness he found not himself more distempered by his preaching, and would mention such experiences, as arguments to move; and induce his friends to yeeld to his preaching when they disswaded him from it as prejudicial to his health.[1]

This is a description of the eminent Presbyterian clergyman Jeremiah Whitaker, rector of St Mary Magdalen's, Bermondsey, from 1643 until his death in 1654, aged 54 or 55. This passage first appeared in Simeon Ashe's funeral encomium of Whitaker entitled *Living Loves betwixt Christ and Dying* (1654), whose characterization of his preaching while ill was attested in various godly sermons, tracts

* E-mail: Robert.W.Daniel@warwickgrad.net.
This essay draws from my article, '"Preached in much pain": Sick Preachers and Sickly Preaching in Seventeenth-Century England', *Bunyan Studies* 24 (2020), 30–47. I am grateful to the *Bunyan Studies* editorial board for allowing me to include material from it.
[1] Simeon Ashe, *Living Loves betwixt Christ and Dying* (London, 1654), 54 (italics original).

 doi: 10.1017/stc.2022.7

and diaries.[2] Whitaker's discomfort was largely the result of the 'violent pain of the Stone', later discovered to have measured an 'inch and an half long, and one inch broad, weighing about two ounces'.[3] Despite his infirmity, Whitaker preached regularly until the end of his life.[4] Though Ashe's account may have embellished, or been overly sympathetic to, the sufferings of a close friend and colleague, such claims deserve further investigation.[5] This article examines whether other clergymen were just as 'able to creep into the Pulpit, or to crawle unto the Congregation' during illness.[6] By exploring occasions of, and motivations for, sermonizing while sick in seventeenth-century England, such a study may reveal that illness played a much larger role in the pulpit performances of England's preachers, especially amongst puritan clerics, than has been hitherto acknowledged.

The term 'puritan' is deployed here to encompass Church of England, and later Nonconformist, ministers who espoused the significance of preaching God's word as a pastoral duty.[7] Recent scholarship supports this broad approach, demonstrating important continuities in 'puritan' and 'nonconformist' experiences.[8] Examining such preaching across the seventeenth century has been deliberately chosen to overcome the popular division in scholarship between

---

[2] For references to Whitaker 'racked with pain' while sermonizing, see Samuel Clarke, *A Collection of the Lives of Ten Eminent Divines* (London, 1662), 164; Henry Newcome, *The Autobiography of Henry Newcome*, ed. Richard Parkinson, 2 vols (Manchester, 1852), 2: 284; Robert Wild, *Iter Boreale with Large Additions* (London, 1668), 32–3; John Wade, *Redemption of Time* (London, 1683), 450.

[3] Ashe, *Living Loves betwixt Christ and Dying*, 51, 52.

[4] Whitaker preached twice weekly at St Mary Magdalen, once a week at Christ Church, Newgate, and provided one of the weekly early morning lectures at Westminster Abbey: Paul S. Seaver, *The Puritan Lectureships: The Politics of Religious Dissent 1560–1662* (Stanford, CA, 1970), 270.

[5] Ashe himself was a long sufferer of 'fits of the Gout': Richard Baxter, *Reliquiae Baxterianae*, ed. Matthew Sylvester (London, 1696), 430.

[6] Ashe, *Living Loves betwixt Christ and Dying*, 51.

[7] For the importance of preaching within English puritanism, see Tom Webster, *Godly Clergy in Early Stuart England: The Caroline Puritan Movement, c.1620–1640* (Cambridge, 1997), 96–100.

[8] See David R. Como, *Blown by the Spirit: Puritanism and the Emergence of an Antinomian Underground in pre-Civil-War England* (Stanford, CA, 2004); Alec Ryrie, *Being Protestant in Reformation England* (Oxford, 2013); Francis Bremer, *Lay Empowerment and the Development of Puritanism* (New York, 2015).

Robert W. Daniel

pre- and post-Restoration sermon praxis.[9] By taking a broader historical view, one encounters surprising continuities in pulpit practices among a range of denominationally diverse ministers. Several of the clergymen discussed here went on to have complicated relationships with conformity after the Restoration that defy easy categorization. The label of 'puritan' is thus suggestive rather than definitive. This is not to suppose that conformist clergymen did not encounter the same bodily strains and pains during their pulpit labours.[10] Rather, because of the puritan emphasis on regular and impactful preaching, godly clergymen were more likely to sermonize when ill.[11] This article, then, provides a case study of the relationship between preaching and ill-health amongst the godly. In order to do so, the focus will fall on several areas: the ailments and illnesses experienced by ministers in their pulpits; the health risks associated with travelling to and speaking at preaching venues (especially during the winter months); and finally, the theological justifications for preaching when sick.

A wave of recent scholarship within the field of medical humanities has expertly charted the various sickbed behaviours, medical practices and recovery rituals of early modern Britain.[12] Some of this research has included a small but important selection of English clergymen such as Ralph Josselin, Henry Newcome and Richard Baxter. When examining the ill-health of the clerical class, however, studies

[9] See Eric Josef Carlson, 'The Boring of the Ear: Shaping the Pastoral Vision of Preaching in England, 1540–1640', in Larissa Taylor, ed., *Preachers and People in the Reformations and Early Modern Period* (Leiden, 2001), 249–96; Arnold Hunt, *The Art of Hearing: English Preachers and their Audiences, 1590–1640* (Cambridge, 2010), 1–18; Peter McCullough, Hugh Adlington and Emma Rhatigan, eds, *The Oxford Handbook of the Early Modern Sermon* (Oxford, 2011), 329–422 (sermons from 1500–1660), 423–516 (sermons from 1660–1720). While there are good reasons for these divisions, the contiguities in preaching styles and habits that occurred across these periods are largely left unobserved.
[10] For a study of conformist and nonconformist attitudes to illness, see Ralph Houlbrooke, *Death, Religion, and the Family in England, 1480–1750* (Oxford, 1998), 160–82.
[11] This is not to suggest, however, that puritan ministers were alone in emphasizing the import and impact of regular preaching.
[12] See Alun Withey, *Physick and the Family: Health, Medicine and Care in Wales, 1600–1750* (Manchester, 2011); Olivia Weisser, *Ill Composed: Sickness, Gender, and Belief in Early Modern England* (New Haven, CT, 2016); Hannah Newton, *Misery to Mirth: Recovery from Illness in Early Modern England* (Oxford, 2018); Robert W. Daniel, '"My sick–bed covenants": Scriptural Patterns and Model Piety in the Early Modern Sickchamber', in Elizabeth Clarke and Robert W. Daniel, eds, *People and Piety: Protestant Devotional Identities in Early Modern England* (Manchester, 2020), 241–58.

have tended to focus on individual men and their households, godly deathbed speeches and generic conventions in writing about illness.[13] This article takes a broader and more holistic approach which allows us to appreciate certain hitherto undiscovered religious and cultural trends that governed clerical experiences of sickness. This reveals that, like ordinary layfolk, clergymen possessed a strong work ethic, undertaking work even when ill.[14] This showcases the convictions and costs associated with puritan preaching, and perhaps preaching more generally. Such investigations also highlight how ministers behaved in their public ministry when ill, as opposed to how they responded to illness in their own homes, a space which has received more scholarly attention.[15] Finally, the article complements the work of Alison Searle, who has recently examined the theology of pain as expressed by puritan women and clergymen's wives during pregnancy, birth and breastfeeding.[16] In particular, this article concurs with Searle's assertion that physical suffering was an 'experiential and conceptual category for Calvinists' that was seen as 'potentially beneficial', and, completing the picture, this study provides a viewpoint from the male perspective.[17] This research also contributes to

---

[13] See Lucinda McCray Beier, 'In Sickness and in Health: A Seventeenth Century Family's Experience', in Roy Porter, ed., *Patients and Practitioners: Lay Perceptions of Medicine in Pre–Industrial Society* (Cambridge, 1985), 101–28; David Harley, 'The Theology of Affliction and the Experience of Sickness in the Godly Family, 1650–1714: The Henrys and the Newcomes', in Ole Peter Grell and Andrew Cunningham, eds, *Religio Medici: Medicine and Religion in Seventeenth-Century England* (Aldershot, 1996), 273–92; Tim Cooper, 'Richard Baxter and his Physicians', *SHM* 20 (2007), 1–19; David Thorley, *Writing Illness and Identity in Seventeenth-Century Britain* (London, 2016), 27–112.

[14] For examples of layfolk attempting to work while ill, see Newton, *Misery to Mirth*, 221–2.

[15] See Ralph Houlbrooke, 'The Puritan Death-bed, *c.*1560–*c.*1660', in Christopher Durston and Jacqueline Eales, eds, *The Culture of English Puritanism, 1560–1700* (Basingstoke, 1996), 122–44; Andrew Wear, 'Puritan Perceptions of Illness in Seventeenth–Century England', in Porter, ed., *Patients and Practitioners*, 55–100; Mary Ann Lund, 'Experiencing Pain in John Donne's *Devotions upon Emergent Occasions* (1624)', in Jan Frans van Dijkhuizen and Karl A. E. Enenkel, eds, *The Sense of Suffering: Constructions of Physical Pain in Early Modern Culture* (Leiden, 2009), 323–46; Andrew Cambers, *Godly Reading: Print, Manuscript and Puritanism in England, 1580–1720* (Cambridge, 2011), 63–71.

[16] See Alison Searle, '"A kind of agonie in my thoughts": Writing Puritan and Non–Conformist Women's Pain in Seventeenth–Century England', *Medical Humanities* 44 (2018), 125–36.

[17] Ibid. 136.

the history of pain and its intersections with religious belief and praxis amongst the godly by reconceptualizing early modern preaching as a total commitment of the body, and not just of the mind or soul, incorporating the somatic into the sermonic.

Printed conduct literature of the period was vague on whether preaching while sick was to be prescribed or prohibited. George Herbert argued that though the country parson 'preacheth constantly' whereby 'the pulpit is his joy and his throne', if he 'at any time intermit, it is … for want of health', and that in all things a minister should never 'overdo it, to the loss of their quiet, and health'.[18] Churchmen across the religious spectrum, such as Lancelot Andrewes, William Perkins and Jeremy Taylor seemed to concur, omitting any meaningful discussions on preaching when ill in their popular conduct manuals.[19] In contrast, others such as the ejected minister Edward Lawrence asserted that '[t]hey must be sick, that they may the better teach you to prepare for sickness', and that those clergymen who had never experienced ill-health 'are like to be no lively feeling Preachers'.[20] This acknowledged that illness helped ministers write relatable sermons, but said nothing of whether those sermons were expected to be delivered during an illness. Despite the common maxim of the period, adapted from Vespasian, that '[i]t becommeth best a Bishop to die preaching in the pulpit', the absence of a clear consensus regarding preaching while unwell shows that such an eventuality was either ignored, discouraged or taken for granted.[21] This is surprising, given the number of contemporary debates surrounding whether ministers should stay with or flee from their flocks during times of plague.[22]

---

[18] George Herbert, *The Country Parson* (London, 1652), 21, 61–2.

[19] See Lancelot Andrewes, *A Manual of Directions for the Sick* (London, 1642); Jeremy Taylor, *The Rule and Exercises of Holy Dying* (London, 1651). Perkins, in particular, would not have deemed sick clergymen acceptable in the pulpit. He was adamant that proper sermon gestures were for the 'stalke of the bodie being erect and quiet', and the voice should be 'not jagged and abrupt', not easy to do when ill. William Perkins, *The Arte of Prophecying* (London, 1607), 143, 147.

[20] Edward Lawrence, *Christ's Power over Bodily Diseases* (London, 1672), sigs B1v–B2r.

[21] See Robert Bolton, *The Foure Last Things* (London, 1632), sig. C8v; Clarke, *Ten Eminent Divines*, 81; Wade, *Redemption of Time*, 248; Edmund Calamy, *A Funeral Sermon for Mr. Love* (London, 1651), 1; Lawrence, *Christ's Power over Bodily Diseases*, 102.

[22] See Kevin Killeen, *The Political Bible in Early Modern England* (Cambridge, 2017), 95–6.

Though advice was somewhat lacking in print, the practice of preaching when sick was not infrequent. Dedicated to spreading the gospel, puritan ministers sometimes preached whilst suffering from minor or major ailments. The Essex clergyman Ralph Josselin records 'this Sabbath day I preached thrice', despite being 'ill in my stomacke' which caused 'great looseness and griping of my body'.[23] Isaac Archer could 'scar[c]e study, or preach but with pain' when he endured a searing 'toothach[e]' and persistent 'rhewme' in the winter of 1679.[24] Pulpit ailments included accidental injuries. After a serious 'fall backward' in 1683, Thomas Jolly suffered something like a concussion. He described in his notebook how 'weakness seized on my head' and 'empair[ed] my sight'. Despite experiencing 'much pain and sickness', Jolly continued to 'work in my study and preaching', continuing to exercise his ministry as normal, even though the symptoms only abated weeks later.[25] Some illnesses were more common than others. It was not unusual to see ministers enter the pulpit exhibiting influenza-like symptoms. In 1645 the usually valetudinarious Josselin 'preach[e]d 2 sermons. very ill with my cold'.[26] 'I preached in much pain by the chollick through a cold I took', Jolly declared in 1678.[27] It must be remembered that early modern colds laid low many a hardy preacher.[28] Preaching with an 'ague' was also not unusual.[29] The Flintshire minister Philip Henry records in his

---

[23] Ralph Josselin, *The Diary of Ralph Josselin, 1616–1683*, ed. Alan Macfarlane (London, 1976), 121–2. 'Looseness' was one of the commonest terms for diarrhoea at this time: ibid. 58 n. 1.

[24] Isaac Archer, 'The Diary of Isaac Archer, 1641–1700', in Matthew Storey, ed., *Two East Anglian Diaries 1641–1729* (Woodbridge, 1994), 41–200, at 157.

[25] Thomas Jolly, *The Note-Book of the Rev. Thomas Jolly, A.D. 1671–1693 …* , Chetham Society n.s. 33 (Manchester, 1894), 57.

[26] Josselin, *Diary*, 45.

[27] Jolly, *Note-Book*, 86; see also Henry Newcome, *The Diary of the Rev. Henry Newcome, from September 30, 1661, to September 29, 1663*, ed. Thomas Heywood, Chetham Society o.s. 18 (Manchester, 1849), 87, 89, 91.

[28] In 1668, Philip Henry confessed in his diary: 'Ill of ye cold, which provok't other distempers, insomuch that for a time I despayr'd even of life': Philip Henry, *Diaries and Letters of Philip Henry, M.A. of Broad Oak, Flintshire, A.D. 1631–1696*, ed. Matthew Henry Lee (London, 1882), 217.

[29] Early modern 'agues' were no light afflictions and tended to describe a multitude of ailments. On 27 September 1670, Samuel Jeake, the namesake and son of a nonconformist minister, recorded his experience of an ague as 'shaking, giddiness, drowziness, headach & inclination to vomit'. Over weeks the malady came and went in 'fits' whose symptoms usually included: 'first cold, then shaking, then giddiness, lastly headach'. Samuel Jeake, *An Astrological Diary of the Seventeenth Century: Samuel Jeake of Rye, 1652–1699*, ed.

diary on 29 February 1680: 'I quakt of ye Ague from 8. to 11. *yet preached*, neither eat nor drank betw'.[30] So 'exceedingly weak' was Henry Newcome from 'a fit of an ague' that he needed assistance getting to church and with administering communion.[31]

The pain threshold of these men is both harrowing and astonishing. The sixty-six-year-old nonconformist minister Samuel Jeake preached at a meeting in the port town of Rye, Sussex, on 31 August 1690. He did so with a gangrenated finger, swollen arm and gout in each foot.[32] Jeake died a month later. Other older ministers preached with infected limbs. In the spring of 1675, the fifty-nine-year-old Josselin preached in 'sorenes' with a 'sweld leg brake ... gangrening by the blacknes of it'.[33] At the turn of the eighteenth century, the Cumberland clergyman Richard Gilpin preached his final sermon with '*pneumonia*' whereby, 'his lungs being at that time too tender for his work', he 'rather groaned than spake'.[34] The ability (or inability) of ministers to preach God's word while sick was only matched by their capacity to endure pain and discomfort. There was, however, a notable downside, as the example of Gilpin aptly demonstrates: preaching while ill was at times counterproductive as congregants struggled to hear the sermon and digest its message.[35]

Some pulpit illnesses manifested themselves in dramatic ways. The vicar of Wormingford, Essex, Thomas Pilgrim, suffered a seizure in

---

Michael Hunter and Annabel Gregory (Oxford, 1988), 108. For this reason, the symptoms of an 'ague' resembled those of influenza, malaria, or an intermittent fever.

[30] Henry, *Diaries and Letters*, 285 (italics mine).

[31] Newcome, *Autobiography*, 1: 48.

[32] Jeake, *Diary*, 207. Jeake, like other nonconformist ministers who suffered with gout, presumably sat rather than stood when he delivered his sermonic exhortations: see Edmund Calamy, *The Nonconformist's Memorial*, ed. Samuel Palmer, 3 vols (London, 1775), 1: 367.

[33] Josselin, *Diary*, 584.

[34] Calamy, *Nonconformist's Memorial*, 1: 302. Italics original. The New England clergyman John Cotton preached with the same illness: see Clarke, *Ten Eminent Divines*, 81.

[35] Similarly, in 1692, Evelyn recorded that one minister, a 'Mr Smith', had 'such a Cold as he hardly could be heard' by the congregation: John Evelyn, *The Diary of John Evelyn*, ed. E. S. de Beer, 6 vols (Oxford, 2012), 5: 84. A sick minister's coughs and splutters were part of the wider soundscape of early modern churches. For the groaning prayers of godly congregants during service time, see John Craig, 'Psalms, Groans and Dogwhippers: The Soundscape of Worship in the English Parish Church, 1547–1642', in Will J. Coster and Andrew Spicer, eds, *Sacred Space in Early Modern Europe* (Cambridge, 2005), 104–23, at 109–13.

1644 and 'fell down dead in his pulpit'.[36] A year later, the Newbury pulpiteer William Twisse fainted while preaching at St Andrew's, Holborn.[37] While preaching at Copley Chapel in the 1650s, Oliver Heywood was 'taken so ill one sabbath in the pulpit', that he was obliged to 'break off the service abruptly and return home'. For the next three weeks he remained bedridden with a 'severe fever' which made him 'sick nigh unto death'.[38] Heywood was no old man: he was in his mid-twenties. There was widespread panic in July 1691 when an elderly Richard Baxter exhibited a 'great weaknes, fainting, or sinking in the Pulpit' and, 'not able to pronounce the blessing', it was assumed he was 'in all probability near to Death'.[39] On this occasion Baxter lived up to his reputation as being one who 'preach[ed] as a dying man to dying men'; he perished on 8 December the same year.[40] If the illness of a clergymen proved serious enough, however, they could arrange for regular and ready replacements. A commitment to uninterrupted Sabbath preaching ensured that throughout the seventeenth century sick ministers called on their colleagues to preach in their stead.[41] This practice even crossed religious divides after the Restoration, whereby conformists occasionally filled in for

---

[36] Josselin, *Diary*, 18.

[37] E. C. Vernon, 'Twisse, William (1577/8–1646)', *ODNB*, online edn (2004), at: <https://doi.org/10.1093/ref:odnb/27921>, accessed 11 March 2020.

[38] Heywood, *Works*, 1: 29.

[39] N. H. Keeble and Geoffrey F. Nuttall, eds, *Calendar of the Correspondence of Richard Baxter*, 2 vols (Oxford, 1991), 2: 324. The exact date of this sermon is unknown. From February 1687, Baxter acted as Matthew Sylvester's assistant preacher to his congregation in Rutland House, Charterhouse Yard, every Sunday and Thursday morning, where he continued 'for about 4 Years and Half', that is, until the summer of 1691: ibid. 4: 376. From then on, Baxter was quite 'disabled from Publick service by his Growing weakness', and only continued to preach 'in his own House … Morning and Evening every Day': ibid. This must therefore have been one of the last (perhaps the last) public sermons Baxter gave. I am grateful to N. H. Keeble for this information.

[40] Richard Baxter, *The Practical Works of Richard Baxter*, 4 vols (Ligonier, PA, 1990–1), 3: 1030. Such imagery also gives new meaning and poignancy to the skulls that appeared in the portraits that fronted the printed funeral sermons of some godly ministers: see Ann Hughes, 'Print and Pastoral Identity: Presbyterian Pastors Negotiate the Restoration', in Michael Davies, Anne Dunan–Page and Joel Halcomb, eds, *Church Life: Pastors, Congregations, and the Experience of Dissent in Seventeenth-Century England* (Oxford, 2019), 152–71, at 157.

[41] In 1616, 'John Boulte', an unbeneficed clergyman of Ludham, Norfolk, was said in Great Yarmouth to have 'supplied the place during the time of their preachers sicknes, which was nye about 20 weeks': H. W. Saunders, ed., *The Official Papers of Sir Nathaniel Bacon* (London, 1915), 195. Occasionally, however, a suitable replacement could not be found in time: see Evelyn, *Diary*, 2: 389.

Robert W. Daniel

nonconformist preachers (and vice versa) when they found themselves ill or incumbered.[42] Although clergymen routinely fell ill
during this period, such contingencies ensured that congregants did
not have to go without regular preaching.

Instances of preaching when sick were recorded and remembered
by the godly to evidence commitment to God, the physical perils of
preaching, the need to value it and the work of preachers and, more
generally, the bodily cost of faith which was to be imitated by all.
Sometimes pulpit fatalities were also used to admonish the irreligious
behaviour of congregants. When John Oakes died in the middle of
preaching a sermon in London in 1689, his eulogist asked of his
congregation: 'Was he not thus stricken for your rebellion against
his calls?'[43]

If ministers preached while sick, could preaching make them sick?
Delivering a sermon worthy of respect and admiration in early modern England, whether in church or chapel, was no easy feat.[44]
Ministers had to demonstrate the rhetorical skills of *elocutio* and
actio, and were advised to commit their sermon notes to memory,
not to hug the pulpit and to ensure their sermons were topical rather
than overly historical; in short, they had to provide a lively and mem-
orable performance.[45] While scholars have examined how the godly

[42] See Crawford Gribben, 'The Experience of Dissent: John Owen and Congregational
Life in Revolutionary and Restoration England', in Davies, Dunan–Page and Halcomb,
eds, *Church Life*, 119–35, at 126; Newcome, *Autobiography*, 1: 96, 112; Calamy,
Nonconformist's Memorial, 3: 276; Heywood, *Diaries*, 4: 140; John Rastrick, *The Life of
John Rastrick, 1650–1727*, ed. Andrew Cambers (Cambridge, 2010), 123.
[43] Quoted in William Gibson, 'The British Sermon 1689–1901: Quantities,
Performance, and Culture', in Keith A. Francis and William Gibson, eds, *The Oxford
Handbook of the British Sermon, 1689–1901* (Oxford, 2012), 3–30, at 13.
[44] See Alexandra Walsham, *Providence in Early Modern England* (Oxford, 1999), 281–
325; Kate Armstrong, 'Sermons in Performance', in McCullough, Adlington and
Rhatigan, eds, *Early Modern Sermon*, 120–37; Hunt, *Art of Hearing*, 187–228; Mary
Morrissey, 'Ornament and Repetition: Biblical Interpretation in Early Modern English
Preaching', in Kevin Killeen, Helen Smith and Rachel Willie, eds, *The Oxford
Handbook of the Bible in Early Modern England, c.1530–1700* (Oxford, 2015), 303–16.
[45] See Newcome, *Autobiography*, 1: 10. William Perkins, the influential puritan lecturer
of Great St Andrew's Church, Cambridge, made similar recommendations: see Raymond
A. Blacketer, 'The Rhetoric of Reform. William Perkins on Preaching and the Purification
of the Church', in Maarten Wisse, Marcel Sarot and Willemien Otten, eds, *Scholasticism
Reformed: Essays in Honour of Willem J. van Asselt* (Leiden, 2010), 215–37, at 225–7, 229–
31. Such instructions were tempered by frequent references to St Paul's plain-style preaching, his 'bodily presence weak, and his speech contemptible [or ineloquent]': Francis
Smith, *Symptomes of Growth & Decay to Godlinesse* (London, 1660), 29.

preached, scant attention has been paid to how hard this was on the preacher's body. The work of God's pulpiteers was exhausting: with some sermons lasting two or three hours, it was an exercise in physical endurance. Strenuous pulpit exertions were highly demanding on the throat, lungs and voice, and took a physical toll. The Cambridgeshire clergyman Isaac Archer confessed that if his sermons went on for too long, or he had to preach before a large audience, 'it spent mee too much, and would soon have killed me'.[46] Sapped of energy, ministers often felt bereft of strength after sermonizing. The Presbyterian clergyman Henry Newcome wrote plaintively one Sabbath in 1674: 'I preached twice and repeated at night, and was abundantly tired'.[47] Itinerant preachers, ejected from their livings after the Restoration, suffered particularly with bodily strain, some preaching as much as ten times in twelve days, finding the exercise 'toylsom if not so usefull'.[48] It is safe to assume that even those clergymen who preached shorter sermons, or less regularly, still felt this duty to be a physically demanding one. The physical 'wear and tear' caused by such constant preaching did not go unnoticed by auditors. Thomas Holborough observed of the nonconformist preacher Samuel Blackerby (a godly stalwart of Stowmarket, Suffolk), 'I have seen him divers times in the Pulpit, when he had more need to have been in his Bed', adding ominously that Blackerby was, 'seeming to me, reduced almost into his Socket, having spent his Lamp in giving light to others'.[49] Medical practitioners concurred. The physician of the West Country clergyman Samuel Crooke informed him that 'he might live longer if he would preach seldomer'.[50]

There were also environmental factors which greatly affected the health of godly ministers. Before even entering the pulpit, some clerics had to run the gauntlet of getting there. Routinely exposed to the elements, clergymen risked injury or infection on their travels. The winter months were the hardest, and arguably the most hazardous. Oliver Heywood remarked in his diary, 'According to promise I was to goe preach at Idle chappel Jan 11 [16]82 and though it

---

[46] 'Introduction', in Storey, ed., *Diaries*, 1–38, at 23–4. Although Archer was a Church of England clergyman, he only read the Prayer Book out of bare necessity and, tellingly, he obtained a licence to hold a Presbyterian meeting at his home in Chippenham after the short-lived Declaration of Indulgence in 1672.

[47] Newcome, *Autobiography*, 2: 209.

[48] Jolly, *Note-Book*, 53.

[49] Samuel Blackerby, *Sermons Preached on Several Occasions* (London, 1674), sig. A4v.

[50] Clarke, *Ten Eminent Divines*, 34.

was an exceeding stormy morning of wind and snow and the ways deep and dangerous, yet I went, because of my promise'.[51] Heywood's initial reservations were not unfounded. In mid-August 1688, at a neighbour's request, John Bunyan went to Reading to mediate in a quarrel between father and son. On the way Bunyan was drenched in a storm and soon 'fell sick of a violent Feavor'. On 19 August, likely suffering from the onset of this fever, Bunyan preached a rousing sermon at the congregation of John Gammon in Boar's Head Yard, London. Succumbing to his *'sweating Distemper'*, Bunyan perished on 31 August 1688. He probably died of influenza, or pneumonia, as a result of his undertaking this journey.[52] Travelling in inclement weather was often blamed by ministers for their colds, fits, agues and fevers.[53] If journeying in the cold did not hamper health, then preaching in cold churches was almost certainly injurious. Alice Thornton's experience of one wintry Sunday in 1661 was surely typical: 'I was in the church, when it was a frost and snow, sitting in the minister's pewe, I feltt myselfe exceeding cold, and by fitts continued till the Tuesday following, very ill'.[54] Cold churches were clearly a concern for godly clergymen. After recovering from a 'cold' in the winter of 1647, Josselin recorded: 'I preached twice through mercy, and found no prejudice though the day was bitter cold … in the open Church'.[55] Simeon Ashe, however, was

---

[51] Heywood, *Diaries*, 4: 34. See also Jolly, *Note-Book*, 97. By contrast, the godly antiquarian Ralph Thoresby pointed out the tendency for some congregants to be fair-weather sermon attenders, exclaiming in his diary: 'will not an ill morning keep thee from church': Ralph Thoresby, *The Diary of Ralph Thoresby, 1677–1724*, ed. Rev. Joseph Hunter, 2 vols (London, 1830), 1: 209. Ralph Josselin confirmed such behaviours, recording that on the first Sunday of February 1662, 'a snow covering the ground. gods worship is most sadly neglected': Josselin, *Diary*, 495.

[52] Richard Greaves, *Glimpses of Glory: John Bunyan and English Dissent* (Stanford, CA, 2002), 597–9. Italics original.

[53] During the 1660s, Henry Newcome, then in his early thirties, caught a cold from his 'journey to Warrington in so sharp a season in January', forcing him to observe the next Sabbath at home. Venturing out later that month he records there 'being a thin sharp wind, I had a sharp fit of an ague, and was gotten much out of health … was forced to keep in two Sabbaths': Newcome, *Autobiography*, 1: 119. See also Henry, *Diaries*, 188; Archer, 'Diary', 154; Adam Martindale, *The Life of Adam Martindale*, ed. Richard Parkinson (Manchester, 1845), 236.

[54] Alice Thornton, *The Autobiography of Mrs. Alice Thornton* (Durham, 1875), 132.

[55] Josselin, *Diary*, 116. These examples modify Arnold Hunt's assertion that 'attendance at sermons tended to be highest on winter evenings, which may suggest that many people who could not afford fuel in their own houses went to church in order to keep warm':

not so lucky. In August 1662, Ashe, preparing to give his lecture at St Peter Cornhill, 'took cold in the Vestry'. Thinking it would have proved but 'one of his old fits of the Gout', Ashe travelled to Highgate only to die of fever a few days later.[56] It is likely that many more clergymen fell dangerously ill when travelling and preaching in such conditions.[57]

Regular preaching also took a considerable bodily toll as a preacher grew older. The puritan luminary William Gouge, 'being then about Seventy three years old', was described as having 'spent himself so far' in his sermons during the Civil Wars that he 'strained a veyn in his lungs' and was found to be 'spitting blood'.[58] This greatly diminished the frequency and quality of his preaching.[59] Similar fatigues were felt by the ejected clergymen of the Restoration period. Preaching at his home in Stoke Newington in February 1669, the fifty-three-year-old Independent minister John Owen admitted to his auditors that though he had hoped to have 'added a word or two of direction how to put this counsel into execution', he must relent because 'my strength is gone'.[60] These and similar difficulties meant that ageing godly ministers eventually had to accept their physical limitations. Nearing the end of his life during the late 1670s, the veteran John Angier of Denton (father-in-law of Oliver Heywood) resigned himself to the fact that his ministry was coming to a close, as he was 'scarce able to get into the Pulpit for Age, and Weakness accompanying it'.[61] Seniority brought mental as well as physical deterioration. Alongside his 'bodily frailty', the sixty-one-year-old Jolly discovered that he was losing his memory recall. In 1690 he lamented experiencing 'unusuall dullness in mine head as I was preaching'. This continued into his

---

Hunt, *Art of Hearing*, 205–6. Though this may have been true for London parishes, rural and more northern regions were a different matter.

[56] Baxter, *Reliquiae Baxterianae*, 430.

[57] See Jolly, *Note-Book*, 86; Archer, 'Diary', 173. This also applied to high-ranking Church of England clerics. Tobie Matthew, archbishop of York, then in his seventies, recorded in his diary that he could not preach for several months over the winter of 1621–2 because he was 'sore afflicted with rheum and cough, diverse months together': quoted in Rosamund Oates, *Moderate Radical: Tobie Matthew and the English Reformation* (Oxford, 2018), 235.

[58] Clarke, *Ten Eminent Divines*, 144.

[59] See Thomas Fuller, *The Worthies of England*, ed. John Freeman (London, 1952), 394.

[60] Quoted in Gribben, 'Experience of Dissent', 131.

[61] Vincent Alsop, *A Reply to the Reverend Dean of St. Paul's* (London, 1681), 12.

Robert W. Daniel

administration of the Lord's Supper whereby his 'memory was taken away in great measure'. Dotage was a clear sign that Jolly's 'spirits, strength, and gifts [were] failing'.[62] Congregants also complained that elderly ministers, no longer able to project their voices, delivered inaudible sermons. In 1682 the diarist John Evelyn remarked of Benjamin Whichcote, the seventy-three-year-old vicar of St Lawrence Jewry, that he 'spake so very low, & was so feeble an old man, that I could by no meanes hear what he saied'.[63] Effective and affecting preaching, it seems, was either a young or middle-aged man's game.

There were several reasons why puritan pulpiteers risked their lives for (and in) the pulpit. Godly clergymen took their cue from early rarefied reformers such as John Knox who, as Oliver Heywood wrote, set the bar high, in that he frequently 'rose off from his sick and death-bed, and would needs go to the pulpit'.[64] There was also a providential impetus for preaching when ill. The day he was due at a baptism in 1678, Heywood felt 'desperately sick', his 'head akt very bitterly' and he 'vomited', unable to keep his food down. Despite his condition, Heywood attended the event and was able to preach 'extempore for a full hour'. Returning home, and feeling much recovered, Heywood surmised this moral lesson: 'o[h] wonder of mercy! preaching and praying hath helpt my soul and body, both at once'.[65] Seen this way, clergymen preached not just in spite of, but because of, their fevers, colds, agues and distempers. Doing God's work, as opposed to enjoying a period of restful convalescence, was why, Heywood averred, he had been 'perfectly cured'.[66] Preaching

[62] Jolly, *Note-Book*, 103.

[63] Evelyn, *Diary*, 3: 282. Whichcote, who had sided with Parliament during the Civil War, but conformed after the Restoration, died the next year in 1683. The connection between infirmity and inaudibility when preaching was something ministers were all too aware of. In 1701, due to a harsh winter, the seventy-one-year-old Oliver Heywood recorded being 'greatly afflicted with shortness of breathing', but was thankful that when he 'got into the pulpit, I could pray and preach audibly, a long time together': Heywood, *Diaries*, 4: 168.

[64] Heywood, *Works*, 2: 167. Another example may have been John Jewel, bishop of Salisbury, who died shortly after having given a sermon at Lacock, Wiltshire, in September 1571. Though no friend to puritans, Jewel's will noted 'my werye bodie broken and consumed in his werye laboures' of preaching: Kew, TNA, PROB 11/53, fols 309v–310r.

[65] Oliver Heywood, *The Rev. Oliver Heywood, B.A., 1630–1702; His Autobiography, [and] Diaries*, ed. J. Horsfall Turner, 4 vols (Brighouse: 1882), 3: 146.

[66] Ibid.

was curative, its honest labour was healing labour.[67] As Josselin avowed, 'I ventured abroad and preacht twice, knowing my strength belongd to god that gave it and he could preserve my body from danger while I was in his service'.[68] Similarly, Isaac Archer declared: 'went to preach, when scar[c]e able to goe, my health being chiefly to serve God in'.[69] Whether sick or well, clergymen trusted that God's divine will was manifest in either condition. Theologically speaking, to Reformed Englishmen and women, the presence of pain among the saints was also seen as God's cure for sin and selfishness.[70] In continuing, rather than postponing, their sermons when ill, ministers hoped to receive a double blessing by way of spiritual and physical cleansing, 'soul and body, both at once'.[71]

Long-suffering pulpiteers were also meant to be exemplars themselves, showing congregants that certain kinds of illness were not an excuse for church or chapel absenteeism. If the preacher could preach while ill, then the laity could sit and listen while ill. In this, godly ministers created a kind of double obligation for church attendance. Not only was church attendance a devotional duty – and before 1650 and after the Restoration a legal one – but godly clergymen taught that God sometimes sent illness to individuals as an admonition for neglecting Sabbath sermons.[72] If one abandoned church services, especially when sick, one risked becoming even sicker. But if one attended church, even when sick, one had the chance of being physically and spiritually healed. This helps to explain the sermon attendance rates of some of the godly, and sickly, laity.[73] Preaching with pain was also believed to make sermons more arresting. The ejected Worcestershire minister Thomas Baldwin was said to have been much 'troubled both with gout and stone, and often preached with those pains upon him; which some of his auditors thought excited the

---

[67] This was part of a wider cultural and medical belief in the curative properties of movement, fresh air, and exercise: see Samuel Pepys, *The Diary of Samuel Pepys*, ed. H. B. Wheatley, 10 vols (London, 2008), 7: 208; Newton, *Misery to Mirth*, 87.

[68] Josselin, *Diary*, 113.

[69] Archer, 'Diary', 163.

[70] Cooper, 'Richard Baxter and his Physicians', 14.

[71] This supports scholarship on the 'double cure' God's healing was thought to produce: see Newton, *Misery to Mirth*, 131–64.

[72] See Harley, 'Theology of Affliction', 278.

[73] See Rastrick, *Life*, 60–1; Mary Franklin, 'The Experience of Mary Franklin', in Vera J. Camden, ed., *She being Dead yet Speaketh: The Franklin Family Papers* (Toronto, ON, 2020), 131–2, at 151; Clarke, *Ten Eminent Divines*, 506, cf. 429.

greater earnestness, and made his expressions the more affecting'.[74] For all these reasons, preaching when sick was a logical activity, if not an inescapable duty, amongst puritan clergymen.

There is no space here to discuss the plethora of other pastoral duties that might affect the health of godly preachers, such as visiting the sick, administering the Lord's Supper to a large congregation, officiating at baptisms and burials and leading thanksgivings, the headaches and nausea from fasting or night-long prayer sessions, not to mention the strains of facilitating family worship and prayers.[75] Some ministers were so busy that they sacrificed family devotions for a devotion to church work.[76] Occasionally, we even glimpse frustrations at the onerous 'worke enough to doe' by which conscientious clergymen felt overwhelmed.[77] Puritan preachers performed honest work, but it was also hard work, which took a toll on their bodies and on their families.

The wealth of admissions and confessions, in print and manuscript, to the health hazards of sermonizing, tells us that such experiences were widespread amongst the godly clerical class. This radically changes the way we think about early modern preaching, not just as an intellectual and spiritual exercise, but as a physically onerous one. The importance of a robust preaching ministry amongst puritan clerics was, then, not simply a theological notion. Those who campaigned for and practised it knew they did so to the detriment of their bodies, but believed it was for the betterment of souls. Ministers tended to their flocks, despite their physical frailties and disabilities, with resilience, patience and enthusiasm. Their generosity of spirit and courage cautions us not just to focus on what or how they preached, but how they were feeling when they preached, because that will tell us a great deal about why they preached.

---

[74] Calamy, *Nonconformist's Memorial*, 3: 389.

[75] For the heavy pastoral and parish workload of conscientious divines, see Seaver, *Puritan Lectureships*, 131–2.

[76] See Heywood, *Diaries*, 3: 225; Richard Baxter, *A Breviate of the Life of Margaret ... Wife of Richard Baxter* (London, 1681), 101–2.

[77] See Martindale, *Life*, 104; Newcome, *Autobiography*, 1: 73; Henry, *Diaries*, 94. There is no room here to discuss the mental-wellbeing of ministers. There are suggestive examples of godly clergymen suffering from bouts of depression and mental anguish: see Heywood, *Diaries*, 4: 166, 170; Newcome, *Autobiography*, 1: 112, 181–2; Rastrick, *Diary*, 101–2.

This essay's findings have broader implications for the 'lived religion' of English Protestantism and its relationship to sickness during the seventeenth century. Preaching while unwell was noble in theory, but precarious, arduous and potentially dangerous in practice. If ministers preached with colds, agues and fevers, they risked infecting others and exacerbating their own pain and discomfort, or worse. When congregants followed their example, attending church with all manner of ailments, they too risked making themselves and others sicker. A belief in divine providence, the power of preaching and strict sabbatarianism superseded modern notions of communal health and safety and held a powerful sway throughout the seventeenth century. Preaching while ill also illustrates the practical and bodily difficulties clergymen had to overcome when sermonizing, which highlights the need to examine the performativity, not just the literariness, of early modern sermons. True, preaching when unwell could hamper a sermon's audibility, but the physical presence of an ill minister could have a powerful impact and leave a lasting impression. This also tells us something about the work ethic of God's shepherds. Experience of sickness was an accepted part of a clergyman's vocation; his sufferings were to be seen publicly rather than concealed privately, to build faith and serve as a living exemplar. Consequently, puritan clerics frequently exchanged their sickbeds for their pulpits, for various reasons and in a variety of contexts, which both problematizes and enriches our conception of the nature and role of early modern preaching and preachers.

Healthcare and Catholic Enlightenment in the Polish-Lithuanian Commonwealth

Stanisław Witecki*
Jagiellonian University

In the eighteenth century, the ideal of the priest in society was reformed by Polish and Lithuanian Catholic bishops. Instrumental in these reforms were Ignacy Massalski (1726–94), bishop of Vilnius (1762–94) and Michał Poniatowski (1736–94), bishop of Płock (1773–85), then archbishop of Gniezno (1785–94), and simultaneously administrator of the diocese of Kraków (1782–90). Their programmes included making clergy responsible for medical education and the organization of healthcare, and seeking to reform customs which were viewed as detrimental to health. The article draws on pastoral letters, popular educational books and administrative decrees to ascertain what ideas reformers imposed on the clergy. Episcopal visitation protocols, sermons and parish school textbooks are analysed to verify the effects of reforms and ascertain what was taught about health in the parishes. The examination of the relatively rare egodocuments of priests sheds light on how they experienced their afflictions. The article concludes that healthcare was an important topic for Catholic enlighteners in the Polish-Lithuanian Commonwealth, and that priests played a significant role in promoting it. Reforms were driven by humanitarian and physiocratic principles, and were facilitated by an optimistic belief in the benefits of medicine. Nonetheless, many enlightened programmes failed because priests were unwilling or unable to implement changes that interfered with lived religion.

In the summer of 1785, the parish clergy of the diocese of Kraków and archdiocese of Gniezno received a letter signed by Michał Jerzy Poniatowski, recently appointed primate of Poland and the king's younger brother.[1] Some priests may already have heard about the

* Institute of History, Jagiellonian University, ul. Gołębia 13, 31-007 Kraków. E-mail: stanislaw.witecki@uj.edu.pl.

The research is founded by the National Science Centre, Poland, under the project PRELUDIUM 16, no 2018/31/N/HS3/02079.

[1] Michał Poniatowski, *Zalecenie względem niektórych okoliczności ochrony zdrowia ludu roboczego w czasie letnim* [*Recommendation on Certain Circumstances of the Protection of the Health of Workers during Summer*] (Warsaw, 1785).

Studies in Church History 58 (2022), 150–172   © The Author(s), 2022. Published by Cambridge University Press on behalf of Ecclesiastical History Society
doi: 10.1017/stc.2022.8

reforms Poniatowski had implemented in the diocese of Płock since 1773, but even for them this letter must have been utterly surprising.[2] Poniatowski demanded that the clergy see themselves as responsible for the people's health and requested that all landowners do the same. He set out some rules which were to be preached every year before harvest. Firstly, people were to be discouraged from eating unripe fruit and from baking bread or preparing gruel from unripe grain. Since the obvious reason for doing this was hunger, landlords were to provide their subjects with sufficient food. Moreover, people were to be told not to wear any form of headgear or to drink cold water while working in hot weather on the grounds that this would prevent sickness and death. Poniatowski asserted that priests were responsible not only for their people's heavenly life but also their earthly life. He also pointed out that serfs who became ill or died had an adverse effect on agricultural revenues.

Before the end of the eighteenth century, then, Polish and Lithuanian clergy were officially tasked with taking care of the health of the faithful. This request may therefore be treated as a sign of a deeper historical change, which raises several questions. Firstly, what other evidence is there for what Catholic elites thought about the health of the people, and what they were doing about it? Secondly, why did they start at this period to take an interest in healthcare? Finally, given that several of Poniatowski's proposals ran counter to both lived religion[3] and the social model of priesthood which had long defined clergy-parish relationships, to what extent were these proposals owned and adopted by the parish clergy?

Late eighteenth-century healthcare has been widely described in the literature on the social history of medicine. Emerging in the course of the Enlightenment, it encompassed the optimistic belief that health was natural state of the body and that diseases would eventually be eradicated, new physiological theories, the development of institutional healthcare and the mercantilist politics of bureaucratic states.[4] On the other hand, in the developing field of the study of

---

[2] Stanisław Witecki, *Przekaz kulturowy w parafiach katolickich na obszarze Rzeczypospolitej Obojga Narodów czasów stanisławowskich* [*Cultural Transmission in Catholic Parishes in the Polish-Lithuanian Commonwealth during the Stanislavian Period*] (Kraków, 2018), 58–83, 127–95.

[3] This article uses the term 'lived religion' as an alternative to the older concept of 'popular religion'.

[4] Guenter B. Risse, 'Medicine in the Age of Enlightenment', in Andrew Wear, ed., *History of Medicine in Society: Historical Essays* (Cambridge, 1992), 149–96; Jonathan

Stanisław Witecki

Enlightenment religion, health issues are marginal. Historians of that movement tend to focus on political ideas such as freedom and equality, or on theological concepts such as toleration, moderation of ritual, rationalization of faith, and charity.[5]

This article argues that health issues were an important aspect of the reforms proposed by Catholic enlighteners in the Polish-Lithuanian Commonwealth. Their programmes made clergy responsible for medical education, organization of healthcare and the reform of customs which might have been harmful to health. These reforms had a humanitarian and economic rationale and were facilitated by an optimistic belief in the benefits of medicine. However, many enlightened programmes failed because priests were unwilling or unable to implement changes that interfered with lived religion.

CATHOLIC CLERGY AND ENLIGHTENMENT

Individual Catholic priests influenced healthcare through holding a range of posts in the Polish-Lithuanian Commonwealth. Clergy were present in all divisions of the government. That is especially true of the Komisja Edukacji Narodowej (Commission of National Education), founded in 1773. Its first president was Ignacy Massalski, bishop of Vilnius or Wilno, and its second from 1786

Andrews, 'History of Medicine: Health, Medicine and Disease in the Eighteenth Century', *Journal for Eighteenth-Century Studies* 34 (2011), 503–15; James Kelly, 'John Cunningham (ed.), Early Modern Ireland and the World of Medicine: Practitioners, Collectors and Contexts', *SHM* 33 (2019), 330–1.

[5] Stanisław Janeczek, *Oświecenie chrześcijańskie: z dziejów polskiej kultury filozoficznej* [*Christian Enlightenment: The History of Polish Philosophical Culture*] (Lublin, 1994); Jerzy Lukowski, 'Recasting Utopia: Montesquieu, Rousseau and the Polish Constitution of 3 May 1791', *HistJ* 37 (1994), 65–87; S. J. Barnett, *The Enlightenment and Religion: The Myths of Modernity* (Manchester, 2003); David Sorkin, *The Religious Enlightenment: Protestants, Jews, and Catholics from London to Vienna* (Princeton, NJ, 2008); Jeffrey D. Burson, 'The Crystallization of Counter-Enlightenment and Philosophe Identities: Theological Controversy and Catholic Enlightenment in Pre-Revolutionary France', *ChH* 77 (2008), 955–1002; Ulrich Lehner and Micheal O'Neil Printy, eds, *A Companion to the Catholic Enlightenment in Europe* (Leiden, 2010); Rafał Szczurowski, *Zaradzić potrzebom doczesnym i wiecznym: idee oświecenia w Kościele katolickim w Polsce (do 1795r.)* [*Addressing Temporal and Eternal Needs: Ideas of Enlightenment in the Catholic Church in Poland to 1795*] (Kraków, 2014); Ulrich Lehner, *Catholic Enlightenment: The Forgotten Story of the Global Movement* (Oxford, 2016).

was the primate, Michał Poniatowski.[6] Priests also formed the majority of school teachers.

Most members of the Catholic episcopate in the Commonwealth at the end of the eighteenth century were not reformers. Some, such as Wojciech Skarszewski (1743–1827; bishop of Chełm and Lublin 1791–1805, bishop of Lublin 1805–24, archbishop of Warsaw 1824–7), carried out ecclesiastical reform according to the principles of the Council of Trent. Others, such as Ignacy Krasicki (1735–1801; prince-bishop of Warmia 1766–95, archbishop of Gniezno 1795–1801), Józef Kossakowski (1738–94; bishop of Livonia 1781–94) and Adam Naruszewicz (1733–96; bishop of Smoleńsk [now in Russia] 1775–88 [coadjutor], 1788–90 [diocesan], bishop of Luts'k or Łuck [now in Ukraine] 1790–6), promoted the ideas of the Catholic Enlightenment but as writers and politicians rather than in their episcopal capacity. In contrast, Massalski and Poniatowski used their episcopal authority to apply their ideas to people's daily lives.[7]

The success or otherwise of these reforms depended on the parish clergy. Most late eighteenth-century priests had been educated in seminaries. The younger clergy had graduated from the colleges of the Jesuits and the Piarists, which after mid-century reform were teaching modern languages, history, geography and natural sciences. These graduates were supposed to be patriotic citizens, aware of the need for political and economic reforms.[8] At the same time, parish priests had to take into account the reality of lived religion, often incompatible with reforms proposed by the enlighteners.[9] The

---

[6] Danuta Gorecki, 'The Commission of National Education and Civic Revival through Books in Eighteenth-Century Poland', *Journal of Library History* 15 (1980), 138–66.

[7] Michał Grzybowski, *Kościelna działalność Michała Jerzego Poniatowskiego biskupa płockiego 1773–1785* [*The Church Activity of Michał Jerzy Poniatowski, Bishop of Płock 1773–1785*] (Warsaw, 1983); Tadeusz Kasabuła, *Ignacy Massalski biskup wileński* [*Ignacy Massalski, Bishop of Vilnius*] (Lublin, 1998); Richard Butterwick, *Polish Revolution and the Catholic Church, 1788–1792: A Political History* (Oxford 2011).

[8] Janina Rosicka, 'Ekonomia a Oświecenie chrześcijańskie: pijarzy i fizjokratyzm' ['Economy and Christian Enlightenment: Piarists and Physiocracy'], in Irena Stasiewicz-Jasiukowa, ed., *Wkład pijarów do nauki i kultury w Polsce XVII–XIX wieku* [*The Contribution of the Piarists to Science and Culture in Poland in the 17th–19th Centuries*] (Warsaw and Kraków, 1993), 151–71; Kazimierz Puchowski, *Jezuickie kolegia szlacheckie Rzeczypospolitej Obojga Narodów: studium z dziejów edukacji elit* [*Jesuit Colleges for Nobility in the Polish-Lithuanian Commonwealth: A Study in the History of Education of the Elite*] (Gdańsk, 2007).

[9] Tomasz Wiślicz, 'Shepherds of the Catholic Flock: Polish Parochial Clergy, Popular Religion, and the Reception of the Council of Trent', in Luise Schorn-Schütte, ed.,

polarization was not always between subjects and nobility but rather between theologically and philosophically educated individuals, mostly priests, and other Catholics. For peasants and nobility alike, lived religion was based on custom rather than on the Roman Catechism and the canons of the Council of Trent.[10]

Most Catholic priests were not enlighteners, but Catholic clergy played a dominant role in the Polish and Lithuanian Enlightenment. This is one reason why the radical Enlightenment as defined by Jonathan Israel was represented in Poland-Lithuania only by individuals.[11] Enlightenment in the Commonwealth had different shades but almost all were religious. Richard Butterwick has proposed a distinction between Enlightened Catholicism and Catholic Enlightenment. The first refers to Catholicism which included some features of the Enlightenment. It was characterized by an emphasis on education, the reform of popular piety and a cognitive distancing from superstitions. The second encompassed all Enlightenment ideas formulated by Catholics, including those not directly related to religion or modifying the previously accepted functions of religion. Catholic enlighteners changed the social model of parish priesthood significantly by openly enjoining priests to be attentive to the earthly, physical wellbeing of their people.[12] In this way

---

Gelehrte Geistlichkeit – Geistliche Gelehrte: Beiträge zur Geschichte des Bürgertums in der Frühneuzeit, Historische Forschungen 97 (Berlin, 2012), 25–52; Tomasz Wiślicz, *Earning Heavenly Salvation: Peasant Religion in Lesser Poland, Mid-Sixteenth to Eighteenth Centuries* (Berlin, 2020).

[10] Tomasz Wiślicz, 'Religijność wiejska w Rzeczpospolitej szlacheckiej' ['Rural Religiosity in the Republic of Nobles'], *Barok* 11 (2004), 97–118; Anna Niedźwiedź, 'Od religijności ludowej do religii przeżywanej' ['From Popular Religiosity to Lived Religion'], in Barbara Fatyga and Ryszard Michalski, eds, *Kultura Ludowa. Teorie. Prkatyki. Polityki* [*Popular Culture. Theories. Practices. Policies*] (Warsaw, 2014), 327–38; Kim Knibbe and Helena Kupari, 'Theorizing Lived Religion: Introduction', *JCR* 35 (2020), 157–76.

[11] Jonathan Israel, *A Revolution of the Mind: Radical Enlightenment and the Intellectual Origins of Modern Democracy* (Princeton, NJ, 2010).

[12] Richard Butterwick considers this to be the trait of Enlightened Catholicism, rather than Catholic Enlightenment: 'What Is Enlightenment (Oświecenie)? Some Polish Answers, 1765–1820', *Central Europe* 3 (2005), 19–37; idem, 'Between Anti-Enlightenment and Enlightened Catholicism: Provincial Preachers in Late Eighteenth-Century Poland-Lithuania', in idem, Simon Davies and Gabriel Sánchez Espinosa, eds, *Peripheries of the Enlightenment*, Studies on Voltaire and the Eighteenth Century (Oxford, 2008), 201–28; Maciej Janowski, 'Warsaw and Its Intelligentsia: Urban Space and Social Change, 1750–1831', *Acta Poloniae Historica* 100 (2009), 7–77; Martyna Deszczyńska, *Polskie Kontroświecenie* [*The Polish Counter-Enlightenment*] (Warsaw,

they imposed further duties on priests in addition to the wide-ranging responsibilities already imposed by the Council of Trent, which included not only worshipping God, securing the salvation of souls and promoting charity, but also keeping parish registers and guarding the church's economic interests.[13]

This new social obligation had humanitarian as well as economic reasons. It was based on a new understanding of the value of human life and a conviction that there existed a moral necessity to provide support to those who needed it. The reformers were also concerned with improving the economy of the Polish-Lithuanian Commonwealth. Although this was growing during the second half of the eighteenth century, it had not yet fully recovered from the crisis caused by wars between 1648 and 1721. Agricultural underdevelopment was obvious to landowners, who included priests, and such men were often early adherents to physiocracy. For example, Ignacy Massalski established personal relations with the proponents of the new economic theories, visiting Honoré Gabriel Riqueti, count of Mirabeau, and inviting Nicolas Baudeau to Lithuania.[14]

The Polish and Lithuanian nobility had traditionally believed that the wealth of nations derived solely from agriculture, but physiocrats

---

2011); Richard Butterwick, 'Między oświeceniem a katolicyzmem, czyli o katolickim oświeceniu i oświeconym katolicyzmie' ['Between the Enlightenment and Catholicism, or, on Catholic Enlightenment and Enlightened Catholicism'], *Wiek Oświecenia* 30 (2014), 11–55; Witecki, *Przekaz kulturowy*, 51–7.

[13] Luise Schorn-Schutte, 'The Christian Clergy in the Early Modern Holy Roman Empire: A Comparative Social Study', *SCJ* 29 (1998), 717–31; Ian Green, '"Reformed Pastors" and Bons Curés: The Changing Role of the Parish Clergy in Early Modern Europe', in W. J. Sheils and Diana Wood, eds, *The Ministry: Clerical and Lay*, SCH 26 (Oxford, 1989), 249–86; Robert Muchembled, *Popular Culture and Elite Culture in France, 1400–1750* (Baton Rouge, LA, 1985); J. Michael Hayden and Malcolm R. Greenshields, 'The Clergy of Early Seventeenth-Century France: Self-Perception and Society's Perception', *French Historical Studies* 18 (1993), 145–72, at 145; Peter Burke, *Popular Culture in Early Modern Europe* (London, 2009); Magdalena Ślusarska, 'Oświeceniowe modele biskupa, plebana i parafii: kontynuacja czy zmiana tradycji?' ['Enlightenment Models of the Bishop, Priest and Parish: Continuation or Change of Tradition?'], in eadem, ed., *Dwór – plebania – rodzina chłopska* [Manor House – Vicarage – Peasant Family] (Warsaw, 1998), 37–53.

[14] Rafał Szczurowski, 'Jubileuszowe kazania księży Michała Karpowicza (1744–1803) i Wilhelma Kalińskiego (1747–1789) w zmiennych ocenach badaczy' ['The Jubilee Sermons of Priests Michał Karpowicz (1744–1803) and Wilhelm Kaliński (1747–1789) in the varying Assessments of Researchers'], *Folia Historica Cracoviensia* 10 (2004), 347–60, at 352.

elevated that belief to the level of a law of nature. The physiocratic economic school argued for free trade and provided a practical solution for increasing land revenues. This was attractive to landowners, whose income was generated from the sale, and often the export, of agricultural goods.[15] Physiocracy was preferred to mercantilism or cameralism which focused on the trade in manufactured goods and the role of central government and did not fit well with the highly decentralized commonwealth.[16]

In Poland and Lithuania, there was an abundance of land, but the workforce was both scarce and unproductive. Physiocratic principles resulted in the pragmatic understanding that healthy serfs might be economically beneficial. Before the end of the eighteenth century this had few practical implications, since there was little faith in physicians. However, progress in medicine fuelled optimism about the effectiveness of healing and the utility of organized healthcare. The newest medical theories were summarized in an article 'Uwagi o lekarskiej sztuce' ('Remarks on the Art of Medicine') published in the journal *Zabawy przyjemne i pożyteczne (Enjoyable and Useful Activities)* in 1774.[17] It was most probably authored by Grzegorz Piramowicz, a former Jesuit

[15] Ambroise Jobert, *Magnats Polonais et Physiocrates Français (1767–1774)* (Paris, 1941); Janina Rosicka, ed., 'Fizjokratyzm w Polsce' ['Physiocracy in Poland'], in eadem, ed., *Physiocracy Yesterday and Today* (Kraków, 1996), 157–70; Ewa Ziółek, 'Fizjokrata na sejmie wielkim, czyli o poglądach biskupa Józefa Kossakowskiego w sprawie włościan' [*A Physiocrat at the Grand Seym: On the Views of Bishop Józef Kossakowski regarding the Peasantry*], in Urszula Borkowska et al., eds, *Peregrinatio Ad Veritatem: studia ofiarowane profesor Aleksandrze Witkowskiej OSU z Okazji 40-Lecia Pracy Naukowej [Peregrinatio Ad Veritatem: Studies presented to Professor Aleksandra Witkowska OSU to mark 40 Years of Scholarly Work]* (Lublin, 2004).

[16] Franz A. J. Szabo, 'Cameralism, Josephinism, and Enlightenment: The Dynamic of Reform in the Habsburg Monarchy, 1740–92', *Austrian History Yearbook* 49 (2018), 1–14; Ilona Bažantová, 'Cameralism, so called Political Sciences, and the Rationale behind the Austrian Economic and Administrative Reforms in the Second Half of 18th Century, focusing on the Czech Lands', *Journal on European History of Law* 9 (2018), 129–39.

[17] Grzegorz Piramowicz, 'Uwagi o Lekarskiej Sztuce' ['Remarks on the Art of Medicine'], *Zabawy Przyjemne i Pożyteczne [Enjoyable and Useful Activities]* 10/2 (1774), 209–24. In the same issue, he recommended a reading of the Polish translation of Samuel Tissot's medical work, *Avis au peuple sur sa santé* (Lausanne, 1761); Grzegorz Piramowicz, 'List pewnego nauką znakomitego męża do tłumaczów księgi doktorskiej pana Tissot, pod tytułem: Rada dla pospólstwa względem zdrowia jego, po wydanym dziele pisany, Die 25. Jan: 1774' ['A Letter from a certain Eminent Man to the Translators of the Medical Book of Mr Tissot under the Title: Advice for the People regarding their Health, written after Publication of the Book, 25. Jan: 1774'], *Zabawy Przyjemne i Pożyteczne* 10/2 (1774), 354–61.

and chairman of the Towarzystwo do Ksiąg Elementarnych (Society for Elementary Textbooks), which sought to provide such works for elementary schools.[18] Piramowicz presented the natural and optimistic concept of health as desirable and as achievable by secular means. Neither God nor any other *sacrum* was mentioned. Illness was presented as a natural abnormality which should be limited by prevention and might be eradicated with the help of professional physicians. A healthy lifestyle should therefore be taught to all people, peasants included. Piramowicz recommended proper nutrition and outdoor activities, emphasizing the need for fresh air and improved hygiene and cleanliness. His proposals were in line with the latest medical theories, which Piramowicz reviewed critically, arguing that the systematists who were developing general theories could not and should not exclude the achievements of nosologists who gathered empirical data, and vice versa.[19]

MEDICAL EDUCATION

New medical theories might have been accepted by individuals and described in the press, but before 1763 there was only one medical faculty in the whole of Poland-Lithuania: located in the University of Kraków, it had just two professors.[20] In 1774, Stanisław August Poniatowski initiated the establishment of the Królewska Szkoła Lekarska (Royal Medical School) in Гродна / Hrodna or Grodno (now in Belarus). It was organized by the French physician Emmanuel Gilibert and equipped with facilities which included a hospital, a botanical garden and a dissecting room.[21]

---

[18] For more on healthcare publications in the Commonwealth, see Jakub Węglorz, 'Metody terapeutyczne stosowane w medycynie nowożytnej na terenach Rzeczypospolitej w XVII i XVIII w. w kontekście charakterystyki wykorzystanych źródeł' ['Therapeutic Methods used in Early Modern Medicine in the Territory of the Polish-Lithuanian Commonwealth during the 17th and 18th Centuries in the Context of the Characteristics of the Sources used'], *Historyka. Studia Metodologiczne* 48 (2018), 95–109; Jarosław Barański, 'Cnoty lekarza w polskiej lekarskiej myśli filozoficzno-moralnej w XVIII i XIX wieku' ['The Virtues of Physicians in Polish Medical, Philosophical and Moral Thought during the 18th and 19th Centuries'], *Medycyna Nowożytna* 25 (2019), 27–49.

[19] Risse, 'Medicine in the Age of Enlightenment', 155–71.

[20] Weronika Kocela, *Trudna sztuka babienia: kultura medyczna Polski drugiej połowy XVIII wieku* [*The Difficult Art of Midwifery: Polish Medical Culture in the Second Half of the 18th Century*] (Warsaw, 2020), 14–31.

[21] Adam Wrzosek, 'Założenie Królewskiej Szkoły Lekarskiej w Grodnie za Stanisława Augusta' ['The Foundation of the Royal Medical School in Grodno under Stanisław

Stanisław Witecki

The improvement of medical education was overseen by the Komisja Edukacji Narodowej (Commission for National Education). The University of Kraków was reformed by the rector, Hugo Kołłątaj, with the help and support of Poniatowski.[22] The University of Vilnius was transformed by the rector, Marcin Poczobut, with the backing of Massalski.[23] Both schools had similar facilities to those established in Grodno and employed well educated staff, mainly from abroad. Lectures covered anatomy, botany and chemistry, pathology, medical practice, midwifery and surgery.

Reformed universities were training increased numbers of physicians, but prevention was believed to be better than cure. In 1785, the Komisja Edukacji Narodowej published an *Elementarz dla szkół parafialnych narodowych* (*Elementary Textbook for National Parish Schools*), including a chapter about moral science by Piramowicz.[24] This presented the physiocratic notion that taking care of one's own health was a moral duty and a social responsibility, which guaranteed the effectiveness of labour. Children were instructed to seek help from physicians or educated landlords, and never from quack doctors or fairies. Pupils were also taught about proper diet, home ventilation, physical education and the necessity of smallpox inoculations, and provided with some basic rules for treating the sick.

Whilst the Komisja Edukacji Narodowej would have liked schools in every parish to base their teaching on this text, the reality was very different. Even in dioceses overseen by Poniatowski and Massalski, who fully supported educational reform, many parishes had schools which were not organized or barely functioning. Landlords and serfs alike opposed the reforms, worrying that educated children would not want to work in agriculture. In existing schools, teachers often used older texts, the content of which was limited to reading

August'], *Archiwum Historji i Filozofji Medycyny oraz Histoji Nauk Przyrodniczych* 2 (1925), 149–68, at 164.
[22] Mirosława Chamcówna and Kamilla Mrozowska, *Dzieje Uniwersytetu Jagiellońskiego w latach 1765–1850* [*The History of the Jagiellonian University in the Years 1765–1850*], 2 vols (Kraków, 1965), 2: part 1.
[23] Janina Kamińska, 'Szkoła Główna Wielkiego Księstwa Litewskiego jako uczelnia oświeceniowa' ['The Main School of the Grand Duchy of Lithuania as an Enlightenment University'], *Kwartalnik Historii Nauki i Techniki* 60 (2015), 55–67.
[24] Andrzej Gawroński, Onufry Kopczyński and Grzegorz Piramowicz, *Elementarz Dla Szkół Parafialnych Narodowych* [*Elementary Textbook for National Parish Schools*] (Warsaw, 1785).

lessons and the catechism. Nevertheless, there were some parishes where children were taught according to the physiocratic ideas of Piramowicz.[25] Poniatowski not only supported the reorganization of parish education, but also made priests responsible for preaching about health. Before he sent the letter described above, as bishop of Płock (1773– 85), he ordered priests to advise parents not to sleep in the same bed as an infant, in order to avoid the all-too-common risk of suffocation.[26] Poniatowski presented this medical knowledge in two pastoral letters; in contrast, Massalski as bishop of Vilnius made it an element of the diocesan preaching programme. In his persuasive book *Kapłan Sługa Boży (The Priest, Servant of God)*, anonymously published in Vilnius in 1793, he tasked the clergy with the civic obligations of serving the Commonwealth and the people. Priests should not only teach the truths of faith necessary for salvation, but should also offer advice which would make earthly life happier and render individuals more useful to their fellow Christians and their country.[27] *Kapłan Sługa Boży* was published late in Massalski's career. However, it was a recapitulation of the programme he had been advocating for many years.

In 1776 Massalski organized the Jubilee which had been proclaimed for all Catholics by Pope Clement XIV in 1775. This had been envisaged by the pope as a traditional public expression of piety and a chance to gain an indulgence. In Massalski's diocese of

---

[25] Tadeusz Mizia, *Szkolnictwo parafialne w czasach Komisji Edukacji Narodowej* [*Parish Education during the Time of the Commission for National Education*] (Wrocław, 1964); Przemysław Jędrzejewski, 'Szkolnictwo parafialne województwa krakowskiego w dobie Sejmu Wielkiego (1788–1792)' ['Parish Education in the Krakow Voivodeship during the Time of the Great Sejm (1788–1792)'], in Katarzyna Dormus, ed., *Komisja Edukacji Narodowej: kontekst historyczno-pedagogiczny* [*Commission for National Education: Historical and Pedagogical Context*] (Kraków, 2014), 251–78.
[26] Michał Poniatowski, 'List Pasterski Do Oboyga Stanów Dyecezyi Płockiey tak Duchownego, yako i Swieckiego wydany' ['Pastoral Letter to both States of the Diocese of Płock, Clergy as well as Laity'], in *Rozrządzenia Y Pisma Pasterskie Za Rządów J. O. Xięcia JMci Michała Jerzego Poniatowskiego Biskupa Płockiego &tc. &tc. Do Dyecezyi Płockiey Wydane: Dla wygody teyże Dyecezyi zebrane, i do Druku podane* [*Ordinances and Pastoral Letters of Michał Jerzy Poniatowski, Bishop of Płock, to the Diocese of Płock: Issued for the Convenience of the Diocese, collected and submitted to Print*], 4 vols (Warsaw, 1785), 1: 391–589, at 449.
[27] *Kapłan Sługa Boży y Pasterz Dusz, Czyli List Xiędza Plebana do Xiędza Brata Swego Zamykaiący w Krótkim zebraniu obowiąski Kapłańskie i Pasterza Dusz* [*The Priest, Servant of God and Shepherd of Souls, that is, a Letter from the Priest to his priestly Brother, briefly describing the Duties of the Priest and Shepherd of Souls*] (Wilno, 1793).

Vilnius, it was turned into a programme of public preaching on centrally defined topics, set down by Wilhelm Kaliński at the bishop's request.[28] These topics included the obligation to take care of one's body, as well as rules to be followed during illness and convalescence. The sermons were supposed to encourage individuals to learn about the body as well as the soul; they also advised landlords about helping peasants to improve their diet, houses and clothing for medical reasons. In addition, the bishop required any religious order which wished to organize rural missions to preach about these topics during the Jubilee.[29] In 1785, he requested the deans of the diocese to submit reports on the realization of this educational programme.[30]

The obligation to preach about health was not supposed to undermine belief in God's providence. During an outbreak of plague in 1771, Massalski issued a pastoral letter proposing standard preventative measures such as specific medications, the isolation of individuals and entire villages, the use of protection against the breath of those infected, and the cleaning of houses where people had been taken ill.[31] However, his practical advice constituted an appendix to a theological interpretation of the plague as a punishment for

---

[28] Magdalena Ślusarska, 'Ku odnowie życia religijno-moralnego wiernych i poprawie ich obyczajów: duchowieństwo diecezji wileńskiej w okresie pontyfikatu biskupa Ignacego Jakuba Massalskiego (1762–1794) a oświeceniowa reforma katolicka' ['Towards the Renewal of the Religious and Moral Life of the Faithful and the Improvement of their Mores: The Clergy of the Vilnius Diocese during the Pontificate of Bishop Ignacy Jakub Massalski (1762–1794) and Enlightened Catholic Reform'], *Senoji Lietuvos Literatūra* 33 (2010), 171–210, at 181. The programme of the Jubilee and other relevant documents were published as Tomasz Hussarzewski, ed., *Książka Jubileuszowa na Diecezyą Wileńską z Rozkazu Jasnie Oswieconego Pasterza Roku 1776* [*Jubilee Book for the Year 1776 for the Diocese of Vilnius, by Order of the Illustrious Shepherd*] (Wilno, 1776).

[29] For more about rural missions, see Louis Châtellier, *The Religion of the Poor: Rural Missions in Europe and the Formation of Modern Catholicism, c.1500–1800* (Cambridge, 1997).

[30] Vilnius, Vilniaus universiteto biblioteka, F57-B53-1414, 'Protocollum actorum curiae … Dni Ignatii Jakobi principis Massalski, episcopi Vilnensis … sub auditoriatu D. Antoni Kruszewski … 1785 … inchoatum' (Wilno, 1785), 161.

[31] Jan Kracik, *Pokonać czarną śmierć: staropolskie postawy wobec zarazy* [*Overcoming the Black Death: Polish Attitudes towards the Plague in the Early Modern Period*] (Kraków, 1991); Andrzej Karpiński, *W walce z niewidzialnym wrogiem: epidemie chorób zakaźnych w Rzeczypospolitej w XVI–XVIII wieku i ich następstwa demograficzne, społeczno-ekonomiczne i polityczne* [*The Fight against the Invisible Enemy: Epidemics of Infectious Diseases in the Polish-Lithuanian Commonwealth in the 16th–18th Centuries and their Demographic, Socio-Economic and Political Consequences*] (Warsaw, 2000); Katarzyna Pękacka-Falkowska, *Dżuma w Toruniu w trakcie III wojny północnej* [*Plague in Toruń during the Third Northern War*] (Lublin, 2019).

sin.[32] The primary way of ending the plague was to propitiate God. To this end, priests should focus on improving the morality of the faithful, organizing traditional rituals such as the Forty Hours' Devotion, processions to village crosses and a voluntary three-day fast. Priests were also strictly forbidden to leave their parishes and instructed to provide sacramental ministry to the sick: this seems to have been a response to the common practice of avoiding contact with sick parishioners.

In the city of Vilnius, the Jubilee programme was put into practice by Massalski's chosen preachers, among whom were Michał Karpowicz and Wilhelm Kaliński, who published books related to the programme, thus achieving national fame.[33] Kaliński's personal diary also provides evidence of how he internalized a naturalistic understanding of health. He recorded every illness or even discomfort he suffered; despite the high frequency of these entries, he always interpreted illness as an abnormality, and also as an excuse for not fulfilling his duties as professor at the University of Vilnius. He also speculated about the causes of his ailments, generally attributing them to bad diet.[34]

Parish clergy reacted in different ways. The records of parish visitations reveal that some priests in the diocese of Vilnius bought and read collections of Jubilee sermons. In his memoires, Jędrzej Kitowicz, parish priest in Rzeczyca, in the archdiocese of Gniezno, and author of the *Opis obyczajów za panowania Augusta III* (*Description of Customs during the Reign of August III*) ridiculed Poniatowski's pastoral letters.[35] Moreover, in a survey undertaken by the bishop's officials in the diocese of Płock, none of the parish clergy reported preaching about healthcare, and none had purchased a medical book or even sermons with physiocratic content.[36] The single exception seems to be a sermon entitled 'O obowiązkach lekarzów'

---

[32] Ignacy Jakub Massalski, *Incipit: Nie Przestaje Nas Dotykać Ręka Boska ...* [*Incipit: The Hand of God does not cease to touch us ...*] (Wilno, 1771).

[33] Rafał Szczurowski, 'Jubileuszowe kazania'.

[34] Wilhelm Kaliński, *Dziennik 1787–1788* [*Journal 1787–1788*], Archiwum Dziejów Oświaty 4 (Wrocław, 1968). For more about experiencing health, see Michael Stolberg, *Experiencing Illness and the Sick Body in Early Modern Europe* (London, 2011).

[35] Richard Butterwick, 'Catholicism and Enlightenment in Poland-Lithuania', in Lehner and Printy, eds, *Companion to the Catholic Enlightenment*, 297–358, at 317.

[36] Witecki, *Przekaz kulturowy*, 142–69, 249–50. See also idem, 'The Base of the Parochial Book Collections of the Catholic Church in the Polish-Lithuanian Commonwealth during the Stanislaus Era' [database], 20 September 2018, online

('Concerning the Duties of Doctors'), by Jan Kaczyński, of the parish of Gaworów.[37] This was printed in a collection of exemplary texts, by parish clergy as well as by the diocesan elite, chosen by the theologians appointed by Poniatowski, who shared the belief that disease might be an indicator of the divine will. Kaczyński condemned healers who had no professional training as immoral. He did not name them specifically, but he might have been referring to quack doctors. Against the backdrop of recent developments in medicine, he was particularly critical of those who, perhaps out of pride, did not listen to the advice given by younger but better educated colleagues. Noting the presence of a multitude of diseases, he demanded adequate specific treatments for each one, implicitly rejecting the effectiveness of alleged panaceas. At the same time, he did not interpret health simply as a natural phenomenon. Diseases were caused by air (the miasma theory), the weakness of the human body, a bad lifestyle, or, most importantly, the will of God. God, Kaczyński claimed, sends disease to punish, admonish and warn. Therefore the first prerequisite for recovery was for the sick person to turn to God, asking him for direct or indirect help, through prayer and treatment by physicians.

HEALTHCARE AND LIVED RELIGION

The Council of Trent had several times discussed responsibility for the care of the poor and sick, which it recognized as one of the most important aspects of the Church's mission.[38] In the Polish-Lithuanian Commonwealth, King Zygmunt August accepted its decrees as early as 1564, and clergy did the same in 1577 during

---

at: <http://ksiegozbioryparafialne.omnino.com.pl/?action=geoQuery>, accessed 28 January 2021.

[37] Jan Kaczyński, 'Kazanie o Obowiązkach Lekarzów Względem Chorych, Przez Xiędza Jana Kaczynskiego Altarzystę Goworowskiego' ['Sermon on the Duties of Physicians towards the Sick, by Father Jan Kaczynski, Altarist of Goworów'], in *Kazania Niektóre ICHMć Xsięży Diecezyi Płockiey. z podawanych co rocznie dwiema ratami w Maju i w Październiku do Kancelaryi Zadwornej Biskupiej 1782. Teraz z teyże Kancelaryi Wydane i do Druku Podane* [*Sermons of some of the Priests of the Diocese of Płock, from those submitted to the Bishop's Chancellery twice a Year in May and October*]. (Warsaw, 1785), 131–47.

[38] *The anons and Decrees of the Sacred and Oecumenical Council of Trent, celebrated under the Sovereign Pontiffs, Paul III, Julius III and Pius IV*, transl. James Waterworth (London, 1848), ch. 8, session 25, 262-4.

the synod of the province of Gniezno in Piotrków.[39] Later diocesan synods and bishops in pastoral letters required clergy to organize charitable provision in their parishes. These norms provided the basis for the development of parish hospitals during the seventeenth and eighteenth centuries, intended to provide food and shelter for the use of the infirm, aged and poor, but not to provide professional medical treatment.[40] During the late eighteenth century, between 40 and 45 per cent of Polish and Lithuanian parishes had such hospitals, but usually they were in a bad condition. Many were financed from separate benefices, including land and capital donated by rich benefactors. Benefice revenues were often irregular, or too low or devalued, or impossible to collect. Moreover, some hospitals had no property at all, leaving them completely dependent on the goodwill of parishioners.[41] Real change did not occur until Catholic enlighteners in the late eighteenth century proposed a new method of funding and tried to transform them into healing institutions.

The bishop of Livonia, Józef Kossakowski, in a novel published in 1786, *Xiądz Pleban* (*The Parish Priest*), depicted the ideal parish priest, who instructed his parishioners to employ a full-time physician, to build isolation homes for those suffering from infectious diseases, and to establish hospitals for invalids. The book's hero initiated the training of midwives, not only to assist women during labour but also to give smallpox inoculations. Kossakowski's ideal priest believed that prevention was the most reliable way of securing health. He encouraged parishioners to build new, dry and well-ventilated houses

---

[39] Stanisław Litak, *Od Reformacji Do Oświecenia: Kościół Katolicki w Polsce Nowożytnej* [*From the Reformation to the Enlightenment: The Catholic Church in Early Modern Poland*] (Lublin, 1994), 58–61.

[40] Bolesław Kumor, 'Opieka społeczna Kościoła w świetle ustawodawstwa synodalnego w Polsce (do 1795)' ['Church Social Care in the Light of Synodal Legislation in Poland to 1795'], in Urszula Augustyniak and Andrzej Karpiński, eds, *Charitas. Miłosierdzie i opieka społeczna w ideologii, normach postępowania i praktyce społeczności wyznaniowych w Rzeczypospolitej XVI–XVIII wieku* [*Charitas. Charity and Social Care in the Ideology, Standards of Conduct and Practice of Religious Communities in the Polish-Lithuanian Commonwealth during the 16th–18th Centuries*] (Warsaw, 1999), 11–18.

[41] Stanisław Litak, *Parafie w Rzeczypospolitej w XVI–XVIII wieku: struktura, funkcje społeczno-religijne i edukacyjne* [*Parishes in the Polish-Lithuanian Commonwealth during the 16th–18th Centuries: Structure, Social, Religious and Educational Functions*] (Lublin, 2004), 329–60; Marian Surdacki, *Opieka społeczna w Polsce do końca XVIII wieku* [*Social Welfare in Poland to the End of the 18th Century*] (Lublin, 2015).

to prevent them from catching coughs, to make and wear boots and hats to prevent fevers, and to eat ripe fruit to prevent scurvy. In the novel, these improvements were all financed by parishioners, landlords alongside serfs.[42] That ideal was based on the programme of reforms realized by the priest Paweł Brzostowski in his estate village of Merkinė or Merecz. However, in the diocese of Vilnius this was an exception, albeit a well-known one.[43]

Poniatowski tried to bring some of these ideas to life. In an ordinance of 1773, he required priests not only to offer their parishioners spiritual counsel and to perform the sacrament of the anointing of the sick, but also to provide any available physical treatment.[44] This general principle became enshrined in systemic reform in 1777. Poniatowski ordered that a Brotherhood of Mercy be organized in every parish, consisting of laymen under the supervision of priests, who were to maintain the parish hospitals by means of membership dues and alms. The Brothers were obliged to find the best medically educated person in the neighbourhood, and to use only his services. Sick people were to be transferred to the hospitals. If that was impossible, the Brothers were to help them at home. Severe cases were to be treated in one of three larger hospitals run by religious orders in bigger towns, and these became central diocesan institutions.[45] Moreover, Poniatowski subordinated all religious fraternities to the Brotherhood of Mercy. Members of these older fraternities were expected to continue their previous ritual duties, but the bishop declared that material help as an expression of charity was a more reliable way to achieve salvation than pure worship. He also banned the customary funeral receptions, instead encouraging people to donate food to the parish clergy, who were to distribute it to the poor and sick. Poniatowski introduced the same reforms in the diocese of Kraków in 1784 and the archdiocese of Gniezno in 1786.

---

[42] Józef Kossakowski, *Xiądz Pleban* [*The Parish Priest*] (Warsaw, 1786).

[43] Mieczysław Motyka, '"Ksiądz Pleban" Józefa Kossakowskiego wobec doświadczeń Rzeczypospolitej Pawłowskiej' ['"The Parish Priest" by Józef Kossakowski in the Light of the Experience of the Republic of Pawłów'], *Roczniki Naukowo-Dydaktyczne WSP w Rzeszowie* [*Scientific and Didactic Yearbooks of the WSP in Rzeszów*] 4 (1969), 7–17.

[44] Poniatowski, 'List Pasterski Do Oboyga Stanów', 453.

[45] Idem, 'Ustanowienie Bractwa Miłosierdzia po Parafiach w Diecezyi Płockiey' ['The Establishment of the Brotherhood of Mercy in the Parishes of the Diocese of Płock'], in *Rozrządzenia Y Pisma Pasterskie*, 2: 426–504.

Parish clergy from the diocese of Kraków reacted to this reform in various ways. A Brotherhood of Mercy was indeed created in most parishes, but parishioners often refused to contribute to its funding. In some parishes, contrary to the bishop's decree, the Brotherhood of Mercy was subordinated to already existing devotional sodalities.[46] The ban on funeral receptions had no effect, and the custom has remained very much alive to this day.

In rural areas, those who were ill often had to cope without the help of physicians, who were almost exclusively based in bigger cities or in courts. The best strategy, advocated by clergy of every rank as well as most doctors, was asking for God's help. There was, however, a multitude of ways to obtain divine assistance. Prayers in which the faithful relied humbly on God, as recommended in Kaczyński's sermon, were theologically the ideal. However, asking saints for help in exchange for prayers, pilgrimage or a votive offering was much more popular. In the case of the wealthy, this would often involve the endowment of an altar, chapel or church.[47] Evidence for the prevalence of such a transactional attitude to spiritual healing is provided by the growing popularity of miracle sites during the seventeenth and eighteenth centuries and a significant increase in the number of devotional books published by the guardians of such sanctuaries. Most were written by members of religious orders, but the existence of images depicting miracles and votive offerings in parish churches indicates that secular clergy also supported such practices. Clergy themselves sought the help of the saints. The parish priest of Słaboszów in the diocese of Kraków, author of an exceptionally detailed personal diary written between 1693 and 1701, went on pilgrimage to Jędrzejów each time he recovered from gout; there he expressed his gratitude to St Wincenty Kadłubek for his intercession.[48]

---

[46] Jan Kracik, 'Oświeceniowa dobroczynność w sarmackim świecie? Bractwo Miłosierdzia prymasa Poniatowskiego w diecezji krakowskiej' ['Enlightenment Charity in the Sarmatian World? The Brotherhood of Mercy of Primate Poniatowski in the Diocese of Krakow'], *Studia Historyczne* 32 (1989), 201–12, at 208–12.

[47] Tomasz Wiślicz, 'Ex-Votos in the World of Objects of Polish Peasants in the Early Modern Times', *Acta Poloniae Historica* 102 (2010), 133–46.

[48] Kraków, Biblioteka Jagiellońska, 2433, Kazimierz Jan Kanty Dziuliński, 'Diariusz potocznych rzeczy i wydatków na różne domowe potrzeby' ['Diary of Everyday Things and Expenses for various Household Needs'] (1693).

The French Catholic Church of that time, in the words of Robert Muchembled, 'redoubled its prudence concerning possible miracles tied to devotional sites and more generally to the very ancient cult of healing saints'.[49] By contrast, in the Polish-Lithuanian Commonwealth, the church disapproved only of the numerous unauthorized miracle sites, such as trees, fountains or other places where saints were said to have appeared and instructed sick people what to do in order to be healed. Usually, after detailed scrutiny, bishops or archdeacons forbade people from gathering at such sites under penalty of excommunication.[50] Until the late eighteenth century, bans were motivated by the fear of uncontrolled and potentially idolatrous popular practices, and by the assumption that unauthorized miracle sites were competing with official sanctuaries. Poniatowski warned against miracle sites that lacked official church endorsement, labelling them superstitious and unreliable.[51]

In many sanctuaries, priests encouraged the faithful to describe their experiences in a book of miracles.[52] Stories approved and written down by clergy (naturally) ended in miraculous recovery; other healing practices were presented as ineffective. Such accounts can, however, provide information about popular medicine. Usually, people would first try to heal themselves, or would turn to relatives, neighbours and local quacks, using not only herbal remedies but also magical rituals and spells. Such symbolic actions were considered practical and morally neutral by the laity but were not approved by the clergy.[53]

[49] Muchembled, *Popular Culture and Elite Culture in France*, 218.

[50] Some priests, however, had supported such local cults and had initiated their authorization: Tomasz Wiślicz, '"Miraculous Sites" in the Early Modern Polish-Lithuanian Commonwealth', in Thomas Wünsch, ed., *Religion und Magie in Ostmitteleuropa: Spielräume Theologischer Normierungsprozesse in Spätmittelalter und Früher Neuzeit* (Berlin, 2006), 287–99.

[51] Poniatowski, 'List Pasterski Do Oboyga Stanów', 476.

[52] Tomasz Wiślicz, 'Dziwne, przypadkowe i nadzwyczajne: zbiory miraculów z XVII i XVIII wieku jako źródło do badań kulturowych' ['Strange, Accidental and Extraordinary: 17th- and 18th-Century Miracula Collections as a Source for Cultural Research'], in Iwona Dacka-Górzyńska and Joanna Partyka, eds, *Staropolska Literatura Dewocyjna. Gatunki, Tematy, Funkcje* [*Old Polish Devotional Literature: Genres, Themes, Functions*] (Warsaw, 2015), 225–34.

[53] Małgorzata Delimata-Proch, 'Konflikt czy współzawodnictwo? O zakresie, metodach oraz skuteczności działania cyrulików i niebieskich uzdrowicieli w świetle polskiego piśmiennictwa mirakularnego (XVII–XVIII w.)' ['Conflict or Competition? On the Scope, Methods and Effectiveness of Barber Surgeons and Heavenly Healers in the

Jan Wujkowski, author of the catechism most frequently used by parish clergy at the end of the eighteenth century, *Chleb duchowny (Spiritual Bread)*,[54] interpreted magical healing as indirectly idolatrous. He believed that such practices were supernatural, and that since they did not draw power from divine or ecclesiastical blessing, they must result from an older pact with the devil. He did not see this as conscious idolatry, but rather as arising from ignorance, and advised clergy to warn about this rather than punish it. It was only direct dealing with the devil which Wujkowski interpreted as witchcraft and deserving of the death penalty.[55] Poniatowski and Massalski also criticized popular magical medicine, but for them rituals, spells and amulets were not idolatrous but simply expressions of ignorant superstitious belief.[56] Their view was similar to that of Ludovico Muratori in his *Della forza della fantasia umana (Of the Strength of the Human Imagination)*, translated into Polish by someone in Massalski's circle.[57] It is clear that no eighteenth-century Polish Catholic priest openly undermined belief in witchcraft, defined as dealing with the devil. Enlighteners did, however, refute the idea that non-maleficent symbolic folk practices such as healing constituted witchcraft.[58]

Fasting was another practice which reformers tried to modify for medical reasons. In the Polish-Lithuanian Commonwealth, it was treated as a national custom, distinguishing Poles from other

---

Light of Polish Miracular Literature (17th–18th Centuries)'], *Medycyna Nowożytna* 24 (2018), 139–52; Kathryn Edwards, ed., *Everyday Magic in Early Modern Europe* (Farnham, 2015).

[54] Witecki, *Przekaz kulturowy*, 330.

[55] Jan Stanisław Kostka Wujkowski, *Chleb duchowny, wszytkim chrześćianom na pośiłek w drodze, do nieba idącym wystawiony albo raczey Katechizm na świat polski wychodzący: krotkie nauki chrześćiańskiey z rożnemi w sobie zebranie maiący ...* [*Spiritual Bread for all Christians, for a Meal on the Way to Heaven, or, the Catechism for the Polish World: A Collection of short Christian Teachings ...*] (Kalisz, 1733), 298–305.

[56] Witecki, *Przekaz kulturowy*, 303–9.

[57] Lehner, *Catholic Enlightenment*, 144–5; Butterwick, 'Catholicism and Enlightenment', 318.

[58] Tomasz Wiślicz, 'Czary przed sądami wiejskimi w Polsce w XVI–XVII w.' ['Witchcraft before Rural Courts in Poland in the 16th and 17th Centuries'], *Czasopismo Prawno-Historyczne* [*Journal of Legal History*] 49 (1997), 47–63; Jacek Wijaczka, 'Procesy o czary w Polsce w dobie Oświecenia: zarys problematyki' ['Witchcraft Trials in Poland during the Enlightenment: An Overview of the Issues'], *Klio* 7 (2005), 17–62; Małgorzata Pilaszek, *Procesy o czary w Polsce w wiekach XV–XVIII* [*Witchcraft Trials in Poland in the 15th–18th Centuries*] (Kraków, 2008).

Stanisław Witecki

Christians, who were accused of taking this obligation too lightly. It was a boastful stereotype that was propagated by seventeenth- and eighteenth-century preachers, but many Polish and Lithuanian Catholics, regardless of their social origins, refrained from eating meat and dairy, not only when it was required by the church, but also voluntarily on other days. Others, however, observed only formal restrictions, at the same time overeating on fish and confectionery.[59] Like other Christian enlighteners,[60] Poniatowski found both the overly strict and the merely formal observance of fasts to be unhealthy and impious. In the diocese of Płock, he lifted the prohibition on dairy consumption on 12 November 1777, arguing that a person's piety should be judged according to their willingness to limit the quantity of food they consumed, and required people to reflect on what their conscience was saying rather than to refrain from eating only one category of food. He also explained that in the Commonwealth of Poland-Lithuania, where olives were an expensive imported product, butter and cream were the most important source of fat, and necessary for health, especially that of hard-working peasants.[61] Poniatowski based his decision on the permission issued by Clement XIV in 1773. He claimed that consumption of dairy had been allowed in other dioceses, but no documentary confirmation is known to exist. Massalski did not

[59] Jan Kracik, 'Post po staropolsku' ['Fasting in the old Polish Style'], in idem, *Paradoksy z Dziejów Kościoła* [*Paradoxes in the History of the Church*] (Kraków, 2012), 202–11; Jędrzej Kitowicz, *Opis Obyczajów Za Panowania Augusta III* [*A Description of Customs during the Reign of August III*] (Warsaw, 2003), online at: <https://literat.ug.edu.pl/kitowic/k0007.htm>, accessed 28 January 2021. The observance of fasts had much deeper reasons than those portrayed by opponents. Dietary restrictions not only have pious purposes, but also play a role in community building and identity construction. They appear to constitute one of the universal features of human culture. Polish and Lithuanian discussions of the loosening of fasts therefore require more attention and the adoption of a holistic and comparative anthropological perspective: see David Freidenreich, *Foreigners and their Food: Constructing Otherness in Jewish, Christian and Islamic Law* (Berkeley and Los Angeles, CA, 2011).
[60] Sydney Watts, 'Enlightened Fasting: Religious Conviction, Scientific Inquiry, and Medical Knowledge in Early Modern France', in Ken Albala and Eden Trudy, eds, *Food and Faith in Christian Culture* (New York, 2011), 105–24; Julia Herzberg, 'Faith on the Menu: Conflicts around Fasting in Muscovy', *Kritika: Explorations in Russian and Eurasian History* 21 (2020), 371–400.
[61] Michał Poniatowski, 'Pozwolenie dla Diecezyi Płockiey z mocy Stolicy Apostolskiej zażywania w dni postne potraw maślnych' ['Permission for the Diocese of Płock, issued by the Holy See, for eating Dairy Products on Fast Days'], in *Rozrządzenia Y Pisma Pasterskie*, 2: 420–5.

lift the prohibition for the diocese of Vilnius as a whole, but he had been giving individual dispensations from dairy restrictions for nobility, monks and nuns throughout his episcopate.[62] In 1760 Primate Władysław Łubieński, on behalf of the bishops' conference, had asked Clement XIII to lift the prohibition on dairy consumption throughout the Polish-Lithuanian Commonwealth, but was not successful.[63] One reason might have been a lack of unanimity among bishops. Wacław Sierakowski (1699×1700–80; bishop of Kamieniec 1739–40, bishop of Przemyśl 1742–60, archbishop of Lviv or Lwów [now in Ukraine] 1760–80), opposed liberalization in his book *Prawo Święte Kościoła Chrystusowego o Postach* (1759).[64] Wojciech Skarszewski, in pastoral letters as Roman Catholic bishop of Chełm and Lublin, recommended fasting as a mean of securing God's protection for the commonwealth.[65] At the same time, his Greek Catholic counterpart, Porfiriusz Skarbek-Ważyński (1730×32–1804; bishop of Chełm 1790–1804), took diocesan synods as an opportunity to defend strict fasting.[66]

Parish clergy did not have a uniform attitude to fasting. In his best-selling catechism, Jan Wujkowski presented a nuanced attitude. Limitations on the quantity of food consumed did not apply to pregnant women, wet nurses or hard-working people. Sick people were even allowed to eat dairy.[67] Parish priests who used this catechism would have been lifting the prohibition of dairy consumption, an

[62] Michał Kurdybacha, 'Wstęp' ['Introduction'], in Kaliński, *Dziennik 1787–1788*, 11. For example, on 15 February 1785 he allowed dairy products to be eaten during a fast: Vilnius, Vilniaus universiteto biblioteka, F57-B53-1414, Protocollum, 34.
[63] Stanisław Librowski, 'Konferencje Biskupów XVIII Wieku Jako Instytucja Zastępująca Synody Prowincjonalne. Cz. 1: Obrady w Sprawach Kościoła i Szczątkowa Po Nich Dokumentacja' ['Eighteenth-Century Episcopal Conferences as the Substitute for Provincial Synods. Part 1: Debates on Church Affairs and Residual Documentation'], *Archiwa, Biblioteki, i Muzea Kościelne* [*Archives, Libraries and Church Museums*] 47 (1983), 239–311, at 279.
[64] Wacław Hieronim Sierakowski, *Prawo Święte Kościoła Chrystusowego o Postach* [*The Holy Law of the Church of Christ regarding Fasting*] (Lwów, 1761); Andrzej Kraśnicki, 'Posty w Dawnej Polsce' ['Fasts in Old Poland'], *Collectanea Theologica* 12 (1931), 190–235, at 195–6. I would like to thank Kilian Harrer for informing me of the request of Łubieński and the work by Sierakowski.
[65] See, for example, Lublin, Archiwum Archidiecezjalne Lubelskie, Rep 60A, 170, Protocollum actorum curiae episcopalis (1791–1802), 318–21.
[66] Edward Likowski, ed., *Synody dyecezyi chełmskiej ob. wsch* [*Synods of the Chełm Diocese of the Eastern Rite*] (Poznań, 1902).
[67] Wujkowski, *Chleb duchowny*, 399–407.

exception which had hitherto been reserved for the sick and which Poniatowski wanted to make into a general rule that would prevent weakness and illness among serfs. However, there is evidence that such liberalization of fasting was not successful: diarists and folklorists during the nineteenth century noted that dairy prohibition was strictly observed, and the custom was depicted again in the Nobel Prize-winning novel *Chłopi* (Peasants), by Władysław Reymont (1904–9).[68]

In the eighteenth century, new ideas about cleanliness and its relation to sickness also emerged.[69] Human corpses were considered particularly unclean and dangerous to health. Catholic enlighteners therefore began to oppose the custom of locating cemeteries around and under churches. In the Polish-Lithuanian Commonwealth, this debate can be traced back at least to 1770, when the Grand Marshal of the Crown, Stanisław Lubomirski, proposed that churchyards should no longer be used as burial grounds. Another supporter of this policy was Massalski, who proposed similar measures during the 1771 plague epidemic. During the Jubilee of 1776, he announced that both the commonwealth and the church were planning to put an end to 'improper' cemeteries in churchyards, and obliged priests in his diocese to support this.[70] This order was strikingly opposed to lived religious practice. Sanctity of space was believed to be dependent on proximity to holiness, and the holiest objects in the parish were the relics kept in the churches. People wanted to be buried as close to the centre of the sacred space as possible, but this depended on a person's social position. The richest were buried under the church floor, the less well off in the churchyard close to the church walls, and the poorest next to the churchyard fence. Nobody wanted to be buried outside the churchyard, let alone outside the village. Massalski was aware of this and did not seek to render the division between sacred and profane obsolete; indeed, he emphasized that the new graveyards would be blessed. In 1792, these measures were incorporated into law by the newly established Komisja Policji Obojga Narodów (Police Commission for both Nations), but they did not become a reality until shortly before the collapse of the Polish-Lithuanian Commonwealth in 1795.[71]

[68] Kracik, 'Post po staropolsku', 178–9.
[69] Georges Vigarello, *Concepts of Cleanliness: Changing Attitudes in France since the Middle Ages* (Cambridge, 2008).
[70] *Ksiąszka Jubileuszowa na Diecezyą Wileńską*, unpaginated.
[71] Penny Roberts, 'Contesting Sacred Space: Burial Disputes in Sixteenth-Century France', in Bruce Gordon and Peter Marshall, eds, *The Place of the Dead: Death and*

CONCLUSION

Public health was an important concern of Polish and Lithuanian Catholic enlighteners. Numerous theoretical works by Catholic priests argued that medical education and the organized provision of healthcare were moral obligations as well as necessary steps for improving agricultural productivity. Their conviction was derived from humanitarian as well as physiocratic principles and was facilitated by an optimistic belief in benefits of medicine. They were aware of recent advances in science and believed that diseases could be prevented and even eradicated with the help of professional physicians. Without that confidence, reform would not be worth the effort.

Belief in medicine did not mean that Catholic enlighteners rejected the possibility of divine intervention in health matters or denied that diseases might be indicators of the divine will. It was God who established the laws of nature, and it was God who acted through these laws and who could suspend their operation. Prayer remained the best strategy for securing health, and it was advocated by clergy of every rank, including the reforming bishops Michał Poniatowski and Ignacy Massalski. Belief in the healing power of the saints' intercessions remained intact; however, enlighteners were sceptical of the authenticity of new miracle sites, particularly those reported by local people.

Massalski and Poniatowski, as well as the Komisja Edukacji Narodowej, tried to organize healthcare and medical education by enforcing new rules for parish clergy. Priests were made responsible for organizing parish schools with medical knowledge as part of the curriculum, teaching about health in sermons, supporting sick parishioners and changing the status of parish hospitals from charitable to healthcare institutions. In addition, enlighteners attempted to modify elements of lived religion which were detrimental to health. Some

---

Remembrance in Late Medieval and Early Modern Europe (Cambridge, 2000), 131–48; Will J. Coster and Andrew Spicer, eds, *Sacred Space in Early Modern Europe* (Cambridge, 2005); Mateusz Wyżga, 'Funkcjonowanie wiejskich cmentarzy parafii katolickich w dobie przedrozbiorowej na przykładzie dekanatów Nowa Góra, Skała i Proszowice z okolic Krakowa' ['The Functioning of Rural Cemeteries of Catholic Parishes in the Pre-Partition Era as exemplified by the Deaneries of Nowa Góra, Skała and Proszowice in the Vicinity of Krakow'], *Kwartalnik Historii Kultury Materialnej* [*Quarterly Journal of the History of Material Culture*] 62 (2014), 441–62.

customs, such as rigorous fasting and churchyard burial, came to be considered harmful. Others, such as healing with magic or spending money on a funeral wake rather than on helping the poor and sick, were condemned as ineffective, superstitious or impractical.

The parish clergy did not form a homogeneous group, and it is difficult to generalize about their attitude to these reforms. Some preached with the help of collections of physiocratic sermons as recommended by Massalski, and others organized the Brotherhood of Mercy as intended by Poniatowski. Many renewed or established parish schools according to the principles of the Komisja Edukacji Narodowej. However, numerous priests did not do any of these things. Some simply rejected additional, often burdensome, tasks, while others encountered obstacles, such as lack of funding or resistance from nobles or peasants. There is little direct evidence of individual priests rejecting the idea that charity is more important than devotion. However, the fact that many reforms failed or were only realized much later suggests that parish clergy either did not want to interfere with lived religion or generally failed in doing so.

Moral Sick Notes: Medical Exemptions to Religious Fasting in the Eighteenth-Century Spanish World

George A. Klaeren*

University of St Andrews

Eighteenth-century moral theologians in Spain expressed concern that many Catholics were obtaining permission to avoid fasting and abstinence from meat by claiming that they were ill and required medical dispensations. This article examines the theological and medical debate which occurred over a series of treatises and essays in which physicians and moral theologians sought to come to a common understanding of when a Spaniard was infirm enough to be medically excused from fasting and, perhaps more importantly, who had the authority to make this decision. Throughout the eighteenth century in Spain, this responsibility continued to be shared by priests and physicians. The debate highlights the contest for medical authority, mitigated by doubt. It also suggests that any understanding of early modern medical pluralism must include members of the theological community as well as health professionals.

INTRODUCTION: AVOIDING FASTING IN EIGHTEENTH-CENTURY SPAIN

It was common knowledge in eighteenth-century Spain that some Catholics would fake an illness in order to avoid the religious obligation of fasting and abstaining from meat, two practices which the church commanded them to observe on specified days throughout the year. The Catholic Church in Spain had traditionally made allowances for those who, for medical reasons, needed to be excused from fasting; but by the eighteenth century, moral theologians had begun to complain that too many individuals were wrongly claiming medical exemption. Indeed, by 1834, this fact had become the source of a familiar phrase that John Collins included in his book of Spanish proverbs for English speakers:

> *Achaques al Viernes para no ayunar.* – 'Ailments on Friday in order to avoid fasting.' – Applied to Catholics who pretend indisposition, to be

* St Mary's College, School of Divinity, University of St Andrews, South St, St Andrews, KY16 9JU. E-mail: gak6@st-andrews.ac.uk.

Studies in Church History 58 (2022), 173–195   © The Author(s), 2022. Published by
Cambridge University Press on behalf of Ecclesiastical History Society
doi: 10.1017/stc.2022.9

dispensed from abstaining from eating flesh on fasting days; – also to those who find excuses and raise difficulties against doing any thing not agreeable to them.'[1]

Far more than a proverb, medical excuses from fasting were a serious concern for early modern Spaniards. When was it morally permissible to break religious dietary laws on medical grounds? Perhaps more importantly, who had the authority to determine these boundaries and grant permission to be excused from fasting? These questions, which had been raised for centuries, became particularly important for theologians and physicians in the mid-eighteenth century. From 1727 to 1786, at least fourteen different essays or treatises were written defining the parameters of fasting within the Spanish world alone. Many of these were written specifically in response to instructions and changes to the religious practices concerning dietary restrictions in Lent introduced by Clement XII (1730–40), Benedict XIV (1740–58) and Clement XIII (1758–69), changes which were not unanimously enforced or welcomed in Spain.

This article examines the debate over medical exemptions and considerations relating to religious fasting and abstinence from meat in eighteenth-century Spain, focusing on discussions which articulated who had the expertise and authority to verify illnesses and grant dispensations on medical grounds. After summarizing the 'rules' of fasting in eighteenth-century Spanish Catholicism and the ways in which a person could receive a dispensation, this article highlights the arguments between theologians, physicians and other intellectuals who sought to determine the cause underlying the abuse of medical exemptions. Two fundamental questions are emphasized: what constituted a sickness worthy of a dispensation, and who had the authority and knowledge to discern such cases? To conclude, this article uses this discussion to demonstrate how the medical and theological communities engaged one another in the early modern Hispanic world, contextualizing these discussions in the broader field of 'medico-moralism' and arguing for a more inclusive understanding of medical pluralism which incorporates the impact of

---

[1] John Collins, *A Dictionary of Spanish Proverbs, compiled from the best Authorities in the Spanish Language* (London, 1834), 6. The proverb is sometimes presented as 'Achaques al jueves, para no ayunar el viernes' ('Ailments on Thursday in order not to fast on Friday'): Regino Etxabe, *Diccionario de refranes comentado* (Madrid, 2012), 23. All translations are my own, unless otherwise noted.

theology and religion in determining the parameters of sickness and health in early modernity. This article helps us to understand better how the church had an active role in defining what constituted 'sickness'. It helps to elucidate how the church negotiated the meaning and evaluation of both 'sickness' and 'health'. These were shared concepts that were used by the theological and medical communities of early modern Spain. Discussions of moral theology involving fasting necessarily raised questions about health and illness. What is seen in the debate over medical exemptions to fasting is that these ideas, far from being static, were malleable terms which required theologians constantly to engage with, and incorporate knowledge from, medical experts and authorities. Clergy were not only part of discussions about what was considered true 'sickness', but were also questioning who had the privilege of determining these concepts in the first place.

THE RULES: THE TRADITION OF FASTING AND ABSTINENCE FROM MEAT IN EARLY MODERN SPAIN

Fasting and abstinence from meat have a long history of observance both in Christianity and in other religions.[2] Christian fasting has been linked with several biblical precedents and was advocated by many Church Fathers, including Augustine, Basil, Gregory the Great and Athanasius.[3] In the medieval and early modern periods, its Catholic proponents included Thomas Aquinas and Fray Luis de Granada.[4] Religious scholars in the early modern period knew and referenced this tradition to underscore the importance of fasting and

---

[2] Michael Dietler, 'Feasting and Fasting', in Timothy Insoll, ed., *The Oxford Handbook of the Archaeology of Ritual & Religion* (Oxford, 2011), 179–94, at 187–8; Aaron S. Gross, Jody Myers and Jordan D. Rosenblum, eds, *Feasting and Fasting: The History and Ethics of Jewish Food* (New York, 2020).

[3] Among many other verses, see Ps. 35: 13; Joel 2: 12; Matt. 4: 2, 6: 16–18; Acts 13: 2, 14: 23: S. H. Mathews, *Christian Fasting: Biblical and Evangelical Perspectives* (Lanham, MD, 2015); José Francisco de Malpica Diosdado, *Alexipharmaco de la salud, antidoto de la enfermedad, favorable dietetico instrumento de la vida. Dissertacion medico-moral, que trata del ayuno, y accidentes, que escusan de él, y que hacen licito el uso de las carnes á los enfermos, y valetudinarios. En un copioso cathalogo, sacado de tres autores contra el sentir de los hereges, que lo improbaban, y tambien para desterrar los vanos miedos de la opinion vulgar* (Mexico, 1751), 39.

[4] Malpica Diosdado, *Alexipharmaco*, 39. See, for example, Thomas Aquinas, *Summa Theologica*, II–II. q. 147.

George A. Klaeren

abstinence.[5] One author wrote that while some early Church Fathers believed it possibly a divine law, it was 'at the very least … a precept of Apostolic canon law and the transgression of it is a moral sin'.[6] Similarly, Benedict XIV described Lenten fasting as:

> among the principal cornerstones of right doctrine. [It was] once sketched for the first time by the Law and the Prophets, somewhat consecrated through the example of Our Lord Jesus Christ, handed down from the Apostles, prescribed everywhere by Sacred canons, and [it is] accepted and observed by all of the Church since its inception.[7]

Rules governing fasting existed in Spain as early as the Council of Toledo in 655; by the eighteenth century, however, the manner and customs of abstinence and fasting had changed significantly from the practice described by the Church Fathers or even by medieval

[5] 'Desde el principio del mundo se halla en las Escrituras indicado; se figuró en la Ley, y los Profetas; y esta santificado con el exemplo de la Magestad Divina. Solemnizaron su observancia los Apostoles; està notificada por los Sagrados Canones. Los Santos Padres, y Doctores lo observaron, y la Universal Iglesia lo tiene recevido' ('From the beginning of the world it has been found indicated in the Scriptures, figured in the Law and the Prophets, and sanctified by the example of the Divine Majesty. The Apostles solemnified its observance; it is notified in the Sacred Canons. The Holy Fathers and Doctors observed it, and the Universal Church has received it'): Joseph [José] Vicente Diaz-Bravo, *El ayuno reformado segun practica de la primitiva iglesia, por los cinco breves de Nuestro Santissimo Padre Benedicto XIV. Obra historica, canonico-medica, necessaria à los señores obispos, curas, confessores, medicos, sanos, y enfermos* (Pamplona, 1754), 1–2. Quotations are replicated in their original use of accents, although the use of alternative letters and some spelling (such as the long 's', z/c and y/i) have been modernized.
[6] 'Pero á lo menos es precepto de derecho canonico Apostolico. Y la transgression de él, es pecado mortal, como que es en materia grave': Malpica Diosdado, *Alexipharmaco*, 39.
[7] Translated from the Italian: 'fra i principali capisaldi della retta dottrina, il digiuno quaresimale. Abbozzato un tempo per la prima volta nella Legge e nei Profeti, quasi consacrato dall'esempio di Nostro Signore Gesù Cristo, tramandato dagli Apostoli, prescritto ovunque dai Sacri canoni, è accolto ed osservato da tutta la Chiesa fin dai suoi primordi': Benedict XIV, *Non ambigimus*, Papal Breve, 30 May 1741, Libreria Editrice Vaticana, online at: <https://www.vatican.va/content/benedictus-xiv/it/documents/breve–i-non-ambigimus–i–30-maggio-1741–il-pontefice-ricorda.html>, last accessed 11 January 2022. The Latin text of this document reads: 'inter præcipua Orthodoxæ disciplinæ capita perpetuò adnumeratum retineri Quadragesimale Jejunium; quod olim in Lege, & Prophetis primitùs adumbratum, ipsius Domini nostri Jesu-Christi exemplo veluti consecratum, ab Apostolis traditum, à Sacris Canonibus ubique præscriptum, & ab universali Ecclesia ab ipso sui primordio retentum, & observatum est': Manuel Ezquerro Perez, *Explicacion de las bulas novissimas de Nuestro S[anctissimo] Padre Benedicto XIV. Sobre el ayuno, complice, y sigilistas; y suplemento al elenco moral de Castropalao, en las materias del ayuno, y penitencia* (Madrid, 1758), 196–7.

theologians such as Thomas Aquinas.[8] The basic rules articulated by Spanish catechisms at the end of the seventeenth and beginning of the eighteenth centuries can be summarized in two parts:

1. Adult Catholics, by command of the church, were expected on given days throughout the liturgical year to practice abstinence from meat. Furthermore, on many of these days of abstinence, Catholics between the ages of 21 and 60 were additionally required to fast.

2. When fasting, one could drink non-nutritive beverages, but could consume only one meal at midday (around eleven o'clock) and a modest, light meal (*refección, collation*) later in the evening.[9]

Although these rules remained roughly consistent in Spain throughout the eighteenth century, exceptions abounded. For example, in Spain, abstinence from meat during Lent also extended to abstaining from eggs and dairy products.[10] However, most Spaniards purchased a special bull known as *la bula de la Santa Cruzada* ('the bull of the Holy Crusade').[11] These licences were a privilege gifted to Spain to sell in order to raise funds for 'crusades'

---

[8] Fasting practices developed regionally, determined by local councils or synods, and were often implemented on a diocesan level. Traditions changed over time; for example, Manuel Villodas, who held a chair of theology at the University of Valladolid in the eighteenth century, wrote that initially the Lenten fast did not start until the Monday following the first Sunday in Lent in order 'that the tithe of the year is composed of thirty-six days, and not forty' ('que el diezmo del año se compone de treinta y seis dias, y no de quarenta'): Manuel Villodas, *Analisis de las antiguedades eclesiásticas de España para instruccion de los jovenes. Comprehende los sucesos mas notables de los once siglos primeros*, 2nd edn, 2 vols (Valladolid, 1802), 2: 400. Even as far back as the Council of Toledo, however, provisions for excuses from the fast had been made for 'those with inevitable necessity, illness, or impossibility of age' ('los que sin inevitable necesidad, enfermedad ó imposibilidad de la edad'): ibid. 399. Such individuals were instructed by Canon IX of the council to request a dispensation from their bishop: ibid. 399–400.

[9] Pedro de Lepe, *Catecismo Catholico, en el qual se contiene la explicacion de los principales mysterios de Nuestra Santa Fe Catholica, y las demas cosas, que debe el Christiano saber para su salvacion* (Madrid, 1699), 280–1; Rafael Lasala y Locela, *Catecismo mayor de la doctrina Christiana, en que se comprehende el menor, y se da una instruccion mas cumplida de las verdades de Nuestra Santa Religion Catolica* (Cervera, 1791), 310–11.

[10] Lepe, *Catecismo*, 281. Sources various described *cosas de leche*, or more often *lacticinios*.

[11] Jose Fernandez Llamazares, *Historia de la bula de la Santa Cruzada* (Madrid, 1859); Patrick J. O'Banion, 'For the Defense of the Faith? The Crusading Indulgence in Early Modern Spain', *ARG* 101 (2013), 164–85; María Pilar Martínez López-Cano, *La iglesia, los fieles y la corona: La bula de la Santa Cruzada en Nueva España, 1574–1660* (Mexico City, 2017).

(liberally interpreted) and granted the purchaser certain privileges, including in some cases the permission to eat dairy products, eggs or even meat in certain circumstances during days of fasting and abstinence.[12] Generally, however, Spaniards were meant to abstain from meat on Fridays and Saturdays throughout the year and supposed to fast for a handful of solemnities and observances throughout the year, as well as before partaking of the eucharist.[13] By some estimates, days which involved some degree of abstinence or fasting could constitute around one-third of the year for an observant Catholic in the early modern period.[14] Most debates on the subject, however, focused on the Lenten practices of abstinence and fasting which occurred in the forty-day liturgical season between Ash Wednesday and Easter Sunday. Other observances ranged in duration from a half-day to a few days in a row, but none had as much potential for impacting human health as the forty near-consecutive days of Lenten abstinence and fasting.[15]

Fasting could serve several purposes.[16] It could be a preparatory practice (as before the eucharist or in Advent), a way of 'elevating minds' and intensifying devotion, committing oneself to prayer, an expression of grief or mourning or a practice of mortification and self-sacrifice.[17] Fasting could also be prescribed as a penitential act

[12] On the popularity of these bulls, see: O'Banion, 'For the Defense', 168; 'An Officer of the United States Navy' [William Samuel Waithman Ruschenberger], *Three Years in the Pacific; Containing Notices of Brazil, Chile, Bolivia, Peru* (London, 1835), 1: 209–10. Ruschenberger describes how in post-independence Peru it was still routine for everyone to purchase this licence; furthermore, because these *bulas* lapsed after two years, they were a 'lucrative branch of the church revenue': ibid.

[13] For example, fasting was required on the four Fridays of Advent, at the Christmas vigil (on Christmas Eve), on the Ember days and, most importantly, during Lent. Moreover, Catholics were required to observe a pre-eucharistic fast in which they did not eat or drink anything between midnight and the reception of the host the next morning.

[14] Regina Grafe, *Popish Habits vs. Nutritional Need: Fasting and Fish Consumption in Iberia in the Early Modern Period*, University of Oxford Discussion Papers in Economic and Social History 55 (Oxford, 2004), 17. This estimate may be conservative: in the first half of the eighteenth century, the average Spaniard without a bull may have been expected to fast on at least 57 days, and to abstain from meat on approximately 92 additional days, totalling about 41 per cent of the year.

[15] 'Near-consecutive' because one did not fast on Lenten Sundays (other than the eucharistic fast).

[16] For an overview, see Bridget Ann Henisch, *Fast and Feast: Food in Medieval Society* (University Park, PA, 1976); Caroline Walker Bynum, *Holy Feast and Holy Fast: The Religious Significance of Food to Medieval Women* (Berkeley, CA, 1987), 34.

[17] '[M]entem elevas', found in the preface for Lent. Campbell supports Hillaire Kallendorf's notion that fasting was a 'preferred method for early modern Spaniards to

in the belief that 'we mortify [the body] with fasting, which subdues the carnal and luxurious appetites ... we deprive ourselves of the delights of the body'.[18] Fasting was part of the fabric of early modern Spanish society. It was a unitive experience that everyone would have known and experienced, and its impact can be traced socially, culturally and even economically. Scholars have demonstrated, for example, the effect which fasting had in promoting the sale of fish and offal, both of which were permitted on days of abstinence.[19]

It is clear, however, that fasting was also a practice that needed explanation and enforcement. One way to problematize fasting in the early modern period, for example, was to question the definition of 'food' or 'meat'. Were milk, wine or hot chocolate nutritive beverages which could be considered to break fasting? Was smoking tobacco permissible? Did turtles count as 'meat' (which was not allowed) or as 'fish' (which was)?[20] These questions were certainly debated, but an equally important and problematic issue concerned the legitimate circumstances in which a person could be excused from fasting, either partially or totally.[21]

---

display their religiosity': Jodi Campbell, *At the First Table: Food and Social Identity in Early Modern Spain* (Lincoln, NE, 2017), 137; see also Anon., *The Golden Manual: Being a Guide to Catholic Devotion, Public and Private, compiled from Approved Sources* (London, 1850), 227.

[18] '[L]a mortificamos con el ayuno, que sujeta los apetitos carnales y de luxuria: ... nos privamos de los deleites del cuerpo': Lasala y Locela, *Catecismo mayor*, 405.

[19] Grafe, *Popish Habits*; Campbell, *First Table*, 37, who describes 'an uncertain zone between foods that were clearly prohibited on fast days and those that were allowed'. Among these was offal, discussed in Carolyn A. Nadeau, *Food Matters: Alonso Quijano's Diet and the Discourse of Food in Early Modern Spain* (Toronto, ON, 2016), 106–7.

[20] Beth Marie Forrest and April L. Najjaj, 'Is Sipping Sin Breaking Fast? The Catholic Chocolate Controversy and the Changing World of Early Modern Spain', *Food and Foodways: Explorations in the History and Culture of Human Nourishment* 15 (2007), 31–52. See also selected primary sources, including some referenced by Forrest and Najjaj: Antonio de Leon Pinelo, *Question Moral si el chocolate quebranta el ayuno eclesiastico. Tratase de otras bebidas i confecciones que se usan en varias provincias* (Madrid, 1636); Daniel Concina, *Theologia Christiana Dogmatico-Moral*, transl. Joseph Sanchez de la Parra, 2 vols (Madrid, 1770), 1: 326; Christoval [Christobal] Nieto de Piña, *Discurso Medico Moral. Los que usan leche medicinal deben considerarse entre los dispensados al ayuno eclesiastico* (Seville, 1779).

[21] Forrest and Najjaj, 'Sipping Sin?'; David Gentilcore, *Food and Health in Early Modern Europe: Diet, Medicine and Society, 1450–1800* (London, 2016); Campbell, *First Table*; Nadeau, *Food Matters*.

According to canon law and most Spanish theologians, there were three exceptions, besides age, which excused someone from fasting, or in some cases from abstaining from meat: piety, labour and infirmity.[22] Piety allowed those who could not fast and undertake a religious office to be excused, for example, those preaching or confessors. Labour exempted those whose employment required significant physical exertion, such as farm labourers, blacksmiths and soldiers. Both categories were subject to nuanced disputes, but the third category created serious debates.[23] 'By illness', one theologian explained, 'are excused from fasting those that suffer serious pain that is evidently incompatible with fasting'.[24] Another stated that 'by illness, here it is not only understood as those who have a serious illness, but also those with ailments that make the precept notably most difficult'.[25]

These ambiguities in definition created a serious issue for theologians and physicians in the eighteenth century. And indeed, fasting was a serious topic, for, as many theologians pointed out, it was a mortal sin to break a fast without just cause. Moreover, the visibility of breaking a fast made it a useful marker of heterodox (and Protestant) behaviour; Catholics could use fasting as a litmus test in their efforts to counter such non-Catholics.[26] For example, the Carmelite theologian José Vicente Díaz-Bravo (1708–72) described fasting as 'the character which distinguishes the Catholic from the enemies of the Cross of Jesus Christ'.[27] Similarly, the Capuchin moral theologian Jaime de Corella (1657–99) wrote that only

---

[22] Francisco Larraga, *Prontuario de la Teología Moral*, ed. Francisco Santos y Grosin (Madrid, 1801), 407.

[23] Ibid. 407–8.

[24] 'Por razon de enfermedad se excusan del ayuno los que padecen grave dolencia, que evidentemente es incompatible con el ayuno': Josef Faustino Cliquet, *La flor del moral: esto es lo mas florido, y selecto qué se halla en el jardin ameno, y dilatado campo de la Theologia Moral*, 3 vols (Madrid, 1791), 3: 114.

[25] 'Y por enfermedad, aqui no solamente se entienden los que estàn con enfermedad grave, sino con achaques, que hacen notablemente dificultoso el precepto': Lepe, *Catecismo*, 286.

[26] This was also true outside Spain: Jane K. Wickersham, *Rituals of Prosecution: The Roman Inquisition and the Prosecution of Philo-Protestants in Sixteenth-Century Italy* (Toronto, ON, 2012), 112.

[27] 'A Observancia sacrosanta del Ayuno, es el caracter, que distingue al Catholico, de los enemigos de la Cruz Jesu-Christo': Diaz-Bravo, *El ayuno reformado*, 1; Balbino Velasco Bayón, 'José Vicente Díaz-Bravo', in Real Academia de la Historia, *Diccionario Biográfico Electrónico*, n.d., online at: <http://dbe.rah.es/biografias/22420/jose-vicente-diaz-bravo>, accessed 30 January 2021.

'nonbelievers, insane people, and children' ate meat on fasting days, and even in the eighteenth century the Inquisition continued to hear accusations, albeit very rarely, regarding those breaking fasts in conjunction with committing other spiritual abuses.[28] Scorning the practice of fasting was not meant to be a casual endeavour.

THE PROBLEM: THE DECLINE OF FASTING IN EIGHTEENTH-CENTURY SPAIN

Spanish Catholics were, therefore, supposed to be regularly observing days of fasting and abstinence from meat, with occasional exceptions in Spanish society being granted for illness and other reasons. In reality, however, this appears to not have been the practice of many Spaniards. Many eighteenth-century writers, both physicians and theologians, complained that almost all Spaniards seemed to be breaking the fast by claiming medical exemptions which were granted to them by priests and doctors. Take, for example, the testimony of Diego de Torres Villarroel (1694–1770), a renowned writer of the Spanish Enlightenment, who described his frustrations in a publication in 1730.[29]

> By experience I have seen, it is rare … [that a house] serves fish on the tables on fast days, and in all the eating halls I have seen healthy, fat, and robust people; and they have the nerve to say that Lent was made for fools and Friars. The ailments to avoid fasting are many, but not all are legitimate.[30]

---

[28] 'A los infieles, à los locos, y à los niños, que no han llegado al uso de la razon, se les puede dàr carne en dia prohibido': Jayme de Corella, *Suma de la theologia moral*, 5th edn (Madrid, 1694), 156; Miguel Anxo Pena González, 'Jaime de Corella', in Real Academia de la Historia, *Diccionario Biográfico Electrónico*, n.d., online at: <http://dbe.rah.es/biografias/17513/jaime-de-corella>, accessed 30 January 2021. In 1790, for example, the tribunal in Valencia heard accusations against Luis Cheli, a French widower and hosier; one of Cheli's neighbours claimed that both he and his mother 'ate meat on Fridays, [that] he did not fast on precepted days, nor did he pray the Mass on half-feast days' ('comia de Carne los dias viernes, que no ayunaba los dias de precepto, ni ora misa los dias de media fiesta'): Madrid, Archivo Histórico Nacional, Inquisición 5312, Exp. 121 (1790), Santo Oficio de la Inquisición, Tribunal de Valencia, 'Proceso de Fe de Luis Cheli y María Cheli', 18.

[29] I. L. McClelland, *Diego de Torres Villarroel* (Boston, MA, 1976), 13.

[30] '[P]or experiencia he visto, que es rara la casa de la Corte, y de las Ciudades populosas en que se sirven à las mesas pescados en dias de ayuno; y à todos los comedores los he visto sanos, gordos, y robustos, y tienen por estrivillo decir, que la Quaresma se hizo para los bobos, y los Frailes. Los achaques para no ayunar son muchos; pero no todos son

It appears that many Spaniards were avoiding fasting, not by openly rejecting the practice, but by claiming that they should be excused from fasting or abstinence because of illness or infirmity. To be clear, it is difficult to ascertain definitely whether there was an empirical or quantitative decline in the observance of fasting and religious dietary restrictions in eighteenth-century Spain. While there is widespread discussion in works published in this period, it is nevertheless possible that these reflect an unsubstantiated or merely apparent decline which existed more in the discussion of learned authors and printed sources than in reality. However, given the number and the variety of sources which addressed this topic, including writings by local clergy, well-known Spanish intellectuals and religious authorities and papal brevia, it is reasonable to assume that they reflect not only a perceived decline but also a real change in practices of fasting during the eighteenth century. Additional quantitative analysis of the purchasing of *bulas Cruzadas* could support this thesis. This tension between the regulations for fasting and the actual practice of it may have been exacerbated by the widespread use of the *bulas Cruzadas* in Spain; one liberty often granted by the bull was the permission to consume dairy products, eggs and even meat during days of fasting and abstinence, provided the holder of the bull had consulted both a medical expert and a spiritual advisor. One reproduction of the bull from the mid-seventeenth century affirmed:

> Also conceded to all persons who hold this Bull, [is that] during all the aforementioned year, they can, on the advice of both Physicians, spiritual and corporal, eat meat during Lent, and other times of fasting, and prohibited days for eating meat throughout the year. And that likewise they can eat freely as they wish eggs and things made from milk ...[31]

---

legitimos': Diego de Torres Villarroel, *Vida natural, y catholica: Medicina segura para mantener menos enferma la organizacion del cuerpo, y assegurar al alma la eterna salud* (Madrid, 1730), 88.

[31] 'Item concede a todas la personas que tomaren esta Bula, que durante el dicho año, puedan de consejo de ambos Medicos, espiritual, y corporal, comer carne en Quaresma, y otros tiempos de ayunos, y dias prohibidos de comer carne por todo el año. Y que ansimismo pueden libremente a su albedrio comer huevos, y cosas de leche': Bernabe Gallego de Vera, *Explicacion de la bula de la Santa Cruzada. Muy necessaria para confessores, y de grande utilidad, y provecho para todo genero de personas* (Madrid, 1652), 28r, 207–8. Gallego de Vera provided the text in both Castilian and Latin; of importance is the phrase 'de consilio utriusque Medicis', which Gallego de Vera translated as 'de consejo de ambos Medicos, espiritual, y corporal'.

The treasured *bulas Cruzadas* did not give individuals *carte blanche* dispensation from dietary restrictions; rather, they required that those seeking such dispensation demonstrate a legitimate medical reason for being excused.[32] The apparent result was the phenomenon of Friday ailments.

This crisis came to a head in 1741, when Benedict XIV issued two papal brevia on the laxity of fasting in the Catholic world. He lamented in *Non ambigimus* that 'the most sacred observance of the Lenten fast has been almost completely eliminated by the excessive ease of dispensing it everywhere in [an] indiscriminate manner for futile and non-urgent motives'.[33] He urged the clergy to exhort and guide their parishioners to observe the Lenten fast faithfully and emphasized that dispensations should not be given except in cases of 'legitimate cause' which had been subjected to 'the counsel of each of two Physicians' (*utriusque Medici consilio*).[34] The papal language should have been familiar to Spanish readers, because the *bulas* employed the same phraseology of 'legitimate cause' and 'the counsel of two Physicians'.[35]

Almost immediately, it seems, objections and qualifications were raised in response to this bull, questioning whether it applied to corporate and public dispensations or only to private ones and whether an absolute mandate from the pope had been given. In response, Benedict XIV issued *In suprema universalis* three months later, which clarified that his commands concerning dispensations applied

---

[32] Claudio Ferlan, *Ayuno Eclesiástico (DCH) (The Ecclesiastical Fast (DCH))*, Max Planck Institute for European Legal History Research Paper Series No. 2018–09, online at: <https://papers.ssrn.com/sol3/papers.cfm?abstract_id=3260582>, last accessed 11 January 2022, 10.

[33] '[C]he la sacritissima osservanza del digiuno quaresimale, per l'eccessiva facilità di dispensare ovunque, in modo indiscriminato, per futili e non urgenti motivi, sia stata quasi completamente eliminata': Benedict XIV, *Non ambigimus*.

[34] '[S]ine legitima causa, & de utriusque Medici consilio': Ezquerro Perez, *Explicacion*, 199; Benedict XIV, *Non ambigimus*; cf. the Italian translation of this phrase 'il consiglio di due medici' ('the advice of two physicians'). Similarly, 'de utriusque Medici consilio' and 'dell'uno e dell'altro medico' in Benedict XIV, *In suprema universalis*, Papal Breve, 22 August 1741, Libreria Editrice Vaticana, online at: <https://www.vatican.va/content/benedictus-xiv/it/documents/breve–i-in-suprema-universalis—i–22-agosto-1741–nei-giorni-.html>, last accessed 11 January 2022. Compare also 'giusta motivazione' and 'sine legitima causa'.

[35] As will be demonstrated, this phrase was interpreted by Spanish authors to mean a spiritual physician (such as a priest or a confessor) and a corporal physician (such as a medical doctor).

183

Klaeren

George A. Klaeren

to every single Catholic.[36] Here the language was exact and emphatic: to receive a dispensation from fasting, any Catholic would need 'legitimate cause', which was granted by 'the counsel of each of two Physicians'.[37]

THE DEBATE: DOUBTS ABOUT MEDICAL EXEMPTIONS TO FASTING

However, although the brevia were meant to give clarity, many doubts remained in Spanish society concerning medical exemptions to fasting, evidenced by the number of publications devoted solely to the task of explaining and understanding the bulls, brevia and canons on fasting. Much of this doubt can be attributed to two points: a lack of clear consensus on *what* constituted an excuse-worthy illness and arguments about *who* was allowed to determine this. Canon law and moral theologians were not often explicit on what defined illness; likewise, the language of 'legitimate cause' was also not explicit. Some categories were clear (pregnant women, for example, were automatically exempt) but because of the subjectivity of experiencing pain and illness and the variety of such experiences, this was left largely to interpretation on a case-by-case basis. 'Casuist theologians have signalled so many [reasons for dispensation]', complained Díaz-Bravo, 'that there is hardly anyone to whom abstinence applies.'[38] He outlined four categories of medical excuses: supposed causes (*supuesta*), doubtful causes (*dudosa*), legitimate causes (*legitima*) and certain causes (*cierto*).[39] The first two, based on hypothetical or potential dangers, were insufficient grounds for receiving a dispensation, while the final category of certain causes applied to those circumstances such as pregnancy in which it was 'notorious and manifest ... of such a manner that no one to this point has doubted [it]'.[40] The problematic area was the third category, which applied to those health concerns regarding which 'it is prudently feared that if one does not dispense [a person] from fasting or abstinence ... one could occasion some grave

---

[36] Benedict XIV, *In suprema universalis*.
[37] See the Latin text of *In suprema universalis* in Ezquerro Perez: '[N]on vero singulis ob legitimam causam, & de utriusque Medici consilio dispensatur': Ezquerro Perez, *Explicacion*, 203.
[38] 'Los Theologos Casuistas señalan tantas, que apenas hay sujeto à quien obligue la abstinencia': Diaz-Bravo, *El ayuno reformado*, 127.
[39] Ibid. 128.
[40] '[D]e modo, que ninguno hasta aqui ha dudado': ibid.

184

harm to the health of the body [of the sick person] ... Not all sickness is legitimate cause, but only a notable sickness and that which could be dangerous.'[41]

The instructions mandated the advice of both a spiritual and a corporal physician. But who had the authority to determine cases of 'legitimate cause'? As Díaz-Bravo noted, 'Canonists and Physicians travel on contrary paths.'[42] While, in the past, bishops had been responsible for granting dispensations to parishioners in their dioceses, this task had now been shifted to a cast of figures drawn from both the medical and the theological communities.[43] In Paris, for example, authority for granting dispensations had been reassigned from priests to physicians in 1657.[44] In Spain, however, this responsibility continued to be shared by clergy and physicians. Physicians had been added to the list of individuals who could grant a dispensation, but they did not replace parish priests and confessors.

Despite the papal instructions, it seems that there were instances where two experts were not consulted. In some cases, individuals consulted authorities from the medical community, mostly physicians (*médicos*) and surgeons (*cirujanos*), while in other cases, individuals sought the advice of authorities from the theological community, priests and confessors. One moral theologian explained, for example, that obvious illnesses (similar to Díaz-Bravo's 'certain cause') did not need to be verified by a physician, 'but when the aforementioned evidence is lacking, one is excused from fasting if a Physician, or lacking one, a Surgeon, a Parish Priest, a Confessor, or a prudent person declares that the sufferer cannot fast without serious detriment to his health'.[45] While this ranking seems to privilege the medical authorities over the local parish priest, most theologians were clear to assert that it was the right of a confessor or a priest, 'not having a physician with whom to consult', to grant dispensations entirely

---

[41] '[S]e teme prudentemente de ella, que si no se dispensa el ayuno, o abstinencia, puede ocasionar algun daño grave à la salud del cuerpo, ... No toda enfermedad es causa legitima, sino es la enfermedad notable, y que fuere peligrosa': ibid. 128, 130.

[42] 'Los Canonistas y Medicos vàn por caminos contrarios': ibid. 127.

[43] Villodas, *Analisis*, 2: 399.

[44] Sydney Watts, 'Enlightened Fasting: Religious Conviction, Scientific Inquiry, and Medical Knowledge in Early Modern France', in Ken Albala and Trudy Eden, eds, *Food and Faith in Christian Culture* (New York, 2011), 105–24, at 111–12.

[45] 'Pero quando falta la dicha evidencia, si el Medico, ò en su defecto el Cirujano, el Pàrroco, el Confesor, ò un varon prudente, declara que el doliente no puede ayunar sin grave detrimento de su salud': Cliquet, *La Flor*, 3: 114; see also Larraga, *Prontuario*, 408.

on their own.[46] In some parts of the Spanish empire, access to a physician or health professional may have been difficult to obtain, but on the Iberian peninsula, this would not have been a logistical concern; other factors could have included a general societal scepticism or disdain for physicians or a reluctance to incur the cost of consulting one.[47]

Nor did an academy-trained and licensed professional physician have to be consulted as the representative for health professionals. Manuel Ezquerro Perez, a chaplain and synodal examiner in Logroño, wrote:

> Who is meant by spiritual Physician? ... the Confessor approved by the Ordinary ... Who is meant by corporal Physician? ... One that has been examined and approved by the Royal *Protomedicato* to cure sick persons, and graduates with licences from the University of Salamanca in the Faculty of Medicine, and where there is no Physician nor is there easy recourse to where there is one, a wise or intelligent man in the art of healing will suffice ...[48]

As a chaplain and a confessor in his diocese, Ezquerro may have been safeguarding what he viewed as his own responsibility. His explanation reveals a loose interpretation of 'physician'; Ezquerro includes practitioners licensed by the *protomedicato* (a governmental council responsible for overseeing the licensure of medical professionals) and 'academic' medical experts, as well as local individuals who had some knowledge of healing and of illnesses.[49] As the historian María Luz López Terrada has shown, Spanish society was medically

---

[46] '[N]o habiendo médico con quien consultarlo': Antonio Covian, *Manual de curas o breve compendio del ministerio parroquial* (Granada, 1815), 36.

[47] Bjørn Okholm Skaarup, *Anatomy and Anatomists in Early Modern Spain* (Farnham, 2015), 214; Barbara Mujica, 'Healing on the Margins: Ana de San Bartolomé, Convent Nurse', *Early Modern Studies Journal* [online journal] 6: *Women's Writing / Women's Work in Early Modernity* (2014), 128–65, at 137, at: <https://earlymodernstudiesjournal.org/wp-content/uploads/2014/10/5.-Mujica.pdf>, last accessed 11 January 2022.

[48] 'P. Quièn se entiende por Medico espiritual? R. Que el Confessor aprobado por el Ordinario; ... P. Quièn se entiende por Medico corporal? R. Que el que està examinado, y aprobado por el Real Protomedicato, para curar enfermos, y los graduados de Licenciados en la Universidad de Salamanca en la Facultad de Medicina; y donde no hubiere Medico, ni es facil el recurso adonde lo hay, bastarà el consejo de varon prudente, è inteligente en el arte de curar': Ezquerro Perez, *Explicacion*, 73–4.

[49] John Tate Lanning, *The Royal Protomedicato: The Regulation of the Medical Profession in the Spanish Empire*, ed. John Jay TePaske (Durham, NC, 1985).

pluralist, drawing on non-exclusive resources for health from academic and extra- or para-academic professionals, including pharmacists and apothecarists, university-trained physicians, barbers and surgeons and even local healers who employed magic or religious healing.[50] The interpretations in theological handbooks of this point indicate that many of these para-professionals were considered capable of providing the expertise required by the 'corporal physician'.

Some writers argued that the medical community was at fault here for underestimating the seriousness of the theological issues at hand. Benito Jerónimo Feijóo (1676–1764), perhaps the most famous writer of the Spanish Enlightenment, authored at least five different essays which discussed fasting. In one, he complained about '[t]he ease of the Physicians in declaring people exempt from the obligation of observing the Lenten abstinence who suffer some habitual indisposition'.[51] Additionally, some critics argued that the 'professionals' from the medical community were actually poorly informed when it came to the science of health and nutrition. Feijóo and others were particularly dismayed that many granting dispensations were doing so based on outdated and incorrect medical theories regarding nutrition which asserted that a vegetarian diet created weakness and a proclivity to become ill. He commented: 'Those physicians who indifferently [examine] sick people, both actual and habitual, proceed irrationally [when they] excuse the Lenten abstinence. Many are gravely harmed by this dispensation.'[52] Díaz-Bravo, while arguing that physicians should determine the seriousness of an illness, also cautioned that 'it is convenient that Physicians should undo the [false] impression that Lenten foods are notably harmful ... Although fasting foods may

---

[50] María Luz López Terrada, 'Medical Pluralism in the Iberian Kingdoms: The Control of Extra-Academic Practitioners in Valencia', *MH* 53, Supplement S29: *Health and Medicine in Hapsburg [sic] Spain: Agents, Practices, Representations* (2009), 7–25.

[51] 'La facilidad de los Médicos en declarar exentos de la obligación de observar la abstinencia Cuaresmal a los que padecen alguna indispoción habitual': Benito Jerónimo Feijóo, *Teatro crítico universal*, vol. 8 (Madrid, 1779; first published 1739), TCU VIII.11§XI¶58, online at: <https://www.filosofia.org/bjf/bjft800.htm>, accessed 17 January 2022. References to Feijóo here include the numbers of the volume, discourse or essay, section and paragraph.

[52] '[Q]ue proceden irracionalísimamente aquellos Médicos, los cuales indiferentemente a todos los enfermos, ya actuales, ya habituales, excusan de la abstinencia Cuaresmal. A muchísimos dañan gravemente con esa dispensación': Feijóo, *Teatro crítico universal*, vol. 7 (Madrid, 1778; first published 1736), TCU.VII.9§VII¶25, online at: <https://www.filosofia.org/bjf/bjft700.htm>, accessed 17 January 2022.

George A. Klaeren

[cause] harm, it is not as much as many physicians think.'⁵³ Díaz-Bravo cited the work of Feijóo, Paolo Zacchia and Jorge Baglivo as medical authorities who supported this position.⁵⁴

Likewise, at a meeting of the Royal Academy of Medicine in Seville, Josef Alonso y Saenz, a theologian at the University of Seville, mentioned in one address 'the defects with which a physician can damage the *spiritual good* of a sick patient ... the excessive liberty with which they usually dispense the obligations of *hearing Mass, fasting, and abstaining from eating meat*'.⁵⁵ Saenz conceded that the physician's job was made harder by 'finicky' patients who exaggerated their ailments, and several other authors also blamed those who consulted physicians and gave false accounts of their illness.⁵⁶ Joaquin Antonio de Eguileta, a chaplain in Madrid, railed against such patients in a sermon for the first Sunday in Lent:

> Who does not tremble ... upon seeing Lent draw near, knowing that he has to undertake the fast? Who does not seek out the opinions and liberal judgments of Physicians in order to free himself of the obligation of fasting? In the Divine Judgment the truth of these reports will be examined ...⁵⁷

Still others during the eighteenth century argued that due to their lack of medical knowledge members of the theological community were at fault for giving dispensations so frequently. In 1751, the *criollo* physician Joseph Francisco de Malpica Diosdado blamed not only the 'bad' religiosity of Mexican Catholics, but also the willingness of priests to grant dispensations out of their general ignorance of the health sciences. '[I believed] that on the matter of Fasting and

---

⁵³ '[E]s conveniente, que los Medicos se desimpressionen de que son notablemente nocivos los alimentos Quadragesimales; ... Aunque dañen los alimentos de ayuno, no es tanto como piensan muchos medicos': Diaz-Bravo, *El ayuno reformado*, 130–1.
⁵⁴ Ibid. 131.
⁵⁵ '[L]os defectos con que el médico puede perjudicar *el bien espiritual* de los enfermos ... Demasiada libertad con que, suelen dispensar en las obligaciones de *oir Misa, ayunar, y abstenerse de comer carnes*': Josef Alonso y Saenz, 'Disertacion Médico-Teológico-Canónico-Legal: De los casos principales en que el Médico es reo en el fuero interno y externo, canónico y civil', in *Memorias Académicas de la Real Sociedad de Medicina, y demas Ciencias de Sevilla*, vol. 10 (Seville, 1792), 530–1.
⁵⁶ Ibid. 531.
⁵⁷ '¿Quién es el que al ver cerca de sí la Quaresma no tiembla, ...juzgando que el ayuno le ha de tragar? Quién es el que no busca pareceres de Médicos y opiniones anchas par librarse de la obligacion del ayuno? En el Juicio divino se exâminará la verdad de los informes': Joaquin Antonio de Eguileta, *Sermones para todas las Dominicas del año*, 3 vols (Madrid, 1800), 1: 295.

188

concessions to meat, the Theologians were stricter than the Physicians. Upon verification I found that it is the contrary: both the narrowest and most rigid were the Physicians who wrote on the proposition of Fasting, [rather] than the Theologians.'[58] Malpica Diosdado outlined nine reasons which he believed were most central to the decline of the practice of fasting, including the relaxed stance of popular Spanish works on moral theology, the work of 'interloping' city physicians and the fears that were commonly held about the perils of fasting and abstaining from meat, which, according to Malpica Diosdado, were based on bad science and ignorance.[59] He not only argued against liberal or casuist moral theology, but also pointed to the culpability of the medical community at all levels, including 'not only the local healers (*curanderos*), but also the expert Physicians (*Medicos peritos*)'.[60] If a medical opinion was to be given on fasting, he asserted, it should be 'from the mouth of a Wise, expert, and discreet Professor ... not from the mouth of an interloper lacking the necessary science and requisite faculties'.[61] Malpica Diosdado dedicated the second part of his work to a 'catalogue of sicknesses ... whose *dictamina* should be consulted along with the experts of the Medical faculty' when reviewing cases of medical exemption.[62] Diosdado provided a collation of advice from three medical authorities, including passages on fevers and heart ailments.[63]

[58] '[D]e que en materias de Ayuno, y concessiones de carne, eran los Theologos mas estrictos, que los Medicos: y de su averiguacion hallo, que es al contrario: mas estrechos, mas rigidos son uno, û otro Medico, que escribieron de proposito de Ayuno, que los Theologos': Malpica Diosdado, *Alexipharmaco*, 8.

[59] Ibid.

[60] '[Q]ue no solo los curanderos, sino los Medicos peritos': ibid. 14–15.

[61] '[P]or la boca de un Sabio, perito, y discreto Professor, ... No assi de a boca de un intrunso; pues faltandole la ciencia necessaria, y las facultades requisitas': ibid. 15.

[62] 'Catalogo de enfermedades ... cuyos dictamenes deben consultrase con los Peritos de la Facultad Medica': ibid. 77.

[63] Ibid. The three medical authorities included the Cistercian medical-moral scholar Antonio José Rodríguez (1703–77), the papal physician Paolo Zacchia (1584–1659) and Juan Alonso de Los Ruices y de Fontecha (1560–1620), professor of medicine at the Universidad de Alcalá de Henares. Malpica Diosdado also often cited Feijóo: Gema Rivas Gómez-Calcerrada, 'Antonio José Rodríguez', in Real Academia de la Historia, *Diccionario Biográfico Electrónico*, n.d., online at: <http://dbe.rah.es/biografias/19961/antonio-jose-rodriguez>, accessed 31 January 2021; Jacalyn Duffin, 'Questioning Medicine in Seventeenth-Century Rome: The Consultations of Paolo Zacchia', *Canadian Bulletin of Medical History = Bulletin canadien d'histoire de la médecine* 28 (2011), 149–70, at 150–1; Ana María Rodríguez González, 'Juan Alonso de Los Ruices y de Fontech', n.d., Lucio Anneo Séneca Instituto de Estudios Clásicos sobre la Sociedad y la Política, online at: <http://

Feijóo, who had earlier noted the free hand of physicians, conceded that theologians should recognize that fundamentally medical professionals carried more authority in these discussions because of their ability to understand and define illness:

> much more depends on the knowledge of the Physician than on the Theologian. All that the Theologian contributes to the question is only the maxim ... which is that one is given dispensation from the fast whose health would be seriously injured by abstinence ... All the rest that is needed for the resolution, which is to know: when the abstinence [is], and what [type of] abstinence; to whom, and in which cases does it do serious harm to health, pertains to Medicine and not to Theology. With that it is found much more proportionate for a Physician to decide the doubt, than a Theologian.[64]

The recommendations of Feijóo and Malpica Diosdado indicate a growing awareness that, despite doubt and uncertainty among the medical community, a class of true medical expertise could be recognized in those physicians who had trained in medical science and who followed an established canon of medical authorities. This supports historical arguments that the medical sphere experienced trends of professionalization in the eighteenth century.

Conclusion: Medico-Moralism, Doubt and Authority in a Medically Pluralist Society

Despite the flurry of publications throughout the eighteenth century, the questions surrounding medical dispensations to fasting, namely the definition of a 'legitimate cause' and the uncertainty about

---

portal.uc3m.es/portal/page/portal/inst_lucio_anneo_seneca/bases_datos/bvhe/biblioteca/a_b/juan_alonso_de_los_ruices_y_de_fontecha>, accessed 31 January 2021.

[64] '[M]ucho más pende del conocimiento Médico, que del Teológico. Todo lo que la Teología contribuye a la cuestión, es únicamente una máxima ... esto es, que está dispensado de ayuno aquél, a cuya salud hace grave daño la abstinencia ... Todo lo demás que se necesita para la resolución, que es saber, cuándo la abstinencia, y qué abstinencia; a quiénes, y en qué casos hace grave daño a la salud, pertenece a la Medicina, y no a la Teología. Con que se halla mucho más proporcionado para decidir la duda un Médico, que un Teólogo': Benito Jerónimo Feijóo, *Cartas eruditas y curiosas*, 5 vols (Madrid, 1777), vol. 1, CE.I.xv.10, online at: <https://www.filosofia.org/bjf/bjfc000.htm#t1>, accessed 17 January 2022.

whose expertise to seek, persisted in Spain.[65] Although no definitive answer emerged, the discussion reveals that a dialogue was taking place, even if it was sometimes contentious, between two communities: the medical and the theological. The issues of fasting required cooperation between these two groups because the definitions and questions involved knowledge of Catholic theology and apostolic and canon law as well as detailed information about nutrition, illness and the human body. To address the challenges of medical exemptions to religious fasting, eighteenth-century Spanish thinkers realized that it was necessary to approach the subject as an area of overlap area between faith and medicine.

In 1748, in a published exposition on the brevia, Antonio José Rodriguez, who was both a Cistercian monk and a renowned author on medicine, argued that cooperation was needed between medicine and theologians because the subject of fasting belonged to both.[66]

> The point is perfectly Moral and perfectly Medical ... [for] a just determination, it is necessary [that the] subject is equally instructed in Moral Theology and in Medicine. Neither the Physician, however grand he may be, knows all the nature ... of all that is Christian, nor does the Theologian ... know what there is in the nature of diets and of illnesses ...[67]

Rodriguez suggested that either cooperation was necessary or theologians would need to recognize that the field of medicine represented an area of knowledge which needed to be incorporated into moral theology and studied more thoroughly. Feijóo praised Rodríguez's approach and argued that he embodied the type of scholar who was needed to address such issues, 'for ... he knows

[65] See early nineteenth-century manuals, for example Francisco Echarri, *Directorio Moral*, Tercera Vez Ilustrado, vol. 2 (Madrid, 1805), 289–323.

[66] Gómez-Calcerrada, 'Antonio José Rodríguez'; Antonio José Rodriguez, *Reflexiones theologico-canonico-medicas, sobre el ayuno eclesiastico, que establecen su practica, después de los breves de Nuestro Santissimo Padre Benedicto XIV* (Madrid, 1748).

[67] 'Es el punto perfectamente Moral, y perfectamente Medico: por esso para la determinacion justa, es preciso sujeto, que estè igualmente instruìdo en la Theologìa Moral, y en la Medicina. Ni el Medico, por grande que sea, sabe toda la naturaleza, ... todo Christiano; ni el Theologo ... sabe lo que hay en la naturaleza de los alimentos, de las enfermedades': Rodriguez, *Sobre el ayuno eclesiastico*, 251.

the subject matter which a Theologian knows and he knows also that which pertains to the Physician'.[68]

What emerges from this discussion is a more complex way of thinking about how illness was constructed, defined, contested and resolved in the eighteenth-century Spanish world. Fasting represented a tangled nexus of medical and moral-theological interests. As a religious practice, it was asserted to have spiritual impact and significance, but insofar as it involved the human body, it was also governed by medical and anatomical knowledge. It was, as Rodríguez argued, both medical and theological; as such, it was one of many topics in early modern Spain which was included in the category of 'medico-moralism', that is, those issues which shared the interests and methodologies of both the theological and the medical communities. While 'medico-moralism' may seem to be limited to writings of moral theology, the debates over fasting show that medicine and theology were actively engaging one another and cooperating in the generation of new policies toward fasting and understanding illness, nutrition and anatomy. Two important ramifications of the debate merit special attention: firstly, the impact of doubt and lack of consensus in establishing medical authority; and secondly, the role of religion and of the patient in enriching understandings of medical pluralism.

Firstly, the debates clearly suggest that authority on the matter was negotiated between 'two Physicians', that is, between confessors and priests on the one hand and physicians and other medical professionals on the other. While many sources affirmed that the ultimate power of dispensation resided with the church, especially the papacy and the bishops, in most cases the decisions of dispensation were constructed in tandem between the clergy and a medical professional. Several writers also suggested that the opinion and advice of the medical expert gained authority in these questions during the eighteenth century. Feijóo, Rodríguez, Malpica Diosdado and Díaz-Bravo, for example, all emphasized the importance of the clergy consulting learned and professional medical practitioners or undertaking to understand the medical matters themselves. This growing authority is countered, however, by the presence of dissension, a lack of consensus among the medical community, and the reliance by many on

---

[68] '[Q]ue sabe en la materia lo que sabe el Teólogo, y sabe también lo que pertenece al Médico': Feijóo, *Cartas Eruditas*, CE.I.xv.10.

outdated (for example, Galenic) medical theories. Uncertainty, so central to the epistemology of Enlightenment Spain, also shaped opinions on the value and verisimilitude of medical knowledge.[69] These issues contributed to a mistrust and scepticism about the veracity of medical expertise in eighteenth-century Spain and may have allowed for dispensations to be granted in the grey area of doubt.

Secondly, the debate challenges our understanding of early modern Spain as a medically pluralist society. López Terrada has argued that to study the history of medicine in early modern Spain, one needs to employ a comprehensive approach that appreciates the 'medical pluralism' which included both academic physicians and 'unofficial' health providers. Moreover, she asserts, 'in order to understand the relationships among the different medical systems that coexist in a society during a certain historical moment, we must take into account not only academic medicine and its professionals, but also society collectively'.[70] The discussion about medical exemptions to fasting demonstrates that the medical pluralism of Spanish society was indeed complex. First, publications related to fasting show that the requirement to consult a 'corporal physician' was freely interpreted to include a wide range of figures in the medical community beyond physicians, including surgeons, barbers and other healers. Second, the case of fasting demonstrates that understanding society 'collectively' involves understanding and appreciating the importance of the theological community and of religious ideas in determining the boundaries of illness and health.[71] In order to understand what it meant to be sick enough to be excused from fasting, more than a physician's definition was needed, although, as has been noted, there is evidence to suggest that professional medical opinion was already gaining epistemic weight during the Spanish Enlightenment.

The fasting debates also highlight the importance of the lay patient as part of the medically pluralist Spanish society. As recent studies in medical anthropology and sociology have indicated, the narratives of those suffering illnesses are valuable sources of experiential knowledge, not least for the way that they reveal differences between expert

[69] Ivy Lilian McClelland, *Ideological Hesitancy in Spain 1700–1750* (Liverpool, 1991).
[70] López Terrada, 'Medical Pluralism', 8.
[71] Carolin Schmitz, 'Barberos, charlatanes y enfermos: La pluralidad médica de la España barroca percibida por el pícaro Estebanillo González', *Dynamis* 36 (2016), 143–66.

authority and patient perspective.[72] In the debate about valid medical excuses for exemption from fasting, a great deal of authority was granted to the person who was claiming to be ill: he or she, after all, was the one who was experiencing the conditions and ailments that were exacerbated by fasting. Even the medical professionals of Spain acknowledged this experiential authority which was the privilege of the patient. Regrettably, recovering the patient 'voice' in the discussion of medical exemptions to religious fasting may prove impossible. This article examines sources written by learned authors and by clergy rather than by those individuals seeking medical exemptions to fasting. It nevertheless remains aware of the fact that the layperson played an important role in the process; future research may yield ways of highlighting how individuals seeking dispensation thought about medical exemptions (for example, from sources such as letters).[73]

Torres Villarroel, who was so perturbed by the lack of faithful fasting in Spain, recognized that authority, and therefore culpability, in this matter rested ultimately with the ailing layperson. He wrote that, in the end, the decision to grant a medical dispensation was not given by either a physician or by a priest, but by the individual seeking the dispensation:

> They [the Physician and Confessor] do not give this licence; the one who gives it is the one who is suffering an ailment; and thus, he should inform faithfully about his illness, without deleting nor adding circumstances to the gravity of the pain which he suffers, because if he informs sinisterly [with an aim to deceive], the devil will carry him off along with the licence of the Physician and Confessor.[74]

---

[72] Gareth Williams and Jennie Popay, 'Lay Knowledge and the Privilege of Experience', in David Kelleher, Jonathan Gabe and Gareth Williams, eds, *Challenging Medicine*, 2nd edn (Abingdon, 2006), 122–45, at 122.

[73] For a work elevating the patient in the history of Spanish medicine, see Carolin Schmitz, *Los enfermos en la España barroca y el pluralismo médico: Espacios, estrategias, y actitudes*, Estudios sobre la Ciencia 71 (Madrid, 2018).

[74] '[Q]ue ellos no dan esta licencia, que el que la da es el que padece el achaque; y así, debe fielmente informar de su enfermedad, sin quitar ni poner circunstancia á la gravedad del daño que padece, porque si informa siniestramente se lo llevará el diablo con la licencia del Médico y el Confesor': Diego de Torres Villarroel, *Tratados físicos, médicos y morales, vida natural y católica: medicina segura para mantener menos enferma la organizacion del cuerpo, y asegurar al alma la eterna salud*, vol. 4 (Madrid, 1794), 143.

Similarly, the priest and friar Josef Jacobo Gonzalez recommended in a 'crusade bull sermon' that 'in order that the Physician and the sufferer, both of them together, should not perish, the sufferer should inform the Physician entirely truthfully and the Physician should resolve [it] without the least flattery'.[75] Although the advice of experts was required, these authorities also recognized their reliance on the patient's perspective and the patient's definition of illness and suffering. This suggests that early modern Spanish health professionals recognized that the definition of illness included what philosopher S. Kay Toombs has described as the 'decisive gap' between the 'qualitative immediacy' of an infirmity as experienced by the patient and the textbook definition of an ailment.[76] In this way, the patient became an important part of determining health and illness in eighteenth-century Spain.

The controversy over medical exemptions to fasting thus requires historians to understand the relationship between theology and religion and the production of medical knowledge. Discussions about sickness and health in Spain occurred within a historical context in which theological and religious considerations had an important role in determining definitions and establishing accepted traditions. This is especially clear in medico-moral topics which rendered it necessary that the theological and medical communities should cooperate. The decision to seek a 'sick note' excusing one from fasting was a perfect example of this: it was not only a medical question, but also a moral question. Fasting, and the ensuing discussion over these 'moral sick notes', emphasizes the need to study the realm of medico-moralism and to understand the relationship between theology and the health sciences in Spain and in the early modern Catholic world more broadly.

---

[75] '[P]ara que el Medico, y el doliente, ambos juntos, no perezcan, debe el doliente informar al Medico con toda verdad, y resolver el Médico sin la menor lisonja': Josef Jacobo Gonzalez, *Sermon, que en la publicacion de la bulla de la Santa Cruzada para el año de mil setecientos setenta y seis* (Madrid, 1776), 14. 'Crusade bull sermon' is O'Banion's term for sermons preached to encourage the purchase of the *bulas Cruzadas*; 'For the Defense', 173.
[76] S. Kay Toombs, *The Meaning of Illness: A Phenomenological Account of the Different Perspectives of Physician and Patient* (Dordrecht, 1993), 12.

Pain as a Spiritual Barometer of Health: A Sign of Divine Love, 1780–1850

Angela Platt*

Royal Holloway, University of London

A popular nineteenth-century spiritual barometer displays the steps one might take in the Christian life to bring oneself closer to either 'glory' or 'perdition'. Near the top of the barometer, nearing 'glory' is the bearing of painful tribulations, connected to the cross of Christ. Whilst pain was undeniably an undesired presence in life, it was also a hallmark of spiritual progress. The denouement of Christian health, therefore, was often to be in pain. Looking at pain narratives of six evangelical Dissenters, this article explores how pain was perceived by these individuals through the lens of the atonement. As the atonement was a loving aspect of God's providence, so too was pain in the Christian life a quotidian display of divine love. The meaning and purpose of pain was sanctification, understood as a retributive, though mainly redemptive, implement of God's fatherly love. Whilst sharing a common framework of atonement, case studies from different denominations display nuanced differences in their pain narratives: the Baptists and Congregationalists examined here emphasized the sin that required the atonement, whereas the Quakers emphasized suffering with or alongside Christ.

A popular nineteenth-century spiritual barometer found in evangelical magazines displays the steps one might take in the Christian life towards (or away from) spiritual health. This barometer is classified as 'a Scale of the Progress of Sin and Grace'. It assesses behaviours and character traits on a sliding scale, showing whether readers are closer to glory (at the top), treading in the dangerous territory of indifference (in the centre), or nearing perdition (at the bottom). At the top of the barometer, listed as the penultimate category towards 'glory', immediately preceding 'desiring to be with Christ' and 'death', is pain and tribulation as a cross an individual must bear in the Christian life.[1] Whilst pain was undeniably an

---

* E-mail: Angela.platt@stmarys.ac.uk.

[1] 'A Spiritual Barometer; or, a Scale of the Progress of Sin and of Grace', *The Christian's Penny Magazine and Friend of the People* 6 (1851), 7.

Studies in Church History 58 (2022), 196–216 © The Author(s), 2022. Published by Cambridge University Press on behalf of Ecclesiastical History Society
doi: 10.1017/stc.2022.10

undesired presence in life, it was also a hallmark of spiritual progress. The denouement of Christian health was ostensibly to be in pain.

Such 'barometers of spiritual health' were common amongst evangelically inclined Dissenters throughout the late eighteenth and early nineteenth centuries, and they took diverse forms. The Quaker Elizabeth Fry developed her own 'spiritual barometer' which was republished in her memoirs. She provided three points to measure spiritual health, the second of which concerned the manner in which one handled affliction: 'every time that trial or temptation assailed thee, didst thou endeavour to look steadily to the Delivering Power – even to Christ who can do all things for thee?'[2] Unsurprisingly, affliction or pain was an expected component of life on earth for many. Pain was not only expected in the Christian life but for many it was integral to it. Conversely, as will be discussed below, pain could also be an indicator of spiritual demise. The aforementioned barometer named the penultimate stage before 'perdition' as 'disease and death', reflecting the Christian's belief that non-believers endured earthly pain as a foreshadowing of eternal misery. This article will present several examples of pain narratives, which aimed to assist sufferers to comprehend, process and prepare for the experience of pain, and will show how pain was conceived as a stage in Christian spiritual growth.

An example of this interconnection can be seen in the interpretation of a biblical passage by Jane Saffery Whitaker. The daughter of the popular Particular Baptist minister John Saffery, Jane led a women's Bible study in the 1820s. During one meeting, she expounded Matthew 20, in which the mother of James and John requested that Jesus grant them seats of power in his coming kingdom. Jesus replied: 'Ye know not what ye ask. Are ye able to drink of the cup that I shall drink of, and to be baptized with the baptism that I am baptized with?'[3] Jane Saffery interpreted Jesus's response as a lesson in pain. James and John would only become worthy of such an elevated position in the kingdom if they endured extensive pain and suffering on earth. She asserted: 'No one is fit to sit on thrones judging others till he has served & suffered. I shall only reach My throne by the way

---

[2] Elizabeth Fry, *Memoir of the Life of Elizabeth Fry with Extracts from her Journal and Letters*, ed. Katharine Fry and Rachel Elizabeth Cresswell, 2 vols (London, 1847–8), 1: 147–8.
[3] Matt. 20: 21–2 (KJV).

of the Cross. Are your sons ready to go the same way?'[4] Jane's lesson inculcated an important perspective on the Christian life: for her, pain was not only inevitable; it was also necessary.

Jane's words are an example of a 'pain narrative'. Such 'pain narratives' attempted to build a framework to understand pain; as patients articulated their pain, they found meaning.[5] Affliction was therefore 'crucial in shaping the self'.[6] 'Pain narratives', therefore, offer historians useful insights into the identity of individuals, denominations and wider culture. For sufferers, pain was a part of daily life. It was also beset with a tension: pain was anxiously avoided as well as submissively welcomed. Pain was processed by Dissenters not only as an endemic aspect of life, but also as a necessary one, which led to growth and sanctification. Undeniably, pain and its interpretation as redemptive has been a significant aspect of the Christian faith throughout much of Christian history. What is characteristic in these narratives, however, is the relationship of pain to divine love and its connection to the atonement.

These experiences of pain will be explored through an examination of six evangelical Dissenters, four women and two men: David Everard Ford (Congregationalist), Sarah Pearce (Baptist), Elizabeth Saffery (Baptist), James Backhouse (Quaker), Hannah Backhouse (Quaker) and Elizabeth Fry (Quaker). These pain narratives are found in personal papers of both men and women, but no crucial differences are noted between their experiences. Harvey notes that gender was not the main factor in her research on forms of embodied pain using middle-class letters from 1726 to 1827. Rather than gender, religion was the most important factor shaping their experience.[7] Likewise, religion takes centre stage in this research into the process of pain. The six Dissenting evangelicals examined here all reached adulthood during what has been described by interpreters such as Boyd Hilton as the 'Age of Atonement', lasting from *c*.1785 to 1865. Their writings illustrate how they understood pain as an aspect of

---

[4] Oxford, Bodl., Reeves Collection, Box 2/C, 'Pocket Diaries of Jane Saffery Whitaker'.
[5] Lisa Wynne Smith, '"An Account of an Unaccountable Distemper": The Experience of Pain in Early Eighteenth-Century England and France', *Eighteenth-Century Studies* 41 (2008), 459–80.
[6] Dorothy Porter and Roy Porter, *In Sickness and in Health: The British Experience, 1650–1850* (London, 1988), 3–13.
[7] Karen Harvey, 'Epochs of Embodiment: Men, Women and the Material Body', *Journal for Eighteenth-Century Studies* 42 (2019), 455–69.

God's loving work in their lives. Perhaps drawing from Bentham's utilitarianism,[8] these Dissenters came to understand the short-term earthly pains they suffered as acceptable losses which would result in eternal spiritual gains.

This analysis will first consider the nature of pain recounted in these papers before, secondly, assessing how pain was interpreted through reference to the providential will of God. As the atoning work of Christ was a pain-filled example of God's providence, so too was day-to-day pain in the Christian life. Thirdly, it will examine the extent to which pain was viewed as part of God's loving sanctification. Understood as a display of God's love, pain was an essential element of the authors' spiritual growth and sanctification, although they struggled to accept this interpretation. Analysing the personal papers of this selection of Dissenters reveals nuances of interpretation when comparing the Quakers to the Congregationalists and Baptists. Whilst all of these evangelicals emphasized the atonement-centred view of pain, the Quakers understood pain in terms of an identification with Christ's sacrifice, while the Baptists and Congregationalists focused on the need for repentance.

METHODOLOGY

The intersection of religion and pain is a growing focus of research. Religion offers an important lens through which to interpret and process pain, serving as a form of spiritual 'record-keeping', or a guide for religious conduct.[9] Thus experience of pain was often viewed as a central trait of religious identity; early modern Quakers, for instance, saw suffering as a part of their public testimony.[10] Conversely, pain has also been given an important role for those identified as non-believers. Eternal suffering was perceived as the ultimate purpose of hell, the destination for non-believers, according to many evangelical Dissenting groups. Research on pain is also a burgeoning field within

---

[8] Boyd Hilton, *The Age of Atonement: The Influence of Evangelicalism on Social and Economic Thought, 1785–1865* (Oxford, 1988), 31–2.
[9] Harvey, 'Epochs of Embodiment'; Alan H. Cadwallader, 'Pedalling the Death of a Life: A Late Victorian Variation on dealing with Grief', *JRH* 38 (2014), 35–52; Joanna Bourke, *The Story of Pain: From Prayer to Painkillers* (Oxford, 2017), 90–109.
[10] Amanda E. Herbert, 'Companions in Preaching and Suffering: Itinerant Female Quakers in the Seventeenth- and Eighteenth-Century British Atlantic World', *Early American Studies: An Interdisciplinary Journal* 9 (2011), 100–40.

Angela Platt

the wider framework of the history of emotions. Emotions, including pain, were constituted in both social and individual terms. Pain was constituted by the interplay of the community framework (in which cultural and communal mores developed) and personal characteristics. This combination inspired individual experiences of pain which were articulated by sufferers-in-pain through sharing pain narratives. By recording these experiences, individuals found a space to process their pain and grow in self-understanding.[11] This article examines the social and cultural interpretations of pain, particularly focusing on the 'numinous' character of pain. Pain, while importantly affecting the body and the mind, also has a spiritual dimension.

Scholarship on the emotions more generally also proves helpful in this research. Rosenwein's approach to viewing feelings through 'emotional communities' offers a helpful approach, enabling the analysis of shared language and contexts, to understand how pain was conceived. This article will make use of this method, as it articulates how pain in religious communities was broadly conceived and differentially experienced. Glucklich identifies pain as operating in a space 'in between' the body and the mind.[12] Boddice argues in favour of a 'biocultural' view of emotions in which the body and mind are not separate from and the cultural influences, nor are these mutually exclusive.[13] I want to extend Boddice's corpus of experience to include the spiritual dynamic of identity. Echoing Glucklich, I suggest that pain is found somewhere 'in between', but that this is within the corpus of individuals' biocultural experience. Using personal papers in conjunction with didactic literature, this article employs a 'discursive analysis',[14] which draws out how pain is described and conceived in authors' letters, diaries, memoirs and sermons. The article expands on the growing field which analyses intersections between religion and the emotions by looking at how pain was conceived both similarly and distinctly by a small sample of evangelicals from three Dissenting denominations: Baptists, Congregationalists and Quakers.

[11] Smith, 'Account of an Unaccountable Distemper'; Joanna Bourke, 'Pain Sensitivity: An Unnatural History from 1800 to 1965', *Journal of Medical Humanities* 35 (2014), 301–19.
[12] Ariel Glucklich, *Sacred Pain: Hurting the Body for the Sake of the Soul* (New York, 2001), 11–39.
[13] Rob Boddice, *The History of Emotions* (Manchester, 2018), 107–29.
[14] 'Discursive analysis' is helpfully clarified further by Callum G. Brown, *The Death of Christian Britain* (London, 2009), 1–15.

This is a very small set of Dissenters, and the findings presented here will not apply to every Baptist, Congregationalist or Quaker identified in this period. However, this study does suggest potential distinctions between the denominations in the understanding of pain, which may offer a framework for further comparative research.

THE NATURE OF PAIN

The definition of pain has been a subject of much debate. Pain can be viewed as a sensory phenomenon as it relates to the physiological response of neurons which deploy signals to the brain. Beyond this, there are also important psychological and emotional attributes of pain which cannot be severed from this discourse. Pain is a multi-faceted experience in which the physiological, emotional and mental aspects are inextricably linked. Sense and emotions thus coalesce in experience and ought to be considered in concert.[15] This article will explore pain by focusing particularly on spiritual manifestations of this experience.

The personal papers of these Dissenters evince many types of pain. Sometimes identified as affliction, suffering, sickness or grief, pain presented in many forms: physical, emotional, mental and spiritual. What seems to run throughout these narratives is the synonymity of pain with loss. Pain was often conceived in terms of loss, whether it was the loss of energy and vigour which permitted an individual to engage actively in ministerial activity, or the loss of motor skills which permitted individuals to eat, drink and dress themselves. Pain was also felt in the grief of losing a loved one.

David Everard Ford (1797–1875) was a Congregationalist minister, hymn writer, author and speaker for the British Mission (the Congregationalist Home Missionary Society). In April 1836 his father died as the result of a botched eye surgery to remedy cataracts. When Ford developed eyesight issues of his own in 1846, he avoided a surgical remedy for fear of repeating his father's fate. Indeed, anxiety marked much of Ford's experience with pain, as his ministerial work did not bring in sufficient income for his family.[16] James Backhouse (1794–1869) was a botanist and Quaker minister. As a teenager, James had desired to become a chemist, but was stymied by poor

[15] Boddice, *History*, 107–29.
[16] Cambridge, King's College Library, Box FB/2/5, 'Diaries of David Everard Ford'.

health. He developed a keen interest in natural history and botany and in 1816 purchased a botanical nursery with his brother. In 1822 he married Deborah Lowe, another Quaker minister, but she died in December 1827. Thereafter, James dedicated himself vigorously to Quaker ministry. He travelled to Australia in 1832, where he explored his botanical interests and advocated for evangelical prison reform.[17] Hannah Backhouse (1787–1850) was a Quaker minister and the wife of minister Jonathan Backhouse. The excerpts from her journal as recorded in her memoirs are replete with pain, especially grief, caused by the death of close relatives and friends. The first such bereavement was recorded in 1804, when Hannah lost her sister Mary. Her journal is full of further episodes of grief and associated anxiety occasioned by the loss of other family members, including her son Jonathan.[18] Elizabeth Fry (1780–1845) is one of the best-known evangelical Quakers of the nineteenth century. Her letters, diaries and memoirs recount multiple episodes of grief at the loss of family members and friends. The first significant loss she recalled was that of her mother in 1792. Her diaries are full of further accounts of grief, including the loss of her daughter, also named Elizabeth. Struggle with personal illness was also recorded, as she declined in health during the last few years of her life.[19] Elizabeth Saffery (1762–98) was a Particular Baptist, married to minister John Saffery. During the final months of her life, she recorded her struggles in her journal. Her last entry was in April 1798; she died the following month. Throughout this discourse, she lamented the loss of her mobility as sickness repeatedly prevented her from attending church.[20] Sarah Pearce (c.1760–1804) was a Particular Baptist whose husband Samuel was a well-known minister. Sarah's pain is recorded in her short memoirs, detailing her grief after her husband died unexpectedly in 1799, followed by the death of her youngest son, also named Samuel, in 1800.[21]

By focusing on these six evangelical Dissenters, this article elucidates how pain was constituted and experienced. Whilst 'Dissenter'

[17] Sarah Backhouse, *Memoir*.

[18] Hannah Backhouse, *Extracts from the Journal and Letters of Hannah Chapman Backhouse* ([London], 1858).

[19] Fry, *Memoir*, 2: 532–6.

[20] Timothy Whelan, *Nonconformist Women Writers, 1720–1840* (London, 2011).

[21] Sarah Pearce, 'Memoirs of Mrs. Pearce, Widow of the Late Rev. Samuel Pearce of Birmingham', in Thomas Gibbons, ed., *Memoirs of Eminently Pious Women*, new edn, rev. Samuel Burder (London, 1827), 3: 198–207.

can be understood easily to refer to those Protestants who were not part of the Church of England, 'evangelical' is a slightly more nebulous term. Definitions tend to have vague boundaries, and a rigid approach might be accused of being overly exclusive or too porous. The evangelical Dissenters considered in this article may be denoted as such in terms of Bebbington's evangelical 'quadrilateral': crucicentrism, activism, conversionism and biblicism,[22] with some variety in emphasis. This evangelical label might most nebulously be attributed to Quakers of this group, whose views on the Bible differed from those of other evangelicals, not least because of their understanding of how the Holy Spirit (or 'inner light') related to Scripture. However, some Quakers took approaches which differed little from other evangelicals: Timothy Larsen suggests that, for Elizabeth Fry, the 'inner light' was essentially a 'text prompter' drawing from the Bible.[23] James Backhouse, on the other hand, asserted that the Bible should not take precedence over the leadings of the Spirit. In a letter included in his memoirs, Backhouse happily described reading the Bible to prisoners in Australia but expressed bemusement that anyone should 'regard the bible ... above the teachings of the Holy Spirit'.[24] Thus, whilst these individuals could fairly be called 'evangelical', distinctions in their views must be acknowledged. Their similarities, however, are most significantly manifested through their shared prioritization of the atonement. As noted above, this era has been characterized as an 'Age of Atonement' owing to the centrality of the atonement of Christ in evangelical life.[25] The atonement was crucial to understanding the cause of pain. Individual pain in Christian lives was viewed as a corollary to this atoning work. This crucicentrism drives the understanding of pain expressed by these Dissenters, which was viewed in connection with God's love for them. Through this lens, they understood the cause and purpose of pain in their lives.

---

[22] David Bebbington, *The Dominance of Evangelicalism* (Downers Grove, IL, 2005).
[23] Timothy Larsen, *A People of One Book: The Bible and the Victorians* (Oxford, 2011), 177–80.
[24] Sarah Backhouse, *Memoir*, 75.
[25] Apart from Hilton, see Jan-Melissa Schramm, *Atonement and Self-Sacrifice in Nineteenth-Century Narrative* (Cambridge, 2015); Timothy Gorringe, *God's Just Vengeance: Crime, Violence, and the Rhetoric of Salvation*, Cambridge Studies in Ideology and Religion 9 (Cambridge, 1996), 193–222.

The Cause of Pain: Loving Providence

Most important to the experience of pain was the search for meaning. How did the experience of sickness fit into the cosmic agenda for their lives? Why was pain a prevalent aspect of life? Such questions demanded answers. The providence of God has long been a popular explanation for the cause of painful situations. Pullin, in her research on early modern Quakers, suggests that providential punishment was a lens through which Quakers viewed the suffering of their oppressors. Viewing their persecutors receiving what they saw as 'providential punishment' gave them collective reassurance that they found favour with God.[26] In research on the abolition of the slave trade, Coffey asserts that 'judicial providentialism' was levied against nations who supported slavery. British abolitionists feared that divine wrath would be released on sinful nations because of slavery. It was a sin which rivalled those committed by Sodom and Gomorrah.[27]

However, pain was not only seen in terms of providential punishment. The providential lens through which the Dissenters in this article interpreted their particular experience of pain was the love of God as exemplified in the atonement. Joseph John Gurney suggested that the atonement, whilst accomplished by suffering (of Christ), was unequivocally a demonstration of love. 'The Christian doctrine of atonement, has often been misrepresented ... the gift and sacrifice of [God's] only begotten Son, is the glorious result, not of wrath, but of LOVE.'[28] David Everard Ford echoed this idea in his sermon expounding God's love, entitled *The Greatness of the Love of Christ*. Firstly, he suggested that suffering through sacrifice was evident throughout Bible history, reaching its climax in the work of Christ: 'the institution of sacrifices was designed to prepare the way for a suffering and atoning Saviour'. Ford then linked this suffering narrative to God's love: 'In tracing the history of redemption ... every step of its explanation was a fresh display of *the greatness of the love of Christ.*'[29] By

[26] Naomi Pullin, 'Providence, Punishment and Identity Formation in the Late Stuart Quaker Community, *c.*1650–1700', *SC* 31 (2016), 471–94.
[27] John Coffey, '"Tremble, Britannia!": Fear, Providence and the Abolition of the Slave Trade, 1758–1807', *EHR* 127 (2012), 844–81.
[28] Joseph John Gurney, *A Letter to the Followers of Elias Hicks, in the City of Baltimore and its Vicinity* (Baltimore, MD, 1840), 11.
[29] David Everard Ford, *The Greatness of the Love of Christ: A Sermon* [on John 11: 36] (London, 1826), 10.

interpreting the cause of pain through this lens of the atonement, these evangelicals understood that pain was an act of love, albeit only effective for believers. In contrast, for unbelievers the atonement remained a reminder of the eternal wrath to come.

God's atoning love provided a framework to understand providential pain for these evangelical Dissenters. The Porters note that sufferers-in-pain would attribute their pain to God; they often thanked God for their affliction. They suggest that this removed the 'sinister unknown aura' of pain. Knowing that God would never bestow sickness without a purpose (even if unknown), sufferers clung to this hope.[30] Suffering was viewed as an integral part of God's plan. As the atonement was part of God's divine plan, so was the suffering of Christians. However, pain was not always welcomed, and this produced a tension. On one hand, pain was anxiously avoided. Indeed, anxiety about anticipated pain could be as all-consuming as the reality. On the other hand, pain was also accepted and submitted to as part of God's providential dealings. Such a tension is prevalent in these Dissenting documents. Dissenters who felt their submission to pain to be inadequate would often plead (either with God or by scolding themselves) that they should trust God's loving providence by accepting this period of pain. Perhaps this might be viewed as a version of 'speech act theory' as discussed by William Reddy. Whilst the submissive emotions (fuelled by love to God) might be lacking, through speech and prayers they might become activated and, in some cases, actualized.[31] It was in the context of this tension between the desire to submit lovingly to God and the desire to avoid pain that considerable anxiety was expressed.

Missives exchanged between loved ones were often replete with details about the health and well-being of physically distant family members. Diaries recounted thoughts and feelings of illness, sometimes on a daily basis. Affliction was often reported in conjunction with anxiety, as individuals struggled to reconcile their feelings with their sense that they should submit to God's will. Whilst Elizabeth Saffery was documenting her final month of decline, her pain was severe enough for her to wish for an imminent death. However,

---

[30] Porter and Porter, *In Sickness*, 170–1.
[31] William Reddy, *The Navigation of Feeling* (Cambridge, 2001), 64–111. Reddy suggests that emotions might be latent and 'activated' by speech, or they might not exist before speech and 'actualized' (generated into existence) by speech.

despite considerable suffering, her journal is defined by the desire to submit to God's will through her pain. While she wishes explicitly that the pain would leave her, she also tries to persuade herself to 'cheerfully bear it'. On 19 October 1797 she wrote: 'The will of the Lord be done when contrary to our own but I trust I desire if affliction & disappointment is my lot to cheerfully bear it. I know it best yet murmur at it still.'[32] She echoed this on 12 November: 'Submission to the will of God in all things ... I shall never want anything contrary to his will.'[33] Saffery seemed to hope that loving submission would be activated through her desire for its actualization. Her diary entries up to her death show her negotiating the tension between her resistance to pain and her will to submit to God's providence. Elizabeth Fry's experience of submission was similar. Her daughters, Katharine and Rachel, suggested that their mother's 'health suffered from all her sorrows' in 1844 with the 'threatenings of the return of some of her most painful symptoms'.[34] In July 1845, Fry commented on her illness in a letter to Katharine: 'I have felt very poorly ... I have felt unusually low', yet Fry still concluded: 'I desire in my heart to say, "not as I will, but as Thou wilt"'.[35] Enduring the death of her youngest son Samuel in 1800, Sarah Pearce wrote a letter to a friend, passionately mourning her loss. She concluded that this must be part of God's plan, even if she was not privy to the reasons for it: 'Be still, then, ever tumultuous passion, and know, that he who hath inflicted these repeated strokes, is God; that God whom I desire to reverence under every painful dispensation, being persuaded that what I know not now, I shall know hereafter.'[36] In December 1836 Ford was consumed with anxiety owing to the afflictions suffered by his son Everard. 'In the dead of the night ... my dear wife woke me, exclaiming that he was dying in her arms.' In the following months, Ford's diary demonstrates that he was possessed by anxiety about his son, as he simultaneously sought to submit to God's will. On 28 January he asserted a reconciliation of these feelings: 'I think that I have surrendered him into the hands of God. It has been a painful struggle, but I trust that divine grace will bear me through.'[37]

---

[32] Whelan, *Nonconformist Women*, 410.
[33] Ibid. 415.
[34] Fry, *Memoir*, 2: 504.
[35] Ibid. 2: 520.
[36] Pearce, 'Memoirs', 201.
[37] 'Diaries of David Everard Ford'.

When Hannah Backhouse lost her eight-year-old son Jonathan in 1820, the grief and its indelible memory permeated her parenting. 'On this period I do not know how to dwell ... our dear eldest child became very ill'; after the best medical treatment 'he expired in a convulsion fit in my arms. I seemed at the time hardly sensible of the depth of the sorrow.'[38] When illness affected her other children, Hannah found herself sick with anxiety. A few weeks after Jonathan's death, her son Henry became ill, and her sister aided with his care: 'inexpressibly kind and tender was my dear sister in this my deeply-tried state of mind; for the illness of my beloved child made me tremblingly alive to every touch'.[39] Nonetheless, Hannah submitted to these experiences of pain as being part of God's will for her life. Indeed, when her second son, Gurney, died in November 1824, she concluded: 'It is the Lord's doing, and it is marvellous in my eyes!'[40]

Elizabeth Saffery, Fry, Pearce and Ford all hoped that their desire for submissive feelings, catalysed by their love to God, would activate their sense of submission to God's will. Pain was a source of much anxiety for these Dissenters, both in its hypothetical and its actual forms. This anxiety created a tension between their submission to God and their desire to avoid pain. Whilst pain was to be avoided, it was also seen as having significant benefits in terms of spiritual health. Pain was interpreted primarily in spiritual terms, by which Dissenters sought to understand how pain could be a loving part of God's providential plan. The key question of theodicy, which often arises in religious communities with regard to pain, asks how a loving God can permit so much pain, especially amongst those who love him. Still a difficult issue today, it was no less so for eighteenth- and nineteenth-century Dissenters. Rather than viewing pain as antithetical to divine love, these Dissenters identified it as an extension of divine love. God's providential inclusion of pain was for the purpose of sanctification: a provision of spiritual health.

THE PURPOSE OF PAIN: LOVING SANCTIFICATION

Determining the purpose of pain was the most crucial aspect of these pain narratives. Scholars such as Gorringe and Bending have

---

[38] Hannah Backhouse, *Extracts*, 41.
[39] Ibid. 42.
[40] Ibid. 54.

suggested that a debate arose in the nineteenth century regarding the constitution of pain. Some considered it an extension of the redemptive process, whilst others saw it as a retributive manifestation of God's wrath. Gorringe suggests a link between nineteenth-century penal reform and atonement theology. Debates regarding the purpose of imprisonment (whether it was rehabilitative or punitive) were widespread.[41] Bending contrasts literature by prominent religious figures of the day, suggesting that a tension existed between theologies of pain as a redemptive process and those identifying it as retributive. However, for these Dissenters at least, these two purposes would not have been mutually exclusive. Pain could be both retributive and redemptive; it could be a punishment but it could also be an experience which was rooted in Christ's atoning work.

That pain could be retributive was noted by J. J. Gurney, who suggested that pain was a direct consequence of sin: 'pain and misery are the ultimate and inevitable consequences of vice'. He asserted that pain was part of the 'retributive system constituted by the moral government of God'.[42] Such experience in isolation, however, was confined to unbelievers, whose retributive punishment would culminate in an eternal hell. Conversely, for believers, pain could be a retributive punishment, but it was also an agent for curative sanctification. This was also affirmed by Gurney: 'pains and afflictions ... are so overruled for good, that they are often the means of curing that very evil out of which they originate'.[43] Thus it was through the atoning work of Christ that believers avoided eternal pain while simultaneously enduring earthly pain for their sanctification. It is important to clarify here that in theological terms pain functioned differently in the lives of believers and those of unbelievers, as already noted. The redemptive love-saturated aspects of pain would only be available to the former. Bending evinces this distinction when she discusses the retributive theory, as emphasized by the Anglican J. C. Ryle. In the era of the cholera pandemic, Ryle believed that this disease was a part of God's chastising judgment: '"the Hand of the Lord!" working on earth'. He viewed the situation of unbelievers as especially poignant since the disease was so painful that deathbed conversions were not

---

[41] Gorringe, *God's Just Vengeance*, 193–222.

[42] Joseph John Gurney, *Essays on the Evidences, Doctrines, and Practical Operation, of Christianity*, 5th edn (London, 1833), 131.

[43] Ibid. 137.

physically possible. Only those who were already redeemed before contracting it could expect the pain to draw them closer to God.[44]

In the early nineteenth century, then, these personal documents demonstrate how pain could be considered a redemptive gift from God, which was intended to sanctify. Indeed, pain was often viewed as a 'therapeutic progress': pain indicated that one was improving in health. This view applied to physical as well as spiritual sickness.[45] In 1823, Hannah Backhouse ruminated upon the nature of suffering in her journal a few years after losing her son: 'I believe there is never high attainment without much suffering.' She interpreted her suffering as preparation for her subsequent ministry.[46] James Backhouse expressed similar sentiments when he first felt an impression to speak in a meeting in 1816: 'my heart overflowing with gratitude to God, who, after permitting me to feel my own weakness, had strengthened me thus openly to avow myself in His service'.[47] Elizabeth Fry suggested in July 1803 that suffering was a crucial aspect of spiritual progress: 'No cross, no crown, has been rather a stimulus to me', she wrote in her journal.[48] In October 1797, Elizabeth Saffery noted in her journal her conviction that suffering was a preparation: 'shall I cheerfully leave this Lump of Clay that engages so much of my attention at present, to be food for worms for a season[?] blessed be God[,] its only to be refined, while my spirit shall fly beyond the Grave'.[49]

In this era, pain was often viewed as a form of divine chastisement. That is, pain was viewed as part of God's loving sanctification manifested through fatherly discipline. Ford's *Laodicea* (1844) indicates this connection. Focusing on Revelation 3: 19, 'As many as I love, I rebuke and chasten', Ford argued that God applied chastising love to believers who were 'backsliding' in their faith. Moreover, 'the design of Christian discipline is the correction rather than the

---

[44] Lucy Bending, *The Representation of Bodily Pain in Late Nineteenth-Century English Culture* (Oxford, 2004), 19–20.

[45] Porter and Porter, *In Sickness*, 98–112; Heather D. Curtis, *Faith in the Great Physician: Suffering and Divine Healing in American Culture, 1860–1900* (Baltimore, MD, 2007), 26–50.

[46] Hannah Backhouse, *Extracts*, 49.

[47] Sarah Backhouse, *Memoir*, 9.

[48] Fry, *Memoir*, 1: 119.

[49] Whelan, *Nonconformist Women*, 435.

punishment of the offender'.[50] Similarly, after Pearce had endured the death of her husband and her firstborn son, she concluded that this pain was much-deserved chastisement which would be perpetuated until she learned her lesson. In a letter to a 'Mrs F.', she wrote in December 1800: 'Oh, my rebellious passions! ... though he smote me ... in wrath, yet hath [he] remembered mercy ... He is a God full of compassion, who does not afflict willingly; and I believe I shall see in the end, that all that hath befallen me is for my profit.'[51]

Elizabeth Fry echoed this in November 1811 when she lamented the loss of her daughter. She considered this pain to be a loving example of God's chastening: 'although it pleases my Heavenly Father thus to chastise me yet I am permitted to feel that He doth love those whom He chasteneth. I feel His love very near, and like a tender parent that may see right to inflict the rod, rather, perhaps than spoil the child.'[52] Fry believed that suffering was indicative of God's love; a view she clearly expresses in an annotation to her Bible at 1 Thessalonians 1: 4–5: 'Which is a manifest token of the righteous judgment of God, that ye may be counted worthy of the kingdom of God, for which ye also suffer.'[53] Her note reads: 'Their tribulations a token of his love.' Similar sentiments were expressed by her husband Joseph Fry. During their courtship in 1800, he wrote her a letter trusting that their future marriage might be marked by a mutual duty and 'resignation to suffer into Blessing'.[54]

Importantly, however, suffering was not always viewed as positive or redeeming, as shown by the case studies in this article. The Unitarian Harriet Martineau, for example, experienced serious sickness in the 1840s. During this period, she expressed the sentiments that pain was God's fatherly chastisement, 'an instrument for good', although she also acknowledged that some were 'soured by suffering'. This 'souring' was a condition, she suggested, in which the residual 'ideas' of pain remain long after the painful episode has passed.[55] Indeed, Harriet's own attitude to pain soured as she abandoned her Unitarian faith. This was clear by the time her memoirs were

[50] David Everard Ford, *Laodicea; or, Religious Declension: Its Nature, Indications, Causes, Consequences, and Remedies* (London, 1844), 102.
[51] Pearce, 'Memoirs', 201.
[52] Fry, *Memoir*, 103.
[53] London, BL, Add. MS 73528, Elizabeth Fry's annotated Bible.
[54] BL, Add. MSS 3672–3675, Letters between Elizabeth Gurney and Joseph Fry.
[55] Harriet Martineau, *Life in the Sick-Room* (London, 1844), 8–9.

published in 1855, by which point she had turned to natural (scientific) explanations for lived experiences.[56] Experiences of pain may have led to questioning one's assurance of God's love, rather than securing it.[57]

In general, however, suffering reminded these Dissenters of their need for redemption and caused them to be refined, as though in a 'fiery furnace'.[58] That is, pain was used as a spiritual corrective for believers. Poor habits were gradually changed through pain. Pain influenced moral actions and catalysed spiritual growth. It strengthened individuals and developed character. Pain of various types reminded individuals of their need for redemption. Pain was central to God's chastising fatherhood. The connection between God's loving fatherhood and pain would become weaker in the latter half of the nineteenth century as the chastising motif was supplanted by an image of God as a tender or sentimental father, for whom pain was increasingly unwelcome.

DENOMINATIONAL DISTINCTIVES

For the evangelical Dissenters considered here, pain was a manifestation of God's love, viewed through the lens of the atonement. However, there were some nuanced experiential differences in their pain narratives. I do not wish to suggest that these differences represented distinct boundaries in experience, but it is clear that the extant Dissenting accounts demonstrate some divergent emphases. The two Baptists and one Congregationalist considered here focused more on repentance from sin and God's chastising love through pain. Their participation in God's atoning love was fundamentally a matter of realizing how unworthy they were and how necessary was Christ's sacrifice. Moreover, they often suggested that the cause of this discipline was their over-focus upon 'earthly objects'. In 1797 the Baptist

[56] Odile Boucher-Rivalain, 'Harriet Martineau (1802–1876), from Unitarianism to Agnosticism', *Cahiers Victoriens et Édouardiens* [online journal] 76 (Autumn 2012), 27–43, at: <https://doi.org/10.4000/cve.520>, last accessed 25 January 2022.
[57] Recent scholarship has noted a gap in both Protestant and Catholic provision for those contending with suffering in the twenty-first century, demonstrating how the link between pain and religious life remains an important issue in discussion: see, for instance, Armand Leon Van Ommen, *Suffering in Worship: Anglican Liturgy in relation to Stories of Suffering People* (London, 2019).
[58] Bourke, *Story of Pain*, 90–109.

Elizabeth Saffery was concerned that her decline might be attributable
to an over-attachment to 'earthly objects' in contrast to her love for
God: 'Now much Sin dwells in my heart[.] when shall I love the
Creature as I ought[?] Can Christ be altogether lovely while I feel
those attachments to earthly Objects[?] Lord thou knowest my
heart altogether[.] I Desire to Love thee supremely.'[59] She later suggested that her suffering was intended to wean her from earthly pleasures: 'These 2 past days been very ill in body but blessed be God not
uncomfortable in my soul, it is the Lord & I know he does all things
well. I need these trials to wean from ye world & live more on a
Covenant keeping God.'[60]

In 1801 Sarah Pearce, also a Baptist, wrote to 'Mrs H.' asserting
that her recent pain, following the loss of her son and husband, had
been caused by an over-affection for earthly things. It ought to continue, she suggested, until she had remedied this over-attachment.
Her response was not marked by anger towards God, who, she
believed, had removed her loved ones in his providence. Instead,
she directed ill-feelings towards herself, castigating herself for her
inadequate faith:

> When shall I feel my will absorbed in the will of God, and have none
> but his? I want to live above this fading dying world, and wonder I
> should be so attached to it, when it has so frequently disappointed
> me. Oh how I envy those who have learnt that useful lesson, deadness
> to the creature, and life in God![61]

This theme is repeated by other Baptists and Congregationalists.
Pain, while a manifestation of God's providence, is blamed on the
self. When the family income of the Congregationalist Ford was
insufficient to support his family in July 1838, he suggested it was
a consequence of his earthly focus: 'Perhaps I have been getting too
fond of the world, & this chastisement is sent to humble me; or perhaps it is to prepare me for a greater trial.'[62]

It does not appear that the 'earthly objects' to which these three
authors referred were objects of material culture. Rather, they chas-
tised themselves for being inordinately interested in earthly

[59] Whelan, *Nonconformist Women*, 407.
[60] Ibid. 417–18.
[61] Pearce, 'Memoirs', 201–2.
[62] 'Diaries of David Everard Ford'.

relationships, and especially for their fondness for children and partners. Their concern was that these relationships had disrupted their affection for God. This is clearly indicated in *The Baptist Manual* (1838). An article on holy living cautioned readers: 'We are to beware lest we should love even a wife, husband, or a child to such a degree as to forget that God requires the chief place in our affections.'[63] In a sermon on Colossians, the Baptist preacher Octavius Winslow (1808–78) presented the imminent danger of loving a family member too much: it would result in a transfer of affections from God to that family member: 'her affections have been inordinately set upon an *earthly object*, – her love to Jesus has, in consequence, waned. Her zeal for his glory has cooled; her walk with God has been less close.'[64] In this particular section of his sermon, Winslow was referring to a mother loving her nursing child more than God. Indeed, pain could serve as a disciplinary reminder of their need for atonement, and one which would continue until they had repented of the 'earthly object' sins which had ensnared them. For these Baptists and Congregationalists, pain appears to be a side effect of the sin which necessitated the atoning work of Christ.

By contrast, for the three Quakers considered here, the sanctifying nature of pain was seen more often in terms of an identification with Christ's afflictions. This is not to suggest that Quakers were not concerned that earthly pleasures or sin might divert their attention from God. This was certainly the case for Elizabeth J. J. Robson, who agonized over such feelings in July 1844: 'I have not thought enough of Jesus; my mind has not been fixed on heavenly things as it used to be[;] … my mind has been filled with the things of this world so much as to leave no room for better things.'[65] However, when it came to the practical experience of pain, whether mental or physical, Quakers often drew analogies with the suffering of Christ. On 13 December 1842, Hannah Backhouse wrote a letter to Maria Fox lamenting the death of her beloved husband, Joseph. She reflected upon how

---

[63] Baptist General Tract Society, 'No. 10. The Grace of God, and a Holy Life', in *The Baptist Manual: A Selection from the Series of Publications of the Baptist General Tract Society designed for the Use of Families: And as an Exposition of the Distinguishing Sentiments of the Denomination* (Philadelphia, PA, 1838), 7.

[64] Octavius Winslow, *The Glory of the Redeemer in his Person and Work* (London, 1844), 286.

[65] Elizabeth J. J. Robson, *A Memoir of Elizabeth J. J. Robson, late of Saffron Walden, who died 15th of 10th Month, 1859* (London, 1860), 5.

these afflictions were shared with Christ: 'Oh, the sufferings that have been passed through from generation to generation! We hear of them in part, but the fulness of them is only known by Him who tasted death for every man, and who, in all our afflictions, is afflicted.'[66] Similarly, as Fry was reaching the end of her life, she repeatedly identified her suffering with that of Christ. In a letter to a friend on 31 December 1844, she wrote: 'May our afflictions be sanctified to us, not leading us to the world for consolation, but more fully to cast ourselves on Him who died for us, and hath loved us with an everlasting love.'[67] This was reiterated in her journal on 29 January 1845: 'I have passed through deep baptisms of spirit in this illness. I may say, unworthy as I am to say it, that I have had to drink in my small measure of the Saviour's cup, when he said, "My God! My God! Why hast Thou forsaken me!"'[68] One of Fry's adult daughters recalled a conversation with her mother near the end of her life. Fry opened the Bible in her daughter's company and read the text: 'Beloved, think it not strange concerning the fiery trial which is to try you' (1 Peter 4: 12). She then discussed enthusiastically how, through her sickness, she was participating as a 'disciple in the suffering of [the] Lord'.[69]

These views show considerable continuity with medieval practice, wherein pain was often marked by a concentration on the passion of Christ. Christ's suffering body was a 'site of imitation' in late medieval sermons, enabling listeners to identify with Christ through their own pain.[70] Such suffering has been identified as crucial to female Quaker experience. Amanda Herbert, in her research on eighteenth-century female Quaker itinerants, suggests that, for Quaker women, suffering was a 'testimony of their gender': suffering was viewed as part of their public testimony as missionaries. Analysing William Sewell's *History*, Herbert suggests that bodily pain was connected to female virtue. However, the identification with Christ's suffering was not exclusive to Quaker females. Indeed, among eighteenth-century Quakers, Herbert asserts that men emphasized resilience and suffering with Christ, whilst women described their

---

[66] Hannah Backhouse, *Extracts*, 254–5.
[67] Fry, *Memoir*, 2: 507.
[68] Ibid. 508.
[69] Ibid. 528.
[70] Shannon Gayk, 'The Form of Christ's Passion: Preaching the *Imitatio Passionis* in Late Medieval England', *Yearbook of Langland Studies* 31 (2017), 231–56, at 246.

pain in terms of embodiment and victimhood.[71] Whilst these themes are not absent in this selection of Quaker women, the interpretive emphasis has shifted to atonement and suffering with Christ, a theme expressed by both women and men.

In final years of his life (1868–9), as James Backhouse suffered from a serious chest illness, he compared his experience to that of the suffering Christ. As his sister notes, Backhouse 'recounted his mercies, saying, how different was his condition to that of his dear Saviour; He when nailed to the cross for our sins, could not in His sufferings obtain relief by a change of posture, whilst to himself there was every alleviation that affection could suggest'.[72] As Backhouse continued to deteriorate, he felt encouragement from the suffering Christ had endured. Through this solidarity, he found comfort in his pain: 'Surely it was permitted in great mercy that He, who was perfect in holiness, should thus be tried, for the encouragement of His poor feeble followers.'[73]

Quaker suffering has received much attention from scholars of the seventeenth and early eighteenth centuries. Suffering has been linked historically with Quaker experience; accounts of their suffering were regularly published into the nineteenth century after a weekly 'Meeting for Sufferings' was first established in 1676. Whilst a steady stream of research has been published on their early modern sufferings, research on nineteenth-century Quaker suffering is sorely lacking. Research on early modern Quaker suffering notes its endemic nature in Quaker experience. Although their pain was perceived as virtuous, they identified their persecutors' suffering as a result of God's judgment.[74] A century and a half later, these authors reveal, suffering was still regarded as a form of virtue, through the lens of the atonement.[75]

[71] Herbert, 'Companions', 87–8.
[72] Sarah Backhouse, *Memoir*, 229.
[73] Ibid. 239.
[74] John Miller, '"A Suffering People": English Quakers and their Neighbours *c.*1650–1700', *P&P* 188 (2005), 71–103; John R. Knott, 'Joseph Besse and the Quaker Culture of Suffering', *Prose Studies* 17 (1994), 126–41.
[75] Importantly, this narrative of suffering with Christ has been studied in other denominations. In her research on pain and religiosity amongst Catholic convents in the nineteenth century, Mangion notes the connection between bodily pain and salvation: pain was part of the 'quest for spiritual perfection'. Pain was something which connected individuals to Christ through their sanctification, as they 'imitated' Christ in their pain: Carmen Mangion, '"Why, would you have me live upon a gridiron?": Pain, Identity,

Conclusion

The study of these six Dissenters has revealed that narratives of pain, and indeed the experience of pain itself, were linked to the theme of divine love, viewed through the lens of the atonement. In this 'Age of Atonement', the cross was central to manifestations of God's love; conceptions of pain were no exception. Pain was connected to the atonement through the great suffering of Christ, which was, according to these Dissenters, a result of 'love not of wrath'. Importantly, the loving application of the atonement was only available to those who were believers: God's wrath was still reserved for unbelievers. The cause of pain for these believers was, ultimately, divine love. As the atoning work of Christ was a loving manifestation of God's providence, so too was quotidian Christian pain a loving manifestation of God's providence. This resulted in a tension between anxious avoidance of pain and submission to providence.

Whilst pain has been identified as psychological and physiological in its constitution, it must also be understood through the spiritual experience of these religious Dissenters. Key to understanding pain was the meaning which was constructed within this experience. To this end, pain was often constructed as part of God's sanctifying work, initiated by the atonement. This painful sanctification was seen as part of God's loving fatherhood. Denominational distinctives were noted as sufferers identified pain with the atonement, either through expressing their sense of need for it, or through their identification with Christ's suffering. The Baptists and Congregationalist considered here seemed to place greater emphasis on their sin as a cause for their pain, whilst the Quakers emphasized their pain as virtuous through solidarity with Christ's suffering. This is a common theme in Quaker theology, but more work needs to be done to explore whether these distinctions were characteristic of denominational approaches. Experiences of pain cut across gendered boundaries, as men and women both curated narratives of their pain interpreted through the lens of the atonement. For these Dissenting evangelicals, pain was expected, avoided and ultimately embraced as part of spiritual growth and health.

---

and Emotional Communities in Nineteenth-Century English Convent Culture', *Interdisciplinary Studies in the Long Nineteenth Century* [online journal] 15 (2012), at: <https://doi.org/10.16995/ntn.652>, last accessed 24 January 2022.

Caring for the Sick in Hamburg: Amalie Sieveking and the 'Dormant Strength' of Christian Women

Andrew Kloes*

Washington DC

Following an outbreak of cholera in Hamburg in 1831, Amalie Sieveking founded the Weiblicher Verein für Armen- und Krankenpflege (Women's Association for the Care of the Poor and the Sick). This was the first Protestant religious voluntary society in Germany organized and led by a woman. Sieveking's conception of the Christian life of faith and the contemporary needs of the kingdom of God convinced her that Protestant women needed to assume a more active role in German society. The Women's Association visited the homes of those who were sick or in other difficult personal circumstances. They attempted to promote the comprehensive well-being of those whom they assisted by providing food, clothing and other necessities of life, paid employment, housing and opportunities to cultivate their spiritual life.

Throughout the spring and summer of 1831, government officials in the German city-state and North Sea port of Hamburg were closely monitoring the spread of cholera westwards across Europe. Between May and July, Hamburg authorities received news that cholera, the bacteriological disease endemic to the Bengal delta of the Indian subcontinent, had broken out in cities along the Baltic Sea, the Red Sea and the White Sea coasts. In response, they ordered into quarantine all arriving ships that had departed from those ports before they could unload their cargoes in Hamburg.[1] Likewise, after cholera had reached the inland population centres of Warsaw, Berlin and Vienna between June and September, Hamburg placed restrictions on the entrance into the city of goods and people travelling from these cities. In June, Hamburg's medical doctors began to meet weekly to discuss cholera and its treatment. At the end of July, before any cases of cholera had been reported in Hamburg, the city council

---

* E-mail: andrew.kloes@gmail.com.
[1] Frank M. Snowden, *Epidemics and Society: From the Black Death to the Present* (New Haven, CT, 2019), 233.

ordered the creation of two cholera hospitals. Each could accommodate two hundred patients and both were made ready within ten weeks.[2] As Hamburg braced itself for the arrival of cholera, on 10 September 1831, Amalie Sieveking, a thirty-seven-year-old upper-class woman, whose late father had been a merchant and senator of Hamburg, issued an appeal in one of the city's newspapers.[3] With the anticipated appearance of cholera in mind, Sieveking addressed her 'beloved brothers and sisters in the Lord' and invited them to join her in volunteering to nurse the 'members of the poorer classes of our father city'. Sieveking continued:

> We now live in a world that lies in a pitiful condition, a veritable show-place of sufferings and sorrows. We are living in so-called Christendom, but we are surrounded by those to whom 'Christianity' is just an empty word, those who have not experienced the sanctifying and quickening power of the gospel in their own hearts. Dare we boast that we have had such an experience of the gospel? If we have, regardless of whether we are men or women, must we then not all consider ourselves to be missionaries in a certain sense? Have we thus not become those who are commanded to proclaim the glorious goodness of Christ, who has called us to into his wonderful light, so that through our witness other souls may not drift away, but rather, be returned to him who is their faithful shepherd? Perhaps a few of the lost may be called to Christ through the witness of our words, but the greater witness of a life that is delighted in God and active in works of love is a sacred duty that is incumbent upon all Christians together.[4]

[2] Friedrich Wolter, *Das Auftreten der Cholera in Hamburg in dem Zeitraume von 1831–1893 mit besonderer Berücksichtigung der Epidemie des Jahres 1892* (Munich, 1898), 217–22.
[3] Carl Bertheau, 'Amalie Sieveking', in Albert Hauck, ed., *Realencyklopädie für protestantische Theologie und Kirche*, 22 vols (Leipzig, 1906), 18: 324–8, at 324.
[4] 'Wir leben ja in einer Welt, die im Argen liegt, und die eben deshalb der Schauplatz mannigfachen Elends und Jammers sein muss; wir sehen uns mitten in der Christenheit von solchen umgeben, denen das Christentum noch ein leeres Wort ist, welche die heiligende und beseligende Kraft des Evangeliums noch immer nicht am eigenen Hertzen erfuhren. Dürfen wir nun solcher Erfahrung uns rühmen, müssen wir dann nicht auch alle auf gewisse Weise als Missionare und Missionarinnen uns ansehen, verordnet zur Verkündigung der herrlichen Tugenden des, der uns berufen hat zu seinem wunderbaren Lichte, ob nicht durch solches Zeugnis eine oder die andere Seele sich treiben lasse, auch sich hinzuwenden zu ihm, dem treuen Hirten und Bischof unserer Seelen? Wenige mögen berufen sein zu dem Zeugnisse durch das Wort; das höhere Zeugnis

Despite her plea, no one joined Sieveking at the new cholera hospital that Hamburg city officials had set up in the Ericus Bastion, one of the city's old fortifications near the harbour district.[5] However, the following May, in the middle of a second cholera outbreak in Hamburg, twelve women did support Sieveking in founding the Weiblicher Verein für Armen- und Krankenpflege (Women's Association for the Care of the Poor and the Sick). Over the next twenty-seven years, Hamburg endured fourteen further outbreaks of cholera, which altogether claimed the lives of nearly eight thousand city residents and infected tens of thousands of others. Every year, the members of the Women's Association re-elected Sieveking to serve as their president, until her death in April 1859.

Notwithstanding her significance to the histories of social work, Protestantism and women's empowerment in Germany, Amalie Sieveking remains an understudied figure. There is no modern scholarly biography of her in German and little has been written about her work in English. She has, however, been the subject of five studies published between 1985 and 2013 by Rainer Postel, Theodor Kuessner, Jutta Schmidt, Inge Grolle and Inge Mager.[6] These have analysed different aspects of her life and work, including the influence of the historic pietist tradition and the early nineteenth-century Awakening (*Erweckung*) movement on the development of her theological views, her opposition to the theological rationalism of the Protestant religious Enlightenment, and her vision for her association's ministry. To complement these previous studies, after first

---

eines gottseligen, liebetätigen Wandels ist eine heilige Verpflichtung für alle Christen insgemein': Amalie Sieveking, 'Amalie Sievekings Aufruf an christlichen Seelen', in Martin Hennig, ed., *Quellenbuch zur Geschichte der Inneren Mission* (Hamburg, 1912), 165–9, at 165–6. All translations from the German are my own.

[5] Emma Poel, *Denkwürdigkeiten aus dem Leben von Amalie Sieveking in deren Auftrage von einer Freundin derselben verfaßt* (Hamburg, 1860), 179.

[6] Theodor Kuessner, *Die Erweckungsbewegung in Hamburg im Spiegel der Briefe, Tagebücher und theologischen Schriften Amalie Sievekings* (Hamburg, 1986); Rainer Postel, 'Amalie Sieveking', in Martin Greschat, ed., *Gestalten der Kirchengeschichte*, 12 vols (Stuttgart, 1985), 9/i: 233–42; Jutta Schmidt, *Beruf: Schwester. Mutterhausdiakonie im 19. Jahrhundert* (Frankfurt, 1998), 36–60; Inge Grolle, 'Amalie Sieveking (1794–1859)', in Adelheid M. von Hauff, ed., *Frauen gestalten Diakonie*, 2 vols (Stuttgart, 2006), 2: 120–31; Inge Mager, 'Weibliche Theologie im Horizont der Hamburger Erweckung. Amalie Sieveking (1794–1859) und Elise Averdieck (1808–1907)', in eadem, ed., *Hamburgische Kirchengeschichte in Aufsätzen*, 4 vols (Hamburg, 2013), 4: 339–76.

examining Hamburg's decades of public health struggles against cholera, which prompted the work of the Women's Association and formed its social context, this article concentrates on Sieveking's leadership of her association and the administrative procedures she developed to foster the health of those whom it served in various practical ways. It concludes by considering the legacy of her example in stimulating other women to become publicly active in Christian work.

This research is based on the annual reports of the Women's Association and examines how the public health crisis that cholera created in Hamburg during the middle decades of the nineteenth century catalysed a group of Protestant women in the city to take unprecedented public action in the pursuit of their religious and humanitarian goals. The scholarship on Protestant social reform initiatives in nineteenth-century Germany has long emphasized the transformative influence of the revolutionary movements of 1848 on church leaders' attentiveness to the struggles of the urban poor. However, it is demonstrated here that the recurring outbreaks of cholera in Hamburg in the 1830s prompted a small group of Protestant women to address the needs of vulnerable urban residents in their city. These women pioneered a new organizational form of women's public Christian service that spread widely within German-speaking Europe and to Protestant communities in other countries.

The ways in which Amalie Sieveking sought to respond to the immediate physical danger of cholera were inextricably related to her conception of the Christian life of faith, her concerns for the spiritual condition of Hamburg (especially the welfare of its most vulnerable residents), and her conviction that both the gospel and the contemporary needs of the kingdom of God made it necessary for Protestant women to take up a more active role in German society. While cholera gave the initial impetus to her work, Sieveking soon developed a holistic conception of health that was more than the mere absence of sickness. In addition to arranging nursing and medical care for those who were ill, the Women's Association attempted to promote the comprehensive well-being of those whom they assisted by supporting their access to a healthy diet, employment with regular wages, adequate housing and opportunities to cultivate their spiritual life.

Sieveking was not alone in undertaking this new type of religious voluntary work. During the early decades of the nineteenth century,

Protestants in large cities and small towns throughout German-speaking Europe founded numerous religiously motivated associations and societies to pursue various evangelistic and social reform goals. These included societies to support the distribution of Bibles and booklets on religious topics to lower-income people, as well as societies that had formed out of concern for the spiritual life and physical well-being of vulnerable people in German society, whose circumstances were believed to have estranged them from Christian faith.[7] German Protestant voluntary societies were formed to care for (among others) orphans, men and women who had been recently released from prison, and women who were leaving prostitution. Indeed, according to Ernst Huth, a German pastor in Mecklenburg-Schwerin, in 1845 there were '1,457 Protestant associations for Christian purposes in Germany and German-speaking Switzerland', while the prominent Hamburg Christian social reformer Johann Hinrich Wichern believed that Huth had considerably undercounted and that there were more than six thousand such associations in German-speaking Europe.[8] That Protestants founded so many new voluntary associations to pursue their various religious goals, instead of attempting to accomplish them through already existing churches, marks a major development within German Protestantism. Hamburg was a locus of this activity: Protestants (most of whom were Lutherans) founded twenty-five new religious voluntary societies in the city between 1814 and 1844.[9] To put this in context, in 1842 there

[7] Andrew Kloes, *The German Awakening: Protestant Renewal after the Enlightenment, 1815–1848* (Oxford, 2019), 187–222.

[8] '[I]m Ganzen 1457 evangelische Vereine mit christlichen Zwecken in Deutschland und der deutschen Schweiz': Johann Hinrich Wichern, 'Neue Zeitschriften und Bücher, welche sich auf das Gebiet der inner Mission beziehen. Evangelischer Vereinskalender Deutschlands und der protestantischen Schweiz für das Jahr 1845', *Fliegende Blätter aus dem Rauhen Hause zu Horn bei Hamburg* 2 (1845), 123–5, at 124.

[9] Johann Hinrich Wichern, 'Die in den letzten 25 Jahren gestifteten christlichen Vereine und Anstalten zur Hebung leiblicher und geistlicher Not unter Wittwen, Waisen, Armen, Gefangenen in Hamburg', *Fliegende Blätter aus dem Rauhen Hause zu Horn bei Hamburg* 1 (1844), 186–8, at 187. On the religious and social context of the Women's Association for the Care of the Poor and the Sick in Hamburg, see also Rudolf Kayser, 'Henri Merle d'Aubigné und die Anfänge der Erweckung in Hamburg', *Zeitschrift des Vereins für Hamburgische Geschichte* 30 (1929), 106–35; Kurt Detlev Möller, *Hamburger Männer um Wichern. Ein Bild der religiösen Bewegung vor hundert Jahren* (Hamburg, 1933); Georg Daur, *Von Predigern und Bürgern. Eine hamburgische Kirchengeschichte von der Reformation bis zur Gegenwart* (Hamburg, 1970), 169–240; Ulrich Heidenreich und Inge Grolle, *Wegbereiter der Diakonie: Johann Wilhelm Rautenberg, Amalie Sieveking*

Andrew Kloes

were just forty-four clergy ministering to the 161,238 parishioners of the seventeen Lutheran parishes in Hamburg and its surrounding suburbs. Hamburg at this time was overwhelmingly Lutheran, with 94 per cent of its inhabitants belonging to a Lutheran parish. The remaining 6 per cent of the city's residents (10,416 people) belonged either to one of six other Christian churches (Church of England, English Reformed, French Reformed, German Reformed, Mennonite and Roman Catholic) or to the city's Jewish community.[10]

In an attempt to conceptualize all of these new endeavours, the Göttingen University professor of theology Friedrich Lücke intro-duced a new term into the German Protestant lexicon in a November 1842 lecture to the Göttingen Missionary Society: 'the inward mission' or 'home mission' of the Protestant church (*die innere Mission der Evangelischen Kirche*).[11] By this expression Lücke emphasized that, parallel to the 'outward mission' or 'foreign mission' (*äußere Mission*) of the church 'to send the gospel outwards, and spread Christian truth and Christian life among non-Christians', there was an equally imperative need to do the same in German soci-ety.[12] Lücke called for a corresponding 'inward mission' to the many in Germany who, by virtue of being born in a historically Christian country, were considered church members, but for whom, according to him, personal Christian faith did not characterize their lives. More recently, historians Michael Häusler and Ulrike Gleixner have iden-tified the considerable proliferation of Protestant voluntary societies at this time as part of the 'bourgeois transformation of church life' (*die Verbürgerlichung des kirchlichen Lebens*), by which economically

(Bremen, 2005); Inge Mager, 'Weibliche Theologie'; Hartmut Lehmann, 'Die Arbeit der dienenden Liebe, oder: Zweierlei Emanzipation. Beobachtungen und Fragen zu einer Geschichte der weiblichen Diakonie', in Rainer Hering and Manfred Jakubowski-Tiessen, eds, *'Erinnern, was vergessen ist': Beiträge zur Kirchen-, Frömmigkeits- und Gendergeschichte. Festschrift für Ruth Albrecht* (Husum, 2020), 241–53.

[10] Franz Heinrich Neddermeyer, *Zur Statistik und Topographie der Freien und Hansestadt Hamburg und deren Gebietes* (Hamburg, 1847), 358.

[11] Friedrich Lücke, *Die zwiefache innere und äußere Mission der Evangelischen Kirche, ihrer gleiche Nothwendigkeit und nothwendige Verbindung; eine Rede in der Missions-Versammlung zu Göttingen den 13. Nov. 1842* (Hamburg, 1843).

[12] 'Die Christliche Mission ist zuächst und ursprünglich die Sendung des Evangeliums nach Außen, die Verbreitung der Christlichen Wahrheit und des Christlichen Lebens unter den Nichtchristen': ibid. 7.

ascendant members of the middle class were beginning to transform the public religious landscape of German-speaking Europe.[13] Amongst this plethora of new, extra-ecclesiastical German Protestant organizations, the Women's Association for the Care of the Poor and the Sick in Hamburg was nonetheless unique. Following the precedent of the German women's patriotic associations which had been formed during the Napoleonic wars under the aegis of Princess Marianne of Prussia in March 1813 to raise money, collect materials that were needed by the army, and nurse sick and wounded soldiers, Sieveking's association was the first religious voluntary society in Germany to be founded by a woman and to have an exclusively female membership.[14] For the first time in post-Reformation Germany, upper- and middle-class urban women had organized themselves into a religious voluntary society that was independent of any church, for the purpose of carrying out a public Christian ministry.[15] While in Roman Catholic areas and territories of Germany women's religious orders had long looked after the physical and spiritual needs of the poor in their local

[13] Michael Häusler, 'Vereinswesen / Kirchliche Vereine I', in Gerhard Müller, ed., *Theologische Realenzyklopädie*, 36 vols (Berlin, 2002), 34: 639–54; Ulrike Gleixner, *Pietismus und Bürgertum. Eine historische Anthropologie der Frömmigkeit* (Göttingen, 2005), 393.

[14] Wilhelm Baur, *Prinzess Wilhelm von Preussen, geborne Prinzess Marianne von Hessen-Homburg. Ein Lebensbild aus den Tagebüchern und Briefen der Prinzess* (Hamburg, 1886), 154–6, 187–90. These were established in the context of the wholesale closure in 1802 and 1803 of religious communities in areas of Germany that came under Napoleonic rule. These included three ancient German women's religious houses (*Damenstifte*) that had adopted Protestantism during the sixteenth century, thereby losing the autonomous constitutional status (*Reichsunmittelbarkeit*) that they had held within the Holy Roman Empire for over eight hundred and fifty years: Hans Peter Hankel, *Die reichsunmittelbaren evangelischen Damenstifte im Alten Reich und ihr Ende* (Berlin, 1996), 186–95. In 1844, Sieveking's society voted to appoint four men to act alongside her as trustees of the property that the society had acquired, C. C. Crasemann, G. C. Gorissen, W. Hübbe and H. M. Waitz; also in that year, Hamburg senator G. C. Lorenz Meyer began to advise the association on its financial accounts: Heinrich Sieveking, *Der weibliche (Sieveking'sche) Verein für Armen- und Krankenpflege in Hamburg* (Hamburg, 1932), 44–5, 95; Amalie Sieveking, *Zwölfter Bericht über die Leistungen des weiblichen Vereins für Armen- und Krankenpflege* (Hamburg, 1844), 24. [Hereafter annual reports of the Women's Association are referred to as *Bericht* with the corresponding report number and year.]

[15] Ingrid Lahrsen, *Zwischen Erweckung und Rationalismus. Hudtwalcker und sein Kreis* (Hamburg, 1959), 115–16; Postel, 'Amalie Sieveking'; Ute Gause, 'Frauen und Frömmigkeit im 19. Jahrhundert: Der Aufbruch in die Öffentlichkeit', *Pietismus und Neuzeit* 24 (1998), 309–27.

community, and had directly inspired Sieveking, her Protestant association did not require its members to make the degree of commitment that taking vows in a religious order entailed.[16] It permitted married women with children and other family responsibilities to participate fully in the association's work. As such, its activities, which included visiting the homes of those in need, providing jobs to unemployed men and women, and operating residential housing for low-income families, proved historically significant within the history of German Protestantism.

Another important context of Sieveking's decision to establish a religious voluntary association to practise Christian charity was the question of whose Christian duty it was to care for the sick and other vulnerable members of Hamburg society. While in other Protestant states in Germany, kings or dukes acted as the supreme bishop (*summus episcopus*) of the church in their lands, in Hamburg it was the city-state's Council (referred to as the Senate after 1814) that held the highest ecclesiastical authority; as a condition of holding public office, members had to promise to uphold the Lutheran Formula of Concord.[17] As part of Enlightenment-era

[16] Schmidt, *Beruf: Schwester*, 47–54. In her 1842 annual report, Sieveking commented that because the Women's Association was a 'Protestant confraternity', and not a Catholic religious order, an oath of obedience 'naturally, cannot and may not be introduced' ('Ein Gelübde des Gehorsams, wie es in den barmherzigen Schwesterschaften der katholischen Kirche Statt findet, kann und darf in eine protestantische Genossenschaft näturlich nicht eingeführt werden'): Sieveking, *Zehnter Bericht* (1842), 30–1. While Sieveking again emphasized her Protestant identity in the report for 1852, the Women's Association's statutes never introduced specific confessional requirements for membership, which is unsurprising given how homogeneously Lutheran Hamburg was: Sieveking, *Zwangzigster Bericht* [1852], 60. Moreover, Sieveking was not sectarian, but rather ecumenically oriented, recommending to the readers of her annual reports the writings of the Catholic priest Johann Michael Feneberg, and those of the Lutheran pastor Ludwig Hofacker: Sieveking, *Siebzehnter Bericht* [1849], 28; Sieveking, *Sechsundzwangzigster Bericht* [1858], 60. Remarking upon the vibrant Catholic faith of one man to whom the Women's Association had provided assistance, Sieveking wrote: 'Wie es mich freut, auch unter unsern Armen manchen Beleg zu finden zu dem, das freilich schon längst meine innigste Ueberzeugung: daß der seligmachende Glaube nicht gebunden ist an diese oder jene äussere Confession, daß der Herr Christus vielmehr in allen Confessionen seine unsichtbare Kirche hat' ('How it pleases me to find, even among our poor, some proof of what, admittedly, has for long been my most heartfelt conviction: that saving faith is not tied to this or that external confession, but, to the contrary, that the Lord Christ has, in all confessions, his invisible church'): Sieveking, *Einundzwangzigster Bericht* [1853], 58.
[17] Hans Georg Bergemann, *Staat und Kirche in Hamburg während des 19. Jahrhunderts* (Hamburg, 1958), 14–15.

ecclesiastical reforms (discussed below) that were adopted in 1788 with strong support from the city's Lutheran clergy, the Council decided to transfer responsibility for providing for the poor (and also the associated funds) away from the five main parish churches of Hamburg and invest them instead in a newly created General Foundation for Poor Relief (*allgemeine Armenanstalt*).[18]

Eighteenth-century Hamburgers did not regard this development as an act of aggressive secularization, but as one of social progress animated by Christian social concern for the poor. In December 1791, Joachim Christoph Bracke, pastor of the Hauptkirche Sankt Nikolai, one of the principal parish churches in Hamburg, emphasized this in comments he addressed to officers of the General Foundation during a sermon:

> Your foundation for the poor is the greatest, most comprehensive, and in the opinion of experts, the most consummate work in our German fatherland up until now. Over four thousand poor families find through your arrangement and supervision housing, work, sustenance, care, and the children of these poor receive education and help for their further advancement. May this monument of Christian patriotism, which you have established and built, remain the ornament of our city![19]

The historian Hans Otte has argued that the establishment of the General Foundation reflected a belief among Hamburg's patricians that the city's clergy lacked the expertise to administer on their own poor relief for a city of 130,000 inhabitants. After the enactment of these reforms in Hamburg, according to Otte, 'the church no longer had a function of its own in caring for the poor'.[20] These reforms shifted to civil authorities responsibilities for poor relief that had long

---

[18] Hans Otte, 'Kirchliche Armenpflege in norddeutschen Städte zwischen Aufklärung und Erweckung: Hamburg, Braunschweig, Osnabrück', *Pietismus und Neuzeit* 25 (1999), 125–57, at 131–4.

[19] 'Ihr Armen-Institut ist das größte, weitläuftigste und, nach dem Urtheil der Kenner, bis jetzt das vollkommenste Werk in umserm deutschen Vaterlande. Ueber vier tausend arme Familien finden unter Ihrer Anordnung und Aufsicht Wohnung, Arbeit, Unterhalt, Pflege, und die Kinder dieser Dürftigen Erziehung und Hülfe zu ihrem weitern Fortkommen. Dies Denkmahl des christlichen Patriotismus, das Sie gegründet und errichtet haben, bleibe die Zierde unserer Stadt!': Joachim Christoph Bracke, *Ermahnungs-Rede bei Eröffnung der Sonntagsschulen für die Armenkinder* (Hamburg, 1792), 15.

[20] Otte, 'Kirchliche Armenpflege', 134.

been the purview of Hamburg's church officials. By founding her voluntary society, Sieveking asserted that, in addition to the church and the state, individual Christians, too, including women, were also responsible to God for caring for the most vulnerable members of society. Sieveking came to this conclusion through her reading of Isaiah 58: 6–12 and Matthew 25:31–46: these admonitions to feed the hungry, clothe the naked, shelter the poor and care for the sick, she argued, gave a biblical mandate to her association's activities.[21]

THE FIRST CHOLERA OUTBREAK IN HAMBURG

After all the city's preparatory efforts, the first case of cholera in Hamburg was detected in early October 1831, only a few days after the new hospitals were furnished and made ready to receive patients. On 6 October, the medical examiner of Hamburg reported the first cholera fatality to the police, a sixty-seven-year-old man who, decades earlier, had been a sailor.[22] Prior to his death, the man had been living underground, twenty-four steps below street-level, in badly overcrowded conditions near the waterfront. He was one of forty-one men, women and children living together in living quarters that had been converted from a former dance hall, public house and bowling alley. The second person to die from cholera in the city was a twenty-eight-year-old woman, who had lived at the same location as the first victim for the past fifteen years. According to the medical examiner, both had lived lives of considerable hardship. The man had been a beggar for thirty-one years, the woman had worked as a prostitute since the age of eighteen, and both suffered from alcohol addiction.[23]

While the deprivations of the first two victims' housing conditions were severe, they were not atypical in Hamburg at that time, when the city was home to a reported 145,363 residents.[24] In November 1831, Johann Carl Georg Fricke, a physician, member of the city's

---

[21] Amalie Sieveking, 'Anrede an die Mitglieder des weiblichen Vereins für Armen- und Krankenpflege, den 23. Mai 1832', in *Zehnter Bericht* (1842), 56–68, at 56–8; Sieveking, *Zwangzigster Bericht* (1852), 23–68; Sieveking, *Zweiundzwangzigster Bericht* (1854), 39–58.

[22] Johann Carl Georg Fricke, *Geschichtliche Darstellung des Ausbruchs der asiatischen Cholera in Hamburg* (Hamburg, 1831), 23–7.

[23] Ibid. 27–8.

[24] Wolter, *Das Auftreten der Cholera*, 222.

board of health and founder of a medical school in Hamburg, authored a report on the cholera outbreak in which he discussed the city's housing stock.[25] According to Fricke,

> Hamburg has a large number of small, gloomy, damp alleyways, passages and courtyards in which numerous people dwell. Very many of them are only able to see the sun when they leave their homes. Very many of them, in fact, a numerous class of poor but hardworking, citizens, who are employed in the trades, live along larger alleys, but in low, gloomy and damp cellars ...[26]

Fricke explained that the nearby Elbe river flooded these cellar apartments several times each year for six to eight hours at a time. Residents were forced to shovel out the sediment deposited by the flood waters before they could reoccupy their homes. Fricke estimated that between 30,000 and 40,000 working class inhabitants of Hamburg, plus an additional 6,000 to 7,000 people in poverty, lived in such inadequate housing. Three or four generations residing together in one apartment was not uncommon. The dearth of quality housing in Hamburg and the accompanying social problems persisted for decades as the city-state's population increased at a higher annual rate than any of the other thirty-four states that belonged to the German Confederation, rising by 53 per cent between 1831 and 1858, when it reached 222,379.[27]

During the 1831 cholera epidemic in Hamburg, those who lived close to the harbour, the river and the canals, and those who worked as manual labourers, tradesmen and seamen, were especially, but not exclusively, affected by the disease.[28] While an estimated 10,000 people experienced some symptoms of cholera infection, Hamburg officials noted 937 particularly severe cases, of which approximately two-

---

[25] 'Johann Karl Georg Fricke', in Hans Schröder, ed., *Lexikon der hamburgischen Schriftsteller bis zur Gegenwart*, 8 vols (Hamburg, 1854), 2: 380–4.

[26] 'Hamburg hat eine große Anzahl kleiner, dumpfer, feuchter, Gäschen (Twieten), Gänge und Höfe, in denen eine Ueberzahl Menschen wohnen. Sehr viele von ihnen können nur dann die Sonne sehen, wenn sie ihre Wohngegend verlassen, sehr viele von ihnen, und zwar eine zahlreiche Classe geringer, aber fleißiger, gewerbtreibender Bürger, wohnen zwar in grösseren Gassen, aber in niedrigen, feuchten und dumpfen Kellern': Fricke, *Geschichtliche Darstellung*, 18.

[27] Georg von Viebahn, *Statistik des zollvereinten und nördlichen Deutschlands*, 2: *Bevölkerung, Bergbau, Bodenkultur* (Berlin, 1862), 40.

[28] Wolter, *Das Auftreten der Cholera*, 233–9; Karl Gottfried Zimmermann, *Die Cholera-Epidemie in Hamburg während des Herbstes 1831* (Hamburg, 1831), 40–1, 44–5, 51–2.

thirds were men and boys. Of these more severely ill cholera patients, 439 recovered and 498 died.[29] Following two months of declining numbers of new cases in December 1831 and January 1832, on 1 February 1832, 119 days after the first reported case in the city, government officials pronounced Hamburg free of cholera. The city's Lutheran, Reformed, Catholic, Mennonite and Anglican churches were asked to give thanks to God for preserving the city through the plague during their services on Sunday, 12 February 1832.[30]

However, the officials' assessment that the city was free of the disease proved to be premature. Cholera reappeared just two months later. Between 1 April and 22 December 1832, Hamburg endured a much worse outbreak than it had suffered in 1831. Over these thirty-eight weeks, there were 3,349 severe cases of cholera (2.3 per cent of Hamburg's population) resulting in 1,652 deaths (1.1 per cent of Hamburg's population).[31] Further outbreaks occurred in fourteen out of the next twenty-seven years, from 1833 to 1859, which cumulatively claimed the lives of 5,833 further residents of Hamburg.[32]

Hamburg's decades of public health struggles against cholera, its urban misery resulting from overcrowding and inadequate housing, to say nothing of the consequences of the great fire of May 1842, which, according to contemporary reports, killed 51 and left 19,995 men, women and children (approximately 11 per cent of the city's population) homeless, formed the social setting in which Amalie Sieveking founded and led her association.[33]

The Activities of the Women's Association for the Care of the Poor and the Sick

From 13 October to 6 December 1831, Amalie Sieveking lived at the cholera hospital and nursed its male and female patients. During the preceding eighteen years, she had worked in girls' education, having decided not to marry. Her interest in girls' welfare had been shaped in

[29] Wolter, *Das Auftreten der Cholera*, 38, 234.
[30] Richard Baker, *A Sermon on the Cessation of the Cholera in Hamburg* (Hamburg, 1832), 5.
[31] Wolter, *Das Auftreten der Cholera*, 244.
[32] Ibid. 254–6, 273–8, 282–95.
[33] Heinrich Schleiden, *Versuch einer Geschichte des großen Brandes in Hamburg vom 5. bis 8. Mai 1842* (Hamburg, 1843), 219–24.

Table 1. Cholera Deaths in Hamburg, 1831–59

Year	Cholera deaths
1831	498
1832	1,652
1833	46
1834	155
1835	8
1837	142
1848	1,772
1849	593
1850	440
1853	301
1854	311
1855	204
1856	78
1857	491
1858	7
1859	1,285

Source: Wolter, *Das Auftreten der Cholera*, 254–6, 273–8, 282–95.

part by her experience of losing her own mother at age five and her father at age fifteen. The trade embargo against Britain that Napoleon had introduced in November 1806 ruined her father's business and, as a result, following his death, she and her two brothers were all separated from each other.[34] After a period spent privately tutoring girls who came from a similar social milieu, in 1815 she co-founded a charity school that provided free education to girls from working class backgrounds.[35] In 1823 Sieveking published, anonymously, a collection of reflections on texts from the Old and New Testaments.[36] After receiving encouragement to write more on the Bible from Claus Harms, a prominent Lutheran pastor in nearby Kiel, and Johannes Geibel, an influential Reformed pastor in neighbouring Lübeck, she published a second volume of essays in 1827, again anonymously.[37]

[34] Grolle, 'Amalie Sieveking', 121.
[35] Ibid. 122.
[36] [Amalie Sieveking], *Betrachtungen über einzelne Abschnitte der heiligen Schrift* (Hamburg, 1823).
[37] [Amalie Sieveking] *Beschäftigungen mit der heiligen Schrift* (Hamburg, 1827); Kuessner, *Die Erweckungsbewegung in Hamburg*, 97. Sieveking later published a third

While the doctors in the hospital and the members of Hamburg's General-Gesundheits-Commission (General Health Commission) had initially been dismissive of Sieveking's abilities and sceptical of her commitment, during her eight weeks of voluntary work in autumn 1831 she was able to gain their respect, to the extent that upon her departure five of them presented her with their written thanks for her service.[38] As she wrote in a letter dated 16 March 1832 to her former governess, Wilhelmine Hösch, it was during her time in the hospital that she refined her plans for founding 'a women's association for the care of the poor and the sick'. Its purpose would be 'frequently and regularly to visit the poor sick in their own homes, to provide closer oversight of them than it is possible for the officials of the poor relief service to do, to show concern for their order and cleanliness, and for whatever else, by which they may be helped spiritually and physically'.[39] Sieveking further confided to Hösch that she had shared a draft of her plans for her envisaged association with two of the doctors from the hospital, Friedrich Siemssen and Joachim Friedrich Siemers, who had encouraged her and promised her their future support.[40]

On 23 May 1832, twelve other women, six married and six unmarried, met with Sieveking in the home of Anna Brunnemann, with whom she had lived after the death of her parents.[41] This

book, *Unterhaltungen über einzelne Abschnitte der heiligen Schrift* (Leipzig, 1855). Her references to August Hermann Francke and to the hymns of Paul Gerhardt, Gerhard Tersteegen, Christian Gellert and Philipp Spitta indicate how her own spirituality had been shaped by the Lutheran and pietist traditions.

[38] Poel, *Denkwürdigkeiten aus dem Leben*, 206.

[39] 'Daß mir dieses nun ziemlich allgemein eingeräumt wird, und man mir von dieser Seite mit Vertrauen entgegenkommt, ist mir jetzt insbesondere wichtig für die Ausführung eines neuen Planes, der mich seit meinem Aufenthalte im Hospital ernstlich beschäftigt, die Stiftung nämlich eines weiblichen Vereins für Armen- und Krankenpflege. Der Zweck desselben ist häufiger, regelmäßiger Besuch der armen Kranken in ihren Wohnungen, eine genauere Beaufsichtigung derselben, als diese der allgemeinen Armenordnung möglich ist, Sorge für Ordnung und Reinlichkeit und alles übrige, wodurch ihnen geistig und leiblich aufgeholfen werden mag': Amalie Sieveking, 'Aus einem Briefe von Amalie Sieveking an Minchen Hösch vom. 16.3.1832 über ihre Schule, den Dienst im Cholera-Hospital 1831 und den Entwurf des Vereins', in Heinrich Sieveking, *Der weibliche (Sieveking'sche) Verein*, 75–9, at 78.

[40] Ibid. 78.

[41] Poel, *Denkwürdigkeiten aus dem Leben*, 209, 215.

gathering marked the first meeting of the Women's Association for the Care of the Sick and the Poor. Sieveking opened with prayer:

Lord, our Saviour, we thank you, that you have guided us together, and united us in a work, that, we hope, will glorify your name! ... Kindle within us the fervour of your love, and make us ready to be instruments of blessing. Yes, allow your kingdom to be advanced by the undertaking for which we have now come together![42]

Sieveking next spoke about some of the obstacles she anticipated that they would face: the distress they might feel from seeing the miserable conditions in which some people in Hamburg lived, the mockery of those who thought the women foolish or vainglorious for what they were trying to do, and the frustration of being rebuffed or disrespected by the people whom they were trying to help. Sieveking also stressed that the members of the association ought to be humble and respectful in their interactions with those who had already for many years been providing services to the poor, Hamburg's relief officers (*Armenpfleger*) and the physicians who worked closely with them (*Armenärzte*).

Under the Enlightenment-era reforms introduced in Hamburg in 1788, whose proponents had included Amalie Sieveking's uncle, Georg Heinrich Sieveking, the administration of all the city's poor relief services had been reorganized under the General Foundation for Poor Relief (*allgemeine Armenanstalt*). Supervising these efforts was a board (*Großes Armen-Collegium*) that consisted of church treasurers, state officials and prominent citizens, of whom seventeen functioned as an executive council (*Kleines Armen-Collegium*).[43] This council oversaw the poor relief efforts in five districts (*Haupt-Armenbezirke*). The two superintendents (*Armenvorsteher*) of each district sat on the executive council, along with five members of the city

---

[42] 'Herr, unser Heiland, wir danken Dir, dass Du uns, zusammengeführt, zu einem Werke, uns vereinigt hast, davon wir hoffen, daß Dein Namen dadurch verherrlicht werden solle! ... Entflamme in uns die Gluth Deiner Liebe, und bereite uns so zu Werkzeugen des Segens. Ja, laß auch durch dieses Unternehmen, dazu wir jetzt zusammengetreten, Dein Reiche gefördert werden!': Sieveking, 'Anrede an die Mitglieder', 56–7.

[43] 'Neue Hamburgische Armen-Ordnung, beliebt durch Rath- und Bürger-Schluß den 18 Februar und 7 Juli 1788', in Johann Arnold Günther, ed., *Vollständige Einrichtungen der neuen Hamburgischen Armen-Anstalt*, 4 parts (Hamburg, 1788), 1: 7–48, at 7–22; Mary Lindemann, *Patriots and Paupers: Hamburg, 1712–1830* (Oxford, 1990), 111–34.

council, and two lay church officers (*Oberalte*). Each of the five districts was further subdivided into twelve quarters (*Armen-Quartiere*) and each quarter was served by three relief officers (*Armenpfleger*). The boundaries of the quarters were drawn so that each encompassed an area with roughly fifty needy families.[44] Additionally, the five districts were each served by at least one physician and one surgeon to whom the relief officers could refer poor residents for medical care.[45] Clergy (*Pfarrer*) were permitted to serve neither on the board nor on the council of the General Foundation for Poor Relief; nor might they function as relief officers.[46] By 1832, the number of relief officers per city quarter had been reduced from three to two, even as a sixth district with eight new city quarters had been added. That year there were twenty-one superintendents, 136 relief officers, twelve physicians, seven surgeons, and thirty-three apothecaries providing care for the poor of Hamburg.[47]

Sieveking's association was in no way intended to supplant the work of the General Foundation for Poor Relief in Hamburg. Sieveking recognized that the latter provided financial and practical assistance on a far greater scale than her association ever could. For example, in 1832, when the average weekly wage of a factory worker was approximately eight Hamburg marks a week, the General Foundation received an income of 299,133 Hamburg marks (215,500 in state funding, plus 83,633 from private donations) and, drawing upon its capital reserves, disbursed 336,872 Hamburg marks in various services to the poor.[48] Sieveking's was a far smaller operation: the annual reports show that between 1833

---

[44] Werner von Melle, *Die Entwicklung des öffentlichen Armenwesens in Hamburg* (Hamburg, 1883), 70.

[45] 'Des großen Armen-Collegii näher Erläuterung für die Herren Armen-Pfleger, über die Grundsätze und Einrichtungen der neuen Armen-Anstalt, und über die nach Maasgabe der neuen Armen-Ordnung von ihnen zu übernehmenden Geschäfte', in Günther, ed., *Vollständige Einrichtungen*, 4: 1–176, at 82–98.

[46] Otte, 'Kirchliche Armenpflege', 133.

[47] 'Personale der Hamburgischen allgemeinen Armen-Anstalt für das Jahr 1832, mit beygefügter Eintheilung sämmtlicher Armen-Quartiere, und einem topographischen Register', in J. C. Köster, ed., *Hamburgischer Staats-Kalender auf das Schalt-Jahr 1832* (Hamburg, 1832), 81–8.

[48] Johann Christoph Friedrich Nessmann, 'Ein Beitrag zur Statistik der Löhne und Preise', in *Statistik der Hamburgischen Staats* 8 (1876), 114–18, at 115; Caspar Freyherr von Voght, *Gesammeltes aus der Geschichte der Hamburgischen Armen-Anstalt während ihrer funfzigjährigen Dauer* (Hamburg, 1838), 140.

and 1858 the average annual income of her association was 12,600 Hamburg marks, and the most income it received in any one year was 30,593 Hamburg marks. Rather, Sieveking saw the task of her association as supplementing the aid that the civil authorities were able to provide by focusing on individuals who had been overlooked by the poor relief system but would benefit from personal attention.[49] Moreover, Sieveking regarded her association's activities as a public, collective expression of its members' Christian faith, one which she likened to the ministrations of the deaconesses in the ancient churches.[50] As she wrote in the association's first annual report, by befriending people who were sick, who were living in difficult circumstances or who were on their deathbeds, they sought to reconcile to God those whose bitterness and despair had estranged them.[51]

Sieveking relied on written recommendations from the city's poor relief officers, district physicians and other individuals whose judgement she trusted when identifying whose who would benefit from a visit.[52] If a poor person applied directly for assistance, Sieveking would first speak with them. Once convinced that the association could help, she coordinated with the relevant district physician and requested information about the person's living situation and their family's circumstances, provided on a form. Questions included: what support the family was already receiving from the General Foundation, what illnesses the members of the house suffered from, what kind of diet the physician recommended to help them with their illness, and whether they 'belonged to the class of the honourable poor', by which Sieveking meant that they did not abuse alcohol, 'make a living from begging' or live out of wedlock.[53] The Women's Association helped both those who were already receiving support from the General Foundation and those who were not. In 1840, the association amended its statutes to limit the eligibility for new cases of assistance to those in which a formerly '[wage-]earning member of the family is seriously ill'.[54]

[49] Amalie Sieveking, *Bericht über die Leistungen des weiblichen Vereins für Armen-und Krankenpflege* (Hamburg, 1833), 7–8.
[50] Sieveking, *Dritter Bericht* (1835), 35–6; Sieveking, *Sechster Bericht* (1838), 21.
[51] Sieveking, *Bericht* (1833), 19–20.
[52] Ibid. 2–3.
[53] Sieveking, *Zweiter Bericht* (1834), 2; Sieveking, *Dreizehnter Bericht* (1845), 27.
[54] '[V]or allen übrigen, da in der Regel nur Familien aufgenommen werden, in denen ein erwerbendes Mitglied ernstlich erkrant ist': Sieveking, *Achter Bericht* (1840), 1.

Once the association had accepted a family for assistance, Sieveking was generally the first member of the society to visit them in their home. Thereafter, according to their level of need, a rota of between three to six women from the association took turns visiting the family twice weekly, weekly or twice monthly. There were two reasons for this policy. Sieveking believed that the association could better evaluate how best to address the family's needs by having multiple perspectives on their situation. Additionally, she hoped that each member of the society would become more adept at assessing how to help the poor by visiting multiple families. Sieveking hoped that through receiving these visits, the family would be encouraged that there were people who cared about their welfare and who were working to help them obtain food, other necessities that they lacked and employment. In becoming a member of the association, the women visitors also promised to foster the Christian faith of those whom they visited, by engaging them in spiritual discussion and encouraging them to read the Bible and edifying Christian books, attend church worship services and find enjoyment in taking holy communion.[55]

After each visit, the members of the association were required to write a report, again using a form designed by Sieveking. These reports, submitted to and collated by her, served as the basis for discussions at the association's weekly meetings. These were held on Wednesday afternoons in a room in the Hamburg government administration building (*Stadthaus*) that had been procured for them by senator Martin Hieronymus Hudtwalcker, who sat on the

[55] Sieveking, *Zweiter Bericht* (1834), 3; Sieveking, *Neunter Bericht* (1841), 47–81. Regarding the association's efforts to encourage those whom they visited to read the Bible and Christian literature, historians estimate that the literacy rate in the German Confederation in the 1840s was approximately 80 to 85 per cent; according to Prussian Army statistics, 91 per cent of the men conscripted in 1841 could read and write at a basic level. While Hamburg city officials did not include statistics on literacy rates in their contemporary reports, 304 church-affiliated, state-sponsored and private schools served an urban population of 209,823 in 1848, while only 180 schools operated in 1846 in Berlin, where the population was 389,308: Thomas Nipperdey, 'Mass Education and Modernization: The Case of Germany 1780–1850', *TRHS*, 5th series 27 (1977), 155–72, at 161; Peter Flora, *Indikatoren der Modernisierung: Ein historisches Datenhandbuch* (Wiesbaden, 1975), 67; 'Zahl und Gattung der Unterrichtsanstalten', in *Statistik des Hamburgischen Staats* (Hamburg, 1872), 20–4, at 23; 'Statistische Uebersicht des öffentlichen Unterrichts im preußischen Staate im Jahre 1816 und in Jahre 1846', *Mittheilungen des statistischen Bureau's in Berlin* 1 (1849), 33–51.

executive council of the General Foundation for Poor Relief.[56] Using the money that it received from its donors, and gifts in kind from butchers, bakers, grocers and other benevolent people, the association distributed the necessities of life to those whom they visited. For example, according to its accounts for 1835, the association administered weekly donations of meat and bread, provided vouchers for peat fuel for home heating, and paid for other foodstuffs, clothing, clean bedding for the families of tuberculosis patients, medicines, transportation to the doctor and children's school fees. Inspired by the society, other women in Hamburg also began to invite the families whom the society visited for weekly meals in their homes. Additionally, each member received two Hamburg schillings per family visit, per week, that she could use at her discretion to purchase items for the family.[57] Sieveking determined that any greater expenditure of the association's funds had to be discussed as a group. All the association's annual reports record such expenditure and disbursements of food and other needed items.

Most of the association's funds were devoted to creating opportunities for employment. In its second annual report, Sieveking argued forcefully that the saying 'one only has to want to work, in order to find work in Hamburg' was simply not true.[58] Sieveking had seen first-hand evidence during her visits that some people were unemployed not because of any character fault, but because they were overburdened by their caring duties for sick or disabled family members. Others experienced financial difficulties when their wares did not sell at the expected time or for the desired price, while still others simply had genuine difficulties finding suitable employment. Like many from her class background, Sieveking believed that the poor could improve their living conditions by adopting 'the virtues of middle-class life: industriousness, good housekeeping, order, cleanliness, faithfulness and integrity'.[59] However, Sieveking also had compassion for the apparent absence of these qualities in those whom the association visited, and she believed that they could be nurtured by providing employment opportunities.

---

[56] Sieveking, *Bericht* (1833), 4–5
[57] In Hamburg, sixteen schillings were equivalent to one mark.
[58] 'Wer in Hamburg nur arbeiten will, der kann auch Arbeit finden': Sieveking, *Zweiter Bericht* (1834), 16–17.
[59] '[D]ie Tugenden des bürgerlichen Lebens: Betriebsamkeit, gutes Haushalten, Ordnung, Reinlichkeit, Treue und Wahrhaftigkeit': Sieveking, *Fünfter Bericht* (1837), 17.

Andrew Kloes

In accordance with this conviction, from 1833 to 1858, between 49 per cent and 74 per cent of the association's annual expenditure was dedicated to paying the wages of poor men and women employed to undertake a variety of types of work. For example, the association hired some of its clients to do the laundry of other families who were too sick to do it themselves; they paid others to nurse sick people or to clean their homes while they convalesced. Among those the association engaged were carpenters, metalworkers, potters, shoemakers and tailors, who were supported to ply their trades for the benefit of others for whom the association was caring. The association also employed people to process and spin silk, flax and wool, to knit garments or to make feather beds or cushions and seagrass mattresses.[60] Some of these products were intended for commercial sale, but most, particularly shoes, were produced for the families whom the association visited. Sieveking believed that not only having work, but having the security of regular guaranteed wages formed an integral part of a person's health and well-being.[61]

In 1837, the Women's Association received a large donation of 10,300 Hamburg marks, from an anonymous man whom Sieveking described as 'a ninety-year-old foreign Christian philanthropist'.[62] This enabled the association to expand the scope of its activities and to provide accommodation to families in need of housing. Using these funds, and land donated by the government, the association built a complex of nine simple flats of three and four rooms each; the first families were welcomed on 15 November 1840, paying below market-rate rents of between 30 and 36 Hamburg marks per year. Known as the Amalie Home (*Amalienstift*), the building was equipped with shared facilities for cooking, laundry and storage, and a common room in which residents could gather for morning and evening readings from the Bible and Johann Arndt's devotional work, *True Christianity*.[63] On the first floor were two larger and two smaller rooms, out of which two physicians in partnership with the association, Otto Moraht and Adalbert

[60] Sieveking, *Dritter Bericht* (1835), 14; Sieveking, *Fünfundzwanzigster Bericht* (1857), 10; Sieveking, *Siebzehnter Bericht* (1849), 10.
[61] Sieveking, *Neunter Bericht* (1841), 19.
[62] '[E]inem jetzt schon 90jährigen auswärtigen christlichen Menschenfreunde': ibid. 25.
[63] Ibid. 22–45.

Rambach, operated a children's hospital.[64] Starting with this building, the association acquired other proprieties, and by 1901 it was
operating five homes that provided accommodation for a total of
105 families.[65]

CONCLUSION

From one perspective, the achievements of the Women's Association
were modest. According to the statistics included in the twenty-six
annual reports that Sieveking wrote before her death in April 1859,
the members and income of the association grew from 20 women and
1,322 Hamburg marks in 1833, to 61 and 7,827 in 1843, to 80 and
12,852 in 1853. Altogether, between May 1832 and May 1858, a
total of 193 different women joined the association and visited a
total of 1,192 impoverished families in Hamburg. During the nearly
three decades that Sieveking led the organization, it addressed the
physical needs of several thousand vulnerable people in Hamburg
and attempted to encourage them in the Christian life of faith.
This was a small proportion of the needy poor in Hamburg in
these years. However, the association's broader historical significance
lies in the fact that it demonstrated for the first time that Protestant
women could organize and operate an effective public ministry in
German society.

On 25 October 1841 Sieveking discussed her inseparable concerns
for the welfare of the poor, the evangelization of Germany and the
social agency of women, when, at the invitation of Georg
Treviranus, the pastor of a Reformed congregation in Bremen, she
spoke to three hundred men and women gathered in a public hall.
After recounting how Jesus's exhortation in Matthew 25 that
Christians should care for the vulnerable members of society had
motivated her to establish her association, Sieveking elaborated on
what she hoped her association would do for women in German society, particularly those who came from the burgeoning middle class:

> I had two things in mind with the idea that I was seeking to bring to
> life. I certainly hoped it would be a blessing to the poor and those in

[64] Otto Moraht and Adalbert Rambach, 'Die Krankensäle im Amalienstifte', in
Sieveking, *Zehnter Bericht*, (1842) 93–6.
[65] Theodor Schäfer, 'Stifte und Heime', in Daheim-Schriftleitung, ed., *Daheim-Kalender
für das Deutsche Reich auf das Gemeinjahr 1901* (Leipzig, 1901), 241–63, at 255.

need, however, my attention was not directed towards that alone. At least as important to me was the blessing that I hoped it would bring to those of my fellow sisters who would join me in such words of love. The higher interests of my sex lay close to my heart …[66]

Sieveking lamented the attitudes that disrespected and disregarded widows and older women who did not have husbands or children as being unable to make a useful contribution to society. At the same time, she criticized the amount of time that young unmarried women were encouraged to dedicate to the 'fineries and vanities' of embroidery, dressmaking and dances. Empathizing with these young women from middle- and upper-class backgrounds, Sieveking considered it unavoidable that 'feelings of emptiness so often take hold of them, the vague yearning, the longing to get out of their circumstances'.[67] In response to these and other limitations that society had placed on women, it had been her goal to create alternative opportunities for women to exercise leadership and undertake meaningful responsibilities in public life through Christian service: 'How to unite all this dormant strength in common work for the Kingdom of God, that was the task I set myself, the solution to which I began to deliberate, as soon as I left the cholera hospital.'[68]

Sieveking's association met with a positive reception across northern and western Europe largely due to the wide readership of her detailed, published annual reports. In addition to financial information on the association's income and expenditures, these included lengthy essays on practical, social, political and theological topics related to their work. Among the readers of Sieveking's reports were Queen Caroline Amalie of Denmark and Queen Elisabeth of Prussia, who corresponded with her and later received her when

---

[66] 'Bei der Idee, die ich jetzt ins Leben zu rufen suchte, schwebte ein Zweifaches mir vor. Wohl hoffte ich davon einen Zeugen für die Armen und Notleidenden; aber nicht darauf allein hatte ich mein Augenmerk gerichtet; wenigstens eben so wichtig war mir der Segen, den ich mir davon für diejenigen meiner Mitschwestern versprach, die sich zu solchem Liebesworte mit mir verbinden würden. Die höheren Interessen meines Geschlechts lagen mir am Herzen': Amalie Sieveking, 'Vortrag von A. W. Sieveking gehalten am 25. October 1841 im Saale der Seefahrt in Bremen', in Sieveking, *Zehnter Bericht* (1842), 69–93, at 73.
[67] '[D]aher das Gefühl der Leere, das sich ihrer so oft bemächtigt, das unbestimmte Sehnen, das Hinausverlangen aus ihren Verhältnissen': ibid. 75.
[68] 'Alle diese brachliegenden Kräfte zu einem gemeinsamen Wirken für das Reich Gottes zu vereinigen, das war die Aufgabe, die ich mir gestellt, und auf deren Lösung ich Bedacht nahm, sobald ich das Cholera-Hospital verlassen': ibid.

she visited Copenhagen in 1843 and Berlin in 1849.[69] However, her
initiative inspired many other women, and also some men. By 1842,
other women's religious voluntary societies modelled on Sieveking's
had been formed in twenty-six cities and towns across Europe,
including Bern, Bonn, Bremen, Danzig, Frankfurt-am-Main,
Hannover, London, Paris, Potsdam, Rotterdam, Stuttgart, Tallinn
and Zürich.[70] Sieveking's pioneering work in Hamburg also encouraged the growth of the modern German Protestant deaconess movement, established in October 1836 when Theodor and Friederike
(née Münster) Fliedner opened a hospital and deaconess-training
institute (*Diakonissen Bildungs-Anstalt*) in Kaiserswerth. After
Friederike Fliedner died in childbirth, Theodor Fliedner married
Caroline Bertheau, a former pupil of Sieveking's. By 1878, deaconess
institutes founded on the model of Kaiserswerth had been established
in another twenty-seven cities in the German empire and twenty cities in Britain, Europe and the United States. In aggregate, these institutes had trained 3,908 deaconesses, who worked in 1,095 locations,
including asylums, hospices, hospitals, orphanages, prisons and
schools.[71] However, unlike Sieveking's association, the institutes
that followed the model of Kaiserswerth did not permit married
women to serve as deaconesses.

Sieveking continued to be an influential figure among German
Protestant women long after her death in 1859. Emma Poel, to
whom Sieveking had entrusted her personal papers, published a biography in 1860, which was quickly translated into English, Danish,
Dutch and French. Among those in the twentieth century to be
inspired by Sieveking was Eva Hoffman-Aleith. After receiving her
doctorate in church history from the University of Berlin in 1937,
Hoffmann-Aleith later functioned as the emergency pastor of a
Confessing Church congregation in Brandenburg during the
Second World War. Hoffmann-Aleith introduced her own biography
of Sieveking in 1940 by noting:

[69] Poel, *Denkwürdigkeiten aus dem Leben*, 278–9, 310–12.
[70] Johann Hinrich Wichern, 'Vorwort', in Poel, *Denkwürdigkeiten aus dem Leben*, iii–xii,
at vii–viii. Others women's associations were located in Altona, Celle, Göttingen, Jülich,
Lübeck, Ratzeburg, Gotha, Osnabrück, Stade, St Gallen, St Georg (a suburb of
Hamburg), Weimar and Wernigerode.
[71] Theodor Schäfer, *Die Geschichte der weiblichen Diakonie*, 2 vols (Hamburg, 1879), 1:
234–7.

Anyone who immerses themselves in the writings of Amalie Sieveking, becomes gripped by the words of this woman of great character. Here one finds, the rare integration of person and work, Protestant faith and conscientious deeds. What she has to say to German girls and German women about true womanhood, which unites in a harmonious whole, empathy, clarity of understanding and resoluteness of character, remains of everlasting importance.[72]

Arguably the greatest testimony to Sieveking's legacy is that in 2021, the association she founded over 189 years ago continues to assist vulnerable people in Hamburg.[73]

While Sieveking has long been admired for her Christian social conscience, the sources examined in this article illustrate how her association's achievements rested not only on her ability to articulate a compelling theological vision for their work, but also on her skills as organizer and administrator. In addition to building rapport with those on whose behalf she organised aid for over twenty-five years, Sieveking's public ministry required her to be able continually to inspire other women to join her, to evaluate many applications for assistance, to assess numerous reports of her members' visits to clients, to oversee and coordinate the different committees of her association, to make decisions about the association's finances, to manage relationships with government officials and those who contributed funds and needed items to her association, and to prepare yearly reports on the association's activities to give account to donors and publicize the work to a wide readership in Hamburg and beyond. In all these ways, Sieveking worked to rouse the 'dormant strength' of Christian women and create new possibilities for their participation in German society.

---

[72] 'Jeder, der sich in die Schriften von Amalie Sieveking vertieft, wird innerlich gepackt von den Worten dieser charaktervollen Frau. Hier decken sich, wie selten, Person und Werk, evangelischer Glaube und verantwortungsbewußtes Tun. Von unvergänglicher Bedeutung bleibt, was sie dem deutschen Mädchen und der deutschen Frau über echte Weiblichkeit zu sagen hat, in der sich ein weiches Gefühl, Klarheit des Verstandes und Festigkeit des Charakters zu einem harmonischen Ganzen verbinden sollen': Eva Hoffmann-Aleith, *Amalie Sieveking. Die Mutter der Armen und Kranken* (Göttingen, 1940), 3.
[73] Amalie Sieveking-Stiftung, 'Mehr als 185 Jahre Engagement in Hamburg-St. Georg', 9 January 2021, online at: <https://www.sieveking-stiftung.de/>, accessed 4 August 2021.

Health and Sickness as Reality and Metaphor in the Oratory Parish of F. W. Faber, 1849–63

Melissa Wilkinson*

Welwyn Garden City

This article examines the first London Oratory, located in King William St, London between May 1849 and March 1854, during the provostship of its founder F. W. Faber (1814–63). Beginning with a discussion of the physically unhealthy climate at the Oratory and the situation of its congregation, it then considers Faber's health while provost before examining his use of words such as sickness, illness, health and infection in written works and analysing his use of these as metaphors for the spiritual life. The metaphorical concepts of health and sickness are linked to his pessimism about humanity and his preoccupation with the four last things, obtaining eternal salvation, and the relationship between the individual Christian and God. The article thus highlights something of the spirituality, health and teaching of an individual priest, as well as the preoccupations of a parish in mid-nineteenth-century London.

Frederick William Faber (1814–63) was the founder and first provost of the London Oratory. Initially based at King William St (now William IV St), Strand, from 31 May 1849, the congregation moved to Brompton on 1 March 1854. Drawing on Faber's correspondence and preaching, this article discusses health and sickness as reality and metaphor. It falls into three parts. After a brief biographical sketch of Faber, it introduces the reality of the parish based at King William St, which spans the years before and after the restoration of the Roman Catholic hierarchy in England and Wales in November 1850, and the creation of the diocese of Westminster, to which the Oratory subsequently belonged. We see how Faber responded to parishioners and the preoccupations of the parish, including its response to the poverty in the area. Secondly, the article discusses the reality of sickness and health in the lives of Faber and his community. Thirdly, it examines metaphors of sickness, suffering, illness, infection and health as they were used by Faber in discussing

* E-mail: dr.m.j.wilkinson@btinternet.com.

Studies in Church History 58 (2022), 241–261   © The Author(s), 2022. Published by
Cambridge University Press on behalf of Ecclesiastical History Society
doi: 10.1017/stc.2022.12

the spiritual life in letters and sermons between his foundation of the London Oratory in May 1849 and his death at Brompton in September 1863. This will highlight something of Faber's spirituality, teaching and theology, and show how the metaphorical concepts of health and sickness are linked to his pessimism about humanity and his preoccupation with the four last things, obtaining eternal salvation and the relationship between the individual Christian and God.

This article provides a glimpse into ideas which will be developed more fully and extended in my current research project, a study of the London Oratory at King William St and Brompton. Its aim is to add to the relatively small body of work on Faber by presenting Faber and the London Oratory in a broader historical and social context.

THE LONDON ORATORY AT KING WILLIAM STREET

Frederick William Faber was born at Calverley, Yorkshire, on 28 June 1814. After attending Harrow School and University College, Oxford, he was ordained priest in the Church of England in 1839, becoming vicar of Elton, Huntingdonshire, in 1842. In November 1845 he became a Roman Catholic. His hope was to bring the Oratory, an order of secular priests living together without vows and founded in Rome by St Philip Neri (1515–95), to England, but because Bishop (later Cardinal) Wiseman[1] rejected the idea he founded a religious order, the Brothers of the Will of God (also known as Wilfridians), in Birmingham.[2] The community moved to Cotton, Staffordshire, in October 1846 at the request of John Talbot, the sixteenth earl of Shrewsbury (1791–1852), who lived nearby at Alton Towers. However, in January 1849 Faber and his community returned to Birmingham in order to join the newly formed English Oratory established by John Henry Newman (1801–90). Faber moved to London on 15 April 1849 to become founder and first provost of the London Oratory.

---

[1] Faber knew Nicholas Wiseman (1802–65) as bishop of the Central District, which included Birmingham, and later as vicar apostolic of the London District. After the restoration of the Roman Catholic hierarchy in England and Wales in November 1850, Wiseman became the first cardinal archbishop of Westminster.

[2] Melissa Wilkinson, *Frederick William Faber: A Great Servant of God* (Leominster, 2007), 124.

Faber's letters immediately after his arrival in London are concerned with the difficulties of starting a new parish. On 29 April he was able to write to Newman, who was living at the Birmingham Oratory, which had been founded in January 1849: 'Your sons are at last safely housed, amid dirt and disorder, but very happy and comfortable.'[3] One month later, on 31 May, the new Oratory was officially opened with high mass at which Bishop Wiseman preached.[4] The building, which had not yet been redecorated from its former use as a 'gin shop',[5] was situated on one side of a wedge-shaped group of buildings bordered by King William St and Agar St, both of which led out onto the Strand, and Chandos St.[6] Reference to a map of 1843 reveals its surroundings to have been a mixture of residential, commercial and civic buildings, including the church of St Martin-in-the-Fields and its workhouse, while the Oratorians' immediate neighbours were Charing Cross Hospital and the Royal Westminster Ophthalmic Hospital.[7] The 1851 census records that individuals and families living in King William St had been born in diverse parts of the country, and formed part of the general migration to cities such as London during the nineteenth century. Their occupations included printer, accountant, military outfitter, lead seller, bookseller, architect, watchmaker, bricklayer, coffee house keeper, musician and carriage painter. Many of the buildings that Faber would have known were demolished and rebuilt from the 1860s onwards.

Faber seems to have had a good relationship with members of his congregation at King William St[8] and the large attendance at services indicates that they responded positively to his preaching and to his community's apostolate in general. Faber's letters reveal that those who attended the Oratory came from all strata of society, including

---

[3] Raleigh Addington, ed., *Faber – Poet and Priest: Selected Letters by Frederick William Faber 1833–1863* (London, 1974), 188–9 (F. W. Faber to J. H. Newman, 29 April 1849).

[4] London, London Oratory [hereafter: LO], MSS 2, no. 3, Faber to Newman, 2 May 1849.

[5] Addington, ed., *Faber*, 185 (Faber to Newman, 16 April 1849).

[6] B. R. Davies, *London, 1843* (London, 1843), online at *David Rumsey Map Collection*: <http://rumsey.geogarage.com/maps/g0890184.html?lat=51.509082704910874&lon=-0.12380046007774759&zoom=17>, accessed 31 October 2020.

[7] 'The Royal Westminster Ophthalmic Hospital' (n.d.), online at *Lost Hospitals of London*: <https://www.ezitis.myzen.co.uk>, accessed 30 October 2020.

[8] Wilkinson, *Faber*, 134.

titled or well-off individuals, identifiable because they were those whom Faber asked for money to support the Oratory, as well as English and Irish poor. Many of the latter arrived in London as a result of the potato famine in 1846, and Faber wrote to Lord Arundel: 'We live among the lowest poor; our whole lives are sacrificed to the Irish.'[9] Faber's letters to Newman are full of bravado, intended to impress the community in Birmingham. Thus, at the beginning of June he wrote: 'Confessions are increasing, and the numbers at the weekday masses, and we have worshippers before ye tabernacle all day, and quite thick towards evening.'[10] In July: 'The chapel is always crammed. Confessions increase. Our Communions average at present 250 a week, i.e. 13000 per annum.'[11] In August: 'I wish we had counted the penitents of the last two days; they must have been several hundreds. I think I absolved 60 at one sitting last night; the communions have been marvellous'.[12]

The darker side to this bravado is that Faber wrote of opprobrium from other clergy in London because members of Roman Catholic parishes in the city and converts from the Church of England were attending the Oratory.[13] Faber opined: 'We are hearing on all sides about ourselves and ye hatred against us. Persons coming to say they can come here no more, because Revd Mr so and so says he won't visit them when dying if they do and such things.'[14] Also, 'I think also a *little* jealousy has been created by the retreat from the flux of coronetted [*sic*] carriages, so you must be prepared to hear we do not care for the poor.'[15] Faber's letters give the impression that some came to King William St because of its novelty whereas others came because they were being given something spiritual that they were not receiving elsewhere.

Although Faber's community was situated in the middle of a city where poverty, cholera, disease and unsanitary conditions were constantly present, it was also a time of change, the result of legislation that included the Public Health Act (1848). In a sermon published under the title 'Our Lord's Choice of Poverty', Faber preached that 'there is no dignity or poetry about poverty, as about other

---

[9] Addington, ed., *Faber*, 242 (Faber to Lord Arundel, 11 March 1852).
[10] LO, MSS 2, no. 41, Faber to Newman, 6 June 1849.
[11] Addington, ed., *Faber*, 196 (Faber to Newman, 6 July 1849).
[12] Ibid. 200 (Faber to Newman, 15 August 1849).
[13] LO, MSS 2, no. 213, Faber to Newman, 15 January 1850.
[14] Ibid., no. 127, Faber to Newman, 18 October 1849.
[15] Addington, ed., *Faber*, 211 (Faber to Newman, 6 March 1850).

suffering',[16] and in the similarly titled 'Poverty the Choice of Jesus', he identified the 'discontent of a poor man' and 'ill temper' which arise when such a man compares himself with those who are rich. Here Faber's aim was to contrast the poverty of Jesus, by implication authentic, with the 'comforts of poor men in general'. He preached: 'However dark your way may seem, however multiplied your hardships and your woes, you are what Jesus chose to be, and is not that fortune enough to make you richer than all this poor perishing world can give?'[17] Faber did not ignore poverty, which he was unable to relieve, but created a scriptural framework through which his poor parishioners could view their predicament.

As well as poverty, parishioners brought sickness into the church, together with dirt, fleas and smells which were reportedly so disgusting that they made other parishioners and community alike nauseous, leading to liberal use of incense during mass. During the painting[18] of the church one month after its opening in June 1849, Faber wrote, 'The house is dreadful; the paint has driven the fleas out of the chapel and so they have come into the house. Brother Chad [Strickson] catches them by handfuls.'[19] Later he complained: 'The frontals of ye altars it appears are filled with bugs, and ye room in which they were put is swarming with them; and alas! so is ye altar linen.' Another reason for the fetid atmosphere was bad sanitation. However, although Faber indicates that he had a lavatory in his room, inherited from its days as a gin shop,[20] he gives no further details as to the presence or efficacy of further hygiene facilities. A month later, Faber wrote of cholera in the Oratory house and wider area, including Charing Cross Hospital next door.[21] Faber, who also had cholera and was 'very much out of spirits',[22] wrote to Newman: 'We are all giddy, sick and tired, in great measure from ye heat and effluvia of ye chapel'.[23] This continued into August, during

---

[16] F. W. Faber, 'Our Lord's Choice of Poverty', in John Bowden, ed., *Notes on Doctrinal and Spiritual Subjects*, 1: *Mysteries and Festivals*, 3rd edn (London, 1866), 127.

[17] Ibid. 129.

[18] Although the church was painted in June, it was not fitted with a permanent altar, organ and pews until its formal opening in October.

[19] Addington, ed., *Faber*, 198 (Faber to Newman, 2 July 1849).

[20] LO, MSS 2, no. 109, Faber to Newman, 6 September 1849.

[21] Ibid., no. 91, Faber to Newman, 19 July 1849; no. 101, Faber to Newman, 14 August 1849.

[22] Ibid., no. 105, Faber to Newman, 18 August 1849.

[23] Ibid., no. 103, Faber to Newman, 15 August 1849.

which time Faber wrote that he had 'chronic inflammation of the bowels',[24] probably as a result of having had cholera. Part of the problem was the building itself:

> All considered our chapel dangerous in respect of cholera. Some police courts, much better ventilated than the Oratory, have been closed by the sanitary commissioners. It is madness ... to have sermons and crowded services in the lower chapel. It is very low, underground, and almost without ventilation. I proposed keeping on the low Masses and the Confessionals, but no services.[25]

The unhealthy atmosphere had the effect of turning actual and potential worshippers away. The more nasally discerning, particularly those from the higher classes, stopped coming because the stench of unwashed bodies and dirty clothes repulsed and alienated them. Faber wrote to Newman: 'at present there are, what F[ather] Bernard [Dalgairns] happily names, immovable <u>belts</u> of stink in ye chapel, no wonder people faint or go off in epileptic fits'.[26] The following day, Faber reported that 'Mr Wickwar of Oxford Street has called today to apologise for leaving our chapel. He says he came last Sunday ... but could not breathe and became giddy, and in company with 2 other gentlemen who felt ill at the chest through the effluvia he left the chapel.'[27] Faber opined: 'I maintain that people of a certain class in England are made physically ill by contact with stench and filth.'[28] This was problematic because the presence of the poor depleted the income of the embryonic Oratory, which would have been boosted by richer parishioners. Faber wrote to Newman: 'I regret this, because I am sure a great part of our mission ought to be to ye higher classes; and yet ye poor turn them out even from ye afternoon lectures which are specially directed to the educated'.[29] He also reported Fr Dalgairns's comment that 'ye English love of cleanliness is only part of our pride and national exclusiveness'.[30]

The formal opening of the Oratory church took place on 30 October 1849. Its interior, completed just in time for the inaugural

[24] Ibid., no. 97, Faber to Newman, 3 August 1849.
[25] Addington, ed., *Faber*, 200 (Faber to Newman, 15 August 1849).
[26] Faber to Newman, 14 August 1849.
[27] Faber to Newman, 15 August 1849.
[28] Faber to Newman, 14 August 1849.
[29] LO, MSS 2, no. 69, Faber to Newman, 9 July 1849.
[30] Faber to Newman, 14 August 1849.

mass, is illustrated in a painting reproduced in Chapman's monograph *Father Faber*, which illustrates the community at vespers and benediction in the church in front of a prosperous-looking congregation. Large gilt-framed paintings of Mary and St Philip Neri hang above maroon curtains, one on the left and one to the right of the altar, while a side chapel houses a life-sized crucifix, paintings and statues.[31] In his sermon at the opening, Wiseman praised Faber's community and preached that 'from hence you go forth as apostles of love each of you into the dismal city'; the following day Faber wrote to Newman: 'Our function last night went off most gloriously ... the bishop was extremely eloquent, and gave us his imprimatur in the most unqualified terms.'[32]

FABER'S HEALTH WHILE AT KING WILLIAM ST

Faber suffered from ill-health throughout his life due to Bright's disease, and also took Blue Pills, which caused mercury poisoning.[33] His condition deteriorated markedly from 1849 onwards, affecting his ability to function as provost, although he remained in charge. The bravado of his letters to Newman is accompanied by a sense of overpowering suffering. Newman's letters were sympathetic and encouraging towards the new venture, and he wrote: 'We are very much distressed about your illness, and won't forget you.'[34] Illness made Faber an outsider because he was unable to participate fully in the life of his community, and his letters illustrate that he was very much on his own, receiving little compassion from members of his community, who were frequently too busy or too ill themselves.[35] In October 1849, Faber had influenza.[36] In the same month he was depressed by Newman's unsympathetic comments,[37] attributable either to insensitivity (perhaps a foretaste of their future difficult relationship) or to the fact that Newman was simply too far away in Birmingham to understand Faber's predicament fully. Ill-health continued throughout the year and in November he wrote:

---

[31] Ronald Chapman, *Father Faber* (London, 1961), 166.
[32] Addington, ed., *Faber*, 203 (Faber to Newman, 31 October 1849).
[33] Wilkinson, *Faber*, 57.
[34] LO, MSS 8, no. 160, Newman to Faber, 25 December 1849.
[35] LO, MSS 2, no. 183, Faber to Newman, n.d.
[36] Ibid., no. 115, Faber to Newman, n.d. ('end of October 1849' added in pencil).
[37] Ibid., no. 183, Faber to Newman, n.d.

'Today I have such a rheumatism in my face and one side of my head that I am quite floored simply by having to endure ye pain, which is a cut above my usual power of pain bearing.'[38] In December he described being 'so ill that I can hardly grapple with your letter. I get worse daily.'[39] Letters to Newman are filled with comments such as: 'Here is ye 5 days illness out of eight', and '3 hours per diem of Irish confessions' to deal with whilst feeling desperately unwell.[40] In December he wrote: 'I am so wretchedly ill with constant vomiting on Saturday and rheumatism in ye hand I can barely write.'[41] On Christmas Eve he was ill in bed and depressed, complaining: 'The rheumatism seized ye side of my head and face, eye to ear, where ye Friday's headache had been. I was nearly delirious … with ye pain.'[42] In January 1850 Faber had cholera.[43] He was briefly better later in the month, but his doctor warned that a stroke was likely, due to hemiplegia, a form of temporary paralysis. Faber wrote: 'I lock my door when I feel it coming on; but it is merely transient. I was told a slight portion of my brain has softened as it is only on the right side.'[44] Faber was ill later in January and in April[45] and explained to Newman: 'I have been so ill for 4 or 5 days that I can hardly keep my temper in ye confessional, and I have no appetite and sleep badly.'[46] As he recounted: 'It is painful to say mass and I have little or no sleep at nights from it. Ye right wrist is failing; I feel ye act of writing, if I keep much to it. I am afraid I am very much out of spirits about myself; I am so weak, and have such odd sensations inside.'[47] In October, Faber observed: 'I can't apply my head in ye very least, and feel as if I was slightly drunk.'[48] He was often either confined to his room or carrying out his ministry with great difficulty, reporting: 'I can hardly ever say mass, people are near and they see my face, and I get flurried and break ye rubrics … I have left out glorias

[38] Ibid., no. 145, Faber to Newman, 20 November 1849.
[39] Ibid., no. 157, Faber to Newman, 1 December 1849.
[40] Ibid., no. 147, Faber to Newman, 29 November 1849.
[41] Ibid., no. 171, Faber to Newman, n.d. [December 1849].
[42] Ibid., no. 176, Faber to Newman, Christmas Eve 1849.
[43] Ibid., no. 185, Faber to Newman, 1 January 1850.
[44] Ibid., no. 189, Faber to Newman, 3 January 1850.
[45] LO, MSS 3, no. 30, Faber to Newman, 13 January 1851, ibid., no. 49, Faber to Newman, 30 April 1851.
[46] Ibid., no. 71, Faber to Newman, 8 August 1851.
[47] Ibid., no. 74, Faber to Newman, 25 September 1851.
[48] Ibid., no. 82, Faber to Newman, 22 October 1851.

even and credos … and I am never very well when I haven't said mass.'[49] It is perhaps unsurprising that he told Newman: 'I find invalidism anything but sanctifying to me. It seems to me suffering doesn't make saints, but polishes them up when once made.'[50]

Faber was aware of the effect that illness had on his spiritual discipline and frequently mentions the burden that it placed on his prayer life. It is, however, significant that in writing of himself he often dismissed suffering in a flippant manner. In this way, Faber's writing about his own ill-health is frequently, but not always, impersonal, as though he believed that the experience was being used by God as a moral chastisement or as something with which to challenge him. Thus Faber dismissed his suffering as punishment for over-reliance on himself and too little reliance on God.[51] Furthermore, Faber often seems to have regarded any form of sickness as being part of a spiritual discipline in which he, and humanity in general, must become proficient. The problem, he wrote, was that '[o]ne gets effeminized so quickly, especially when valetudinarianism keeps up a running fight with penance.'[52]

Whether consciously or unconsciously, concerns about his own health and the reality of taking medications such as Blue Pills, mercury, laudanum, opium, alcohol and iron, which together were slowly poisoning him, leaches into everything that Faber wrote, recurring constantly in books, letters, lectures and sermons. He was the target of experimentation from his doctors and endured constant changes in treatment. For instance, he told Newman: 'Last week [my doctor] took a different view of my case, and would have it was deficiency of acid, not excess of it, and gave me hydrochloric acid, which made me ill; so he gives me iron which makes me drunk and clogs my head up with silliness.'[53] Iodine gave Faber headaches,[54] and chloroform made him so unwell that he was unable to do anything.[55] He complained: 'My health gets worse and worse, tho' I look so well.'[56] In his biography, John Bowden writes that Faber was

[49] Ibid., no. 83, Faber to Newman, 31 December 1851.
[50] Ibid., no. 108, Faber to Newman, Easter Day [27 March] 1853.
[51] LO, MSS 2, no. 70, Faber to J. B. Morris, 17 July 1844.
[52] LO, MSS 1, no. 130, Faber to Morris, 20 August 1850.
[53] LO, MSS 2, no. 107, Faber to Newman, 27 August 1849.
[54] LO, MSS 3, no. 75, Faber to Newman, 30 September 1851.
[55] Faber to Newman, Christmas Eve 1849.
[56] Faber to Newman, 27 August 1849.

recommended to apply a relic of the Carmelite mystic St Mary Magdalene of Pazzi (1566–1607) to his head. He reported that doing so cured his headache on two occasions, but that he never tried it again because the experience frightened him.[57]

It seems probable that the experience of illness and isolation changed Faber's idea of God, and that it became more profound because he had time in which to be susceptible to religious experience. Illness, the claustrophobic experience of being shut in, the climate of sickness around the Oratory and medication, coupled with his intensely religious nature, clearly affected Faber's spirituality, making it more contemplative,[58] as well as shaping the way in which that experience was passed on to other people. Writing this article during the COVID-19 pandemic has provided insight into Faber's isolation and the fragile, sickness-filled environment in which he lived. In contrast to the angst surrounding the COVID pandemic, religious experience provided spiritual freedom from illness for Faber and a sense of companionship in his suffering, although this does not mean that he was not aware of the problematic nature of suffering. In addition, medication, particularly opiates, may have caused an altered mental state or visions, and there are trance-like passages in some of Faber's writings. We cannot, however, say conclusively whether or how his imagination was affected.

ILLNESS AS METAPHOR AND REALITY IN BOOKS, SERMONS AND PUBLIC LECTURES

Words such as illness, sickness and suffering are used by Faber in two ways, either as metaphor or for their own sake as literal description, but however used they have both physical and spiritual connotations. Faber's spirituality is intensely imaginative and poetical and influenced by his practice of Ignatian spirituality.[59] He frequently uses words such as fragility, melancholy, illness, infection, pain, darkness, loss, ungodliness, absorption, sickness, dirt, devil and damnation, silence and lost to make his point in connection with illness.

---

[57] John Bowden, *The Life and Letters of Frederick William Faber*, 5th edn (London, 1869), 323.
[58] See Wilkinson, *Faber*, 118.
[59] See ibid. 121.

The most common use of these terms is for the spiritual life of the individual and for states within the spiritual life, and Faber uses them equally when discussing his own problems in letters and when preaching to his congregation. In this context, illness is frequently used as an excuse for lack of religious discipline, and Faber uses words relating to illness in criticism of individuals. For example, it is always their fault that they are spiritually unwell, because they do not care or are lazy. The spiritually ill individual is not doing something in their spiritual life, or doing something wrong, or doing it with the wrong attitude, particularly refusing to take their relationship with God seriously. Faber's attitude is contradictory, because he expects everything from the individual spiritually whilst telling them that they will achieve nothing. He is frequently cynical about the individual's ability to progress spiritually and he seems to weigh them down with problems, perhaps because he did not have the ability to encourage them to a higher level of holiness.[60] The individual in a state of spiritual illness was one who was constantly making excuses, either consciously or unconsciously. There is an element of moral blindness and ineptitude present in this idea which, for Faber, is the state of the majority of people, even those who claim to be religious and who attend church regularly. Excuses in the spiritual life are, for Faber, a malady that impinges upon an individual's relationship not only with their contemporaries but also with the church, God, angels, saints and Mary. This is particularly serious for Faber, because they are not only avoiding the advantages of the everyday practice of Christianity but also missing out on a profound relationship with God, the only relationship worth cultivating because it is eternal. Faber also uses illness in a wider context, to describe the relationship of Great Britain as a whole towards God, and he is concerned with the spiritual health of the British Empire. It is significant that he consistently contrasts the British Empire unfavourably with Catholic countries, arguing (albeit with questionable logic) that the latter were always superior because they had remained loyal to Roman Catholicism, even if they were poor and inefficient compared to the British Empire.[61]

The character of Faber's discussion of illness in books and sermons is fairly consistent. He creates a straightforward image that is

---

[60] Ibid. 244.
[61] Ibid. 144, 236.

uncomplicated and easily understandable to his listeners or readers, especially those living in a setting where illness, accidents and early deaths were everyday occurrences. Thus, although popularly viewed as a rather colourful character given to excessive poetical flights of fancy, Faber's view of the world and of humanity in general was in reality often profoundly pessimistic.[62] This shows itself in his sermons and books, in which again he was often cynical about the individual's ability to be spiritual, a streak of pessimism that frequently becomes sarcasm. In his *Spiritual Conferences*,[63] written in 1850, Faber contrasted the excuses of humanity with the truth of God with reference to suffering. Thus, in a chapter entitled 'Self Deceit', Faber explored the notion of suffering in conjunction with the capacity of the individual for deluding themselves. This functions as an example of Faber's penchant for realism and his lack of sentimentality when discussing illness or suffering, and it is noticeable that he does not try to dress up the discussion of illness in an idealistic or Romantic guise. Rather, he suggests that there is no true suffering in the world, and he mocks individuals for their covert or overt self-centredness while undergoing what they describe as suffering.[64] Faber's particular sarcasm is reserved for those whose suffering is accompanied either by the expectation that God will or must do something to alleviate their suffering or by a sense of peevishness towards God for not doing so. This is because Faber viewed this as evidence of a wrong relationship between the individual and God.[65] Furthermore, Faber was of the opinion that people tend to 'exaggerate the misery of the world' and that what individuals describe as suffering is inconsequential, nothing more than a flea-bite. In the spiritual life, Faber is concerned that suffering functions as a series of excuses for moral and spiritual laziness and disregarding the sovereignty of God.

Occasionally it is difficult to tell whether Faber really meant what he said, or whether it was either a throwaway comment or medication-induced hyperbole. However, whatever its source, cynicism regarding suffering is one of the most important ideas in Faber's books and sermons. Thus he writes of an archetypal individual: 'They have had a modicum of pain, an allowance of annoyances, a

---

[62] Ibid. 244.
[63] F. W. Faber, *Spiritual Conferences*, 9th edn (London, 1858).
[64] Ibid. 216–17.
[65] Ibid. 218.

sprinkling of dissatisfactions and disappointments. But this does not amount to suffering.'[66] We can hypothesize that rather than intending to patronize or discourage individuals, Faber wishes to make their suffering authentic, part of a genuine and deep spirituality which is sensitive to a higher ideal.[67] This is because he believed that suffering should not cause individuals to move away from God but should draw them into a deeper appreciation of Jesus's redemptive suffering, although he acknowledges that such an attitude is rare. For Faber, authenticity is fundamental to the individual's spiritual life; in particular, as he writes, '[o]ut of God all is unreal. Away from God all is untrue.'[68] It is not only that true suffering is rare, but also that a spirit of disinterested willingness to suffer is rarer: 'in these smooth times a great proportion of men go to their graves, without having had what could rightly be called suffering'.[69]

Faber's discussion of suffering changes its meaning subtly depending on its context. It is as though his primary aim was to produce an active, practical response in his listeners, because the majority would not have been familiar with the theological niceties of his argument. In a letter to the duchess of Argyll, written in 1857, Faber highlighted the idea of suffering experienced by an individual within the Roman Catholic Church, writing 'How different suffering is in the Church and out of it! It seems to have so much more meaning, and to do its work so much more straightforwardly when one is in the true Fold.'[70] Here he seems to offer a nuanced view of suffering as a work, a springboard for action or amendment of life for the individual who suffers.

For Faber, everything about life, humanity and the world is dangerously orientated away from God, and humanity is always unwilling to change. In preaching, he frequently uses the idea that sickness is a common state in life. In this context he associates sickness with the idea that life is sad and deeply melancholy when it is without faith, and when the individual is alienated from God due to lack of faith or not knowing about Christianity. In a sermon preached on the Feast of the Epiphany, 6 January 1861, Faber uses this notion in the context of the Incarnation, as the historical event which gives life its

---

[66] Ibid. 216.
[67] Ibid. 217.
[68] Ibid. 221.
[69] Ibid. 216.
[70] Addington, ed., *Faber*, 282 (Faber to the duchess of Argyll, [May 1857]).

only meaning. Faber asked: 'What is life without God, without Jesus? How it passes away in joy; How it lingers in sorrow.'[71]

Faber commonly used the word 'infection' to mean something contrary to faith, which is to be shunned by the individual Christian, and writes of danger even from those who he describes as reformed heretics, by which he means converts who bring in ideas from outside the church.[72] He discusses the restrictions of existing on earth and in time, as contrary to heaven, eternity and God. These are interlinked for Faber, inasmuch as what individuals do while on earth affects the quality of, or their alienation from, their eternal vision of God. Thus heresy is described as a source of infection because it spreads ideas which are contrary to Roman Catholic doctrine. In a lecture entitled 'The Church at War with Heresy' (1851), Faber writes of Mary: 'Devotion to her preserves men from infection.' Later in the same lecture he writes of the 'evils of living among heretics' but also claims that 'by fervour [Mary] destroys heresy by limiting its infection'.[73] Faber's use of language is that of infection and contamination versus purity. It perhaps is significant that there was cholera in the area around the Oratory at the time that this lecture was given.

Health is mentioned by Faber in contrast to sickness. For example, a sermon for New Year's Eve 1849 refers to 'pleasure in living, especially if we have health'.[74] However, the idea of physical health is more often used by Faber in a negative than a positive sense and is frequently viewed as something which ensures that the individual becomes too comfortable and satisfied with things such as gossip or fashion, and therefore complacent and further away from God. Faber writes of the relationship between bodily health and spiritual health in *Spiritual Conferences* (1850). In the chapter 'Weariness in Welldoing', Faber expresses concern that individuals are obsessed with material things and creating a climate of ease and well-being to the detriment of their spiritual life, asserting: 'We are all of us too much inclined to

---

[71] LO, MSS packet 1, part 2, doc. 1, F. W. Faber, Sermon, 'The Epiphany', 6 January 1861.

[72] F. W. Faber, *The Precious Blood*, 3rd edn (Philadelphia, PA, 1959; first published 1860), 180.

[73] LO, MSS packet 3.4, doc. 12, F. W. Faber, Lecture 4: 'The Church at War with Heresy'.

[74] LO, MSS packet 1, part 2, doc. 30, F. W. Faber, 'The View which ye Saints take of the World as a Howling Wilderness', 31 December 1849.

make concessions to our bodies.' This idea is significant for Faber. It recurs throughout his mature thought in a variety of guises related to the irrevocability of time that has been wasted or frittered away, because time spent away from religion is wasted. For that reason, for Faber, '[r]eliance on comforts is quite incompatible with true liberty of spirit.'[75] In *Growth in Holiness* (1854), he observes those for whom sensuality is a ruling passion, describing 'persons of soft ... nature, sensitive and sentimental, loving bodily comforts'.[76] Faber highlights the relationship between physical health and spiritual well-being using the notion that both health and ill-health can be, and often are, used as an excuse for lack of action, almsgiving or prayer.[77] Here he seems to be criticizing a form of sickness within health, one that is merely fashionable or part of a trend (or both), the enjoyment of poor health rather than authentic sickness or suffering. Faber is concerned that '[t]he worship of health is one of the most efficient and extensive causes of lukewarmness and indevotion' in the spiritual life.[78] 'We must not forget that many of the phenomena of the spiritual life spring from physical causes.'[79] He is concerned to point out that many individuals attribute positive feelings to God and temptations to 'Satan, what is really a matter of nerves or of digestion'. In contrast, Faber attributes a moral dimension to feelings of good, as opposed to bad, health: 'The reaction after hard work, different seasons of the year, individual constitution, very slight atmospherical disturbances, all of them tend to bring forth many moral results, without the intervention of actual pain or positive malady.'[80]

In Faber's mind, illness can be harnessed to concentrate the collective mind on what is important by bringing people back to attendance at church and the practice of religion. This was demonstrated for Faber by a cholera epidemic in September 1854, the horror of which he described in a letter to George Talbot:

> Last week we had an awful outburst of it, which has been carefully concealed in the newspapers; and which passed away in four days. There were 400 corpses lying in Broad Street the afternoon I was there; black

[75] Faber, *Spiritual Conferences*, 246.
[76] F. W. Faber, *Growth in Holiness*, new edn (London, n.d.), 79.
[77] Faber, *Spiritual Conferences*, 247.
[78] Ibid. 246–7.
[79] Ibid. 246.
[80] Ibid. 247.

flags in Silver Street and Pulteney Street to warn passengers away; and lime laid down in several streets. The deaths in town exceeded the usual average last week by 2193, all cholera cases. This outburst has subsided; but the pestilence still rages. We have cholera sick calls daily.[81]

However, the horror had its positive side: 'The cholera is preaching a capital mission. Our confessionals are crowded, and with gentry of 10, 20, 30 years without sacraments.'[82] Faber does not mention prayers for those who were unwell, but that does not mean that he did not use them. Likewise, he does not question whether or not God was with people or helped them in times when disease or epidemics were present. Thus although he refers to suffering as an 'empire, which original sin has created',[83] he does not seem to have viewed illness or epidemics as forms of divine punishment.

Faber's book *The Precious Blood* was written during 1860 for the Confraternity of the Precious Blood, which had been established at the Oratory ten years earlier. In it, he dwells on the prevalence of physical pain in the life of the individual. It seems that his knowledge stems not only from meditation and study of Scripture and theology, but also from practical reflection on his own experience of sickness. In a chapter entitled 'The Necessity of the Precious Blood', which is a meditation on philanthropy, he reflects: 'Every one whose lot it is to lead a life of pain knows too well how little medical science avails to alleviate this particular kind of human suffering',[84] and comments: 'how feeble and how limited is the jurisdiction of medical science'.[85] Faber points out 'the limits of scientific and medical discovery' and asks: 'how often have the remedies themselves brought new pains along with them?'[86] In addition, '[a]n immense amount of the world's misery consists of bodily pain', yet '[t]here are few things more hard to bear. It is one of our unrealities that we write and speak lightly of it. We think it grand to do so. We think to show our manliness.'[87]

[81] Addington, ed., *Faber*, 266 (Faber to Monsignor George Talbot, 15 September 1854).
[82] Ibid.
[83] Faber, *Precious Blood*, 61.
[84] Ibid. 60–1.
[85] Ibid. 61.
[86] Ibid.
[87] Ibid. 60.

In a meditation entitled 'The Solitariness', preached in 1859, Faber discussed the solitary, inward nature of suffering as experienced by humanity and by Jesus in his passion and writes as an aside: 'Sickness is a drawing of us into still farther solitude – yet kind ministries are around.'[88] In *The Precious Blood*, Faber interprets pain and suffering as important aspects of the relationship of the individual Christian with Jesus. Faber uses the consideration that Jesus is the only one who truly understands because he has suffered and shares not only Faber's suffering, but also the suffering of those who will read the book. He writes: 'What is the meaning of pain, except the purification of our soul.'[89]

> The long, pining, languishing sick bed, with its interminable nights and days, its wakeful memories, its keen susceptibilities, its crowded and protracted inward biography, its burdensome epochs of monotony – what would this be, if we knew not the Son of God, if Jesus had never been man, if his grace of endurance had not actually gone out of his Heart into ours.[90]

In a sermon whose subject is mental suffering in purgatory, Faber states that 'Pain is a desperately difficult thing to bear', and asks 'is bodily or mental pain worst?'[91] In *The Precious Blood* Faber is also concerned with mental suffering. This is something which occupies less of his thought than physical suffering, and he seems to show less sympathy towards it. He writes: 'The excesses of mental anguish, while they visit chiefly the rarer and more sensitive minds, are always of brief duration.'[92] Faber's meditation leads him to the conclusion that '[i]t is the characteristic of mental suffering to be for the most part beyond the reach of philanthropy',[93] opining: 'Who has not often wondered at the most invariable irritation produced in unhappy persons by ... formal soothing?'[94] In discussing the relationship between the mind and the body and the relationship between the

---

[88] F. W. Faber, Sermon, 'The Solitariness', in Bowden, ed., *Notes*, 1: 193–6, at 193.
[89] Faber, *Precious Blood*, 48.
[90] Ibid. 49.
[91] F. W. Faber, Sermon, 'Devotion to the Passion', in Bowden, ed., *Notes*, 2: 361–3, at 361.
[92] Faber, *Precious Blood*, 61.
[93] Ibid. 62.
[94] Ibid. 61.

purely mental and the spiritual within life, if indeed such a distinction can be made, in his book *Bethlehem* (1860), Faber was concerned to inculcate a spirit of spiritual cheerfulness, a positivity which contrasts with melancholy or sadness. He writes: 'Sadness is a sort of spiritual disability. A melancholy man can never be more than a convalescent in the house of God',[95] and he contrasts sadness with joy: 'Joy is the freshness of our spirits. Joy is the life-long morning of our souls, an habitual sunrise out of which worship and heroic virtue come.' This notion is also part of Faber's view of the relationship between the individual Christian and God, in which the onus is on the individual not to ask questions or expect answers from God. He writes of the melancholy individual's mind: 'He may think much of God, but he worships very little. God has rather to wait upon him as infirmarian, than he to wait on God as his Father and his King. There is no moral imbecility so great as that of querulousness and sentimentality.'[96] Here Faber once again mentions physical health as a contrast to sickness. He is very plain and forthright, presenting health in a straightforward way: 'We must rejoice, because he loves to see us rejoice. Melancholy in a creature is a kind of inglorious reflection on the creator.'[97]

For Faber, the idea of spiritual illness or sickness has a moral dimension that is linked to the notion that religion is also a public duty. This is indicated in *Bethlehem*, in which Faber describes saints 'whose way of worshipping His glory is to tell the wonders which He has let them see'. Thus the Christian must ensure that other people are also saved and understand the purpose of Christianity in daily life, rather than treating religion as purely a personal matter. For Faber, '[h]e who lies down at full length on life, as if it were a sick-bed, – poor languishing soul! What will he ever do for God?'[98] This activism is an important part of Faber's thought, which may be attributable to the Evangelicalism of his early life. It is also associated with the sense of sarcasm and chivvying that is present throughout his mature works, but to a greater degree in his later writing. Writing of the worship of God, he opines: 'Is religion a private luxury – a simple sofa of sweet soft thoughts for conscience to lie down upon

[95] F. W. Faber, *Bethlehem*, new edn (London, n.d.; first published 1860), 200.
[96] Ibid.
[97] F. W. Faber, 'God's View of our Past Sins', in Bowden, ed., *Notes*, 2: 70–2, at 70.
[98] Faber, *Bethlehem*, 200.

and take its ease?'[99] This notion also occurs in his preaching; thus in a sermon entitled 'God so little Loved', Faber wrote: 'Is your piety to go to sleep while the world is perishing?' This alludes to the gospel, probably that set for that Sunday, in which Jesus, asleep in a boat in a storm with his disciples, is woken by them asking: 'Teacher, do you not care that we are perishing?'[100] Faber is concerned to suggest that it is the responsibility of individual Christians to do the work of Jesus and save those around them. '[D]ead and dying souls' are a spiritual rather than a physical reality, but also a spur to action. Faber asks: 'Driven by a holy despair at the awful sense of dead and dying souls around you, what sacrifices are you making for Him who sacrificed himself on the cross for you?'[101]

In Faber's thought, individuals, although in need of healing, become the instrument of their own destruction or sickness, a spiritual sickness, perversity or error which leads away from God. In this context the metaphorical concepts of health and sickness are linked to Faber's preoccupation with the four last things: death, judgment, heaven and hell. It is as though he believed that lack of love for God saps vital moral and physical strength from humanity: he suggests that 'all the miseries of this life' come about 'because of God not being loved'[102] and expresses the concern that 'Hell [is] … filling hourly.'[103] In sermons and books Faber is always concerned with sin, the nearness of hell and the ever-present possibility of separation from God and personal damnation. For this reason, he views the personal wants of the individual as secondary to the necessity of doing everything possible to ensure salvation. Furthermore, because he views the encounter with God as the only significant encounter, he assumes that individuals will want to consider their salvation as their highest priority. In this context, time is against the individual because the time and day of death are always unknown, particularly during times of sickness or epidemic. In a sermon entitled 'The Legacies of Jesus', Faber wrote: 'If life be bright and smiling, Jesus is the

---

[99] LO MSS, packet 1, part 1, section 1, doc. 18, F. W. Faber, 'God so little Loved' (sermon), n.d.; see also idem, Sermon, 'God so little Loved', in Bowden, ed., *Notes*, 1: 35–7, at 35.
[100] Mark 4: 39 (NRSV).
[101] Faber, 'God so little Loved'.
[102] Ibid.
[103] F. W. Faber, 'Eternity', in Bowden, ed., *Notes*, 2: 339–42, at 339.

brightness and the smile.'[104] For Faber, God is the only cure for spiritual sickness; however, individuals are passive and disinterested and allow themselves to be destroyed by the world, many only waking up later in hell after their death, where all is irrevocable. Faber contrasts time and eternity, presenting the latter as a luminous ever-present reality. In the sermon on 'Eternity', he writes: 'Picture a life, all classes living, scheming, building, planning, as if all was to go on the same without end. An Angel comes down ... proclaims, no more time! We fall into the arms of eternity.'[105]

Conclusion

Three broad conclusions can be drawn from these findings. Firstly, the Oratorians were unprepared for the reality of poverty, disease and sickness in London, which overwhelmed the parish from the outset. Faber's vocation was to create a series of parishes, becoming a valued part of the wider community, before moving on a whim, often leaving opprobrium in his wake.[106] The Oratorians moved away from King William St despite the reality that they were needed and parishioners wanted them to stay. They moved ostensibly because they could not develop the parish as an oratory; however, it seems likely that it was also Faber's reluctance to be in charge of a poor parish and his wish to move in higher social circles and to be distinctive which led to the creation of the Oratory at Brompton in March 1854. Secondly, sickness was part of Faber's everyday existence; his ailments, together with (and perhaps especially) the medication he took for them, thwarted both his career as a priest and his plans for the King William St Oratory. Thirdly, Faber was a priest whose physical struggles infected his whole language and mindset; he used the twin metaphors of sickness and health as an edifice within which to place his understanding of theology. Moreover, Faber's character was austere, shunning pretension and moral sickness in favour of true healthy asceticism. Perhaps for that reason, the metaphor of sickness became more useful to Faber than the reality of sickness and health, as it provided a structure within which to instruct his parishioners. Furthermore, his pessimism about the society in which he lived led

[104] LO, MSS packet 1.2.1, doc. 7, F. W. Faber, 'The Legacies of Jesus', 6.
[105] Faber, 'Eternity', 339.
[106] Wilkinson, *Faber*, 127.

him to highlight humanity's worrying propensity for sickness in the form of abandoning the practice of Christianity for meaninglessness and frivolity. This glimpse of the life of the Oratory at King William St has not only shown something of Faber's religious response to people and surroundings in mid-nineteenth-century London, but has also highlighted themes which are, in one sense, universal.

Ministering to Body and Soul: Medical Missions and the Jewish Community in Nineteenth-Century London

Jemima Jarman*

Birkbeck, University of London

From 1879, evangelical missions aimed specifically at Jews began providing free medical services to the newly arrived immigrant community in London's East End. This article focuses on three specific medical missions to Jews belonging to the London Society for Promoting Christianity among the Jews, the British Society for the Propagation of the Gospel amongst the Jews and the Mildmay Mission to the Jews. It considers the particular attractions of these medical missions in terms of what they were able to offer the immigrant Jew that existing state and voluntary medical services did not provide, alongside the cost and possible risk posed by attendance. The article questions whether the popularity of evangelical medical missions within the Jewish East End is as surprising as it may first appear, if the limited health care options available to the nineteenth-century poor are considered in conjunction with the additional obstacles facing Jewish immigrants, such as cultural and religious differences, anti-Jewish prejudice and most notably the language barrier.

In the closing decades of the nineteenth century, a number of medical missions directed specifically at Jews were established, run and supported by evangelical Christians. Their establishment across Britain corresponds with the rapid growth in the country's Jewish population as a result of the mass migration from Eastern Europe brought about by discriminatory laws, economic hardship and violent attacks. The Jewish immigrant, a newcomer in a foreign land with few resources or established networks, faced additional barriers in accessing health care beyond those experienced by the native poor. The vast majority of Jewish immigrants would not have known English or any other European language apart from their native Yiddish. In addition to

* E-mail: jemimajarman@outlook.com.
I wish to thank CMJ UK for granting permission to publish their archival material, as well as the Special Collections team at the Bodleian Libraries for their mediated copying service during the pandemic.

Studies in Church History 58 (2022), 262–283   © The Author(s), 2022. Published by Cambridge University Press on behalf of Ecclesiastical History Society
doi: 10.1017/stc.2022.13

this significant language barrier, many East European Jews would naturally have had difficulty navigating the English health care system (such as it was), due to an unfamiliarity with the workings of Poor Law provision or the bureaucracy surrounding many voluntary hospitals.

The established Anglo-Jewish community worked with both the state and voluntary medical establishments to ensure that basic provisions were made to cater for Jewish patients, such as the provision of kosher food.[1] However, the Anglo-Jewish communal body, the Jewish Board of Guardians, took the line that there was nothing specifically Jewish about the provision of medicine and so saw no need to set up separate or additional medical services within the community.[2] This left England's rapidly expanding immigrant Jewish population with few options for treatment in times of sickness outside admittance to the dreaded workhouse infirmaries or, if they qualified for such charity, the wards of a voluntary hospital, which required long waits of up to seven hours and intrusive questioning to determine whether the patient was a deserving or undeserving recipient of charity.[3] Outdoor medical care, that is, assistance granted outside of an institution, was kept to a minimum by Poor Law guardians, and some parishes (including Whitechapel) aimed to abolish its provision completely.[4] Home medical missions are situated against this background of limited state and voluntary medical services. The history of the home medical mission movement will be outlined, the specific theological arguments that developed in support of Jewish medical missions discussed, and the importance of medical missions in facilitating access to quality health care for society's poor and vulnerable, in this case Jewish immigrants in London's East End, considered.

[1] Gerry Black, 'Health and Medical Care of the Jewish Poor in the East End of London, 1880–1914', *Jewish Historical Studies* 36 (1999–2001), 93–111.
[2] Laurie Magnus, *The Jewish Board of Guardians and the Men who made it, 1859–1909: An Illustrated Record* (London, 1909), 119.
[3] Gerry Black, *Lord Rothschild and the Barber: The Struggle to establish the London Jewish Hospital* (London, 2000), 35; Black, 'Health and Medical Care, 1880–1914', 101.
[4] While the Poor Law medical officer could still make recommendations for outdoor treatment of the sick, it was the Poor Law guardians who had the power to grant or withhold this aid: P. F. Aschrott, *The English Poor Law System: Past and Present*, transl. Herbert Preston Thomas (London, 1902), 262; Jeanne L. Brand, 'The Parish Doctor: England's Poor Law Medical Officers and Medical Reform 1870–1900', *BHM* 35 (1961), 97–122, at 106.

Despite the fact that medical missions were heavily used by Jews in the East End, they have barely been recognized in Anglo-Jewish scholarship. One factor possibly contributing to this neglect is the relatively recent introduction of the study of health, illness and medicine within the humanities. A second contributing factor may be the continued practice among historians of Anglo-Jewry of downplaying and dismissing the significance of evangelical missionary activity within Jewish communities. Therefore, this subject, involving as it does both medical history and missionary history, has received very little scholarly attention to date.

There are a few exceptions to this general absence of scholarship, thanks to the pioneering work of Gerry Black and Lara Marks, both of whom have highlighted the significance of medical missions in the provision of healthcare services to Jews in nineteenth-century London.[5] However, the scope of their research is much broader than that of medical missions specifically, and so naturally the subject occupies only a peripheral place in their studies. More recently, Ellen Ross has written on the subject of medical missions and Jews, with a focus on how women resisted the proselytizing element of the missions.[6] However, this single article is necessarily limited in scope. When writing about medical missions to Jews, all three authors rely heavily upon sources created by the established Anglo-Jewish community, who openly criticized evangelical missionary activities, while voices from other contemporary perspectives are not given an equal hearing.[7] In response to this imbalance, this article will give serious and considered attention to the beliefs and motivations of the

---

[5] Gerald David Black, 'Health and Medical Care of the Jewish Poor in the East End of London, 1880–1939', (Ph.D. thesis, Leicester University, 1987); Black, 'Health and Medical Care, 1880–1914'; Black, *Lord Rothschild*; Lara Marks, 'Irish and Jewish Women's Experience of Childbirth and Infant Care in East London, 1870–1939: The Responses of Host Society and Immigrant Communities to Medical Welfare Needs' (D.Phil. thesis, University of Oxford, 1990); eadem, *Model Mothers: Jewish Mothers and Maternity Provision in East London, 1870–1939* (Oxford, 2001).

[6] Ellen Ross, "'Playing Deaf": Jewish Women at the Medical Missions of East London, 1880–1920s, *19: Interdisciplinary Studies in the Long Nineteenth Century* [online journal] 13 (2011), at: <http://doi: https://doi.org/10.16995/ntn.622>, last accessed 14 January 2022.

[7] Scholarship has relied heavily upon Anglo-Jewry's primary newspaper, the *Jewish Chronicle* (hereafter: *JC*), founded in 1841, for information on medical missions; in addition to its own articles, it reproduced reports of Anglo-Jewish communal and religious bodies such the Jewish Board of Guardians, the Jewish Board of Deputies and the United Synagogue.

missionaries themselves, going beyond the reductive label of 'conversionist',[8] as recorded in both published and unpublished missionary records. It will introduce the medical provisions in London that were accessible to the poor and highlight some of the most significant barriers that immigrant Jews faced in making use of these.

The focus here is on three medical missions to Jews operating in East London during the closing decades of the nineteenth century. These were supported by the British Society for the Propagation of the Gospel amongst the Jews (hereafter: BSPGJ), the Mildmay Mission to the Jews (MMJ) and the London Society for the Promotion of Christianity among the Jews (LSPCJ). After introducing each of these medical missions, the question of why they were popular among Jewish immigrants in need of health care will be considered. Finally, the cost of attending these missions upon the immigrant Jew, socially and psychologically rather than financially, will be weighed. The study of these missions promises to offer new perspectives and fresh contributions to our current understanding of the churches' response to religious plurality, and of the developments within Christian-Jewish relations more particularly, in nineteenth-century England.[9]

MEDICAL CARE IN NINETEENTH-CENTURY LONDON

The options available for the sick poor towards the end of the nineteenth century were provided primarily by the state, through the workings of the Poor Law, or through philanthropic agencies operating voluntary hospitals and dispensaries.[10] Turning to the Poor Law first, despite having undergone a number of reforms over the century, infirmaries remained underfunded, understaffed and in some cases

---

[8] This term was used by Anglo-Jewish contemporaries to make derogatory references to the missionaries in the press, mainly the *JC*, and has been subsequently adopted by Anglo-Jewish historians, including Eugene Black, Israel Finestein, Todd Endelman, David Feldman and Ellen Ross.

[9] See Charlotte Methuen, Andrew Spicer and John Wolffe, eds, *Christianity and Religious Plurality*, SCH 51 (Woodbridge, 2015), in particular John Wolffe, 'Plurality in the Capital: The Christian Responses to London's Religious Minorities since 1800', ibid. 232–58; W. M. Jacob, 'Anglican Clergy Responses to Jewish Migration in late Nineteenth-Century London', ibid. 259–73.

[10] Valuable studies on Victorian health care systems include Keir Waddington, *Charity and the London Hospitals, 1850–1898* (New York, 2000); Gwendoline Ayers, *England's First State Hospitals and the Metropolitan Asylum Board, 1867–1930* (London, 1971).

grossly mismanaged.[11] A royal commission recorded that as late as 1909 patients still felt that they were treated grudgingly by Poor Law Medical Officers and seen as 'only a shade above criminals'.[12] Poor Law Guardians, not wishing to reward the feckless poor by providing medical care of equal quality to that available to the prudent, paying patient, aimed to ensure that their medical services were the least attractive option. For these ideological reasons, and for the more practical reasons of keeping costs down, Poor Law infirmaries offered a very basic standard of health care service provision.

The second option available to the sick poor in London was provided by the voluntary hospitals and their outpatient departments. The hospitals, superior to Poor Law infirmaries in the quality and standard of the care provided, were dependent on the donations of philanthropists, the income of subscribers and goodwill funds raised by the public. For this reason, they never became the main providers of healthcare in London, working instead in tandem with the workhouse infirmaries.[13] Unable to provide beds for all those in need, preference was given to those who could pay something towards their treatment; of those who could not, it was only the medically interesting cases, or those useful for teaching, who were not sent on to the Poor Law infirmary.[14] Moral character was also considered when deciding who would receive treatment, with those judged immoral or undeserving considered unfit beneficiaries of charity. For example, unmarried mothers would not be admitted to maternity wards, and those with venereal diseases could be refused treatment.[15] Even those whose appearance identified them as being from the 'pauper class' could be barred from entering the hospital by porters, who were instructed to send such cases straight to the Poor Law authorities.[16]

Those in need of medical care who were unable to pay for a doctor therefore had the option of either trying their luck at an inpatient

---

[11] It has been argued convincingly that the Poor Law system created an inherently negligent medical service: Kim Price, *Medical Negligence in Victorian Britain: The Crisis of Care under the English Poor Law, c.1834–1900* (London, 2016).

[12] *Report of the Royal Commission on the Poor Laws and Relief of Distress, 1909*, quoted in Black, 'Health and Medical Care, 1880–1939', 139.

[13] Waddington, *Charity*, 9.

[14] A. E. Clark-Kennedy, *The London: A Study in the Voluntary Hospital System, 2: 1840–1948* (London, 1964), 104.

[15] Marks, 'Irish and Jewish Women', 146–7.

[16] F. B. Smith, *The People's Health, 1830–1910* (London, 1979), 252.

department of a hospital or applying directly to the Poor Law relieving officer. At a voluntary hospital, there was the risk of being turned away. Even if entry was granted, the average wait to be seen at the London Hospital was seven hours, at the end of which the patient might still be sent to the Poor Law infirmary.[17] Those who went directly to the Poor Law, at least in districts such as Whitechapel, would be offered indoor relief only, meaning dreaded institutionalization, with no option to receive treatment at home.[18]

IMMIGRANT JEWS IN STATE AND VOLUNTARY HEALTH INSTITUTIONS

Historically, the Jewish community in Britain had cared for its sick through its synagogues, which would raise and distribute funds primarily among their own membership. By 1862 this function was taken over by a centralized body, the Jewish Board of Guardians (JBG),[19] but by 1879, the JBG had dropped the provision of medical relief entirely.[20] The justification given for cutting this traditional welfare service within the community was that sufficient provision existed outside it. The Anglo-Jewish community were ratepayers and contributed to the upkeep of Poor Law provisions, and it was argued that duplicating these services and paying twice over for them was unjustifiable. What is more, as the 'Guardians' of the Jewish community, they did not wish to be seen as pauperizing the poor by catering too comfortably to their needs;[21] nor did they wish

---

[17] Ibid. 255.

[18] William Vallance, clerk to the guardians of Whitechapel Union, gave evidence of the scant outdoor medical relief available in the district: *Select Committee of the House of Lords on Poor Law Relief. Report, Proceedings, Minutes of Evidence, Appendix* (London, 1888), 493, 513.

[19] The JBG was a voluntary body formed in 1859 in an effort to rationalize the distribution of charitable aid within the community. It adopted the Poor Law philosophy of 'least desirability' when dealing with the poor and sought to separate the 'deserving' from the 'undeserving' cases. Aid was primarily given in the form of small business loans, assistance to secure apprenticeships and help to emigrate or be repatriated. Members of Anglo-Jewry's elite sat upon the board, with the role of president remaining within a single family from 1869 into the twentieth century. For more on the JBG, see Vivian D. Lipman, *A Century of Social Service: 1859–1959: The Jewish Board of Guardians* (London, 1959); Mordechai Rozin, *The Rich and the Poor: Jewish Philanthropy and Social Control in Nineteenth-Century London* (Brighton, 1999); Alysa Levene, *Jews in Nineteenth-Century Britain: Charity, Community and Religion, 1830–1880* (London, 2020).

[20] Lipman, *A Century of Social Service*, 62.

[21] Rozin, *The Rich and the Poor*, 126.

to be seen as providing services superior to those available to non-Jews, which might have had the undesirable effect of stirring up anti-Jewish feeling or of encouraging and attracting more Jewish immigrants to English shores.[22] These attitudes were in keeping with wider Victorian attitudes on the proper treatment of the poor, which came under much criticism, from both contemporaries and subsequent scholars of the period.

As difficult as it was for the native poor to access the welfare services they required in times of need, and as resistant as they were to using the harsh, impersonal and punitive system of the Poor Law, for the newly arrived immigrant Jew, there would have been additional barriers to navigating the system and additional reasons for dreading the prospect of entering an institution. It was these factors, specific to the immigrant Jew's position in a foreign environment, for which the JBG failed to make provision.[23]

The first of these factors, and perhaps the most obvious, is the language barrier. The vast majority of Jewish immigrants would have spoken Yiddish, with no knowledge of the English language prior to settling in the East End. However, Anglo-Jewry's communal leaders consistently resisted making any acknowledgement that language posed a significant barrier for immigrant Jews in accessing health care: 'We do not think the language barrier is a very real one ... Moreover we think interpreters are unnecessary.'[24] How it was expected that a non-English speaker would communicate his or her ailments, or understand the advice and instructions given by an English-speaking doctor in return, can only be imagined. Such concerns were expressed by the wider Jewish community, who reproached the JBG communal leaders: 'The want of a Jewish Dispensary, or a person who can speak Yiddish to attend the parochial ones, has been brought before the community more than once, but, to their shame, the want has never been remedied.'[25] Despite such appeals, it is clear from a reported fatal case of misdiagnosis at the

---

[22] On the ideology of the JBG, see ibid. 113–61, especially 122–3, 135–40, 147–9.

[23] A combination of strained finances and a commitment to deter further Jewish immigration to England meant the JBG was unwilling to make special provisions. These dual concerns are repeatedly voiced in its annual reports during the years 1879–1900.

[24] United Synagogue, *Mission Committee Report* (London, 1912), 17 (§58), quoted in Black, 'Health and Medical Care 1880–1939', 215.

[25] *JC*, 1 December 1893, 10.

London Hospital in 1901, the direct result of miscommunication due to language barriers, that adequate action was not taken.[26]

Secondly, the immigrant Jewish community was subject to prejudice as foreigners and to antisemitism as Jews. They became the scapegoats for low wages and high rents, in an East End of London suffering from mass unemployment, and were at risk of receiving unfavourable treatment as a result of these negative perceptions.[27] An example of these prejudices affecting medical care can be found within the records of the Poor Law Unions, with a Whitechapel medical officer named Braye receiving a number of complaints due to his behaviour towards Jewish patients.[28] Even in the voluntary London Hospital which had made the most accommodations for Jews, 'Jews were not particularly welcome'.[29]

The third factor to consider is that of cultural difference. The Jewish immigrant did not arrive in England without prior experience of medicine or medical practices and institutions, and this prior experience of health care provision would naturally have shaped the way that the healthcare options available in the new country were evaluated and navigated. Whether the cold mechanics of the Poor Law, the paternalistic bureaucracy of the voluntary hospital, or the combination of medical treatment with religious instruction at the medical mission, felt culturally closer to the immigrant Jew's own traditions and former experiences is an area awaiting further research.

Having highlighted the additional factors of language, anti-Jewish prejudice and cultural difference effecting the immigrant Jew's ability to access and utilize existing state and voluntary provision in the field of medical care, the JBG's assertion that there was 'nothing of a specially Jewish character in dispensing drugs and giving medical advice' is difficult to apply to the case of new immigrants.[30] It is in light of the inadequacy of existing medical provision, and in acknowledgement of

---

[26] London Hospital House Committee Minutes, 25 March 1901, cited in Black, 'Health and Medical Care, 1880–1939', 214.

[27] For more on the reception of alien Jewish immigrants in England, see, for example, Bernard Gainer, *Alien Invasion: The Origins of the Aliens Act of 1905* (London, 1972); David Feldman, *Englishmen and Jews: Social Relations and Political Culture, 1840–1914* (London, 1994).

[28] Examples of Braye's abusive behaviour are given in Marks, 'Irish and Jewish Women', 246.

[29] *JC*, 6 November 1896, 11.

[30] Magnus, *Jewish Board of Guardians*, 119.

the particular barriers facing London's immigrant Jewish community, that the establishment of evangelical medical missions directed at Jews in London's East End needs to be considered.

The Emergence of Medical Missions in Nineteenth-Century Britain

'Some may ask, are Medical Missions needful and useful at home? I answer, I believe there is a medical necessity for them, neither hospitals nor dispensaries nor parochial medical relief can fully meet the need.'[31] Medical missions for Jews did not develop in a silo but were part of a larger medical missionary movement in Britain with its origins during the 1840s in Edinburgh, spearheaded by Dr William Burns Thomson, a medical doctor engaged in the work of the Edinburgh Medical Missionary Society. Inspired by the combined medical and evangelistic work that was undertaken in foreign mission fields, Thomson saw an opportunity to apply this mode of operation to domestic home missions.[32] But whereas abroad it often happened that a missionary with no training in medical work was compelled by circumstance to treat the sick, Thomson's vision was to create a professionalized medical mission with qualified doctors and nurses who combined a passion for bodily healing with a desire to evangelize.[33]

When setting his new model of mission work before a primarily evangelical audience, Thomson was required to provide compelling evidence of the biblical nature of, and scriptural sanction for, such work. As a result, theological arguments emerged that confirmed the existence of a special interconnectedness between the body and the soul, and a new emphasis was placed on the healing ministry of Christ and his disciples:

> Now it is very evident that there is a natural kinship between medicine and the gospel. What the one professes to do for the body, the other professes to do for the soul. Indeed, because of the strange, strong

---

[31] *Medical Missions at Home and Abroad: The Quarterly Magazine of the Medical Missionary Association* (hereafter: *MMHA*), October 1878, 29.
[32] Kathleen Heasman, 'The Medical Mission and the Care of the Sick in Nineteenth-Century England', *HistJ* 7 (1964), 230–45, at 232–3.
[33] *MMHA*, [July] 1878, 1.

union which subsists between body and soul, the health of either can hardly be promoted alone – certainly cannot be perfected alone.[34]

Every instance of healing in the gospels was drawn upon as evidence of how Christ himself had set an example for medical missionary work, warranting the Church to do the same.[35] Jesus was held up as the 'Great Physician' and the book of Acts was described as 'the first report of the first Medical Missionary Society'.[36] By showing the model of the medical mission to have its origins in the New Testament, this entirely new and pioneering method of evangelism would have been quickly adopted by bibliocentric evangelicals.[37]

Underpinning all medical missions was the scriptural instruction to 'proclaim the Kingdom of God and to heal';[38] but those aimed especially at Jews were motivated by additional convictions. One was that Christians owed a debt of gratitude to the Jews as the originators of their religion, and that medical missions could provide a practical way to repay this debt.[39] Another was that Christians owed a debt of reparation to the Jew for the past wrongs that had been done to them under the broad banner of Christianity.[40] This belief was particularly influential for Jewish medical missions, established as they were at the same moment when East European Jews were leaving their homelands due to persecution. As the Jews had physically suffered as a result of discriminatory laws and violent attacks in Christian countries, it was argued that reparations were required, and what could be more suitable than attending to the illnesses and injuries of the Jewish immigrants themselves? In the words of the Mildmay Mission to the Jews: 'As so-called Christians had inflicted on the Jews enormous physical injury, it was surely the right thing for true Christians to render them bodily help and

[34] Ibid. 7.
[35] '[I]t is to the Gospels themselves, the record of our Lord's life and work, that we have to look for the chief exemplar, and the chief warrant for medical missions': *MMHA*, January 1882, 231.
[36] John Lowe, *Medical Missions: Their Place and Power* (London, 1886), 17.
[37] 'Biblicism' is one of the four defining characteristics of evangelicalism, according to David Bebbington's definition in *Evangelicalism in Modern Britain: A History from the 1730s to the 1980s* (London, 2015), 1–19.
[38] Luke 9: 2 (NRSV).
[39] For an expression of these ideas, see for example, *Jewish Herald* (hereafter: *JH*), July 1882, 75. This was the magazine of the BSPGJ.
[40] *JH*, June 1882, 71.

healing.'[41] Taking this standpoint, medical missions were promoted within evangelical circles as a practical means of removing the barriers of suspicion and mistrust separating Jews from Christians and increasing receptivity to the gospel message, although whether this was achieved in reality is an entirely separate matter.

An awareness of the convictions that motivated Christians to conduct medical missionary work among the Jews of the East End is crucial for understanding the dynamics between the medical missionary and the patient. The established Jewish community was loud in its criticisms of medical missions and these Anglo-Jewish voices have formed the primary source of reference for the few scholars who have addressed the work of these medical missions.[42] For a more accurate and more nuanced understanding of this snapshot in the history of Jewish-Christian relations, the voices of all parties need to be heard and considered, particularly given the absence of material recording the thoughts and experiences of the immigrant Jews who used these missions themselves.

JEWISH TREATMENT IN MEDICAL MISSIONS

The first medical mission established by evangelicals for Jews began operations in 1879 in Church St (now Fournier St), Spitalfields. It belonged to the BSPGJ, a non-denominational, pan-evangelical society founded in 1842. The medical aspect of their mission work was under the management of John Reid Morrison, LRCP, who dispensed free advice and medicine on Tuesday afternoons between 2 and 4 p.m., during which time approximately thirty patients would be seen by him. Demand was higher than the capacity of Morrison's clinic, and by 1882, the medical mission work had expanded to meet this, opening two afternoons a week (Tuesdays and Fridays), with the doctor making home visits to patients on other days when required.[43] In its first year of operation, the medical mission recorded 960 Jewish attendants. By 1889, almost a decade on, it recorded an attendance of 1,900 patients.[44] The work of the medical mission was deemed to be

[41] *Service for the King*, February 1884, 38.
[42] Criticisms of the medical missions can be found in *JC*.
[43] Information on this medical mission compiled from *JH*, April 1879, 40; August 1879, 89; January 1882, 9; June 1888, inner cover.
[44] *JH*, July 1880, 75; September 1889, 167.

'invariably most successful'[45] by those who carried it out, and if success is measured by the take-up of such services among the local Jewish population of Spitalfields, it was indeed successful.

The second medical mission for Jews, and the most significant in terms of the scope of its work, opened in 1880 as part of the MMJ. This was a non-denomination, evangelical, independent mission founded and overseen by the Rev. John Wilkinson in 1876. Its medical branch, supervised by John Dixon (a Bachelor of Medicine and Master of Surgery), became (and remained) the largest medical mission for Jews in London, operating from 10 a.m., Monday to Saturday. The staff included not only a number of qualified doctors, but also a team of trained deaconess nurses, a separate dispenser and later a skin specialist and a dentist.[46]

The medical mission of the MMJ eventually operated from a purpose-built hall on Philpot St, but as part of a larger network of missions associated with the annual Mildmay Conference, the MMJ was also able to make use of other Mildmay institutions, including their hospital at Turville St (which later moved to Austin St) and various convalescent homes. In its first year of operating, the MMJ recorded a total of 1,966 cases seen. By 1900, after two decades of unbroken work, the recorded number of cases seen in one year was 28,376.[47]

The third medical mission under consideration here was established at the comparatively late date of 1891 and was part of the LSPCJ, founded in 1809, the earliest mission to be aimed exclusively at evangelizing the Jewish people. The LSPCJ ran its medical mission from Goulston St, Aldgate, which opened to patients on Mondays, Thursdays and Saturdays from 10.30 a.m. It was first staffed by a Dr Chaplin with the assistance of a Dr Benoly.[48] In the first four

---

[45] *JH*, January 1882, 9.

[46] On Dixon's early commitment to working as a medical missionary for the Jews, see Harriette Cooke, *Mildmay, or, the Story of the First Deaconess Institution* (London, 1893), 164–5; for information on the medical mission's early operations, see *MMHA*, July 1883, 335; January 1887, 185. A dentist was added to the staff by 1900: *Trusting and Toiling* (hereafter: *TT*), December 1900, 182; this magazine was issued by the MMJ. A skin department followed in 1906: *MMHA*, February 1906, 73.

[47] *MMHA*, November 1885, 19; *TT*, December 1900, 182.

[48] *Jewish Missionary Intelligence* [hereafter: *JMI*], December 1891, 177–8.

years of its operation, the medical mission recorded 59,530 attendances, an annual average of 14,882.[49]

Each of these three medical missions was located within the Jewish
quarter of the East End, was open at convenient hours and could be
attended without an appointment, a medical order or a subscription
letter. The medical missionaries did not carry out interrogations to
determine eligibility for support or to ascertain whether those who
came to them were 'deserving' or 'undeserving' poor. What is
more, in addition to giving advice and dispensing medication at no
financial cost to the patient, the missionaries also distributed essential
items such as coal, blankets, nourishing food and even toys for
children.[50] The medical missions were thus unique in recognizing
and responding to the fact that many of the Jews who came to the
practice were suffering from conditions caused by absolute poverty,
rather than any diagnosable illness. As an article in the *Jewish
Herald* observed: 'Alas there are thousands of Jewish men, women
and children living around our Mission House ... in a most heart-
rending condition of poverty and want. They came for advice and
medicine, and it was found that what was best for them was
bread.'[51] Beyond the draw of such charitable offerings, the particular
attractions of the medical mission to the Jewish immigrant will be
examined in more detail below, while the possible negative consequences resulting from these missionary-patient interactions will
also be considered.

THE ATTRACTION OF MEDICAL MISSIONS

Yiddish-speaking Staff

Newly arrived immigrant Jews without knowledge of the English
language faced a significant barrier in effectively accessing health
care; particularly as Yiddish, unlike other European languages,
would have been unknown to British natives, whether Jewish or
Gentile. Therefore, in order to communicate with the new community, it was necessary for non-Yiddish speakers either to learn Yiddish

---

[49] W. T. Gidney, *At Home and Abroad* (London, 1900), 51.
[50] For example, *MMHA*, March 1889, 262, reports 'giving milk, tea, coca, beef-tea, rice,
warm clothing, socks, cuffs, comforters, boots, trusses, elastic stockings etc.' *MMHS*,
February 1902, 74, describes Jewish children being cheered by 'a dolly or a scrap book'.
[51] *JH*, June 1883, 63.

(a popular option among missionaries) or to find a mediatory language in which both Yiddish and English speakers could try to make themselves understood. German was the imperfect mediatory language, Yiddish having its origins in Middle High German, and for this reason the established Anglo-Jewish community directed Yiddish-speaking Jews to the German Hospital.[52]

It is difficult to determine exactly which languages were known by the individuals who worked within these three medical missions and to what degree of proficiency, but that a concerted effort to learn Yiddish was made is certain.[53] As a result, Jewish patients were able to communicate in their native language and be understood in a medical setting. The fact that this was the case was much lamented in the Anglo-Jewish press. It was reported that 'sick people are driven to the Missionary Dispensary ... because it is only there they are properly understood by the doctors';[54] that in the medical missions the foreign poor could 'speak with doctors who really understand them';[55] and that there medical advice was given 'in their own tongue'.[56] That medical mission staff were able to communicate directly with immigrant Jews in their 'own tongue' and did not need to rely on translators, was an important factor since, according to a report given by the United Synagogue, intermediary communicators were not trusted: 'Interpreters have been tried at the Hospital, but they were not a success. It is said that the foreign Jews are suspicious of them and thought they were police spies.'[57]

Sympathetic and Effective Treatment

A further attraction of the medical mission was the quality of the treatment received and the sympathetic and friendly manner in

[52] *JMI*, December 1891, 178, describes 'voluntary workers who can speak German' as 'much needed' in the medical mission. The JBG made arrangements made with the German Hospital: Black, *Lord Rothschild*, 31.

[53] An account of a man interested in becoming a missionary with the MMJ tells how he was told 'kindly but plainly' that he 'must have a knowledge of Yiddish': *TT*, [July 1896], 137; and the LSPCJ ran bi-weekly Yiddish classes for all who worked in their medical mission: Oxford, Bodl., Papers concerning the London Mission, CMJ d.38-2.

[54] 'Mr Oppenheim on Mr Schewzick', *JC*, 1 December 1893, 10.

[55] Rev. S. Singer, 'Conversionist Activity and its Perils', *JC*, 20 November 1903, 16.

[56] 'Proposed Free Dispensary for the Jewish Poor', *JC*, 6 November 1896, 11.

[57] United Synagogue, *Mission Committee Report*, quoted in Black, 'Health and Medical Care, 1880–1939', 215.

which it was given. Medical missions considered their work to be a practical display of Christian love and 'the best of all methods for removing distrust and unbelief'.[58] Medical missionaries were advised to call men by their first names to increase the sense of intimacy, to take notes when the patient spoke and to repeat back the patient's sentiments using their own words as much as possible so that the patient felt understood and listened to.[59] At the medical missions, waiting times were not long and the time spent on an individual patient averaged between six and fourteen minutes (see Table 1 below), compared to the average of thirty seconds in big hospitals such as the London Hospital.[60]

Indeed, Redcliffe N. Salaman, a doctor at the London Hospital, complained of the medical missions in the *Jewish Chronicle*, accusing them of 'pandering to the ailments of the people' who were allowed to enter 'minutely into all their symptoms, real or alleged'.[61] The use of the word 'pandering' here and the suspicion implied in the reference to a patient's 'alleged' symptoms shows a marked lack of sympathy from Salaman as both a British co-religionist and a medical professional.

In listening actively to, and showing sympathy with, the patient, treating them as a person rather than simply a medical case, the medical missionaries built trust and won the confidence of their Jewish patients, as seen in the positive responses to medical mission recorded in missionary periodicals: 'a man affirmed to me, "in the hospital they cut you anyhow, but when you do it, it is done with mercy." Or a woman's words, "I like to attend here rather than at hospital, because your hands are so full of love."'[62]

But it was not just on the basis of kindly treatment that the medical missions became popular among Jews, it was due also to the skill of the doctors and the effectiveness of their treatments.[63] John Dixon, doctor at the MMJ, had a particularly good reputation in the East

[58] *MMHA*, March 1886, 63.
[59] W. Thomson Crabbe, 'Medical Missions: The Importance of Individual Dealing', *MMHA*, October 1880, 148–50.
[60] Marks, 'Irish and Jewish Women', 321.
[61] *JC*, 7 October 1904, 173.
[62] *JH*, February 1904, 74.
[63] Heasman, 'Medical Mission', 239, notes that the standard of qualification was higher among missionary doctors than it was generally among the district medical officers.

Table 1: Average Length of Patient Consultations at Medical Missions, estimated according to Missionary Records

BSPGJ	LSPCJ	MMJ
Medical mission open 2 days a week, 2 hours a day for approximately 48 weeks a year = 192 hours or 11,520 minutes.1 doctor saw 1,900 patients, averaging 6 minutes spent on each patient.[64]	Medical mission open 3 days a week, 6 hours a day for approximately 48 weeks a year = 864 hours or 51,840 minutes.2 doctors saw 14,882 patients between them, giving each doctor an average of 7 minutes to spend on each patient.[65]	Medical mission open 6 days a week, 6 hours a day for approximately 48 weeks a year = 1,728 hours or 103,680 minutes.At least 4 members of staff (2 doctors, 2 nurses) saw 28,376 patients between them, giving each missionary medic an average of 14 minutes to spend on each patient.Doctors saw 16,822 cases: 12 minutes per case. Nurses saw 6236 cases (including home visitations): 33 minutes per case.[66]

End and developed a loyal patient base.[67] Unusually, evidence in support of Dixon's popularity can be found in both Jewish and

[64] Opening times were Tuesdays and Fridays, 2–4 p.m.: *JH*, June 1888, inner cover. Dr Woodroffe saw 1,900 new cases 'during the past year': *JH*, September 1889, 167.

[65] The mission opened with two doctors, Dr Chaplin and Dr Benoly, working Mondays, Thursdays and Saturdays from 10.30 a.m.: *JMI*, December 1891, 177–8. A six-hour work day is recorded in the archival reports of medical missionaries, from 10.30 to 1.30 and 2.30 to 5.30: Bodl., CMJ d.38-2.

[66] For statistics on numbers of patients seen that year, see *TT*, December 1900, 182. For the dates and times of medical mission operating, see ibid., July 1898, 123. Workers included Drs Dixon and Marshall (Samuel Hinds Wilkinson, *The Life of John Wilkinson: The Jewish Missionary* [London,1908], 199) and deaconesses Miss Athill and Mrs Tang (*A Summary of the Lord's Work: In witnessing for Jesus to the Jews; and on their behalf … during the Year 1887* [London, 1888], 26). Eleven medical workers were employed in the London mission, not only doctors and deaconesses but also those who gave scriptural addresses or short sermons, or attended the waiting room: *TT*, January 1896, 16.

[67] Dr Dixon was reported to be a household name among East End Jews: *TT*, December 1889, 183.

missionary writings, as well as sources external to these communities. The *Jewish Chronicle* reports that Jewish attendance at the Mildmay Mission was 'due to the reputation of its doctor as an able practitioner' and as one who possessed 'a reputation for efficacious treatment of various ailments'.[68] The evangelical publication *Medical Missions at Home and Abroad* records that when active attempts were made to dissuade Jews from using the medical mission, the arguments would fall upon deaf ears: 'the patients only smile and shake their heads and say they like to come to Dr. Dixon'.[69] After thirty-one years of service to medical missions among Jews, Dixon's popularity among the Jewish community was also acknowledged in his obituary.[70]

A heymishkeyt?

Scholars have yet to consider how a Jewish immigrant's previous experience of medical care in Eastern Europe and how pre-existing cultural approaches towards medicine and medical practitioners would have informed the way a Jewish immigrant navigated the various health care options in nineteenth-century London. This subject deserves dedicated research of its own, but here I wish only to suggest briefly and tentatively that London's medical missions may in some ways, despite their proselytizing element, have felt less alien to an immigrant Jew than the environment of the state infirmary or voluntary hospital.

Firstly, medical missions offered care in the community. Jews were not required to be institutionalized to receive treatment, as those who sought help from the Poor Law had to be (if the rules of not granting outdoor relief were being strictly adhered to); nor were they obliged to wait hours in an outpatient department of a voluntary hospital if medical care could be better administered at home through the visitation of doctors and nurses. The MMJ had a particularly well-organized schedule of visitations, hiring a separate doctor to undertake home visits: over two thousand each year, with around two-thirds

---

[68] 'Jewish Board of Guardians', *JC*, December 12, 1890, 12.
[69] *MMHA*, April 1888, 103.
[70] 'Obituary: Dr John Dixon', *British Medical Journal* 2, no. 2647 (23 September 1911), 714.

of these being to children.[71] Hospitals as institutions were generally feared due to their associations with destitution, poverty and medical harm rather than healing; but even the best hospital would have had its frightening aspects for a new immigrant, due to its unfamiliar environment and the alien language spoken by its staff.[72]

Moreover, medical missions were the only medical facilities in London where a Jewish patient would not be the conspicuous 'foreign Jew', a minority among a possibly hostile majority, but would be surrounded by their neighbours, friends and fellow immigrants. Describing the medical mission's waiting room for a child reader, the missionary Miss Wilkinson wrote:

> Look for a few minutes in our medical mission room; you will see it is quite full of men, women, and children whose faces are very different from those you are in the habit of seeing, for they are the children of Abraham, Isaac and Jacob and their features are all Jewish. Listen to their talk, can you understand it? No, for they most of them come from other countries and they have learned to mix up two or three languages and thus formed a talk which is often called 'Jewish jargon' and which most Jews understand but not many Gentiles.[73]

In such a waiting room, where a patient's native tongue could be freely spoken and understood and in which they were surrounded by others who were also struggling to settle and survive in a harsh new environment, a feeling of *heymishkeyt* (being at home) was surely closer than it was in the interrogatory office of the Poor Law relieving officer or in the uncomfortable outpatient department of a voluntary hospital.[74] Despite the presence of the missionaries and their evangelistic efforts, the Jewish patients at the medical mission would have always been the majority party and psychologically this was no doubt reassuring.

Finally, it is worth remembering that East European Jews were already accustomed to making pragmatic choices when it came to medical care, particularly in the Russian Pale of Settlement, where restrictions on Jews entering universities meant that the vast majority

---

[71] *TT*, November 1899, 183.
[72] Black, *Lord Rothschild*, 46.
[73] 'The Children's Corner', *MMHA*, January 1888, 62.
[74] 'God bless you for all your that you do us poor Jews … you understand us here, and we feel "heimlich"': 'Mrs Rocha's Report', *MMHA*, July 1902, 154.

of professional doctors would have been Gentiles. By necessity there had developed a culture in which religious and political differences could be set aside in the interest of health, and this allowance seems to have been transferred across to life in the East End.[75]

THE COST OF ATTENDANCE

Even with the attractions and benefits outlined above, attendance at the medical mission came with a cost of sorts. While the medical missions did not require the Jewish patient to profess a conviction, or even an interest, in Christianity to access their medical services, there was still a process to which Jewish patients were expected to submit prior to seeing the doctor. This process was similar across all medical missions, whatever their clientele, and consisted primarily of a short address, a prayer and in some cases also a hymn in the waiting room prior to the commencement of the day's medical business. After this, the doctor would begin consultations with patients but, while waiting their turn, attendees could be approached by missionary staff for individual conversation on matters of faith and religion.[76]

The inconvenience of having to engage with eager evangelicals on matters of religion at a time when their immediate concern was for their health was a cost to be weighed and balanced against the advantages of the medical mission by the individual seeking aid. Judging from the significant numbers of Jews attending the East End medical missions consistently over the twenty-year period under consideration here, it would appear that the quality of the medical care received at the medical missions outweighed the inconvenience of having to listen to sermons or hymn singing.

In addition to the personal compromises inherently required of a Jew attending a Christian medical mission, those who sought medical aid also ran the risk of being penalized by the JBG. The MMJ reported that officers from the JBG would stand at the door of their premises threatening those who went inside with a permanent

---

[75] Lisa Epstein, 'Caring for the Soul's House: The Jews of Russia and Health Care 1860–1914' (Ph.D. thesis, Yale University, 1995). 113; see also eadem, 'Health and Healing', in *YIVO Encyclopedia of Jews in Eastern Europe*, 27 October 2010, online at: <https://yivoencyclopedia.org/article.aspx/Health_and_Healing>, accessed 24 November 2020.
[76] *JMI*, December 1891, 177; *TT*, December 1898, 186; *JH*, January 1894, 5.

8111

111

11111

1 111

11 11

111 1

11111

1111

ban on receiving any Jewish charity.[77] The BSPGJ made a similar report in 1883, describing the anxiety with which patients entered the mission, 'in fear lest they should be detected by the Jewish Authorities!'[78]

THE RESULT OF ATTENDANCE

The *Jewish Chronicle* was vocal in condemning the work of the medical missions in the East End. Within its pages, the missionary doctor was accused of being 'an enemy in disguise' whose primary work is to ensnare 'unwary Jews'.[79] The mixing of medical aid with proselytizing activity was considered to be 'the least defensible of all the methods employed by Christians to "propagate the Gospel among the Jews"'.[80] But despite such accusations and attacks, the medical missionaries were bolstered by their faith and were prepared for the world to misunderstand them: 'some will call us proselytisers, trap-layers, men who are trying to gain a mean advantage over our patients when their minds are enfeebled by disease etc.; we must be prepared to be misunderstood',[81] because that which may be considered 'guile in the eyes of the scoffer' is in the sight of God 'heavenly wisdom'.[82]

One historical defence against the accusation that the missionaries laid traps for the unsuspecting is the honesty and openness with which they shared their very lack of success in altering the beliefs of the Jews who used their services. The medical missionaries found that 'the patients are for the most part ... very indifferent to their souls' needs',[83] and frankly admitted that they saw few 'signs of a transformed life as a result of the medical mission work'.[84] The emphasis on seeking proof of a transformed life rather than lip-service was crucial to an evangelical, sincere in their desire to see genuine religious conversions. Needless to add, the spiritual

---

[77] *MMHA*, July 1883, 335.
[78] *JH*, October 1883, 121.
[79] *JC*, 6 November 1896, 16.
[80] *JC*, 18 November 1887, 5.
[81] *MMHA*, December 1891, 37.
[82] James Miller, *Medical Missions: An Address to Students introductory to a Course of Lectures on this Subject undertaken by Members of the Edinburgh Medical Missionary Society* (Edinburgh, 1849), 32.
[83] *TT*, January 1897, 6.
[84] *TT*, December 1898, 186.

'indifference' observed here relates to the measure of interest Jewish patients showed in the missionary doctors' evangelistic overtures and it took no account of the actual religious life of the patient.

CONCLUSION

Medical missionaries were resigned to being misunderstood in the times in which they practised and they have continued to be largely misunderstood in the scholarship. This is certainly true for the case of medical missions in Anglo-Jewish history. Previous scholarship that has engaged with medical missions to Jews has relied heavily upon sources originating from within the Anglo-Jewish community, which have generated a one-sided and under-researched story. This article has drawn on a wider range of existing sources, including those of the missionaries themselves, who have until now been largely left out of their own history, and the experiences of those who used the services.

It has explored the unique offerings of medical missions and identified the ways in which the specific needs of the newly arrived immigrant Jewish community were met. Compared with other health care services available on the nineteenth-century medical market, medical missions did the most to provide the East End Jewish community with free, easy to access medical services with Yiddish speaking staff and a *heymish* environment. By focusing attention on domestic medical missions to Jews, this article highlights the complexity not only of Christian-Jewish interaction but also of immigrant-Anglo Jewish relations, as well as contributing to the history of medical services in the nineteenth century.

The article has demonstrated how a more nuanced picture of Jewish-Christian relations is revealed when the practical and charitable actions of the Christian missions are analysed in the light of the theology underpinning these actions and when the motivations for mission work, as expressed by the missions themselves, are given credence. This study of medical missions has also contributed to our understanding of how churches responded to religious plurality. In establishing domestic missions to non-Christians 'at home', churches provided tailored welfare services that met the specific needs of the 'other', in this case immigrant Jews, that were not catered for elsewhere. Moreover, while the evangelistic nature of mission work was in theory intended to reduce, if not to eliminate, religious plurality, this research has shown that conversion was not the sole aim of medical missions. This case study has illustrated the complex and multi-faceted character of Christian missions towards the Jews in the nineteenth century.

The Church's Promotion of Public Health in the Southern Part of the Nineteenth-Century Austro-Hungarian Empire

Branka Gabrić* and Darija Damjanović Barišić*
Institute for Global Church and Mission / Frankfurt am Main

Then part of the Austro-Hungarian Empire, the kingdom of Slavonia was characterized in the nineteenth century by constant political and administrative changes. After its liberation from Ottoman conquests, the rural area of the kingdom, already underpopulated, was left with damaged and poor infrastructure. In such circumstances, and as the most educated figures within their communities, Catholic bishops from the diocese of Đakovo and Srijem oversaw the reorganization and reform of local society, providing the foundations for further social development. They renewed and modernized local infrastructure and the production of basic goods, while also providing access to clean water and introducing hygiene measures in cemeteries to prevent the spread of infectious diseases. In addition, they played a crucial role in the opening of hospitals and schools in the region. In such work, one can detect elements of the approach later known as public health.

In the eighteenth and nineteenth centuries, potentially life-threatening issues included unsanitary conditions, contaminated water supplies, defective sewage systems and waste disposal, inadequate housing, poor nutrition and bad working conditions. Illness was regarded as an indicator of poor social and environmental conditions and cleanliness was thus embraced as a path to health. Public health in this period focused on attempts to deal with unacceptable living conditions through legislation or population policies.[1] In fact, it was in this period that many European governments started to promote health initiatives. The nineteenth century has been described as

* E-mails: gabric@iwm.sankt-georgen.de; d.damjanovic@gmail.com.
We wish to thank Ankica Landeka from the Central Archdiocesan and Faculty Library of the Catholic Theological Faculty in Đakovo and Vlatko Dolančić from the Archdiocesan Archive of the Đakovo-Osijek Archdiocese, who supported us in gathering sources and materials for this article.

[1] Joy Ladurner et al., eds, *Public Health in Austria: An Analysis of the Status of Public Health* (Copenhagen, 2011), 1–3.

Studies in Church History 58 (2022), 284–305   © The Author(s), 2022. Published by Cambridge University Press on behalf of Ecclesiastical History Society
doi: 10.1017/stc.2022.14

the period of 'the great sanitary awakening',[2] due to progress in public health and the so-called sanitary revolution.[3] 'Sanitation changed the way society thought about public responsibility for citizens' health.'[4] Indeed, 'protecting health became a social responsibility',[5] and disease control was increasingly oriented toward prevention measures.

Public health scholars recognize that 'religious and societal beliefs influenced approaches to explaining and attempting to control communicable disease by sanitation, town planning, and provision of medical care'. However, they also note that 'where religious and social systems repressed scientific investigation and the spread of knowledge, they were capable of inhibiting the development of public health'.[6] Religious and social attitudes could significantly influence a population's outcomes in terms of health and this article aims to investigate whether the local Catholic Church had a positive impact on raising the quality of life in the southern part of the nineteenth-century Austro-Hungarian Empire. In order to consider the role of bishops in this regard and recognize aspects of their work as a commitment to public health, this article will offer an overview of the territory of Slavonia and Srijem, investigating the state's public health provision in this period. It will also examine specific actions by the local church, both in terms of the various measures undertaken by the bishops in the areas of infrastructure improvement and hygiene, as well as in their investment in health care[7] and education. This article contributes to research on the history of the dioceses of Đakovo and Srijem through the prism of engagement in the field of public health.

---

[2] This phrase was used by one of the fathers of public health, Charles-Edward A. Winslow, in 1923: Institute of Medicine, *The Future of Public Health* (Washington DC, 1988), 58.

[3] The term is applied to the set of policies implemented in Europe in the last third of the nineteenth century after discovering that polluted water and food could transmit cholera and several other infectious diseases. The provision of safe drinking water and better hygiene measures led to a decline in deaths from diarrheal diseases: 'Sanitary Revolution', *Oxford Reference*, online at: <https://www.oxfordreference.com/view/10.1093/oi/authority.20110803100440898>, accessed 5 July 2021.

[4] Institute of Medicine, *Future of Public Health*, 58.

[5] Ibid.

[6] Theodore H. Tulchinsky and Elena A. Varavikova, *The New Public Health* (Oxford, 2009), 1.

[7] In this article, the term 'healthcare' is used to designate systems of healthcare provision; while 'health care' is used to describe those actions oriented toward improving health and caring for people or populations.

Branka Gabrić and Darija Damjanović Barišić

POLITICAL AND ECCLESIASTICAL CIRCUMSTANCES

Today's areas of Slavonia (in Croatia) and Srijem (in Serbia) had been under Habsburg rule from 1527 until 1867, when they became a part of the Austro-Hungarian Empire. The territory of the kingdom of Slavonia consisted of three counties (Požega, Virovitica and Srijem), and the Military Frontier (Croatian: *Vojna Krajina*, German: *Militärgrenze*), a borderland of the Habsburg monarchy. The kingdom had been established by a peace treaty in Srijemski Karlovci in 1699, which brought liberation from a hundred and fifty years of Ottoman occupation. With the withdrawal of the Ottoman army and population at the end of the Great Viennese War (1683–91), Slavonia was further destroyed and neglected, and its population displaced. The late seventeenth-century census of Slavonia, undertaken by Don Ferdinand Carl, count of Caraffa di Stigliano, a member of the Court Chamber of Vienna, shows that this area had between seventy and eighty thousand inhabitants, and that 50 per cent of settlements were uninhabited.[8] The area of Slavonia and Srijem was rural and agrarian, with only about 30 per cent of the population living in urban areas; a large part of the territory of Slavonia, about 70 per cent of its total area, was made up of forest and marshland.[9] The 'Opis stanja katoličkih župa 1733/34' ('Description of the Condition of Catholic Parishes in 1733/34'), a document drawn up by the Franciscans of the province of Bosna Srebrna who ran the parishes in Slavonia, notes the small number of families who remained in these areas, and the hunger and poverty which they suffered.[10] These families struggled to cover the cost of living, and parish priests were often paid with local agricultural

---

[8] Antun Lešić, 'Stranovništvo Slavonije krajem 17. i početkom 18. stoljeća' ['The Population of Slavonia at the End of the Seventeenth and Beginning of the Eighteenth Centuries'], *Essehist* 6 (2004), 84–94. All translations from Croatian into English are the authors' own.
[9] Robert Skenderović, 'Ekološko–geografska determiniranost koloniziranja Slavonije u 18. stoljeću' ['Ecological-Geographical Determinism of the Colonization of Slavonia in the Eighteenth Century'], *Radovi – Zavod za hrvatsku povijest* [*Transactions of the Institute of Croatian History*] 51 (2019), 181–99; Anđelko Vlašić, 'Iskorištavanje šuma u Slavoniji u Osmanskom razdoblju (1526–1691)' ['Forest Exploitation in Slavonia in the Ottoman Period (1526–1691)'], *Scrinia Slavonica* 16 (2016), 71–90.
[10] Stjepan Sršan, 'Katoličke župe u đakovštini početkom 18. stoljeća' ['Catholic Parishes in Đakovo at the Beginning of the Eighteenth Century'], *Zbornik Muzeja Đakovštine* [*Proceedings of the Museum of the Đakovo Region*] 4 (1997), 83–99.

produce and firewood and were not invited to officiate at burials due to lack of means.

In terms of its ecclesiastical organization, the kingdom of Slavonia was divided between several dioceses. After its liberation, its small Catholic population and the high number of destroyed churches led the Viennese administration to unite the two dioceses of Bosnia and Srijem. This was confirmed by Pope Clement XIV with the unification provision *Universi orbis Ecclesiis* in 1773.[11] The united diocese, Ðakovo or Bosnia and Srijem,[12] initially had sixteen parishes with affiliated churches; in 1782 its territory was increased to include eighty-seven diocesan priests across forty-eight parishes.

This expansion reflected the demographic changes that occurred after the Great Viennese War: by the middle of the eighteenth century, more than four hundred thousand Christians from Bosnia, led by Franciscans, had migrated to liberated Slavonia and Srijem in order to escape Ottoman repression. Other people from within the Austro-Hungarian Empire also contributed to the new settlement of this area.[13] These population changes created new challenges in terms of the provision and maintenance of adequate living conditions and hygiene measures.

PUBLIC HEALTH MEASURES IN THE EIGHTEENTH AND NINETEENTH CENTURIES

The eighteenth and nineteenth centuries saw a number of states begin to tackle issues relating to healthcare. Important new provisions were outlined; however, although there was growing awareness of the role of the state, the practical implementation of these measures was very slow due to a lack of human and material resources. This partly explains the importance of episcopal engagement with social and health care issues, which this article will explore.[14]

---

[11] Mato Cepelić and Milko Pavić, *Josip Juraj Strossmayer, biskup bosansko–dakovački i srijemski, god. 1850–1900* [*Josip Juraj Strossmayer, Bishop of Bosnia-Ðakovo and Srijem, 1850–1900*] (Ðakovo, 2013), 4.

[12] Its Latin name is *Bosniensisseu Diacovensis et Sirmiensis*. Hereafter we will refer to this diocese by the abbreviated name of Ðakovo and Srijem.

[13] Lešić, 'Stranovništvo Slavonije' ['Population of Slavonia']; Skenderović, 'Ekološko–geografska determiniranost' ['Ecological-Geographical Determinism'].

[14] For a broader historiographical context, see Alfons Labish and Reinhard Spree, eds, *Einem jeden Kranken in einem Hospitale sein eigenes Bett* (Frankfurt am Main and

It was the plague epidemic that appeared at the borders of the Habsburg monarchy in 1700, and from 1708 spread to the territory of Hungary, that led Emperor Joseph I (1705–11) to establish the first integrated state-level Court Sanitary Commission (*Sanitäts-Hofkommission*) in 1710.[15] In the same year, Joseph I published the 'pest patent for the Military Frontier', which marked the beginning of the organization of an anti-epidemic defence as another important function of the Military Frontier.[16] With these provisions, the organization of a 'sanitary cordon system' began.[17] This was the first element of organized healthcare to be implemented in the area of Slavonia; it fell under the jurisdiction of the Viennese authorities and was also organized by the army. Located along the border with the Ottoman Empire, this 'sanitary cordon' was overseen by its own medical staff who monitored the flow of travellers, the maintenance of quarantine measures and the identification of infectious diseases, especially the plague. From 1730, sanitary commissions were formed in Osijek and Karlovac to monitor conditions in the Slavonian Military Frontier (*Slavonska vojna krajina*) and within the Karlovac General Command (*Karlovac Generalate*),[18] one of the regiments

---

New York, 1996); George Rosen, *A History of Public Health* (Baltimore, MD, 2015); Michael Pammer, 'Vom Beichtzettel zum Impfzeugnis. Beamte, Ärzte, Priester und die Einführung der Vaccination', *Österreich in Geschichte und Literatur* 39 (1995), 11–29; Michel Foucault, *The Birth of the Clinic* (London and New York, 1973); Virginia Berridge, Martin Gorsky and Alex Mold, *Public Health in History* (New York, 2011).

[15] Erna Lesky, 'Die österreichische Pestfront an der k. k. Militärgrenze', *Saeculum* 8 (1957), 82–106, at 86; Franciscus Xav. Linzbauer, *Codex sanitario-medicinalis Hungariae*, 3 vols (Budae, 1852), 1: 409; Robert Skenderović, 'Epidemije kuge u Banskoj Hrvatskoj i Slavoniji krajem 17. i početkom 18. stoljeća kao povod za početak organiziranja javnozdravstvenoga sustava' ['Plague Epidemics in Banská Bystrica, Croatia and Slavonia in the late Seventeenth and early Eighteenth Centuries as the Motivation for the first Attempts to organize the Public Health System'], *Povijesni Prilozi* [*Historical Contributions*] 60 (2021), 77–96, at 83–4.

[16] Franz Vaniček, *Specialgeschichte der Militärgrenze aus Originalquellen und Quellenwerken geschöpft*, 4 vols (Vienna, 1875), 1: 162.

[17] This line of defence against the plague also existed within the monarchy. It aimed to isolate and control the flow of travellers from areas where the epidemic was present.

[18] The Military Frontier in present-day Croatia had two parts. The first, the Croatian Military Frontier (*Krabatische Graenitz*) was the western part of the Military Frontier. In the sixteenth century, it belonged to the territory of the kingdom of Croatia. The second part, the Slavonian Military Frontier (*Slawonische Graenitz, Windische Graenitz*) was the part of the Military Frontier that belonged to historical Slavonia. For more on the Croatian and Slavonian Military Frontiers in the Habsburg monarchy, see Gunther

on the Croatian Military Frontier (*Hrvatska vojna krajina*).[19] However, until the reign of Maria Theresa (1740–80), the Habsburg monarchy had no state healthcare system as such. The lack of educated doctors was compensated for by trained surgeons, monks and so-called *feldshers* (*ranari*).[20] Significant changes occurred in 1770 when Maria Theresa passed the first general health law, the *Generale Normativum Sanitatis*, which, according to Robert Skenderović, 'was intended for the entire Habsburg monarchy'; this 'regulated all elements of healthcare and the system of state supervision of local medical institutions and medical staff, so that from the time of Maria Theresa we can talk about an organized state healthcare system'.[21] The law prescribed compulsory education for medical staff (doctors, surgeons, feldshers, pharmacists and midwives) and defined their work; its second part regulated the sanitary cordon. In 1766, Maria Theresa's request for the introduction of more educated doctors, along with the passing of additional legislation, led to further legal changes in Slavonia.[22]

The monumental *System einer vollständigen medicinischen Polizey* (*Complete System of Medical Policy*, 9 vols, 1779–1817), by the German scholar Johann Peter Franck, offers an example of strong governmental action in healthcare reform and regulation. It outlined a comprehensive and coherent approach to public health, based primarily on authoritative governmental rules and medical policy, in which municipal authorities were responsible for keeping towns clean and for monitoring infectious diseases and hospitals.[23]

Erich Rothenberg, The Austrian Military Border 1740–1881 (Chicago, IL, and London, 1966).

[19] Vlatka Dugački and Krešimir Regan, 'Povijest zdravstvene skrbi i razvoja zdravstvenih ustanova na hrvatskom prostoru' ['History of Healthcare and Development of Healthcare Institutions in Croatian Territory'], *Studia lexicographica: časopis za leksikografiju i enciklopedistiku* [*Journal of Lexicography and Encyclopaedic Studies*] 13 (2019), 35–74, at 46.

[20] The term *feldsher* had been coined in the fifteenth century to refer to barber surgeons trained through apprenticeships, rather than at a university medical faculty.

[21] Robert Skenderović, 'Zdravstvene reforme Marije Terezije u slavonskom Provincijalu i *Generale normativum sanitatis* iz 1770' ['Health Reforms of Maria Theresa in the Slavonian Province and the *Generale normativum sanitatis* from 1770'], *Scrinia Slavonica* 5 (2005), 115–43, at 142.

[22] Ibid. 133.

[23] Tulchinski and Varavikova, *New Public Health*, 11; Dorothy Porter, *Health, Civilization and the State* (London and New York, 1999), 53. While Franck's work was very influential in Russia, and he acted as director general of the principal hospital of

Branka Gabrić and Darija Damjanović Barišić

The nineteenth century saw further changes introduced. In 1850, the principles of public medical management implemented across the entire Habsburg territory sought to establish the employment of county doctors, rather than municipal doctors, better suited to the needs of local populations.[24] As a result of the Croatian-Hungarian settlement in 1868, Croatia gained independence in regulating healthcare, paving the way for the 1874 Health Insurance Act in the kingdoms of Croatia and Slavonia. In addition, the National Health Council was established as an advisory body on health issues. As a result, health authorities were established in cities and municipal areas, and doctors were employed at the county level. In the same year, the first medical associations were founded, including one in Osijek.[25]

A further reorganization of healthcare was also carried out in 1894 on the basis of the Law for the Regulation of Healthcare in the Kingdoms of Croatia and Slavonia,[26] which extended responsibility for public health service provision to municipalities. This included special measures concerning midwives: each city was required to have one or more midwives whose work was supervised by a county

---

Vienna and was employed in the regulation of the sanitary service of the Austro-Hungarian army, the extent of his influence on the development of public health in other European countries remains unclear.

[24] Dugački and Regan, 'Povijest zdravstvene skrbi i razvoja zdravstvenih ustanova' ['History of Healthcare and Development of Healthcare Institutions'], 50. Four phases can be observed in the development of public health in the Habsburg monarchy. The first half of the eighteenth century was marked by a concentration on preventative measures to prevent plague epidemics. The second phase can be recognized in the building of public health institutions and of institutional networks at the local level. The third phase is seen in ensuring the availability of healthcare and increasing the number of professional staff. The fourth phase was the period after the system had already been formally developed, when public health policy focused on the general health of the population and preventative measures: see Ivana Horbec, *Zdravlje naroda-bogatstvo države. Prosvijećeni apsolutizam i počeci sustava javnog zdravstva u Hrvatskoj* [*The Health of the People, the Wealth of the State: Enlightened Absolutism and the Beginnings of the Public Health System in Croatia*] (Zagreb, 2015), 56.

[25] Dugački and Regan, 'Povijest zdravstvene skrbi i razvoja zdravstvenih ustanova' ['History of Healthcare and Development of Healthcare Institutions'], 51.

[26] Hrvatski Sabor, *Zakon od 24. siečnja 1894. o uredjenju zdravstvene službe u kraljevinah Hrvatskoj i Slavoniji* [*Act of 24 January 1894 regarding the Organization of the Health Service in the Kingdoms of Croatia and Slavonia*] (Zagreb, 1894); Jozo Ivčević, 'Javna uprava zdravstvom u (sjevernoj) Hrvatskoj 1868–1928. godine' ['Public Health Administration in (Northern) Croatia 1868–1928'], *Arhivski Vjesnik* [*Archival Herald*] 36 (1993), 117–30.

physician, depending on the number of inhabitants. Despite these changes, it was not until 1913 that the first Croatian Society for the Preservation of Public Health (Hrvatsko društvo za čuvanje narodnoga zdravlja) was founded.[27] These measures were intended to achieve radical change in both the nature of healthcare and the approach taken by practitioners. The majority of healthcare institutions in the territories of the Habsburg monarchy had been run by religious orders and the church until the period of Habsburg 'enlightened absolutism' during the eighteenth and early nineteenth century, when – as in many other parts of Europe – the state became the main actor in issues regarding healthcare provision.[28]

Although the Habsburg monarchy developed a significant and realistically enforceable health monitoring system throughout its territory, it did not invest enough resources to implement it effectively, especially in the southern areas. There continued to be a lack of doctors throughout the nineteenth century, particularly in the region of Slavonia. Since there was little public investment in the realization of royal decisions and laws in Slavonia and Srijem, health care there continued to be provided by the church. Successive bishops of Đakovo and Srijem invested considerable material resources into measures intended to ensure better social and hygiene conditions for the population within their diocese. With poverty and disease being seen as synonymous in this period, caring for the poor became a part of public health policy. However, such care had always been an important

---

[27] Dugački and Regan, 'Povijest zdravstvene skrbi i razvoja zdravstvenih ustanova' ['History of Healthcare and Development of Healthcare Institutions'], 52–3. In 1919, Dr Andrija Štampar was appointed head of the Ministry of Public Health. Štampar, later the first president of the World Health Organization, devised an institutional form of primary health care in Croatia, the first of its kind in the world.

[28] In early nineteenth-century France, the new Paris Health Council addressed a wide range of public health concerns, such as sanitation, food control and occupational health, and in 1848 a central national health authority was established. In Britain, a Central Board of Health was founded in 1805 with the purpose of overseeing quarantine regulations in order to prevent the spread of yellow fever and cholera; over the course of the nineteenth century, other public health provisions were also introduced, such as sanitation, lighting, iron water pipes and water filtration. 1881 was a significant year for public health in Germany: Otto von Bismarck, the chancellor, introduced legislation that provided mandatory insurance for injury and illness, and survivor benefits for industrial workers. Two years later, social insurance to fund the healthcare of workers and their families was introduced, based on mandatory payments from workers' salaries and employer contributions. See Tulchinski and Varavikova, *New Public Health*, 13.

part of the church's charitable activity. In that spirit, and under these particular circumstances, the bishops sought to offer more systematic provision in the challenging context of the renewal of a devasted territory.

THE ACTIVITY OF THE LOCAL CHURCH FROM THE PERSPECTIVE OF PUBLIC HEALTH

Considering one of the earliest classical definitions of public health, dating from 1920,[29] it is apparent that many of the efforts undertaken by the bishops of Đakovo fall within this category. The definition, published by Charles-Edward A. Winslow, founder of the Yale Department of Public Health, only five years after the death of Bishop Strossmayer, provides a good overview of the efforts and work of the Slavonian bishops. Winslow defines public health as:

the Science and Art of (1) *preventing disease*, (2) *prolonging life*, and (3) *promoting health* and efficiency through organized community effort for:

(a) sanitation of the environment,

(b) control of communicable infections,

(c) *education* of the individual in personal hygiene,

(d) organization of medical and nursing services for the early diagnosis and preventive treatment of disease, and

(e) development of *social machinery* to ensure a standard of living adequate for the maintenance of health for everyone, so organizing these benefits as to enable every citizen to enjoy his birthright of health and longevity.[30]

This definition summarizes broader efforts in the field of public health, as well as the new discoveries and guidelines developed in the nineteenth century, and provides a more coherent way of assessing and interpreting the different actions undertaken by the local church in Slavonia during this period. The remainder of this article will focus on three main areas in which the local church acted to protect and improve public health: investment in infrastructure,

---

[29] For more on the most influential definitions of public health, see Angus Dawson and Marcel Verweij, 'The Meaning of "Public" in "Public Health"', in eidem, eds, *Ethics, Prevention, and Public Health* (Oxford, 2007), 13–29.

[30] As quoted in Tulchinski and Varavikova, *New Public Health*, 45 (italics ours).

measures intended to improve hygiene, and the provision of general health care and education.

The Importance of Infrastructure Improvement and Hygiene Measures

Throughout the eighteenth century, the rural population in the kingdom of Slavonia cultivated the land by hand without draught animals. Fertile fields were located along rivers that often flooded, destroying crops.[31] Houses were made of mudbricks or wood with earth floors and reed roofs; brick buildings were rare and generally found only in urban settlements.[32] As a result, conditions were often highly unhygienic.

After the liberation of Slavonia from the Ottomans, the first bishops in this area, Juraj III Patačić (1703–16), Petar IV Bakić (1716–49), Josip Antun Ćolnić (1751–73) and Matej Franjo Krtica (1773–1805), sought to restore the neglected areas by cutting down forests, establishing pastures, buying cattle, dredging ponds and planting vineyards.[33] Considerable efforts were made to resettle the abandoned villages on the diocese's territorial estates, which stretched from the Sava to the Drava river, east of the city of Brod, all the way to Petrovaradin and Zemun. The main obstacle to the colonization of these areas was the dense forests, which were difficult to clear to provide space for new settlements, pastures and arable land, as well as for the roads necessary to connect these settlements.

Another ecological problem was the presence of many marshlands in Slavonia and Srijem, especially along the rivers, which required draining.[34] Infectious diseases were frequent, notably malaria,

[31] Milan Vrbanus, 'Ratarstvo u slavonskoj posavini krajem 17. stoljeća' ['Farming in the Slavonian Posavina at the End of the Seventeenth Century'], *Scrinia Slavonica* 2 (2002), 202–60.
[32] Aleksandra Muraj, 'Svakodnevni život u 19. stoljeću' ['Everyday Life in the Nineteenth Century'], in Vlasta Švoger and Jasna Turkalj, eds, *Temelji moderne Hrvatske. Hrvatske zemlje u „dugom" 19. stoljeću* [*Foundations of modern Croatia. The Croatian Lands in the 'long' Nineteenth Century*] (Zagreb, 2016), 309–39.
[33] Cepelić and Pavić, *Strossmayer*, 847–99; Marin Srakić, 'Ponovna uspostava i uređenje vlastelinstva bosansko–đakovačke biskupije (Prema dokumentima Dijecezantskog arhiva u Đakovu)' ['Re-establishment and Arrangement of the Manor of the Bosnian-Đakovo Diocese (According to the Documents of the Diocesan Archives in Đakovo)'], in Dušan Čalić and Đuro Berber, eds, *Peti znanstveni sabor Slavonije i Baranje* [*Fifth Scientific Congress of Slavonia and Baranja*] (Osijek, 1991), 151–61.
[34] Skenderović, 'Ekološko-geografska determiniranost' ['Ecological-Geographical Determinism'], 188–91.

which was endemic in the area until the beginning of the twentieth century. Because of the prevalence of diseases such as malaria, typhus, plague, dysentery and smallpox, along with other infectious illnesses, these areas of the Habsburg monarchy were considered unhealthy. The most frequent causes of death recorded in parish registers included fever, diarrhoea, diphtheria and smallpox.[35] Unhygienic living conditions were conducive to infections that often proved fatal, especially for mothers and newborn babies.[36]

One of the most important figures in public and ecclesiastical life in the early nineteenth century was Bishop Antun Mandić (b. 1740; bishop 1815–16). Born in Slavonia, Mandić succeeded a series of bishops who came from Zagreb and the surrounding dioceses. A native of the city of Požega, Mandić knew the people, their language and customs, and understood the problems facing his compatriots and the country more generally. Educated in Požega, Zagreb, Bologna and Vienna, he held several secular posts and responsibilities in addition to his clerical ministry, including appointment as secret adviser to the imperial court and commissioner for Slavonia during the Napoleonic Wars. He also contributed to the publication of numerous works in the Croatian language, and was an advocate for the development of a programme of instruction in Slavonian and Croatian orthography which was used from 1779 in schools across the kingdom of Slavonia.[37]

Mandić envisioned the development of the whole diocese, looking to modernize his homeland along the lines of other parts of the monarchy. In order to improve diet and nutrition, he ordered the digging of fishponds, dredging of riverbeds and rebuilding of mills for grinding grain, providing local people with easier access to flour. Mandić also bought cattle, horses and oxen, and restored vineyards, creating employment opportunities for the population on the diocesan estates.

[35] Skenderović, 'Zdravstvene reforme Marije Terezije' ['Health Reforms of Maria Theresa'], 122–4; idem, 'Ekološko–geografska determiniranost' ['Ecological-Geographical Determinism'].
[36] Skenderović, 'Zdravstvene reforme Marije Terezije' ['Health Reforms of Maria Theresa'], 122–4.
[37] Marin Srakić, 'Biskup Antun Mandić – „zamišljatelj svega boljega i uzvišenijega u biskupiji"' ['Bishop Antun Mandić: "The Inventor of everything better and more sublime in the Diocese"'], *Diacovensia* 24 (2016), 229–46; Zlatko Vince, 'Antun Mandić kao kulturni i prosvijetni radnik' ['Antun Mandić as a Cultural and Educational Worker'], *Diacovensia* 1 (1996), 155–66.

Another important investment was the building of a silk mill in the city of Đakovo for the production of mulberry silk, which provided employment for young people. He later established a brewery, as well as a large water fountain which was of great importance for the city population, since clean water was key to stopping the spread of epidemics and improving hygiene conditions. Another of Mandić's tactical moves was his settlement of a colony of German craftsmen and traders in Đakovo. Their arrival provided an opportunity for the development of crafts and the founding of guild associations. His efforts and investment also led to the restoration of the village of Pridvorje, which had earlier been destroyed by fire.[38]

In his short but very active period as bishop of Đakovo and Srijem, Mandić contributed to the development of local communities and helped, in numerous ways, to ease the hardships of rural life. He did not overlook the relevance of health care provision alongside his improvement of living standards. His successors continued these efforts, particularly Josip Juraj Strossmayer (b. 1815; bishop 1850–1905), a native of Osijek. Strossmayer was well acquainted with the situation in the kingdom of Slavonia. He completed his doctorate at Vienna's *Augustineum*, an institute of higher education for diocesan priests, where he later became one of the directors and a court chaplain. From 1849 he was professor of canon law at the University of Vienna. Alongside his bishopric, Strossmayer entered public political life in 1860 and became the head of the Croatian National Party. He held this post until the so-called revision of the Croatian-Hungarian settlement in 1873, after which he withdrew from public political life. During this period of political engagement, he was a member of the Croatian parliament, president of the Croatian Royal Committee and, from 1861 to 1862, the district prefect of Virovitica County.[39]

As bishop, Strossmayer reorganized the work of the diocesan estates. After the abolition of serfdom in 1849, these possessions were divided between different towns and villages, and the diocese lost about two-thirds of its territory, resulting in a significant

---

[38] Cepelić and Pavić, *Strossmayer*, 15.
[39] Nikša Stančić, 'Josip Juraj Strossmayer u hrvatskoj politici' ['Josip Juraj Strossmayer in Croatian Politics'], *Rad Hrvatske akademije znanosti i umjetnosti. Razred za društvene znanosti* [*The Work of the Croatian Academy of Sciences and Arts. Department of Social Sciences*] 535 (2018), 11–36.

depletion of the revenues which its bishops had previously used to rebuild the diocese and help those in need. The diocesan office's financial records include a list of the pious foundations (*pia fondatia*) established by individual bishops, which indicates the works they had financed, using both revenues from the diocesan estates and their own money. Such initiatives included foundations for poor school children and seminarians, the widows of estate officials and estate residents, as well as for orphans or poor people from Đakovo. Other foundations were set up to finance schools and teachers. Most of the funds, however, went to foundations for hospitals, shelters and houses for the elderly in the towns of the diocese, Đakovo, Osijek, Mitrovica, Kamenica and Petrovaradin.[40]

Despite the considerable depletion of income arising from the reorganization of the formerly feudal estate, Strossmayer continued to support a number of projects. In addition to management of the diocese and pastoral care of the people entrusted to him, Strossmayer's work aimed at improving the overall health and social situation of the residents of the diocese.[41] His episcopal motto, 'all for the faith and for the homeland', articulates his understanding of his role and his commitment to caring – in the broadest sense, both spiritually and physically – for the people entrusted to him. He later added 'enlightenment leads to freedom' to his motto, underlining the importance of knowledge. His Enlightenment interests help to explain his broader involvement in the development of the region and his desire to modernize the economy and agriculture of the diocesan estates, in line with the modernization of production across Europe during this period.

One of his first investments was the replacement of the old mill in Đakovo with a modern steam mill in 1877. The diocesan properties included several brickfields, which he modernized, also opening a new one.[42] He built bridges and a new public steam bath in Đakovo in 1894. Keenly aware of the importance of clean water,

---

[40] Đakovo, Archdiocesan Archive (NAĐ), 12 Diocesan Council, books II (1874–97), IV (1824–92), V–VIII (1874–97); II–VI (1898–1926).

[41] Because of his involvement in many secular spheres, Strossmayer had a good knowledge of the political, social, educational and pastoral problems of the kingdom of Slavonia, and indeed of the whole of Croatia, at that time. He was best known for his speeches at the First Vatican Council (1869–70), opposing the dogma of papal infallibility. He acknowledged the dogma, but never officially endorsed it.

[42] The new brickfield provided the bricks for the new cathedral in Đakovo (1866–82).

The Church's Promotion of Public Health

he also built wells for drinking water. He invested in new equipment to make the cultivation of the land and vineyards more efficient. Oak forests covered a large area of the diocesan estates; their wood was used in the production of wooden barrel staves which were sold all over Europe.[43] With this and other income from the estates, Strossmayer was able to finance further economic, construction, cultural-educational and humanitarian projects.

Strossmayer insisted that the clergy, 'for the love of science and administration', should also record statistics in registers, as required by Croatian and Slavonian authorities. In addition to recording marriages, births and deaths, clergy were required to enter lists of young men undertaking military service (1887), school children (1889), children due for vaccination against smallpox (1873) and other parish statistics.[44] In his circulars to diocesan clergy, Strossmayer often emphasized the need for clergy to be kind to people, as Jesus had always been merciful and open to others. Trust opened up a space for mutual cooperation. In the many difficulties facing the poor of the diocese, Strossmayer believed they should be able to find refuge and help in the clergy and the church.[45]

The Provision of Health Care

When examining the church's activity in providing health care in this area, it is worth looking back to the sixteenth and seventeenth centuries, when the historical sources clearly show the support and help offered to people by religious orders. After the Ottoman incursions, medical treatment of the Muslim population was undertaken mostly by *hodjas* (teachers), while Franciscan friars played a major role among the non-Islamized population. They were especially popular during outbreaks of plague: advising on cleanliness, isolation of patients and the burning of clothes; giving medications against fever; and implementing hygiene measures after a death. In these ways, they contributed significantly to the fight against this vicious disease.[46]

[43] Cepelić and Pavić, *Strossmayer*, 905–11.
[44] Ibid. 186. Today, these registers are an invaluable resource for research in many areas, including public health and education.
[45] Ibid. 178–9.
[46] Dugački and Regan, 'Povijest zdravstvene skrbi i razvoja zdravstvenih ustanova' ['History of Healthcare and Development of Healthcare Institutions'], 43–4.

Branka Gabrić and Darija Damjanović Barišić

In the first half of the eighteenth century, health care remained, for the most part, in the hands of priests (mostly Franciscans and Jesuits), alongside trained *feldshers* and barbers. Franciscans and Jesuits often established pharmacies, and their larger communities included monks who specialized in medicine and pharmacy, as was the case with the friaries and monasteries in Virovitica, Osijek and Požega.[47] Nonetheless, a large proportion of the population was left to fend for themselves, dependent on herbal remedies and folk medicine.[48]

The restoration of the kingdom of Slavonia, along with that of the possessions and settlements of the Bosnian and Srijem dioceses was a long and slow process. Mandić described Đakovo, the seat of the diocese, to the Archbishop Palatine at the beginning of his episcopate in 1806 as 'such a miserable city with no Sunday fair, no suitable house where necessary people would live, no doctor, no pharmacy'.[49] After his arrival in the diocese, he tried to provide adequate medical care in Đakovo. In 1809, he brought in the pharmacist Torkvat Manastir from Pecs, initially providing him with accommodation in the seminary before having an apartment and a pharmacy built for him.[50] It seems that Mandić also arranged for a doctor to be made available, but the sources do not indicate this person's name or when he arrived. It is probable that, as was customary at that time, the pharmacist

[47] The oldest medical book in the Croatian language was published by the Franciscans in Buda in 1768; it is a bilingual Croatian-Latin translation of the book *Flos medicinae / Cvit likarije*. In many areas, the Franciscans were the only doctors available: Fr Petar Dombaj Saboljević worked in Vukovar, and in Virovitica Fr Bonifacije Gerber, a trained *feldsher*, established a small pharmacy. Its importance is evidenced by the fact that in the entire Virovitica County, from Osijek to Koprivnica, there was no other doctor or pharmacy. This situation alone testifies to the great lack of healthcare in Slavonia: Skenderović, 'Zdravstvene reforme Marije Terezije' ['Health Reforms of Maria Theresa'], 117.
[48] The experience of folk healers and herbalists is preserved in books called '*Ljekaruše*': Dugački and Regan, 'Povijest zdravstvene skrbi i razvoja zdravstvenih ustanova' ['History of Healthcare and Development of Healthcare Institutions'], 43–4.
[49] 'Đakovo je tako bijedan grad, da u njemu nema ni nedjeljnog sajma, ni prikladne kuće u kojoj bi stanovali potrebni ljudi, ni liječnika, ni apoteke': Marin Srakić, 'Antun Mandić, biskup, realizator školskih reforma u Hrvatskoj' ['Antun Mandić, Bishop, Implementer of School Reforms in Croatia'], in Dragutin Tadijanović, ed., *Zbornik radova o Marijanu Lanosoviću* [*Collected Papers relating to Marijan Lanosović*], Posebna izdanja, Zavod za znanstveni rad Osijek 6 [Special Editions of the Osijek Institute for Scientific Research 6] (Osijek, 1985), 87–97, at 92.
[50] Cepelić and Pavić, *Strossmayer*, 17; Željko Lekšić, 'Kratka povijest ljekarništva u Đakovu do Drugog svjetskog rata' ['A Brief History of Pharmacy in Đakovo until the Second World War'], *Zbornik muzeja đakovštine* [*Proceedings of Đakovo Museum*] 13 (2017), 127–44.

Manastir also offered medical services. A doctor is first mentioned in 1829, visiting a home for retired priests.[51] Aware of the importance of health care in the large area of his diocese, Mandić established a foundation to start a hospital in Đakovo. At this time, the construction of hospitals was not financed by the state, so the financial burden of founding and maintaining hospitals in Slavonia was borne by counties and cities, which generally meant that they were managed by religious foundations and funded by money bequeathed by citizens.[52] Mandić's original idea was to build a monastery, a girls' school and a hospital in Đakovo.

Mandić succeeded in establishing a foundation, the endowment of which was increased by his successors, Bishops Raffay (1816–30), Sučić (1828–34) and Kuković (1834–49). It was Kuković who, in 1840, finally began the construction of a dormitory and school for girls, as well as a hospital.[53] He was also the patron of the Zagreb branch of the *Gospodarsko društvo* (the 'Economic Society', founded in 1845) and the author of articles on the economy, published in the *Osiječki kalendar* ('Osijek Calendar') and intended to educate local people.[54] Mandić's successors continued working on improving education and promoting health care for the inhabitants of Slavonia and Srijem, taking an approach that could be characterized as holistic care. The diocese also organized a hospital for wounded and sick Croatian soldiers involved in the quelling of the Hungarian uprising (1848–9), in the seminary building in Đakovo. This ran for three months in 1849, and the army subsequently offered financial assistance to restore the building.[55]

It was Bishop Strossmayer who finally completed the construction of the hospital in Đakovo. The first private hospital in Slavonia, it existed from 1859 to 1947. From 1868 it was run by the order of the Sisters of Mercy of St Cross, who were invited to Đakovo by Strossmayer. Ten sisters lived in the convent, two of whom were in charge of the hospital, which at first had twenty beds in two rooms, for female and male patients. Although originally intended to provide

---

[51] This was opened in 1829 by Mandić's successor, bishop Raffay.
[52] Skenderović, 'Zdravstvene reforme Marije Terezije' ['Health Reforms of Maria Theresa'], 136–7.
[53] Vince, 'Antun Mandić', 155.
[54] Cepelić and Pavić, *Strossmayer*, 22.
[55] NAĐ, 10 Diocesan Ordinariate, 371/1849; 641/1849; 136/1850; 371/1850; 1052/1850; 1070/1850, official correspondence of the military authorities with the diocese in Đakovo.

health care for patients from the episcopal estates, many other patients were also treated there: civilians and priests, foreigners who were in Đakovo for work or travel, as well as soldiers before their transfer to the military hospital in Osijek.[56] During the occupation of Bosnia and Herzegovina in 1878, the hospital was made available to the wounded; they were taken care of by the sisters, while the monastery provided food. The monastery cooperated with the secular authorities, and always accepted requests from the municipality and Red Cross for use of the hospital during epidemics.

Reports on the hospital's work, including the numbers of patients and other statistics, were regularly submitted to the Royal Provincial Government in Zagreb. The hospital was located next to the convent and girls' school until 1886, when it was moved to a new diocesan building. In 1898, a sanitary inspection of the hospital was carried out, which showed the hospital to be clean and tidy, and stated that it had a steam disinfector for the laundry and bedding.[57] Besides the Sisters of Mercy, two nurses, and at one time three, worked in the hospital. Only one doctor is mentioned in the records: Dr Miroslav Weiss, who came to Đakovo in 1883. He also oversaw the health of the pupils at the girls' school, including vaccinations and regular check-ups, and was responsible for ordering classes to be cancelled during outbreaks of contagious diseases such as measles, diphtheria or typhus.[58] The convent had a garden and kept cattle to help feed both the nurses and the sick in the hospital. From the monastery's financial reports, it is evident that if a patient died in the hospital, the hospital staff took care of the organization of the funeral, for instance by liaising with the undertaker and ordering a coffin.[59] The hospital was funded by the foundation established by Bishop Mandić, while the costs for patients not from the episcopal estates were borne by the patients themselves, their relatives, or in some cases the municipality. This was not a hospital in the modern sense of the word: it did not perform surgery, and it had neither an infirmary nor its own pharmacy. However, it did take care of patients from many different

[56] Estera Radičević, 'Bolnica biskupskog vlastelinstva – bolnica Milosrdnih sestara sv. Križa u Đakovu' ['The Hospital of the Episcopal Estate, the Hospital of the Sisters of Mercy of the Holy Cross in Đakovo'], *Zbornik muzeja đakovštine* [*Proceedings of Đakovo Museum*] 13 (2017), 47–66.

[57] Ibid. 58–61.

[58] Ibid. 63.

[59] Ibid. 56.

backgrounds and with various diagnoses. It was a small but not unimportant health institution at the very centre of the diocese, where those in need could seek medical help.

Another important medical institution in the diocese was the hospital in Osijek. Since 1862, Strossmayer had been applying for money from the Huttler-Kohlhoffer-Monsperger foundation[60] for the construction of an orphanage; however, he was only able to open it in 1870.[61] Having finally succeeded, he used the remaining funds to open a hospital. There had been a military hospital in Osijek since 1730 due to the large number of soldiers stationed at the Military Frontier. After an outbreak of plague in 1749, the city also established a civilian hospital, although this was more of an almshouse or home for the elderly. By the end of the eighteenth century, it was augmented by Georg Ritter's surgical practice,[62] becoming a real medical institution; it functioned as such until 1874, when Bishop Strossmayer began the construction of a new Huttler-Kohlhoffer-Monsperger foundation hospital with three hundred beds, run by the Sisters of Charity of St Vinko Pavlov from Zagreb. In 1893, Vatroslav Schwarz became head of the hospital,[63] and its ownership passed into the hands of the Royal Provincial Government.[64] We can therefore see how bishops took the

---

[60] Two citizens of Osijek, originally from Germany, Johann Kohlhoffer and Josef Huttler, bequeathed all their possessions in 1782 to a religious foundation for neglected children. The executor of their wills, the Jesuit Cristian Monsperger, also left his property to the foundation, which was placed under the royal protection and administration of the Hungarian Council of Governors in Pest.

[61] The orphanage housed sixty children, male and female. In 1899, its management was entrusted to the Styrian province of the Merciful Sisters of St Vinko Pavlov. Children could train in craft schools, while gifted students were provided with further education: Cepelić and Pavić, *Strossmayer*, 254–5.

[62] Georg Ritter is the first surgeon mentioned in the historical accounts of the institution: Željko Vranješ and Krešimir Glavina, 'Od Zakladne bolnice do Kliničkog bolničkog centra u Osijeku' ['From the Foundation Hospital to the Clinical Hospital Centre in Osijek'], *Medicinski vjesnik* [*Medical Journal*] 41 (2009), 27–40; Zlata Živaković–Kreže, 'Razvoj zaštite zdravlja u Slavoniji, posebni osvrt na Osijek' ['The Development of Healthcare in Slavonia, a Special Review of Osijek'], *Hrvatski časopis za javno zdravstvo* [*Croatian Journal of Public Health*] 1 (2008), 14–18.

[63] Kamilo Firinger and Vladimir Utvić, *Povijest bolničkih ustanova u Osijeku od 1739 do 1930* [*History of Hospital Institutions in Osijek from 1739 to 1930*] (Osijek, 1970); Vladimir Utvić, *Povijest bolničkih ustanova u Osijeku od 1874 do 1974: II dio* [*History of Hospitals in Osijek from 1874 to 1974: Part 2*] (Osijek, 1974); Aleksandar Včev, 'Prva klinika Kliničkog bolničkog centra u Osijeku' ['The First Clinic of the Clinical Hospital Centre in Osijek'], *Medicinski Vjesnik* [*Medical Journal*] 41 (2009), 41–6.

[64] Cepelić and Pavić, *Strossmayer*, 245–55.

initiative in opening medical institutions in the territory of their diocese and made them available to those in need.

Preventative health measures were also important for the Slavonian bishops, as is evident from the provisions made by Raffay and Strossmayer regarding sanitary conditions in cemeteries, which could easily become sources of epidemic outbreak and infectious disease. Strossmayer instructed his clergy in the management of cemeteries, highlighting the importance of having a morgue (1851), promulgating orders from the Vienna Ministry that the deceased undergo a post-mortem examination (1885–93), and ordering that cemeteries and tombs be properly ordered (1867).[65] In 1887 he also circulated a notice relating to a ban issued by the Department of Internal Affairs of the kingdom of Dalmatia, Croatia and Slavonia on the transfer of dead bodies from one place to another in order to avoid the transmission of infectious diseases.[66]

Strossmayer's commitment to education and his openness to both science and faith can be seen in his recommendation that clergy read the journal *Zdravlje* [*Health*].[67] He also issued a circular during an outbreak of cholera asking priests to pray that God might preserve them from infection,[68] and ordered that, if possible, they should celebrate a special mass 'for the avoidance of mortality or times of plague' (*collecta e missa de vitanda mortalitate vel tempore pestilentiae*).[69] In 1883, the *Bulletin of the Dioceses of Bosnia and Srijem* published a pastoral-medical article on how to prevent cholera and how to act if it occurred, based on the recommendations of a certain Dr Klenke. The article offers very practical advice about disinfection measures and encourages parish priests and school-teachers to promulgate this guidance.[70] Priests were not expected to rely solely on prayer, but were provided with medical facts about the disease, its spread and prevention.

[65] Ibid. 188.

[66] Josip Juraj Strossmayer, 'Okružnica' ['Circular'] and 'Naredba' ['Order'], *Glasnik biskupija Bosanske i Srijemske* [*Bulletin of the Dioceses of Bosnia and Srijem*] 9 (1881), 173–4.

[67] NAĐ, 10 Diocesan Ordinariate, 379/1880.

[68] NAĐ, 10 Diocesan Ordinariate, 1890/1893: the bishop recommends the clergy pray to God so that they do not become infected with cholera.

[69] Josip Juraj Strossmayer, 'Okružnica' ['Circular'], *Glasnik biskupija Bosanske i Srijemske* [*Bulletin of the Dioceses of Bosnia and Srijem*] 21 (1893), 18–19.

[70] N. N., 'Preventivna sredstva proti koleri i vladanje za vrieme iste' ['Cholera Prevention Measures and Behaviour during a Cholera Epidemic'], *Glasnik biskupija Bosanske i Srijemske* [*Bulletin of the Dioceses of Bosnia and Srijem*] 11 (1883), 183–4.

The Provision of Education as the Prerequisite for further Health Education

There is now empirical evidence that educational programmes and policies act as crucial public health interventions. Public health researchers have examined the relationship between education and health, and two points are worth mentioning in particular. First, health is a prerequisite for education: hungry or sick children cannot listen and study well.[71] Second, education about health within schools is a central tool of public health.[72] The concepts of education and health are interconnected; in fact, education is a fundamental social determinant of health.[73]

It is evident that the bishops of Đakovo and Srijem were also aware of the importance of education. They contributed to the expansion of both primary education, by founding schools, and higher education, by founding faculties and supporting the establishment of universities. Mandić was a supervisor of Croatian public schools in the kingdom of Croatia and Slavonia; once he became bishop, he financed the construction and equipping of schools in five other parishes.[74] His successor, Kuković, began the construction of the school in Đakovo, later run by the Sisters of Mercy, while Strossmayer continued to build and equip schools in other parishes of the diocese. The opening of new schools in the diocese allowed for the expansion of primary education, but also made it possible to offer basic health education. Nineteenth-century reports indicate that every parish in the diocese had a school, and the vast majority of these were run by the church.[75] In 1852, the Croatian 'ban'[76] asked the diocese in

---

[71] Charles E. Basch, 'Healthier Students are Better Learners: A Missing Link in School Reforms to close the Achievement Gap', *Journal of School Health* 81 (2011), 593–8.

[72] Louk W. H. Peter et al., 'Effective Elements of School Health Promotion across Behavioral Domains: A Systematic Review of Reviews', *BMC Public Health* 9 (2009), 182–95.

[73] Robert A. Hahn and Benedict I. Truman, 'Education improves Public Health and promotes Health Equity', *International Journal of Health Services* 45 (2015), 657–78.

[74] Cepelić and Pavić, *Strossmayer*, 15.

[75] Ibid. 15, 239. Except in the military district, where schools came under military administration, the vast majority of schools in the diocese were overseen by the church.

[76] 'Ban' was a noble title used in several states in central and south-eastern Europe between the tenth and twentieth centuries, primarily in the territory of Croatia. From the eighteenth century, a ban presided over the Croatian parliament and headed the executive branch. He was directly subordinate to the king, enforcing the ruler's orders: Leksikografski zavod Miroslav Krleža, *Hrvatska enciklopedija, mrežno izdanje* [Miroslav

Branka Gabrić and Darija Damjanović Barišić

Đakovo to approve a booklet on health entitled *Zdravstvoslavlje* [*Healthcare*], by a Dr Bock, which had been translated from German into Croatian for students of the final (third) grade of elementary school. Strossmayer gave his approval for its use in all schools in the diocese.[77]

Strossmayer also argued in parliament for the establishment of a modern Croatian university in Zagreb, and financially supported its foundation, which took place in 1874. He was also aware of the importance of establishing a medical faculty in the university, which he advocated although it was not established until 1917. In addition, between 1861 and 1866 Strossmayer played a crucial role in the opening of another academic institution, the Yugoslav Academy of Sciences and Arts. All these institutions contributed to improving the educational level of the general population, and thus to the development and wellbeing of wider society.

CONCLUSION

In this period of important social and political changes across the nineteenth-century territory of the southern Austro-Hungarian Empire and kingdom of Slavonia, we have seen the fruitful and multifaceted activity of the local church in providing the population with better living conditions. This article is the first analysis of the activity of the bishops of Đakovo and Srijem in the domain of public health. Moreover, it provides a significant contribution to understanding the development and implementation of public health measures in eastern Croatia.

In line with nineteenth-century understandings of public health and the need to improve basic living conditions and hygiene, the engagement of bishops in this territory was ultimately aimed at the population's well-being and, in this particular political context, had a huge significance. These Slavonian bishops had the sense and vision to facilitate the provision of better living conditions and improve the quality of life and health, not only of individuals, but of whole

Krleža Lexicographic Institute], *Croatian Encyclopedia*, online edition, at: <https://enciklopedija.hr/natuknica.aspx?ID=5627>, accessed 23 May 2021.
[77] NAĐ, 10 Diocesan Ordinariate, 852/1852, official letter about the Croatian ban to the diocesan administration, 23 August 1852; Cepelić and Pavić, *Strossmayer*, 240.

hamlets, villages and towns, indeed of the entire territory entrusted to them.

According to the regulations of both the Habsburg monarchy and the kingdom of Croatia and Slavonia, the provision of health care was left to local authorities who lacked sufficient funds. It was at this local level that the church had more material resources and, accepting state provisions, bishops attempted to implement them. Bishops also held certain secular powers, although further research is needed to determine whether, or to what extent, their political function played a role in their episcopal work promoting public health.

Finally, this article contributes to understandings of the church's engagement in the field of health, looking at a part of Europe that was affected by repeated conquest and destruction, and about which there are almost no historical-ecclesiastical studies in the field of health. This study shows how the local church played a significant role in deploying proper resources to implement measures promoting public health during the nineteenth century. We can see that the efforts of religious communities in the prevention of infectious diseases, infrastructure improvement and the provision of medical services not only influenced public health approaches, as underlined by Tulchinsky and Varavikova, but could also make a significant contribution to the public health of a whole region.

'It is well with the child': Changing Views on Protestant Missionary Children's Health, 1870s–1930s

Hugh Morrison*

University of Otago

Esme Cleall observes that for nineteenth-century British missionary families ill-health was constructed as being 'reflexive of and contributory to a specifically missionary identity'. This article argues that while this was a persistent theme, a new and significantly different discourse emerged emphasizing missionary families' health. Children were central to this discursive shift. The article focuses on missionary children's health, using selected Anglo-American cases. There was an uneasy overlap of religiously motivated rhetoric that still expected illness and death to be part of missionary childhood experience, and a professionalized discourse that redefined missionary families as sites of health and well-being. This culminated in medical and academic literature within religious and missionary circles that constructed missionaries' children as a new category. Thus churches responded both to the development of the medical profession and to the development of modern child-centred thinking and practices, in the process developing a new missiological or theological response to childhood.

The archives of missionary families' lives are full of letters documenting the health or ill-health of their children. The following extract is typical, both in its occurrence and its appeal to theological language in the midst of grief. In 1895 James and Honor Newell of the London Missionary Society (LMS) reported the death from pneumonia of their infant daughter in Samoa, with these words: '"It is well with the child." May her parents have faith in the Good Shepherd's love, and themselves learn in suffering how to help and comfort others.'[1] Yet when we turn to scholarship this refrain is less typically heard. While illness and death are common themes in both the

* College of Education, University of Otago, PO Box 56, Dunedin 9054, New Zealand. E-mail: hugh.morrison@otago.ac.nz.
[1] London, School of Oriental and African Studies Special Collections, Archives of the London Missionary Society (hereafter: CWM/LMS), Personal South Seas, Boxes 2, 11, 12, J. E. Newell Papers.

Studies in Church History 58 (2022), 306–329   © The Author(s), 2022. Published by Cambridge University Press on behalf of Ecclesiastical History Society
doi: 10.1017/stc.2022.15

historical details of missionaries' lives and the general historiography of the modern missionary movement, this has mainly been narrated as an adult story with little focus to date on the place, experiences and significance of missionary children's health and well-being. This article brings the spotlight to bear more precisely on missionary children, both to indicate directions for further scholarship and to argue that missionary children were central to significant shifts in wider thinking about missionary families' health over the late nineteenth and early twentieth centuries.[2]

Nineteenth-century missionary experiences and depictions cast a long shadow on public perceptions of a missionary's life as difficult and potentially dangerous, and illness figured largely in this respect. English historian Esme Cleall writes, with reference to British LMS missionaries in southern Africa and India, that in general over the long nineteenth century:

> illness was a chronic part of the missionary experience. Sickness and health preoccupied a huge proportion of missionary correspondence as missionaries detailed their own illnesses and those of their colleagues and loved ones; applied to take leave, or to return to Britain; outlined and justified medical expenses; explained slow work, or lack of work; and suggested health risks connected with particular areas or seasons to those with little experience of their location. Chronic illness patterned everyday life. … Illness and health shaped perceptions of the self and of others and channelled social relationships. It helped to construct difference because of its power to inscribe itself onto the body and the mind, shaping imagined worlds and social performances.[3]

Missionary health was a cause for increasing concern for missionary boards and, by the end of the nineteenth century, ranked highly in how they selected candidates for service.[4] Yet as Cleall reflects further

---

[2] This article forms part of a larger research project on Protestant missionary children, with a geographical focus on South and East Asia, Melanesia and southern Africa. The selection of cases is constrained by the researcher's archival time, access, choices and sampling decisions. I acknowledge that not all the points made here will necessarily apply to all mission contexts and that the 1920s and 1930s differed greatly from much of the nineteenth century with respect to missionary experiences.

[3] Esme Cleall, *Missionary Discourses of Difference: Negotiating Otherness in the British Empire, 1840–1900* (Basingstoke, 2014), 99–100.

[4] Ibid. 101–2; Brooke Whitelaw, 'A Message for the Missahibs: New Zealand Presbyterian Missionaries in the Punjab, 1910–1940' (MA thesis, University of Otago, 2001), 57–60.

for the missionary context, illness had a persistent and deep-seated 'potency' as a 'formative or valid experience in its own right'. Prolonged or repeated experiences of sickness in particular acted to 'embed themselves in identity'. This apparent association of missionaries and illness over the nineteenth century led ultimately to illness becoming 'reflexive of and contributory to a specifically missionary identity' wherein 'illnesses were constructed as a specifically missionary experience'.[5]

In the longer term this accepted association was sustained through public representations of missionaries through books, magazines and newspapers, and this enduring perception carried over to representations of their children. Thus, when Ernest Burt, of the English Baptist Missionary Society (BMS), later wrote his memoir of forty years in China, in hindsight he appeared to express less surprise and grief over the death of an infant daughter (and the near-death of least one other child) than he did over the death of his wife Helena in 1904.[6] Such views were historically persistent well into the first half of the twentieth century. Pat Booth, growing up in northern India in a New Zealand Baptist family, recounts her brother's attack of malaria in 1949 in these simple terms: 'I remember watching the sun go down; it was a brilliant orange, no doubt because of the dust in the air. John survived.'[7] This was not solely a British or indeed Anglo-American phenomenon. From a different national perspective, but in the same vein and period, illness and death among Danish missionary families in southern India was such an issue that considerable 'emotional labour' was expended in managing parents' responses as mediated through their published communications with church audiences back home. 'Emotional labour' can be understood as work that 'requires one to induce or sustain the outward countenance that produces the proper state of mind in others' and which involves 'the management of feeling to create a publicly observable facial and bodily display'. For Danish missionaries, Karen Vallgårda contends, this contributed to their public missionary identity well into the early 1900s as they worked to manage their own grief and represent

[5] Cleall, *Missionary Discourses of Difference*, 98, 112.
[6] Oxford, Angus Library and Archive, Baptist Missionary Society Archives (hereafter: BMS), CH/56, Ernest Whitby Burt, '[Unpublished] Autobiography of Revd. E. W. Burt (China 1892–1933)', 30–2.
[7] Patricia Booth, *Pat's India: Memories of Childhood* (Wellington, 2017), 26.

themselves appropriately to Danish audiences who increasingly
expected families and households to be companionate and safe places
for children.[8]

That Danish public perception was significant. During this same
period the prevailing nineteenth-century image of missionary identity
began to shift, even though the sad reality was that children continued to get sick or to die. Just fifteen years after the death of baby
Newell in Samoa, Commission V at the Edinburgh Missionary
Conference in 1910 received a submission arguing strenuously that
in mission work 'there is a morbid pride in being overworked and
run down' and that 'much of the loss of health in the past and
many deaths' was wasteful and increasingly preventable.[9] The extent
to which this began to be taken seriously was amply demonstrated in
medical surveys and reports written for American missionaries in the
1920s and 1930s, indicating that good health was now a priority and
an expectation for both adults and children.[10] Thus there existed an
uneasy overlap of religiously motivated rhetoric that still accepted illness and death as part of missionary childhood experience and an
emerging professionalized discourse that redefined missionary families as sites of health and well-being, reflecting: a general decline of
child mortality across Western societies; significant improvements
or advancements in both general and children's medicine; a growing
emphasis that the well-being of the child benefitted children, families
and the nation;[11] and missionary parents' expectations in particular.
This culminated in a growing body of medical and academic

[8] Karen A. A. Vallgårda, *Imperial Childhoods and Christian Mission: Education and
Emotions in South India and Denmark* (Basingstoke, 2015), 12, building on A. R.
Hochschild, 'Emotion Work, Feeling Rules, and Social Structures', *American Journal of
Sociology* 85 (1979), 551–75; and idem, *The Managed Heart: Commercialization of
Human Feeling* (Berkeley and Los Angeles, CA, 1983).
[9] World Missionary Conference 1910, *Report of Commission V: The Training of Teachers*
(Edinburgh and London, 1910), 112–13.
[10] William G. Lennox, 'Wasted Lives', *Chinese Recorder*, 1 September 1920, 608; idem,
The Health and Turnover of Missionaries (New York, 1933).
[11] For the British context, see in particular Harry Hendrick, *Child Welfare: Historical
Dimensions, Contemporary Debate* (Bristol, 2003), especially 19–86, 87–98; Stephanie
Olsen, *Juvenile Nation: Youth, Emotions and the Making of the Modern British Citizen,
1880–1914* (London, 2014). For broader discussions of childhood in relation to the
state and medical advances during the early to mid-twentieth century, see Kriste
Lindenmeyer and Jeanine Graham, 'The State', in Joseph M. Hawes and N. Ray
Hiner, eds, *A Cultural History of Childhood and Family in the Modern Age* (London,
2014), 135–59; Doug Imig and Frances Wright, 'Health and Science', ibid. 179–94.

literature within religious and missionary circles that began to construct missionaries' children as a new category. Churches responded
to advances in the medical profession and its attendant wisdom and in
modern child-centred thinking and practices, in the process developing a new missiological or theological response to childhood. Thus
childhood, as a category and a set of experiences, emerged as a pivotal
element of wider changes in attitudes towards missionary health and
well-being.

This article focuses on this transition of church and missionary
organization attitudes to the health and well-being of missionary children through the late nineteenth and early twentieth centuries, utilizing selected examples from the history of Anglo-American missions,
but with a particular focus on South and East Asian and South Pacific
settings. The sources used are a mix of official, published and unpublished materials, with many that are adult-produced but also some
that derive from children, albeit often in hindsight.[12] This reflects
two things. On the one hand its wide use of such sources reflects
the article's intention to articulate how childhood became a focus
for official organizations, agencies and churches and therefore calls
upon a range of sources written by, and intended for, adults. On
the other hand, reflecting further the importance of children's voice
in historical analysis, it at least introduces the sense that children were
at the heart of these experiences and sometimes had something to say
about them. In relation to children's experiences of death within the
family, for instance, English historian John Burnett notes that the
'emotional effect of such losses on parents and surviving children is
often not recorded and is incalculable'.[13] It is interesting to note,
for example, the relative lack of references to illness and death to
be found in published missionary children's memoirs.[14] Likewise,
even though children's religious magazines contain many instances

---

[12] On the efficacy of, and issues surrounding, the use of adult memoirs of childhood, see
Mary Jo Maynes, 'Age as a Category of Historical Analysis: History, Agency, and
Narratives of Childhood', *JHCY* 1 (2008), 114–24.
[13] John Burnett, ed., *Destiny Obscure: Autobiographies of Childhood, Education and Family
from the 1820s to the 1920s* (London, 1982), 35.
[14] Stephanie Vandrick, *Growing up with God and Empire: A Postcolonial Analysis of
'Missionary Kid' Memoirs* (Bristol and Blue Ridge Summit, PA, 2019), particularly 48.
Wider literature on methodologies around children's voice and focusing on children's
response to global crises such as the Spanish Flu pandemic is exemplified in the range
of essays in Kristine Moruzi et al., eds, *Children's Voices from the Past: New Historical
and Interdisciplinary Perspectives* (Cham, 2019); Charlotte Bennett, '"Now the War is

of missionary children's writing, these almost never contain references to hardship, illness or death (presumably excised or redacted by parents or editors). Overall, then, this article introduces a story with potential for much more research and reflection. It is a story of persistent problems and public perceptions (of mortality and morbidity as an inescapable childhood or mission location reality), and of changing attitudes or expectations (on behalf of both missionary parents and the denominations or societies employing them) that gradually began to shift the status quo by the 1940s.

MISSIONARY CHILDREN AND HEALTH IN CONTEXT

In Britain, publicity around the violent deaths of such missionaries as Anglican bishop John Patteson (New Hebrides, 1871) and Congregationalist James Chalmers (Papua, 1901) helped to make notions of 'heroic martyrdom' and the 'martyr hero' acceptable among late Victorian and early Edwardian supporters of foreign missions, and thus to normalize the idea that some degree of suffering was intrinsic to the missionary experience.[15] Multiple literary representations of these events boosted a broader public perception that missionary life was inherently dangerous and life-threatening. This was not the same everywhere; there were, for example, demonstrable differences in context and experience between missionary settings and clear changes over time. While East Asia might be deemed less problematic by the early 1900s, parts of Africa continued to present a daunting challenge, unchanged in some settings from the early to mid-nineteenth century. This was particularly so for those missionaries in tropical zones where death rates were noticeably higher. 'In the early years', notes Norman Etherington, 'a "call" to tropical Africa or South Asia could be a death sentence'. For example, 69 per cent of missionaries sent to Sierra Leone between 1804 and 1825 died in missionary service, as did just over a quarter of all Wesleyan Methodist missionaries in West Africa between

---

over, we have something else to worry us": New Zealand Children's Responses to Crises, 1914–1918', *JHCY* 7 (2014), 15–41.
[15] Judith Rowbotham, '"Soldiers of Christ"? Images of Female Missionaries in Late Nineteenth-Century Britain: Issues of Heroism and Martyrdom', *GH* 15 (2002), 82–106, at 85–6. See further Thorgeir Kolshus and Even Hovdhaugen, 'Reassessing the Death of Bishop John Coleridge Patteson', *Journal of Pacific History* 45 (2010), 331–55.

1835 and 1907.[16] As such, missionaries in tropical Africa 'fought a constant struggle against the ravages of disease' and accepted that 'missionary service involved not only a sacrifice of health, but potentially of life too'.[17] Many of the pioneering ventures experienced high rates of mortality as a consequence, and illness proved to be a major and persistent drain on resources and progress. The grief of Edith and Walter Stapleton (English Baptists) in 1904, over leaving a baby boy buried 'in the sacred piece of ground behind the church' in the Congo Free State, was sadly typical.[18] Perceptions, too, may have differed from realities, as noted by Diane Langmore for missionaries and their families in Papua, where by the early 1900s the dangers displayed lavishly and prosaically in missionary or popular fictional literature sat somewhat at odds with actual experience.[19] She cites very small numbers of adult deaths in this period and a discernible improvement in death rates compared with earlier decades in both Melanesia and Polynesia. At the same time, she notes variable rates between missions, with a higher rate among single male missionaries of both the Anglican Mission and the Roman Catholic Sacred Heart Mission.

To date, missionary children[20] have tended to be left out of this picture, even though they were much more numerous in a range of geographical settings by the end of the nineteenth century. While these children are now more prominent in scholarship,[21] closer

---

[16] Norman Etherington, 'Education and Medicine', in idem, ed, *Missions and Empire* (Oxford, 2005), 261–84, at 277–8.

[17] Michael Jennings, '"This mysterious and intangible enemy": Health and Disease amongst the Early UMCA Missionaries, 1860–1918', *SHM* 15 (2002), 65–87, at 66.

[18] Jane Marshall, *Mama* (Milton Keynes, 2008), 48.

[19] Diane Langmore, 'Exchanging Earth for Heaven: Death in the Papuan Missionfields', *JRH* 13 (1985), 383–92, at 384, 386.

[20] While the words 'children' and 'childhood' are used most commonly in this article, for the sake of brevity these terms cover infants, children and young people, unless otherwise specified.

[21] Examples of recent research include Vallgårda, *Imperial Childhoods*; Emily J. Manktelow, *Missionary Families: Race, Gender and Generation on the Spiritual Frontier* (Manchester, 2013); Linda Devereux, 'Narrating a Congo Missionary Childhood (1958–1964): Memory and Meaning examined through a creative Non-Fiction Text and Exegesis' (Ph.D. thesis, Australian National University, 2015); Joy Schulz, *Hawaiian by Birth: Missionary Children, Bicultural Identity, and U.S. Colonialism in the Pacific* (Lincoln, NE, 2017); Hugh Morrison, '"It's really where your parents were": differentiating and situating Protestant Missionary Children's lives, c.1900–1940', *Journal of Family History* 42 (2017), 419–39; idem, 'Three Variations

analysis and conceptualization of their health and mortality has only just begun. Again, Langmore makes two observations for Papua that further highlight missionary children's potential significance in this regard: that missionary children's mortality statistics appear higher at the end of the nineteenth century than for the countries from which they came, thus reinforcing a public perception that they inhabited endemically dangerous spaces; and that for 'many Protestant missionaries, their most intimate experience of death was amongst their children ... [wherein their] faith did not render the missionary or his wife immune to the grief and pain of such an experience'.[22]

There is a growing focus on health and death within the broader field of childhood and youth history, signified, for example, by monographs on the history of child death in Victorian Britain and on early modern English children, illness and death,[23] and further represented by at least three edited collections for the pre-modern and modern eras.[24] The religious contexts and contours of childhood illness and death, however, are variously and not always satisfactorily present, and deserve further examination precisely because of their interconnectedness. For example, Hannah Newton rightly argues that early modern religion and medicine were intricately linked, but notes that they have 'attracted only a limited amount of attention in the historiography'. Because 'sickness was largely a spiritual experience' for children, and 'religious acts were also a part of the preparation of death', that historiographical neglect needs to be redressed.[25] Likewise, Lydia Murdoch, in her discussion of child deaths during

on a Theme: Writing the Lives of Scottish and New Zealand Missionary Children, *ca.*1900–1950', *JHCY* 12 (2019), 199–218; David A. Hollinger, *Protestants Abroad: How Missionaries tried to change the World but changed America* (Princeton, NJ, and Oxford, 2017).
[22] Langmore, 'Exchanging Earth for Heaven', 385.
[23] Laurence Lerner, *Angels and Absences: Child Death in the Nineteenth Century* (Nashville, TN, 1997); Hannah Newton, *The Sick Child in Early Modern England, 1580–1720* (Oxford, 2012).
[24] Gillian Avery and Kimberley Reynolds, eds, *Representations of Childhood Death* (Basingstoke and New York, 2000); Katie Barclay and Kimberley Reynolds with Ciara Rawnsley, eds, *Death, Emotion and Childhood in Premodern Europe* (Basingstoke, 2016); Kathleen Jones, Lydia Murdoch and Tamara Myers, eds, *JHCY* 8, no. 3 (Fall 2015), special issue on childhood and death. The volume by Barclay et al. lists at least twenty-six entries in the bibliography on childhood, health and death.
[25] Newton, *Sick Child*, 6.

the 1857 Indian Rebellion, clearly elucidates the ways in which childhood, death and its memorialization point to the complex entanglements of religion and culture (especially parental expectations about childhood death integral to British imperial culture in that period).[26] In similar fashion Kevin Murphy makes important links between children's literature, evangelical religion, class and race for antebellum America.[27] While not exhaustive, a survey of scholarship that now more specifically references religious elements in the British context reveals an emphasis on the period from about the mid-seventeenth to the mid-nineteenth centuries, covering topics such as puritan or pietistic spirituality and its influence on how children's death experiences might be conceptualized; child and parental emotions involved with illness and death; and the relationship between evangelicalism, literary production and representations of death.[28] Such a survey, however, further reveals little scholarship on the early twentieth century, especially on missionary children as a subset of religious childhoods defined more generally.[29] They are the focus of the following discussion.

Missionary children lived where they lived as a consequence of their parents' religious dispositions, motivations and decisions; albeit shaped further by their various imperial or colonial contexts.[30] In this regard John W. de Gruchy insightfully links parents' religious

[26] Lydia Murdoch, "'Suppressed grief': Mourning the Death of British Children and the Memory of the 1857 Indian Rebellion', *JBS* 51 (2012), 364–92, at 380–2.
[27] Kevin A. Murphy, 'Providing Models of Dying: Middle-Class Childhood, Death and American Juvenile Fiction, 1790–1860', *JHCY* 11 (2018), 169–87.
[28] Ralph Houlbrooke, 'Death in Childhood: The Practice of the "Good Death" in James Janeway's *A Token for Children*', in Anthony Fletcher and Stephen Hussey, eds, *Childhood in Question: Children, Parents and the State* (Manchester and New York, 1999), 37–56; Alec Ryrie, 'Facing Childhood Death in English Protestant Spirituality', in Barclay et al., eds, *Death, Emotion and Childhood*, 109–28; Katie Barclay, 'Grief, Faith and Eighteenth-Century Childhood: The Doddridges of Northampton', ibid. 173–89; Merete Colding Smith, 'Child Death and Children's Emotions in Early Sunday School Reward Books', ibid. 229–44; Elisabeth Jay, "'Ye careless, thoughtless, worldly parents, tremble while you read this history!": The Use and Abuse of the Dying Child in the Evangelical Tradition', in Avery and Reynolds, eds, *Representations of Childhood Death*, 111–32. See also Anthony Fletcher, 'The Death of Charlotte Bloomfield in 1828: Family Roles in an Evangelical Household', in John Doran, Charlotte Methuen and Alexandra Walsham, eds, *Religion and the Household*, SCH 50 (Woodbridge, 2014), 354–65.
[29] One exception is David Maxwell, 'The Missionary Home as a Site for Mission: Perspectives from Belgian Congo', in Doran, Methuen and Walsham, eds, *Religion and the Household*, 428–55.
[30] Morrison, 'It's really where your parents were', 426–8.

vocation with children's health experiences, among other things, when he asks what children might have thought about their parents' motivations: 'That is surely an interesting subject for consideration and research, not least because of everything children had to endure for the sake of the missionary cause, many not surviving to tell the tale.'[31] As overall missionary numbers surged from the late nineteenth century,[32] so too did the numbers of their children. By 1925 there were an estimated 29,000 Protestant missionaries worldwide, around half from North America.[33] While there are no comprehensive statistics of missionary children, some examples give a sense of their presence. In China there were an estimated 3,800 children born to Protestant missionaries between 1868 and 1949, nearly fifty each year.[34] LMS records reveal some 650 children born to missionary parents in India and the South Pacific in the same period (around eight per year).[35] Presbyterian sources for Scotland and New Zealand show that there were at least 890 missionary children born between 1870 and 1940 (more than twelve per year), living in such diverse regions as southern Africa, China, India, the Caribbean and Melanesia.[36] This burgeoning child population reflected a wider trend for the imperial

[31] John W. de Gruchy, '"Who did they think they were?" Some Reflections from a Theologian on Grand Narratives and Identity in the History of Missions', in Andrew Porter, ed., *The Imperial Horizons of British Protestant Missions, 1880–1914* (Grand Rapids, MI, and Cambridge, 2003), 213–25, at 217.
[32] Kenneth Scott Latourette, *A History of the Expansion of Christianity*, 7 vols (London, 1938), 4: 2; 7: 16.
[33] Jeffrey Cox, *The British Missionary Enterprise since 1700* (New York and London, 2008), 213–15, 267; Gerald Anderson, 'American Protestants in Pursuit of Mission, 1886–1986', *IBMR* 12 (1988), 98–118, at 102, 105.
[34] Sarah A. Mason, 'Missionary Conscience and the Comprehension of Imperialism: A Study of the Children of American Missionaries to China' (Ph.D. dissertation, Northern Illinois University, 1978), 6.
[35] Calculated from CWM/LMS, 'London Missionary Society Register of Missionaries' Children up to 1940', vols 1–2; see also the *Chronicle of the London Missionary Society*, 1889–1939.
[36] Data for Scottish and New Zealand Presbyterian missionary families are compiled from the following sources: (1) Scotland: annual reports to the General Assemblies of the Church of Scotland, the Free Church of Scotland and the United Free Church of Scotland, 1860–1940; Hew Scott, *Fasti Ecclesiae Scoticanae: The Succession of Ministers in the Church of Scotland from the Reformation*, vol. 7 (Edinburgh, 1928); John Alexander Lamb, *The Fasti of the United Free Church of Scotland, 1900–1929* (Edinburgh, 1956); (2) New Zealand: annual reports to the General Assemblies of the Synod of Southland and Otago, 1866–1901, and of the Presbyterian Church of New Zealand, 1869–1940; *The Break of Day*, a children's monthly magazine; individual missionaries' staff files; and the 'Register of New Zealand Presbyterian Ministers, Deaconesses

era. From about the 1860s, the numbers of British children in the various non-white settler colonies increased markedly. In Hong Kong the numbers of children designated 'British or other Europeans' aged under fifteen doubled between 1891 and 1906. Similar growth rates occurred in Singapore, and also in Hanoi and Saigon under the French.[37]

ILL-HEALTH: EXPERIENCES AND REPRESENTATIONS

Stories of missionary children's illnesses or deaths, commonly couched in religious language, spanned the entire length of the modern Protestant missionary movement across a plethora of published and unpublished sources. Mary Moffat wrote to her father from South Africa in 1832 that 'our beloved and interesting child Betsy is no longer an inhabitant of this lower world. Her freed spirit took its happy flight on the night of 4th January. As parents we do feel, and it is necessary that we should feel, for He does nothing in vain who has afflicted us.' Prior to Betsy's death the Moffats had lost at least one other infant, in 1825.[38] A century later Dr Adam Harvie commented that 'growing up in India is no joke', when reporting on a neighbouring missionary child's battle with life-threatening dysentery.[39] These were real-life situations that had an impact on the parents and siblings involved, irrespective of time or place, as well as on those who read about them. As such their representations regularly combined emotional and theological elements. This was typified in the case of five-year old Lancely Griffin, the only child of LMS New Zealanders Harry and Evelyn, who died from influenza in Samoa in 1919. His post-funeral memorial card included lines translated from a Samoan hymn: 'Anywhere with Jesus is good; / When with him I am at rest. / For any work of my Master, / I am willing, choose me.' The card noted that this hymn 'in the vernacular was often sung by Lancely

---

& Missionaries 1840 to 2015', last major update 2009, online at <http://www.archives.presbyterian.org.nz/page143.htm>, accessed 22 January 2021.

[37] David Pomfret, *Youth and Empire: Trans-Colonial Childhoods in British and French Asia* (Stanford, CA, 2016), 23.

[38] John S. Moffat, *The Lives of Robert and Mary Moffat* (London, 1885), 165, 124–5.

[39] Dunedin, Presbyterian Research Centre (hereafter: PRC), Archives of the Punjab Mission (Punjab), Punjab Mission Staff Papers 1901–1930, Series 6.11, Adam Harvie to George Jupp, 26 December 1927.

and for that reason was the favourite hymn of the family at evening prayers'.[40]

The public perception, promulgated through literature, that life was generally or typically difficult for missionary families, and that some parts of the world were more dangerous than others, pertained equally to depictions of children. The nineteenth-century prominence of Africa, and especially the exigencies of tropical Africa, seems to have been particularly influential in this respect, alongside pietistic elements of contemporary Protestant evangelicalism with their focus on sacrificial service.[41] However, while Africa featured highly in this regard, other regions were represented similarly. Among these was the Pacific, and by the late 1800s particularly Papua and New Guinea, with many references in popular literature to cannibals, tribal violence and exigencies of climate or terrain.[42] The biographer of LMS missionary William Lawes recorded the mission community's struggle with malaria in New Guinea, which in 1877 took the lives of fifteen 'Polynesian teachers and their wives' and also his younger son Percy, before the family evacuated to northern Australia. As a result, William and Fanny decided that she and their elder son should return to England while he remained.[43] Published stories of family struggles around health in such locations heightened the long-held view that children were not suited for tropical climates and bolstered missionary parents' demands that their organizations provide better support for their children's health as well as their education. Ideas about the dangers of tropical climates for the young, particularly the effect of heat on children's rate of maturation, were cemented in both scientific and popular rhetoric by the second half of the nineteenth century for a range of imperial settings, and endured

---

[40] CWM/LMS, South Seas, Incoming Correspondence 1919, Box 59, Harry Griffin, Lancely Griffin memorial card.

[41] See, for example, Andrew Porter, 'Cambridge, Keswick and Late Nineteenth-Century Attitudes to Africa', *JICH* 5 (1976), 5–34; Dagmar Konrad, 'Lost in Transition: Missionary Children of the Basel Mission in the Nineteenth Century', *IBMR* 37 (2013), 219–23.

[42] See, for example, James Chalmers, *Adventures in New Guinea* (London, 1886); W. P. Nairne, *Greatheart of Papua (James Chalmers)* (London, 1920); James Paton, *The Story of John G. Paton told for Young Folks, or, Thirty Years among South Sea Cannibals* (London, 1892).

[43] Joseph King, *W. G. Lawes of Savage Island and New Guinea* (London, 1909), 91–4; CWM/LMS, W. G. and Fanny Lawes Papers, Box 1, Folder 10, W. G. Lawes to 'My Dear Sister in Christ', 18 September 1877.

into the twentieth century with respect to children of missionary and imperial families more generally.[44] Ironically, as statistics suggest for the LMS, the Pacific and parts of Africa had become the least dangerous regions by the early 1900s, with the lowest juvenile death rates, and a further marked decline after 1900.[45]

Experiences of illness or death were not limited to the regions in which families lived. They also occurred during transition periods such as seasonal holidays in the hill stations, going to or from school, en route from mission fields to metropole and while children were in their home countries. These were simply the accepted hazards of travel or new contact: seasickness, illness at the start of a new school term, or a young child contracting the normal range of illnesses in the home country. At the same time, deeper tragedies occurred. Again in 1838, the Moffats suffered the further loss of six-year-old Jim, who 'went to the dimly-known world about which his child-mind was already so busy', at the beginning of a return trip to Britain. On that voyage tragedy and joy were juxtaposed, with the birth of another daughter.[46] Such health experiences could dominate the voyage itself and their impact be deeply felt, with physical illness and mental or spiritual anguish sometimes unhelpfully conflated. Six-year-old Joyce Wilkins was sick with fever for most of the voyage from India to England in 1908, and remembered vividly that while bed-bound she felt that she 'was being punished for all my wickedness'.[47] For the LMS, of all the child deaths reported for the period 1890–1939, two occurred at sea and nineteen while the children were domiciled in England, Scotland or Australia for their education. In the 1930s, mental health issues impacted on Presbyterian children,

[44] See, for example, Elizabeth Buettner, *Empire Families: Britons and Late Imperial India* (Oxford, 2004), 29–45; Cleall, *Missionary Discourses*, 59–60, 104–7; Ryan Johnson, 'European Cloth and "Tropical" Skin: Clothing Material and British Ideas of Health and Hygiene in Tropical Climates', *BHM* 83 (2009), 530–60; Ann Laura Stoler, *Carnal Knowledge and Imperial Power: Race and the Intimate in Colonial Rule* (Berkeley and Los Angeles, CA, 2002), 66–75.
[45] LMS missionary percentages are calculated from Norman Goodall, *A History of the London Missionary Society 1895–1945* (Oxford, 1954), 595–623; children's deaths from announcements in the *Chronicle of the London Missionary Society*, 1889–1939.
[46] Moffat, *Robert and Mary Moffat*, 209, 211.
[47] Joyce Wilkins, *A Child's Eye View, 1904–1920* (Brighton, 1992), 34. The larger story of the Wilkins children, involving their being domiciled in England at residential schools for missionaries' children, is outlined in Vyvyen Brendon, *Children of the Raj* (London, 2006), 189–93.

with the apparent suicides of at least three young American college students, recently repatriated from India and struggling to adjust to their new cultural settings.[48] These kinds of experiences were not unique to missionary families. Nineteenth-century British migrants' diaries and shipping records contained regular cases of children's illness and, at times, tragically high rates of child mortality at sea.[49] At the same time, long-held fears and myths about health in the tropics lay at the heart of the Western discourse about children and shaped policies and practices of child repatriation to the metropole for education well into the interwar period. This was neatly caught in Ada Harvie's observation that, on returning to India in 1933, her children had 'lost some of their [New Zealand] colour but they are still much more rosy & healthy looking than the children here'.[50] The 'children here' were European, not Indian.

Amidst the great slew of literature that compounded public perceptions about missionary families, these children were sometimes the subject of books in their own right, wherein their tragically premature deaths were a major feature, even into the early 1900s. These included such children as Lucy Thurston in Hawai'i (1842), Charles Dwight in Constantinople (1853), Emily Lillie in Jamaica (1865), the Lee children in India (1899) and Carol Bird, also in India (1910).[51] These works sat within a broader category of religious literature and also hymnody for both adults and children.[52] In the main, this corpus reflected contemporary Protestant literary tropes of the exemplary Christian child and their death. In the Anglo-American context, these narratives had their origins in the seventeenth century, exemplified in the narration of thirteen child deaths in James Janeway's *A Token for Children*, published in many editions

---

[48] PRC, Punjab, Series 6.27, Thomas Riddle to William Mawson, 4 November 1934.

[49] Lyndon Fraser, 'Memory, Mourning and Melancholy: English Ways of Death on the Margins of Empire', in idem and Angela McCarthy, eds, *Far from 'Home': The English in New Zealand* (Dunedin, 2012), 99–122, at 105–9.

[50] PRC, Punjab, Series 6.10, Ada Harvie to William Mawson, 18 January 1933.

[51] A. P. Cummings, *The Missionary's Daughter: A Memoir of Lucy Goodale Thurston of the Sandwich Islands* (New York, [1842]); Anon., *Charles Dwight: or, the Missionary's Son* (London, [1853]); Anon., *The Missionary's Daughter: A brief Memoir of Emily Judson Lillie* (London, [1865]); Ada Lee, *Seven Heroic Children: A Great Sorrow and a Great Victory* (London, 1903); Handley H. Bird, *Carol, 'A sweet savour of Christ': The Memoir of a Missionary Child* (London, Edinburgh and New York, 1910).

[52] Alisa Clapp-Itnyre, *British Hymn Books for Children, 1800–1900: Re-tuning the History of Childhood* (London and New York, 2018), 227–54.

from 1671.[53] Prevailing evangelical thinking 'took its authority from the Bible and deduced from Jesus's words: "Except ye be converted, and become as little children, ye shall not enter the kingdom of heaven" (Matthew 18: 3) that dying children must therefore represent the supreme example and test of the Christian profession of faith'. From the early nineteenth century, emergent and sustained literature either about or for children 'showed both how to elicit evidence of "the principle of faith" having taken root and how the death-bed itself could be used as a premature opportunity for exhibiting "the fruits of holiness"'.[54]

This literature had at least two broad purposes, being simultaneously consolatory and didactic. As such, it endured well into the twentieth century in terms of both its appeal and its discursive impact. Alisa Clapp-Itnyre, writing about children's hymns in a way that represents wider literature, provides helpful context in arguing that in the case of children 'surrounded by death', who therefore 'struggled with the meaning of life and death', it was 'not morbid to present hymns to them which tackled these weighty issues head-on. Undoubtedly what hymns offered to children were consolation and clarity of a Christian kind'; they 'offered children Christian answers to "the next chapter": eschatological principles in the traditional Four Last Things – heaven, hell, death, and judgement'.[55]

Accounts of missionary children's illness and deaths followed this approach. The narrative of sixteen-year-old Charles Dwight's illness and death in Constantinople, for example, showcased a boy who previously had 'yielded to [God's] power', who had 'put his trust in the Saviour' and who 'now entered a new life'. As a result, he exemplified what young readers should value: 'Prayer was his delight. The Bible was a precious book. He aimed to do right and to make everybody happy.'[56] However, Dwight's narrative also pointed children to broader horizons. Readers were told that while at peace with the prospect of death, Charles still hoped to live, so that he could 'do good' in his life. In particular 'his heart was set on being a missionary', to follow his father's footsteps in Constantinople. 'It was this that seemed to him even more desirable than to go at once and be with

[53] Houlbrooke, 'Death in Childhood', 37–8, 52; Ryrie, 'Facing Childhood Death', 112, 125.
[54] Jay, 'Use and Abuse of the Dying Child', 112–13, quoting William Wilberforce.
[55] Clapp-Itnyre, *British Hymn Books*, 239.
[56] Anon., *Charles Dwight*, 3.

Christ.'[57] Similar accounts of other missionary children's deaths, exemplified through the posthumous accounts of the six Lee children who tragically died in a mudslide in Darjeeling in 1899, struck this same balance of mourning, eschatological hope and inspiration, encouraging their readers to live full and devoted lives here and now. What is striking about Ada Lee's account of her children, for example, is that it focuses not so much on their deaths as on their lives. Her children emerge as exemplars of Christian childhood and faith; not perfect but spiritually aware and active. Their deaths were therefore not central, but rather the *raison d'être* for representing their exemplary lives to a wider reading public. Ada and her editors made it abundantly clear that they wanted to see tangible results from the book's publication, in the form of various philanthropic projects.[58] Later newspaper reports, from such places as Newcastle in Australia, indicate that children and adults alike learnt about the events of 1899 and, moved by the immensity of the tragedy, wrote letters to the Lees and contributed financially to a range of projects over a sustained period of time.[59]

HEALTH AND WELFARE: CHANGING EXPECTATIONS

Reference to the three young adults who committed suicide during their physical and emotional transitions from India to America in the 1930s forms a turning point in this discussion, anticipating a discourse that has been more dominant since 1945 and which brings children and childhood more to the centre of its concern. In 2009 an article appeared in the journal *Mental Health, Religion and Culture*, focused on understanding the struggles that missionary children as young adults reportedly have with 'repatriation' to the home culture and 'lower levels of well-being'. It sought to apply analytical rigour to the anecdotal problems accruing from the struggle of these individuals, who, while 'looking like an insider', were internally struggling because they felt 'completely on the outside ... lost in the slang or idioms', and who had 'acquired different tastes in food', struggled 'to maintain foreign customs' and were 'unfamiliar with the pop

[57] Ibid. 5–6.
[58] Lee, *Seven Heroic Children*, v–ix, 147–55.
[59] 'A Terrible Night: Darjeeling Disaster of 1899', *Newcastle Morning Herald and Miners' Advocate*, 20 August 1924, 10.

culture'.[60] The article appeared within a now well-established field of research on third culture children, with a special focus on 'missionary kids'. While the authors rightly identify the influential work of American sociologist Ruth Hill Useem in the 1960s (who coined the phrase 'third culture kids'),[61] the seeds of this approach are actually to be found in changing professionally articulated attitudes during the 1920s and 1930s. Particularly important were foundational studies of missionary children's health, education and development. Herein lies the transition from accepting the status quo, outlined in the previous discussion, to new ways of thinking about missionary children as a category of concern and analysis in their own right.

This transition needs to be set against a larger canvas in at least two respects. One is the overall improvements in child mortality and morbidity in Western societies from the late nineteenth century onwards. Apparent declines in LMS children's deaths in this period (either from Britain or the settler colonies), for example, while context-specific and not everywhere the same, need to be understood within a general decline in infant and child mortality rates.[62] Colin Heywood notes a 'rapid decline' in infant mortality from about 1895 to 1905 in most Western European nations, and the same for overall child mortality from the second half of the nineteenth century.[63] This varied in different British contexts during the period: while infant mortality rates in New Zealand and Australia were declining, they were higher for white infants in the Cape Colony and among Dublin's Roman Catholic families. Even in England rates were (and indeed still are) clearly differentiated by geography and class.[64]

---

[60] Michael J. Klemens and Lynette H. Bikos, 'Psychological Well-Being and Sociocultural Adaptation in College-Aged, Repatriated, Missionary Kids', *Mental Health, Religion and Culture* 12 (2009), 721–33, at 721.
[61] Ibid. 722–3.
[62] LMS statistics are derived from the same sources as for n. 35. These indicate an overall decline in the death-rate of children across all LMS locations between the 1890s and 1930s.
[63] Colin Heywood, *Childhood in Modern Europe* (Cambridge, 2018), 221–2.
[64] See further Langmore, *Missionary Lives*, 75; David Thorns and Charles Sedgewick, *Understanding Aotearoa / New Zealand: Historical Statistics* (Palmerston North, 1997), 40–1; S. E. Duff, *Changing Childhoods in the Cape Colony: Dutch Reformed Church Evangelicalism and Colonial Childhood, 1860–1895* (Basingstoke, 2015), 17; Charles Simkins and Elizabeth van Heyningen, 'Fertility, Mortality, and Migration in the Cape Colony, 1891–1904', *International Journal of African Historical Studies* 22 (1989), 79–

The second consideration is the emergence of intersecting medical
professionalization and a focus on child welfare, particularly at the
state level. Medical science made noted advances through the nineteenth century and was one factor, among others, in declining rates
of child mortality; in particular, significantly lower rates of infant
mortality were a noted feature across a range of Anglo-American societies.[65] For this reason, British parents, for example, had much higher
expectations of their children's health by the early twentieth century.[66] This expectation was increasingly echoed by missionary parents both in situ and in respect to their children domiciled at 'home'
for education. Moreover, in this period children were increasingly to
the fore of the evolving medical sciences, with an explicit focus on
vaccines for diseases such as diphtheria and tetanus, and on paediat-
rics more generally.[67] As a result, children's health and general welfare
were increasingly linked, both in the public mind and in state-led policies, as was reflected in the growing array of institutional responses to
childhood problems across Anglo-American societies and the application of new developmental thinking in child psychology.[68] These
same developments were mirrored within nineteenth-century missions, with a more concerted focus on 'medical missions' by

111, at 89; Dylan Shane Connor, 'Poverty, Religious Differences, and Child Mortality in
the Early Twentieth Century: The Case of Dublin', *Annals of the American Association of
Geographers* 107 (2017), 625–46, at 625–6. For infant mortality, see, for example, Alison
Clarke, *Born to a Changing World: Childbirth in Nineteenth-Century New Zealand*
(Wellington, 2012), 213–25; Philippa Mein Smith, *Maternity in Dispute: New
Zealand, 1920–1939* (Wellington, 1986); Stephen Mintz, *Huck's Raft: A History of
American Childhood* (Cambridge, MA, and London, 2004), 173–4.
[65] Lynne Curry, *Religion, Law, and the Medical Neglect of Children in the United States,
1870–2000: 'The Science of the Age'* (Basingstoke, 2019), 2–3; Heywood, *Childhood in
Modern Europe*, 222–6.
[66] Siân Pooley, '"All we parents want is that our children's health and lives should be
regarded": Child Health and Parental Concern in England, c.1860–1910', *SHM* 23
(2010), 528–48.
[67] Curry, *Religion, Law, and Medical Neglect*, 157; Jeffrey P. Brosco, 'Pediatrics', in Paula
Fass, ed, *Encyclopedia of Children and Childhood in History and Society*, 3 vols (New York,
2004), 2: 657–61, at 659–61; Richard Meckel, 'Health and Science', in Colin Heywood,
ed, *A Cultural History of Childhood and Family in the Age of Empire* (London and
New York, 2010), 167–87, at 182–5.
[68] For context, see Heywood, *Childhood in Modern Europe*, 223–9; James Schmidt,
'Children and the State', in Paula Fass, ed, *The Routledge History of Childhood in
Western Europe* (London and New York, 2015), 174–90; Stephen Lassonde, 'Age,
Schooling, and Development', ibid. 219–24.

1900.[69] While medical missionaries potentially 'acquired an outsize reputation as conveyors of European medical science' (due to the influence of individuals such as Albert Schweitzer and David Livingstone),[70] the establishment of mission hospitals and growing employment of medically qualified personnel brought medical expertise physically closer to missionary families and thus raised parental expectations of their children's welfare.

Reflecting these broader developments, new voices emerged with respect to missionary children, especially in the years following the First World War. Their tone was not necessarily new, in that adult concerns about the particular needs of parents or children had started to be aired some years previously. At the 1900 New York missionary conference, for example, the Hon. J. B. Arnold (president of the University of Michigan) highlighted the problem that

> comes upon the father and mother when that sad day arrives that they must send their children home for education when they so need the companionship of father and mother, and when father and mother even more, perhaps, need the companionship of their children. We can do something to help in this matter by caring in all ways possible to us for the comfort and help of the children at home.[71]

Over the long nineteenth century such concerns had been raised in different places leading, for instance, to the establishment of a variety of missionary children's residential homes together with schools in both metropole and mission settings, a range of annually budgeted denominational funds to support children's education, and parental costs being properly recognized in missionaries' working conditions. At the same time, they were often piecemeal, and the fundamental dilemma – family separation or cessation of missionary service due to children's needs – remained a key unresolved problem for many families. As Allen Parker, an educator of missionary children in India, stated as late as 1936, the '[o]ne great difficulty which remains

---

[69] Etherington, 'Education and Medicine', 274–84; Christopher Grundmann, 'Medicine', in Jonathan Bonk, ed., *Encyclopedia of Missions and Missionaries* (New York and London, 2007), 238–42; Andrew Walls, *The Missionary Movement in Christian History: Studies in the Transmission of Faith* (Maryknoll, NY, 1996), 199–210.

[70] Etherington, 'Education and Medicine', 274.

[71] Editorial Committee, *Ecumenical Missionary Conference New York, 1900: Report of the Ecumenical Conference on Foreign Missions, held in Carnegie Hall and Neighbouring Churches, April 21 to May 1*, 2 vols (New York, 1900), 1: 320–1.

is that of the education and development of the children and the pain of separation from them.'[72] Likewise William Hocking, in his critical report *Re-thinking Missions* (1932), acknowledged family separation as a key issue, one that burdened both parents and organizations with 'the expense of tuition and travel'. In his opinion, separation often occurred 'at a time when children are going through difficult periods of adjustment to different modes of living, to different countries, and to different peoples. The anxiety and strain of these separations and the financial responsibilities incident to them are very great.'[73] Such voices represented a new discourse around missionary children's welfare that came from two directions, reflecting the greater professionalization of Western medicine, but also the increasing role of the state in protecting childhood, refracted through a more specifically religious and missionary lens.

In the first instance, there was a clear and explicit medical voice which by the 1920s echoed the arguments raised at the Edinburgh Conference in 1910 that losses due to death and illness were 'wasteful' and 'preventable' elements of missionary economy, especially in the light of contemporary medical knowledge. An article in the *Chinese Recorder* began: 'Dysentery has caused 19% of all known deaths of missionary children. ... This issue of the *Recorder* will reach missionaries just at the beginning of the danger season. Therefore a few facts and suggestions may be in order.' The article concluded with a list of twelve 'Rules to avoid contracting dysentery (cholera and typhoid fever)'.[74] The subtext for parents was clear: you have the knowledge, so it is your responsibility to apply it. This same message was conveyed in William Lennox's formal 1933 report on American missionaries' health, focused mainly on East Asia. A chapter on 'The Health of Missionary Children' emphasized children's health and raised their profile, yet tied their well-being to broader concerns:

> In most fields children remain with their parents, and many a capable missionary has been forced to leave his assignment because of the ill

---

[72] Allen Ellsworth Parker, 'An Analysis of the Factors in Personality Development of the Children of Missionaries' (M.A. thesis, University of Chicago, 1936), 1.

[73] William Ernest Hocking, *Re-Thinking Missions: A Layman's Inquiry after One Hundred Years* (New York and London, 1932), 297.

[74] W. W. Peter, 'Guard your Health: How to avoid Dysentery', *Chinese Recorder*, 1 July 1921, 495.

health of a child. Further, these children are an important source of
new recruits. Finally, in most communities the health of the children
is a barometer of the health of the community.[75]

His conclusions were double-edged. On one hand, missionary children's lives in East Asia were by now thought to be no less dangerous,
disease-wise, than those of their contemporaries at home, based on
known mortality and morbidity statistics. On the other hand, the
onus was on parents to make sure that this was sustained, urging
them to be medically trained or at least scientifically knowledgeable
about the basics of hygiene and prevention. He concluded: 'when
intelligence and care are applied to the problem it is possible for children of missionaries ... to be reared without undue loss'.[76] The overall sense emerging in this period was that the health of missionaries
and their families was seen increasingly as a 'social good', perhaps one
that had economic value but which was also tied to broader goals. As
such it was 'not an isolated value in life', but rather one that had 'significance and meaning only in relation to other values', including
theological and spiritual ones, and which had its 'ideal in the sound
mind in a healthy body fitted to carry on physical, mental and spiritual work and to meet with wholesome spirit the many crises of life.
Health as an ideal implies more than freedom from disease.'[77]

In the second instance, an educational voice began to assert itself,
one that emphasized or echoed this more holistic view of missionary
children and thus placed them more centrally as a key focus in their
own right. Primarily this was articulated through two postgraduate
theses from the University of Chicago, completed by past or present
staff at Woodstock School, established at Landour in northern India
for missionary and expatriate children.[78] To some extent, these had

[75] Lennox, *Health and Turnover*, 175.
[76] Ibid. 180.
[77] Reginald M. Atwater, 'What Place does Hygiene deserve in the Christian Missionary
Enterprise?', *Chinese Recorder*, 1 July 1925, 421.
[78] Parker, 'Analysis'; Robert L. Fleming, 'Adjustment of India Missionaries' Children in
America' (Ph.D. dissertation, University of Chicago, 1947); 'Woodstock School', online
at: <www.woodstockschool.in/wp-content/uploads/2016/03/History-of-Woodstock-
School.pdf>, accessed 31 January 2021. There was a third thesis presented in this period,
which I have not been able to access: Louise Van Evera, 'A Study of the Problems involved
in the Education of Children of Missionaries serving under the Board of Foreign Missions
of the Presbyterian Church, U.S.A., as revealed in the Experience of a Selected Group of
Undergraduate Students' (M.A. thesis, Presbyterian College of Christian Education,
1940).

been prefigured by slightly earlier broad survey observations about missionary children, influenced in part by eugenicist thinking.[79] What the Chicago theses contributed, however, was academic rigour and a more sustained conceptualization of what it meant to be a missionary child at that point in time.

This research presented two apparently contradictory views, with a simultaneous focus on the potential and problems surrounding missionary children. Positively the focus was on their character, the supposed advantages accruing from being in a Christian family, their broad outlooks on life from living in multi-cultural contexts and evident educational or vocational success. Negative issues revolved around perceived problems of mission location (climate, isolation and context-specific factors such as dependence on servants), family separation and cultural adjustments. Both studies also highlighted problems (and solutions) differentiated by national origins; for example, British children were deemed to need different educational solutions than those for Americans.[80] Both writers pointed to the same emphasis in the medical discourse around missionary children, namely that parents had a critical role in addressing these issues. In this respect, Parker clearly differentiated between 'faith missionaries' and those from the denominational missions, perceiving in the latter a higher quality of missionary parent due to educational backgrounds and selection processes. He differentiated further between those parents who were vaguely aware of problems, those who did not take these seriously and those who did but needed support. His findings were aimed as much at missionary 'committees and boards in America' as they were at parents themselves.[81]

The research projects of Parker and Fleming appear to be the first attempts systematically and reflectively to talk to, and learn from, missionary children. Here were the recorded memories, thoughts and feelings of 184 ex-missionary children, albeit from the hindsight of young adulthood. Also significant were the principles underlying or informing the research. While Fleming noted that '[o]ne should see the individual in relation to the sum total of his experience', he

[79] In particular Ellsworth Huntington and Leon F. Whitney, *The Builders of America* (New York, 1927); Ellsworth Huntington, 'The Success of Missionary Children', *Missionary Review of the World*, February 1935, 74–5; Dan B. Brummitt, 'The Fate of Missionaries' Children', *Missionary Review of the World*, January 1934, 37–8.
[80] Parker, 'Analysis', 59–60.
[81] Ibid. 36, 39–41, 101.

proceeded to argue that two equally important principles were to '[a]pproach the individual from his own point of view' and to understand that across cohorts of missionary children '[s]everal personality types seem to exist'.[82] It was important to him that younger people were allowed to speak for themselves without fear of being spoken for by older adults. As a result, children's lives were described not just in terms of factors such as health or education, but also more affective elements, including (among others) speech, clothing, sexuality, relationships, leisure and religious identity.[83] In essence the research began to add colour and diversity to public representations of missionary children's lives; it gave them an identity and allowed their experiences to be differentiated from those of adults and from one another.

A broad reading of Christian history indicates that children have always been important, albeit for different reasons or to fit particular agendas.[84] Through the nineteenth century this was epitomized in the Protestant Sunday school movement and the various educational projects and child-focused sodalities of Roman Catholicism. In the context of the missionary movement this was nowhere clearer than in the myriad educational projects among indigenous or colonized children. Missionary children emerge as one particular subset of these 'religious childhoods', but one that has often been hidden within more adult-centric discourses. This article has sought to bring to light the role that illness, death and advancing medical understanding played in slowly turning the gaze of churches towards missionary children as a distinct and influential group, within the wider trope of 'imperial children'. In that process, children's experiences and childhood as a category took on a more central role as churches and missionary organizations recalibrated their thinking about missionary well-being. Illness and death continued to be a childhood reality, but by the 1930s this was no longer the defining factor in public perceptions or representations of missionary children's lives. Or at least, it did not need to be, and that was the point. Rather, missionary children's lives, with respect to health

---

[82] Fleming, 'Adjustment', 5–7.

[83] Ibid. 13–19, 23–4, 25–41, 44–50.

[84] The complexities of children as historical religious actors, subjects and agents are canvassed, for example, in Diana Wood, ed., *The Church and Childhood*, SCH 31 (Oxford, 1994); Hugh Morrison and Mary Clare Martin, eds, *Creating Religious Childhoods in Anglo-World and British Colonial Contexts, 1800–1950* (London and New York, 2017).

and welfare, began to be understood in more holistic terms, in a manner that more than hinted at the expectation of a new status quo. This contention, broadly explored here, now needs fleshing out for a range of comparative national contexts.

Caring for the Sick and Dying in Early Twentieth-Century Anglo-Catholic Parishes

Dan D. Cruickshank*

University of Glasgow

This article explores the evidence given to the Royal Commission on Ecclesiastical Discipline (1904–6), to examine how Anglo-Catholic clergy and parishes across England were caring for the sick and dying at the beginning of the twentieth century. It considers why Anglo-Catholic clergy and parishes had come by that point to believe that the existing provisions for the care of the sick and the dying provided by the Book of Common Prayer were not wholly satisfactory. Through the replies of clergy to the commission, it discusses the extent to which these practices were born out of a need to find new ways to reach the sick and the dying in twentieth-century England, and to what extent they were seen as demonstrating an allegiance to a more 'catholic' theology.

Studies of Anglo-Catholicism[1] have long held in esteem the pastoral work of priests in parishes often neglected by other strands of churchmanship in the Church of England.[2] Recently questions have been raised regarding the reality of this work.[3] The Royal Commission on Ecclesiastical Discipline, which was convened between 1904 and 1906, provides a unique insight into the nature of services in Anglo-Catholic parishes at the beginning of the twentieth century.

---

* Theology and Religious Studies, No. 4 The Square, University of Glasgow, G12 8QQ. E-mail: d.cruickshank.1@research.gla.ac.uk.

[1] There is a debate to be had about terminology, over whether 'ritualist' or 'Anglo-Catholic' best describes the practices of those active at the beginning of the twentieth century. 'Ritualist' is a rather loaded term, full of derogatory connotations, and one perhaps better fitted to the nineteenth century than the twentieth. As this article is concerned solely with the twentieth century, it will show preference for the term 'Anglo-Catholic'.

[2] For a recent example, see James Pereiro, 'The Oxford Movement and Anglo-Catholicism', in Rowan Strong, ed., *OHA, 3: Partisan Anglicanism and Its Global Expansion 1829–c.1914* (Oxford, 2017), 187–211, at 208–9.

[3] The idea that the pastoral care offered by Tractarian priests was significantly different from that of their non-Tractarian brethren has been challenged, quite convincingly, by George Herring in his *The Oxford Movement in Practice: The Tractarian Parochial Worlds from the 1830s to the 1870s* (Oxford, 2016), 150–65.

Studies in Church History 58 (2022), 330–351   © The Author(s), 2022. Published by Cambridge University Press on behalf of Ecclesiastical History Society
doi: 10.1017/stc.2022.16

Through an evidence-gathering process that took place in 1904 and 1905, the commission created the most comprehensive survey of the conduct of worship at Anglo-Catholic parishes produced up until that point.[4] This article will use the commission's evidence to consider how such parishes provided for the sick and the dying during the period. In doing so, it will consider what was novel about the approaches of Anglo-Catholic parishes towards caring for the sick and dying, exploring how they differed from the approaches sanctioned by the Book of Common Prayer. By examining the responses of Anglo-Catholic clergy to the commission, it will consider how pastoral need as well as a belief in a 'catholic' theology influenced their decision to use, and their justification of, non-Prayer Book provisions for the sick and dying.

The Royal Commission on Ecclesiastical Discipline was the culmination of an almost decade-long anti-ritualist campaign which had raged both inside and outside parliament.[5] This of course was not the first royal commission called to examine the issues raised by the ritualist movement, the Royal Commission on Ritualism having met from 1867 to 1870. It was that commission which led to the anti-ritualist legislation of the late nineteenth century.[6] The ineffectiveness of this legislation in 'solving' the ritualist question, and the unhappiness about the prosecutions which resulted from the legislation and affected those on both sides of the ritualist debate, were the real inspirations for the new commission.[7] Carrying out its duty, the Royal Commission on Ecclesiastical Discipline became the largest officially sanctioned central gatherer of information regarding liturgical practice which the Church of England had seen in modern times.[8]

---

[4] Guides such as *The Tourist's Church Guide*, the first edition of which came out in 1874, whilst providing information on the location of ritualist churches, give rather scant information on the practice of those churches: Nigel Yates, *Anglican Ritualism in Victorian Britain, 1830–1910* (Oxford, 1999), 386–414.

[5] For a thorough overview of this campaign, see G. I. T. Machin, 'The Last Victorian Anti-Ritualist Campaign, 1895–1906', *VS* 25 (1982), 277–302.

[6] Dan D. Cruickshank, 'Debating the Legal Status of the Ornaments Rubric: Ritualism and Royal Commissions in Late Nineteenth- and Early Twentieth-Century England', in Rosamond McKitterick, Charlotte Methuen and Andrew Spicer, eds, *The Church and the Law*, SCH 56 (Cambridge, 2020), 434–54, at 441–8.

[7] Ibid. 448.

[8] Unofficial 'guides' to churches, such as *Mackeson's Guide*, sometimes covered a larger number of churches, but these were unofficial and often gave scant information: John Shelton Reed, *Glorious Battle: The Cultural Politics of Victorian Anglo-Catholicism* (Nashville, TN, and London, 1996), 267.

John Shelton Reed claimed that the commission considered evidence from 8,689 out of the 14,234 Church of England churches that the commission identified as currently existing in England.[9] Donald Gray, however, gave the much more conservative number of 687 services held at 559 churches across England:[10] 559 was the number that the report of the Royal Commission used, and although not as impressive as 60 per cent of churches, 3.9 per cent of all churches was not an insignificant number by any means.[11]

The report of the Royal Commission, which directly led to the failed attempt to revise the Book of Common Prayer, which in turn ushered in the 'Prayer Book Crisis', has been the focus of most who have considered the commission.[12] There have been a few accounts of the evidence contained within the report. The evidence was considered briefly, and colourfully, by Donald Gray in his study of the 'Prayer Book Crisis'.[13] Bethany Kilcrease has also considered the commission, focusing mainly on how it was a culmination of the conflict between ritualists and anti-ritualist groupings, with both organizing to help or hinder the commission.[14] Nigel Yates, in his study of ritualism, was cautious about using the evidence of the commission, which he considered 'relies very heavily on the observations of hostile, and sometimes not very well-informed, witnesses'.[15] Such a view ignores the fact that the priests of all churches mentioned by witnesses were given the chance to respond, that the vast majority did, and that all witnesses were thoroughly questioned by the commissioners, who, as Grey points out, were selected to bring a sense of balance and a lack of partisanship.[16] As this article will demonstrate, commissioners were not afraid to push witnesses in order to satisfy themselves that their statements

[9] Ibid. 255. Reed seems to have confused here the number of churches included in the English Church Union's *The Tourist's Church Guide*, 25th edn (London, 1901), which was 8,689, with the number of churches on which the Royal Commission heard evidence.
[10] Donald Gray, *The 1927–28 Prayer Book Crisis: (1) Ritual, Royal Commissions, and Reply to the Royal Letters of Business*, Joint Liturgical Studies 60 (London, 2005), 25–6.
[11] *Report of the Royal Commission on Ecclesiastical Discipline*, Cd 3040 (London, 1906), 20.
[12] See Dan D. Cruickshank, *The Theology and Ecclesiology of the Prayer Book Crisis, 1906–1928* (Cham, 2019).
[13] Gray, *1927–28 Prayer Book Crisis: (1)*, 25–8.
[14] Bethany Kilcrease, *The Great Church Crisis and the End of English Erastianism, 1898–1906* (London and New York, 2017), 147–61.
[15] Yates, *Anglican Ritualism*, 327.
[16] Gray, *1927–28 Prayer Book Crisis: (1)*, 25.

were unambiguous and reflected the actual situation within a parish. I have previously considered the evidence of the Royal Commission, but have only scratched the surface of the material covered in the three substantial volumes of evidence.[17] What unites the work of Kilcrease, Yates and myself is the use of ecclesiological questions to interrogate the evidence and the consideration of how this evidence demonstrates the tension between the hierarchy of the church and the competing theological movements within it. In contrast, this article will use the evidence to build a picture of how certain aspects of pastoral care were conducted within Anglo-Catholic parishes at the beginning of the twentieth century.

Three main currents emerging from the evidence presented to the commission were seen by witnesses as unique to how Anglo-Catholic parishes cared for the sick and dying: reservation of the consecrated elements, the use of a sanctus bell, and organized prayers for the sick, dying and (in extreme cases) dead. Through an examination of these practices, the article will explore both how they were implemented in churches across England and also the pastoral reasons priests gave to explain these non-Prayer Book actions. In doing so it will consider how pastoral concern and Anglo-Catholic theology led to novel approaches to caring for the sick and dying.

In the 1552 Book of Common Prayer, reservation had implicitly been made illegal within the Church of England, with a rubric in the order for communion stating that 'if any of the bread or wine remain, the Curate shall have it to his own use'.[18] In 1552 and 1559, no distinction was made between bread and wine that had been upon the Lord's table during the service and any surplus which had been unused, part of Cranmer's conscious omission of any idea of consecration within his eucharistic theology as expressed in his Prayer Books.[19] Since the 1662 Book of Common Prayer, the reservation of consecrated elements after a communion service had been explicitly made illegal in the Church of England. The new communion rubric regarding any bread or wine not consumed by communicants allowed for the curate to take home the remaining elements which

---

[17] See Dan [D.] Cruickshank, *From the Sublime to the Ridiculous: Ritualism and Anglo-Catholicism in the Evidence of the Royal Commission into Ecclesiastical Discipline, 1904–6* (London, 2018); idem, 'Debating the Legal Status'.

[18] *The First and Second Prayer Books of Edward VI* (Goring Heath, 1999), 392.

[19] Gordon P. Jeanes, *Signs of God's Promise: Thomas Cranmer's Sacramental Theology and the Book of Common Prayer* (London and New York, 2008), 110–12.

were 'unconsecrated'. Any consecrated elements were not to 'be carried out of the Church, but the Priest and such other of the Communicants as he shall call unto him, shall immediately after the blessing, reverently eat and drink the same'.[20] This rubric was a suggestion by John Cosin, drawn from his *Durham Book*, prepared in advance of the Savoy Conference of 1661, in order to bring the rules surrounding the consumption of the leftover elements more into line with the Laudian understanding that these had been fundamentally changed through their use in the communion service.[21] However, through the latter half of the nineteenth century, reservation had been adopted by some in the Anglo-Catholic wing of the Church of England.[22] The Royal Commission gives some insight into how widespread the practice was, geographically speaking. The majority of cases of reservation of the elements reported to the commission came, perhaps unsurprisingly, from London and, perhaps more surprisingly, the south-west of England. In the south-west, the most reports of reservation appeared to come from Devon, where cases were reported in a number of seaside resorts and urban centres, including Babbacombe, Paignton and Plymouth.[23] It seems, then, that there was a concentration of advanced Anglo-Catholicism in London and the south-west at the start of the twentieth century. Nigel Yates, considering the spread of ritualist priests in the 1870s, found there was an 'above average concentration' of such priests in the dioceses of London, Bath and Wells and Exeter.[24] This trend was continuing into the twentieth century.

Overall, thirty churches in which reservation took place were presented to the commission.[25] Yates has questioned the reliability of this number, stating that it is 'certainly inaccurate and indicates

[20] *The Book of Common Prayer and Administration of the Sacraments and other Rites and Ceremonies of the Church according to the Use of the Church of England [1662]* (London, 1992), 265.
[21] G. J. Cuming, *A History of the Anglican Liturgy* (London and Basingstoke, 1982), 124.
[22] Ian Machin, 'Reservation under Pressure: Ritual in the Prayer Book Crisis, 1927–1928', in R. N. Swanson, ed., *Continuity and Change in Christian Worship*, SCH 35 (Oxford, 1999), 447–63, at 447–8.
[23] *Minutes of Evidence taken before the Royal Commission on Ecclesiastical Discipline: Volume One*, Cd 3069 (London, 1906), 25, 326, 350; *Minutes of Evidence taken before the Royal Commission on Ecclesiastical Discipline: Volume Two*, Cd 3070 (London, 1906), 243.
[24] Yates, *Anglican Ritualism*, 84–5.
[25] *Royal Commission: Report*, 37.

that the precautions taken by parishes to disguise reservation were remarkably effective'.[26] However, this is based on his assumption that churches tried hard to disguise reservation, a supposition not borne out by the evidence of the commission. Furthermore, Yates does not question any of the other statistics drawn from the evidence of the commission. Without clear evidence of why this data is unreliable, there seems no obvious reason not to accept the number of thirty churches practising reservation. Of these, the commission found only thirteen in which reservation took place 'publicly in the church itself or in a chapel to which the public had access, or which was so arranged that the place of reservation was visible from outside the chapel'.[27] In the public evidence, moreover, only in one church, St Peter's, Plymouth, was it explicitly stated that reservation took place in public.[28] St Peter's was one of the first cases heard by the Royal Commission, forming part of the evidence of the first two evidence-givers: the Revd William Edward Bowen and Henry Charles Hogan. Bowen, a priest who did not 'hold any cure',[29] had become an anti-ritualist campaigner. In 1902 he had produced a small book, *Contemporary Ritualism: A Volume of Evidence*, specifically for the use of parliamentarians,[30] and in 1904 he followed this up by circulating an anti-ritualist pamphlet amongst them.[31] Gray identified this pamphlet as having had an 'explosive effect on the Prime Minister', thus making the formation of the Royal Commission inevitable.[32] Bowen, then, was an obvious choice as the first witness to the commission. Instead of relying on his previously published evidence, Bowen presented evidence from Anglo-Catholic churches gathered since May 1903, relying heavily on the work of his 'chief reporter', Henry Hogan.[33] Hogan had decided which churches to visit based on the English Church Union (ECU)'s *Tourist's Church Guide*, using the edition published in 1901.[34]

[26] Yates, *Anglican Ritualism*, 328.
[27] *Royal Commission: Report*, 37.
[28] *Royal Commission: Volume One*, 25.
[29] Ibid. 1.
[30] W. E. Bowen, *Contemporary Ritualism: A Volume of Evidence* (London, 1902).
[31] Gray, *1927–28 Prayer Book Crisis: (1)*, 23.
[32] Ibid. 23–4.
[33] *Royal Commission: Volume One*, 2.
[34] *Tourist's Church Guide*, 25th edn; *Royal Commission: Volume One*, 2.

It was Hogan who gave evidence about St Peter's, after attending a Monday service on 25 January 1904. He had been keen to visit after seeing a piece in the *Western Morning News* about the first sermon by the new incumbent, the Revd H. M. Downton.[35] In the sermon, Downton had referred to the bishop's visit to the parish, which seems in part to have been caused by the public reservation of the consecrated elements in the church. Downton commented that the people of the parish:

> could not fail to have been impressed with the tone of paternal affection and sympathy which prevailed throughout the whole of the bishop's sermon, and though most of them, if not all, regretted his decision, regarding the public reservation of the Blessed Sacrament and the curtailment of other ritual acts, yet they could thankfully accept the liberty the bishop gave to reserve the Blessed Sacrament for the purpose of communicating the sick and dying, and for not curtailing in any greater degree than he had done the traditional ritual of that church.[36]

It is clear from this that public reservation had been practised in the church, but the bishop of Exeter, Herbert Ryle, had intervened to ensure that the elements were only reserved privately for the use in communicating 'the sick and dying'. Since this decision, Downton made clear, 'the Blessed Sacrament had ceased to be reserved publicly in open church'.[37] However, the bishop had not completely stopped the practice of reservation. It was this claim, that reservation formed part of the pastoral care for the sick and dying in a parish, which was to be mentioned repeatedly when reservation was raised before the commission.

From the evidence given to the commission, London seems, unsurprisingly, to have had the highest incidence of reservation. The bishop of London, Arthur Winnington-Ingram, informed the committee that from an inquiry in his diocese, he found that thirty-four churches were practising reservation, of which fifteen practised perpetual reservation, whilst nineteen practised occasional reservation, in which the elements were 'reserved for a particular sick person and then taken almost immediately to the sick person'.[38]

---

[35] *Royal Commission: Volume One*, 25.
[36] Ibid.
[37] Ibid.
[38] *Royal Commission: Report*, 38. This number is of course higher than the total number of churches the commission found practising reservation, which suggests that the numbers

Overall this was a small, but not insignificant, number of churches. Winnington-Ingram told the commission he believed there were 640 churches in his diocese, although the commission believed there were 607: so around 5 per cent of London churches were practising reservation.[39] Those priests from London who either wrote to the commission after a witness spoke about their church, or who appeared as witnesses themselves, all claimed that they practised reservation out of pastoral necessity. Frederick C. Holiday, the church-warden at St Augustine's, Kilburn, claimed that reservation was not practised at his church. However, upon further questioning he informed the committee that 'sometimes' some of the consecrated elements were reserved after the service to be 'taken at the end of the service to a sick person'. This occurred 'immediately' after the service was concluded, and thus the elements were not 'reserved in the church'.[40] The Revd Canon C. E. Brookes, the incumbent at St John the Divine, Kennington, spoke of a similar practice at his own church, with the reserved elements being 'taken straight from the church, and taken directly after a celebration'. Brookes was adamant that he would allow no delay to take place, telling the commissioners that he 'was asked only the other day, for instance, to allow the Blessed Sacrament to be reserved from our 7 o'clock celebration to half past 10, and I said no – that it could not be done'.[41] This, then, was not reservation as is typically understood. The consecrated elements were 'reserved', in that they were retained without being consumed from those consecrated at the communion service in the church, but they were taken directly from that celebration to the communicant in the parish. There was, strictly speaking, no reservation taking place within the church building.

St Frideswide's, Poplar, pushed the boundaries of how this type of reservation could take place. The priest at St Frideswide's, the Revd C. P. S. Clarke, appeared before the commission in January 1905. In 1932 Clarke would write a history of *The Oxford Movement and After*, in anticipation of its centenary, in which he depicted the commission

produced by the commission should be seen as a minimum number, and as a sample, rather than suggestive of the total number of churches using a practice.
[39] *Minutes of Evidence taken before the Royal Commission on Ecclesiastical Discipline: Volume Three*, Cd 3071 (London, 1906), 259.
[40] *Royal Commission: Volume Two*, 443.
[41] Ibid. 276.

337

as a fruit of Davidson's early archiepiscopate, when he needed 'time to free himself of the notion that force was a remedy [to the practices of] Ritualists'.[42] As an evidence giver, Clarke informed the commission that it was the practice at St Frideswide's to reserve the elements 'for a few hours' usually when 'there is a person, who may be likely to die at any minute'. For those few hours between service and distribution, the reserved elements were not held in the church, but instead in the 'Sisters' Chapel', presumably one designated or built for the Sisters of Mercy, who operated in the parish.[43] Clarke informed the commission that the usual practice was for a priest to leave with the elements, accompanied by a verger who carried a lit candle. When pressed by Michael Hicks Beach, the chairman of the committee, over whether this was 'desirable', Clarke responded that he thought it was, as 'one wants to shows some respect and reverence, to the Blessed Sacrament; and I think it is good for the people too. Of course, one might put on an overcoat over one's surplice and go secretly, but I think it is good for the people in the street to know.' Perhaps inadvertently, he had admitted that the elements were carried to the chapel in a proper ceremonial procession, with a priest in surplice led by a verger with candle. It was hard to argue that all these elements were a necessity for communicating the sick; instead, the main audience for this procession were passers-by, whom Clarke said would occasionally 'take off their hats or would show some mark of reverence'. It was, he claimed, 'a witness'.[44]

The majority of churches where the commission found evidence of reservation pleaded that it was done out of pastoral necessity. At most of these churches, the priests were keen to point out that the reserved elements were carried almost immediately from the service to the sick person. In these cases, it is hard to argue that reservation was really taking place for devotional reasons. How could a congregation adore the reserved sacrament when it was never held in public, or if it was immediately taken from the church? Although it was not a main feature of theological writings of the period, the fact that reservation was almost exclusively for the communion of the sick and

[42] C. P. S. Clarke, *The Oxford Movement and After* (London and Oxford, 1932), 277.
[43] *Royal Commission: Volume Two*, 326. The Devonport society of the Sisters of Mercy was one of the first Anglican religious orders founded after the Reformation, in 1848: see Thomas J. Williams, 'The Beginnings of Anglican Sisterhoods', *Historical Magazine of the Protestant Episcopal Church* 16 (1947), 350–72, at 353–6.
[44] *Royal Commission: Volume Two*, 326.

dying is not wholly surprising from the sparse discussion of the matter by Anglo-Catholic theologians.[45] For example, Edward Bouverie Pusey had argued that although Article 28 of the Thirty-Nine Articles appeared to condemn reservation, it did not in fact condemn reservation for the practice of communicating the sick as this was a practice of the early church and 'there is no instance, in which the Church of England has condemned any practice of the Primitive Church'.[46] However, the generation of Anglo-Catholic theologians who were emerging at the start of the twentieth century would soon come to defend reservation for devotional purposes.[47] Moreover, the case of St Frideswide's, Poplar, demonstrates that even with immediate removal of the elements from the church for distribution to the sick there was still opportunity for the priest to encourage adoration. It is tempting to give the priests the benefit of the doubt, and say that reservation was born out of the necessity of pastoral care rather than from theological reasoning. However, this begs the question of why reservation was seen as more appropriate to early twentieth-century pastoral needs than the existing Prayer Book service for the communion of the sick.

An order for the communion of the sick had first appeared in the 1549 Book of Common Prayer. The order in the first Prayer Book offered two options: the first was a short service which would take place immediately after the communion service in the church, using consecrated elements from that service, distributed after a general confession and absolution.[48] The second provided for a communion service to be held in the house of the sick person, when there was not a service in the church on that day.[49] In the 1552 Prayer Book only the latter option was envisaged; although it did not explicitly rule out the use of pre-consecrated elements, the fact that the Prayer Book

---

[45] Although the doctrine of the real presence was a central issue for post-Oxford Movement theological writers, the question of reservation was rarely seen as part of this discussion. For an overview, see Peter Nockles, *The Oxford Movement in Context: Anglican High Churchmanship, 1760–1857* (Cambridge, 1994), 235–49.

[46] E. B. Pusey, *The Real Presence of the Body and Blood of our Lord Jesus Christ: The Doctrine of the English Church with a Vindication of the Reception by the Wicked and of the Adoration of our Lord Jesus Christ truly Present* (Oxford and London, 1869), 313–14. Article 28 states: 'The Sacrament of the Lord's Supper was not by Christ's ordinance reserved, carried about, lifted up, or worshipped.'

[47] See, for example, Darwell Stone, *The Reserved Sacrament* (London, 1917).

[48] *First and Second Prayer Books*, 266.

[49] Ibid. 266–8.

provided a collect, epistle and gospel suggested a full communion service was to be held within the sick person's home.[50] This service was repeated in the books of 1559 and 1662 without alteration.[51] The addition of the 1662 rubric discussed above, which directed that any leftover consecrated elements from the main communion service were to be consumed 'reverently' immediately after the service, and not to be 'carried out of the Church', made clear that pre-consecrated elements were not to be used in the communion of the sick.[52] The use of reservation thus went against the rubrics of the 1662 Prayer Book, but could find precedent in that of 1549. The question remains why Anglo-Catholic priests were turning to an illegal practice rather than the legal service provided by the Prayer Book.

Many of those priests who discussed reservation before the commission were keen to stress that it complemented the Prayer Book service for the sick, rather than replacing it. Clarke said they 'always' tried to hold the communion service for the sick 'but there are cases where the sick person cannot bear even a short service'.[53] Hicks Beach asked if Clarke had ever 'found a difficulty in celebrating the Communion Service for the Sick in a private house' on account of the 'surroundings', a not very subtle euphemism for the poverty and slum housing which characterized much of Poplar.[54] Clarke answered that he had not 'because we have Sisters of Mercy, and they always go beforehand and get the room ready'. Also, he added, he was 'not so easily affected' by his surroundings, and was of the view that 'ritual and the surroundings do not make much difference' to the conduct of the service.[55] When the revision process of the Book of Common Prayer took place in the aftermath of the Royal Commission, there were some claims that the communion service for the sick had fallen into disuse due to priests' dislike of being in the houses of poor parishioners.[56] Clarke seems to have pre-emptively dismissed that as a reason.

---

[50] Ibid. 422–3.
[51] John E. Booty, ed., *The Book of Common Prayer 1559: The Elizabethan Prayer Book* (Charlottesville, VA, and London, 2005), 307–8; *Book of Common Prayer [1662]*, 328–30.
[52] *Book of Common Prayer [1662]*, 265.
[53] *Royal Commission: Volume Two*, 326.
[54] Drew D. Gray, *London's Shadows: The Dark Side of the Victorian City* (London and New York, 2010), 119–32.
[55] *Royal Commission: Volume Two*, 326.
[56] Cruickshank, *Theology and Ecclesiology of the Prayer Book Crisis*, 39.

Arthur Eglington, priest at St John's, East Dulwich, claimed that when he had arrived in the parish 'there was no actual Celebration for the Sick according to the Book of Common Prayer'. Rather, he found that the parishioners had been 'educated up to the practice of reservation'.[57] In some parishes, reservation seems to have supplanted the Prayer Book service for the sick, not out of necessity but on theological grounds. Eglington was attempting to reintroduce the Prayer Book service, and informed the commission that over the previous three years he had taken around a hundred and forty services for the sick, of which twelve had involved using the reserved elements.[58] Even in what was a quite advanced parish, the priest had managed to reduce the number of services using reservation substantially. By contrast, Ernest Charles Atherton, the priest at St James the Great, Keyham, Devonport, reported that of the seventy-four visitations to the sick he had taken in the past year, around forty-five or forty-six were private celebrations; thus the remainder, nearly thirty, involved reservation.[59] Brooks, from St John the Divine, Kennington, claimed that 'I very much prefer celebrating, and I very much prefer my colleagues doing the same, but I suppose that more often they are communicated with the Reserved Sacrament than with a celebration.'[60] The people's churchwarden at St Mary Magdalene, Paddington, Charles E. J. Twisday, claimed that as doctors often 'impose regulations as to rest and absence of excitement' it was often impossible to conduct the Prayer Book service without going against doctors' orders.[61]

Of the priests who spoke about the Prayer Book service for the communion of the sick, if we are to take them at their word, all apparently preferred conducting that service to communicating the sick with the reserved elements. Reservation was seen as a necessity arising partly from the need not to disturb the extremely sick with a communion service. Although reservation can be portrayed as a clear token of Anglo-Catholicism, the evidence of the commission suggests that those using reservation did so because of perceived pastoral need. The concentration in London, especially in the East End of

---

[57] *Royal Commission: Volume Two*, 199.
[58] Ibid. 202.
[59] Ibid. 243.
[60] Ibid. 276.
[61] Ibid. 278.

London, seems to reflect a practice adopted to suit a growing population. But a growing population alone does not fully account for the growth in demand for communicating from a sick bed. The adoption of the practice across Devon shows a growing demand within Anglo-Catholic parishes that were not subject to high population growth, suggesting a growing demand from Anglo-Catholic parishioners to receive when sick or close to death. The Prayer Book service for the sick, whilst shorter than the full communion service, was still considerably lengthier than communicating with the reserved elements. At a time of growing demands on their time, reservation was one way Anglo-Catholic priests could ensure that they met all their pastoral commitments within the hours of a day.

We now turn from perhaps the most obvious Anglo-Catholic practice to occur in the evidence to two more obscure ones. One of the most intriguing elements covered in the Royal Commission's final report was the use of church bells. The report stated that 'it would appear from the evidence that the practice of ringing the church bell at the time of the consecration, is valued as a method of enabling the sick persons to join in the service at which they are unable to be actually present'.[62] The use of a sanctus bell had been growing amongst Anglo-Catholics towards the end of the nineteenth century. Percy Dearmer, in *The Parson's Handbook*, had suggested that 'perhaps the bell in the tower will toll three times at each consecration, and a small bell may also be used if it is felt to be desirable'.[63] *Ritual Notes*, another leading Anglo-Catholic manual, also recommended the ringing of a bell at the moment of consecration.[64] This was not a practice contained within, or sanctioned by, any of the Prayer Books, and the evidence of the Royal Commission provides an examination both of the practice and of the pastoral justification many priests used for adopting it.

The evidence presented to the commission suggests that in many Anglo-Catholic parishes, the main church bell, rather than small altar bells, was used as a sanctus bell. This was the case at St Andrew's, Willesden, where the bell was 'tolled always three times after the consecration of each of the elements' as 'those who lie on sick beds, as

[62] *Royal Commission: Report*, 23.
[63] Percy Dearmer, *The Parson's Handbook*, 1st edn (London, 1899), 161.
[64] The Editors of 'The Order of Divine Service', *Ritual Notes on the Order of Divine Service* (Oxford, 1894), 46.

well as those at work, within hearing of it, have often spoken of the comfort of knowing that they are being remembered before God at that most solemn moment of the eucharistic service'.[65] The same occurred at St Frideswide's, Poplar, where Clarke said that it was tolled 'to let people outside, especially the sick, know what is going on'.[66] Similarly at Holy Trinity, Stratford-upon-Avon, the vicar, George Arbuthnot, informed the commission that this was done 'to let persons outside know what was going on, so that they might, if they thought fit, join in the prayers which were being offered'. Arbuthnot went on to say he knew from personal experience 'that sick persons appreciate this'.[67] Percy Gethen, rector of St Benedict, Ardwick, gave a spirited defence of the practice:

> The purpose of this [the sanctus bell] is plain and reasonable. It is a notification to the faithful who cannot be present in church, and especially to the sick, who are thus enable to join with the congregation in saying το αμην επι τη ση ευχαριστια [*sic*; 'the amen to our thanksgiving'].[68]

> It cannot be regarded as a ceremony performed in the church, since the bell and ringer are not in the church, but in the belfry tower.[69]

This last comment, that the ceremony took place not in the church but in the belfry, seems particularly telling and may suggest why in the evidence of the commission there were no real examples of stand-alone sanctus bells in use. Gethen seems to have been aware that the ringing of such a bell would constitute a ceremony, and as it was not contained within any of the Prayer Books of the Church of England, it was not a ceremony legally allowed in a church building.[70] Thus Gethen appears to have been exploiting what he clearly believed to be a loophole, by holding an illegal ceremony outside the church which took place concurrently with the legal service being held inside the church. This was a clever, if legally rather dubious, way to circumvent the use of non-Prayer Book ceremonies within the worship of

---

[65] *Royal Commission: Volume One*, 242.
[66] *Royal Commission: Volume Two*, 325.
[67] *Royal Commission: Volume One*, 529.
[68] 1 Corinthians 14: 16. My thanks to Jonathan How for the translation.
[69] *Royal Commission: Volume Two*, 22.
[70] Using such legal loopholes and questioning the interpretation of rubrics was standard practice across the Anglo-Catholic movement: Cruickshank, 'Debating the Legal Status'.

Anglo-Catholic parishes. Presumably other churches avoided the use of stand-alone sanctus bells so as to avoid making the ceremony too explicit. The use of church bells was not regulated within the Church of England, so this too allowed a certain legal loophole in facilitating their use in ceremonies not envisaged by the Prayer Book.

The problem with all the defences given by priests for the use of the sanctus bell is they rely on what, at best, can be described as hearsay. That priests who supported the practice felt it was appreciated by the sick is not the same as it being demonstrated that the sick felt it was part of the pastoral support offered them by the parish. The pastoral need being met was also directly tied into Anglo-Catholic theology, with priests talking of the desire to make sure sick parishioners knew when the moment of consecration occurred within the eucharistic prayer. Wanting people outside the church to know when the moment of consecration occurs is arguably not, primarily, a pastoral concern. For this practice, unlike reservation, the pastoral needs of the parish seem to be a flimsy defence for a liturgical innovation driven by theological concerns.

The final example, the incorporation of extempore or formal but unauthorized prayer into the services of the Church of England, was an issue almost as old as the church itself.[71] No Book of Common Prayer had ever instituted a way to incorporate prayers for individual parishioners into the life of the local church. Non-Prayer Book prayers had been a hallmark of the Evangelical Revival, both in organized prayer services and to a lesser extent within the conduct of Prayer Book services.[72] Peter Nockles, considering the difference between the Evangelical Revival of the eighteenth century and the Catholic Revival of the nineteenth, spoke of the 'greater emphasis on the corporate idea and life of the church' in the latter.[73] The evidence to the Royal Commission demonstrates how Anglo-Catholic parishes were attempting to personalize the prayers in their parish by

[71] Lori Branch, 'The Rejection of Liturgy, the Rise of Free Prayer, and Modern Religious Subjectivity', *Restoration: Studies in English Literary Culture, 1660-1700*, 29 (2005), 1–28.
[72] David W. Bebbington, *Evangelicalism in Modern Britain: A History from the 1730s to the 1980s* (London and New York, 1989), 55; Gareth Atkins, 'Anglican Evangelicalism', in Jeremy Gregory, ed., *OHA*, 2: *Establishment and Empire, 1662–1829* (Oxford, 2017), 452–73, at 453–4.
[73] Peter B. Nockles, 'The Oxford Movement as Religious Revival and Resurgence', in Kate Cooper and Jeremy Gregory, eds, *Revival and Resurgence in Christian History*, SCH 44 (Woodbridge, 2008), 214–24, at 219.

institutionalizing them. In this way they were able to ensure that all parishioners, sick or not, were visibly or verbally maintained as members of the worshipping church community.

Emily Bruce, who presented first-hand evidence she had gathered on behalf of the leading evangelical group, the Church Association,[74] noted that at the Church of the Holy Innocents, Hammersmith, she found 'near one of the doors ... a framed card with, "Of your charity", etc., and the names of the sick and the dead'.[75] Another witness described at Christ Church, Chester, seeing 'in the porch a copper plate asking for prayers of the dead, "of your charity pray for Jones, Taylor, Peers, Putlans. By thy Cross and Passion, good Lord deliver"'. However, the priest of the parish, J. F. Howson, in his written response to the commission was keen to point out that 'there is a prayer-board, but it includes living people who are sick, and the four names quoted are four sick cases in my parish, who are still living'.[76] There was also a prayer board asking for prayers for 'the sick and departed' in Chislehurst Parish Church.[77] St Stephen's, Lewisham, also had in the porch 'a large framed card ... with three headings, viz., "Sick," – "Travelling" and "Departed," with a list of names under each, and a request at the foot that "prayers, intercessions, etc. be made for all men"'.[78] The same was to be found at All Saints, Newcastle-upon-Tyne.[79] At St Hilda's, Darlington, there was 'a framed notice with the words – "The prayers of the church are desired for [ ] In sickness [ ] Among the faithful departed." Under the latter heading is a list of twenty-three names on the list of the sick, the words "In Pace" have been added.'[80] These notice boards were clearly not static objects, but were continually updated to reflect the health of people across the parish.

Some parishes integrated prayers for the sick and dying into the service itself. The simplest form was perhaps found at St John's, Gainsborough, where during the course of the Sunday morning

[74] The Church Association, founded in 1865, had spearheaded attempts to have ritualist clergy prosecuted in the second half of the nineteenth century: Yates, *Anglican Ritualism*, 216–20.
[75] *Royal Commission: Volume One*, 150.
[76] Ibid. 269.
[77] Ibid. 373.
[78] *Royal Commission: Volume Two*, 119.
[79] Ibid. 303.
[80] Ibid. 298.

'Choral Eucharist', 'the celebrant read out the names of some sick persons to be prayed for, and then some other names'. A prayer board was also to be found in the church.[81] At St Frideswide's, Poplar, a weekly service was held on a Wednesday evening with 'a sermon and intercessions, the congregation sending up petitions for sick friends and other things they wish prayer for'.[82] At All Saints, Walworth, Hogan reported that during the course of a communion service, also held on a Wednesday, 'before the Prayer for the Church Militant he [the priest] asked for prayer[s for] certain sick persons, and for Robert Dolling, and another person departed'.[83] Charles Coard, a former Sunday school teacher in the parish of All Hallows, North St Pancras, claimed there was 'a special Saturday morning celebration in which people are asked to pray for the faithful departed'. The priest, Coard claimed, instructed that the children be taught to pray for the dead.[84] However, the priest, B. S. Lombard, claimed in his written response that Coard's claim was a 'misrepresentation'

> In teaching the children we always try to inculcate the thought that Prayers for the Dead mean Prayers for the living – that death does not end all things, and I have repeatedly told Mr. Coard when he has tried to argue the point that we only teach it as a pious custom, and one which was stated to be not opposed to the law of the Church of England by the late Archbishop Temple.[85]

Frederick Temple, archbishop of Canterbury 1896–1902, whilst no Anglo-Catholic, made public his support for prayers for the dead numerous times during his episcopacy.[86] Anglo-Catholics were now able to use his approval to defend the practice.

Here we seem to be seeing theology informing pastoral practice. This is not necessarily Anglo-Catholic theology; the need for personal prayer was also a concern of evangelicalism. However, in some of these cases, prayers for the dying, and especially the dead, are quite

---

[81] Ibid. 333.
[82] Ibid. 331.
[83] *Royal Commission: Volume One*, 338. Dolling was a leading ritualist priest who had died in 1902: Yates, *Anglican Ritualism*, 282–3.
[84] *Royal Commission: Volume Two*, 202.
[85] Ibid. 204.
[86] Peter Hinchliff, *Frederick Temple, Archbishop of Canterbury: A Life* (Oxford, 1998), 274–5.

clearly informed by Anglo-Catholic theology. To pray for the dying implies that they will need specific graces as they pass from life to death. Shelton Reed sees prayers for the dead as implying the existence of purgatory, and prayers for the dying can be seen to imply the same.[87] However, this ignores the theological context of the nineteenth century. The Tractarians had published James Usher's support for prayers for the dead as practice independent of a belief in purgatory in Tract 72,[88] and Geoffrey Rowell has demonstrated that both the Tractarians and those who followed them held views of the existence of a purgatory-like state after death, whilst distancing themselves from Roman Catholic doctrine on purgatory.[89] Most Anglo-Catholics held a view that there was a perceived 'distinction between the Patristic, and basically purificatory, and the Roman, and basically penal, concepts of purgatory', and tended towards the former.[90] In light of this, it seems unlikely that any Church of England priest offering prayers for the dead in the early twentieth century would see these prayers as being a deciding factor in whether the dead entered hell or heaven; it is much more conceivable that they were understood to help a soul through a stage its purification before it entered heaven.

Of course, if prayers could help the dead, the question had to be asked, could the eucharist? There was limited evidence for the use of requiem masses in Anglo-Catholic parishes. Hogan heard a sermon at St Columba, Kingsland Road, in which the priest informed his parishioners that 'when death had taken place it was far more important that mourners should be present at the Requiem Mass than that they should spend money on wreaths and flowers'.[91] Such a sermon served as an attempt to educate parishioners into new pastoral ways of being: lessening the focus on existing lay pastoral response and replacing them with new ways grounded in a more Anglo-Catholic theology. The only requiem mass actually attended by someone who presented evidence to the Royal Commission was held at St Mary Magdalene, Munster Square, in Camden Town. The priest, the Revd W. H. H. Jervois, came before the commission on 12

[87] Reed, *Glorious Battle*, 89.
[88] 'Tract 72', in *Tracts for the Times: Volume Four* (London, 1839).
[89] Geoffrey Rowell, *Hell and the Victorians: A Study of the Nineteenth-Century Theological Controversies concerning Eternal Punishment and the Future Life* (Oxford, 1974), 99–108.
[90] Ibid. 105.
[91] *Royal Commission: Volume One*, 12.

January 1905 to answer questions about the conduct of his parish. Evidence about the church had been presented to the commission the previous year by Bowen, although there had not been a discussion of the church before the commission.[92] Jervois was unusual as an Anglo-Catholic parish priest in being willing to discuss his church in person with the commission, with most only sending in written responses.[93] He confirmed to the commission that a service was held in his church in which 'before the Prayer for the Church Militant the celebrant read out a long list of names of deceased persons for whom the prayers of the congregation were asked', although he claimed he was not the celebrant at the specific service attended by the evidence gatherer. However, he also confirmed that it was his custom to 'always ask at the offertory, before the Prayer for the Church Militant, for prayers for the sick or any other special object'.[94] We thus see again the adoption of personal prayers into the regular liturgical practice of the church.

The chairman of the commission, Hicks Beach, had done some research on the parish and was keen to enquire about its approach to the subject of prayers for the dead. He told Jervois that he had noted that 'in the publication of the Guild of All Souls your church is noted as having had a service entitled "Vespers of the Dead" on All Souls' Eve'.[95] The Guild of All Souls had been founded in 1873 to attempt to make the practice of intercessory prayers for the dead more widespread across the Church of England; Reed was right to say that by doing so they hoped 'by clear implication, to propagate the doctrine of Purgatory', and the Roman Catholic version of that doctrine.[96] This was an advanced, and fringe, Anglo-Catholic group and thus it is not unsurprising that Jervois attempted to distance himself from the Guild. Jervois replied that the service was an annual one, to which Hicks Beach questioned whether the service was the same as the one published by the Guild. Pushed to name the differences, he said his service 'consisted simply of psalms and scripture antiphons and omitted the words, "Rest eternal grant them O Lord, and let light perpetual shine upon them"'. Hicks Beach asked if they used

---

[92] Ibid. 41.
[93] Most of these written responses adhered to a template apparently produced by the ECU: Cruickshank, 'Debating the Legal Status', 449.
[94] *Royal Commission: Volume Two*, 239.
[95] Ibid.
[96] Reed, *Glorious Battle*, 89.

the two collects written by the Guild in the service, to which Jervois responded they did not, as they 'only used one Collect'. After Hicks Beach gave him copies of the collects, Jervois conceded that they did use one of the collects: 'O God, the Creator and Redeemer of all them that believe, grant unto the souls of Thy servants and handmaids the remission of all their sins, that through our devout applications they may obtain the pardon they have always desired.' Hicks Beach pointedly asked under what authority Jervois held such a service. None, Jervois conceded, and both men agreed that in future he should ask the bishop for such approval. This was not the end of the matter, though, as Hicks Beach had also noted that throughout November the church's parish magazine had advertised a number of services at which 'the Holy Eucharist will be offered for the faithful departed'. He asked what happened at these services. According to Jervois it was the 'ordinary Communion Service with the Collects from the Burial Service'. Hicks Beach then enquired: 'I have no doubt that you do draw a distinction, but could you tell me shortly what distinction you draw between your offering the Holy Eucharist for the faithful departed and the sacrifices of Masses condemned in the Thirty-first Article for the same purpose?' Jervois' response was evasive, focusing on his interpretation of the article, which he took 'to condemn any idea of the repetition of the Sacrifice upon the Cross or any idea, but that of pleading the sacrifice – any idea of fresh sacrifice. That, I conceive, is what is condemned – the various ideas that had arisen with regard to the Eucharist being a separate sacrifice from that on the Cross.'[97] Lewis Dibdin, Dean of Arches, revisited this question during his own questioning of Jervois, asking whether the latter's interpretation of the article was correct or whether 'the Thirty-first Article defines that doctrine for us'? 'It was commonly said,' he added, 'that the priest did offer Christ for the quick and the dead to have remission of pain or guilt.' Jervois agreed, but offered another interpretation again of the article, that it stated 'that the priest apart from our Lord, or apart from the body, the Church, by himself, was offering a fresh sacrifice for the living and the dead; that is the case'. There followed a protracted discussion on the meaning of the thirty-first article. Jervois explained that he prayed for the 'remission of sins of the faithful departed', but not 'the remission of pain'; the latter, he argued, was where 'the whole Romish doctrine concerning purgatory

---

[97] *Royal Commission: Volume Two*, 239.

comes in'. Moreover, Jervois did not 'believe in material pains', which suggested that his not praying for the remission of pain was less to do with a disagreement on the efficiency of such prayers and more about the status of souls after death.[98] This was pastoral care for the dead, with Jervois offering some sort of service to the deceased through a requiem mass. Jervois was unclear about the theology behind this, though it was certainly Anglo-Catholic in nature.

It is important to emphasize that this was the only case of a requiem mass discussed by the commission, and it was not a common pastoral concern in the period. However, as has been demonstrated, praying for the dead and dying was an established practice at numerous churches. Jervois's answers demonstrate how naïve the theological reasoning behind this was. He did not wish to state explicitly a belief in purgatory, although his practices certainly suggested such a belief. The commission evidence cannot reveal the extent to which this was shared by those priests and parishes who prayed for their dead and dying. What we may be seeing is a pastoral action with historical precedents, that Anglo-Catholics were re-adopting whilst not being fully aware of, or comfortable with, the practice's original theological underpinning. Even in this unusual case, pastoral desires seem to be driving developments with theological justifications trying to catch up.

It is of course too simplistic to see pastoral concerns and theological ideas simply as competing elements. As the evidence discussed here shows, the pastoral concerns of Anglo-Catholic priests were often informed by, or at least aligned with, their theological ones. Andrew Atherstone has written of the ritualists as the innovators of what he terms 'party badges'. These were 'visual innovations, obvious to all … accessible symbols of their theology, otherwise only deducible from sermons and tracts'.[99] As this article has shown, this approach is too dismissive. Although a prayer board may have helped identify a church as Anglo-Catholic, it was not constructed as a party badge, but to serve as a pastoral aid. These were novel Anglo-Catholic approaches to existing problems, created as pastoral solutions. A pastoral rationale may have been used as a cover for more obviously

[98] Ibid. 240.
[99] Andrew Atherstone, 'Identities and Parties', in Mark D. Chapman, Sathianathan Clarke and Martyn Percy, eds, *The Oxford Handbook of Anglican Studies* (Oxford, 2016), 77–91, at 81.

ritualistic practices, such as the sanctus bell, but for practices such as reservation and organized prayers, this does not seem to be the case. Instead, we seem to see pastoral actions with historical precedents being adopted without the theological implications having been fully thought through. Whilst the evidence of the Royal Commission can offer a national overview, it cannot show what the introduction of such practices looked like on a local level. Further research is also needed to reveal more about how the pastoral and the theological were linked. Whether for pastoral or theological reasons, the evidence of the Royal Commission shows us that Anglo-Catholicism was changing the ways in which the sick and dying were being cared for in Church of England parishes across the country.

'Alleviating the Sum of Human Suffering': The Origins, Attributes and Appeal of Hospital Sunday, 1859–1914

Roger Ottewill*

Southampton

In many communities, from the mid-Victorian era until well into the twentieth century, one Sunday every year was dedicated to the work of local hospitals and dispensaries. Originating in Birmingham and desig-nated Hospital Sunday, it enabled congregations to remember their responsibilities towards the sick and it raised much-needed funds for what was essentially voluntary provision, prior to the establishment of the National Health Service. In so doing, they were demonstrating their commitment to philanthropy and (for many) the tenets of the social gospel. Hospital Sunday also symbolized an element of interdenominational coop-eration, with most denominations participating, at a time when relations between the established church and the Free Churches on other issues could sometimes be fraught. Moreover, it facilitated the engagement of churches with charitable organizations, such as friendly societies. This article aims to explore the origins of Hospital Sunday, to analyse its key attributes, to assess its appeal and to highlight some of the issues which arose during the Victorian and Edwardian eras.

INTRODUCTION: 'HOSPITALS ARE A FORM OF PHILANTHROPY'[1]

By the end of the nineteenth century, what was known as Hospital Sunday had become a firmly established, and greatly valued, feature of the Christian calendar in many British cities, towns and even villages. Arguably, it was as well recognized as Christmas, Easter, Whitsun and especially Harvest Festival, with which it shared a num-ber of features, such as the principle of charitable donations. Indeed, Hospital Sunday was in keeping with what had become a common practice of setting aside a number of special Sundays each year for a variety of purposes.[2]

* 15 Atherley Court, Southampton, SO15 7NG. E-mail: rogerottewill@btinternet.com.

[1] 'The Editor's Box: Hospital Sunday', *The Bystander*, 17 June 1908, xii.
[2] Examples include Education Sunday, Temperance Sunday, Mission Sunday, Industrial Sunday and a Sunday on which the Sunday School anniversary was celebrated.

Studies in Church History 58 (2022), 352–371   © The Author(s), 2022. Published by Cambridge University Press on behalf of Ecclesiastical History Society
doi: 10.1017/stc.2022.17

Originating in Birmingham in 1859, Hospital Sunday provided an opportunity for churches and chapels not only to raise essential funds for what was at that time primarily voluntary provision but also to remember the suffering of patients and the contributions made by hospital staff to their care and well-being. From its genesis in Birmingham, the idea quickly spread across England as well as other parts of the United Kingdom, and indeed further afield.[3] Although attempts were made to 'nationalize' it by setting a date for its observance throughout the whole country, it remained essentially a grassroots phenomenon with clergy and civic leaders deciding the most appropriate Sunday for their communities, which organizations should be invited to participate, and the beneficiaries of the funds raised. While several medical journals in the late 1860s agitated for 'one Sunday to be set apart throughout the Kingdom', this campaign proved unsuccessful.[4]

Through their engagement with Hospital Sunday, places of worship were able to demonstrate their commitment to philanthropy and altruism and what Hugh McLeod has portrayed as 'the creative role' of religion with respect to 'the impetus it gave to humanitarian activity of many kinds'.[5] For evangelicals, in particular, it can also be seen as a means of aligning themselves with, and a manifestation of, certain tenets of the social gospel. David Bebbington contrasts this with the personal gospel by defining it, perhaps contentiously, as 'an attempt to change human beings by transforming their environment rather than touching their hearts'.[6] In the context of this article, the environment comprises provision for the relief of sickness, not only in hospitals but also in cognate institutions such as dispensaries. Hospital Sunday illustrates the way that physical health was seen as an essential adjunct of spiritual health.

Hospital Sunday also symbolized an element of interdenominational cooperation with most denominations participating, at a time when relations between the established church and the Free Churches could sometimes be fraught. Moreover, Hospital Sunday was an additional means by which churches could engage with the

[3] In 1873, in reference to Australia, the *Edinburgh Evening News* commented: 'Hospital Sunday has now become a colonial as well as a British institution': 'Hospital Sunday in Australia', 18 November 1873, 2.
[4] 'Hospital Sunday', *Cardiff Times*, 18 December 1869, 6.
[5] Hugh McLeod, *Religion and Society in England, 1850–1914* (London, 1996), 7.
[6] David Bebbington, *Evangelicalism in Modern Britain* (London, 1989), 211.

needs and aspirations of the wider community and with charitable organizations, such as friendly societies.

In the academic literature, there is relatively little about Hospital Sunday, beyond that which considers the role of churches and chapels in what may be broadly defined as 'good works' and 'charitable enterprise'. Callum Brown, for example, in his characterization of 'the faith society, 1900–14' makes no mention of this widely adopted initiative.[7] Jeremy Morris, in his study of churches in Croydon between 1840 and 1914, does mention Hospital Sunday. As he puts it, churches functioned 'as fund-raising units for philanthropic work … through the institution of annual hospital sermons … for example, the Croydon general hospital fund could by 1879 raise nearly a quarter of its annual income, which in that year totalled £2,500' from this source.[8] Nevertheless, as Morris points out, there were both ideological and material limits to voluntary activity of this kind. Likewise, Waddington's study of the Metropolitan Hospital Sunday Fund draws upon the discourse of voluntarism and highlights the friction which arose over what was perceived as a threat to the independence of hospitals.[9] Although he adopts what is essentially a secular perspective, as will be indicated later, certain aspects of the religious dimension are acknowledged. Reference can also be made to Kenneth Brown, who draws attention to the role of many Nonconformist ministers in philanthropic activities, including writing about, financial support for, and participating in 'welfare movements, temperance, *hospitals*, libraries'.[10]

In the work of Stephen Cherry, which focuses primarily on the financing of hospitals in the days before the establishment of the National Health Service, Hospital Sunday is located alongside other sources of finance for voluntary hospitals, such as subscriptions, patient payments, workplace collections and investment income.[11]

---

[7] Callum Brown, *Religion and Society in Twentieth-Century Britain* (Harlow, 2006), 40–87.

[8] Jeremy Morris, *Religion and Urban Change: Croydon 1840–1914* (Woodbridge, 1992), 131.

[9] Keir Waddington, 'Bastard Benevolence: Centralisation, Voluntarism and the Sunday Fund 1873–1898', *London Journal* 19 (1994), 151–67.

[10] Kenneth Brown, *A Social History of the Nonconformist Ministry in England and Wales 1800–1930* (Oxford, 1988), 205 (emphasis added).

[11] See, for example, Steven Cherry, 'Before the National Health Service: Financing the Voluntary Hospitals, 1900–1939', *Economic History Review* 50 (1997), 305–26; idem, 'Hospital Saturday, Workplace Collections and Issues in Late Nineteenth-Century Hospital Funding', *MH* 44 (2000), 461–88.

Although by 1900 Hospital Sunday 'only provided between 4 and 7 per cent of hospitals' ordinary income in England and Wales and slightly less in Scotland by the 1890s', it was still highly valued.[12]

From an essentially religious perspective, Hospital Sunday was a tangible response to the gospel imperative of loving one's neighbour, as exemplified by the parable of the Good Samaritan. Thus, it can be seen as, in the words of David Nash, one of 'the numerous ways in which members of British society and their local communities embraced the morality and ideals of the "Good Samaritan" story', which continues to this day.[13] This, he suggests, is one of the 'stories of belief' that might replace or at least modify the dominant narrative of secularization.[14]

That said, religious historians such as Jeffrey Cox have argued that by engaging in welfare provision, churches sowed the seeds of their own demise in the twentieth century, as the state gradually took over this role. Indeed, Hospital Sunday can be seen as a classic example of what Cox characterizes as 'religious philanthropy'.[15] A similar stance is adopted by Frank Prochaska, who has illustrated the extent to which churches were engaged in charitable activities, including those supporting medical and related services, in the nineteenth century.[16] Thus Hospital Sunday is indicative of the manner in which, in his words, 'Christian self-examination predisposed the faithful to charitable conduct and animated piety.'[17]

In seeking to build on these foundations, this article aims to explore the origins of the Hospital Sunday initiative, to analyse its key attributes, to assess its appeal in blurring the boundary between the sacred and the secular with respect to sickness and medical care, and to indicate some of the issues to which it gave rise. Throughout, it is intended to position Hospital Sunday within the moves by churches and chapels during the nineteenth century to demonstrate

[12] Cherry, 'Hospital Saturday', 470.
[13] David Nash, *Christian Ideals in British Culture: Stories of Belief in the Twentieth Century* (London, 2013), 30.
[14] David Nash, 'Reconnecting Religion with Social and Cultural History: Secularization's Failure as a Master Narrative', *Cultural and Social History* 1 (2004), 302–25.
[15] Jeffrey Cox, *The English Churches in a Secular Society: Lambeth 1870–1930* (Oxford, 1982), especially 265–76.
[16] Frank Prochaska, *Christianity and Social Service in Modern Britain: The Disinherited Spirit* (Oxford, 2006), especially 1–27.
[17] Ibid. 7.

their value to the communities in which they were situated by not only addressing the spiritual needs of the population they served but also promoting physical well-being. For primary source material, heavy reliance has been placed on online sources. Although these consist mainly of newspaper reports and journals, such as *The Lancet* and the *British Medical Journal*, they have still facilitated the undertaking of an initial exploration and demonstration of the wide-ranging impact of this 'outward facing' initiative. The resulting narrative, which charts its development during the Victorian and Edwardian eras, is offered as the basis for further investigation.

ORIGINS: 'TO AID IN FREEING THE GENERAL HOSPITAL FROM ITS LOAD OF DEBT'[18]

As Cherry has observed, '[t]he preaching of church sermons, usually followed by an appeal or collection, often promoted or marked the establishment of hospitals in the eighteenth century. Although church and chapel hospital collections were regular or periodic, they were first systematized into an annual Sunday event on an area basis in Birmingham in 1859.'[19] Thus in determining a launch date for Hospital Sunday, at least as far as England is concerned, a strong case can be made for Tuesday, 23 October 1859. On that day, a group of clergy from all the major denominations in Birmingham convened a meeting to consider a response to a financial crisis facing the city's General Hospital. As it was put formally in the public invitation:

> We the undersigned, regretting deeply the crippled finances of the above most valuable institution respectfully invite the attendance of the Ministers of Religion in the town and neighbourhood to a conference ... with the view of considering the practicability and desirableness of setting apart a day on which collections in aid of the Funds of the Hospital shall be made in every place of Public Worship.[20]

The signatories included clergy from a wide variety of denominations: high and low church Anglicans, Independents, Baptists, Wesleyan and Primitive Methodists, Presbyterians, Swedenborgians, Roman

[18] 'A Few Local Notes', *Birmingham Journal*, 22 October 1859, 8.
[19] Cherry, 'Hospital Saturday', 470.
[20] 'General Hospital', *Birmingham Journal*, 22 October 1859, 4.

Catholics and Unitarians. There was also a representative of the Jewish faith. One of the signatories was R. W. Dale, at that time assistant minister at the renowned Carrs Lane Independent / (Congregational) Church. In the 1870s and 1880s he was to become one of the foremost exponents of the civic gospel, which required Christians to engage fully with municipal institutions as a means of enhancing the well-being of their fellow citizens. In a sermon preached in 1884 on 'Political and Municipal Duty', he made the case for 'medicine and not the gospel only' to cure the sick.[21] Among the clergy, a key figure was John C. Miller, the vicar of St Martin in the Bull Ring, Birmingham. Later, however, he was at pains to point out in a letter to *The Times*, published in 1873, that the idea of a Hospital Sunday had not originated with him. As he explained: 'It was suggested in the *Midland Counties Herald* by a good man on the staff of that paper [Thomas Barber Weight] that a simultaneous collection in the churches and chapels would do much to help' in relieving the very heavy debt burden of the General Hospital.[22] Thus the press was seen as having a key role in persuading the town to adopt the idea.

From whomever the idea originated, it is clear that it resonated with the clergy of Birmingham, including those of the Jewish faith, and it was agreed to hold the first Hospital Sunday on 13 November 1859. For the *Birmingham Journal*, 'On no occasion within our rec-ollection ha[d] any event offered an opportunity for a zealous but friendly rivalry between church and chapel, and church and church.'[23] On that Sunday, special sermons were preached in a number of churches, as well as the Roman Catholic cathedral and the synagogue. The total sum raised was £4700 13s 6d.[24] In the light of this, and the initiative's impact in general, it was claimed that 'Hospital Sunday … [would] not soon be forgotten by the people of Birmingham.'[25] This proved to be an accurate prediction and the event became an annual fixture in the life of most places of worship in the town. In 1865, for example, the words of Dr Miller were used by

[21] Quoted in Gerald Parsons, *Religion in Victorian Britain*, 1: *Traditions* (Manchester, 1988), 93.
[22] 'Letter to the Editor: Hospital Sunday', *The Times*, 4 March 1873, 11.
[23] 'The General Hospital Sunday', *Birmingham Journal*, 12 November 1859, 7.
[24] 'The Movement in Aid of the General Hospital', *Birmingham Journal*, 17 December 1859, 6.
[25] 'A Few Local Notes', *Birmingham Journal*, 19 November 1859, 8.

the *Birmingham Journal* to underline the character of the appeal in its editorial columns:

> the heartiness with which the clergy and ministers of religion have thrown themselves into these efforts, year by year, the noble generosity with which the congregations have responded to appeals made from the pulpits – and the all but universal approval with which this prompt, inexpensive, and effective means of supplementing the resources of our charitable institutions has been greeted, render it unnecessary for us to do more than notify the recurrence of Hospital Sunday.[26]

As a result, for many decades Birmingham's Hospital Sunday served as an exemplar for other communities.

As mentioned earlier, the idea was soon taken up elsewhere. In some instances, what had previously been a piecemeal approach was replaced by a more co-ordinated and extensive one. Indeed, as Waddington points out, although 'sympathetic clergy had traditionally dedicated church collections to individual hospitals ... under a fund these contributions were redirected away from a single institution to an organisation that coordinated sermons, universalised support, and redistributed collections as a solution to the medical charities' perceived financial difficulties'.[27] An early adopter was Bristol, which held its first Hospital Sunday on 12 January 1862. A couple of months later, the committee of Bristol's General Hospital praised the initiative:

> The Royal Infirmary and the Hospital are under deep obligation to the ministers of the Gospel in the churches and chapels of the city and surrounding district, who readily responded, with feelings of Christian enthusiasm, to a request for sermons and collections in their places of worship for the second Sunday in January. The handsome sums contributed in this way justify your committee in pressing that a Hospital Sunday shall be sacredly set apart for this excellent manifestation of the spirit of our Common Master, whose works were so eminently directed to the relief of suffering humanity.[28]

Whilst the initial enthusiasm proved hard to sustain, in time the idea became firmly established in the area.

[26] 'Hospital Sunday', *Birmingham Journal*, 21 October 1865, 6.
[27] Waddington, 'Bastard Benevolence', 153.
[28] 'Bristol General Hospital', *Western Daily Press*, 11 March 1862, 3.

During the 1860s hospitals in those communities without a Hospital Sunday often pointed to the example of what was happening elsewhere in making their case for one to be held locally. For example, in December 1864 at a meeting of the Quarterly Court of Governors of Addenbrooke's Hospital in Cambridge, the mayor remarked 'that in many provincial towns there was what was called a Hospital Sunday – a Sunday in the year in which sermons were preached at all the churches and Dissenting chapels … He was sure that much larger collections would be made by having all the sermons on the same Sunday.' He went on to argue for a similar event to be held in Cambridge.[29] However, although 11 June 1865 was suggested it would seem that in Cambridge and district very few churches participated at first, with Hospital Sunday not being formally observed until the summer of 1874.[30]

As a further example, at the annual meeting of the Royal Albert Hospital in Devonport in November 1865 it was explained that:

> Considering the efficient aid which is given to hospitals in many large towns by the institution of a Hospital Sunday, whereon a simultaneous appeal may be made from all places of worship, the committee addressed a circular to the clergy and ministers of religion in Devonport and Stonehouse, asking their aid, and suggesting the second Sunday in November for the purpose.[31]

Evidence as to what happened next is sparse, but it would seem that it was not until 13 November 1870 that a Hospital Sunday was instituted in this part of the country.[32]

Other towns and cities which held their first Hospital Sunday in this period included Sheffield on 31 January 1869,[33] Manchester on 27 February 1870,[34] Cardiff on 27 April 1873[35] and Dublin on 15 November 1874.[36] The situation in Scotland was a little more

[29] 'Cambridgeshire: Addenbrooke's Hospital', *Cambridge Chronicle*, 31 December 1864, 7.
[30] 'Addenbrooke's Hospital', *Cambridge Independent Press*, 4 July 1874, 8.
[31] 'Royal Albert Hospital', *Western Morning News*, 15 November 1865, 4.
[32] 'Hospital Sunday', *Western Morning News*, 12 November 1870, 2.
[33] 'Sermons for our Medical Charities', *Sheffield and Rotherham Independent*, 23 January 1869, 6.
[34] 'Hospital Sunday', *Manchester Courier and Lancashire General Advertiser*, 24 February 1870, 6.
[35] 'Hospital Sunday in Cardiff', *Western Mail*, 28 April 1873, 3.
[36] 'Dublin Hospital Sunday Fund', *Irish Times*, 14 November 1874, 7.

Roger Ottewill

complicated since, in a letter to *The Times* published in 1873, it was claimed by William Carnie, treasurer of the Royal Infirmary in Aberdeen, that 'Hospital Sunday ... [had] been a recognised institution in Aberdeen for well nigh a century ... the first Sunday of every year ... [being] faithfully observed'.[37] That said, other towns in Scotland appear to have followed the pattern elsewhere in the United Kingdom. For example, Dundee's first Hospital Sunday was held on 28 December 1873[38] and Greenock's on 4 May 1879.[39] However, it was not until 1893 that a Hospital Sunday Fund was established in Glasgow.[40]

As far as London was concerned, preliminary steps were taken to promote the idea in the early 1870s. Although the case was forcefully made in an article published in *The Times* on 27 January 1870,[41] it was not until November 1872 that 'a meeting of representatives of many of the unendowed hospitals' of the metropolis was held to promote the idea. At this, the chairman, Richard Martin, the treasurer of St Mark's Hospital:

> gave proofs from the experience of the hospital authorities at Birmingham, Leeds, Newcastle, Manchester, and other places where such an annual collection was made, that not only had the effect been a great increase in the subscriptions, but that very few cases were known where people had excused themselves in the course of the year from subscribing on the ground that they had made their contributions anonymously through the collecting box.

In other words, Martin offered reassurance that Hospital Sunday did not undermine other modes of giving in support of voluntary hospitals. He also indicated that the bishop of London, the Rt Revd John Jackson, and the Roman Catholic archbishop of Westminster, Cardinal Manning, 'had intimated their willingness to co-operate in the scheme'.[42] Indeed, as *The Tablet* reported,

[37] 'Letter to the Editor: Hospital Sunday', *The Times*, 13 March 1873, 10.
[38] 'Hospital Sunday in Dundee', *Edinburgh Evening News*, 29 December 1873, 2.
[39] '"Hospital Sunday" in Greenock', *Glasgow Evening News and Star*, 1 May 1879, 4.
[40] See 'Editorial', *Glasgow Herald*, 3 January 1893, 4; 'Glasgow Hospital Sunday Fund', 20 November 1894, 2.
[41] '"Hospital Sunday"', *The Times*, 27 January 1870, 3 quoting from an article in *The Lancet*.
[42] 'Proposed "Hospital Sunday"', *The Times*, 22 November 1872, 5.

Cardinal Manning 'spoke strongly in favour' of it.[43] Support also came from the lord mayor, who played a key role, and the first Hospital Sunday in the capital was held on 15 June 1873, with further collections on the two subsequent Sundays. Not surprisingly, the sums raised were considerable and for many decades the Metropolitan Hospital Sunday Fund was a major source of income for medical facilities, also receiving support from royalty. For example, King Edward VII and Queen Alexandra attended an afternoon service at St Paul's Cathedral on 7 June 1903, and special Hospital Sunday collections were taken, since they were otherwise engaged on the following Sunday, which had been officially designated for this purpose.[44] The collections that year in London amounted to a record sum of £64,975.[45]

By the turn of the twentieth century, the concept of Hospital Sunday was well established and continued to serve as a financial lifeline for voluntary hospitals and dispensaries until the establishment of the National Health Service after the Second World War. It can also be seen as a providential element of Christian witness in a wide variety of communities, both large and small, since it offered churches an additional means of demonstrating their value to wider society. Moreover, such was its impact that at the end of the nineteenth century controversy arose as to whom credit was due for initiating the term 'Hospital Sunday'. While many considered that Revd J. L. Miller of Birmingham was the originator, others backed the claims of John Henn, rector of St John's Church in Manchester.[46] Whatever the merits of the respective claims of each candidate, the dispute illustrates the sensitivities surrounding this demonstration of philanthropic endeavour.

ATTRIBUTES: 'SIMULTANEOUS SUNDAY COLLECTIONS'[47]

At first sight, Hospital Sunday might be regarded as simply an effective and efficient means of fund-raising for a good cause. This, however, oversimplifies what was, in effect, a multifaceted initiative,

---

[43] 'Hospital Sunday for London', *The Tablet*, 14 December 1872, 761.
[44] 'Hospital Sunday', *The Lancet*, 6 June 1903, 1614–15.
[45] 'Hospital Sunday', *The Lancet*, 11 June 1904, 1665–6.
[46] 'The Early History of the Hospital Sunday and Saturday Funds', *The Hospital*, 1 September 1894, 451–2.
[47] 'Hospital Sunday for Cardiff', *Cardiff Times*, 15 March 1873, 5.

incorporating a variety of features that are worthy of further consideration.

The first is the role of the sermon, which was seen as a vehicle both for offering a theological justification for the appeal and for maximizing the sum raised. As it was put by Waddington, 'the pulpit was co-opted to preach the gospel of hospital funding, systematically publicising medical relief to motivate benevolence'.[48] The comment was made in a *British Medical Journal* article of 1872 that 'the sermons on these occasions are generally evidently most carefully prepared, each minister trying to outvie the others in eloquence upon that always eloquent subject "Charity"'.[49] In the early days, the local press frequently reported the title and sometimes the content of sermons, which were regarded as an essential prerequisite for the collection, together with leaflets in the pews. As the basis for what they had to say, preachers used a wide variety of texts, and from these various themes emerge. For many, Christ's example in healing the sick was to the fore. This was reflected in the titles of three sermons preached at various London churches on Hospital Sunday in June 1893. At St Michael's, London Fields, the title was 'Christ the Healer'; at St Peter's, Greenwich, 'Christ in the Sick Ward'; and at Holy Trinity, Minories, 'Christ healing the Man sick of the Palsy'.[50]

In the circumstances, it was unsurprising that another pervasive theme was the importance of charity as a marker of neighbourliness, or what was often described, in the terminology of the late nineteenth and early twentieth centuries, as 'brotherhood' or 'brotherly love'. Here the notion of support for the poor and disadvantaged was very much in evidence. Take, for example, a sermon preached by Revd J. Bullen at St Matthew's Church in Southampton in April 1874 and based on the text: "Take care of Him, and whatsoever thou spendest more, when I come again I will repay thee" (Luke 10: 35), from the story of the Good Samaritan. As Bullen explained, the text was:

> … part of the answer given to the scribe in reply to the question 'And who is my neighbour?' and went on to observe that if kindness was only shown to the grateful and deserving we should only be rendering them

[48] Waddington, 'Bastard Benevolence', 153.
[49] 'Hospital Sunday', *British Medical Journal* 1, no. 592 (4 May 1872), 480.
[50] 'Hospital Sunday', *The Lancet*, 10 June 1893, 1406–7.

what was their due. When they saw a poor creature in distress let him be relieved at once, without deliberation. Let them not wait to ask the question whether he was a friend … ; let them not wait to see whether the charity given would be appreciated or not, for the voice of God said in all cases of the afflicted, 'Take care of Him'.

He went on to argue that 'no charities were more deserving than those of the Infirmary and the Dispensary', and that their work could be greatly extended 'if more funds were forthcoming.' Moreover, as they 'were chiefly for the benefit of poor persons, that alone rendered them deserving of support' and that they should take the words of the second part of the text about paying whatever was necessary 'literally to themselves'.[51]

In a similar vein, at Manchester Cathedral in 1890, Revd Canon Davenport Kelly based his sermon on the text 'He had compassion on him' (Luke 10: 33). In so doing, 'he pointed out the way in which the word "compassion" had too often fallen from the meaning it first had of suffering with another, to a transient sentiment of pity'. He went on to argue that in professing to 'learn Christ', his congregation 'should see what suffering with others meant to Him'. He ended by expressing the hope that there would be 'a marked increase' in collections.[52]

In their appeals preachers frequently made reference to the role of hospitals in the alleviation of suffering and distress, and the dedication of the medical and nursing staff. For example, in 1889 the vicar of St Giles, Northampton, referred to the town's infirmary as 'that noble institution in their midst', in the context of a sermon based on St Paul's exhortation to present our 'bodies as a "living sacrifice"'.[53] This, he argued, could be demonstrated by giving up something close to their hearts in order to donate to the hospital. Similarly, in 1895, Revd H. S. Mercer of Christ Church, Coventry, 'referred to the great blessings derived from the hospital', by way of encouraging his hearers to assist in the good work it performed.[54] On this occasion, the text is unknown.

[51] 'Hospital Sunday at Southampton', *Hampshire Advertiser*, 29 April 1874, 3.
[52] 'Hospital Sunday in Manchester and Salford', *Manchester Courier and Lancashire General Advertiser*, 10 February 1890, 8.
[53] 'Hospital Sunday at Northampton', *Northampton Mercury*, 13 July 1889, 10.
[54] 'Hospital Sunday', *Midland Daily Telegraph*, 29 April 1895, 3.

The sermons preached on Hospital Sunday served as opportunities to remind congregations of the obligations that their faith imposed. They also reinforced the religious character of the occasion and often gave the impression that hospitals were divinely ordained institutions. Moreover, the message of the sermon was usually underpinned by other features of Hospital Sunday services. As it was put in a report of the first Hospital Sunday celebrations at St Andrew's Church in Cardiff, 'the arrangement of the service had reference to the special character of the day'.[55] From other accounts it is clear that particular attention was given the choice of hymns and anthems. For example, in 1874, at All Saints, Southampton, 'hymns commencing "O thou by whom the healing art", "Divine physician of the soul", and others ... appropriate to the occasion' were selected.[56] With respect to this aspect of the service, a special piece of choral music, 'Let not thine Hand be stretched out to receive: An Anthem for Hospital Sunday or any other Occasion of Almsgiving to the Poor', was composed by John Stainer (1840–1901).[57] Prayers would also have reflected the nature of the occasion.

A second feature was the cross-denominational and inter-faith dimension. This was highlighted in an appeal which appeared in the *Sheffield and Rotherham Independent* in 1869: 'Churchman and Dissenter, Protestant and Catholic, Christian and Jew, are alike called upon to help, for this is the cause of the sick and lame poor [who are] "ever with us", and whose appeal no one will venture to refuse.'[58] Similar remarks were made in respect of Birmingham, where 'all unite in demonstrating that in the sacred cause of charity distinctions of creed lose their disintegrating character'.[59] Such comments could be applied to many communities and can perhaps be regarded as an antidote to the antipathy which could often sour relations between denominations during the second half of the nineteenth century and into the twentieth, over such controversial issues as the marking in 1862 of the two hundredth anniversary of the Great Ejection, the role of ritual in worship, church governance and the church rate, and the provision of primary education. By comparison, the imperative to

[55] 'Hospital Sunday in Cardiff', *Western Mail*, 28 April 1873, 3.
[56] 'Hospital Sunday at Southampton'.
[57] See 'Extra Supplement', *Musical Times and Singing Class Journal* 36, no. 628 (1 June 1895), 1–8.
[58] 'Sermons for our Medical Charities'.
[59] '"Hospital Sunday"', *The Times*, 27 January 1870, 3.

care for the sick and suffering was viewed as relatively unproblematic and could function as a unifying force. Through Hospital Sunday, the churches were enabled to present 'a united front against one of society's more pressing problems'.[60]

Although there is little evidence of united services being held in the early years of Hospital Sunday, later, especially in smaller communities, open-air services were organized. One example comes from the Hampshire village of Hook, where 'Church and Chapel ... pulled together for the common good.' In 1907, an innovation was the 'free distribution of a tastefully printed "Order of Service" containing all the hymns'. This meant that 'all were able to follow the service throughout, obviating the difficulty of lending hymn books which usually suffer in their excursion to an open air service'.[61]

A third attribute was the manner in which the idea spread. In this respect, it can be seen as an example of the 'diffusion of innovation'. As mentioned in the Introduction, what was essentially a local initiative mushroomed, in part because of the publicity it received from a generally sympathetic press as well as its evident success in monetary terms. Indeed, the *British Medical Journal* regarded 'the aid of the press' as one of the factors 'necessary for success'.[62] However, Hospital Sunday remained a local phenomenon 'owned' by individual communities and focused on their health care institutions. As indicated earlier, attempts to establish one dedicated Sunday in each year for this purpose, to be observed throughout the country, were unsuccessful.

APPEAL: 'GREATER MORAL WEIGHT'[63]

Apart from the attributes considered above, the appeal of Hospital Sunday for individual churches was that it enabled them to benefit from being part of a more extensive initiative. This was reflected in remarks made by one of the early advocates, the vicar of Leeds, Canon James Woodford, who claimed that by having the collections simultaneously on the same Sunday the town's ministers were 'relieved of the burden of a coming collection, the date of which might be

---

[60] Waddington, 'Bastard Benevolence', 154.
[61] 'Hook Hospital Sunday', *Hants and Berks Gazette*, 6 July 1907, 8.
[62] 'Hospital Sunday', *British Medical Journal* 1, no. 592 (4 May 1872), 480.
[63] 'Leeds General Infirmary', *Yorkshire Post*, 8 December 1869, 3.

regulated or postponed by many circumstances – by the presence or absence of some influential person, and by other reasons of a similar nature'. By implication they could concentrate on their message from the pulpit. It also, he claimed, attached 'greater moral weight' to the appeal when all the chapels and churches were acting in unison.[64]

Also of importance was its role in enabling churches, chapels and synagogues to reach out to the wider community and in particular to secular institutions. Put a little differently, it blurred the boundary between the sacred and the secular. This was evident not only in the raising of money within the context of acts of worship which was to be donated to temporal, albeit charitable, institutions but also through engaging with members of friendly societies and related organizations and inviting them to attend a church service. Thus in many communities church parades gradually became a distinctive component of Hospital Sunday. For example, in 1890 in the small Hampshire town of Alresford, the leading member of the local branch of the Ancient Order of Foresters[65] suggested that since they did not 'habitually attend divine service on their feast day' they should do so on Hospital Sunday and invited other societies to join with them in doing so. This received a favourable response and after processing down the main street, Foresters and members of the Hampshire Friendly Society, the Unity Order of Oddfellows, the Hand-Held Friendly Society, the George Club and the Bighton Friendly Society attended a service at the parish church, when Revd A. A. Headley 'preached a most suitable sermon'.[66]

Another example comes from the north Hampshire town of Whitchurch, with its Hospital Sunday attracting many visitors. As reported in 1909, 'thousands of people crowded into the town from Basingstoke on the one side to Stockbridge on the other. Both railways gave extra facilities in the way of cheap tickets but the majority of the visitors came by road and the various inns and stable yards were more than over-crowded.'[67] In a similar manner to Alresford there was a procession comprising a wide variety of organizations, one of which was the Salvation Army band. There was an open-air service conducted by Revd Thomas Davies, who was 'in

[64] Ibid.
[65] His formal title was 'Chief Ranger of Court "Princess Alexandra"'.
[66] 'Alresford: Hospital Sunday', *Hampshire Chronicle*, 9 August 1890, 5.
[67] 'Whitchurch: Hospital Sunday', *Hants and Berks Gazette*, 11 September 1909, 6.

charge of the parish during the vicar's absence', with the sermon being based on the parable of the Good Samaritan. Throughout 'the afternoon collecting boxes were carried round, not only by the official collectors of each society, but also by a number of young ladies, whose persuasive appeals were all but irresistible'.[68]

The Alresford and Whitchurch examples were by no means exceptional and were replicated in many communities throughout the country. They illustrate how Hospital Sunday had become part of what has been conceptualized as 'civic ritual',[69] and in the process could be said to have lost some of its religious significance. In other words, it had become more of a civic festival and less of a religious celebration. This, however, was by no means the only issue which arose for those of a religious disposition with even such an ostensibly benign concept as Hospital Sunday.

Issues: A Sensitive Initiative

An early indication of the problems which could arise was seen in Liverpool. Here in 1870 initial steps to launch a simultaneous collection in all churches and chapels were in danger of being blown off course by what were dubbed as 'unfair clerical proceedings'.[70] These were steps taken by Church of England clergy to protect their charitable endeavours, which for twenty years had taken the form of collections for a variety of denominational causes, including some non-medical charities. In seeking protection for these, the clergy wanted to 'ring-fence' some of the money collected, thereby undermining one of the key principles of Hospital Sunday. As it was put in editorial comment in the *Liverpool Daily Courier*: 'The strangest incident in the bitter controversy is that every one is bent on doing good, and that one man differs from his neighbour only in the means of achieving the common end.'[71] Thanks to the efforts of the lord mayor, together with a willingness to compromise, agreement was

---

[68] Ibid.
[69] Ben Roberts, 'Entertaining the Community: The Evolution of Civic Ritual and Public Celebration, 1860–1953', *UH* 44 (2017), 444–63.
[70] 'General Intelligence: Unfair Clerical Proceedings', *Glasgow Evening Citizen*, 24 October 1870, 3.
[71] 'The Charity Quarrel', *Liverpool Daily Courier*, 22 October 1870, 6.

reached and Liverpool's first Hospital Sunday went ahead in early 1871.

In larger towns and cities, such as Liverpool, where health care provision was spread across a number of institutions clergy were given the opportunity to participate in decisions regarding the distribution of funds raised, through membership of committees established to oversee Hospital Sundays. Such involvement, however, was by no means unproblematic. Deciding which institutions should receive financial support could also give rise to disagreements and accusations of unfairness. Thus engagement with the secular world could be a double-edged sword. As Waddington observes, in 1874 the Metropolitan Sunday Hospital Fund was involved in 'an acrimonious and public debate as those concerned with the position of the specialist hospitals attempted to hijack the movement by imposing their own views on distribution, threatening collections until a compromise was reached'.[72]

Another issue was that of sectarianism, which has been explored by Carmen Mangion, primarily in the context of the institutional culture of voluntary hospitals. She highlights a case from 1885 when an applicant to train as a nurse at University College Hospital (UCH) in London, a supposedly non-sectarian institution, was rejected because she was a Nonconformist. As Mangion observes, in considering the resulting controversy from the perspective of the funding of voluntary hospitals, 'the Metropolitan Hospital Sunday Fund took the claim of sectarianism seriously[;] they feared it would damage the credibility of all voluntary hospitals and could lead to a decline in donations'.[73] One of those who took exception to the action of UCH was a Congregational minister and a member of the Metropolitan Hospital Sunday Fund Committee, Henry Allon. In a letter to *The Times*, he argued for the holding of an inquiry to establish the facts in this case. In so doing he was motivated by what he described as his 'earnest deprecation of sectarian exclusiveness'.[74] In the end, the fund 'with the support of the Hospitals Association opted out of defining sectarianism and supported

---

[72] Waddington, 'Bastard Benevolence', 157.
[73] Carmen M. Mangion, '"Tolerable Intolerance": Protestantism, Sectarianism and Voluntary Hospitals in Late Nineteenth-Century London', *MH* 62 (2018), 468–84, at 480–1.
[74] 'Letter to the Editor: University College Hospital and the Hospital Sunday Fund', *The Times*, 3 August 1885, 4.

'tolerable intolerance', with respect to nurse-hiring policies in this instance, 'in order to maintain its role in the funding of voluntary hospitals'.[75] Consequently, when hiring nurses, UCH could continue to discriminate on grounds of denominational affiliation without forfeiting its entitlement to financial support from the Metropolitan Hospital Sunday Fund.

From the perspective of the churches, there were also issues associated with the occasion's becoming too secularized. One manifestation of this was the establishment of a Hospital Saturday to complement Hospital Sunday. Originating in Liverpool in 1870, this was seen as a means of securing contributions from those who would not be in church on Hospital Sunday. Again the concept spread rapidly to other towns. Taking Southampton as an example, in 1874 it was decided that on the Saturday before Hospital Sunday 'a general collection should be made in the various manufactories and workshops of the town as well as amongst the officers and crew of the steamships in the port'.[76] While such a move undoubtedly increased the amount collected, it could be argued that by extending the scope of the appeal its character as a practical outworking of the Christian gospel was weakened. Thus, although most clergy and their congregations were sympathetic towards, and keen to support the aims of, Hospital Sunday, they could be troubled and constrained by the more 'worldly' aspects.

A final issue was associated with a gradual decline in the amount collected in many of the larger centres of population, a frequent cause for concern. This was attributed to a variety of factors. In 1910, for example, the leading Congregationalist and minister of Lyndhurst Road Church in Hampstead, Revd Dr R. F. Horton, drew attention to 'the fact that the people who used to contribute now go out of town for the weekend. They spent Sunday in the country. The habit of Sunday worship in church was dying out ... [in] England.'[77] More prosaically, in some communities bad weather over the weekend Hospital Sunday was held was blamed for a reduction in donations. A 1910 press report from Leeds, which held its Hospital Sunday in February, indicated that for some years 'congregational collections had been of diminishing quantity' and although 'a

---

[75] Mangion, 'Tolerable Intolerance', 483.
[76] 'Hospital Sunday at Southampton'.
[77] 'Hospital Sunday', *Daily News*, 13 June 1910, 6

special effort' had been made that year 'unfortunately bad weather interfered with the attendances'.[78] In Sheffield, which also held its Hospital Sunday in the winter, the local paper commented that 'a stormy Sunday mean(t) empty churches and empty churches mean(t) attenuated collections'.[79] There were, therefore, signs that maintaining the momentum was a particular challenge, with frequent references in the press to a decline in the sums raised and the need for appeals to be more robust and assertive.

CONCLUSION: 'WITH MUCH VIGOUR AND EARNESTNESS'[80]

From its inception in 1859, Hospital Sunday symbolized what might be termed a symbiotic relationship between spiritual and physical health. Altruism was seen as a marker of spiritual well-being, especially when it was directed towards alleviating the plight of those, especially the poor, whose physical health required attention, either in hospital or the community. As it was put in 1900 by the minister of Lake Road Baptist Church in Portsmouth, 'it was the duty of the Christian Church to emulate the spirit of philanthropy shown by our Master, and to assist the afflicted and the poor by giving to the institution which brought help and succour to them'.[81] However, while at one level such sentiments were laudable, constant vigilance was required to ensure that the spiritual dimension was not eroded as secular pressures grew and practical issues emerged.

These became increasingly apparent since, during the late Victorian and Edwardian eras, Hospital Sunday can be said to have incorporated elements of both 'embodied' and 'diffusive religion', a distinction drawn by Bishop Talbot in his charge to the diocese of Rochester when first appointed to the see in 1903, and one appropriated by Jeffrey Cox.[82] Embodied religion was exhibited by those who had internalized Christian formularies and creeds and sought to put their faith into practice through church membership and good works. As applied to Hospital Sunday, it meant that they attended the

[78] 'Hospital Sunday in Leeds', *Yorkshire Post*, 21 February 1910, 8.
[79] 'Hospital Sunday', *Sheffield Daily Telegraph*, 2 February 1910, 6.
[80] 'Hospital Sunday', *Manchester Courier and Lancashire General Advertiser*, 24 February 1870, 6.
[81] 'Hospital Sunday', *Portsmouth Evening News*, 29 October 1900, 2.
[82] Cox, *English Churches*, 93–5.

requisite service(s), engaged fully with the sermon(s) and donated generously. However, in many communities, with its parades, street collections and civic services, Hospital Sunday had become, in some respects, an epitome of 'diffusive religion'. This meant that, in the words of Stuart Mews, it was one of 'the many signs that the English people did have elemental conceptions of right and wrong, a willingness to offer help to a needy neighbour, and appreciation of a warm community spirit'.[83] Through participation in the more festive aspects of Hospital Sunday, they aligned themselves with what was generally perceived to be simply a good cause.

Due in part to its diffusive and celebratory character, Hospital Sunday did not end in 1914. It continued into the inter-war years and remained a distinctive component of the Christian calendar until, as indicated earlier, the National Health Service came into being in 1948. Even then, as Robert Piggott cogently demonstrates, the legacy of Hospital Sunday was reflected in many different aspects of health care provision, from fund-raising for extra comforts for patients to (in particular) the work and witness of hospital chaplains.[84] The concept of a Christian festival dedicated to the values inherent in hospitals and health care more generally undoubtedly had deep roots. It was an initiative initially characterized, in words from a Manchester newspaper editorial of 1870, by 'much vigour and earnestness', features that needed to be maintained if it was to retain its appeal.[85] The fact that it spread so rapidly following its Birmingham launch was indicative of its perceived worth as an additional means by which churches, chapels and synagogues could contribute to the well-being of the wider community.

---

[83] Stuart Mews, 'Religion, 1900–1939', in Chris Wrigley, ed., *A Companion to Early Twentieth-Century Britain* (Oxford, 2003), 470–84, at 471.

[84] See, in this volume, Robert Piggott, 'Hospital Sunday and the new National Health Service: An End to "The Voluntary Spirit" in England?', 372–93.

[85] 'Hospital Sunday', *Manchester Courier and Lancashire General Advertiser*, 24 February 1870, 6.

Hospital Sunday and the new National Health Services: An End to the 'Voluntary Spirit' in England?

Robert Piggott*

University of Huddersfield

The advent of the welfare state has been seen by some historians as a decisive blow for British traditions of voluntarism, echoing some of the concerns raised in the lead up to the establishment of the National Health Service (NHS). This article examines the practice of Hospital Sunday in England in the post-war period. In doing so it evidences the effect of the nationalization of the voluntary hospitals in 1948 on the relationships between clergy, their congregations and health care. It argues that much greater attention needs to be paid to the continuities evident in Christian-inspired social action in the NHS in the long 1950s and after. Attending to the role of such Christian social action allows historians both to extend our knowledge of the importance of Christianity to social life in the period and to deepen our understanding of the operation of the welfare state.

At the Truro diocesan conference in 1950, the bishop of Plymouth was reported as calling for Christians to 'capture the Welfare State for Christ and his Church … as a way of serving Christ in the 20th century by serving the community'.[1] A term coined by William Temple, the welfare state was welcomed by some as the fulfilment of the aims of Christian social reformers.[2] However, whether Christians were able to continue to influence the character of the welfare state after its inception, and if so, to what extent, remains relatively unexplored.[3] In one view, the role of charity was usurped by the state and long-

---

* Department of History, English, Linguistics and Music, University of Huddersfield, Huddersfield, HD1 3DH. E-mail: r.piggott@hud.ac.uk. The author would like to thank Rob Ellis, as well as the anonymous reviewers, for their insightful advice on an earlier draft of this article. He is also grateful to Roger Ottewill for his support during the revision process, and to Barry Doyle for advice and guidance along the way.
[1] 'Capture Welfare State for the Church', *The Cornishman*, 26 October 1950, 4.
[2] Matthew Grimley, *Citizenship, Community and the Church of England* (Oxford, 2004), 1; Adrian Hastings, *A History of English Christianity* (London, 2001), 422.
[3] Though see Daniel S. Loss, 'The Institutional Afterlife of Christian England', *JMH* 89 (2017), 282–313.

Studies in Church History 58 (2022), 372–393   © The Author(s), 2022. Published by Cambridge University Press on behalf of Ecclesiastical History Society
doi: 10.1017/stc.2022.18

standing traditions of voluntary service simply discarded.[4] This article examines the effect of the establishment of the National Health Service (NHS) on the practice of Hospital Sunday in order better to understand the role of Christian charity in the first decade and a half of the NHS's existence.

Hospital Sunday had linked faith communities with voluntary hospitals through fund-raising and worship in a variety of urban places, becoming widespread by the 1870s.[5] Voluntary hospitals, a vital part of health care provision prior to the NHS, were locally based charitable initiatives drawing their income from donations, endowments and subscription schemes.[6] By the inter-war period, they were funded by a combination of charity and contributory schemes, as well as some limited payment by patients.[7] Hospital Sunday, a yearly event, contributed a small proportion of hospitals' annual income. By the 1930s it had, in many places, become an elaborate festival, marked by parades, brass bands and civic worship, and was supported by medical professionals. However, when the National Health Service Act (1946) turned control of Britain's voluntary hospitals over to central government, fund-raising for medical care was no longer necessary and the primary object of Hospital Sunday was eliminated.

The historiography on Hospital Sunday is not extensive and the custom has received little attention from historians of religion.[8] As well as providing evidence of the links between congregations and health care prior to the establishment of the welfare state, examining the history of Hospital Sunday after 1948 helps to illuminate the impact of the momentous changes in the role of religion in public life and society after the Second World War. The literature in this field is too extensive to recapitulate here, but the subject remains contested.[9] While Adrian Hastings was able to

---

[4] Frank Prochaska, *Christianity and Social Service in Modern Britain* (Oxford, 2006).

[5] See, in this volume, Roger Ottewill '"Alleviating the Sum of Human Suffering": The Origins, Attributes and Appeal of Hospital Sunday, 1859–1914', 352–71.

[6] For a recent survey, see George C. Gosling, *Payment and Philanthropy in British Healthcare, 1918–48* (Manchester, 2017), 4–9, 19–22.

[7] Martin Gorsky and John Mohan with Tim Willis, *Mutualism and Health Care: British Hospital Contributory Schemes in the Twentieth Century* (London, 2005), 31–7.

[8] Though see Ottewill, '"Alleviating the Sum of Human Suffering"'.

[9] For an overview, see Clive Field, *Britain's Last Religious Revival? Quantifying Belonging, Behaving, and Believing in the Long 1950s* (London, 2015), 2–6.

produce some very cogent evidence as to why the period might be seen as a one of a 'modest religious revival', the data as analysed by Clive Field offers a very mixed picture indeed.[10] Although this remained a time in which Christianity mattered in both politics and culture, it was also apparently one in which religious leaders 'lost heart', to use Philip Williamson's words.[11] Examining the changing role of the churches in the provision of welfare is one way to help us better understand these changes.

Matthew Grimley identified 'state encroachment' as a 'threat' affecting the Church of England from the late nineteenth century onwards, with the government taking responsibility for welfare provision previously administered by Christians.[12] As a side-effect of this development, he noted the subsidiary role into which voluntary associations had been forced after 1945, and religion's attendant retreat from the public sphere.[13] This story is echoed elsewhere: in an absolutist rendering, Frank Prochaska has implicated the welfare state in a sudden evaporation of Christian-inspired social action.[14] In this version, the welfare state, administered by cold bureaucracy and supported by statist Labourites, pushed the need for Christian charity to the margins, with the Church of England episcopate seemingly complicit in this process.[15] Aspects of Prochaska's thesis are readily open to question and Deakin and Smith have discussed the 'myth' of Labour's hostility to voluntary action.[16] In the same volume, Eliza Filby directly critiqued Prochaska's account of the role of the Church of England in the consensus years and after, arguing that the welfare state presented a 'challenge[;] ... however the story is one of reformulation rather than retreat'.[17] Indeed, following the

[10] Hastings, *English Christianity*, 465; Field, *Britain's Last Religious Revival?*, 99–104.
[11] Hastings, *English Christianity*, 403–580; Philip Williamson, 'National Days of Prayer: The Churches, the State and Public Worship in Britain, 1899–1957', *EHR* 128 (2013), 323–66, at 363.
[12] Grimley, *Citizenship*, 17.
[13] Ibid. 216–17.
[14] Prochaska, *Christianity and Social Service*; Adam Dinham and Robert Jackson, 'Religion, Welfare and Education', in Linda Woodhead and Rebecca Catto, eds, *Religion and Change in Modern Britain* (Oxford, 2012), 272–94, at 273–4.
[15] Prochaska, *Christianity and Social Service*, 152–6.
[16] Nicholas Deakin and Justin D. Smith, 'Labour, Charity and Voluntary Action', in Matthew Hilton and James McKay, eds, *The Ages of Voluntarism* (Oxford, 2011), 69–93.
[17] Eliza Filby, 'Faith, Charity and Citizenship: Christianity, Voluntarism and the State in the 1980s', ibid. 135–57, at 136–9.

work of Daniel Loss, we might see the post-war settlement as in fact accompanied by the incorporation of Church of England personnel and initiatives into the institutions of the state.[18] This is clearly seen in the chaplaincy service, which maintained a role for clergy in the NHS.[19] In light of this scholarship, this article explores further the ways in which Christians adapted to the post-war settlement, focusing on the continued links between faith and voluntarism.

The continued role of voluntarism in the NHS is an emerging theme in medical history. Ramsden and Cresswell have noted the ongoing role of voluntary aid societies in first aid training after 1948.[20] As they put it, 'older traditions of voluntaristic self-sacrifice to a greater communal and national good' remained, despite the state having taken greater responsibility.[21] It is these pre-NHS 'older traditions' that have received the most attention from historians of medicine. A small portion of this has concerned Hospital Sunday, which has been of interest to historians of medicine in the light of its role in hospital funding.[22] Keir Waddington, for instance, put the Metropolitan Hospital Sunday Fund at the 'apex' of the voluntary hospital movement and within the history of the 'rationalisation' of charitable giving in the nineteenth century.[23] In doing so, he noted that the Metropolitan Fund had supported 'interdenominational cooperation' by providing an apolitical focus for ecumenical action.[24] Carmen Mangion has investigated this aspect further, drawing attention to the fund's role in combating sectarianism in London's hospitals.[25] Provincial Sunday funds have also featured in work on hospital

---

[18] Loss, 'Institutional Afterlife'.

[19] Ibid. 298.

[20] Stefan Ramsden and Rosemary Cresswell, 'First Aid and Voluntarism in England, 1945–85', *TCBH* 30 (2019), 504–30, at 509–11.

[21] Ibid. 529.

[22] This generally extends only to brief mentions of the practice: see, for instance, Gosling, *Payment and Philanthropy*, 7, 20, 105.

[23] Keir Waddington, 'Bastard Benevolence: Centralisation, Voluntarism and the Sunday Fund 1873–1898', *London Journal* 19 (1994), 151–67, at 152; he returned to the subject in his monograph *Charity and the London Hospitals, 1850–1898* (Woodbridge, 2000). Geoffrey Rivett, *The Development of the London Hospital System, 1823–1982* (London, 1986), also includes much on the fund.

[24] Waddington, 'Bastard Benevolence', 154.

[25] Carmen M. Mangion, '"Tolerable Intolerance": Protestantism, Sectarianism and Voluntary Hospitals in Late Nineteenth-Century London', *MH* 62 (2018), 468–84.

financing, though generally only briefly.[26] For instance, the work of Hayes and Doyle captured vividly the associational aspects of hospital fund-raising in the inter-war period. This showed the increasing importance of charity appeals, individual giving and a wide variety of associational activities involved in raising money, of which Hospital Sunday was one amongst many.[27]

The first section of this article seeks to extend the existing literature on Hospital Sunday by widening the focus beyond London. However, although Hospital Sunday was held across Britain, in a bid to make the material more manageable, the present article draws its evidence from the English context only. The broad swath of the sources cited has been drawn from digitized local newspapers, although it is hoped these are indicative of wider themes. The article largely assumes the prominence of Anglicans within the public sphere at this time. Williamson has argued that public days of prayer at the start of the twentieth century represented a novel level of 'co-operation between the principal churches' which placed the 'Church of England [in] a new position of leadership'.[28] In doing so, he also noted the continuing desire by Catholic archbishops to maintain 'distinctiveness'.[29] This was also the case in relation to Hospital Sunday. While Catholic clergy joined in its promotion, it was the Protestant churches, and Anglicans in particular, who were at the forefront.

Helen McCarthy has drawn attention to the 'democratising logic at work in the associational cultures of inter-war Britain'.[30] As will be seen in the next section, this logic was clearly present in the fund-raising practices organized as part of Hospital Sunday and continued into the immediate post-war period. The second section evidences the reactions of clergy, medical professionals and representatives of medical charities to the prospect of nationalization of the hospitals. While Prochaska's account assumes that members of the

---

[26] Steven Cherry, 'Hospital Saturday, Workplace Collections and Issues in Late Nineteenth-Century Hospital Funding', *MH* 44 (2000), 461–88; Barry M. Doyle, *Politics of Hospital Provision in the Early Twentieth Century* (Abingdon, 2014), 117, 173.

[27] Nick Hayes and Barry M. Doyle, 'Eggs, Rags and Whist Drives: Popular Munificence and the Development of Provincial Medical Voluntarism between the Wars', *HR* 86 (2013), 712–40.

[28] Williamson, 'National Days of Prayer', 325.

[29] Ibid. 338.

[30] Helen McCarthy, 'Associational Voluntarism in Interwar Britain', in Hilton and McKay, eds, *Ages of Voluntarism*, 47–68, at 67.

clergy embraced these changes wholeheartedly, it is shown here that in fact clergy raised concerns about the erosion of a personal and spiritual connection to health care which they felt a state-run hospital service would cause. The third section will argue that despite limitations being placed on the role of charitable giving, the voluntary spirit did not entirely dissipate. Although the NHS presented new challenges to Christians devoted to sustaining a link between charity and medical care, and these were sometimes insurmountable, there remained a concerted effort to maintain support for the hospitals, even after certain avenues were closed.

HOSPITAL SUNDAY

Linda Woodhead has argued that the advent of the NHS both 'absorbed' and 'erased' aspects of the health care system of the preceding period. She neatly encapsulated the changes as the 'triumph of scientific medicine … of the national over the local; of the male medical profession over voluntaryism; and of secular medicine over religious, or mixed, provision of health or healing'.[31] Although the extent to which the impact of the NHS can be seen in such absolute terms is perhaps questionable, there is no doubt that before the Second World War health care was strongly linked at a local level to religious congregations through both fund-raising and voluntary service. Links to individual hospitals were also maintained by members of the clergy and, in their role as public personages, they served on the committees of the voluntary hospitals, sometimes as governors.[32] Hospital Sunday in particular offered clergy and congregations an opportunity to unite to support the hospitals as part of a local Christian civic culture. Such practices of social service generated social status for their participants in a period in which hospital charity was more democratic and participatory than it had ever been.[33]

Gorsky, Mohan and Willis have argued that the contributory schemes 'undermined the social hierarchies' initially present in the

[31] Linda Woodhead, 'Introduction', in eadem and Catto, eds, *Religion and Change*, 1–33, at 21.
[32] See, for instance, London, Wellcome Collection, b3171562x, West Suffolk General Hospital, *Annual Report* (Bury St Edmunds, 1934); Keir Waddington, 'Subscribing to a Democracy? Management and the Voluntary Ideology of the London Hospitals, 1850-1900', *EHR* 118 (2003), 357–79, at 368.
[33] McCarthy, 'Associational Voluntarism', 48–9.

voluntary hospital administration.[34] These hierarchies continued to be reconfigured after the First World War by individual giving. Evidence presented by Hayes and Doyle underscores this and shows the ongoing vitality of voluntary action between 1919 and 1939.[35] The impressive variety of practices and events that took place in relation to hospital fund-raising included, but was not limited to, the placing of collection boxes in pubs and places of work, summer fetes, concerts, flag days and the award of a silver cup for the subpostmaster collecting the most money for local hospitals.[36] Hayes and Doyle also showed that hospitals in this period became less reliant on elite contributions, and increasingly emphasized small-scale donations, as well as gifts in kind.[37] This growing importance of small donors democratized hospital funding and reconfigured the social hierarchies implicit in fund-raising.

Hospital Sunday sat within these practices. It demonstrated the churches' long-standing commitments to medical care at a local level. The voluntary hospitals often had strong links to local Christian congregations and some hospitals were denominational foundations.[38] Even those without a specific denominational affiliation might have a long-standing association with certain congregations. At Huddersfield, Anglican clergy had been involved in both the laying of the foundation stone and the opening ceremony of the Huddersfield and Upper Agbrigg Infirmary in 1829 and 1831, with the vicar of Huddersfield presiding at the former ceremony.[39] Huddersfield's Infirmary Sunday, held from 1870 onwards, revivified the connection of churches and chapels with the hospital. The result was impressive: their contribution grew from £13 0s 3d in 1868 to £283 17s 8d in the first year.[40] As well as special services, fund-raising events in Huddersfield and its townships connected the various places of worship to the hospitals through entertainment and

[34] Gorsky and Mohan with Willis, *Mutualism and Health Care*, 31.

[35] Hayes and Doyle, 'Eggs, Rags and Whist Drives', 712–13. The classic account is Stephen Yeo, *Religion and Voluntary Organisations in Crisis* (London, 1976).

[36] Hayes and Doyle, 'Eggs, Rags and Whist Drives', 721–4.

[37] Ibid. 727–35.

[38] Joan Higgins, 'American Hospitals in the British Health Care Market', *Medical Care Review* 47 (1990), 105–30, at 106.

[39] 'Huddersfield Infirmary', *Leeds Mercury*, 4 July 1829, 3.

[40] E. D., 'Aid to the Infirmary', *Huddersfield Chronicle and West Yorkshire Advertiser*, 25 July 1868, 8; 'Huddersfield Infirmary Annual Meeting', *Huddersfield Chronicle*, 25 June 1870, 8.

association.[41] Here and across the country, congregations were linked to local hospitals through parades, concerts and other similar practices. As a contributory scheme, the sums raised on Hospital Sunday were variable and even at the height of the event's popularity these generally represented only a small proportion of the hospitals' total income. As Waddington showed, in commanding the support of London's elite, the Metropolitan Hospital Sunday Fund raised £725,647 for London's hospitals and dispensaries between 1873 and 1894. However, this remained a small proportion of the hospitals' income, amounting to just under 6% of the various institutions' incomes in 1891.[42] In addition, Gorsky, Mohan and Willis noted that between 1919 and 1939 the role of charitable contributions declined in importance to the voluntary hospitals.[43] The picture remained the same in the 1940s. For instance, while Hospital Sunday in Preston in 1944 raised £2,197 (a local record), the *weekly* running cost of the hospital amounted to £1,860.[44] Despite its marginal role in funding, however, Hospital Sunday was considered by its participants to provide a 'link between the hospitals and the churches', which itself was viewed as important.[45]

The changing emphasis of fund-raising and the growing importance of individual voluntary action seems to have increased innovation in fund-raising methods. This innovation sometimes conflicted with the ethos of Hospital Sunday: the Royal Portsmouth Hospital's acceptance of the proceeds of a raffle in 1932 led to their exclusion from the local Sunday Fund.[46] Innovation was carried over into the post-war period, and a more eccentric example included the collections from a crossing keeper's garden on the London and North Eastern Railway line between Harrogate and Knaresborough. Ornamented with a miniature boating lake and lighthouse, a bandstand and an array of figures, this was perhaps inspired by the model village at Bourton-on-the-Water, which also donated to a Hospital

[41] Angela Griffiths, 'Yorkshire Sings: A Musical and Social Phenomenon', *Huddersfield Local History Society Journal* no. 11 (Winter 2000/2001), unpaginated.
[42] Waddington, 'Bastard Benevolence', 160.
[43] Gorsky and Mohan with Willis, *Mutualism and Health Care*, 48–53.
[44] 'Hospital Sunday in Preston and District', *Lancashire Evening Post*, 24 January 1946, 3.
[45] G. Brett and A. S. Reeve, 'Hospital Sunday', *Yorkshire Post and Leeds Intelligencer*, 7 May 1948, 2.
[46] 'Hospital Prize Scheme Sequel', *Manchester Guardian*, 13 June 1932, 11.

Sunday fund.[47] For the crossing keeper and his fellow fund-raisers, including those engaged in more prosaic activities such as door-to-door collecting, such exertions could earn them a mention in the local newspaper and thus a modicum of esteem.[48] Even more likely to cement their social standing was an active role on a Hospital Sunday committee, a commitment which was often deemed worthy of mention in an obituary, underlining the links between social service and the social status produced by fund-raising.[49]

Although much of the literature has focused on the role of the Metropolitan Sunday Fund, other urban centres connected the municipality with a Hospital Sunday Fund through a civic service with mayoral patronage. Both Hull and Bristol, for instance, connected the churches, the local authority and the hospitals through a Lord Mayor's Hospital Sunday Fund. This connection transformed the lord mayor into the figurehead of the appeal, responsible for writing an annual letter to the local papers, and, in Hull at least, it entailed a tour of the hospitals to hand over cheques for the proceeds.[50] In both Hull and Bristol, the lord mayor's office became attached to the scheme well after it had come into being.[51] These funds continued after the Second World War. In Hull the fund's events were spread across a range of associational activities including an annual dance, as well as other less regular events such greyhound racing at Craven Park, in addition to a parade and church service collections on the nominated Sunday.[52] A civic service was a regular feature in urban areas, with the choice of venue often, but not always, the parish church.[53] Often too, a local fund would promote interdenominational cooperation, and the event might be a united

[47] 'The Wonders of a Crossing Keeper's Garden', *Harrogate Herald*, 20 August 1947, 1; 'Hospital Sunday Tribute to Legion', *Gloucestershire Echo*, 30 September 1946, 3.
[48] 'Tebay Hospital Sunday Parade', *Penrith Observer*, 20 May 1947, 5.
[49] For example, 'Church Tribute', *Harrow Observer*, 17 April 1947, 5.
[50] James Owen, 'Letter to the Editor: Hospital Sunday', *Western Daily Press*, 6 March 1946, 3; 'Civic Gifts, Greetings for Hull Folk', *Hull Daily Mail*, 27 December 1946, 3.
[51] 'The Talk of Bristol', *Bristol Mercury*, 30 March 1900, 8; 'The Bristol Royal Infirmary and General Hospital', *Bristol Times and Mirror*, 19 January 1861, 6; 'Hospital Sunday in Hull', *The Hospital*, 5 November 1910, 170; 19 September 1914; 'Hull Lady's Offer', *Hull Daily Mail*, 19 January 1861, 4.
[52] 'Fair Prices', *Hull Daily Mail*, 18 October 1946, 1; 'Tonight's Craven Park Greyhounds', *Hull Daily Mail*, 10 October 1946, 6.
[53] 'Mayor at Hospital Sunday Service', *Hastings and St Leonards Observer*, 6 July 1946, 5; 'Hospital Sunday Observance', *Western Morning News*, 21 October 1946, 6.

service.[54] Indeed, the events could also support inter-faith relations.[55] In its ideal-typical form, a band would accompany a parade to a local church for a service in which the friendly and voluntary aid societies, alongside members of the municipality, demonstrated their support for local hospitals.[56] As Tom Hulme and others have shown, the 1920s and 1930s saw a sustained revival of forms of civic ritual, based in a 'civic publicity' movement.[57] Hospital Sunday parades offered similar spectacles and there was an element of local distinctiveness which will have contributed to feelings of civic pride.

The Hospital Sunday service itself continued the association of local government, friendly societies and medical staff inside the church or chapel. In certain places the event held special significance for members of the medical professions.[58] Besides offering an opportunity for a minister to preach on the subject of Christian charity and medical care, medical and administrative staff also, on occasion, offered an address.[59] Such addresses could also underline the connection between the hospitals and the local community. Accordingly, the service might function as part of a recruitment drive for nurses.[60] Medical staff, often in uniform, might also take up the collection and give the reading.[61] The service as much as the parade thus allowed the various constituencies involved in medical care to join together and advance their cause.

In a system of locally managed and voluntarily supported hospital care, Hospital Sunday linked a range of actors and groups to their local hospitals. Although often a minor part of a hospital's yearly budget, these elaborate fund-raising practices connected hospitals and congregations. These practices continued after the National Health Service Act (1946) had been passed. Indeed, in the face of nationalization, Hospital Sunday arguably took on extra significance.

---

[54] 'Towcester', *Northampton Mercury*, 20 September 1946, 2.

[55] 'Call for Hospital Sunday to stay', *Birmingham Daily Gazette*, 27 October 1947, 1.

[56] See 'Banners that may never fly again', *Gloucester Citizen*, 19 October 1949, 4.

[57] Tom Hulme, '"A nation of town criers": Civic Publicity and Historical Pageantry in Inter-War Britain', *UH* 44 (2017), 270–92; for a brief overview of the historiography, see Ben Roberts, 'Entertaining the Community: The Evolution of Civic Ritual and Public Celebration, 1860–1953', *UH* 44 (2017), 444–63, at 447.

[58] 'Our London Letter', *Western Mail*, 26 June 1946, 2.

[59] 'First Clue to Penicillin', *The Times*, 12 June 1944, 2.

[60] 'City Lack of Nurses is "Serious"', *Gloucester Citizen*, 16 July 1946, 4.

[61] 'Nurses Read Lessons in Church', *Shields Daily News*, 27 October 1947, 8; 'Nurses to Collect', *Hull Daily Mail*, 7 November 1947, 3.

Nationalization engendered concerns over the future of specific hospitals and also created a funding cliff-edge.[62] Popular belief that hospitals were already state funded was cited at Hull and elsewhere as the reason for the decline in contributions.[63] To manage this, members of the clergy joined the mayors in letter writing campaigns.[64] At Liverpool this action was both interdenominational and interfaith: the letter was signed by the Anglican bishop of Liverpool, the Catholic archbishop, a senior rabbi and the president of the Free Church Council, among others.[65] As will be seen in the next section, in response to the changes decreed by the 1946 act, clergy looked to defend the voluntary system and to maintain a role for religion in hospital care.

RESPONSES: 'THERE WILL BE A NEED FOR THE VOLUNTARY SPIRIT'[66]

Prochaska's account included a blanket assertion that 'Christian leaders' wholeheartedly embraced the welfare state. In doing so, he asserted, they had 'endorsed a collective secular world … in a culture growing more materialist and national'.[67] Yet there is ample evidence that clergy defended voluntarism both before and after the NHS had come into being. Their defence of the voluntary hospitals drew on a position that privileged democratic participation at a local level and was antipathetic to the centralized state.[68] On an explanatory level, we might see the NHS as a threat to the role of the clergy in medical care and thus to a source of their social esteem. However, they also saw a particular conception of health care as being under threat. Their concerns were the same as Prochaska's: that the loss of voluntarism meant more materialism, and that hospitals would now treat those in need as medical subjects, rather than as individual people.

[62] G. S. James, 'Hospital Sunday', *Western Daily Press*, 6 March 1947, 3.
[63] 'Fund £1,500 less in its Last Year', *Hull Daily Mail*, 22 December 1947, 4; 'One Reason why Hospital "Subs." are down', *Hartlepool Northern Daily Mail*, 11 September 1947, 4.
[64] Brett and Reeve, 'Hospital Sunday'.
[65] 'Help Hospitals', *Liverpool Echo*, 16 October 1946, 4.
[66] 'Day to Day: There will be a need for "The Voluntary Spirit"', *Nottingham Journal*, 11 February 1948, 2.
[67] Prochaska, *Christianity and Social Service*, 151.
[68] Ibid. 153.

Martin Daunton has demonstrated that the 'tension between efficiency and an active, participatory democracy' had been a feature in the debate over medical provision for much of the early twentieth century.[69] Grimley has similarly shown that the privileging of voluntary action had been a key element in the work of Christian social thinkers of the period.[70] This was also evident in the public pronouncements of clergy in their Hospital Sunday sermons in the years prior to 1948.[71] For instance, at St Mary's Church in Nottingham, Canon R. H. Hawkins saw the establishing of the NHS as 'an attack on the voluntary hospitals' and thus on voluntarism itself, and expected the efficiency of the new service to result in a 'very hard and cold' and 'less kindly hospital service'.[72] Similarly at St Paul's, West Hartlepool, Revd J. E. Lee expressed unease; he was reported to have 'observed that active relief was now becoming so much a part of the machinery of State' that 'spontaneous' assistance was being crowded out.[73] Although they are anecdotal evidence, these sermons were probably indicative of widespread ideas about the primacy of voluntarism and the supposedly deleterious effect of state control.

Concerns expressed at Hospital Sunday services immediately prior to the establishment of the NHS reflected a significant section of the public opinion. Hayes has noted that although the public expected greater efficiency to accompany the new service, there were also worries 'that state-run hospitals would be overcrowded – or depersonalised'.[74] Middle-class respondents to social surveys in particular favoured the retention of the voluntary hospital system, citing aversion to 'officialdom and state interference'.[75] Contemporary surveys found a split in public opinion with '[o]nly a little over a half' in favour

[69] Martin Daunton, 'Payment and Participation: Welfare and State-Formation in Britain 1900–1951', *P&P* 150 (1996), 169–216, at 204–5.
[70] Grimley, *Citizenship*, especially 65–102.
[71] Joan Keating, 'Faith and Community Threatened? Roman Catholic Responses to the Welfare State, Materialism and Social Mobility, 1945–1962', *TCBH* 9 (1998), 86–108, at 94.
[72] 'Efficiency is not Everything', *Nottingham Journal*, 13 May 1946, 4; Similar views were expressed by Revd J. C. Poole at Hastings the following year: 'State Hospitals Warning', *Hastings and St Leonards Observer*, 28 June 1947, 3.
[73] 'Hospitals & the Spirit of Service', *Hartlepool Northern Daily Mail*, 17 June 1946, 3.
[74] Nick Hayes, 'Did we really want a National Health Service? Hospitals, Patients and Public Opinions before 1948', *EHR* 127 (2012), 625–61, at 651.
[75] Ibid. 640, 650.

of a 'fully nationalised service'.[76] As members of this social class who had long participated actively in medical fund-raising and organization, it is perhaps unsurprising that clergy voiced their disquiet.[77]

Concerns about the new service were not limited to the clergy. Where Hospital Sunday was strong, local newspapers were vociferous in their objections. The *Hull Daily Mail*, for example, depicted nationalization as a direct seizure by the state of money voluntarily donated by Hullensians.[78] Alongside this, the argument for the role of voluntarism in the new NHS was made not only by clergy, but also by medical professionals and those representing medical charities. The Nottingham Hospital Sunday Fund committee argued that 'there ought to be encouragement and opportunity for Christian people to contribute to the care and comfort of the sick and suffering' in the new service, with the *Nottingham Journal* echoing this sentiment in an editorial.[79] Hospital Sunday addresses by medical professionals also included calls for a continued link between health care and voluntarism. The congregations at the Bristol Hospital Sunday services of both 1947 and 1948 heard doctors speak to this end.[80] The following year, in response to a Ministry of Health circular which banned the participation of medical professionals in fund-raising, a Dr Hellier noted that the rule change had meant he had been 'forbidden to give an address on Hospital Sunday in aid of the Infirmary' and argued that '[t]his spurning of private generosity may, I believe, ultimately affect our whole conception of hospitals, and possibly the spirit in which the work is done there'.[81] Collectively doctors, clergy and the newspapers discussed the need to maintain a role for Christians in support of patient care in the NHS with the aim of retaining a human element to this care.[82]

As a corollary of their long-standing proximity to medical care, both the clergy and the churches sought to influence practices within the new health service. A primary vehicle for this was the Churches' Council of Healing, an ecumenical initiative set up by Archbishop

[76] Ibid. 645.
[77] 'Duke of Devonshire and the Hospitals', *Eastbourne Herald*, 1 June 1946, 12.
[78] 'Hull Infirmary's £475,594 for State', *Hull Daily Mail*, 13 Nov 1947, 1.
[79] '"Sunday Fund" Future', *Nottingham Journal*, 11 February 1948, 4.
[80] 'Revive Spirit of Service', *Western Daily Press*, 10 March 1947, 3.
[81] Quoted in 'Gift Ban may change the Spirit of Hospitals', *Yorkshire Post and Leeds Intelligencer*, 21 March 1949, 6.
[82] 'Hospital Sunday at Rugeley', *Lichfield Mercury*, 5 September 1947, 5.

Temple in 1944, the year of the NHS White Paper.[83] One of its aims was to promote divine healing as opposed to faith healing or miraculous healing, complementary to medical science rather than a substitute for it.[84] The council advocated for the benefits of patients maintaining faith and hope as part of their treatment, and Root has connected the movement with the development of psychotherapy.[85] Its work was supported by the British Medical Association (BMA) and the council offered a continued link between the English churches and medical care. In accordance with these principles, F. S. Sinker, a member of the clergy in Lichfield diocese, took a medical degree with the stated aim of developing 'friendly association between clergymen and doctors'.[86] To this end, the council also held meetings as part of the BMA's annual conferences.[87]

Through its report of 1947/8, the Churches' Council collectively sought to influence the use of medical services. It argued that the NHS Act had made 'the entire nation ... potential patients' and that hospitals were now crowded by those in search of value for money rather than helping themselves, to the detriment of those really in need.[88] It reiterated the argument that the character of care seemed to be at risk, with the sick losing 'personal contact' with the doctor and 'hospitals ... so overcrowded ... that they are no longer the havens of peace and rest they once were'.[89] Similar messages seem to have been being relayed by clergy in the parishes. At Golcar near Huddersfield, the vicar, Edward Clarke, had welcomed the NHS in his letter to the parish magazine of August 1948. However, he took the line that, although those using the service had the right to do so, they should not seek to use it for 'self interest and personal advantage'.[90] Similar points were expressed in a further

---

[83] Sheryl Root, 'The Healing Touch: Spiritual Healing in England, *c.*1870–1955' (Ph.D. thesis, University of Warwick, 2005), 203.

[84] 'Three Divine Healers to aid Lincs Doctors', *Lincolnshire Echo*, 3 June 1948, 3; 'Presbyterians agree Faith Healing has "important aspect"', *Western Mail*, 21 May 1953, 3.

[85] Root, 'Healing Touch', 300–6.

[86] Churches' Council of Healing, quoted in 'Divine Healing', *Tamworth Herald*, 18 October 1947, 4.

[87] 'Church should strike "A Note of Triumph"', *Bognor Regis Observer*, 29 March 1956, 5.

[88] Quoted in '"Help Yourself"', *Coventry Evening Telegraph*, 10 November 1949, 6.

[89] '"Invite to Illness"', *Lincolnshire Echo*, 10 November 1949, 1.

[90] Wakefield, West Yorkshire Archives Service, WDP105/8, *Golcar Parish Magazine*, August 1948, unpaginated.

letter of September 1949, which drew attention to reports of excessive use of day surgeries for care which might reasonably be provided in the home, while also criticizing workers at the Royal Ordnance Factories who had reportedly been drawing sick pay while working elsewhere.[91] This proprietary attitude to health care appears to have been engendered by a long-term association with the hospitals. At Golcar, the congregation had supported Infirmary Sunday to the end, and the parish magazine had previously included information on the implementation of the National Insurance Act (1911).[92]

It is clear, then, that rather than simply 'endorsing' the welfare state, as Prochaska put it, church leaders and clergy sought to influence its character. As will be explored further in the next section, obstacles were placed in their way. However, they continued to look for avenues through which to maintain the role of Christians in medical charity. For instance, the bishop of Birmingham, Ernest Barnes, used a sermon in December 1947 to propose that Hospital Sunday should henceforth support medical missions and hospital amenities.[93] Secular leaders also followed this line: the lord mayors of Hull and London both expressed their support for the continuation of their funds to assist patient welfare.[94] What to do with the day was, however, subject of some public debate. While the repurposing of Hospital Sunday to aid medical missions received support in a letter to *The Times* signed by the president of the BMA, amongst others, opposition to the proposal came from the Metropolitan Fund in particular.[95] In a strongly worded letter, C. J. Holland-Martin, then president of the fund, offered a response indicative of an emerging effort to retain a role for voluntarism in the NHS. In this he drew strongly on notions of Christian charity and denied the ability of an 'Act of Parliament' to 'solve the age old problem of the sick and the needy or absolve the ordinary citizen from his Christian duty to give alms'.[96] As will be seen in the next section, volunteers continued to recognize this duty.

[91] *Golcar Parish Magazine*, September 1949.
[92] Edward Clarke, 'The Infirmaries', *Golcar Parish Magazine,* February 1948, unpaginated; 'Infirmary Sunday', *Golcar Parish Magazine*, February 1913.
[93] 'Hospital Sunday Decision', *Birmingham Daily Gazette*, 24 December 1947, 3.
[94] 'Hospital Fund in New Form?' *Hull Daily Mail*, 16 April 1948, 3; C. M. Wells, 'Hospital Sunday', *The Times*, 26 May 1948, 5.
[95] 'Medical Missions', *The Times*, 15 September 1948, 6.
[96] C. J. Holland-Martin, 'Hospital Sunday', *The Times*, 20 September 1948, 5.

CHANGES AND CONTINUITIES: 'THE VOLUNTARY SPIRIT ... HAS
NEVER DIED'[97]

As we have seen, a core element of Prochaska's argument was to
emphasize the disavowal by the Labour Party of its voluntarist
traditions. In doing so he cited not only Bevan's remarks in
parliament deprecating the practice of nurses fund-raising, but also
the Ministry of Health circular of January 1949, referred to briefly
above.[98] The circular was intended by the ministry to counter the
idea that 'that hospitals ... are still dependent on voluntary financial
help'. Although it allowed volunteers to work in hospitals, it banned
hospital committees from fund-raising.[99] However, Bevan's policy
appears to have been resisted on the ground. It was met with protests
from hospital boards, and within three months the *Daily Mail* was
reporting that 'despite Bevan', half a million subscribers were
contributing to Hospital Leagues of Friends.[100] Indeed it is arguable
that by eliminating the need for fund-raising for medical care, the
ruling opened up space for voluntary action to contribute to
non-medical care in hospitals. In any case, early in 1952 this policy
was effectively overturned by Harry Crookshank as incoming
Conservative Minister of Health.[101] With the Conservatives
concerned about spiralling costs in the health service, both
Crookshank and his successor Iain MacLeod were keen to promote
the contribution of volunteers.[102]

Resistance to the Ministry of Health circular appears to have been
widespread. For instance, although it appeared to some that Hospital
Sunday had thereby been banned, services continued to be held.[103] At
the 1949 Harvest Festival service at Exeter Cathedral, medical staff
circumvented the ban by attending in an 'unofficial' capacity, and
the collection was taken up for the Patient's Extra Comforts

---

[97] K. H. Robbins, quoted in 'League of Hospital Friends formed in Aylesbury', *Bucks Herald*, 7 December 1951, 8.
[98] Prochaska, *Christianity and Social Service*, 123, 152.
[99] 'Hospitals must not appeal for Money', *Sussex Agricultural Express*, 14 January 1949, 5.
[100] 'Rush to aid Hospitals goes on despite Bevan', *Daily Mail*, 4 April 1949, 3.
[101] 'Appeals for Hospital Funds', *The Times*, 23 January 1952, 2.
[102] Charles Webster, 'Conservatives and Consensus: The Politics of the National Health Service, 1951–64', in Ann Oakley and Susan Williams, eds, *The Politics of the Welfare State* (London, 1994), 54–74; Nigel Fisher, *Iain Macleod* (London, 1974), 93–5.
[103] 'Hospital Sundays to end', *Lincolnshire Echo*, 11 January 1949, 3; 'Regional Board Protest to Ministry', *Nottingham Journal*, 11 January 1949, 4.

Fund.[104] As has already been seen, Sunday funds were beginning to be repurposed; often, as with the Metropolitan Fund, they were directed to other areas within the ambit of hospital care in a broad sense. At Bristol, the lord mayor wrote to the *Western Daily Press* praising the approach taken by the Metropolitan Fund, arguing for 'continued voluntary effort' to assist those in need.[105] At the subsequent Bristol Hospital Sunday, the lord mayor's chaplain saw the need for an 'anti-boredom fund' for hospital patients.[106] Subsequently, the fund became the Lord Mayor's Voluntary Services Fund, with money going to hospital comforts and to local charitable initiatives.[107]

Elsewhere, as indicated above, the circular was taken by some as a signal to repurpose Hospital Sunday to support medical missions abroad.[108] The *Liverpool Echo* columnist 'Layman' cast this redirection of the event as resistance to authority in the name of the 'voluntary spirit'.[109] The vicar of Leeds, later bishop of Lichfield, A. S. Reeve, then chair of the Leeds Hospital Sunday Committee, wrote to the *Yorkshire Post* shortly before Hospital Sunday in May 1949 noting the change of object. In his letter he reported that the committee believed this would 'entirely preserve the spirit of Hospital Sunday'.[110] Thus, in line with Filby's characterization of the period as one of 'reformulation', the voluntary spirit was retained by redirecting the funds raised by the services to a variety of causes. In Birmingham, the day became Appeal Sunday, with the first in June 1948 seeing the churches choose the UN Appeal for Children to support instead of the local hospital.[111] In other places, causes such as the British Legion and the British Empire Cancer Campaign were identified as appropriate recipients.[112] For others, closure of the scheme was deemed the simplest response, especially where organizers had faced

---

[104] 'Thanksgiving for Harvest', *Western Times*, 21 October 1949, 8.
[105] C. R. Gill, 'Lord Mayor's Hospital Fund Future', *Western Daily Press*, 15 February 1949, 5.
[106] 'An Anti-Boredom Fund', *Western Daily Press*, 14 March 1949, 1.
[107] 'Sunday Collections for Lord Mayor's Fund', *Western Daily Press*, 9 March 1950, 6.
[108] 'Objection to Leeds Hospital Plan', *Yorkshire Post and Leeds Intelligencer*, 5 January 1949, 4.
[109] Layman, 'Pulpit and Pew', *Liverpool Echo*, 7 February 1949, 5.
[110] A. S. Reeve, 'Hospital Sunday', *Yorkshire Post and Leeds Intelligencer*, 12 May 1949, 2.
[111] 'Churches and the Children Appeal', *Birmingham Daily Gazette*, 5 June 1948, 3.
[112] 'Harleston British Legion', *Diss Express*, 26 November 1948, 6; R. H. Hawkins and R. Angel Wakely, 'Hospital Sunday', *Nottingham Evening Post*, 7 May 1949, 4.

diminishing returns.[113] In some areas, flag days were rededicated to other causes.[114] The Ministry of Health ruling presented an issue for the Manchester and Salford Medical Charities Fund in particular, as with the support of hospital workers it had accumulated funds in the region of £40,000. Following legal advice, the decision was taken not to wind up the fund; the chairman voiced the intention, 'if the law permits', of continuing to support the 'organisations attached to many hospitals'.[115]

It has been mentioned above that the work of friends groups appears to have become more, not less, important following the Ministry of Health circular.[116] These groups present evidence of clear continuities for Christian charity in the period. They were strongly connected to the churches, and hospital chaplains appear to have taken on organizing roles within them.[117] Friends groups participated in Hospital Sunday services, or sometimes organized their own.[118] As with the services prior to the foundation of the NHS, these were used both as a means of raising money and for promotion. At Birmingham, the friends used a Hospital Sunday service as part of a recruitment drive.[119] Friends also made collections at Hospital Sunday services, and, again as with pre-NHS services, these generally raised small amounts, but formed part of a wider fund-raising initiative; proceeds were used to enhance patients' experience, for instance by funding Christmas parties and presents for patients, television sets and contributions to the maintenance of the hospital gardens.[120] The continuing Christian character of these groups can be clearly seen in their chapel appeals, which continued throughout the 1950s.[121] Bevan had promised there would be provision for chapel

---

[113] 'Hospital Sunday Fund closes', *West Sussex County Times*, 19 July 1946, 8; 'Looe to have more Houses', *Cornish Guardian*, 21 July 1949, 6.

[114] 'Worthy Task well done', *Hartlepool Northern Daily Mail*, 26 January 1949, 5; 'Hospitals call in Collecting Boxes', *Worthing Herald*, 14 January 1949, 9.

[115] '£40,000 in Charities Fund: Problem of Disposal', *Manchester Guardian*, 25 January 1949, 8.

[116] 'Those little extra Comforts', *The Cornishman*, 13 January 1949, 4.

[117] 'Hospital Friends', *Kent & Sussex Courier*, 23 October 1953, 4.

[118] 'Hospital Sunday Service', *Warwick and Warwickshire Advertiser*, 15 October 1954, 1.

[119] 'Hospitals need more "Friends"', *Birmingham Daily Post*, 15 September 1956, 22.

[120] 'Over £3,000 in Fund', *Wiltshire Times and Trowbridge Advertiser*, 4 February 1956, 7.

[121] 'Hospital Chapel Appeal', *West Sussex Gazette*, 2 December 1954, 5; 'Hospital Chapel used First Time', *Hampshire Telegraph*, 25 October 1957, 8.

space in NHS hospitals.[122] However, as capital spending was limited before 1962, friends groups ensured that the provision of chapels was supported.[123] Services in the chapels held by these groups and chaplains' sermons on Hospital Sundays in local churches further linked these groups inside and outside the hospital.[124]

Any assessment of the success of those hoping to keep Hospital Sunday alive after 1949 is somewhat confused by moves to revive the practice. In some places, the tradition seems simply to have survived and we might see arguments for revival more as part of a strategy to increase public support for the day.[125] Hospital boards themselves seem to have been keen on a revival, and the National Association of Hospital Management Committees enquired into this possibility.[126] As evidence of 'reformulation rather than retreat', services now had the primary purpose of bringing medical professionals into the churches and enabling congregations to support their work through prayer and thanksgiving. First mooted in the Church Assembly in 1951, a revival was supported corporately by the Church of England, with the idea of a national agreed date of St Luke's Tide (the period around 18 October) receiving considerable support.[127]

The adoption of St Luke's Tide as Hospital Sunday appears to have been somewhat patchy, but the date does seem to have become established in some areas. St John's, Sparkhill, in Birmingham, for instance, appears to have held a Hospital Sunday service each year in October.[128] Such services maintained many features of previous practice. They sometimes took the form of a united ecumenical service, included addresses from medical professionals, and were attended by members of local voluntary aid societies and sometimes also by members of the municipal authorities.[129] However, the day does not appear to have been widely kept. In 1959, A. S. Reeve, now bishop of Lichfield and chairman of the Council of Healing,

[122] 'Chaplains for Hospitals: Bevan's Pledge', *Gloucester Citizen*, 14 May 1948, 4
[123] 'Hospital Helpers want to build a Chapel', *Harrow Observer*, 14 May 1959, 7.
[124] 'League's new Plans inside and outside Torbay Hospital', *Torbay Express and South Devon Echo*, 14 December 1961, 7; 'Shoreham', *West Sussex Gazette*, 22 October 1953, 11.
[125] For another instance, see 'Hospital Sunday', *Bucks Herald*, 19 May 1950, 10.
[126] 'Hospital Sunday may be revived', *Worthing Herald*, 14 September 1951, 2.
[127] An Anglican Correspondent, 'Church adopts Silent Minute', *Manchester Guardian*, 15 November 1951, 5; 'Convocation of Canterbury', *The Times*, 16 October 1952, 3.
[128] 'Hospital Sunday Services', *Birmingham Daily Post*, 22 October 1956, 24.
[129] 'Hospital Sunday Services in Birmingham', *Birmingham Daily Post*, 16 October 1961, 14; 'Hospital Sunday at Burntwood and Hammerwich', *Lichfield Mercury*, 19 May 1961, 10.

was still calling for Hospital Sunday to be revived.[130] Renewing this call in the House of Lords in 1961, Reeve continued to fly the flag for voluntarism and to support a connection between the churches and the hospitals.[131] At a Hospital Sunday service at West Bromwich in 1962, he outlined the many ways in which Christians could continue to support non-medical care in local hospitals, including running the hospital library trolley service, reading to the patients and visiting those without friends or family nearby.[132] Members of the clergy and the Church of England's hierarchy clearly continued to work to promote voluntary action in this period.

Long after the Ministry of Health's apparent ban, Hospital Sunday continued to be celebrated in many places. Thirty years after the foundation of the NHS, Radio 4's 'Morning Service' of 15 October 1978 broadcast Walsall Parish Church's Hospital Sunday service.[133] In this way, Christians continued to show their support for the health service. This support included collections for hospital comforts and gifts in kind.[134] Moreover, they continued to volunteer through Hospital Leagues of Friends. Through the work of the chaplains, these groups linked the state with voluntarism in line with Loss's 'institutional afterlife'. Hospital Sunday also bequeathed institutional structures to medical charity. The Metropolitan Hospital Sunday Fund continued its work and the lord mayor continued to write letters to *The Times* encouraging congregations to participate.[135] As Filby noted, in the latter part of the twentieth century there was a process of rebranding such organizations.[136] Now named London Catalyst, the fund remains in operation, and retains strong links to faith groups.[137]

[130] 'Bishop's Plea for Return of Hospital Sunday', *Birmingham Daily Post*, 18 September 1959, 23.
[131] HL Deb, 26 April 1961 (vol. 230, 896–902).
[132] '"Patients still need Voluntary Aid"', *Birmingham Daily Post*, 15 October 1962, 26.
[133] 'Morning Service', *Radio Times*, issue 2866 (14 October 1978), online at: <https://genome.ch.bbc.co.uk/f40b0a6a9221f150053237546101b2fb>, accessed 30 November 2021.
[134] 'Barton', *Luton News and Bedfordshire Chronicle*, 22 October 1953, 11.
[135] Leslie Boyce, 'Work of Almoners', *The Times*, 6 December 1952, 7.
[136] Filby, 'Faith, Charity and Citizenship', 137–8.
[137] London Catalyst, *Trustees' Report and Annual Accounts* (London, 2019), 3–5.

CONCLUSION

However it is dated, the theme of voluntarism's decline appears to be an attractive one. As McCarthy noted, until recently historians thought of the period between the two world wars as 'mark[ing] an era of associational decline'.[138] Nevertheless, as is clear in relation to Hospital Sunday and other aspects of medical charity, the voluntary impulse remained strong even in the era of the welfare state. Christians set out to defend voluntarism in medical care and when one avenue was closed to them, they looked to support such endeavours in other ways. Of course, their involvement was modulated and even attenuated by these changes. As Grimley puts it, on the definition provided by the likes of Neville Figgis, organizations such as tenants' associations could not be counted as 'free associations, as they existed only in reference to the state'.[139] In this strict sense, Hospital Leagues of Friends were not 'free' either. However, they continued to be vehicles through which Christians 'could serve Christ' through the 1950s and into the 1960s. The extent to which these groups remained Christian in membership requires more research, but Cheshire and Merseyside hospital friends were still holding an annual Hospital Sunday at Liverpool Cathedral in 1970.[140]

Whilst the relevance of Christian charity to medical care was eroded by state funding, Christians sought to remain relevant in other ways, and they did so even as charity appeared to become more secular into the later twentieth century.[141] Medical professionals, congregations and members of the clergy continued to see voluntarism as lending a softening element to state-run medical care long after the NHS had come into operation.[142] In this sense we can see the ongoing importance of religion to welfare, and to wider society, not only in the long 1950s, but long after. Whilst Christians may not have 'captured the welfare state' outright, elements of Christian

[138] McCarthy, 'Associational Voluntarism', 49.
[139] Grimley, *Citizenship*, 217.
[140] 'Looking Around', *Liverpool Echo*, 11 April 1970, 6.
[141] Filby, 'Faith, Charity and Citizenship', 138.
[142] 'Human Element in Hospitals', *Warwick and Warwickshire Advertiser*, 2 November 1956, 1.

charity were supported by its structures, and its structures were also to some extent permeable to charitable impulses. Whilst charities may not have remained overtly Christian in character throughout the century, a range of activities and organizations continued to support the connection between Christians and medical charity. The voluntary spirit lived on.

From Plato to Pentecostalism: Sickness and Deliverance in the Theology of Derek Prince

Brian Stanley*

University of Edinburgh

This article analyses the intellectual sources and global influence of the demonology of Derek Prince (1915–2003), a former philosophy fellow of King's College, Cambridge, who, after his move to the United States in 1963, became a globally influential Pentecostal teacher and author. It argues that his academic expertise in the philosophy of Plato shaped his understanding of the invisible realm of spiritual powers and its impact on the health and material well-being of Christians. Prince's teaching on ancestral curses and the vulnerability of Christians to demonization has been widely received in Africa and other parts of the non-Western world, appearing to provide answers to endemic problems of chronic sickness and impoverishment.

THE RAPPROCHEMENT OF HEALING AND SALVATION

As this article focuses on a figure who will be unfamiliar to many readers of Studies in Church History, it will be appropriate to begin by painting on a broader canvas.[1] Two general and interrelated points need to be made that may be helpful in placing Derek Prince in the context of this volume's theme of the Church, sickness and healing.

The first is to suggest that the evidence points to a tenacious persistence in much of the globe of what many Westerners might describe as pre-Enlightenment cosmological understandings of disease and its remedies, notwithstanding the concurrent adoption

* 13 Carlingnose View, North Queensferry, Inverkeithing, Fife, KY11 1EZ. E-mail: brian.stanley@ed.ac.uk.

[1] This article represents an expansion and development of material first published in my *Christianity in the Twentieth Century: A World History* (Princeton, NJ, 2018), 296–304. I am grateful to the provost and fellows of King's College, Cambridge, for granting me access to the minute books of the Cambridge Apostles and to the fellowship dissertation of Derek Prince, and to Peter Monteith, former assistant archivist of King's College, for his assistance. I also express my gratitude to Allan Anderson, Paul Grant and the anonymous peer reviewers for helpful comments on an earlier draft of this article.

Studies in Church History 58 (2022), 394–414   © The Author(s), 2022. Published by Cambridge University Press on behalf of Ecclesiastical History Society
doi: 10.1017/stc.2022.19

of many aspects of technological modernity. Such persistence is as evident among populations that have become substantially Christian as among those that have not. It also co-exists with the dissemination throughout the globe of a professional ethos of healthcare, founded on biomedicine, scientific techniques of surgery and increasingly tight state regulation of medical practitioners. What began in Europe has spread throughout the rest of the globe, a process in which Christian medical missions played a key role between the late nineteenth century and the post-independence era, when many (though not all) mission hospitals were handed over to the health services of the newly independent states. However, it is a fallacy to suppose that the global diffusion of Western scientific medicine has simply dissolved indigenous conceptions of sickness, healing and their relationship to spiritual power. Walima Kalusa has pointed out that in mid-twentieth-century Zambia, as indeed in Africa generally, the business of delivering medical treatment through mission hospitals and a host of clinics lay largely in the hands of African medical auxiliaries.[2] These African personnel faced the challenge of integrating the new biomedicine with traditional understandings of disease and healing. Moreover, possessing limited facility in English or other colonial languages themselves, they had to resort to indigenous linguistic terms to describe disease, diagnosis and medicine. The result was a form of inculturation of Western medical science which is, in many ways, analogous to the inculturation of Christianity in multiple indigenous forms. Missionary medicine, concludes Kalusa, 'thus came to be comprehended as if it was a variation of African medicine and not a superior system of healing'.[3] Kalusa's conclusion reinforces an argument first made by Terence Ranger in his presidential address to the Ecclesiastical History Society in 1981, when he contended that conversion to Christianity in modern Africa did not move people out of a 'rural, magical, pre-scientific, archaic universe into an urban, rational, scientific and modern one'. Rather, Christianity effected a shift of balance within an African spiritual

---

[2] Walima T. Kalusa, 'Language, Medical Auxiliaries, and the Re-interpretation of Missionary Medicine in Colonial Mwinilunga, Zambia, 1922–51', *Journal of Eastern African Studies* 1 (2007), 57–78.
[3] Ibid. 74.

universe, while reinforcing the continuing reality of a cosmos permeated by unseen spiritual powers.[4] The second, and closely associated, general observation is to suggest that, when viewed in a global perspective, the long, slow separation of the business of healing from the ecclesiastical sphere that was apparent between the Reformation and the nineteenth century now shows signs of going into reverse owing to the extraordinary global explosion of Pentecostal Christianities.[5] If at least some varieties of sickness are once again to be understood as having their roots in malevolence or spiritual conflict, then Christianity, if accepted as the ultimate source of spiritual power, can be expected to bring its superior resources to bear on those afflictions of body and mind that appear to defy obvious explanation. As Ranger put it, what many African peoples describe as 'Diseases of God' – those everyday ailments that form an inevitable part of the human condition – can be dealt with by natural remedies, whether these are traditional herbal ones or modern drugs. The problem lies rather with the 'Diseases of Man', those more deeply rooted maladies that point to the harmful irruption of the invisible realm into the life of the sufferer, as the result of behaviour of a fundamentally antisocial or malign character, whether by some ancestor in the past, or an enemy, or even oneself in the present.[6] For many Christians in the non-Western world today, it is, paradoxically, such 'Diseases of Man' that call for the powerful salvific intervention of the divine, through the charismatic ministrations of the man, or occasionally the woman, of God. The realms of healing and salvation, which the course of European history and theology has forced asunder, are thus being drawn back into a closer relationship that mirrors the world of the gospels, in which a mere choice of how to translate the Greek word *sōzō* determines whether someone is described as having been either 'healed' or

---

[4] Terence Ranger, 'Medical Science and Pentecost: The Dilemma of Anglicanism in Africa', in W. J. Sheils, ed., *The Church and Healing*, SCH 19 (Oxford, 1982), 333–65, at 336, 337. For a more recent exposition of the balance between continuity and discontinuity in the relationship between African indigenous cosmologies and Pentecostal Christianity, see Allan Heaton Anderson, *Spirit-Filled World: Religious Dis/Continuity in African Pentecostalism* (Cham, 2018).

[5] On the long process of separation, Keith Thomas, *Religion and the Decline of Magic* (London, 1971), remains unsurpassed.

[6] Ranger, 'Medical Science and Pentecost', 339.

'saved' by Christ.[7] It is precisely this dimension of Christianity that the exploding Pentecostal Christianities of the southern hemisphere have rediscovered and accentuated to a degree that presents the world of scholarship, framed as it is by Enlightenment assumptions about the irrationality of beliefs in invisible spiritual forces, with something of a problem.

Joel Cabrita has published an important study of the Scottish émigré to Australia and then the United States, John Alexander Dowie (1847–1907), and the international Zionist movement of which he was the progenitor. Cabrita makes a persuasive case that the efflorescence of movements of divine healing in both American and African contexts in the early twentieth century should be interpreted as the product of a single transnational evangelical movement, coursing in various directions through the veins of an increasingly interconnected global Christian body politic. Such movements, she insists, cannot be adequately explained in monochromatic terms, either as the transmission of a distinctively American narrative to Africa, or by the converse claim that African prophet healing movements simply represent the absorption by a Westernized Christianity of typically African indigenous modes of religious expression.[8] A parallel bifurcation in the scholarship between America-centric and Africa-centric perspectives is evident in discussion of the explosion of neo-Pentecostal Christianity in Africa since the 1980s. Should the rapid dissemination of the prosperity gospel and deliverance movements (sometimes loosely termed 'faith healing' movements) in this period be viewed as the product of the deepening dependence of African Christianity on American theological and financial resources, as Paul Gifford suggests (although he rightly stresses that this is not to deny African religious creativity)?[9] Or should they be given a more favourable endorsement as evidence of the Africanization of Western Christian traditions that failed to

---

[7] For example, Mark 5: 34; Luke 8: 48; 17: 19; 18: 42; see Paul Germond and Sepetla Molapo, 'In Search of Bophelo in a Time of AIDS: Seeking a Coherence of Economies of Health and Economies of Salvation', *Journal of Theology for Southern Africa* 126 (2006), 27–47, at 42–3.
[8] Joel Cabrita, *The People's Zion: Southern Africa, the United States, and a Transatlantic Faith-Healing Movement* (Cambridge, MA, 2018), 4–5.
[9] Paul Gifford, *African Christianity: Its Public Role* (London, 1998), 44–7, 308–25; idem, *Ghana's New Christianity: Pentecostalism in a Globalising African Economy* (London, 2004), 197–8.

take bodily well-being seriously, as most African scholars argue?[10] Both contentions have their merits, but are problematic if taken in isolation.

DEREK PRINCE, TRANSNATIONAL APOSTLE OF HEALING AND DELIVERANCE

This article examines a Western Pentecostal teacher, Derek Prince (1915–2003), who provides a more recent parallel to Dowie as a pivotal figure located at the hub of a transnational web of healing and deliverance ministry. Like Dowie, he was British, contrary to the characteristic assumption of some recent commentators that he must have been American.[11] Nevertheless, his most influential ministry, like Dowie's, was exercised from the United States, even though its content was probably most extensively disseminated in Africa. Yet, as with Dowie again, his distinctive teaching cannot be dismissed as merely representative of the eccentric margins of popular American Protestantism; it owed a profound debt to his own intellectual formation in the classical Western philosophical tradition in Cambridge, although a further debt to exposure to African varieties of spiritual experience cannot be ruled out. His teaching, like Dowie's, circulated internationally, but in Prince's case the media of transmission were not merely printed, but also reflected the enhanced possibilities of global interconnection afforded by the modern world.

Neo-Pentecostal deliverance and healing ministry in modern Africa, like its close partner the prosperity gospel, coheres with indigenous understandings of the reality of the spirit world, while also being dependent on external influences. Its rapid diffusion was assisted by technological innovation, air travel, television and video communication, and, above all, by the invention in 1962 of the compact audio cassette tape, a medium that enabled the global circulation, at very low cost, of recorded messages by popular charismatic preachers. Prince's biographer, Stephen Mansfield, aptly observes that 'the

[10] For example, Ogbu Kalu, *African Pentecostalism: An Introduction* (Oxford, 2008).
[11] For example, Claudia Währisch-Oblau, 'Material Salvation: Healing, Deliverance, and "Breakthrough", in African Migrant Churches in Germany', in Candy Gunther Brown, ed., *Global Pentecostal and Charismatic Healing* (Oxford, 2011), 61–80, at 66.

cassette tape defined Charismatic culture. The faithful took tapes the way their secular counterparts took medicine.'[12]

Whereas most of the Pentecostal preachers whose messages circulated on audio cassettes in Africa from the 1980s were American, Derek Prince, perhaps the most influential of all, was British, although he had resided in the United States since 1963. Prince was not simply British; he hailed from the upper echelons of English society. Born in Bangalore in 1915 to a British army family, he was baptized in St John's Church, Bangalore, at that time largely an expatriate Anglican congregation. Educated at Eton College and King's College, Cambridge, he was elected a fellow of King's in philosophy in March 1940. At this point, Prince was very far from being a practising Christian. However, one of his best friends from his undergraduate days was John Earle Raven, later the author of an influential introduction to Plato's thought, as well as a keen amateur botanist.[13] Raven was the only son of Charles Raven, Regius Professor of Divinity at Cambridge from 1932, a leading liberal evangelical and notable writer on science and religion. Prince regularly visited the Raven home, and in 1939 accompanied the family on a botanical summer holiday to Galway. Charles Raven's influence was probably responsible for turning Prince into a pacifist. Whether he also subconsciously imbibed elements of Raven's firm theological conviction that what the church needed more than anything else was to rediscover the experiential power of the Holy Spirit is an intriguing question; Prince's biographer suggests that Raven was the predominant influence on Prince's religious views in the 1930s, but associates the influence more with a rationalistic modernism.[14] Prince was certainly deemed sufficiently ungodly to merit election in October 1938 as a member of the secret, and rather seedy, debating society, the Cambridge Apostles; his fellow members included those

[12] Stephen Mansfield, *Derek Prince: A Biography* (Baldock, 2005), 203–4. Although a popular biography rather than an academic one, it is a very perceptive study.
[13] J. E. Raven, *Plato's Thought in the Making: A Study of the Development of His Metaphysics* (Cambridge, 1965).
[14] Mansfield, *Derek Prince*, 60. On Raven's enthusiasm for the Spirit, see Ian M. Randall, 'Evangelical Spirituality, Science and Mission: A Study of Charles Raven (1885–1964), Regius Professor of Divinity, Cambridge University', *Anglican and Episcopal History* 84 (2015), 20–48.

who would later become notorious for their communist allegiance, Guy Burgess and Anthony Blunt.[15]

Prince refused to serve in a combat role during the Second World War, appealing to none other than Plato for support when he appeared before the tribunal for conscientious objectors.[16] He entered the Royal Army Medical Corps in a non-combatant capacity. In April 1941, while undergoing training with the Corps near Scarborough, Prince came into contact with Pentecostals. Following attendance at an Assemblies of God meeting, he was converted to evangelical Christianity and shortly afterwards was 'baptized in the Spirit' and began to speak in tongues.[17] Although he remained a fellow of King's until 1949, his life was now set in a new direction. In 1974 Prince would inform an academic researcher, 'I know what it costs to be a pentecostal; the pentecostal movement was the child of poverty and rejection'.[18] Prince was far from being a child of poverty himself, but his remark may suggest that his new-found religious allegiance earned this Cambridge philosopher the cold shoulder from many of his former friends and academic associates.

During his war service in Egypt and the Sudan, Prince spent two periods of leave in Palestine. On his first visit in 1942 he was baptized as an adult in the river Jordan – there is remarkably good precedent – by an Assemblies of God missionary. On his second visit, in 1946, he married Lydia Christensen, a Danish Pentecostal missionary nearly twice his age.[19] He witnessed first-hand the birth of the state of Israel. Prince remained a fervent and influential Christian Zionist until his death in 2003. In fact, he spent long periods during his final years living in Jerusalem, worshipping in the Old City at Christ Church, the church established in 1842 by Michael Solomon Alexander, former Jewish rabbi and the first holder of the Anglican-Lutheran Jerusalem bishopric.[20] In 1948 the Princes left Israel and settled in West London, where, from 1949, Derek began

---

[15] Cambridge, King's College Archives, Minute Books of the Cambridge Apostles, volume 17, 1928–47, minutes for 16 October, 23 October and 13 November 1938.

[16] Mansfield, *Derek Prince*, 77.

[17] Ibid. 83–94.

[18] David Edwin Harrell Jr, *All Things Are Possible: The Healing and Charismatic Revivals in Modern America* (Bloomington, IN, 1975), 237, cf. 245.

[19] Mansfield, *Derek Prince*, 110, 125–41.

[20] Ibid. 273.

to assemble a Pentecostal fellowship meeting in his own home at Westbourne Grove; most of the attendees were Jamaicans.[21]

In January 1957 Derek and Lydia were sent as Assemblies of God missionaries to Kisumu in western Kenya, where Prince became principal of the Assemblies of God's Nyang'ori Teacher Training Centre. Arriving in the colony in the aftermath of the Mau Mau anticolonial movement, he became convinced that 'powerful satanic agents and influences' were at work in Kenya, seeking to bring 'hatred, disorder, and bloodshed'.[22] This evaluation of Mau Mau as an explicitly diabolical eruption of 'savagery' and 'pagan witchcraft' directed against Christianity was not some peculiar Pentecostal eccentricity. It was shared by many, perhaps most, of the Anglican missionaries of the Church Missionary Society working in central Kenya.[23] From his location in western Kenya, Prince would have had no first-hand contact with the final stages of Mau Mau, which was a Gikuyu movement that was absent from western Kenya. Nevertheless, it seems likely that Prince's missionary experience in Kenya gave him a newly vivid awareness of the tangible reality of evil forces, though this can be no more than a conjecture. At Kisumu he became involved in healing and deliverance ministry, but mainly in the context of pioneer evangelism. It should be noted that his distinctive teaching that even Spirit-filled Christians might need deliverance from demonic infestation came later, in a North American rather than an African context. It was consequent upon his relocation, first to Vancouver in 1962, where he taught at Western Pentecostal Bible College; then to Minneapolis, where he conducted a teaching ministry in a Pentecostal church pastored by a friend; and finally, in September 1963, to Seattle.

As pastor of Broadway Tabernacle in Seattle in 1963–4, Prince reached the conclusion that some of the most disturbing problems in the congregation's life were the result of 'demonization' of bona fide church members. He reached the conclusion that 'while the

---

[21] Ibid. 174.
[22] Ibid. 191.
[23] See T. F. C. Bewes, *Kikuyu Conflict: Mau Mau and Christian Witness* (London, 1953), 8–9, 43, 52, 54; John Casson, 'Missionaries, Mau Mau and the Christian Frontier', in Pieter N. Holtrop and Hugh McLeod, eds, *Missions and Missionaries*, SCH Subsidia 13 (Woodbridge, 2000), 200–15, at 203.

Spirit of God might live in the spirit of a born-again man, the man's body and soul could still be a haunt of demons'.[24] As a Greek scholar, Prince adhered strictly to New Testament usage in preferring the term 'demonization' to 'possession'. Nevertheless, like many Pentecostals, Prince adhered to a trichotomous anthropology, drawing a sharp distinction between the human spirit (*pneuma*) and soul (*psyche*). He held that while the *pneuma* of a Spirit-filled Christian was inviolable by demonic forces, the *psyche* was not.

Prince's emphasis that even Spirit-filled Christians might be demonized marked a subtle but significant departure from classical Pentecostal teaching. J. A. Dowie had taught that sickness was fundamentally the 'foul offspring of its father, Satan, and its mother Sin'. It followed that the atoning work of Christ included delivering the sinner from sickness as the work of the devil.[25] For the early Zionists and the Pentecostals who followed in their wake, the work of healing in the power of the Spirit necessarily involved contestation with evil forces. However, the majority of Pentecostals throughout the first half of the twentieth century taught that, although truly 'born-again' and Spirit-baptized Christians may still be liable to external torment by demonic forces, they could not become indwelt by demons, for their bodies were the temple of the Holy Spirit and hence, in principle, inviolable. In what may seem a fine and exegetically dubious distinction, they were deemed to be still subject to *oppression*, but not *possession*. The largest white American Pentecostal denomination, the Assemblies of God, formed in 1914, was consistent in teaching that born-again believers cannot be demon possessed.[26] Similarly in West Africa, the appeal of such prophet figures as William Wadé Harris in the Ivory and Gold Coast, or Joseph Babalola in Nigeria, was that they promised those who came to faith in Christ could rest secure in the knowledge that thenceforth they

---

[24] Mansfield, *Derek Prince*, 209.

[25] Gordon Lindsay, *The Life of John Alexander Dowie whose Trials, Tragedies, and Triumphs are the Most Fascinating Object Lesson of Christian History* (n.pl., 1951), 22–5; Philip L. Cook, *Zion City, Illinois: Twentieth-Century Utopia* (Syracuse, NY, 1996), 8.

[26] L. G. McClung Jr, 'Exorcism', in Stanley M. Burgess and Eduard M. van der Maas, eds, *The New International Dictionary of Pentecostal and Charismatic Movements* (Grand Rapids, MI, 2002), 624–8, at 626. For accounts of early American Pentecostals being tormented by demons, see Grant Wacker, *Heaven Below: Early Pentecostals and American Culture* (Cambridge, MA, 2001), 91–2. See also James Robinson, *Divine Healing: The Years of Expansion, 1906–1930* (Eugene, OR, 2014), 146.

would be protected from the power of evil forces. Jesus the healer was also the victor and protector. Thus, converts could with confidence burn their traditional objects of spiritual power ('fetishes') and entrust themselves to the all-surpassing power of God, who would surely protect them from the manifold illnesses and other misfortunes believed to be caused by malign powers.[27]

In Seattle Prince began to question the permanence of the spiritual protection afforded by submission to the lordship of Christ, and commenced his distinctive ministry that employed detailed questionnaires to identify which Christians were indwelt by which demons, or laboured under which specific curses, as a prelude to their deliverance and bodily or inner healing.[28] Subsequently he moved the base of his ministry to Chicago, and then to Fort Lauderdale, Florida, where he became one of a group of charismatic teachers known internationally as 'the Fort Lauderdale Five'.[29] Prince's demonology, then, took its fully developed and distinctive shape in North America, rather than in Africa. The next section will examine the reach of his influence, which, by contrast, extended far beyond the Western world.

THE CHANNELS OF PRINCE'S INFLUENCE

Unlike so many later advocates of deliverance ministry, Prince did not wield his influence primarily through large public crusades or mass healing meetings; David Harrell comments that he was 'never a revivalist', but rather a lecturer and teacher whose refined Cambridge accent, 'education and studious manner always set him somewhat apart' from the Pentecostal mainstream.[30] A prolific popular writer, Prince had published more than forty books by 1984; by his death in 2003, the total had reached over eighty.[31] From 1979 he broadcast an American daily radio programme, *Today with Derek Prince*, which was eventually aired internationally in thirteen languages.

[27] I have argued this case in *Christianity in the Twentieth Century*, 297–8.
[28] Harrell, *All Things are Possible*, 185.
[29] The 'Fort Lauderdale Five' comprised Prince, Don Basham, Bob Mumford, Charles Simpson and Ern Baxter. The group gave particular emphasis to structures of 'shepherding' believers, which aroused controversy on account of their authoritarian tendencies.
[30] Harrell, *All Things Are Possible*, 182, 184–5.
[31] Derek Prince, *Life's Bitter Pool* (Harpenden, 1984), 43; 'About Derek Prince', online at: <https://www.derekprince.org/Groups/1000103610/DPM_USA/About/About_Derek_Prince/About_Derek_Prince.aspx>, accessed 18 January 2021.

Nonetheless, his global influence appears to have been most extensively mediated through the international cassette and book ministry he established late in 1983.[32] It led to a visit to Ghana in 1987, when he was instrumental in securing widespread acceptance for deliverance ministry at a time when it was still controversial, even within Pentecostal circles there.[33] Opoku Onyinah describes Prince as 'the "mentor" of this kind of ministry in Ghana'.[34] He was particularly influential on both Owusu Tabiri, who played a prominent role in developing Ghana's 'prayer camps' (specializing in spiritual warfare) in the early 1990s, and Aaron Vuha of the Evangelical Presbyterian Church.[35]

Prince's influence extended beyond Protestant circles in the United States and reached a broad spectrum of Christians in all continents.[36] Several prominent Roman Catholics acknowledge a specific debt to his teaching. They include Emmanuel Milingo, the controversial archbishop of Lusaka from 1969 to 1983, who was removed from his post by the Vatican because of his alleged encouragement of 'credulity which explains all psycho-physical ills as due to the influence of the devil';[37] later, in 2006, Milingo was excommunicated after his consecration of bishops without papal approval. Other Catholics deeply influenced by Prince include the Nigerian priest and popular author, Stephen Uche Njoku,[38] and the American Dominican pioneer of Catholic charismatic renewal, Francis MacNutt (1925–2020).[39] Prince's relationship with Cardinal Léon-Joseph Suenens of Belgium, the leading European Catholic advocate

---

[32] Prince's obituary in *King's College Cambridge Annual Report* (Cambridge, 2004), 50, notes the particular significance of audio cassettes for the dissemination of his teaching.
[33] Gifford, *African Christianity*, 100, 346–7.
[34] Opoku Onyinah, *Pentecostal Exorcism: Witchcraft and Demonology in Ghana* (Blandford Forum, 2012), 172.
[35] Gifford, *Ghana's New Christianity*, 89; see also Emmanuel Kingsley Larbi, *Pentecostalism: The Eddies of Ghanaian Christianity* (Accra, 2001), 393.
[36] Thomas J. Csordas, *The Sacred Self: A Cultural Phenomenology of Charismatic Healing* (Berkeley, CA, 1994), 41, notes that Prince was one of those primarily responsible for introducing deliverance ministry to American Catholics.
[37] *The Tablet*, 20 April 1996, 525, cited in Gifford, *African Christianity*, 330; see also ibid. 227.
[38] Paul Gifford, *Christianity, Development and Modernity in Africa* (London, 2015), 118–19.
[39] James M. Collins, *Exorcism and Deliverance Ministry in the Twentieth Century: An Analysis of the Practice and Theology of Exorcism in Modern Western Christianity* (Milton Keynes, 2009), 57, 61, 63.

of charismatic renewal, and one of the moderators of the Second Vatican Council, was more ambiguous. On Pentecost Sunday 1977, Prince, along with the other members of the 'Fort Lauderdale Five', was invited to accompany Suenens on a pilgrimage from Mechelen [Malines] to Jerusalem, via Rome and Assisi, to celebrate the fiftieth anniversary of Suenens's ordination. Prince and the other pilgrims presented Suenens with a water goblet as a mark of the friendship formed in the course of the pilgrimage.[40] However, this did not prevent Suenens in a later publication from criticizing Prince (without actually naming him) as a 'Master of Demonology' who was guilty of 'flagrant' exaggerations in attributing 'most, if not all, physical and psychiatric illnesses to demonic influences'.[41] Suenens's accusation had considerable validity. The following section of this article will demonstrate that Prince was prepared to view demonic infestation as the potential cause of a long list of physical and mental afflictions.

Some of the most globally popular charismatic Protestant authors on deliverance ministry trace their understanding of demonization and its remedy in greater or lesser measure to Prince. They include the New Zealand Anglican Bill Subritzky, the British founder of Ellel Ministries Peter Horrobin, and the Southern Baptists Frank and Ida Mae Hammond, authors of the intriguingly titled pastoral handbook, *Pigs in the Parlor: A Practical Guide to Deliverance*, which claims over one million copies sold worldwide.[42] In contrast, Prince himself never produced a full practical guide to techniques of deliverance. The Hammonds' handbook was written at his suggestion, and followed his teaching closely, reproducing verbatim the prayer that Prince recommended for use when conducting an exorcism.[43] It coached deliverance practitioners on how to purge the afflicted of indwelling demons by vomiting them up, a practice

---

[40] Léon-Joseph Suenens, *Memories and Hopes* (Dublin, 1992), 313–15. The Protestant charismatics appear to have asked Suenens for permission to join his pilgrimage, and he agreed. See also Mansfield, *Derek Prince*, 238.

[41] Léon-Joseph Suenens, *Renewal and the Powers of Darkness* (London, 1983), 62.

[42] Collins, *Exorcism and Deliverance Ministry*, 64–5, 87–90; Frank Hammond and Ida Mae Hammond, *Pigs in the Parlor: A Practical Guide to Deliverance* (Kirkwood, MO, 1973).

[43] Hammond, *Pigs in the Parlor*, 154–5. Csordas, *The Sacred Self*, 181–4, reproduces in full the Hammonds' table of types of demonic infestation from *Pigs in the Parlor*, which he terms 'the most comprehensive demonology formulated by practitioners of deliverance' (ibid. 181), but does not trace the classification to its source in Prince.

that bears close parallels with some accounts of exorcism in early modern Europe.[44]

PRINCE, WITTGENSTEIN AND PLATO

Where did Prince's distinctive demonology come from? His experience in Kenya was clearly important in causing him to adopt a spiritualized interpretation of Africa's political problems, but it did not lead him to the conclusion that Christians typically needed deliverance ministry. At least part of the answer lies in Prince's early intellectual formation. At Cambridge he became fascinated with Plato's philosophy, and especially Socrates's insistence in the *Phaedo* that all material things were transitory.[45] Under the influence of Ludwig Wittgenstein, who taught him, Prince also developed an interest in the philosophy of language. As a research student he gave a paper to the Moral Science Club on 16 February 1939 on 'The Use of a Word', part of which Wittgenstein, who had been elected to the Cambridge chair of philosophy a few days previously, 'attacked vigorously'.[46] Prince's paper appears to have stimulated Wittgenstein to pursue the topic further a week later when he himself gave a paper on 'Philosophy' to the Club; the minutes record Prince as questioning Wittgenstein's argument. It appears that Wittgenstein and Prince disagreed quite fundamentally on whether Plato's endeavour to anchor the meaning of ideas in ultimate timeless definitions or 'forms' could be reconciled with Wittgenstein's insistence that language could never yield a coherent or stable account of meaning.[47] While

---

[44] Ibid. 222. For an account of the use of *Pigs in the Parlor* as a deliverance manual in an African American storefront church in Durham, NC, with the use of purging by vomiting, see Catherine Bowler, 'Blessed Bodies: Healing within the African American Faith Movement', in Brown, ed., *Global Pentecostal and Charismatic Healing*, 81–105, at 90. For vomiting as a sign of dispossession in early modern exorcisms, see Philip C. Almond, *Demonic Possession and Exorcism in Early Modern England: Contemporary Texts and their Cultural Contexts* (Cambridge, 2004), 151, 268; Jane P. Davidson, *Early Modern Supernatural: The Dark Side of European Culture, 1400–1700* (Santa Barbara, CA, 2012), 112.

[45] Prince's popular biographer, Stephen Mansfield, is the only commentator who has noted the marked Platonic influence on Prince's cosmology; see his *Derek Prince*, 272.

[46] Brian McGuinness, ed., *Wittgenstein in Cambridge: Letters and Documents 1911–1951* (Oxford, 2008), 294; Theodore Redpath, *Ludwig Wittgenstein: A Student's Memoir* (London, 1990), 80, 82.

[47] McGuinness, ed., *Wittgenstein in Cambridge*, 295; Redpath, *Ludwig Wittgenstein*, 82–3; Mansfield, *Derek Prince*, 74.

self-confessedly influenced by Wittgenstein, Prince remained a more convinced Platonist than his teacher could ever be. Stephen Mansfield rightly notes that, 'Once he became a Christian, [Prince] brought both the scholar's skill and the Platonist's mysticism, perhaps even dualism, to his understanding of Scripture. Thus, he loved language but kept his eye on its spiritual power.'[48] As a Pentecostal practitioner of deliverance in later years, Prince would rely on the capacity of words, invoking the power of the name of Jesus to do precisely what they promised: there was an exact correspondence between the human words and the eternal divine reality that they represented.

In spite of his variance from his teacher on the question of the meaning of words, Prince's fellowship dissertation submitted to King's College in 1940 on 'The Evolution of Plato's Philosophical Method' acknowledged his debt to Wittgenstein three times.[49] It was an attempt to apply the philosophy of language to Plato's analysis and use of Socrates's philosophical method. The dissertation argued for a comprehensive application to all reality of Plato's theory of forms. He cited the judgement of the idealist philosopher A. E. Taylor that, according to Plato's Socrates, philosophy was concerned with those matters that are 'invisible, not merely because our eyes are defective or the bodies we see always composite, but because their nature is spiritual and can only be spiritually discerned'. He reproduced Taylor's judgement that 'The great and imperishable thought of the *Phaedo* is that there are "reals", and those are the most important of all, which are *immaterial*.'[50] However, Prince argued that it was not sufficient to apply the theory, as Taylor did, only to moral qualities such as the beautiful; rather, since 'all words are on the same footing', we should not flinch from applying the principle to 'all Forms without exception'.[51]

What has all this to do with African neo-Pentecostalism? What has Athens to do with Accra? The answer is that Prince's later teaching on deliverance reproduces the language of Plato's *Phaedo* almost verbatim. The *Phaedo* proclaimed a disjunction between two spheres of existence, the changing world of the visible and 'the unchanging

---

[48] Mansfield, *Derek Prince*, 274.
[49] Cambridge, King's College Archives, KCAC/4/11/1, P. D. V. Prince, 'The Evolution of Plato's Philosophical Method' (Fellowship dissertation, n.d. [1940]), 7, 12, 130.
[50] Ibid. 60; citing A. E. Taylor, *Varia Socratica*, first series (Oxford, 1911), 244 (Taylor's italics).
[51] Prince, 'Evolution of Plato's Philosophical Method', 60–1.

things you can only perceive with the mind'.[52] Similarly, Prince, in
one of his most substantial books, *Blessing or Curse: You can Choose*,
taught that 'The things that belong to the visible realm are transitory
and impermanent. It is only in the invisible realm that we can find
true and abiding reality. It is in this realm, too, that we discover
the forces which will ultimately shape our destiny, even in the visible
realm'.[53] Or again:

> A lot of people imagine that what we see, touch, hear and taste are the
> only truly real items. Down through the ages, however, philosophers
> have come to the conclusion that what we see, touch, hear and taste
> are not truly real; they are temporary, and they are very often deceptive.
> These philosophers have warned us that you cannot rely on your
> senses.
>
> And the Bible agrees! Paul said that the things that are seen are fleeting;
> the things that are not seen are eternal. In other words, our sensory
> world is passing away, and therefore only partly real because it does
> not endure.[54]

The message that Prince's African hearers found so attractive was
that the invisible world of contesting spiritual powers was not only to
be taken far more seriously than the mission churches had done, but
was in fact the only enduring reality, infinitely *more* real than the transitory world of physical or material suffering and poverty. His decisive
departure from the tradition of both the Assemblies of God and the
prophet movements of the earlier twentieth century in teaching that
even Spirit-filled Christians could be not simply afflicted by external
demonic attack, but ontologically 'demonized', appeared to eliminate
the ambiguity created by older traditions of Pentecostal
Christianity.[55] If the West African prophets had been fundamentally
mistaken in their assumption that 'once protected, always protected',
then might that not explain why even fervent Christians still fell prey
to sickness and the curse of endemic poverty?

---

[52] Plato, *Phaedo*, transl. David Gallop (Oxford, 1975), 27.
[53] Derek Prince, *Blessing or Curse: You can Choose*, 3rd edn (Baldock, 2007), 36.
[54] Derek Prince, *Lucifer Exposed: The Devil's Plan to Destroy your Life*, new edn (Baldock, 2007), 12.
[55] For precedents in the early Hellenistic church for Prince's belief in the possibility of the
demonization of Christians, see Onyinah, *Pentecostal Exorcism*, 248–51.

According to Prince, from the invisible realm of spiritual reality both blessings and curses flowed down the bloodline from up to four generations back, conveying good (evidenced in health and prosperity) or ill (manifested in hereditary sickness or poverty), a claim that built upon, yet significantly modified, beliefs about the continuing presence and agency of the ancestors that are widely found in Africa, as elsewhere in the non-European world. Prince readily acknowledged that the Bible had more to say about blessings than it did about curses, and taught a moderate version of the prosperity gospel: the blessing of abundance was defined as having all one needed to do the will of God.[56] Nevertheless, the mediating role of ancestors in his teaching on divine blessings was left undefined. In contrast, curses could be traced to errant or malevolent ancestors, and by ultimate derivation to demonic influence. Most African societies venerate ancestors as an essentially beneficent but somewhat unpredictable presence who need to be honoured and conciliated if their descendants and communities are to continue to flourish. In Prince's writings, on the other hand, it is bad rather than good ancestors who need to be brought to the forefront of the memory, and dealt with accordingly. In this respect he conforms to a long-established Protestant missionary tradition, as expounded most notably by Birgit Meyer in her study of nineteenth-century German pietist missionaries to the Ewe of Ghana and their twentieth-century Pentecostal or charismatic Presbyterian Ghanaian successors.[57] Prince was by no means the first effectively to transfer ancestors from the realm of blessing to the malevolent realm of Satan. His distinctive appeal to many African Christians appears to have consisted in the singular prominence that he gave to the notion of ancestral curses as the primary mechanism by which spiritual malevolence extended from the past to the present. 'A curse', he wrote, could be 'likened to a long, evil arm stretched out from the past', resting on a person with 'a dark, oppressive force' inhibiting the full expression of one's personality; it was a vehicle of 'supernatural, spiritual power'.[58]

Prince appealed for biblical support to the long list of blessings and curses in Deuteronomy 28; the repeated pentateuchal warnings about

---

[56] Prince, *Blessing or Curse*, 14, 41–2.
[57] Birgit Meyer, *Translating the Devil: Religion and Modernity among the Ewe in Ghana* (Edinburgh, 1999).
[58] Prince, *Blessing or Curse*, 19, 36.

the iniquity of the fathers being visited on the children to the third and fourth generations were to be taken with absolute seriousness.[59] In *Blessing or Curse: You can Choose*, he listed seven common indications of being under a curse, four of which related to sickness of one kind or another: mental and/or emotional breakdown; repeated or chronic sickness; barrenness, a tendency to miscarry or related female problems; and a history within a family of suicides and unnatural or untimely deaths. If only one or two of these problems were evident, that would not in itself be conclusive evidence of being under a curse, but the concurrence of several suggested that a curse was most likely in operation. Specifically, 'repeated miscarriages or female problems' he regarded as 'automatically' signs of the presence of a curse.[60] Furthermore, Prince insisted that hereditary sickness is 'one of the commonest and most typical marks of a curse at work'.[61] He also taught that an astonishing range of common mental or physical conditions were 'sometimes' caused by demons: 'insanity, insomnia, epilepsy, fits, cramps, migraines, sinus infections, tumors, ulcers, heart disease, arthritis, paralysis, dumbness, deafness, blindness'.[62] It was this depressing catalogue of potential signs of demonic possession that Cardinal Suenens found particularly objectionable.[63] For Prince, the boundary between Ranger's 'Diseases of Man' and the everyday 'Diseases of God' was remarkably porous.

The other three typical indications of being under a demonic curse were marriage breakdown or 'alienation', 'continuing financial insufficiency' and being 'accident prone'.[64] Indeed, when struggling to make ends meet, Prince reached the conclusion that he himself was under a Chinese curse as a result of having in his living room a set of four embroidered dragons brought from China by his maternal grandfather, Major-General Robert Edward Vaughan of the Indian Army, who had been involved in the British suppression of the Boxer Rebellion in 1900.[65] When Prince finally got rid of the

[59] Deut. 28; also Deut. 5: 9; Ex. 20: 5.
[60] Derek Prince, *God's Word Heals* (Baldock, 2010), 177.
[61] Prince, *Blessing or Curse*, 53–5.
[62] Derek Prince, *Expelling Demons*, new edn (Baldock, 2015), 9.
[63] Suenens, *Renewal and the Powers of Darkness*, 62, reproduces this list with only slight amendment.
[64] Prince, *Blessing or Curse*, 53.
[65] For biographical details of Vaughan (1866–1966), see Dix Noonan Webb, 'A Great War C.B. Group of Eight awarded to Major-General Robert Edward Vaughan, Indian

dragons, which he described as 'images of a false god', his income more than doubled and 'a long-delayed legacy' came through.[66]

Such teaching may well strike us as simply bizarre, but it has closer connections with Prince's Platonic studies than is immediately apparent. Plato shared with much Greek thought a belief in the existence and polluting capacity of ancestral curses. In his *Phaedrus* he refers in passing to 'grievous maladies and afflictions', which 'beset certain families by reason of some ancient sin'. For Plato such inherited guilt has its redeeming features, for it can become a source of one type of 'divine madness', expressed in prophesying, prayer and worship, which leads to the purification or 'deliverance' of the possessed sufferer.[67] This paradoxical passage in the *Phaedrus* may have been particularly significant for Prince, but in Plato the link between ancestral curses and demons (which is so central in Prince's Pentecostal theology) appears to be entirely missing. For Plato, as for the early Pythagorean philosophers from whom he borrowed, the 'daemons' are not the villains of the piece, but rather intermediary spiritual beings who usefully protect the gods from polluting contact with matter. They do not represent an absolute cosmological dualism, but rather bridge the chasm between the divine and the human.[68] Prince, by contrast, followed Tertullian in assimilating the whole assembly of ancestral and other spirits into the Pauline concept of evil principalities and powers; cosmological dualism has become absolute.[69]

DEMONOLOGY AND DELIVERANCE

Prince's demonology promised many Christians in Africa and other parts of the non-Western world a total explanation for their

---

Army', auctioneer's catalogue entry, 31 March 2010, online at: <https://www.dnw.co.uk/auction-archive/past-catalogues/lot.php?auction_id=185&lot_uid=182180>, accessed 7 December 2020.

[66] Prince, *Blessing or Curse*, 27–9, 41.

[67] Plato, *Phaedrus*, ed. R. Hackforth (Cambridge, 1952), 57 (244d–e); cf. Robert Parker, *Miasma: Pollution and Purification in Early Greek Religion* (Oxford, 1983), 191–206.

[68] Søren Skovgaard Jensen, *Dualism and Demonology: The Function of Demonology in Pythagorean and Platonic Thought* (Copenhagen, 1966), 60–1, 90–2.

[69] Kwame Bediako, *Theology and Identity: The Impact of Culture upon Christian Thought in the Second Century and Modern Africa* (Oxford, 1992), 108–9, 144–5; see also Mansfield, *Derek Prince*, 272, on Prince's incipient dualism.

continuing predicament in the final years of the twentieth century. Whether in reality it offered them a lasting solution is another question. In practice, an approach that encouraged Christians to be constantly on the hunt for inherited malevolent influences that might account for their physical and material problems inculcated not trust in the power of Christ but enduring fear and mutual suspicion. It is noteworthy that even the Ghanaian neo-Pentecostal churches that formerly derided the so-called *Sunsum sorè* (Spirit-worshipping) churches for their use of herbal medicines are increasingly resorting to herbal remedies themselves, some of which are held to possess exceptional powers of protection against evil forces.[70] A sacramental reliance on certain material objects as weapons of spiritual contestation may be a necessary corrective to Prince's devaluation of the material.

Derek Prince was clearly not the sole source of the teaching on demonology and deliverance that became so popular in many parts of sub-Saharan Africa, as also of Latin America, from the 1980s onwards. Argentina has witnessed a remarkable spread of ministries of deliverance since the 1980s, but the pioneer of such ministry, Carlos Annacondia (b. 1944) appears to have no connection to Prince, and traces his distinctive style of deliverance ministry to the Panamaian evangelist, Manuel Ruiz, under whom he was converted.[71] Deliverance ministry is a ubiquitous feature of contemporary global neo-Pentecostalism, and no single theological lineage can be identified as common to its manifold occurrences. David Maxwell's study of the Zimbabwe Assemblies of God indicates the growing salience, from the 1980s onwards, of a similar preoccupation with deliverance and of analogous ideas of ancestral curses as the likely explanation of the intractable poverty of individuals, but without attempting to construct a genealogy of such ideas.[72] It would require extensive field research to trace more precisely the chronology and geography of Prince's impact in a variety of contexts in Africa, where some local cosmologies were more closely attuned to his stark aetiology of illness than others. It would be necessary to form

---

[70] J. Kwabena Asamoah-Gyadu, 'Therapeutic Strategies in African Religions: Health, Herbal Medicines and Indigenous Christian Spirituality', *Studies in World Christianity* 20 (2014), 70–90, at 86–8.

[71] Norberto Saracco, 'Argentine Pentecostalism: Its History and Theology' (Ph.D. thesis, University of Birmingham, 1989), 243–52.

[72] David Maxwell, *African Gifts of the Spirit: Pentecostalism and the Rise of a Zimbabwean Transnational Religious Movement* (Oxford, 2006), 184–211.

a judgement of his relative significance alongside other leading teachers of demonology, such as the Nigerian Emmanuel Eni. Paul Gifford, Kwabena Asamoah-Gyadu, Opuku Onyinah and Naomi Richman have all identified Prince as being of unusual importance for the growth of deliverance ministry in Pentecostalism in West Africa.[73] Jörg Haustein has similarly identified Prince's teaching that even believers indwelt by the Holy Spirit may be demonized as responsible for a major theological debate among Pentecostals in Ethiopia.[74] However, none of these scholars has formulated any theory of what in particular might account for his enthusiastic reception. My suggestion here is that Prince's unusual synthesis of Platonism and Pentecostalism provides at least part of the answer.

It is frequently asserted that one of the more regrettable legacies of Greek philosophy to the Church from patristic times onwards has been to make Christianity into an immaterial religion preoccupied only with the eternal soul, and notably deficient in the Hebraic emphasis on the body as the object of God's care and even salvation. The emphasis of Pentecostalism on healing the body can then be presented as a necessary corrective to the centuries of Platonization of an originally Jewish faith. Thus, Amanda Porterfield's survey of healing in the history of Christianity cites the early Brazilian Protestant theologian of liberation, Rubem Alves, to the effect that 'the language of the community of faith definitely opposes the platonic negation of the body', but then criticizes Alves for drawing the extreme inference that 'one does not find in this language, consequently, any place or transcendence beyond the world or beyond the body'. Alves, Porterfield plausibly complains, has overlooked 'the demons and spiritual powers that filled the world of Jesus'.[75]

Derek Prince's career points, not to a supposedly typical African understanding of the spirit world radiating outwards to influence global Pentecostalism, but rather to the potential of a neglected aspect

---

[73] Gifford, *African Christianity*, 102, 346–7; idem, *Ghana's New Christianity*, 89; idem, *Christianity, Development and Modernity in Africa*, 31, 69, 118–19; Asamoah-Gyadu, *African Charismatics*, 170; Naomi Richman, 'Machine Gun Prayer: The Politics of Embodied Desire in Pentecostal Worship', *JCR* 35 (2020), 469–83, at 472, 474, 480; Onyinah, *Pentecostal Exorcism*, 172–3, 183.
[74] Jörg Haustein, 'Embodying the Spirit(s): Pentecostal Demonology and Deliverance Discourse in Ethiopia', *Ethnos* 76 (2011), 534–52.
[75] Amanda Porterfield, *Healing in the History of Christianity* (Oxford, 2005), 124, citing Rubem A. Alves, *A Theology of Hope* (Washington, DC, 1969), 149.

of the Western philosophical tradition, when mediated through Prince's popular Christian Platonism, to strike a chord among many who received it in Africa. The irony of the Derek Prince story is that it was precisely the cosmology of Plato that supplied Prince with a lens which enabled him to view the most acute or frequently recurring material ailments of the mind and body as signs of a more fundamental disorder in the realm of the spirit. Crucially, for many of those in Africa and elsewhere who received Prince's message, these material ailments included the curse of chronic poverty. Plato, for all his intellectualist preoccupation with the immortality of the soul, inhabited an enchanted universe populated by diverse spiritual beings, which was the arena for the outworking of ancestral curses. Contemporary Christianity in Africa, many other parts of the developing world, and arguably in some Western contexts as well, locates itself in a similar universe, in a way that much of the Western academy struggles to comprehend.

Masks vs. God and Country: The Conflict between Public Health and Christian Nationalism

Brittany Acors*

University of Virginia

From its inception, the United States Public Health Service (USPHS) has been expressly areligious, aiming to promote the health of the American people during specific crises such as the COVID-19 pandemic, as well as responding to endemic issues such as heart disease, opioid addiction and obesity. However, some Christian nationalists perceive this areligious advocacy of science as a challenge to the moral authority of Christianity and the Bible. Protests against public health guidelines have utilized religious language to defend what participants see as their civil and God-given rights, deepening the divide between science and religion. Yet historically, public health advocates have built relationships with religious community leaders and employed educational campaigns to bridge this gap. Drawing on an analysis of USPHS history, Christian nationalist ideology and recent COVID-19 protests, this article argues that public health has historically used specific strategies to ensure a more favourable response and compliance, and makes the case that it should do so again.

From its inception, the United States Public Health Service (USPHS) has been expressly areligious. Designed to disperse 'reliable information based on the best available public health science, not politics, religion, or personal opinion',[1] the USPHS aims to promote the health of the American people during specific crises such as the COVID-19 pandemic and with respect to more endemic issues such as heart disease, opioid addiction and obesity. However, as sociological research on Christian nationalist responses to masking and social distancing orders has recently demonstrated, this areligious advocacy of science can be perceived as a challenge to the moral authority of Christianity and the Bible. Protests against public health

---

* 2006 Stadium Rd #9, Charlottesville, VA 22903. E-mail: baa9cb@virginia.edu.
[1] David Satcher, 'A Tribute to Surgeon General C. Everett Koop', *Health Affairs*, 1 March 2013, online at: <https://www.healthaffairs.org/do/10.1377/hblog20130301.028767/full/>, accessed 18 January 2021.

Studies in Church History 58 (2022), 415–437   © The Author(s), 2022. Published by Cambridge University Press on behalf of Ecclesiastical History Society
doi: 10.1017/stc.2022.20

guidelines in churches and on state property have utilized religious language to defend what participants regard as their civil and God-given rights, further deepening the divide between science and religion. To bridge this gap, public health advocates have in the past sought to use community engagement strategies and educational campaigns to instil public trust in bacteriology, birth control and safe sexual practices. The following analysis of the history of the USPHS, the ideology and individualism of Christian nationalism, and recent protests against public health policies demonstrates that public health agencies still need to employ such strategies to ensure a more favourable response and compliance in the present pandemic and in future crises.

THE UNITED STATES PUBLIC HEALTH SERVICE

The United States Public Health Service dates nearly to the founding of the United States of America, and it has witnessed every health crisis from smallpox and yellow fever to the opioid epidemic and COVID-19. Founded in 1798 by the Adams administration to care for sick and disabled seamen,[2] the USPHS grew exponentially after the bacteriological revolution of the late nineteenth century, which caused a shift in how disease was regarded, from a moral failing to a societal- and state-level concern.[3] More than two hundred years after its founding, the USPHS is 'the largest public health program in the world' and provides crucial services related to 'healthcare delivery, research, regulation, and disaster relief' for the American people at large.[4] In fulfilling these roles, the USPHS has historically employed a variety of educational strategies adapted to the current situation and needs of American citizens, but it also faces certain impediments which crises exacerbate, as the following analysis demonstrates.

As the chief educational agency for health issues in the United States, the USPHS has relied on the latest scientific evidence and sought to avoid political or religious influence. As the point where medicine meets government, it must tread carefully around the

---

[2] Commissioned Corps of the US Public Health Service, 'Our History', online at: <https://www.usphs.gov/history>, accessed 24 November 2020.
[3] Nancy Tomes, *The Gospel of Germs: Men, Women, and the Microbe in American Life* (Cambridge, MA, 1998).
[4] Commissioned Corps, 'Our History'.

First Amendment of the United States Constitution, which serves to protect citizens' rights from governmental infringement. The First Amendment right to religious freedom has two parts: the establishment clause forbids the creation of a national religion, and the free exercise clause allows people to practise religion according to their consciences. Yet perhaps the context of the Public Health Services' development attests more to its avoidance of religion than to constitutional trepidation, as the body grew out of scientific knowledge about disease and public acceptance of prevention as a social responsibility.[5] The USPHS embrace of bacteriology reflected broader public understanding, in which '[s]cientific measures were seen as replacing earlier social, sanitary, moral, and religious reform measures to combat disease. Science was seen as a more effective means of achieving the same desirable social goals.'[6] In 1988, a Committee for the Study of the Future of Public Health, commissioned by the Division of Health Care Services in the Institute of Medicine, issued a 240-page report on the status of public health services in the United States. This document reflected on the history of these services, assessed their present disorder and inefficacies, and recommended future actions that would enable the public health system to better address immediate crises and enduring problems. Tellingly, the quotation above, about science replacing religion, is the only place in the report where religion is mentioned. This omission arguably made some Christians wary of the authority of public health, as will be seen below.

One of the most common accusations levelled against the USPHS is that it tends to be reactive, rather than proactive, and thus is unable to respond to crises as quickly or efficiently as the public expects. This issue, highlighted both by the 1988 report and by a 2002 *Health Affairs* article entitled 'The Unfulfilled Promise of Public Health: *Déjà vu* all over again', in part reflects governmental priorities, but it also reveals a disjunction between academic analysis and practical implementation. In the *Health Affairs* article, Elizabeth Fee, chief of the History of Medicine Division at the National Institutes of Health's Library of Medicine, and Theodore Brown, professor of community and preventive medicine at the University of Rochester's School of Medicine and Dentistry, trace how events in US history have corresponded with changes (or the lack thereof)

[5] Institute of Medicine, *The Future of Public Health* (Washington DC, 1988), 56.
[6] Ibid. 64.

in public health services.[7] Fee and Brown narrate the constant struggle between progressive reform and conservative reaction regarding the funding and expansion of the USPHS. The USPHS draws national attention and a funding boom during disease crises or times of renewed interest in social inequities, such as the 1930s 'New Deal' and the 1960s 'War on Poverty'. However, during leaner economic times or a New Federalism mentality[8] as seen during the Reagan administration, when attention shifts away from diseases or care for the poor, the government slashes public health funding and the system falls into disarray.[9]

Fee and Brown argue that the United States government and its people should invest in public-health preparedness at all times, and other academics have joined them in advocating consistent investment in national health initiatives. They assert that the boom-and-bust cycle challenges the ability of the USPHS to protect national health from regular stressors such as drug addiction or heart health. The lack of sustained support also inhibits the response of the USPHS to the sudden appearance of new epidemic diseases. In times of relative calm, medical professionals, politicians, sociologists and historians alike call for better preventative health. However, without funding, and with the next crisis always seeming to come too soon, the USPHS has been unable to implement necessary systemic changes.

When COVID-19, the disease caused by the novel coronavirus known as SARS-CoV2, reached the USA late in February 2020, the nation's public health systems were experiencing one of the ebbs in funding that occur regularly under conservative leadership. In an opinion editorial article published in the *Washington Post* on 13 March 2020, Beth Cameron, formerly Senior Director for

[7] Elizabeth Fee and Theodore M. Brown, 'The Unfulfilled Promise of Public Health: *Déjà vu* all over again', *Health Affairs* 21, no. 6 (November-December 2002), 31–43.
[8] The United States government operates as a federalist system, in which the federal or national governing bodies have certain reserved powers, but most other powers are left to the states. American conservatives generally seek to reduce federal powers, resulting in more responsibilities for the states and allowing for idiosyncratic differences in policies based on the opinions of the people in each state. Under the Reagan administration, this shift was called 'New Federalism', and federal involvement in social welfare benefits and other regulations diminished.
[9] Ibid. 41.

Global Health Security and Biodefense in the National Security
Council in the Obama administration, wrote:

> When President Trump took office in 2017, the White House's
> National Security Council Directorate for Global Health Security
> and Biodefense survived the transition intact. Its mission was ... to
> do everything possible within the vast powers and resources of the
> U.S. government to prepare for the next disease outbreak and prevent
> it from becoming an epidemic or pandemic.
>
> One year later, I was mystified when the White House dissolved the office,
> leaving the country less prepared for pandemics like covid-19.[10]

Representatives from the Trump administration explained this elim-
ination as a streamlining of the National Security Council.[11]
However, by the end of Trump's term of office, this decrease in disease prevention preparedness, combined with the rise of Christian
nationalism in the Trump era as discussed below, contributed to
the loss of more than 700,000 American lives.[12]

CHRISTIAN NATIONALISM AND SCIENCE AS AN AFFRONT TO RELIGIOUS MORAL AUTHORITY

Christian nationalists can best be defined as a group of people who
believe that the United States is a Christian nation and should base
its policies on conservative Christian values and the Bible, which they
perceive to be the inerrant word of God. Although Christian nationalists
have promoted such views since the foundation of the USA, they have
become increasingly vocal with the rise of the Religious Right and the
increasing political power of the Moral Majority since the 1970s.[13]

[10] Beth Cameron, 'I ran the White House pandemic office. Trump closed it', *Washington Post*, 13 March 2020, online at: <https://www.washingtonpost.com/outlook/nsc-pan-demic-office-trump-closed/2020/03/13/a70de09c-6491-11ea-acca-80c22bbee96f_story.html>, accessed 18 January 2021.
[11] Tim Morrison, 'No, the White House didn't "dissolve" its pandemic response office. I was there', *Washington Post*, 16 March 2020, online at: <https://www.washingtonpost.com/opinions/2020/03/16/no-white-house-didnt-dissolve-its-pandemic-response-office/>, accessed 18 January 2021.
[12] This article concerns an ongoing health crisis, and statistics are updated to 25 October 2021.
[13] A comprehensive history is beyond the scope of this article, but it can be found in many recent books, including John Fea, *Was America founded as a Christian Nation? A Historical Introduction* (Louisville, KY, 2011); Sam Haselby, *The Origins of American*

Although there is significant overlap between Christian nationalists and evangelicals, Andrew Whitehead and Samuel Perry assert in their study of Christian nationalism, *Taking America Back for God* (2020), that the groups are not to be regarded as one and the same. Whitehead and Perry argue that Christian nationalism must be studied on its own terms, separately from 'Christianity', and that 'understanding Christian nationalism, its content and its consequences, is essential for understanding much of the polarization in American popular discourse'.[14] In subsequent studies, they examine more specifically the contest for moral authority between science and Christian nationalism, a crucial factor for understanding the spread of the COVID-19 pandemic in the United States. By understanding the perspective of Christian nationalists and seeking partnerships with local leaders, public health advocates can create educational campaigns that may better appeal to an otherwise non-compliant population.

People who believe that the USA should be a Christian nation, a position which politicizes religion and theologizes politics, often regard science as a competing authority that cannot be accommodated within the Christian nationalist worldview. Examining why Christian nationalism often corresponds with a rejection of science, sociologists Joseph Baker, Stephen Perry and Andrew Whitehead find: 'Because it provides an alternative source of moral authority beyond divine revelation and, consequently, different narratives regarding human origins, social organization, and humanity's relationship to nature, institutional science is perceived as a threat to the supremacy of Christianity as the moral authority in the public sphere.'[15] Christian nationalist concern with the source of moral authority is not common to all religious people. As Whitehead and Perry identify, liberal Protestants are much more likely to find ways to accommodate religious beliefs and scientific knowledge as dual

Religious Nationalism (New York, 2015); David Hollinger, *After Cloven Tongues of Fire: Protestant Liberalism in Modern American History* (Princeton, NJ, 2013); K. Healan Gaston, *Imagining Judeo-Christian America: Religion, Secularism, and the Redefinition of Democracy* (Chicago, IL, 2019).

[14] Andrew L. Whitehead and Samuel L. Perry, *Taking America Back for God: Christian Nationalism in the United States* (New York, 2020), 16.

[15] Joseph Baker, Samuel Perry and Andrew Whitehead, 'Crusading for Moral Authority: Christian Nationalism and Opposition to Science', *Sociological Forum* 35 (2020), 587–607, at 591.

sources for understanding the world. Many Christian nationalists, however, dispute scientific authority in 'an effort to (re)assert the dominant moral and cultural authority of a white, native-born, straight, masculine, and Christian social order'.[16] Their political, social and religious positions combine to combat both science and scientists, whom they view as detracting from the proper ordering of the USA. It is this stance that has created a significant backlash against public health measures in the current crisis.

While the greatest amount of public opposition between science and Christian nationalism in the past century has concerned evolution and climate change, the disjunction between these two sources of information has also had major consequences for determining responses to the COVID-19 pandemic. Suspicion about science has manifested in non-compliance with public health mandates requiring masking and social distancing as protective measures against COVID-19.[17] Ohio state representative Nino Vitale exemplified this position in a May 2020 Facebook post responding to masking mandates: 'This is the greatest nation on earth founded on Judeo-Christian Principles. One of those principles is that we are all created in the image and likeness of God. That image is seen the most by our face. I will not wear a mask.'[18] In an article which focused on the behaviours of Christian nationalists during the current pandemic, Whitehead and Perry partnered with psychologist Joshua B. Grubbs to understand such responses to public health measures. Specifically, they argue that polls revealing 'religious' Americans as those most opposed to orders such as masking and social distancing are misleading, and that 'Christian nationalism' is a better predictor of

[16] Ibid. 603.

[17] It is important to note here that throughout 2020 states or localities were left to determine their own approaches to preventative measures and mask mandates. Although the Centers for Disease Control and Prevention provided advice, it is not a law-making body. Furthermore, it was unclear whether the federal government had the power to make public health mandates, and conservatives would have seen such actions as a violation of states' rights: Lawrence O. Gostin, I. Glenn Cohen and Jeffrey P. Koplan, 'Universal Masking in the United States: The Role of Mandates, Health Education, and the CDC', *Journal of the American Medical Association* 324 (2020), 837–8.

[18] Elisha Fieldstadt, 'Ohio Lawmaker refuses to wear Mask because he says it dishonors God', NBC News, 6 May 2020, online at: <https://www.nbcnews.com/news/us-news/ohio-lawmaker-refuses-wear-mask-because-he-says-it-dishonors-n1201106>, accessed 7 December 2020.

distrust in scientific expertise.[19] Their study evaluates Christian nationalism as a predictor of the likelihood of undertaking incautious behaviours (attending large gatherings, shopping for non-essentials, eating inside restaurants) and ignoring precautionary recommendations (hand washing, mask wearing, decreased face touching). Their findings indicate that:

> Christian nationalism was significantly and positively related to five indicators of incautious behavior, but unrelated to the frequency with which Americans went to medical appointments, attended church, or went to work outside the home ... Christian nationalism was also negatively associated with each indicator of precautionary behavior except for using more hand sanitizer than normal. Religious commitment, in contrast, was mostly unrelated to incautious behaviors (though it predicted more frequent church attendance) and was positively and powerfully associated with each indicator of precautionary behavior.[20]

These results define a distinction between Christian nationalists and people who can more broadly be categorized as religious. In a webinar on the same topic, Whitehead and Perry shared additional results of their study. They found that rejectors of Christian nationalism were most likely to trust medical experts, scientists and the Centers for Disease Control and Prevention as the most reliable sources of information about COVID-19, while strong Christian nationalists most trusted Donald Trump, religious organizations and the Republican Party.[21] These behaviours and trusted sources further indicate how Christian nationalists view science as a challenge to their moral authority and provide the context for their newsworthy actions during the pandemic.

Although they are a minority, Christian nationalists have garnered a disproportionate number of news articles focused on their lack of compliance with public health orders in 2020 and 2021. At an

---

[19] Samuel Perry, Andrew Whitehead and Joshua Grubbs, 'Culture Wars and COVID-19 Conduct: Christian Nationalism, Religiosity, and Americans' Behavior during the Coronavirus Pandemic', *Journal for the Scientific Study of Religion* 59 (2020), 405–16, at 406.

[20] Ibid. 413.

[21] Andrew Whitehead and Samuel Perry, 'The Fight to Make America Christian Again: Christian Nationalism in National and Texas Politics', Zoom Webinar, Rice University, Baker Institute, 21 September 2020.

April 2020 protest against COVID-19 precautionary restrictions in Michigan, a young white male held a sign that read: 'Even Pharaoh freed slaves during a plague.'[22] This sign combines a biblical narrative with then-president Donald Trump's calls for governors to rescind state restrictions on business operations. It is emblematic of Christian nationalists' methods of depicting public health orders as restrictions of civil – and God-given – liberties. This ideology also appeared as churches across the country refused to comply with government shutdowns. Religious leaders whose churches remained open decried government-mandated cancellation of worship services as a violation of religious freedom,[23] especially as shutdowns coincided with Holy Week and Easter Sunday, and because other organizations such as casinos were permitted to remain open.[24] When Texas Governor Greg Abbott declared churches an essential service, and thus exempted from closures, Pastor Shetigho Nakpodia of Redeemer's Praise Church in San Antonio called him 'the pastor of Texas' and declared, 'I believe he's a man of faith … Maybe that's what the Lord told him to do.'[25] The assertion that government officials should prioritize religion epitomizes Christian nationalism, especially as many of the same voices condemned other officials who prioritized public health and science instead. In the Christian nationalist perspective, Governor Abbott, like the Pharaoh of the Hebrew Bible, set people free during a pandemic. With this action, he earned in their eyes a position somewhere below God and certainly above medical experts who would have everyone remain 'enslaved', as the protest sign asserted.

[22] Photograph by Jeff Kowalsky, in 'Trump and Protesters pressure Governors to start reopening the States', CNBC, 18 April 2020, online at: <https://www.cnbc.com/2020/04/18/trump-and-protesters-pressure-governors-to-start-reopening-the-states.html>, accessed 25 November 2020.
[23] Tom Gjelten, 'Some Religious Leaders defy Shutdown Orders', NPR, 5 April 2020, online at: <https://www.npr.org/2020/04/05/827758335/some-religious-leaders-defy-shutdown-orders>, accessed 25 November 2020.
[24] The unequal treatment of churches in shutdown orders has come to a fore in a recent Supreme Court case, *Calvary Chapel Dayton Valley* v. *Steve Sisolak, Governor of Nevada, et al.* 591 U.S. ___ (2020), online at: <https://www.supremecourt.gov/opinions/19pdf/19a1070_08l1.pdf#page=13>, last accessed 16 November 2021.
[25] Vianna Davila, '"A Church is Hands On:" Why these Texas Churches aren't closing their Doors', *Texas Tribune*, 2 April 2020, online at: <https://www.texastribune.org/2020/04/02/texas-churches-coronavirus-arent-closing-doors/>, accessed 25 November 2020.

Refusal to cancel religious services and charitable operations was not confined to Christian nationalist circles, but also occurred among Catholics, for whom sacraments are crucial and cannot be performed remotely. Jewish and Muslim leaders similarly struggled with the decision, knowing that many community members rely on their synagogues and mosques for food or religious rituals.[26] These concerns for the well-being of people who might go hungry without essential church services differ, however, from Christian nationalist challenges to the authority of public health authorities. Christian nationalist objections to shutdown orders seem to take two contrary paths: either Christians are God's chosen people and God will protect them from any harm, or the virus is not as bad as scientists claim and the government is just using it as an opportunity to suppress churches. Both beliefs lead to the defiance of public health orders and to the view that individual freedom of choice is more important than the societal protection of health.

This individualism may represent a shift with which public health authorities must reckon. While early knowledge of germ theory led to public health measures based on a widespread recognition that disease prevention could protect all citizens, some citizens have come to deny the authority of the underlying science and to prioritize individual liberties. Nicole Bryant, a member of Life Tabernacle Church, which remained open in defiance of Louisiana's closure orders, demonstrates this view:

> There was a time in our history when I feel like we had that religious freedom – everything could have been closed, but people need to worship, religion was top-of-the-line because that was the original reason for [the Founders] coming here ... The beauty of America is you can live your life based on what you prioritize as necessary, and we should be able to do the same.[27]

[26] Ibid.

[27] Michelle Boorstein, 'The Church that won't close its Doors over the Coronavirus', *Washington Post*, 20 March 2020, online at: <https://www.washingtonpost.com/religion/2020/03/20/church-tony-spell-coronavirus-life-tabernacle/?arc404=true>, accessed 25 November 2020. While this article also discusses Orthodox Jewish communities that refused to follow social distancing orders, I believe that these violations of public health guidelines do not represent religious nationalist positions, and therefore they do not fit within the scope of this article, although they deserve further exploration.

In this mythologized version of United States history, Christian nationalists argue that religious freedom, interpreted as the right to unrestricted practice of religious beliefs, originally predominated, but that it has been eroded in recent years. The question is one of moral authority: who has the right to determine how people act in public settings? In this understanding, the medical community, urging groups to stay at home, is pitted against religious communities, who advocate God's protection and the value of gathering for worship. For Christian nationalists, if the choice is between faith in God and fear of death, they know where they stand.

In addition to the rhetoric of individual freedom, race has played an important role in the present pandemic. Throughout their research on Christian nationalists, Perry and Whitehead identify 'Christian nationalists' as white, native-born, culturally Christian people. However, people of colour have not only contracted COVID-19 in disproportionate numbers but have also died of it at higher rates.[28] Individual choices have communal consequences, especially for people who are more likely to occupy service-sector and essential-worker roles due to centuries of systemic racial and economic inequalities. Much like Christian nationalists, many Black communities also distrust medical information.[29] However, for Black communities, this distrust results not from a perception of contested moral authority, but from centuries of unethical experimentation on Black bodies, from the times of slavery[30] through the USPHS-run Tuskegee and Guatemala syphilis studies.[31] Although their distrust results from different experiences and ideologies, and recognizing that Christian nationalist communities have refused to comply with public health standards at greater rates than Black communities, both groups demonstrate the need for the USPHS to intervene and to work to build greater trust in order to serve the American

[28] 'COVID-19 Hospitalization and Death by Race / Ethnicity', Centers for Disease Control and Prevention, 18 August 2020, online at: <https://www.cdc.gov/coronavirus/2019-ncov/covid-data/investigations-discovery/hospitalization-death-by-race-ethnicity.html>, accessed 25 November 2020.
[29] Bernice Roberts Kennedy, Christopher Clomus Mathis and Angela K. Woods, 'African Americans and their Distrust of the Health Care System: Healthcare for Diverse Populations', *Journal of Cultural Diversity* 14/2 (2007), 56–60.
[30] L. Lewis Wall, 'The Medical Ethics of Dr J. Marion Sims: A Fresh Look at the Historical Record', *Journal of Medical Ethics* 32 (2006), 346–50.
[31] Susan Reverby, 'Ethical Failures and History Lessons: The U.S. Public Health Service Research Studies in Tuskegee and Guatemala', *Public Health Reviews* 34 (2012), 1–18.

Brittany Acors

population more fully. The next two sections will explore historical moments when bridges were built between these communities and public health, exemplifying opportunities for future partnerships.

BRIDGING THE GAP BETWEEN RELIGION AND MEDICINE

Community partnerships and educational campaigns have historically instigated a conversion in lifestyle that makes for healthier populations. The bacteriological revolution, the advent of birth control and the explosion of the human immunodeficiency virus (HIV) mark the beginning, middle and end of arguably the most scientifically revolutionary century in human history. Each of these shifts also required a rapid public health response to educate the population as new information became available. Although often driven by private citizens, interventions at these three moments in medical history can serve as models for how the USPHS might respond to increasing distrust in science and medicine in the twenty-first century. These models demonstrate how to build relationships with hesitant communities and ensure greater compliance with future public health measures.

The bacteriological revolution at the turn of the twentieth century was marked by the discovery of several disease-causing vectors and the realization that disease does not discriminate on the basis of race, religion, social class or any of the other factors that people perceive as setting themselves apart from others. In *The Gospel of Germs* (1998), historian Nancy Tomes explores how the American response to the early-twentieth-century 'germ panic' resulted in an obsession with hygiene invading United States culture. While analysing the 'educational crusades that brought women and men from all walks of life to believe in the existence of germs and to alter fundamental aspects of their daily lives to avoid them', Tomes identifies that 'reformers of many stripes promoted this code of behavior with religious fervor and made believing in germs part of the credo of modern living'.[32] The bacteriological revolution provides an example of how both individual beliefs and societal consensus on proper public health behaviours may change, offering a potential remedy for the challenges of disinformation and the assertion of moral authority that underlie public health non-compliance among Christian nationalists.

[32] Tomes, *Gospel of Germs*, xv.

426

Once scientists had identified bacteria and viruses as disease-causing agents, this understanding had to reach the wider public before social behaviour could change substantially. Although originally based on the miasmic theory of disease, which posited that sickness could spread through tainted vapours in the air, many Americans believed that cleanliness was a mark of 'gentility and politeness' among the upper classes, which then trickled down to middle-class people living in urban hotspots of disease.[33] Once diseases began to spread even in these socially powerful circles, however, upper-class Americans quickly grasped the burgeoning bacteriological theory as an explanation, accepting it even before many in the medical community. Part of the reason germ theory caught on so easily, Tomes argues, was that Americans, as a largely religious people, 'had been conditioned to believe in an "invisible world" dominated by unseen forces that held the power of life and death'.[34] Even once scientific researchers identified the invisible agents of disease, people still regarded them with the mix of wonder and fear often reserved for God. They approached information dissemination about germs and bacteria and associated behavioural reform as they had for centuries approached gospel missionizing and ritual activity.

Because effective treatments for diseases did not yet exist, prevention was the best method of ensuring health, and public health campaigns swept through cities. The expansion of public health from 1890 to 1930 occurred for two reasons: first, people came to believe that the government should be responsible for societal well-being through the management of sewage, water supply and food inspection; and second, people recognized that individuals and households were responsible for the policing of 'seemingly innocuous behaviors', like hand-washing and refraining from public expectoration.[35] One way these beliefs spread was through advertising and entrepreneurship, as new products hit the markets promising to protect families from common household germs. A second way they circulated was through union members and African American leaders who took on crucial roles in the tuberculosis crusade, because these two communities were disproportionately affected by what was then known as 'consumption'. A third way information spread was through the

---

[33] Ibid. 3.
[34] Ibid. 7.
[35] Ibid. 6–7.

education of women in 'domestic science' classes and missionary nursing training. As the family members typically most involved in the private sphere, wives and mothers had long run the home and taken a leading role in the religious education of the children. With the advent of germ theory, women took on the extra burden of sanitizing the home against disease vectors, but they also found new careers outside the home as nurses, physicians and home economics teachers.[36] By appealing to the American public at large through advertisements, but also to smaller subsets by addressing their specific concerns, public health crusaders in the early twentieth century enacted a sea change in American beliefs and habits.

As understanding of bacteriology grew widespread, it developed into what Tomes calls the 'gospel of germs', an almost religious 'belief that microbes cause disease and can be avoided by certain protective behaviors'.[37] These behaviours included installing easily sanitized porcelain toilets in the home, preparing food more cautiously, sneezing and coughing into a handkerchief or the elbow, and campaigning against public expectoration. Advertisements in magazines such as *Good Housekeeping* and *Harper's Bazaar*, radio spots, and government mandates about food preparation in restaurants and sanitation practices in hotels combined to make Americans more sanitary and aware of disease. Many of these habits that were new in the early twentieth century – such as washing hands after using the restroom or before eating, keeping raw meat separate from cooked, and using white sheets in hotels because they are more easily washed with bleach – are now standard and unquestioned parts of modern life. Normalizing sanitary practices has not only changed American lifestyles but has also decreased the spread of infectious diseases over time.

Tomes argues that there was a lull in germ consciousness after the incidence of chronic illnesses overtook that of infectious diseases in the 1950s, following the dissemination of antibiotics and the poliovirus vaccine. However, writing in 1998, she contends that 'the gospel of germs has taken on new relevance since 1980'.[38] When HIV-AIDS began killing otherwise healthy young men, initially to the bafflement of medical professionals, a new germ

[36] Ibid. 136.
[37] Ibid. 2.
[38] Ibid. 13.

panic reached the public. Education campaigns were again used, but this time to assure the population that neither handshakes nor nearby sneezes could spread the debilitating new virus. As the fear of AIDS began to abate in the early twenty-first century, however, it seems that germ consciousness has reached a new low. With a widespread view that COVID-19 is not as bad as scientists and the government have made it seem, the United States needs to target its public health information campaign concerning social behaviours such as masking and physical distancing more effectively to hesitant populations. The 'gospel of germs' mindset that was new in 1920 and faded by 2000 has again become necessary in the 2020s, and the way bacteriology entered daily life a century ago provides a model for the present.

However, information campaigns alone no longer seem as effective as they were a century ago. Because most Americans have ready access to the internet, misinformation and disinformation spread more easily than information from legitimate sources such as scientific researchers and the Centers for Disease Control and Prevention (CDC), which are bound by caution and protocols that delay the finding and publicization of research results. After a 2012 outbreak of salmonella, the CDC recognized that this delay could foster disinformation and distrust.[39] Despite this retrospective recognition of the drawbacks of working in accordance with the scientific timeline, the CDC proceeded cautiously in the first few months of 2020, and disinformation often dominated.[40] Between the information delay and the perceived challenge to religion's moral authority described above, the COVID-19 pandemic appears to have come at a challenging time for moderating social behaviours. Historically, in cases when disinformation and distrust have prevailed, partnerships between public health activists and community leaders have proved effective in combating these trends, as can be shown by the case of Margaret Sanger's birth control clinic in Harlem.

When Margaret Sanger (1879–1966) secured funding to open a birth control clinic in Harlem in 1930, she ensured that the clinic

[39] Public Health Matters Blog, 'Public Health: Are we too slow?', Centers for Disease Control and Prevention, 1 May 2013, online at: <https://blogs.cdc.gov/publichealthmatters/2013/05/are-we-too-slow/>, accessed 9 June 2021.
[40] Binxuan Huang and Kathleen M. Carley, 'Disinformation and Misinformation on Twitter during the Novel Coronavirus Outbreak', Cornell University Social and Information Networks, 2020, online at: <https://arXiv:2006.04278>, last accessed 3 February 2022.

would be run under an advisory board consisting of Black community leaders. Sanger realized that working closely with Black leaders, including ministers, could help instil trust in medical and public health measures. The board at the Harlem clinic included social worker James Hubert; May Chinn, the only Black female doctor in Harlem; Baptist pastor William Lloyd Imes; and representatives from the National Association of Colored Graduate Nurses, Harlem Hospital and the National Urban League.[41] W. E. B. Du Bois' magazine *The Crisis* publicized the Harlem clinic, and the Revd Dr Martin Luther King Jr and Coretta Scott King later commended Sanger's work there as well.[42] Mutual relationships underpinned this initiative: while Sanger recognized Black community leaders as crucial for spreading public health initiatives among distrustful populations, Black community leaders recognized Sanger's desire to help people control their bodies and in turn their futures. Working closely with one another enabled shared goal-setting and ultimately led to a healthier population.

In recent years, Planned Parenthood has distanced itself from the legacy of its founder, largely due to Sanger's advocacy of eugenics at home and abroad.[43] Historians, medical doctors and liberal and conservative activists have rightly raised concerns about her beliefs in selective breeding and white maternalism,[44] and this article in no

---

[41] Carole R. McCann, *Birth Control Politics in the United States, 1916–1945* (Ithaca, NY, 1994), 139.

[42] Martin Luther King Jr, 'Family Planning: A Special and Urgent Concern', speech delivered 5 May 1966, Planned Parenthood, online at: <https://www.plannedparenthood.org/planned-parenthood-gulf-coast/mlk-acceptance-speech>, accessed 29 November 2020.

[43] Nikita Steward, 'Planned Parenthood in N.Y. disavows Margaret Sanger over Eugenics', *New York Times*, 21 July 2020, online at: <https://www.nytimes.com/2020/07/21/nyregion/planned-parenthood-margaret-sanger-eugenics.html?auth=login-email&login=email>, accessed 25 January 2021.

[44] For more resources on Margaret Sanger's life and complicated legacy, see David M. Kennedy, *Birth Control in America: The Career of Margaret Sanger* (New Haven, CT, 1970); 'Newsletter #28 (Fall 2001): "Birth Control or Race Control? Sanger and the Negro Project"', The Margaret Sanger Papers Project, online at: <https://www.nyu.edu/projects/sanger/articles/bc_or_race_control.php>, accessed 29 November 2020; R. Marie Griffith, *Moral Combat: How Sex divided American Christians and fractured American Politics* (New York, 2017); Amita Kelly, 'Fact Check: Was Planned Parenthood started to "Control" the Black Population?', NPR, 14 August 2015, online at: <https://www.npr.org/sections/itsallpolitics/2015/08/14/432080520/fact-check-was-planned-parenthood-started-to-control-the-black-population>, accessed 25 January 2021.

way wishes to defend or justify her beliefs or those policies. Rather, the lesson the USPHS may draw from Sanger's work focuses narrowly on her partnerships with community leaders as exemplified through the Harlem clinic's advisory board. Local leaders need to be involved in shaping institutions and determining policies that affect them. This is especially true in communities which preserve strict divisions between insiders and outsiders, whether due to historical wrongs or to a contest for moral authority. Public health partnerships which intentionally include leaders of religious and other organizations can help spread accurate information, instil trust and bridge divides, helping to accomplish mutual goals of health and wellness.

A third example of public health advocacy crossing the religious-scientific divide came through the response of the evangelical Surgeon General C. Everett Koop (1916–2013) to the AIDS crisis in the 1980s. Anthony Petro argues in *After the Wrath of God: AIDS, Sexuality, and American Religion* (2015) that AIDS was not just a social and political issue, but also a moral and religious challenge that required a novel approach to sexual morality. When the Reagan administration appointed Koop as Surgeon General in 1982, AIDS cases had only appeared in the United States within the past year, and it was still known as 'gay-related immune deficiency' (GRID). An evangelical Christian and a paediatric surgeon, Koop had previously published a book making a case against abortion and euthanasia, aimed specifically at Christian audiences, and contributed to a '*Christian Manifesto*, which called for greater evangelical participation in political matters like abortion'.[45] Although the media decried his lack of public health experience, Koop became the nation's guide through one of the most devastating and controversial diseases in American history. While many religious people and even physicians in the last two decades of the twentieth century viewed AIDS as a divine punishment for immoral behaviour and homosexuality, the USPHS under the guidance of Surgeon General Koop responded with an aggressive education campaign designed to encourage the public to reserve judgement, keep them updated on new developments in understanding HIV and ultimately stop the spread of the virus.

[45] Anthony Petro, *After the Wrath of God: AIDS, Sexuality, and American Religion* (New York, 2015), 58.

As already discussed, under a conservative administration in the 1980s, the United States government had been scaling back health care and medical research funding, leaving the country ill prepared for as sudden and horrific a virus as HIV proved to be. Although prevented from speaking publicly about AIDS until Reagan's second term, Koop took charge of the Executive Task Force on AIDS in 1985 and made it one of the administration's top priorities.[46] Recognizing that 'I am the surgeon general of the heterosexuals and the homosexuals, of the young and the old, of the moral [and] the immoral',[47] Koop enacted a campaign for sexual education and condom use that 'surprised his conservative friends and liberal opponents alike, turning many of the former against him while garnering praise from the latter'.[48] Although the campaign attracted a degree of conservative backlash, Koop intended his AIDS reports and other educational publications to appeal broadly to morality.

Recognizing the need for mass public education, Koop parsed his official report on AIDS into a six-page brochure that was mailed to nearly every American household. The pamphlet both corrected misinformation that the virus could spread through casual contact and detailed safe sexual practices that would prevent the virus from spreading.[49] Koop balanced moral appeals for abstinence and monogamy with an educational campaign that went beyond his own religious views, attempting to work with both religious and secular, conservative and liberal, straight and gay people to achieve a healthier and more informed population. He followed the pamphlet with what Petro describes as 'a lecture circuit among religious groups ... that increasingly blurred the lines between the gospel of condoms and the gospel of Jesus, as the surgeon general's sphere of influence came to encompass that of the itinerant public health preacher'.[50] Throughout the AIDS crisis, Koop worked with the gay community and with religious conservatives nationwide. For each audience, he shifted his language slightly to appeal to its worldview, yet he consistently maintained the message that everyone was an important player in the common struggle against AIDS.

[46] Ibid. 69.
[47] Ibid. 53.
[48] Ibid. 55.
[49] Ibid. 75.
[50] Ibid. 82.

Like Sanger, Koop is not a perfect model for public health advocacy. Liberals have criticized the way that his Christian morality often
crept into his public health rhetoric, making certain groups feel ostra-
cized or judged. Others have argued that despite his religious perspective, Koop viewed himself as responsible for the health of the entire
American population. As former Surgeon General David Satcher
eulogized, '[Koop] did not abandon his Christian principles, but he
put the principle of love of one's fellow man above his judgment of
them'.[51] Koop knew how to speak to evangelicals on their own terms,
and he also recognized how crucial education was to alleviate fear and
prevent the spread of a deadly virus. These lessons speak to the present as Christian nationalists fear that science will overtake their
moral authority and advocate for individualistic civil rights in the
midst of a pandemic that has infected over forty-five million
Americans. Language, morality and education matter as much in
the 2020s as they did in the 1980s.

A PROPOSAL FOR THE PRESENT

Historians often worry how involved they should be in the present. I
am not a sociologist, a politician or a healthcare worker, but as an
American historian who studies the intersection of religion and medicine and now finds herself in the middle of a pandemic, I feel a
responsibility to note how the past can help shape our present.
While policy implementation should be left to the experts, the final
section of this article offers a historically informed model for how
community partnerships and attention to language and education
may enable the USPHS to ensure greater compliance with guidelines
that can save lives now and as the COVID-19 vaccines are
distributed.

The US Public Health Service is required to instruct the American
public at large, offering guidance to a diverse population divided by
region, race, education and religion. In the digital age, educational
campaigns may seem moot, as nearly everyone has access to a wealth
of information. However, because people tend to accept the information that supports their beliefs, rather than seeking scientific truth,
there is still a need for public health advocates to increase the

---

[51] Satcher, 'A Tribute to Surgeon General C. Everett Koop'.

effectiveness of their interventions by engaging community leaders and tailoring educational campaign language to their audiences. Yet perhaps a greater issue, especially for populations where infection rates are high, such as among Christian nationalists and Black communities, is trust. Whether these populations view the scientific community as an affront to the moral authority of other sources such as the Bible, or as unreliable due to a historical record of violence and deception towards them, overcoming such breakdowns in trust requires significant work and creative engagement. Through fostering community partnerships and emphasizing shared goals and values, the USPHS could take a proactive, rather than reactive, stance on health issues. This could result in greater compliance with guidelines and vaccinations, and thus in healthier populations, as everyone plays a role in keeping their neighbours safe.

Academics regularly call for the USPHS to be more proactive in facilitating community partnerships in times of relative calm. In 2013, the biomedical scientist and religious studies scholar Jeff Levin published an article advocating for partnerships between public health agencies and religious communities. Levin argues that these partnerships could not only enable better resource sharing, but would also make sense because '(a) these sectors share mutual concerns, (b) the tenets of many religions favor healthy living, (c) congregations provide tangible and emotional resources for health, and (d) religious organizations are able to foster participation among people otherwise hard to reach'.[52] Recognizing that there may be limitations and barriers to this partnership, both from the public health and the religious perspectives, Levin maintains that public health and religious communities share values. A partnership that emphasizes these commonalities would enable preventative measures, social justice and healthier populations both locally and globally.

A group of evangelical doctors has taken this mission to heart during the COVID-19 pandemic. The Christian Medical & Dental Associations (CMDA), an organization whose mission 'is to glorify God by caring for all people and advancing Biblical principles of healthcare within the Church and throughout the world', has issued guidelines for churches to reopen safely, and a plea for Christians to love their neighbours by following public health

---

[52] Jeff Levin, 'Engaging the Faith Community for Public Health Advocacy: An Agenda for the Surgeon General', *Journal of Religion and Health* 52 (2013), 368–85, at 379.

guidelines.[53] Anchoring its 'Plea to our Churches' in love rather than fear, the CMDA reflects the dichotomy Christian nationalists have constructed between the love of God and the fear of death. They also echo the language Surgeon General Koop used when appealing to a similar population. Citing Romans and 2 Corinthians, the CMDA asserts: 'Restricting meeting for a season is not about fear of contracting the virus ourselves. Rather, it is about loving one another and minimizing risk to the vulnerable around us.'[54] Less than two weeks after the article was published, the comment section had divided between those praising the CMDA and saying they would forward it to their church and those advocating conspiracy theories about masking and the government.[55] Although this article and the positive responses to it demonstrate the benefits of a partnership between religious community leaders and public health advocates, the fact that it was not published until November 2020, combined with the spread of disinformation since March 2020, highlights the need to foster these partnerships before crises strike. Establishing effective partnerships before the pandemic, which requires regular funding outside of crises, might have permitted earlier dissemination of information, and thus prevention of disinformation. Nonetheless, it is better to form these relationships now than not at all.

In addition to partnerships with religious community leaders, public health language and communication are crucial to how the pandemic will continue to be regarded, and to how the USPHS can prepare for future moments of crisis and calm. Most importantly, educational campaigns should follow the model of the bacteriological revolution and Surgeon General Koop's response to AIDS. Quick and public response to misinformation and disinformation, along with repetition of scientifically based facts, should circulate to every household, and these days also across the internet. A study of the

[53] 'Courage in the Crisis: CMDA and COVID-19', Christian Medical & Dental Associations, 16 November 2020, online at: <https://cmda.org/coronavirus/>, accessed 30 November 2020.
[54] Jeffrey Barrows, 'A Plea to our Churches', CMDA, 19 November 2020, online at: <https://cmda.org/a-plea-to-our-churches/>, accessed 30 November 2020.
[55] One example of the latter concludes: '[Y]ou are urging Christians to love one another by not loving one another, to isolate and die in misery instead of rejoicing with loved ones to celebrate and give thanks for the birth of Christ ... Hopefully, you will take this message to heart and look into these issues I have raised if you are a real Christian and not some political agent pretending to be a Christian (wolf in sheep's clothing). Be blessed': Gum Drops, comment on Barrows, 'A Plea', posted 23 November 2020.

El Paso Morning Times during the 1918 influenza pandemic reveals that although most media downplayed the virus to prevent alarm, newspapers also highlighted the lives of the dead, circulated the USPHS's preventative guidelines and recognized mutual support and altruism among the population.[56] Some media outlets have followed suit today, as exemplified by the *New York Times* making all articles on the pandemic open access, or by famous journalists such as Katie Couric featuring the 'Faces of COVID-19' and bringing life to the numbing number of dead each day.[57] What is needed is a more aggressive educational campaign by the USPHS and the Surgeon General that draws on the themes of historical public health campaigns as well as current news media. Furthermore, the USPHS, which has commissioned an increasing variety of healthcare professionals and academic scientists in the past century,[58] should consider enlisting both communications professionals and humanities academics. This expansion of the range of expertise would not only foster better informational campaigns, but also has the potential to resolve tensions and prevent further strife between the USPHS and racial and religious minorities.[59]

The successful implementation of a COVID-19 vaccine programme also requires each of the above strategies. Republicans and white evangelicals on the one hand and Black Americans on the other are the two groups most hesitant about receiving a vaccine.[60] Yet they are also two of the groups most at risk of contracting the virus, the former due to engaging in risky behaviours and the latter

[56] Ana Martinez-Catsam, 'The Spanish Influenza of 1918: The Function of the *El Paso Morning Times* to a Community in Crisis', *Journal of the West* 52 (2013), 65–71.

[57] Katie Couric, 'Faces of COVID-19', KCM, online at: <https://katiecouric.com/category/covid-19/faces-of-covid-19/>, accessed 30 November 2020.

[58] Katherine Berry, 'Historical Review of the Commissioning of Health Care Disciplines in the USPHS', *Journal of Dental Hygiene* 85 (2011), 29–38.

[59] See Anne Fadiman, *The Spirit catches you and you fall down* (New York, 1997) for arguments about the necessity of increased cultural competence in medical settings.

[60] Cary Lynne Thigpen and Cary Funk, 'Most Americans expect a COVID-19 vaccine within a year; 72% say they would get vaccinated', Pew Research Center, 21 May 2020, online at: <https://www.pewresearch.org/fact-tank/2020/05/21/most-americans-expect-a-covid-19-vaccine-within-a-year-72-say-they-would-get-vaccinated/>, accessed 30 November 2020; James Doubek and David Greene, 'Black People are more hesitant about a Vaccine. A leading Nurse wants to change that', NPR, 24 November 2020, online at: <https://www.npr.org/sections/coronavirus-live-updates/2020/11/24/938440381/black-people-are-more-hesitant-about-a-vaccine-a-leading-nurse-wants-to-change-t>, accessed 30 November 2020.

due to an often precarious social position. Although vaccinating hesitant populations remains a challenge at the time of writing in October 2021, continued implementation is essential for stopping the spread of the virus and minimizing infection and death rates among vulnerable populations. As they have done historically, public health advocates must combine community partnerships, educational campaigns and tailored language to ensure compliance, trust and healthier populations going forward.

Over its history, the United States Public Health Service has witnessed and responded to every crisis from smallpox to coronavirus, and every endemic issue from venereal disease to heart disease. Regular challenges due to lack of funding or distrust among religious and racial minorities have hampered its efficacy. It is only recently that Christian nationalists have come to view science as an affront to the moral authority of the Bible, and they have subsequently disregarded and disobeyed public health orders designed to slow the spread of COVID-19. Historical examples of how public health advocates partnered with community leaders, implemented educational campaigns and tailored language to ensure better compliance offer important models for the USPHS to consider during the present pandemic and in those still to come. It should especially hone these skills in times of calm going forward, aiming to be more proactive rather than reactive, and thus be better prepared for the inevitable next crisis. For the current crisis, however, a change in mindset and behaviour will be crucial as the pandemic continues to show its tragic power. Rather than masks *versus* God and country, the USPHS should foster strategies that shift American culture to believing in masking – or being vaccinated – *for* neighbour, country and God.